Handbook of
Organizational Justice

Handbook of
Organizational Justice

Jerald Greenberg
The Ohio State University

Jason A. Colquitt
University of Florida

Psychology Press
Taylor & Francis Group

New York London

First Published by Lawrence Erlbaum Associates, Inc., Publishers
10 Industrial Avenue
Mahwah, New Jersey 07430

Published 2008 by Psychology Press
711 Third Avenue, New York, NY 10017
27 Church Road, Hove, East Sussex, BN3 2FA

First issued in paperback 2014

Psychology Press is an imprint of the Taylor & Francis Group, an informa business

Cover design by Kathryn Houghtaling Lacey

Library of Congress Cataloging-in-Publication Data

Handbook of organizational justice / edited by Jerald Greenberg, Jason
    Colquitt.
            p. cm.
        Includes bibliographical references and index.
ISBN 0-8058-4203-9 (cloth : alk. paper)
1. Organizational justice.   I. Greenberg, Jerald.   II. Colquitt, Jason.
HD6971.3.H36   2005
658.3'14—dc22   20040564220
                                                            CIP

ISBN 13: 978-0-8058-4203-6 (hbk)
ISBN 13: 978-1-138-01273-8 (pbk)

To Carolyn.

*Nothing in this book
even begins to capture your fairness.*

—J. G.

To Catherine.

*For all those late nights keeping me company
as I wrote about this subject.*

—J. A. C.

Contents

     Organizational Justice?
       D. Ramona Bobocel and Agnes Zdaniuk

17 How Can Training Be Used to Foster Organizational   499
     Justice?
       Daniel P. Skarlicki and Gary P. Latham

Part VI   Generalizability Issues

18 How, When, and Why Does Outcome Favorability   525
     Interact with Procedural Fairness?
       Joel Brockner and Batia Wiesenfeld

19 How Generalizable Are Justice Effects Across Cultures?   555
       Kwok Leung

Part VII   Integration

20 Organizational Justice: Where Do We Stand?   589
       Jason A. Colquitt, Jerald Greenberg, and Brent A. Scott

     Author Index   621

     Subject Index   641

Preface

Visit any place where people work and ask individuals how they feel about their organizations—their jobs, bosses, coworkers, pay, working conditions, company policies—things in general. What do they like? What annoys them? In short order, the conversation inevitably will turn to issues of fairness and unfairness. Some may proclaim, "You always get a fair shake around here," or "They treat you pretty good," whereas others may grouse, "I don't get paid enough," or "Someone's always out to get you." The attitudes underlying these remarks reflect concerns about fairness, or lack thereof.

As these comments suggest, matters of perceived fairness—or justice, a term with which it is used interchangeably by most social scientists (including the contributors to this book)—run deep in the workplace. Workers are concerned about being treated fairly by their supervisors, managers generally are interested in treating their direct reports fairly, and everyone is concerned about what happens when these expectations are violated. All of this is the stuff of which this book is made—the topic of *organizational justice*—defined as people's perceptions of fairness in organizations.

Matters of justice arise in all life contexts. Spouses insist on being treated fairly by their partners. Athletes demand "a level playing field." And, of course, litigants seek justice in the courtroom. Although these are interesting and important venues, to be sure, there appears to be something unique about the workplace that gives concerns about justice such a prominent place on people's minds. Perhaps it's that the metrics for assessing justice in the workplace are operationalized routinely by naturally occurring differences in pay and work conditions, as well as differential job performance. Similarly, justice concerns are likely to be triggered on the job by the existence of formal procedures that mandate what to do, whether monumental, such as deciding whose jobs are

to eliminate, or mundane, such as when and where rest breaks may be taken. And, of course, the fact that people spend approximately half their waking hours in close interaction with others also may be sufficient to trigger sensitivities about the propriety of their interpersonal treatment. For these reasons, and countless others that are chronicled on the pages of this book, people are keenly attuned to matters of justice and injustice in organizations.

Not surprisingly, social scientists have found themselves sufficiently intrigued by these matters to examine them in detail in recent years, rendering the study of organizational justice one of the most popular foci of organizational scholars today. Consider, for example, that scientific publications referenced by the key terms "justice" and "fairness" have been rising exponentially in recent years, and this trend shows no sign of leveling off. Even the most cursory look at the journals, textbooks, and presentations at scientific conferences in the fields of industrial–organizational psychology, organizational behavior, and human resource management will reveal that today's scholars are keenly attuned to matters of justice. Because the research, theorizing, and practical applications germane to organizational justice have grown so dramatically in recent years, the need has arisen to assemble what we know about organizational justice in a single comprehensive volume.

This book is intended to address that need. In so doing, we intended to throughly document, critically analyze, and thoughtfully reflect on the state of the field to this point. Specifically, the *Handbook of Organizational Justice* is designed to be a complete, current, and comprehensive reference chronicling the current state of the organizational justice literature. To accomplish this lofty objective, we began by composing a list of key questions that depicted the way the field has been unfolding. We then invited key contributors to the field, some of today's most prolific and influential scholars, to address these questions in their essays. To highlight the interconnections between these themes and to trace the development of ideas, we organized these chapters into seven parts.

- Part I, entitled *Introduction*, consists of a single chapter (1) that introduces the topic of organizational justice from a historical perspective. It is designed to help readers understand how the intellectual traditions from which the various perspectives highlighted in this book were derived.
- Part II examines *Construct Validity Issues*. It contains three chapters that address fundamental issues regarding the nature of organizational justice. These concern the interrelationships between procedural and distributive justice (2), the distinctions between procedural and interactional justice (3), and a discussion of the measurement of justice constructs (4).

- Part III is composed of four chapters that critically examine the *Justice Judgment Process*. Specifically, it addresses such central psychological processes as the roles of control (5), self-interest (6), morality (7), and trust (8) in the formation of justice judgments.

- Part IV, on *Justice Effects*, contains four chapters, each of which takes a different perspective on the consequences of fair and unfair treatment in the workplace. Two of these chapters focus on the underlying processes that account for justice effects by analyzing the fair process effect (9) and the role of interpersonal processes (11). The other two chapters focus more on specific effects, such as those associated with performance, withdrawal, counterproductive behavior (10), and organizational citizenship behavior (12).

- Part V is composed of five chapters examining *Justice Applications*. Three of these contributions focus on such key issues as promoting justice in the workplace in ways that help manage stress (13), improve employee selection (14), and reduce discrimination and prejudice (15). The remaining two of the chapters in this section focus on the underlying processes that account for the effectiveness of justice applications—one that examines the role of explanations (16) and another that focuses on training managers to behave fairly (17).

- Part VI consists of two chapters addressing *Generalizability Issues*. One of these chapters examines the generalizability of the widely found interaction between processes and outcomes (18), and the other focuses on the notion of cross-cultural differences in justice effects (19).

- Part VII concludes the book with an *Integration* of the various themes addressed throughout this volume. Specifically, the final chapter (20) presents an effort to summarize and integrate the various issues raised in this book. In so doing, it summarizes the state of the science of organizational justice and presents various issues for future research and theorizing.

We intend this handbook to be a useful guide for professors and graduate students—primarily in management and its subdisciplines (e.g., organizational behavior, and human resource management) and psychology and its subdisciplines (e.g., industrial–organizational psychology and social psychology). This book also is highly relevant to the work of professionals in the fields of communication, sociology, legal studies, and marketing—all of which have received considerable recent attention from scholars interested in matters of justice. We intend for the *Handbook of Organizational Justice* to be a useful desk reference for professionals for years to come. By integrating the fragments representing the state of our knowledge about organizational justice to date, we hope to have produced not only a book that will describe the current state of

the science of organizational justice, but one that also will stimulate future research and theory development.

In conclusion, we with to thank the many scholars who have contributed to this ambitious project. These individuals have defined this field as we know it, and as such have made this book possible. Without their present contributions, this book would not exist, and without the body of work they developed, the topic of organizational justice would not exist. We also wish to thank our various students and colleagues who have helped us with this book at various points along the way. At Ohio State, these include Kyra Sutton and Ed Tomlinson. At the University of Florida, these include John Shaw, Brent Scott, and Cindy Zapata-Phelan. Finally, Jerald Greenberg wishes to acknowledge the family of the late Irving Abramowitz, whose generous endowment to the Ohio State University supported his work for over a decade.

—Jerald Greenberg
—Jason A. Colquitt

About the Contributors

Maureen L. Ambrose is Professor of Management in the College of Business at the University of Central Florida. She received her PhD from the University of Illinois at Urbana-Champaign. Dr. Ambrose's research interest concerns employee's perceptions of organizational justice. Her work examines antecedents and consequences of individual fairness perceptions for a variety of organizational issues (e.g., drug testing, arbitration, employee monitoring, promotion). Additionally, her research has addressed issues such as distinguishing between different types of organizational justice and exploring the moderating influences of contextual and individual variables. Her work has been published in such outlets as the *Academy of Management Journal*, *Academy of Management Review*, *Administrative Sciences Quarterly*, *Journal of Applied Psychology*, *Journal of Management*, and *Organizational Behavior and Human Decision Processes*. Professor Ambrose served as Associate Editor of the *Academy of Management Journal* and was co-editor of a special issue on organizational justice appearing in *Organizational Behavior and Human Decision Processes*. She has served on editorial boards for the *Academy of Management Journal*, *Journal of Applied Psychology*, *Journal of Management*, *Organizational Behavior and Human Decision Processes*, and *Journal of Managerial Issues*. Professor Ambrose also has served on a variety of Academy of Management committees and as Representative-at-Large and Program Chair of the Organizational Behavior Division.

Anke Arnaud has an MBA from the University of Central Florida and is currently a doctoral candidate in organizational behavior at the University of Central Florida's College of Business. She has published several articles on leadership and justice. Her research focuses on ethics, leadership and organizational justice.

Robert J. Bies, PhD, is Professor of Management at Georgetown University's McDonough School of Business. As a researcher, Dr. Bies is best known for his groundbreaking work on organizational justice, and, more specifically, his work on interactional justice. He has published extensively on this topic and related organizational phenomena (e.g., the delivery of bad news, conflict dy-

namics) in academic journals such as *Academy of Management Journal, Academy of Management Review, Human Relations, Journal of Applied Psychology, Journal of Business Ethics, Journal of Management, Journal of Social Issues, Organization Science*, and *Organizational Behavior and Human Decision Processes*, as well as in the prestigious annual series of analytical essays, *Research in Organizational Behavior*. In addition, Dr. Bies co-edited a book of analytical essays, entitled *The Legalistic Organization*. He also was a co-editor of the *Research on Negotiation in Organizations* series. Dr. Bies currently serves on the editorial boards of *Journal of Applied Psychology, Journal of Organizational Behavior*, and the *International Journal of Conflict Management*.

Steven Blader received his BA in Psychology from the University of Pennsylvania in 1994 and his PhD in Social Psychology from New York University in 2002. He currently is on the faculty of the Stern School of Business at New York University. His research focuses on understanding how employees assess their social and relational standing in their work organizations, and the influence of those judgments on their behavior at work. He is currently investigating these issues by examining employee's perceptions of the fairness they experience at work, their judgments about status in their organizational lives, and the extent to which their work organizations constitute an important part of how they think and feel about themselves. Professor Blader has published his research in a number of leading organizational and psychology journals, including *Organizational Behavior and Human Decision Processes, Journal of Applied Psychology*, and *Personality & Social Psychology Bulletin*. In addition, he has presented his research at many prominent national and international conferences, has written several book chapters. He also has authored a book, *Cooperation in Groups* (with Tom Tyler).

D. Ramona Bobocel, PhD, is an Associate Professor in the Department of Psychology at the University of Waterloo. Dr. Bobocel's research focuses on the study of fairness and unfairness in work organizations. Her research has appeared in top-tier scientific journals, such as the *Journal of Applied Psychology, Journal of Personality and Social Psychology*, and *Journal of Management*. This work has been funded by grants from the Social Sciences and Humanities Research Council of Canada and an industry-research collaborative grant from Bell Canada. In recognition of her scientific contributions, Dr. Bobocel received a Premier's Research Excellence Award from the Ontario government of Canada, providing additional research funding for five years. She has served on the Editorial Board of the *Journal of Organizational Behavior* and is currently Associate Editor of *Social Justice Research*. Dr. Bobocel also is past Chair of the Canadian Society for Industrial and Organizational Psychology, a division of the Canadian Psychological Association.

Jeanne M. Brett is the DeWitt W. Buchanan Jr. Distinguished Professor of Dispute Resolution and Organizations and Director of the Dispute Resolution Research Center (DRRC) at the Kellogg School of Management, Northwestern University. Her PhD is in psychology from the University of Illinois. Dr. Brett is the editor of the DRRC's Teaching Materials for negotiations and dispute reso-

lution and decision making used by business, law, psychology and public policy professors around the world. An author of nine books and over 90 journal articles and book chapters, Dr. Brett's work has been published in premier journals, including *AMR, AMJ, OBHDP, JPSP, JAP, Strategic Management Journal, Journal of Management*, and others. Brett's current research investigates how negotiation strategy develops over time. She is especially interested in conflict and disputing, the intervention of third parties and the effects of culture. Her book, *Negotiating Globally* (Jossey Bass, 2001), won the International Association for Conflict Management's Outstanding Book Award in 2002. In 1989 Dr. Brett received the David L. Bradford Outstanding Educator Award in Organization Behavior for "outstanding contributions to pedagogy and teaching in the field of organizational behavior" from the Organizational Behavior Teaching Society; and in 2003 she received the Academy of Management's Outstanding Educator Award. Among Brett's books are *Causal Modeling* (with James and Mulaik) and *Getting Disputes Resolved* (with Ury and Goldberg). She also is co-editor (with M. Gelfand) of the *Handbook of Negotiation and Culture* published by Stanford University Press in 2004.

Joel Brockner is the Phillip Hettleman Professor of Business at Columbia Business School. Professor Brockner's research interests include organizational justice, self-processes in work organizations, decision making, organizational change, and cross-cultural effects on work attitudes and behaviors. He has published two books—one on decision making in "sunk cost" situations, and the other on employees' self esteem. In addition, he has published numerous articles and book chapters in a variety of prestigious outlets, including *Administrative Science Quarterly*, the *Journal of Applied Psychology*, and the *Journal of Personality and Social Psychology*. He has served, or is currently serving, on the Editorial Board of major journals in the fields of management and psychology including the *Academy of Management Journal*, the *Academy of Management Review*, *Organizational Behavior and Human Decision Processes*, and the *Journal of Personality and Social Psychology*. Professor Brockner is a Fellow of both the Academy of Management and the American Psychological Association. Joel is the Faculty Director of the highly regarded executive education program at Columbia Business School, entitled *High Impact Leadership*. He also has served as an expert witness, and he has consulted to a variety of organizations about the planning and implementation of significant organizational change, leadership development, decision making, and negotiation behavior.

Zinta S. Byrne is an assistant professor of psychology at Colorado State University, where she received her MS and PhD degrees. Her double–major BS degree was in Computer Science and Mathematics from California State University at Hayward. She worked for Hewlett-Packard Company as a software engineer, manager, and marketing engineer for 10 years prior to attending graduate school. Before joining the faculty at Colorado State in 2002, she worked as the Western Regional Manager for the Global Products Division of Personnel Decisions International. Current research interests include studying the antecedents, consequences, and underlying psychological mechanisms explaining perceptions of organizational justice within employee–employee, employee–

supervisor, and employee–organization relationships. Additional research interests include citizenship behaviors, organizational politics, teams, leadership, and perceived support. She has made approximately 25 presentations at professional conferences, including the Society for Industrial/Organizational Psychology and the Academy of Management. In addition, Professor Byrne has co-authored six book chapters, and appears in the *Journal of Applied Psychology, Journal of Business and Psychology, Human Resources Management Review, Personality and Individual Differences*, and the *Journal of Vocational Behavior*.

Jason A. Colquitt is an Associate Professor of Management at the University of Florida's Warrington College of Business. He earned his PhD in Business Administration at Michigan State University's Eli Broad Graduate School of Management. He earned his BS in Psychology at Indiana University. Dr. Colquitt's research interests include organizational justice, team effectiveness, and personality influences on task and learning performance. He has published several articles on these and other topics in the *Academy of Management Journal, Academy of Management Review, Journal of Applied Psychology, Personnel Psychology*, and *Organizational Behavior and Human Decision Processes*.

Don E. Conlon is a Professor in the Department of Management, Eli Broad Graduate School of Management, Michigan State University. He received his PhD in business administration from the organizational behavior group at the University of Illinois. Professor Conlon's justice research typically examines perceptions of fairness in a wide variety of situations, including interorganizational disputes, person-organization disputes, and interpersonal disputes. Other research interests include intragroup conflict, negotiation, and managerial decision making, in particular the role project completion information plays in escalation of commitment. His work has been published in a variety of journals including the *Academy of Management Journal, Academy of Management Review, Administrative Science Quarterly, Organizational Behavior and Human Decision Processes*, and the *Journal of Applied Psychology*. Professor Conlon also has received awards from both the Academy of Management and the International Association for Conflict Management. In addition, he has served as Chair of the Conflict Management Division of the Academy of Management, and as President of the International Association for Conflict Management.

Russell Cropanzano (PhD, Purdue University) is the Brien Lesk Professor of Organizational Behavior in the Department of Management and Policy at the University of Arizona's Eller College of Management. His research focuses on perceptions of organizational justice as well as on the experience and impact of workplace emotion. Dr. Cropanzano serves, or has served, on the editorial review boards of *Academy of Management Journal, Journal of Applied Psychology, Journal of Management, Journal of Personality and Social Psychology, Organizational Behavior and Human Decision Processes*, and *Social Justice Research*. He has edited or authored five books, presented over 60 papers and published roughly 75 scholarly articles and chapters. Dr. Cropanzano is a fellow of the Society for Industrial/Organizational Psychology and Representative-at-Large for the Organizational Behavior Division of the Academy of Management. In addition, he

is a co-author (with Robert Folger) of the book *Organizational Justice and Human Resources Management*, which won the 1998 Book Award from the International Association of Conflict Management. Dr. Cropanzano also was a winner of the 2000 Outstanding Paper Award from the *Consulting Psychology Journal*. He is also active internationally, having given talks in Australia, France, New Zealand, the Netherlands and the United Kingdom.

Robert Folger is the Gordon J. Barnett Professor of Business Ethics in the College of Business at the University of Central Florida. He is a Fellow of the American Psychological Association, the Society of Industrial and Organizational Psychology, and the Society for Personality and Social Psychology. He has been a Member-at-Large for the Conflict Management and Organizational Behavior divisions of the Academy of Management. His honors and awards include the New Concept and Best Paper awards from the latter division. His research funding includes grants from the National Science Foundation and the National Institute of Mental Health. Professor Folger has authored over 100 publications that include articles in the *Academy of Management Journal*, *Academy of Management Review*, *Psychological Bulletin*, and *Psychological Review*, on topics such as layoffs, trust, perceived unfairness, employee retribution, and workplace violence. He has served on the editorial boards of the *Journal of Management*, the *Journal of Organizational Behavior*, and the *Academy of Management Review*, and (currently) *Organizational Behavior and Human Decision Processes* and *Social Justice Research*. He edited *The Sense of Injustice* (Plenum, 1984) and co-authored *Controversial Issues in Social Research Methods* (Springer-Verlag, 1988). The International Association for Conflict Management named his co-authored *Organizational Justice and Human Resources Management* as its 1998 "Book of the Year."

Jennifer Z. Gillespie is completing a PhD in industrial/organizational psychology from Michigan State University, and is currently a member of the Psychology Department faculty at Bowling Green State University. Her research interests include organizational justice, as well as the role of the self in organizations. She has published in the *Journal of Applied Psychology*.

Stephen W. Gilliland is the Eller Professor and Chair of the Management and Policy Department in the Eller College of Management at the University of Arizona. He previously served as Vice Dean for the Eller College. Prior to moving to Arizona, Stephen received degrees from the University of Alberta and Michigan State University and was on faculty at Louisiana State University. Stephen's research examines the justice and fairness of management practices and policies, particularly as they relate to hiring issues. Through this merging of social, legal, and managerial issues, he has authored over 40 journal articles and book chapters. Stephen has edited four books (*Theoretical and Cultural Perspectives on Organizational Justice*, *Emerging Perspectives on Managing Organizational Justice*, *Emerging Perspectives on Values in Organizations*, and *What Motivates Fairness in Organizations?*) in the series *Research in Social Issues in Management*. He has served on the editorial boards of the *Journal of Applied Psychology*, *Personnel Psychology*, and the *Academy of Management Journal*. Stephen was the 1997 recipi-

ent of the Ernest J. McCormick Award for Early Career Contributions from the Society for Industrial and Organizational Psychology.

Barry Goldman, JD, PhD, is the Peter Kiewit, Jr. Fellow and an Associate Professor in the Department of Management & Policy at the University of Arizona's Eller College of Business. His primary area of research involves issues of conflict management and justice, particularly legal-claiming by employees. Dr. Goldman practiced law prior to getting his PhD, and his research often focuses on the managerial implications of legal decisions in organizations. He has published in the *Academy of Management Journal, Journal of Applied Psychology, Personnel Psychology, Journal of Management,* and the *Journal of Organizational Behavior,* among other outlets. His research also has been featured in *The Wall Street Journal.* He is presently an officer of the Conflict Management Division of the Academy of Management, from which he has received its Best Paper Award. He also has received the 2004 Best Paper Award from the *Journal of Management* . He teaches classes on negotiations, human resources, and organizational behavior, and has received numerous teaching awards.

Jerald Greenberg, PhD, is the Abramowitz Professor of Business Ethics and Professor of Organizational Behavior at the Ohio State University's Fisher College of Business. Professor Greenberg is co-author of one of the best-selling college texts on organizational behavior, *Behavior in Organizations,* which is in third decade of publication. As a researcher, Dr. Greenberg is best known for his pioneering work on organizational justice. He has published extensively on this topic, with over 150 professional journal articles and books to his credit, including *Advances in Organizational Justice, Equity and Justice in Social Behavior, Justice in Social Relations,* and a compilation of his work, *Quest for Justice on the Job.* Acknowledging his research contributions, Professor Greenberg has received numerous professional honors, including: a *Fulbright Senior Research Fellowship,* and the *William Owens Scholarly Contribution to Management Award* (for the best publication in I/O psychology in 2000). From the Organizational Behavior Division of the Academy of Management, Professor Greenberg has won the *New Concept Award* (for procedural justice), and twice has won the Best Paper Award. In recognition of his life-long scientific contributions, Dr. Greenberg has been inducted as a Fellow of the American Psychological Association, the American Psychological Society, and the Academy of Management. Professor Greenberg also is Past-Chair of the Organizational Behavior Division of the Academy of Management and currently Associate Editor of the journal, *Organizational Behavior and Human Decision Processes.*

Jeff Hale has a master's degree in Management and Policy and an MBA from the Eller College of Management at the University of Arizona. He is currently developing affordable housing for low-income families and individuals.

Gary Latham, PhD, is the Secretary of State Professor of Organizational Effectiveness in the Joseph L. Rotman School of Management, University of Toronto, and a Past President of the Canadian Psychological Association. He is a Fellow of the Academy of Management, American Psychological Association, Ameri-

can Psychological Society, and the Canadian Psychological Association. He is the only person in his field to be made a Fellow of the Royal Society of Canada. Dr. Latham is the first recipient of the award for Distinguished Contributions to Industrial Psychology from the Canadian Psychological Association, and the only person to receive the awards for both the Distinguished Contributions to Psychology as a Profession and as a Science from the Society of Industrial Organizational Psychology. He received the Distinguished Scholar–Practitioner Award from the Academy of Management. In addition he received the Herbert Heneman III Award for Career Achievement in Human Resources from the Human Resources Division of the Academy.

Kwok Leung (PhD in Psychology, University of Illinois) is Professor of Management at City University of Hong Kong. He has published widely in the areas of justice and conflict, culture and business, and cross-cultural research methods. His latest books include *Handbook of Asian Management* (co-edited with Steven White) and *Cross-Cultural Management: Foundations and Future* (co-edited with Dean Tjosvold). He is the Editor of *Asian Journal of Social Psychology* and a departmental editor of *Journal of International Business Studies*. He is also on the editorial board of several journals, including *Journal of Applied Psychology*, *Applied Psychology: An international Review*, and *Journal of Cross-Cultural Psychology*. He is a fellow of the International Academy of Intercultural Research and the President-Elect of the Research Methods Division of the Academy of Management.

Roy J. Lewicki is the Dean's Distinguished Teaching Professor and Professor of Management and Human Resources at the Max M. Fisher College of Business, The Ohio State University. Professor Lewicki received his BA in Psychology from Dartmouth College and his PhD in Social Psychology from Columbia University. Prof. Lewicki maintains research and teaching interests in the fields of negotiation and dispute resolution, managerial leadership, organizational justice and ethical decision making. He is an author or editor of numerous research articles on trust, negotiation and conflict, and twenty-eight books, including *Negotiation* (Irwin/McGraw Hill, 1985, 1994, 1999 and 2003); *Research on Negotiation in Organizations* (JAI, 1986, 1990, 1991, 1994, 1996, 1997 and 1999); *Making Sense of Intractable Environmental Conflicts: Concepts and Cases* (Island Press, 2003) and *Organizational Justice* (Free Press, 1992). These last two books have won awards from the International Association of Conflict Management. He served as Founding Editor of the *Academy of Management Learning and Education* (2000-2004), as Associate Editor of the *Academy of Management Executive* (1992-1996), and is on the editorial boards of several leading research journals. His is a former President of the International Association of Conflict Management, and a Fellow of the Academy of Management.

Christopher J. Meyer is a doctoral candidate in organizational behavior at the Eli Broad Graduate School of Management at Michigan State University. He has published chapters on team decision-making and third parties in negotiation. His research focuses on organizational justice, conflict in organizations, including negotiation, coalitions, third parties, as well as emotions in organizations.

Robert H. Moorman, PhD, is the Robert Daugherty Chair and Professor of Management at Creighton University's College of Business Administration. Dr. Moorman also is the founding director of the Anna Tyler Waite Center for Leadership and coordinator of the Waite Leadership Scholars Program. Dr. Moorman received his PhD from Indiana University and has published extensively on how perceptions of fairness relate to organizational citizenship behavior (OCB) and why employees engage in OCB. His current research also includes the study of the fairness of electronic performance monitoring systems and the work motives of temporary employees. He recently has begun studying the nature of leader honesty and integrity in business organizations. Dr. Moorman has been honored as an Outstanding Teacher and Researcher at both West Virginia University and Creighton University. He is on the Editorial Review Boards of the *Journal of Organizational Behavior*, the *Journal of Leadership and Organizational Studies*, and he reviews extensively on an ad hoc basis for the leading organizational behavior and management journals. Dr. Moorman teaches undergraduate and graduate classes in management, leadership, human resources, and entrepreneurship. He also is an active executive trainer leading sessions on leadership and management skills, both nationally and internationally.

Jaclyn Nowakowski is a doctoral candidate in the Department of Psychology at Michigan State University. She has a master's degree in Industrial/Organizational psychology from the same institution. Her research interests include counterproductive work behavior, ethics in the workplace, and organizational justice. Her work has been presented at conferences and been published in *Organizational Behavior and Human Decision Processes*.

Brent A. Scott is currently a doctoral student in organizational behavior at the University of Florida's Warrington College of Business. He earned his BS in Psychology at Miami University. His research interests include organizational justice, personality, mood, and emotion.

Debra L. Shapiro (PhD, Northwestern University), formerly the Willard J. Graham Distinguished Professor of Management at the University of North Carolina (where she was a faculty member from 1986–2003 and Associate Dean for PhD Programs from 1998–2001), is professor of Management & Organization at the Robert H. Smith School of Business at the University of Maryland. Dr. Shapiro is the author of over 60 journal articles and book chapters in leading academic journals such as *Administrative Science Quarterly*, *Academy of Management Journal* (AMJ), *Academy of Management Review* (AMR), *Organizational Behavior and Human Decision Processes*, *Journal of Applied Psychology*, *Journal of Personality and Social Psychology*, and others. She is a Best Paper Award winner from the Academy of Management (AOM) in 1991, 1992, 1996 and from the International Association for Conflict Management in 1999. She also is an elected member of the Society of Organizational Behavior and of the Academy of Management's (AOM's) Board of Governors, and past- or current-editorial board member of many primier management and international management journals (e.g., *AMR*, *AMJ*, *Journal of Organizational Behavior*, *Journal of International Business Studies*, and *International*

Journal of Conflict Management). Additionally, Dr. Shapiro guest-edited (with Richard Steers and Richard Mowday) a 2004 special-issue of *AMR* on "The Future of Work Motivation Theory." A past Chair of the AOM's Conflict Management Division, Shapiro's research and executive teaching/training regards how to effectively manage conflict in situations involving perceptions of injustice, resistance to organizational change, negotiations, and cultural differences.

John C. Shaw is an Assistant Professor in the Department of Management and Information Systems at Mississippi State University. He earned his PhD at the Warrington College of Business Administration at the University of Florida. He attended Swarthmore College as an undergraduate, where he earned his BA in English Literature. His research focuses on the effects of explanations on attitudes and behavior in organizations.

Daniel Skarlicki holds the Sauder School of Business Professorship in Organizational Behavior at the University of British Columbia. He received his PhD from the University of Toronto. His research focuses on organizational justice, organizational citizenship behavior, and workplace retaliation, and articles reporting this work have appeared in many of the leading scholarly journals, including *Academy of Management Journal, Administrative Science Quarterly, Journal of Applied Psychology,* and *Personnel Psychology.* Prof. Skarlicki serves as co-editor of *Journal of Social Issues in Management,* consulting editor of *Journal of Organizational Behavior,* and is a member of the editorial board of *Journal of Management.* In 2000, Professor Skarlicki received the Ascendant Scholar Award from the Western Academy of Management. He has served as the representative-at-large for the Organizational Behavior Division of the Academy of Management.

Herman Steensma, PhD, is an associate professor of social and organizational psychology at Leiden University, the Netherlands. He also has worked at several other universities and research institutes, and he was a visiting professor at Université Dauphine (Paris) and at the University of Amsterdam. He also has worked as a management consultant. Prof. Steensma was a co-initiator of the first biennial conference on Social Justice Research in the mid-1980s, and he was one of the founders of the Leiden Center for Social Justice Research (with Vermunt). He also co-founded the Dutch Association of Explanatory Sociology; the Association of Social & Organizational Psychology students and alumni, an interdisciplinary network of consultants and researchers specialized in aggression in the workplace; and, with Vermunt, the Journal *Gedrag & Organisatie.* Dr. Steensma's research interests include social justice, leadership and management, organizational change, quality of working life, job satisfaction and work motivation, total quality management, complex decision-making processes, group dynamics, and violence in the workplace. He has published extensively on these topics, both in scientific and professional journal articles and in books. Professor Steensma also has directed over 350 master's theses.

Dianna L. Stone received her PhD from Purdue University and is currently a Professor of Management and Psychology at the University of Central

Florida. Her research focuses on unfair discrimination in organizations, the effects of race, disability and culture on personnel decision-making, electronic human resources systems, and privacy in organizations. Results of her research have been published in the *Journal of Applied Psychology*, *Personnel Psychology*, the *Academy of Management Review*, *Organizational Behavior and Human Decision Processes*, the *Journal of Management*, *Research in Personnel/Human Resources Management*, *Journal of Social Issues*, and *Applied Psychology: An International Review*. She is a Fellow of the American Psychological Association, and the Society for Industrial and Organizational Psychology (SIOP). She has also served as Chair of the Human Resources Division of the Academy of Management, and Financial Officer of SIOP. In addition, she is Co-Director of a Research Center at the University of Central Florida along with Eugene Stone-Romero named PRIMO, Partnership for Research on the Influence of Multiculturalism in Organizations.

Eugene F. Stone-Romero (PhD, University of California-Irvine) is a Professor of Psychology and Management at the University of Central Florida. He is a Fellow of the Society for Industrial and Organizational Psychology, the American Psychological Society, and the American Psychological Association. He previously served as the Associate Editor of the *Journal of Applied Psychology* and on the editorial boards of it, the *Academy of Management Journal*, and the *Journal of Management*. He is now on the editorial boards of *Personnel Psychology*, *Organizational Research Methods*, and the *Asian Journal of Business and Information Systems*. The results of his research have been published in such outlets as *Journal of Applied Psychology*, *Organizational Behavior and Human Performance*, *Personnel Psychology*, *Journal of Vocational Behavior*, *Academy of Management Journal*, *Journal of Management*, *Educational and Psychological Measurement*, *Applied Psychology: An International Review*, *Journal of Applied Social Psychology*, *Journal of Educational Psychology*, *International Review of Industrial and Organizational Psychology*, and *Research in Personnel and Human Resources Management*. In addition, he is the author of a book titled *Research Methods in Organizational Behavior* (Scott, Foresman, 1978) and the co-author of a book titled *Job Satisfaction: How People Feel About Their Jobs and How It Affects Their Performance* (Lexington Books, 1992).

Edward C. Tomlinson is a member of the management faculty at the Boler School of Business at John Carroll University. He holds a BA in economics and business from Virginia Military Institute and an MBA from Lynchburg College as well as a Masters in Labor and Human Resources and a PhD in organizational behavior from The Ohio State University. His primary research interests include the role of trust in professional relationships, negotiation and dispute resolution, and employee deviance.

Tom R. Tyler is a Professor at New York University. He teaches in the psychology department and the law school. His research explores the dynamics of authority in groups, organizations, and societies. In particular, he examines the role of judgments about the justice or injustice of group procedures in shaping legitimacy, compliance and cooperation. He is the author of several books, in-

cluding *The Social Psychology of Procedural Justice* (1988); *Why People Obey the Law* (1990); *Trust in Organizations* (1996); *Social Justice in a Diverse Society* (1997); *Cooperation in Groups* (2000); and *Trust in the Law* (2002).

Riël Vermunt, PhD, is Associate Professor of Social and Organizational Psychology at Leiden University, the Netherlands. Dr. Vermunt's research focuses on organizational justice and its application to economic games, stress reduction, self-esteem threat and boosting of self-esteem. He has authored or co-authored about 100 journal articles on these issues. These have appeared in such journals as the *Journal of Applied Psychology, Journal of Applied Social Psychology, Journal of Personality and Social Psychology,* and the *Journal of Experimental Social Psychology.* He is one of the founders of the International Society of Social Justice Research and he has founded the Dutch journal, *Behaviour and Organization.* For five years, he was Director of Education of the Social Psychology Graduate School "Kurt Lewin Institute" in the Netherlands. Through 2006, Dr. Vermunt is Högskolan professor at the Department of Psychology at University of Skövde, Sweden.

Kees van den Bos is Professor of Social Psychology, including the Social Psychology of Organizations, at the Department of Social and Organizational Psychology at Utrecht University, the Netherlands. His research interests focus on integrating insights from both social and organizational psychology to understand the psychology of fairness judgments and how people react to events they consider fair or unfair. To explore these interests, he developed the uncertainty management model and expanded insights of theories like fairness heuristic theory, the group-value and relational models, referent cognitions theory, and terror management theory. Other research interests include human decision-making, social cognition, and organizational behavior. His research on these various topics has been reported in 60 professional publications, some of which have included as coauthors such scholars as Riël Vermunt, Robert Folger, Joel Brockner, David de Cremer, Russell Cropanzano, Ramona Bobocel, and, most notably, Allan Lind. He is a consulting editor of the *Interpersonal Relations and Group Processes* section of the *Journal of Personality and Social Psychology.* Professor Van den Bos received his PhD summa cum laude, won a dissertation award from the Association of Dutch Social Psychologists, and obtained a fellowship from the Royal Netherlands Academy of Arts and Sciences. He also has been awarded several competitive research grants, including a prestigious VICI innovational research grant from the Dutch national science foundation (NWO), enabling him to develop a center of excellence for justice research at Utrecht University.

Carolyn Wiethoff, PhD, is Clinical Assistant Professor of Management in the Kelley School of Business at Indiana University-Bloomington. Dr. Wiethoff's research focuses on the role of interpersonal trust in organizations, particularly as it relates to diversity management and team cohesion. Her work has been published in outlets ranging from *Journal of Homosexuality* to *Organizational Behavior and Human Decision Processes.* Dr. Wiethoff teaches negotiation and organizational behavior courses in the undergraduate, graduate, and executive

education programs within the Kelley School of Business. She is the recipient of numerous teaching awards at Indiana University, including the Student Alumni Association's Student Choice award in 2002 and the Trustee's Teaching Award in 2004.

Batia M. Wiesenfeld is an Associate Professor of Management at the Stern School of Business, New York University. Her research interests include esteem and identity processes in organizational contexts, organizational justice and change. Dr. Wiesenfeld's work appears in many top journals, including *Psychological Bulletin*, *Journal of Personality and Social Psychology*, and *Organizational Behavior and Human Decision Processes*. Dr. Wiesenfeld has received grants and awards from the Society for Human Resources, and the Organizational Behavior Division of the Academy of Management, as well as from IBM and NCR. She serves on the editorial boards of *Administrative Science Quarterly* and *Organizational Behavior and Human Decision Processes*. Dr. Wiesenfeld received her PhD from Columbia Business School, Columbia University.

Cindy P. Zapata-Phelan is a graduate student at the University of Florida's Warrington College of Business. She earned her BS in Psychology at the University of Florida. Her research interests include organizational justice, team role development, motivation, and team composition.

Agnes Zdaniuk received her master's degree in industrial/organizational psychology from the University of Waterloo and is currently a doctoral student there. Her research focuses on understanding people's opposition to affirmative action and understanding the motivation for revenge.

I

INTRODUCTION

1

What Is Organizational Justice?
A Historical Overview

Jason A. Colquitt
University of Florida

Jerald Greenberg
The Ohio State University

Cindy P. Zapata-Phelan
University of Florida

We present a historical review of the field of organizational justice. Our analysis focuses on "the modern era" of the literature, beginning with research on relative deprivation in 1949 and extending to the present day. Specifically, we organize our discussion with respect to four waves of research and theorizing that have contributed to the development of organizational justice. These include: (a) the distributive justice wave, in which scholars focused on the subjective process involved in judging equity and other allocation norms; (b) the procedural justice wave, in which scholars focused on rules that foster a sense of process fairness; (c) the interactional justice wave, in which the fairness of interpersonal treatment was established as a unique form of justice; and (d) the integrative wave, in which successors to earlier theories provided frameworks for integrating the various justice dimensions. We highlight the ways in which various perspectives influenced one another, and identify seminal contributions graphically in the form of timelines.

The concept of justice has interested scholars over millennia. Dating back to antiquity, Aristotle was among the first to analyze what constitutes fairness in the distribution of resources between individuals (Ross, 1925). This theme was rejuvenated in the seventeenth century by Locke's (1689/1994) writings about human rights and Hobbes's (1651/1947) analysis of valid covenants, and was revisited in the 19th century by Mill's (1861/1940) classic notion of utilitarianism. Despite some differences, these philosophical approaches share a common prescriptive orientation, conceiving of justice as a normative ideal. Although this orientation continues to flourish in contemporary philosophy through the influential work of Rawls (1999, 2001) and Nozick (1974), today's scholarly discourse about justice is supplemented by the descriptive approach of social scientists (for a comparison, see Greenberg & Bies, 1992). These conceptualizations focus on justice not as it should be, but as it is perceived by individuals. In this sense, understanding matters of justice and fairness (terms that tend to be used interchangeably) requires an understanding of what people perceive to be fair.

This descriptive orientation has been of keen interest to social scientists from many disciplines focusing on a wide variety of issues and contexts (Cohen, 1986). Concerns about fairness, for example, have featured prominently in treatises on the acquisition and use of wealth and political power (Marx, 1975/1978), opportunities for education (Sadker & Sadker, 1995), and access to medical care (Daniels, Light, &

Caplan, 1996). Fairness issues also are discussed in research on methods used to resolve disputes (Brams & Taylor, 1996), the interpersonal dynamics of sexual relations (Hatfield, Greenberger, Traupmann, & Lambert, 1982), and even the evolution of mankind (Sober & Wilson, 1998). Our concern—and the focus of this book as a whole—is on justice in a different context, the workplace.

Although attention to matters of justice in the workplace was of at least passing interest to classical management theorists such as Frederick Winslow Taylor (Kanigel, 1997) and Mary Parker Follett (Barclay, 2003), it wasn't until the second half of the 20th century—when social psychological processes were applied to organizational settings—that insights into people's perceptions of fairness in organizations gained widespread attention. Fueled by early conceptualizations such as balance theory (Heider, 1958), cognitive dissonance theory (Festinger, 1957), psychological reactance (Brehm, 1966), and the frustration–aggression hypothesis (Dollard, Doob, Miller, Mowrer, & Sears, 1939; see Homans, 1982), the burgeoning fields of organizational behavior and human resources management found the conceptual tools required to investigate the fundamental matter of justice in the workplace.

Concerns about organizational justice are reflected in several different facets of employees' working lives. For example, workers are concerned about the fairness of resource distributions, such as pay, rewards, promotions, and the outcome of dispute resolutions. This is known as *distributive justice* (Homans, 1961; see also Adams, 1963, 1965; Deutsch, 1975; Leventhal, 1976a). People also attend to the fairness of the decision-making procedures that lead to those outcomes, attempting to understand how and why they came about. This is referred to as *procedural justice* (Thibaut & Walker, 1975; see also Leventhal, 1980; Leventhal, Karuza, & Fry, 1980). Finally, individuals also are concerned with the nature of the interpersonal treatment received from others, especially key organizational authorities. This is called interactional justice (Bies & Moag, 1986; see also Greenberg, 1993a). Collectively, distributive justice, procedural justice, and interactional justice are considered forms of *organizational justice*, a term first used by Greenberg (1987b) to refer to people's perceptions of fairness in organizations.

These organizational justice dimensions are important to people on the job for a variety of reasons. For example, fair treatment provides support for the legitimacy of organizational authorities (Tyler & Lind, 1992), thereby discouraging various forms of disruptive behavior (Greenberg & Lind, 2000) and promoting acceptance of organizational change (Greenberg, 1994). Perceptions of fairness also reinforce the perceived trustworthiness of authorities, reducing fears of exploita-

tion while providing an incentive to cooperate with one's coworkers (Lind, 2001). On a more personal level, fairness satisfies several individual needs (Cropanzano, Byrne, Bobocel, & Rupp, 2001), such as the need for control (Thibaut & Walker, 1975) and the needs for esteem and belonging (Lind & Tyler, 1988). And, of course, behaving in ways perceived to be fair also satisfies people's interest in fulfilling moral and ethical obligations (Folger, 1998).

In our quest to address the question raised in the title of this chapter, "What is organizational justice?," we present a history of the field. Given that considerable attention has been paid to organizational justice in the literature of late (as attested to by the size of this book, if nothing else), we believe it would be useful to trace the development of the major lines of intellectual thought that have led the field to where it is today (see also, Byrne & Cropanzano, 2001; Cohen & Greenberg, 1982; Colquitt & Greenberg, 2003; Cropanzano & Randall, 1993). By pointing out the major themes and milestones that have directed scholarship over the last 50 years, our intent in this chapter is: (a) to help readers of the *Handbook of Organizational Justice* appreciate how the field's major ideas unfolded, and (b) to give researchers new insight by allowing them to learn lessons from the past.

To achieve these objectives, we have organized the history of organizational justice into four major waves that have defined research and theory development. These four waves appear together in Fig. 1.1, with the darker areas representing more intense periods of research activity within each wave. First, the distributive justice wave, spanning the 1950s through the 1970s, focused on fairness in the distribution of resources. The procedural justice wave, which took root in the mid-1970s and continued through the mid-1990s, shifted the primary focus to the fairness of the procedures responsible for reward distributions. Then, beginning in the mid-1980s and continuing today, attention was paid to the interpersonal aspects of justice, defining the interactional justice wave. Simultaneously with this interactional wave, another stream of theory and research sought to combine aspects of the various organizational justice dimensions. This stream, which has gained dominance in the first few years of the 21st century, we refer to as the integrative wave.

By using the metaphor of waves to present these four intellectual themes, we are acknowledging the surge of interest that defined them as well as their ebb and flow of scholarship along the conceptual shoreline. Our presentation of each wave is organized with respect to a timeline that identifies various landmark contributions, papers and publications that shaped the development of the field. Each wave is divided into multiple sections, with the key contributions to each section appearing at the same altitude within each timeline (see Figs. 1.2 to 1.5).

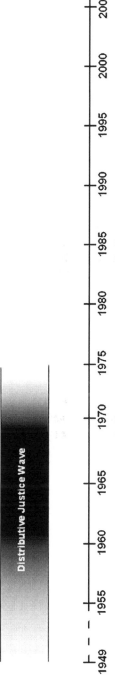

FIG. 1.1.   The four waves of organizational justice theory and research.

7

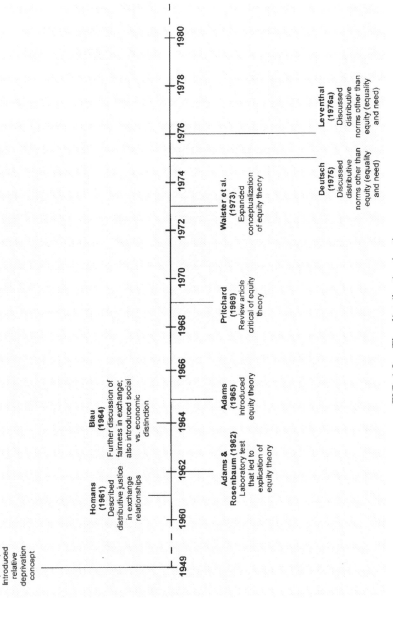

FIG. 1.2.　The distributive justice wave.

Stouffer et al.
(1949)
Introduced
relative
deprivation
concept

Homans
(1961)
Described
distributive justice
in exchange
relationships

Blau
(1964)
Further discussion of
fairness in exchange;
also introduced social
vs. economic
distinction

Adams &
Rosenbaum (1962)
Laboratory test
that led to
explication of
equity theory

Adams
(1965)
Introduced
equity theory

Pritchard
(1969)
Review article
critical of equity
theory

Walster et al.
(1973)
Expanded
conceptualization
of equity theory

Deutsch
(1975)
Discussed
distributive
norms other than
equity (equality
and need)

Leventhal
(1976a)
Discussed
distributive
norms other than
equity (equality
and need)

1949　1960　1962　1964　1966　1968　1970　1972　1974　1976　1978　1980

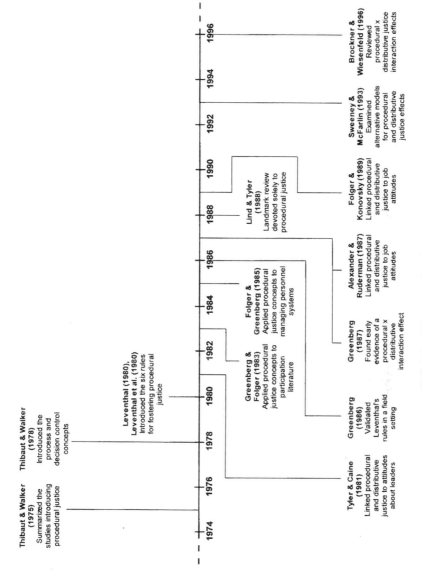

FIG. 1.3. The procedural justice wave.

Thibaut & Walker (1975)
Summarized the studies introducing procedural justice

Thibaut & Walker (1978)
Introduced the process and decision control concepts

Leventhal (1980), Leventhal et al. (1980)
Introduced the six rules for fostering procedural justice

Tyler & Caine (1981)
Linked procedural and distributive justice to attitudes about leaders

Greenberg & Folger (1983)
Applied procedural justice concepts to participation literature

Greenberg (1986)
Validated Leventhal's rules in a field setting

Folger & Greenberg (1985)
Applied procedural justice concepts to managing personnel systems

Greenberg (1987)
Found early evidence of a procedural x distributive interaction effect

Alexander & Ruderman (1987)
Linked procedural and distributive justice to job attitudes

Lind & Tyler (1988)
Landmark review devoted solely to procedural justice

Folger & Konovsky (1989)
Linked procedural and distributive justice to job attitudes

Sweeney & McFarlin (1993)
Examined alternative models for procedural and distributive justice effects

Brockner & Wiesenfeld (1996)
Reviewed procedural x distributive justice interaction effects

1974   1976   1978   1980   1982   1984   1986   1988   1990   1992   1994   1996

9

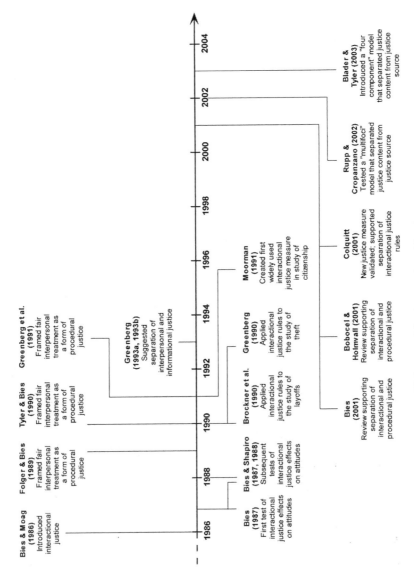

FIG. 1.4. The interactional justice wave.

Bies & Moag (1986) Introduced interactional justice

Folger & Bies (1989) Framed fair interpersonal treatment as a form of procedural justice

Tyler & Bies (1990) Framed fair interpersonal treatment as a form of procedural justice

Greenberg et al. (1991) Framed fair interpersonal treatment as a form of procedural justice

Greenberg (1993a, 1993b) Suggested separation of interpersonal and informational justice

Bies (1987) First test of interactional justice effects on attitudes

Bies & Shapiro (1987, 1988) Subsequent tests of interactional justice effects on attitudes

Brockner et al. (1990) Applied interactional justice rules to the study of layoffs

Greenberg (1990) Applied interactional justice rules to the study of theft

Moorman (1991) Created first widely used interactional justice measure in study of citizenship

Bies (2001) Review supporting separation of interactional and procedural justice

Bobocel & Holmvall (2001) Review supporting separation of interactional and procedural justice

Colquitt (2001) New justice measure validated; supported separation of interactional justice rules

Rupp & Cropanzano (2002) Tested a "multifoci" model that separated justice content from justice source

Blader & Tyler (2003) Introduced a "four component" model that separated justice content from justice source

1986 1988 1990 1992 1994 1996 1998 2000 2002 2004

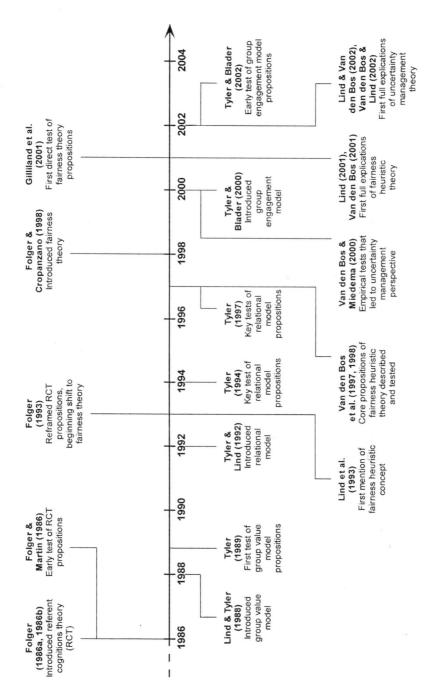

FIG. 1.5. The integrative wave.

11

THE DISTRIBUTIVE JUSTICE WAVE

Inherent in the nature of employee relations is the fact that not all workers are treated alike. At the outset, some get hired for jobs whereas others do not. And, among those who are hired, some enjoy rapid
promotions and the higher pay and status that come with it, whereas
others advance less quickly. The fact that people routinely are differentiated in the workplace lends itself to triggering concerns about fairness. It is not surprising, then, that the earliest attention to matters of
justice in organizations concerned the distributions of rewards. Specifically, such matters were of considerable concern to social scientists
in the three-decade period spanning the 1950s through the 1970s—a period to which we refer as *the distributive justice wave* (see Fig. 1.2).

Stouffer et al.: Relative Deprivation

In an article appearing in the military magazine, *The American Soldier,*
Stouffer, Suchman, DeVinney, Star, and Williams (1949) summarized 4
years of research on the attitudes of U.S. troops during World War II.
One of the questions military researchers asked Army soldiers was,
"In general, have you gotten a square deal in the Army?" (p. 230). The
most prominently occurring category of comments concerned perceived unfairness with the Army's promotion system. The concept of
relative deprivation was expressed first in the following passage fore-
shadowing a surprising and seemingly counterintuitive trend emerging from these data:

> Data from research surveys to be presented will show, as would be ex-
> pected, that those soldiers who had advanced slowly relative to other sol-
> diers of equal longevity in the Army were the most critical of the Army's
> promotion opportunities. *But relative rate of advancement can be based on dif-
> ferent standards by different classes of the Army population.* (Stouffer et al.,
> 1949, p. 250, emphasis in original)

Stouffer et al. (1949) identified an example of this phenomenon with
respect to promotion opportunities among soldiers stationed in the Military Police (MPs) and their counterparts in the Air Corps. Specifically,
although MPs with a high school or college degree had a 34% chance of
being promoted to noncommissioned officer, equally qualified members of the Air Corps had a 56% chance of receiving the same promotion.
Interestingly, however, members of the Air Corps expressed higher levels of personal frustration. Further analysis of this surprising finding
suggested that MPs did not compare themselves to members of the Air
Corps. Instead, MPs who earned promotions felt special because they

were in the top one-third of their peer group, whereas soldiers in the Air Corps who earned promotions felt less special; they achieved merely what the majority of their peers had achieved. Not surprisingly, the denial of promotion among members of the Air Corps was sufficiently rare to trigger feelings of frustration among them.

Another interesting pattern of responses was observed among African American soldiers (Stouffer et al., 1949). Troops stationed in the North and the South were asked to indicate how fairly they were treated by town police, whether they were treated well in the public bus service, and how they would characterize their general adjustment to the Army. Although police treatment and public bus services were regarded to be considerably better in the North, African American soldiers stationed in the South indicated that they were in considerably better spirits. This surprising finding was explained in terms of the different groups against which the soldiers compared themselves. Specifically, the African American soldiers stationed in the South compared themselves not to other soldiers in the North, but to their civilian counterparts in the South, who experienced lower status and income levels. This status and income disparity was less extreme in the North, accounting for the relatively higher satisfaction of Southern soldiers.

These examples of the relative deprivation phenomenon highlight the idea that people's reactions to outcomes depend less on the absolute level of those outcomes than on how they compare to the outcomes of others against whom people judge themselves. This orientation was in keeping with Festinger's (1954) then-burgeoning attention to social comparison processes. Although the notion of relative deprivation continued to be used and further developed soon thereafter (e.g., Davis, 1959; Merton & Rossi, 1957) and expanded some three decades later (Crosby, 1976, 1982, 1984; Martin, 1981), its primary significance in the history of organizational justice is reflected in establishing the importance of social comparison processes in judging satisfaction with outcomes.

Homans: Fairness in Social Exchanges

Homans (1961) built on the notion of relative deprivation in formulating his conceptualization of distributive justice. This is predicated on his earlier conceptualization of social exchange (1958)—the process by which an actor's behavior influences the activities of at least one other individual. For example, a person might help another in exchange for his or her social approval. Over time, Homans noted, people develop exchange histories that create normative expectations for future exchanges. In the case of exchanging help for social approval, to the extent that help results in expressions of thanks in past exchanges, thanks

come to be expected whenever help is given. Moreover, the better established this pattern is, the more strongly it comes to be perceived as normatively appropriate—or, as Homans (1961) put it, "precedents are always turning into rights" (p. 73).

Individuals involved in exchange relationships are sensitive to the possibility that one party may be getting more from the exchange than the other or that one party is not adhering to normative precedents. Importantly, Homans (1961) argued, the participants in an exchange will come to expect a profit that is proportional to their investments and that fairness exists whenever that expectation is met. The distributive justice concept was introduced formally in the following passage:

> Later we shall offer evidence for a general rule of *distributive justice*; here we shall only state it baldly. A man in an exchange relation with another will expect that the rewards of each man will be proportional to his costs—the greater the rewards, the greater the costs—and that the net rewards, or profits, of each man be proportional to his investments—the greater the investments, the greater the profit. (p. 75, emphasis added)

By contrast, distributive injustice occurs whenever profits fall short of investments, which results in anger, and whenever profits exceed investments, which results in guilt. Homans (1961) was not specific about the behavioral consequences of distributive injustice, stating merely that when it occurs, one party may forgo the exchange or attempt to arrive at a new bargain that fulfills expectations.

Importantly, Homans (1961) further noted that the parties involved in a social exchange may reach different conclusions about distributive justice because of the inherently subjective nature of the perceptual processes involved. Specifically, he recognized that people are inclined to disagree about the investments relevant to their social exchange relationships as well as the rewards received and costs incurred when judging profits. This, in turn, depends on the selection of comparison others, thereby highlighting issues of relative deprivation. This theme of subjectivity also would be found in subsequent conceptualizations of distributive justice.

Blau: The Role of Expectations

Many of the themes explored in Homans's (1961) conceptualization of distributive justice also can be found in Blau's (1964) discussion of exchange relationships. Blau (1964) noted that satisfaction with exchange relationships depends in large part on the benefits received relative to the expectations held by the parties. Those expectations are driven by a party's own experiences along with an awareness of the

benefits received by others. Like Homans (1961), Blau (1964) noted that expectations are particularly dependent on the benefits of a particular reference group, making satisfaction with exchanges more relative than absolute.

Central to Blau's (1964) theorizing was the distinction between several different types of expectations. These include *general expectations*, which are driven by prevailing societal norms and standards (cf. Gouldner, 1960), and *particular expectations*, which center on the beliefs that a specific exchange partner will (a) conform to acceptable codes of conduct and (b) provide rewards for association that exceed what could be obtained from other exchange partners. Interestingly, although the latter belief is clearly distributive in nature, the former foreshadows subsequent attention to procedural justice and interactional justice. Blau (1964) also identified *comparative expectations*, which refer to the profits individuals expect to earn from exchange relationships in general—a standard that is used to compare multiple exchange partners. Collectively, these expectations apply to what Blau termed *fair exchange*, which he distinguished from Homans's (1961) conceptualization of distributive justice by arguing that they take into account more general societal norms of fair behavior excluded by Homans (1961). As Blau (1964) put it, "Since fairness is a social norm that prescribes just treatment as a moral principle, third parties in the community will disapprove of a person who deals unfairly with others under his power, whereas the one whose dealings are just and fair earns general social approval" (p. 157).

Although Blau's (1964) discussion of fairness in exchange relationships was similar to those of Homans (1961), another aspect of his theorizing has had a more unique impact on current justice literature. Specifically, Blau (1964) distinguished between two types of exchanges: *economic exchanges*, which are contractual in nature and stipulate in advance the exact quantities to be exchanged, and *social exchanges*, which involve "favors that create diffuse future obligations, not precisely specified ones, and the nature of the return cannot be bargained about but must be left to the discretion of the one who makes it" (p. 93).

Blau (1964) noted as well that social exchange relationships depend on trust that future obligations eventually will be fulfilled over the long term. Blau also suggested that fairness is relevant to the creation of social exchange relationships insofar as "Norms of fairness superimpose a secondary exchange, of fairness for approval, on the primary one" (pp. 157–158). This notion has had a lasting impact in the justice literature, given that the development of social exchange relationships has become one of the most commonly expressed explanations for the effects of justice on work behavior (e.g., Cropanzano, Rupp, Mohler, & Schminke, 2001; Organ, 1990).

Adams: Equity Theory

Many of Homans's (1961) ideas about distributive justice were developed more fully by Adams's (1965) equity theory (see also Adams, 1963), which became the dominant approach for analyzing issues of justice in the workplace for almost two decades. Like Homans, Adams noted that any exchange relationship potentially could be perceived as being unfair to the parties involved. However, Homans (1961) restricted his discussion to the effects of unfairness on satisfaction, whereas Adams (1965) outlined more specific and varied reactions, asking, "Does a man treated unfairly simply express dissatisfaction? Are there not other consequences of unfair exchanges? What behavior is predictable?" (p. 268).

Drawing on Homans's (1961) notions of profits and investments, Adams (1965) framed distributive justice (to which he referred as *equity*) in terms of a perceived ratio of outcomes to inputs. Outcomes include "pay, rewards intrinsic to the job, satisfying supervision, seniority benefits, fringe benefits, job status and status symbols, and a variety of formally and informally sanctioned perquisites" (p. 278). Inputs include "education, intelligence, experience, training, skill, seniority, age, sex, ethnic background, social status, and, of course, the effort he expends on the job" (p. 277).

Adams also incorporated Homans's (1961) idea that these comparisons may result in people perceiving themselves as being inequitably overpaid relative to another, resulting in feelings of guilt, or inequitably underpaid relative to another, resulting in feelings of anger. In keeping with Homans's (1961) discussion of investments, Adams noted that each party to a social exchange infers inputs in terms of their personal relevance and the recognition they bring, acknowledging that the other party may or may not perceive such inputs in similar fashion.

Going beyond Homans (1961), Adams described the mental calculus that underlies outcome/input comparisons. Specifically, Adams (1965) argued that individuals compare their outcome/input ratios to the corresponding ratios of some comparison others or to themselves at an earlier time. This notion of comparison other is borrowed from relative deprivation, acknowledging that different frames of reference will result in different fairness judgments (Stouffer et al., 1949). If an individual's own outcome/input ratio falls below that of the comparison other, then he or she experiences underpayment inequity. If an individual's own outcome/input ratio exceeds that of the comparison other, then he or she experiences overpayment inequity. As in Homans's (1961) conceptualization, underpayment results in feelings of anger whereas overpayment results in feelings of guilt.

The key contribution of equity theory lies in detailing what happens after inequity is perceived. Equity theory's mechanisms were based on Festinger's (1957) cognitive dissonance theory, of which Adams (1963) views equity theory as a special case. Owing to that heritage, the mental and behavioral reactions to inequity described by the theory all have the common goal of restoring balance to the outcome/input ratio comparison. Specifically, the theory argued that inequity creates a sense of psychological tension or distress that motivates individuals to restore balance (Adams, 1963, 1965). This can be accomplished behaviorally, such as by altering one's own outcomes or inputs, acting on the comparison other to alter his or her outcomes or inputs, or withdrawing from the relationship, or cognitively, such as by reevaluating outcomes or inputs or changing the comparison other.

Adams (1965) reviewed the results of earlier empirical studies that supported some of the key propositions of equity theory (e.g., Adams & Rosenbaum, 1962; Homans, 1953). Among those were laboratory experiments in which undergraduate students were hired to conduct interviews (Adams & Rosenbaum, 1962). In one study, the experimenter led the participants to believe either that they were qualified for the interviewing job (hence, equitably paid $3.50/hour wage for that job) or that they would be paid this same amount although they were unqualified to perform that job (hence, they were overpaid). As predicted, the overpaid participants conducted more interviews than those who felt fairly paid. Presumably the feeling that they were getting more outcomes than they deserved motivated them to boost their inputs so as to restore a sense of balance.

Early reviews of equity theory criticized the formulation on several grounds. For example, Pritchard (1969) argued that the definitions of inputs and outcomes were too vague, insofar as some variables (e.g., work responsibility) could fall into either category. Moreover, Adams (1965) neglected to specify exactly who would be chosen as a comparison other, how many others would be chosen, and what criteria would be used to guide those choices. Other criticisms revolved around the testability of the theory. For example, if an overrewarded individual failed to work harder, the lack of input change could disconfirm the theory or point to a cognitive means of restoring balance. Finally, Pritchard (1969) criticized the validity of some of the experimental research supporting the theory. For example, the overpayment manipulation used in Adams and Rosenbaum's (1962) study also could have altered participants' self-esteem, creating behavioral effects for reasons other than input perceptions.

These and other issues have been discussed in subsequent reviews of the equity theory literature (Adams & Freedman, 1976; Goodman &

Friedman, 1971; Greenberg, 1982; Mowday, 1979). Despite these criticisms, equity theory has been regarded to be "among the more useful middle-range theories of organizational behavior" (Weick, 1966, p. 439), and recently has been included in a list of the organizational behavior theories with the highest scientific validity (Miner, 2003).

Although research on equity theory has waned, it has been used in recent years to predict such varied forms of behavior as performance after receiving high status job titles (Greenberg & Ornstein, 1983), assignment to the office of a higher status coworker (Greenberg, 1988), theft in the wake of a pay cut (Greenberg, 1990), and the performance of professional athletes entering free agency (Lord & Hohenfeld, 1979; Harder, 1991; Sturman & Thibodeau, 2001), to name just a few. It also has received renewed attention in the literature on motivation (Mowday & Colwell, 2003). Arguably the most important impact of equity theory was the visibility it brought to the concepts of justice and fairness. That visibility eventually was responsible for the procedural justice wave within the literature.

Walster et al.: Equity Theory Revised

Shortly after Adams's (1965) equity theory became popular, an alternative version was introduced by Walster and her colleagues (Walster, Berscheid, & Walster, 1973; see also Walster, Walster, & Berscheid, 1978). Although it was framed as a more general approach to fairness in social relationships than its predecessor, and it inspired research on a broader range of interpersonal themes beyond the workplace, the Walster et al. version of equity theory retained most of the basic features of Adams's (1965) formulation. This particular version, however, extended Adams (1965) in two basic ways.

First, the Walster et al. version of equity theory noted that Adams's (1965) formula for computing the equity ratio led to counterintuitive predictions when handling negative inputs. Although their allegedly "corrected" formula sparked considerable debate over assumptions concerning ways to combine inputs that remains unsettled (e.g., Farkas & Anderson, 1979; Harris, 1976; Moschetti, 1979; Romer, 1977; Samuel, 1978), these developments were responsive to the admitted problems regarding the quantification of experienced inequity (Adams & Friedman, 1976).

Second, Walster and her associates also distinguished between two forms of inequity restoration that were not developed thoroughly by Adams (1965). These are (a) restoring "actual equity," which involves true modifications to one's own or another's outcomes and/or inputs, and (b) restoring "psychological equity," which involves cognitively

distorting reality in a manner that restores equity. Predicated on the assumption that people are guided by profit maximization, Walster et al. (1973) claimed that people who are overpaid will prefer restoring equity psychologically (thereby allowing them to retain their rewards) whereas those who are underpaid will prefer to restore equity behaviorally, through actual equity restoration (thereby attempting to raise their rewards). Subsequent research has shown that these simple patterns do not hold. Rather, evidence suggests that both behavioral adjustments to work performance (e.g., Greenberg, 1988) as well as psychological distortions of reality (e.g., Greenberg, 1989) occur among both overpaid and underpaid workers.

Today, the Walster et al. (1973) version of equity theory receives little attention by organizational justice researchers. However, several of the issues it raises with respect to the fair distribution of nonmonetary outcomes are important in organizational settings (Greenberg, 1996). In particular, the Walster et al. (1973) analyses of reactions to injustice among victims of exploitative relationships appear to be particularly relevant to organizational settings, given that inherent differences in formal power between parties make opportunities for exploitation considerable. We also note that the matter of if and when people respond to inequities behaviorally, cognitively, or in some combination thereof, highlighted by Walster et al. (1973), is of considerable relevance to those who seek to manage people's behavior in the workplace. After all, to the extent that perceptions of inequity may be difficult to control, the importance of managing reactions to inequity is elevated.

Leventhal and Deutsch: Multiple Allocation Norms

The conceptualizations presented thus far have focused primarily on people's reactions to perceived inequity. In the late 1960s and early 1970s, research by Leventhal and his associates (for a review, see Leventhal, 1976a) took a more proactive perspective by shifting focus from the reactions of reward recipients to the behavior of reward allocators. Specifically, their research asked whether allocators truly followed equity principles—by dividing rewards in proportion to relative inputs—when attempting to divide rewards fairly. In exploring this question, Leventhal (1976a) noted that an allocator uses rewards to direct individuals' efforts toward the fulfillment of group goals. Those rewards are the subject of an *allocation norm*, defined as "a social rule which specifies criteria that define certain distributions of rewards and resources as fair and just" (p. 94).

Leventhal (1976a, 1976b) argued that the equity norm was only one allocation standard that may be followed and that its use was not al-

ways appropriate (see also Leventhal, 1980). Notably, because following the equity norm requires differentiating between the contributions of recipients, it threatens to undermine interpersonal cooperation and to disrupt socio-emotional relations.

Writing around the same time, Deutsch (1975) also cautioned that adherence to standards of equity was inappropriate in non-economic social relations. Although issues of justice still are critical in such contexts, they take alternative forms. Specifically, both Deutsch (1975) and Leventhal (1976a, 1976b) claimed that whenever the primary goal of an exchange is the promotion of group solidarity and harmony, rather than the advancement of individual productivity, equality, rather than equity, is the appropriate allocation norm. Likewise, they considered a need-based allocation rule to be most appropriate whenever the desire to promote personal welfare and development is the primary focus.

By advocating uses of alternative allocation norms, Leventhal (1976b) and Deutsch (1975) significantly broadened the scope and definition of distributive justice. In their terms, a fair outcome resulted whenever an allocation norm benefited the achievement of key goals (e.g., productivity, solidarity, welfare). Both also acknowledged that most allocation decisions could be described more accurately as compromises among multiple allocation norms. For example, the supervisor of a work team may be tempted by prevailing economic standards to adhere to the equity norm by distributing a proportionally greater percent of a lump sum bonus to the most productive group member than to their less productive counterparts. However, with an eye toward promoting group harmony and solidarity and enhancing the welfare of the worst performing member, he or she may be inclined to reduce the variation in rewards within the team to some degree. Indeed, several studies have revealed that reward allocators do, in fact, engage in such compromises (e.g., Greenberg, 1978a, 1978b; Greenberg & Leventhal, 1976; Leventhal, Michaels, & Sanford, 1972).

Following in the traditions of Leventhal (1976a) and Deutsch (1975), who expanded their conceptualizations of justice from one norm (equity) to three (equity, equality, and need), other theorists expanded the list to four (Lerner, 1977), eventually proliferating, at last count, to 17 distinct norms of distributive justice (Reis, 1986). Today, this issue appears to be settled. Although equity remains the dominant conceptualization of distributive justice in the workplace, it is widely acknowledged that most allocation situations are governed by multiple allocation goals served by multiple allocation norms (Elliott & Meeker, 1986; Mannix, Neale, & Northcraft, 1995; Meindl, 1989). Research addressing precisely when each norm will predominate has waned in popularity but has not faded completely (e.g., Aydin & Sahin, 2003; Feather, 2003).

THE PROCEDURAL JUSTICE WAVE

Although notions of fairness in the 1960s and 1970s were dominated by distributive justice, scholars in that area occasionally alluded, at least in passing, to what later became known as procedural justice. Blau (1964), as we noted, referred to acceptable codes of conduct on the part of exchange partners. Similarly, Leventhal (1976b) cautioned that individuals could be influenced not only by an allocation, but also by the framing of the information that led to it, paying passing attention to the notion of "procedural fairness." Likewise, Deutsch (1975) explicitly claimed that the fairness of the procedures used by allocators was an important source of fairness in social relationships. However, it was a question posed by Leventhal (1980)—"What should be done with equity theory?" (p. 27)—that triggered a wave of research on procedural justice that dominated the 1980s and early 1990s (see Fig. 1.3). Leventhal's (1980) critiques noted that equity theory ignores the procedures that result in the outcome distribution. In defining the "concept of procedural fairness" (p. 35), Leventhal (1980) referred to the pioneering work of Thibaut and Walker (1975), which can be credited with introducing the procedural justice construct.

Thibaut and Walker: Fairness in Dispute Procedures

In 1975, Thibaut and Walker published a monograph detailing a 5-year-long stream of research on fairness perceptions in legal dispute resolution contexts. That work represented a unique marriage of social psychology and law. Empirical studies were published in both psychological journals (e.g., LaTour, 1978; Walker, LaTour, Lind, & Thibaut, 1974) and law reviews (e.g., Thibaut, Walker, LaTour, & Houlden, 1974; Thibaut, Walker, & Lind, 1972; Walker, Lind, & Thibaut, 1979). For the most part, Thibaut and Walker's (1975) research contrasted two broad categories of legal procedures: (a) the adversary system (such as used in the United States and Great Britain), in which a judge controls the decision but not the presentation of evidence that leads up to it, and (b) the inquisitorial system (such as used in continental Europe), in which a judge controls both the outcome and the procedure.

Although Thibaut and Walker (1975) compared the ability of adversarial and inquisitorial procedures to create objectively fair decisions (e.g., by minimizing order effects for evidence presentation, by reducing the effects of prior expectancy biases on the part of a judge or juror), their most influential work contribution centered on perceptions of fairness. Of this, Thibaut and Walker (1975) wrote, "This subjective

measure is crucial because one of the major aims of the legal process is to resolve conflicts in such a way as to bind up the social fabric and encourage the continuation of productive exchange between individuals" (p. 67). In this way the study of process fairness mirrored the study of outcome fairness—what is fair depends on what is perceived to be fair.

The perceived fairness of adversarial and inquisitorial procedures first was assessed in a laboratory study in which undergraduates took part in a business simulation (Walker et al., 1974). Participants played the roles of competing advertising companies and were given an "espionage option" that allowed them to steal product names from their competitors. In the event that spying was charged, a trial would determine innocence or guilt, with the winner receiving a cash prize. That trial manipulated procedure (adversarial or inquisitorial), verdict (guilty or innocent), and actual guilt (whether a confederate member of the team actually did or did not spy). In the adversarial condition the participants could choose their attorney from two law students, with the attorney making arguments about the degree of similarity in plaintiff and defendant product names. In the inquisitorial condition the judge instructed a single attorney to make arguments for both sides.

The dependent measures in the study were assessments of satisfaction with the procedure and satisfaction with the verdict. The results revealed significant effects for adversarial versus inquisitorial procedures, with participants preferring the former regardless of the assigned verdict. A main effect of verdict also was observed, with participants being more satisfied with an innocent verdict. However, the procedural main effect was independent of the outcome main effect. This finding was notable because it clearly showed that procedures, not just outcomes, could drive key attitudes, lending legitimacy to process fairness as an area of inquiry. This finding was replicated in further studies that manipulated other elements within the broad categories of adversarial and inquisitorial procedures (e.g., LaTour, 1978).

What explains the beneficial effects of adversarial procedures relative to inquisitorial procedures? Thibaut and Walker (1975) argued that the fundamental difference lies in the control afforded the disputants versus the third-party judge. They formally introduced the concept of procedural justice in the following passage:

> We suggest that the just procedure for resolving the types of conflict that result in litigation is a procedure that entrusts much control over the process to the disputants themselves and relatively little control to the decision maker. There are many correlated and subsidiary elements of *procedural justice*, but the key requirement for procedural justice is this optimal distribution of control. (Thibaut & Walker, 1975, p. 2, emphasis added)

In this connection, the authors described another laboratory study in which participants involved in a hypothetical dispute were asked to rate a number of procedures (including the adversarial procedure and the inquisitorial procedure) with respect to the degree of control they afforded, their perceived fairness, and the degree to which each would be the preferred method for resolving the dispute (Thibaut et al., 1974). They found that participants most strongly preferred the adversarial procedure and that those ratings tended to mirror fairness perceptions and perceptions of the control given to the disputants during the process. Based on these findings, Thibaut and Walker (1975) concluded, "Our research shows that a procedure that limits third-party control, thus allocating the preponderance of control to the disputants, constitutes a just procedure. It is perhaps the main finding of the body of our research" (p. 118).

In their subsequent theory of procedure (Thibaut & Walker, 1978), the authors distinguished between two specific forms of control: *decision control* (the degree to which a disputant can unilaterally determine the outcome of a dispute) and *process control* (the degree to which a disputant can control the development, selection, and presentation of the evidence used to resolve the dispute). The authors went on to assert that the optimal dispute resolution model placed process control in the hands of disputants but reserves decision control for a neutral third party, as in the adversarial model (Thibaut & Walker, 1978). The relative effects of these two forms of control received considerable attention over the next several years (e.g., Lind, Lissak, & Conlon, 1983; Tyler, Rasinski, & Spodick, 1985).

Leventhal: Fairness in Allocation Procedures

In his initial discussion of the limits of equity theory, Leventhal (1976b) noted that the theory failed to address the issues of procedural justice identified by Thibaut and Walker (1975), a theme he revisited in more detail in a later publication (Leventhal, 1980). Leventhal (1976b, 1980) argued that procedural justice should be relevant in allocation contexts, just as it was shown to be relevant in dispute resolution contexts. Although Leventhal's previous work focused on distributive allocation rules, he noted, "Procedural rules constitute the second category of justice rules. A *procedural rule* is defined as an individual's belief that allocative procedures which satisfy certain criteria are fair and appropriate" (Leventhal, 1980, p. 30). He further noted that the fairness of allocation procedures can be judged with respect to seven distinct procedural components: (a) the selection of agents, (b) the setting of ground rules, (c) the gathering of information, (d) the outlining of the

structure for making the decision, (e) the granting of appeals, (f) the building in of safeguards, and (g) the use of change mechanisms.

The most significant contribution of Leventhal's (1980) chapter was his delineation of specific procedural rules that can be used to evaluate the procedural components outlined above. Before discussing his rules, Leventhal (1980) cautioned, "The criteria that define the rules of fair procedure can only be guessed at this time because there have been few studies of procedural fairness. However, the view adopted here is that it is better to have speculative statements about such rules than none at all" (p. 39). With this in mind, Leventhal (1980) identified the following six rules for fair procedures:

- *Consistency.* Procedures should be consistent across time and persons. The former requires some stability in procedural characteristics. The latter requires that no person has special advantage, similar to the concept of equality of opportunity.
- *Bias suppression.* Procedures should not be affected by personal self-interest or blind allegiance to existing preconceptions.
- *Accuracy.* Procedures should be based on as much valid information and informed opinion as possible, with a minimum of error.
- *Correctability.* Procedures must contain some opportunity to modify and reverse decisions by allowing for appeals and grievances.
- *Representativeness.* Procedures must reflect the basic concerns, values, and outlooks of individuals and subgroups impacted by the allocation. This rule embodies Thibaut and Walker's (1975) concept of process control.
- *Ethicality.* Procedures must be consistent with the fundamental moral and ethical values held by the individuals involved. For example, procedures should avoid deception, trickery, invasion of privacy, or bribery.

These six rules also were discussed in a second paper examining allocation rules (Leventhal et al., 1980). Interestingly, even when spelling out these procedural rules, Leventhal et al. (1980) asserted that concerns over procedural justice were likely to be secondary to concerns about distributive justice. They argued that procedures are often complex and difficult to understand, and that they may not be considered when outcomes conform to one's expectations. Leventhal also argued that fairness in general—whether distributive or procedural—often will be only a minor influence on attitudes and behaviors (Leventhal, 1980; Leventhal et al., 1980): "The position adopted in this paper is that an individual's concern about fairness is only one motivational force among many that affect perception and behavior, and that it is often a weaker force than others. In many situations, most individuals probably give

little thought to questions of fairness" (Leventhal, 1980, p. 47). This contention proved to be an interesting point of reference as empirical testing of procedural effects began to emerge.

Procedural Justice Introduced to Organizational Scholars

Greenberg and Folger introduced the construct of procedural justice to the organizational sciences in two chapters. The first chapter (Greenberg & Folger, 1983) applied Thibaut and Walker's (1975) theorizing to the growing literature on participatory management, leadership, and decision-making. Although Thibaut and Walker (1975) described the effects of "decision control" and "process control" in dispute resolutions, Greenberg and Folger (1983) described the effects of "choice" and "voice" on employee reactions (those two sets of labels subsequently were used more or less interchangeably in research and theorizing). The "voice" label was taken from Folger's earlier laboratory work on the effects of procedures that seek participants' opinions (voice) versus procedures that do not (mute), and was based in Hirschman's (1970) analysis of reactions to declining states (Folger, 1977; Folger, Rosenfield, Grove, & Corkran, 1979). Folger et al. (1979) coined the phrase "fair process effect" to refer to "cases in which greater satisfaction results from giving people a voice in decisions" (p. 2254). Greenberg and Folger (1983) applied the fair process effect to various forms of organizational participation, speculated on the psychological mechanisms that underlie the effect, and described potential boundary conditions that could govern its impact on individual reactions.

Their second chapter (Folger & Greenberg, 1985) applied Thibaut and Walker's (1975) concepts and Leventhal's (1980) procedural rules to such human resource management matters as performance evaluation and compensation. In particular, Folger and Greenberg (1985) argued that procedural rules could be used to make performance evaluations fairer by giving employees input into the appraisal process, allowing them to complete self-appraisals, and improving record-keeping procedures. Similarly, they argued that compensation systems could be made fairer by giving employees access to information about pay levels and criteria and by employing "cafeteria-style" benefits plans that offer employees choices. Performance evaluation and compensation systems would go on to join dispute resolutions as the areas to which organizational justice was applied most widely.

One additional work, the book by Lind and Tyler (1988), was particularly instrumental in introducing procedural justice to organizational scholars. At over 250 pages devoted solely to procedural justice, this work was the landmark review that represented many scholars' first introduction to the construct. They reviewed in great detail the seminal

studies of Thibaut and Walker (1975) while also describing the work of
Leventhal (1980) on procedural rules. They also discussed the application of procedural justice in organizations (along with applications to
legal and political arenas), noting that "It is likely that more people encounter formal decision-making procedures in the course of their work
than in any other area of their lives" (p. 173). Their discussion of procedural justice in organizations reviewed the effects of fairness on job satisfaction, compliance with organizational rules, job performance, and
other key outcomes. Notably, Lind and Tyler (1988) also devoted considerable attention to research methods in justice research. Assisting
the field greatly, one chapter described the various designs for conducting justice studies (e.g., laboratory experiments, scenario studies, field
experiments, correlational studies) and the Appendix was devoted to
discussing specific survey measures of procedural justice.

Early Empirical Tests of Procedural Justice

Much of the early empirical testing of procedural justice centered on
establishing it as a construct distinct from distributive justice. One
way of establishing that distinction was by ensuring that the two constructs actually differed in employees' minds, as opposed to being
merely a scholarly invention. An examination of the fairness of performance evaluations by Greenberg (1986) helped address this issue.
Greenberg (1986) asked a sample of middle managers to consider a
particularly fair or unfair performance evaluation and to identify the
most important factor that contributed to that evaluation. Those responses were then grouped by a second sample using a Q-sort procedure, before being cross-validated in a third sample. Seven categories
of experiences emerged, which were used to create survey items assessing the importance of each category. A factor analysis in a fourth
sample yielded two factors for those importance ratings. The first was
a procedural factor composed of process control, correctability, consistency, and accuracy items; the second was a distributive factor reflecting equity concerns. The impact of this study was realized in two
ways. First, it provided empirical support for the existence of the procedural justice rules identified by Thibaut and Walker (1975) and
Leventhal (1980). Second, it showed that employees do, in fact, dis-
criminate between procedural justice and distributive justice.

Another means of establishing a distinct identity for procedural justice was by showing that it explained unique variance in key organizational outcomes beyond the effects of distributive justice. Tyler and
Caine (1981) were among the first to explore this issue by examining
the effects of the justice dimensions on satisfaction with leadership.

Two studies (one using role playing, and the other using retrospective accounts) showed that procedural justice had unique effects on students' evaluations of teachers when controlling for distributive justice. Two additional studies (one using role playing and the other using correlational analyses of questionnaire data) showed that procedural justice had unique effects on satisfaction with political officials—again, controlling for distributive justice. Indeed, the procedural effects in two of the studies were significantly stronger than the distributive effects. It is tempting to speculate that satisfaction with leadership went on to become a commonly assessed dependent measure in procedural justice research as a result of Tyler and Caine's (1981) influential findings.

The first study to demonstrate unique procedural justice effects in organizations was conducted by Alexander and Ruderman (1987). These authors administered to 2,800 federal government employees a survey assessing the fairness of various work policies and outcomes. A factor analysis of survey responses revealed three procedural factors (process control, correctability, and global process fairness) and three distributive factors (promotion equity, punishment equity, and global distributive fairness). Various key outcomes also were assessed, including job satisfaction, turnover intentions, trust, stress, and satisfaction with leadership. As in Tyler and Caine (1981), the results revealed that procedural justice had unique effects on most of the outcomes, and that these were significantly stronger than the effects of distributive justice.

Folger and Konovsky (1989) conducted a similar study in the context of pay raise decisions (see also Konovsky & Folger, 1987). These researchers surveyed 217 employees of a manufacturing plant, and constructed a 26-item measure of procedural justice based in part on Greenberg's (1986) findings. Their measure included items tapping process control, consistency, accuracy, ethicality, correctability, and other fairness dimensions. They also assessed distributive justice, along with three outcomes: satisfaction with raise, organizational commitment, and trust in leader. The results revealed that distributive justice was the primary predictor of satisfaction with raise, whereas procedural justice was the more significant predictor of commitment and trust. Folger and Konovsky (1989) concluded as follows:

> Apart from their desire for fair outcomes, people care a great deal about the justice of decision-making procedures. Moreover, as the issue moves from the level of personal satisfaction with present outcomes to higher-order issues regarding commitment to a system and trust in its authorities, these procedural concerns begin to loom larger than the distributive ones emphasized by equity theory. (pp. 125–126)

The distinction between predicting personal outcomes versus system or authority-referenced outcomes was investigated further by Sweeney and McFarlin (1993) in a sample of engineers working in a public utility company (see also McFarlin & Sweeney, 1992). Using structural equation modeling, these researchers examined alternative models with procedural and distributive justice predicting a personal outcome (pay satisfaction) and a system-referenced outcome (organizational commitment). The best fitting and most parsimonious model was the one in which only distributive justice predicted pay satisfaction and only procedural justice predicted organizational commitment. The authors dubbed this model the "two factor model"—a term that would go on to capture both the statistical independence of procedural and distributive justice, but also the person-referenced versus system-referenced distinction in the types of attitudes they predict.

A final means of establishing the distinction between procedural and distributive justice was by showing that the two have interactive effects on key outcomes. One of the earlier studies identifying such an effect was Greenberg's (1987a), laboratory study in which participants performed a task in exchange for a chance to earn a cash reward. Procedural justice was manipulated by basing the reward on either task performance (fair procedure) or an arbitrary factor (unfair procedure), and distributive justice was manipulated by the allocation of the reward. Significant procedural × distributive justice interactions were found for perceived fairness and intention to complain to the university. Greenberg (1987a) summarized the interaction by noting that "the means justify the ends," (p. 55), as the effects of unfavorable outcomes were mitigated by the presence of high procedural justice.

So many studies in laboratory and field contexts demonstrated similar results that a review was devoted solely to this interaction effect. Brockner and Wiesenfeld (1996) examined 45 independent samples from studies conducted between 1978 and 1996. Many of the studies revealed the same pattern shown in Greenberg (1987a), with high procedural justice neutralizing the effects of outcome distributions. Brockner and Wiesenfeld (1996) used a different phrase to summarize this pattern: "The effects of what you do depend on how you do it" (p. 189). Subsequent research went on to show that the pattern of the effect depended on the nature of the dependent variable. Whereas the aforementioned pattern occurred with system-referenced or agent-referenced criteria, the effects of outcomes on self-referenced criteria were amplified by high procedural justice (Brockner, 2002). In either event, the replicability of significant procedural × distributive interactions clearly demonstrated the utility of separating these two forms of fairness.

THE INTERACTIONAL JUSTICE WAVE

Until the mid-1980s, procedural justice researchers focused primarily on the structural characteristics of formal decision-making procedures and paid little attention to the interpersonal nature of those procedures. Some awareness of interpersonal factors was reflected in items comparing adversarial and inquisitorial procedures by Thibaut and Walker (1975) and in Leventhal's (1980) discussion of the importance of answering questions in a friendly and supportive manner when denying people's requests. However, it was not until Bies and Moag's (1986) analysis of the fairness of interpersonal communication that scientists began paying serious attention to interactional justice. The resulting *interactional justice wave* (see Fig. 1.4), simmered beneath the surface throughout the late 1980s and early 1990s as scholars debated the conceptual status of this third form of justice.

Bies: Fairness in Interpersonal Treatment

Bies became interested in issues of interpersonal treatment as a graduate student. In virtually any graduate program, it is common for PhD students to complain of unfair treatment by faculty members. For example, students may complain that faculty are rude to them or mislead them when describing the terms of a specific project. As Bies experienced more of these shared stories among students, he came to realize that the accounts, although process focused, did not pertain to any formal procedure. Based on this, Bies and Moag (1986) explained that interpersonal treatment is conceptually distinct from the structuring of procedures, an idea they diagrammed as follows: procedure ® interaction ® outcome. Interactional justice, rooted in the interaction step of this diagram, was introduced formally in this passage:

> Concerns about the fairness of interpersonal communication are representative of a set of issues dealing with what we refer to as *interactional justice*. By interactional justice we mean that people are sensitive to the quality of interpersonal treatment they receive during the enactment of organizational procedures. (p. 44, emphasis in original)

If one accepts that interactional justice is distinct from procedural justice, a question arises as to how to foster it. To identify antecedents of fair interpersonal treatment, Bies and Moag (1986) drew on unpublished research by Bies (1985) in which job candidates were asked their opinions about how recruiters should treat job applicants. Four rules governing the fairness of interpersonal treatment were identified.

- *Truthfulness*. Authorities should be open, honest, and candid in their communication when implementing decision-making procedures, and should avoid any sort of deception.
- *Justification*. Authorities should provide adequate explanations of the outcomes of a decision-making process.
- *Respect*. Authorities should treat individuals with sincerity and dignity, and refrain from deliberately being rude to others or attacking them.
- *Propriety*. Authorities should refrain from making prejudicial statements or asking improper questions (e.g., those pertaining to sex, race, age, or religion).

Of these four rules, truthfulness was cited by approximately one-third of the job candidates, whereas the remaining rules were mentioned less frequently. Although these interactional justice rules were derived in a recruitment context, they appear to be relevant to any decision-making setting. As importantly, the four rules are clearly distinct from the procedural justice criteria identified by Thibaut and Walker (1975) and Leventhal (1980). Indeed, one can envision a formal procedure that provides voice, is consistent, unbiased, and accurate, but that is implemented by a supervisor who treats individuals in a rude and dishonest fashion.

Bies expanded the construct of interactional justice in three subsequent chapters coauthored with other so-called "founders of organizational justice" (Byrne & Cropanzano, 2001, p. 3) whose ideas he influenced. Like Bies and Moag (1986), Folger and Bies (1989), Tyler and Bies (1990), and Greenberg, Bies, and Eskew (1991) stressed the importance of considering the way procedures are implemented beyond simply the manner in which they are structured. These analyses expanded the four rules outlined by Bies and Moag (1986) by identifying additional criteria for judging the implementation of procedures. Folger and Bies (1989) identified what they termed "seven key managerial responsibilities" (p. 82), including: (a) truthfulness, (b) justification, (c) respect, (d) feedback, (e) consideration of employee views, (f) consistency, and (g) bias suppression. Tyler and Bies (1990) identified a similar set of principles in discussing the determinants of "proper enactment" (p. 83). Finally, Greenberg et al. (1991) identified six considerations for managers interested in promoting impressions of themselves as fair. These include three structural considerations (e.g., consideration of employees' viewpoints, the appearance of neutrality, and consistent application of rules) and three interpersonally oriented ones (e.g., the timely use of feedback, the use of adequate explanations, and treatment with dignity and respect).

Some of the rules listed by Folger and Bies (1989), Tyler and Bies (1990), and Greenberg et al. (1991) reiterated Bies and Moag (1986), including truthfulness, justification, and respect. However, other rules overlapped with Thibaut and Walker's (1975) procedural criteria (e.g., consideration of employees' viewpoints) and Leventhal's (1980) rules (e.g., consistency, and neutrality/bias suppression). Interestingly, Bies failed to use the term "interactional justice" in any one of these three coauthored chapters. Instead, Folger and Bies (1989) used the phrase "enactment of procedures" (p. 81), and Tyler and Bies (1990) discussed the "interpersonal context of procedural justice" (p. 77) and the "human side of procedural justice" (p. 91). Greenberg et al. (1991) failed to identify the construct using any terminology whatsoever. Clearly, these three chapters were aimed at expanding and clarifying the conceptual domain of procedural justice rather than articulating a new form of justice.

Although it was clear at this point that the enactment of procedures was an important consideration in judging fairness, it remained unclear whether this constituted an entirely different justice dimension or simply another facet of procedural justice. This confusion lead to some inconsistencies in the empirical testing of interactional justice in the years that followed. Although some researchers tested interactional justice propositions without referencing that specific terminology (e.g., Brockner, DeWitt, Grover, & Reed, 1990; Greenberg, 1990), others utilized measures that combined interactional and procedural rules into a single index (e.g., Dailey & Kirk, 1992; Folger & Konovsky, 1989). As we note later, the interactional justice wave did not crest until that confusion was resolved.

Early Empirical Tests of Interactional Justice

In the late 1980s, Bies and his associates conducted empirical studies highlighting the importance of the interpersonal treatment received by individuals as a determinant of attitudinal reactions. For example, Bies (1987) asked employed individuals to recount critical incidents in which they made a request to their boss that was denied. He then assessed the degree to which a justification was given for that denial, along with how much respect and sincerity was shown. His results revealed that justification and respect each had unique effects on fairness judgments. Although Bies (1987) did not refer to "interactional justice" per se, contemperaneous studies by Bies and Shapiro (1987) made use of that term. Specifically, in a role-playing study, these researchers asked participants to imagine that they were in a situation in which their boss accidentally claimed credit for their ideas. The presence or absence of a justification for that behavior was manipulated. The results revealed

significant effects for justification on fairness perceptions and approval of the boss's actions. Similar effects were obtained in a follow-up study using another hypothetical scenario (Bies & Shapiro, 1988).

Although these studies linked interactional justice rules to attitudinal outcomes, researchers had yet to link unfair interpersonal treatment to actual behavioral reactions. Greenberg's (1990) study of theft in manufacturing plants helped to fill this gap. Using three plants assigned to three different conditions (adequate explanation, inadequate explanation, and control group), Greenberg (1990) measured theft before, during, and after a 15% pay reduction was introduced. In the adequate explanation condition, care was taken to incorporate Bies and Moag's (1986) justification and respect rules, whereas in the inadequate condition, employees merely were informed of the pay reduction and were given few details. Both theft and turnover were significantly higher in the inadequate explanation plant relative to the adequate explanation and control plants. As in much of the work that inspired this research, the interactional justice label was not used to identify the phenomenon.

Greenberg did employ the interactional justice terminology a few years later—in fact, arguing that the construct should be separated into two distinct dimensions: interpersonal justice and informational justice (Greenberg, 1993a). *Interpersonal justice* captured the respect and propriety rules from Bies and Moag (1986), whereas *informational justice* captured the justification and truthfulness components. Moreover, Greenberg (1993a) argued that the interactional components were not merely part of the social side of procedural justice, as sincere and respectful treatment can help individuals feel better about decision outcomes as well. Those interpersonal and informational components had been essentially combined in Greenberg's (1990) adequate and inadequate explanation conditions, but were separated in a follow-up laboratory study (Greenberg, 1993b). Participants who took part in that investigation received less than the expected payment, with a justification either given or not given, and sincere, respectful sentiments either expressed or withheld. Greenberg (1993b) found that interpersonal and informational justice each had unique effects on theft, lending credence to the separation of the two interactional facets.

Besides theft, empirical research around this time also began linking interactional justice rules to reactions to layoffs. For example, Brockner et al. (1990) were interested in the conditions under which layoff survivors would remain motivated and committed following downsizing in their organization. One of the independent variables they assessed was whether a justification was received for the layoff. As expected, the presence of a justification was related positively to organizational commitment and work effort among layoff survivors. A

subsequent study also included layoff victims and "lame ducks"— that is, employees who knew they would be laid off in the near future (Brockner et al., 1994). In this investigation, the authors included a three-item interactional justice scale that assessed the degree to which the layoff was justified—a variable that proved to be a significant predictor of support for the organization.

To this point, although research on justification and respect was widespread, most studies failed to frame these concepts as interactional justice. One investigation that triggered a change in that practice was Moorman's (1991) examination of organizational citizenship behaviors. Not only did Moorman (1991) conceptualize interactional justice as a construct separate from procedural justice, he also created the first widely used measure of interactional justice. His results linked interactional justice to four dimensions of citizenship behavior, although these findings were not replicated in a follow-up study using a sample of workers from a different industry (Niehoff & Moorman, 1993).

In retrospect, the measure developed by Moorman (1991) appears to have validated the view that interactional justice was a third form of fairness, reducing the common practice of measuring the concepts discussed by Bies and Moag (1986) without utilizing the interactional justice label (e.g., Brockner et al., 1990; Greenberg, 1990). Despite this, it must be noted that Moorman's (1991) measure adopted the interactional justice conceptualization of Folger and Bies (1989), Tyler and Bies (1990), and Greenberg et al. (1991) rather than assessing Bies and Moag's (1986) four rules. As such, their first item tapped consideration of views ("Your supervisor considered your viewpoint"), whereas their second item tapped bias suppression ("Your supervisor was able to suppress personal biases"). Thus, Moorman's (1991) interactional justice measure actually assessed what we currently regard to be both procedural justice and interactional justice. As a result, scores on Moorman's (1991) procedural and interactional scales were often highly correlated, continuing the common practice of combining the two constructs into a single variable (e.g., Mansour-Cole & Scott, 1998; Skarlicki & Latham, 1997).

Construct Clarification

As the interactional justice wave peaked near the end of the 1990s, several scholars attempted to resolve some of the sources of confusion in the literature. These attempts revolved around (a) the independence of procedural and interactional justice, (b) the merits of splitting interactional justice into interpersonal and informational components, and (c) the potential confounding of justice content with justice source.

For example, both Bies (2001) and Bobocel and Holmvall (2001) argued for separating procedural justice and interactional justice once and for all. They also noted that these two constructs can be defined in conceptually distinct terms because they are based on different rules. They also reviewed empirical support showing that the two constructs have different consequences. For example, interactional justice tends to be related to supervisory-referenced outcomes whereas procedural justice tends to be associated with system-referenced outcomes (e.g., Masterson, Lewis, Goldman, & Taylor, 2000).

Colquitt (2001) explored the merits of separating the interpersonal and informational facets of interactional justice in his study validating a new organizational justice measure. Interactional justice items were created to capture the truthfulness, justification, respect, and propriety rules from Bies and Moag (1986). Confirmatory factor analyses in two independent samples illustrated that the best fit was obtained by separating informational justice (truthfulness and justification) from interpersonal justice (respect and propriety), consistent with Greenberg (1993a). Similar inferences were drawn from a meta-analytic review of the justice literature (Colquitt, Conlon, Wesson, Porter, & Ng, 2001) showing that the relationship between interpersonal and informational justice was similar in magnitude to the distributive–procedural relationship.

Another opportunity for construct clarification occurred when scholars acknowledged that the distinction between procedural justice and interactional justice reflects two distinct factors: differences in justice content (e.g., consistency rule, respect rule) and differences in justice source (e.g., system, agent). Although the alternative conceptualizations of interactional justice advanced by Folger and Bies (1989), Tyler and Bies (1990), and Greenberg et al. (1991) noted correctly that Leventhal's (1980) rules were as much a function of authority behavior as of formalized decision-making procedures, they failed to realize that the interactional rules also could be a function of either organizational systems or individual agents. For example, just as an individual supervisor may treat his or her subordinates in a sensitive and respectful manner, so too may official organizational documents (e.g., memos, newsletters, manuals) be worded in a respectful or disrespectful way, and contain either honest or untruthful information.

Acknowledging that the best way to compare procedural and interactional effects is to fully cross justice content with justice source (Blader & Tyler, 2003; Byrne, 1999; Colquitt, 2001; Rupp & Cropanzano, 2002; Tyler & Blader, 2000), two separate streams of research began to do precisely this. Rupp and Cropanzano (2002), for example, performed a study of "multifoci organizational justice" that

examined supervisor-originating and organization-originating versions of both procedural justice and interactional justice (see also Byrne, 1999). Although the correlations between the two supervisory and two organizational variables were quite high, some support was found for the multifoci perspective. In the same vein, Blader and Tyler (2003) advanced a "four-component model" that distinguished between "formal" and "informal" versions of both procedural and interactional justice (see also Tyler & Blader, 2000).

These efforts at clarification appear to have had a positive impact on the literature, as the popularity of interactional justice has increased dramatically. Although some studies do occasionally assess Bies and Moag's (1986) rules without employing the interactional justice label (e.g., Lind, Greenberg, Scott, & Welchans, 2000) or while using alternative labels (e.g., Blader & Tyler, 2003), such practices have become rare. Instead, it has become quite common for studies to incorporate explicitly all of the major dimensions of organizational justice, often with interactional justice having the most significant effects on key outcome variables (e.g., Ambrose, Seabright, & Schminke, 2002; Aquino, Lewis, & Bradfield, 1999). Other studies are beginning to measure the interpersonal and informational facets of interactional justice separately to determine their unique effects (e.g., Judge & Colquitt, 2003; Kernan & Hanges, 2002). Taking these trends as a guide, the interactional justice wave shows few signs of slowing down.

THE INTEGRATIVE WAVE

We refer to the final phase of the organizational justice literature as the integrative wave—a phase in which scholars began building models and theories that examined the effects of multiple justice dimensions in combination (see Fig. 1.5). Unlike the other three waves depicted in our timelines, the starting point of the integrative wave is open to debate. Although the most intense efforts at integration in justice theorizing have occurred since the beginning of the 21st century, much of that theorizing has built on earlier models that also were integrative in nature. With this in mind, Fig. 1.5 begins with Folger's (1986b) call for an integrative model to replace equity theory.

Much like the interactional wave, the integrative wave simmered beneath the surface for several years before subsequent models and theories integrated multiple justice forms. Specifically, three types of approaches are next identified: counterfactual conceptualizations (e.g., referent cognitions theory and fairness theory), group-oriented conceptualizations (e.g., the group value model, the relational model, and the

group engagement model), and heuristic conceptualizations (e.g., fairness heuristic theory and uncertainty management theory). The interrelationships between these approaches are summarized in Fig. 1.6, which may be considered a "family tree" of contemporary integrative conceptualizations of organizational justice. Note that solid lines convey that a model or theory is a direct successsor to an earlier work, whereas a dotted line illustrates that the approach was a "spin-off" from a prior conceptualization.

Counterfactual Conceptualizations

Folger and his associates have developed two approaches that frame organizational justice in terms of people's perceptions of "what might have been." These conceptualizations, to which we refer collectively as *counterfactual conceptualizations*, include referent cognitions theory and fairness theory.

Referent Cognitions Theory.   In reflecting on the limitations of equity theory, Folger (1986b) suggested that there might be value in reconceptualizing it by more explicitly detailing the cognitive and affective elements that underlie the sense of injustice. Specifically, Folger (1986b) wrote as follows:

> Suppose you do not get what you deserve. Regardless of whether the distributive rule being violated is equity, equality, or need, you are apt to feel resentful. Regardless of which rule was broken, the point is that what happened is not what ought to have happened. When you feel resentful, your thinking is inherently referential—your frame of reference for evaluating what happened consists of a mental comparison to what might have happened instead ... if only things were as they should have been. Such thoughts, then, are *referent cognitions*, involving the psychology of "what might have been." (p. 147, emphasis in original)

Where equity theory (Adams, 1965) focused on a sense of distress, referent cognitions theory (RCT) focused on the feelings of anger and resentment that often accompany relative deprivation (Folger, 1986a, 1986b, 1987). Specifically, RCT argues that resentment about a decision-making event will be maximized when three conditions hold:

1. *Referent outcomes* are high, meaning that a better state of alternative affairs easily could be imagined.
2. The perceived *likelihood of amelioration* is low, meaning that there is little hope that future outcomes will be better.

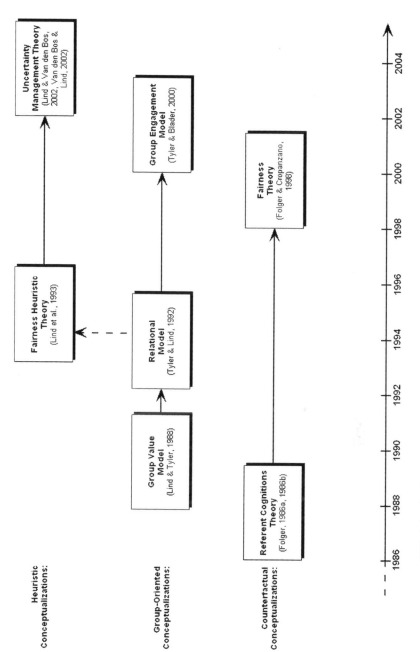

FIG. 1.6. Linkages between integrative conceptualizations of organizational justice.

37

3. *Justification* is low, meaning that the event ought to have occurred
differently.

Referent outcomes reflect distributive justice concerns, whereas justification reflects both procedural justice and the explanations facet of interactional justice.

The effects of the three RCT components have been supported in several laboratory studies. For example, Folger and Martin (1986) manipulated referent outcomes by varying the purported eligibility of participants to take part in a second experiment for additional course credit. In fact, that second experiment did not occur, with justification offered at a high level (an equipment failure resulted in its cancellation) or a low level (the experimenter arbitrarily cancelled it). As predicted, high levels of justification neutralized the effects of referent outcomes on anger and resentment. Other studies yielded similar effects with outcomes other than anger and resentment, such as fairness perceptions, blame, satisfaction, and withdrawal (Aquino, Griffeth, Allen, & Hom, 1997; Cropanzano & Folger, 1989; Folger, Rosenfield, & Robinson, 1983; Van den Bos & Van Prooijen, 2001).

Fairness Theory. In subsequent reflections on RCT, Folger (1993) eschewed the referent cognitions terminology in favor of counterfactual thinking—a process of undoing some event by imagining it otherwise. Folger (1993) also noted that RCT inadequately distinguished between causal responsibility and moral obligation insofar as justifications may be considered unnecessary when some extenuating circumstances are responsible for the negative event. Folger (1993) also avoided the particular jargon of RCT in favor of counterfactual "if onlys" commonly considered when reacting to negative events (e.g., "if only the agent had acted as he or she *should* have, then I *would* have received a better outcome," p. 164).

This shift in framing eventually led to the introduction of fairness theory, which was presented as a successor to RCT (Folger & Cropanzano, 1998, 2001). Fairness theory seeks to explain when an authority will be held accountable for an injustice. In particular, the theory argues that blame will be placed when three counterfactual questions are answered in the affirmative:

1. *Would* I have been better off if a different outcome or procedure had occurred? In other words, have I experienced some injury?
2. *Could* the authority have behaved differently? In other words, were there other feasible courses of action?
3. *Should* the authority have behaved differently? In other words, were moral and ethical standards violated?

The *would* counterfactual extends RCT's referent outcomes component by capturing both outcome and process concerns, whereas the *should* counterfactual spotlights the importance of moral violations, such as interpersonal injustice, bias, or lack of ethicality (for further discussion of morality issues, see Folger, 1998, 2001).

One of the first explicit tests of fairness theory's propositions was conducted in the context of employment rejection letters (Gilliland et al., 2001). The authors reviewed three studies examining the effects of *would reducing* explanations (which clarified the superior qualifications of the individual who was hired), *could reducing* explanations (which attributed the rejection to external factors, such as a hiring freeze), and *should reducing* explanations (which highlighted the reliability and validity of the selection system). The results yielded several main and interactive effects of the three explanation forms for fairness perceptions, intentions to recommend the firm to others, and the decision to apply for another job with the firm. Other studies also used fairness theory successfully as a basis for grounding their predictions (Collie, Bradley, & Sparks, 2002; Colquitt & Chertkoff, 2002).

Group-Oriented Conceptualizations

Recent theoretical statements by Tyler, Lind, and their associates may be considered *group-oriented conceptualizations* because they conceive of justice in terms of the importance of acceptance by (and identification with) the groups to which individuals belong. These include the group value model, the relational model, and the group engagement model.

Group Value Model. In reflecting on Thibaut and Walker's (1975) body of research, Lind and Tyler (1988) suggested that disputants valued procedural justice because it provided some predictability and control over outcomes. Fair procedures suggest that long-term gains will result from exchange relationships with others, whereas unfair procedures suggest that such gains cannot be guaranteed. Lind and Tyler (1988) labeled this perspective the self-interest (or instrumental) model, noting that it can explain many—but not all—of the effects observed in the justice literature. For example, it cannot explain the well-established finding that process control enhances fairness perceptions independently of its ability to influence outcomes (e.g., Earley & Lind, 1987; Kanfer, Sawyer, Earley, & Lind, 1987; Lind, Kanfer & Earley, 1990; Lind et al., 1983; Tyler, 1987; Tyler et al., 1985). Such effects imply that the ability to express oneself has some value irrespective of its ability to fulfill economic self-interest. This effect has been termed the "noninstrumental," or "value expressive," effect of process control or voice.

Lind and Tyler (1988) also noted that the self-interest model was poorly suited to explaining the effects of interactional justice given that respect and politeness do not necessarily affect one's long-term economic outcomes. With this in mind, they introduced the group value model as an alternative to the self-interest model, noting that individuals place a special emphasis on their group memberships and are particularly attuned to their status in the eyes of others and their treatment from fellow group members. They further argued that procedural and interactional justice "specify the authority relations and the formal and informal social processes that regulate much of the group's activity" (p. 231). Put simply, justice says something about the nature of one's group, and one's particular place in it.

With respect to the antecedents of fairness perceptions, Lind and Tyler (1988) argued that fair treatment will be inferred whenever procedures and interactions are in accord with the fundamental values of the group. Thus, process control, consistency, respect, and justifications lead to fairness perceptions not only because of their influence on outcomes, but also because they reaffirm group values. Tyler (1989) highlighted three specific justice criteria that he felt were particularly relevant to the affirmation of group values: (a) bias suppression (which he termed *neutrality*); (b) benevolence (sometimes also labeled *trust* or *trustworthiness*); and (c) interpersonal justice (which he labeled *standing* or *status recognition*). In a random survey of Chicago residents who were asked about their experiences with legal authorities, Tyler (1989) showed that these three justice criteria explained significant variance in fairness perceptions, even after controlling for outcome favorability and control.

Relational Model.   In subsequent theorizing, Tyler and Lind (1992) focused on a fundamental question in any organizational group: "What is needed for authorities to function effectively?" (p. 117). They introduced the "relational model of authority in groups" (p. 115) to answer that question, focusing specifically on the factors that determine the legitimacy of authorities. Borrowing from their group value model, the authors argued that the three factors identified by Tyler (1989) influenced the degree to which individuals view their authorities as legitimate. Tyler and Lind (1992) put it as such:

> People are sensitive to procedural nuances because procedures are viewed as manifestations of basic process values in the group, organization, or institution using the procedure. Because procedures acquire substantial significance as symbols of group values, individuals are concerned as much or more with what happens within the procedure as

with whether the procedure promotes the attainment of some extra-procedural goal. Of key importance, according to this analysis, are the implications of the procedure for one's relationship with the group or authority that enacts the procedure. To the extent that a procedure is seen as indicating a positive, full status relationship, it is judged to be fair. (p. 140)

Except for the relational model's more explicit focus on authority legitimacy, it and the group value model are quite similar, and have been used interchangeably in subsequent research. Thus, although some studies frame predictions using the group value terminology (e.g., Smith, Tyler, Huo, Ortiz, & Lind, 1998; Tyler, Degoey, & Smith, 1996), others use the relational phrasing (e.g., Lind, Tyler, & Huo, 1997; Tyler, 1994, 1997). For example, the three factors identified by Tyler (1989) are often grouped under the heading of "relational judgments" (Tyler, 1994). Like the group value research that preceded it, tests of the relational model have verified that the relational judgments impact fairness perceptions even when controlling for outcome favorability and control (Tyler, 1994), with many of these effects replicated across national cultures (Lind et al., 1997).

Other discussions of the relational model have moved beyond the effects of the three relational judgments on fairness perceptions. For example, studies reviewed by Tyler (1997) explicitly tested a core proposition of the model—that relational judgments predict the legitimacy of authorities. These studies occurred in business, family, education, and political contexts and linked relational judgments to overall authority legitimacy, willingness to accept authority decisions voluntarily, and obedience to authority rules (Tyler, 1997). Additional research has focused on other outcomes of relational judgments. For example, Tyler et al. (1996) linked relational judgments to pride in one's group, felt respect from one's group, and citizenship behavior (see also Smith et al., 1998). These results support the central tenets of the relational model as summarized by Tyler and Lind (1992)—namely, that "a good relationship with authorities promotes feelings of procedural fairness and that this, in turn, leads one to feel valued by the group. This group-value belief is, in turn, a potent determinant of various attitudes and behaviors, including judgments of legitimacy and obedience to authority" (p. 158).

Group Engagement Model.   The most recent theory in this genre focuses on another fundamental question in any organizational group: What causes individuals to perform those behaviors that help the group reach its goals? Put differently, what makes individuals "engaged" in

the groups to which they belong? Tyler and Blader's (2000, 2003) group engagement model focuses on this question. These theorists argued that justice is a key driver of intrinsic forms of motivation (termed *psychological engagement*) and task and citizenship forms of performance (termed *mandatory* and *discretionary* behavior and grouped under the *behavioral engagement* heading). Although many tests of the group-value model and the relational model were concerned with the effects of relational judgments on fairness perceptions and other attitudes, the group engagement model is focused more on behavioral effects.

Specifically, the group engagement model argues that forms of procedural justice and interactional justice originating with supervisors and organizations drive identity judgments (e.g., pride in group, felt respect from group, and identification with group). Although the group-value model and the relational model treat distributive justice primarily as a control variable, its role in the group engagement model is more explicit: Distributive justice influences perceptions of group resources, which in turn impact identity judgments. Finally, identity judgments influence engagement. One of the core propositions of the model is the "social identity mediation hypothesis," according to which, "People's willingness to cooperate with their group—especially cooperation that is discretionary in nature—flows from the identity information they receive from the group. That identity information, in turn, is hypothesized to emanate from evaluations of the procedural fairness experienced in the group" (Tyler & Blader, 2003, p. 353). Although the group engagement model is too new to have been tested fully (for a partial test, see Tyler & Blader, 2002), its focus on explaining the behavioral effects of justice fills an important gap in the literature.

Heuristic Conceptualizations

Recent approaches by Lind, Van den Bos, and their associates have focused on the nature of the mental shortcuts used in forming and using psychological judgments of fairness. Two such *heuristic conceptualizations* have been evident in recent years—fairness heuristic theory, and uncertainty management theory.

Fairness Heuristic Theory.   Fairness heuristic theory (FHT) grew out of tests of the relational model, which conceived of justice as a key determinant of the legitimacy of authority figures (Tyler & Lind, 1992). In a study of litigants' reactions to an arbitration case, Lind, Kulik, Ambrose, and de Vera Park (1993) suggested that people use fairness perceptions to make decisions about whether to accept the directives of an authority. Specifically, they argued that people rely on a "fairness

heuristic" to make such judgments, with that heuristic defined as "a psychological shortcut used to decide whether to accept or reject the directives of people in positions of authority" (p. 225). The results of two studies showed that the fairness heuristic (operationalized in this study as global perceptions of procedural fairness) was positively related to the acceptance of an arbitration award (Lind et al., 1993). That fairness heuristic concept was then developed further in unpublished work by Lind (1992, 1994).

Four years later, Van den Bos, Vermunt, and Wilke (1997) described and tested the first core proposition of FHT—that fairness heuristics are formed quickly, using whatever information is available, so that the heuristic can be used to guide subsequent decisions. In particular, Van den Bos et al. (1997) proposed that there would be a primacy effect, such that information available first would have a greater effect on fairness judgments than information made available later in time. The authors tested their propositions in two laboratory studies in which a series of assessments determined the selection of reward outcome. These studies manipulated procedural justice by making the process either accurate or inaccurate, and also varied outcome favorability, as well as the order in which procedural and outcome information was experienced. When outcome information was presented first, it had a stronger effect on satisfaction and fairness judgments, as well as intentions to protest. The reverse was true when procedural information was presented first. In this case, the procedural information became the key driver of these attitudes and behavioral intentions.

A subsequent study by Van den Bos, Wilke, and Lind (1998) described and tested the second core proposition of FHT—that fairness heuristics are used as a proxy for trust. It was reasoned that the trustworthiness of authorities is a critical concern in organizations, but trustworthiness is more difficult to judge than fairness. In two lab studies, Van den Bos et al. (1998) tested their proposition by varying whether participants received information about an authority's trustworthiness. Both studies revealed that availability of trust information moderated the effects of procedural justice (manipulated here in terms of process control). Specifically, when either positive or negative trust information was present, the effects of procedural justice on satisfaction and fairness ratings were neutralized.

The first full explications of fairness heuristic theory appeared three years later in a series of chapters (Lind, 2001; Van den Bos, 2001a; Van den Bos, Lind, & Wilke, 2001). Drawing on some of the concepts in the relational model, Lind (2001) framed the use of fairness heuristics in the "fundamental social dilemma." That fundamental dilemma is two-sided: On the one hand, there are valued outcomes that can be obtained by identifying with and complying with authority requests; on the

other, complying with such requests leaves one vulnerable to exploitation. Concerns about this dilemma could be alleviated if the authority was known to be trustworthy, but that knowledge takes time to develop and never may be certain. Thus, individuals form fairness heuristics based on their first few encounters with the authority, then rely on them to serve as proxies for trust in negotiating dilemma-related decisions.

Uncertainty Management Theory.   Whereas uncertainty about trust lies at the core of fairness heuristic theory, subsequent studies demonstrated that fairness can be used to cope with other sources of uncertainty. In three laboratory studies, Van den Bos and Miedema (2000) had participants complete a computerized pattern recognition task along with an unseen "other." At the end of the studies, lottery tickets were to be allocated to participants based on their performance, and procedural justice was manipulated by giving participants some process control in that allocation. The studies also manipulated uncertainty by asking participants either to consider their feelings about death (arousing uncertainty) or to reflect on the emotions associated with dental pain (not arousing uncertainty). The results were as predicted: The procedural manipulations had stronger effects on affect ratings when uncertainty was aroused in the participants than when uncertainty was not aroused.

Expanding on Van den Bos and Miedema's (2000) results, Van den Bos (2001b) tested the same sort of effects using less extreme manipulations of uncertainty in three studies. Participants again were asked to perform a computerized pattern recognition task with an unseen other, and again either were given or denied process control in the allocation of lottery tickets. In addition, Van den Bos (2001b) manipulated uncertainty either by asking participants to consider their thoughts and feelings about being uncertain, or to reflect on how it feels to not be in control. Supporting the theory, the same pattern of results was obtained: The effects of the justice manipulations were stronger when uncertainty was made salient for the participants than when it was not made salient.

Building on this research, the first full explications of uncertainty management theory (UMT) appeared in 2002 (Lind & Van den Bos, 2002; Van den Bos & Lind, 2002). Cast as a successor to FHT, UMT views trust as one of a number of factors about which individuals may be uncertain. Although the fairness heuristic can serve as a proxy for trust, it also can help individuals deal with more general sources of uncertainty. In summarizing the core proposition of the theory, Lind and Van den Bos (2002) wrote, "What appears to be happening is that people use fairness to manage their reactions to uncertainty, finding comfort in related or even unrelated fair experiences" (p. 216). Thus, fairness can remove uncertainty re-

lated to an authority figure's trustworthiness, but it also can mitigate the effects of uncertainty that has nothing to do with authority relationships whatsoever. In this manner, UMT builds on some of the core ideas of control-based, or instrumental models of justice (e.g., Thibaut & Walker, 1975), while expanding them beyond the contexts of resource allocation and dispute resolution.

CONCLUSION

As we hope this review has illustrated, the modern era of organizational justice has come a long way in the half century since relative deprivation was introduced (Stouffer et al., 1949). The wave metaphor used to structure our review illustrates the linear progress that has been made within each of the major streams in the literature's history. This progress has better elucidated the subjective process of judging the fairness of outcomes (Fig. 1.2), the power of rules of fair process (Fig. 1.3), the importance of fairness in interpersonal treatment (Fig. 1.4), and the merits of integrating all these orientations (Fig. 1.5). Although the developments within each wave are impressive in and of themselves, the significant evolution of the field is best appreciated by taking a step back and examining the big picture—the effects of the waves in combination (Fig. 1.1). A half century of research has illustrated that justice is a complex, multifaceted phenomenon, as individuals are concerned about fairness for several reasons, judge the fairness of several aspects of decision events, and use fairness perceptions to guide a wide range of key attitudes and behaviors.

In reflecting on the waves reviewed in this chapter, we are reminded of Kuhn's (1963) discussion of the "essential tension" in scientific progress. Kuhn (1963) argued that scientific progress is most often made by individuals who make incremental contributions to traditional areas of inquiry, before using the knowledge and experience gained from such efforts to perform paradigm-shifting works. The essential tension concerns this balance of convergent thinking with divergent thinking—of the need to be both traditionalist and iconoclast. The contributions highlighted in our timelines provide good examples of both sides of that tension, making steady incremental advances within a given wave but also using that knowledge to trigger a new shift in the literature. As Kuhn (1963) would have suspected, such shifts were triggered rarely by individuals new to the literature, but instead, those who were well trained and well versed in the traditional tenets of the current wave of thinking.

Of course, the tempting question with which to conclude this chapter is, "What will be the next wave?" It seems doubtful that the future

of the organizational justice literature will be written solely by further developments in the four waves shown in Fig. 1.1. Of course, it may be that the next wave already has begun, with a triggering point that will come to be appreciated only in hindsight. After all, few scholars in the early 1990s would have identified an interactional justice wave or an integrative wave within the literature, although both were simmering beneath the surface. Alternatively, it may come to pass that an empirical study or theoretical conceptualization will be introduced in the next few years that has the immediate impact of Leventhal's (1980) chapter, or the seminal books by Thibaut and Walker (1975) and Lind and Tyler (1988). The importance of these works became apparent almost immediately, as evidenced by the empirical tests they inspired within a few years of their publication. In either case, the only real answer to the "next wave" question is, "We'll know it when we see it—at least, eventually." And when this occurs, we hope that the contributions to this handbook will have proven inspirational.

REFERENCES

Adams, J. S. (1963). Toward an understanding of inequity. *Journal of Abnormal and Social Psychology, 67*, 422–436.

Adams, J. S. (1965). Inequity in social exchange. In L. Berkowitz (Ed.), *Advances in experimental social psychology* (Vol. 2, pp. 267–299). New York: Academic Press.

Adams, J. S., & Freedman, S. (1976). Equity theory revisited: Comments and annotated bibliography. In L. Berkowitz & E. Walster (Eds.), *Advances in experimental social psychology* (pp. 43–90). New York: Academic Press.

Adams, J. S., & Rosenbaum, W. B. (1962). The relationship of worker productivity to cognitive dissonance about wage inequities. *Journal of Applied Psychology, 46*, 161–164.

Alexander, S., & Ruderman, M. (1987). The role of procedural and distributive justice in organizational behavior. *Social Justice Research, 1*, 177–198.

Ambrose, M. L., Seabright, M. A., & Schminke, M. (2002). Sabotage in the workplace: The role of organizational justice. *Organizational Behavior and Human Decision Processes, 89*, 947–965.

Aquino, K., Griffeth, R. W., Allen, D. G., & Hom, P. W. (1997). Integrating justice constructs into the turnover process: A test of a referent cognitions model. *Academy of Management Journal, 40*, 1208–1227.

Aquino, K., Lewis, M. U., & Bradfield, M. (1999). Justice constructs, negative affectivity, and employee deviance: A proposed model and empirical test. *Journal of Organizational Behavior, 20*, 1073–1091.

Aydin, O., & Sahin, D. N. (2003). The effect of different types of reward allocation on future work partner preferences: An indirect test of the self-interest view. *Social Behavior and Personality, 31*, 133–142.

Barclay, L. J. (2003, April). *Following in the footsteps of Mary Parker Follett: Exploring how insights from the past can advance organizational justice theory and research.* Paper presented at the annual meeting of the Society of Industrial and Organizational Psychology, Orlando, FL.

Bies, R. J (1985). *Individual reactions to corporate recruiting encounters: The importance of fairness.* Unpublished manuscript cited in Bies and Moag (1986).

Bies, R. J. (1987). Beyond "voice": The influence of decision-maker justification and sincerity on procedural fairness judgments. *Representative Research in Social Psychology, 17,* 3–14.

Bies, R. J. (2001). Interactional (in)justice: The sacred and the profane. In J. Greenberg & R. Cropanzano (Eds.), *Advances in organizational justice* (pp. 85–108). Stanford, CA: Stanford University Press.

Bies, R. J., & Moag, J. F. (1986). Interactional justice: Communication criteria of fairness. In R. J. Lewicki, B. H. Sheppard, & M. H. Bazerman (Eds.), *Research on negotiations in organizations* (Vol. 1, pp. 43–55). Greenwich, CT: JAI Press.

Bies, R. J., & Shapiro, D. L. (1987). Interactional fairness judgments: The influence of causal accounts. *Social Justice Research, 1,* 199–218.

Bies, R. J., & Shapiro, D. L (1988). Voice and justification: Their influence on procedural fairness judgments. *Academy of Management Journal, 31,* 676–685.

Blader, S. L., & Tyler, T. R. (2003). What constitutes fairness in work settings? A four-component model of procedural justice. *Human Resource Management Review, 13,* 107–126.

Blau, P. (1964). *Exchange and power in social life.* New York: Wiley.

Bobocel, D. R., & Holmvall, C. M. (2001). Are interactional justice and procedural justice different? Framing the debate. In S. Gilliland, D. Steiner, & D. Skarlicki (Eds.), *Theoretical and cultural perspectives on organizational justice* (pp. 85–108). Greenwich, CT: Information Age.

Brams, S. J., & Taylor, A. D. (1996). *Fair division: From cake-cutting to dispute resolution.* New York: Cambridge University Press.

Brehm, J. (1966). *A theory of psychological reactance.* New York: Academic Press.

Brockner, J. (2002). Making sense of procedural fairness: How high procedural fairness can reduce or heighten the influence of outcome favorability. *Academy of Management Review, 27,* 58–76.

Brockner, J., DeWitt, R. L., Grover, S., & Reed, T. (1990). When it is especially important to explain why: Factors affecting the relationship between managers' explanations of a layoff and survivors' reactions to the layoff. *Journal of Experimental Social Psychology, 26,* 389–407.

Brockner, J., Konovsky, M., Cooper-Schneider, R., Folger, R. Martin, C., & Bies, R. J. (1994). Interactive effects of procedural justice and outcome negativity on victims and survivors of job loss. *Academy of Management Journal, 37,* 397–409.

Brockner, J., & Wiesenfeld, B. M. (1996). An integrative framework for explaining reactions to decisions: Interactive effects of outcomes and procedures. *Psychological Bulletin, 120,* 189–208.

Byrne, Z. (1999, April). *How do procedural and interactional justice influence multiple levels of organizational outcomes?* Paper presented at the annual meeting of the Society for Industrial and Organizational Psychology. Atlanta, GA.

Byrne, Z. S., & Cropanzano, R. (2001). History of organizational justice: The founders speak. In R. Cropanzano (Ed.), *Justice in the workplace: From theory to practice* (pp. 3–21). Mahwah, NJ: Lawrence Erlbaum Associates.

Cohen, R. L. (1986). *Justice: Views from the social sciences.* New York: Plenum.

Cohen, R. L., & Greenberg, J. (1982). The justice concept in social psychology. In J. Greenberg & R. L. Cohen (Eds.), *Equity and justice in social behavior* (pp. 1–41). New York: Academic Press.

Collie, T., Bradley, G., & Sparks, B. A. (2002). Fair process revisited: Differential effects of interactional and procedural justice in the presence of social comparison information. *Journal of Experimental Social Psychology, 38,* 545–555.

Colquitt, J. A. (2001). On the dimensionality of organizational justice: A construct validation of a measure. *Journal of Applied Psychology, 86,* 386–400.

Colquitt, J. A., & Chertkoff, J. M. (2002). Explaining injustice: The interactive effect of explanation and outcome on fairness perceptions and task motivation. *Journal of Management, 28,* 591–610.

Colquitt, J. A., Conlon, D. E., Wesson, M. J., Porter, C. O. L. H., & Ng, K. Y. (2001). Justice at the millennium: A meta-analytic review of 25 years of organizational justice research. *Journal of Applied Psychology, 86,* 425–445.

Colquitt, J. A., & Greenberg, J. (2003). Organizational justice: A fair assessment of the state of the literature. In J. Greenberg (Ed.), *Organizational behavior: The state of the science* (2nd ed.) (pp. 165–210). Mahwah, NJ: Lawrence Erlbaum Associates.

Cropanzano, R., Byrne, Z. S., Bobocel, D. R., & Rupp, D. E. (2001). Moral virtues, fairness heuristics, social entities, and other denizens of organizational justice. *Journal of Vocational Behavior, 58,* 164–209.

Cropanzano, R., & Folger, R. (1989). Referent cognitions and task decision autonomy: Beyond equity theory. *Journal of Applied Psychology, 74,* 293–299.

Cropanzano, R., & Randall, M. L. (1993). Injustice and work behavior: A historical review. In R. Cropanzano (Ed.), *Justice in the workplace: Approaching fairness in human resource management* (pp. 3–20). Hillsdale, NJ: Lawrence Erlbaum Associates.

Cropanzano, R., Rupp, D. E., Mohler, C. J., & Schminke, M. (2001). Three roads to organizational justice. In G. R. Ferris (Ed.), *Research in personnel and human resource management* (Vol. 19, pp. 1–113). New York: Elsevier Science.

Crosby, F. (1976). A model of egoistical relative deprivation. *Psychological Review, 83,* 85–113.

Crosby, F. (1982). *Relative deprivation and working women.* New York: Oxford University Press.

Crosby, F. (1984). Relative deprivation in organizational settings. In L. L. Cummings & B. M. Staw (Eds.), *Research in organizational behavior* (Vol. 6, pp. 51–93). Greenwich, CT: JAI Press.

Dailey, R. C., & Kirk, D. J. (1992). Distributive and procedural justice as antecedents of job dissatisfaction and intent to turnover. *Human Relations, 45,* 305–317.

Daniels, N., Light, D., & Caplan, R. (1996). *Benchmarks of fairness for health care reform.* New York: Oxford University Press.

Davis, J. A. (1959). A formal interpretation of the theory of relative deprivation. *Sociometry, 22,* 280–296.

Deutsch, M. (1975). Equity, equality, and need: What determines which value will be used as the basis for distributive justice? *Journal of Social Issues, 31,* 137–149.

Dollard, J., Doob, L. W., Miller, N. E., Mowrer, O. H., & Sears, R. R. (1939). *Frustration and aggression.* New Haven, CT: Yale University Press.

Earley, P. C., & Lind, E. A. (1987). Procedural justice and participation in task selection: The role of control in mediating justice judgments. *Journal of Personality and Social Psychology, 52,* 1148–1160.

Elliott, G. C., & Meeker, B. F. (1986). Achieving fairness in the face of competing concerns: The different effects of individual and group characteristics. *Journal of Personality and Social Psychology, 50,* 754–760.

Farkas, A. J., & Anderson, N. H. (1979). Multidimensional input in equity theory. *Journal of Personality and Social Psychology, 37,* 879–896.

Feather, N. T. (2003). Distinguishing between deservingness and entitlement: Earned outcomes versus lawful outcomes. *European Journal of Social Psychology, 33*, 367–385.

Festinger, L. (1954). A theory of social comparison processes. *Human Relations, 7*, 117–140.

Festinger, L. (1957). *A theory of cognitive dissonance.* Evanston, IL: Row, Peterson.

Folger, R. (1977). Distributive and procedural justice: Combined impact of "voice" and improvement on experienced inequity. *Journal of Personality and Social Psychology, 35*, 108–119.

Folger, R. (1986a). A referent cognitions theory of relative deprivation. In J. M. Olson, C. P. Herman, & M. P. Zanna (Eds.), *Relative deprivation and social comparison: The Ontario symposium* (Vol. 4, pp. 33–55). Hillsdale, NJ: Lawrence Erlbaum Associates.

Folger, R. (1986b). Rethinking equity theory: A referent cognitions model. In H. W. Bierhoff, R. L. Cohen, & J. Greenberg (Eds.), *Research in social relations* (pp. 145–162). New York: Plenum Press.

Folger, R. (1987). Reformulating the preconditions of resentment: A referent cognitions model. In J. C. Masters & W. P. Smith (Eds.), *Social comparison, justice, and relative deprivation: Theoretical, empirical, and policy perspectives* (pp. 183–215). Hillsdale, NJ: Lawrence Erlbaum Associates.

Folger, R. (1993). Reactions to mistreatment at work. In K. Murnighan (Ed.), *Social psychology in organizations: Advances in theory and research* (pp. 161–183). Englewood Cliffs, NJ: Prentice Hall.

Folger, R. (1998). Fairness as a moral virtue. In M. Schminke (Ed.), *Managerial ethics: Morally managing people and processes* (pp. 13–34). Mahwah, NJ: Lawrence Erlbaum Associates.

Folger, R. (2001). Fairness as deonance. In S. W. Gilliland, D. D. Steiner, & D. P. Skarlicki (Eds.), *Theoretical and cultural perspectives on organizational justice* (pp. 3–34). Greenwich, CT: Information Age.

Folger, R., & Bies, R. J. (1989). Managerial responsibilities and procedural justice. *Responsibilities and Rights Journal, 2*, 79–89.

Folger, R., & Cropanzano, R. (1998). *Organizational justice and human resource management.* Thousand Oaks, CA: Sage.

Folger, R., & Cropanzano, R. (2001). Fairness theory: Justice as accountability. In J. Greenberg & R. Cropanzano (Eds.), *Advances in organizational justice* (pp. 89–118). Stanford, CA: Stanford University Press.

Folger, R., & Greenberg, J. (1985). Procedural justice: An interpretive analysis of personnel systems. In K. Rowland & G. Ferris (Eds.), *Research in personnel and human resources management* (Vol. 3, pp. 141–183). Greenwich, CT: JAI Press.

Folger, R., & Konovsky, M. A. (1989). Effects of procedural and distributive justice on reactions to pay raise decisions. *Academy of Management Journal, 32*, 115–130.

Folger, R., & Martin, C. (1986). Relative deprivation and referent cognitions: Distributive and procedural justice effects. *Journal of Experimental Social Psychology, 22*, 531–546.

Folger, R., Rosenfield, D., Grove, J., & Corkran, L. (1979). Effects of "voice" and peer opinions on responses to inequity. *Journal of Personality and Social Psychology, 37*, 2253–2261.

Folger, R., Rosenfield, D., & Robinson, T. (1983). Relative deprivation and procedural justifications. *Journal of Personality and Social Psychology, 45*, 268–273.

Gilliland, S. W., Groth, M., Baker, R. C. IV, Dew, A. F., Polly, L. M., & Langdon, J. C. (2001). Improving applicants' reactions to rejection letters: An application of fairness theory. *Personnel Psychology, 54,* 669–703.

Goodman, P. S., & Friedman, A. (1971). An examination of Adams' theory of inequity. *Administrative Science Quarterly, 16,* 271–288.

Gouldner, A. W. (1960). The norm of reciprocity: A preliminary statement. *American Sociological Review, 25,* 161–178.

Greenberg, J. (1978a). Equity, motivation, and effects of past reward on allocation decisions. *Personality and Social Psychology Bulletin, 4,* 131–134.

Greenberg, J. (1978b). Effects of reward value and retaliative power on allocation decisions: Justice, generosity, or greed? *Journal of Personality and Social Psychology, 36,* 367–379.

Greenberg, J. (1982). Approaching equity and avoiding inequity in groups and organizations. In J. Greenberg & R. L. Cohen (Eds.), *Equity and justice in social behavior* (pp. 389–435). New York: Academic Press.

Greenberg, J. (1986). Determinants of perceived fairness of performance evaluations. *Journal of Applied Psychology, 71,* 340–342.

Greenberg, J. (1987a). Reactions to procedural injustice in payment distributions: Do the means justify the ends? *Journal of Applied Psychology, 72,* 55–61.

Greenberg, J. (1987b). A taxonomy of organizational justice theories. *Academy of Management Review, 12,* 9–22.

Greenberg, J. (1988). Equity and workplace status: A field experiment. *Journal of Applied Psychology, 73,* 606–613.

Greenberg, J. (1989). Cognitive re-evaluation of outcomes in response to underpayment inequity. *Academy of Management Journal, 32,* 174–184.

Greenberg, J. (1990). Employee theft as a reaction to underpayment inequity: The hidden cost of paycuts. *Journal of Applied Psychology, 75,* 561–568.

Greenberg, J. (1993a). The social side of fairness: Interpersonal and informational classes of organizational justice. In R. Cropanzano (Ed.), *Justice in the workplace: Approaching fairness in human resource management* (pp. 79–103). Hillsdale, NJ: Lawrence Erlbaum Associates.

Greenberg, J. (1993b). Stealing in the name of justice: Informational and interpersonal moderators of theft reactions to underpayment inequity. *Organizational Behavior and Human Decision Processes, 54,* 81–103.

Greenberg, J. (1994). Using socially fair procedures to promote acceptance of a work site smoking ban. *Journal of Applied Psychology, 79,* 288–297.

Greenberg, J. (1996). *The quest for justice on the job.* Thousand Oaks, CA: Sage.

Greenberg, J., & Bies, R. J. (1992). Establishing the role of empirical studies of organizational justice in philosophical inquiries into business ethics. *Journal of Business Ethics, 11,* 433–444.

Greenberg, J., Bies, R. J., & Eskew, D. E. (1991). Establishing fairness in the eye of the beholder: Managing impressions of organizational justice. In R. Giacalone & P. Rosenfeld (Eds.), *Applied impression management: How image making affects managerial decisions* (pp. 111–132). Newbury Park, CA: Sage.

Greenberg, J., & Folger, R. (1983). Procedural justice, participation, and the fair process effect in groups and organizations. In P. B. Paulus (Ed.), *Basic group processes* (pp. 235–256). New York: Springer-Verlag.

Greenberg, J., & Leventhal, G. S. (1976). Equity and the use of overreward to motivate performance. *Journal of Personality and Social Psychology, 34,* 179–190.

Greenberg, J., & Lind, E. A. (2000). The pursuit of organizational justice: From conceptualization to implication to application. In C. L. Cooper & E. A. Locke (Eds.), *I/O psychology: What we know about theory and practice* (pp. 72–105). Oxford, England: Blackwell.

Greenberg, J., & Ornstein, S. (1983). High status job title as compensation for underpayment: A test of equity theory. *Journal of Applied Psychology, 68,* 285–297.

Harder, J. W. (1991). Equity theory versus expectancy theory: The case of major league baseball free agents. *Journal of Applied Psychology, 76,* 458–464.

Harris, R. J. (1976). Handling negative inputs: On the plausible equity formulae. *Journal of Experimental Social Psychology, 12,* 194–209.

Hatfield, E., Greenberger, D., Traupmann, J., & Lambert, P. (1982). Equity and sexual satisfaction in recently married couples. *Journal of Sex Research, 18,* 18–32.

Heider, F. (1958). *The psychology of interpersonal relations.* New York: Wiley.

Hirschman, A. O. (1970). *Exit, voice and loyalty: Responses to declines in firms, organizations, and states.* Cambridge, MA: Harvard University Press.

Hobbes, T. (1947). *Leviathan* (M. Oakeshott, Ed.). Oxford: Basil Blackwell. (Original work published 1651)

Homans, G. C. (1953). Status among clerical workers. *Human Organization, 12,* 5–10.

Homans, G. C. (1958). Social behavior as exchange. *American Journal of Sociology, 63,* 597–606.

Homans, G. C. (1961). *Social behaviour: Its elementary forms.* London: Routledge & Kegan Paul.

Homans, G. C. (1982). Foreword. In J. Greenberg & R. L. Cohen (Eds.), *Equity and justice in social behavior* (pp. xi–xviii). New York: Academic Press.

Judge, T. A., & Colquitt, J. A. (2004). Organizational justice and stress: The mediating role of work-family conflict. *Journal of Applied Psychology, 89,* 395–404.

Kanfer, R., Sawyer, J., Earley, P. C., & Lind, E. A. (1987). Participation in task evaluation procedures: The effects of influential opinion expression and knowledge of evaluative criteria on attitudes and performance. *Social Justice Research, 1,* 235–249.

Kanigel, R. (1997). *The one best way: Frederick Winslow Taylor and the enigma of efficiency.* New York: Viking.

Kernan, M. C., & Hanges, P. J. (2002). Survivor reactions to reorganization: Antecedents and consequences of procedural, interpersonal, and informational justice. *Journal of Applied Psychology, 87,* 916–928.

Konovsky, M. A., & Folger, R. (1987). Relative effects of procedural and distributive justice on employee attitudes. *Representative Research in Social Psychology, 17,* 15–24.

Kuhn, T. S. (1963). The essential tension: Tradition and innovation in scientific research. In C. W. Taylor & F. Barron (Eds.), *Scientific creativity: Its recognition and development* (pp. 18–30). New York: Wiley and Sons.

LaTour, S. (1978). Determinants of participant and observer satisfaction with adversary and inquisitorial models of adjudication. *Journal of Personality and Social Psychology, 36,* 1531–1545.

Lerner, M. J. (1977). The justice motive: Some hypotheses as to its origins and forms. *Journal of Personality, 45,* 1–52.

Leventhal, G. S. (1976a). The distribution of rewards and resources in groups and organizations. In L. Berkowitz & W. Walster (Eds.), *Advances in experimental social psychology* (Vol. 9, pp. 91–131). New York: Academic Press.

Leventhal, G. S. (1976b). Fairness in social relationships. In J. W. Thibaut, J. T. Spence, & R. C. Carson (Eds.), *Contemporary topics in social psychology* (pp. 211–239). Morristown, NJ: General Learning Press.

Leventhal, G. S. (1980). What should be done with equity theory? New approaches to the study of fairness in social relationships. In K. Gergen, M. Greenberg, & R. Willis (Eds.), *Social exchange: Advances in theory and research* (pp. 27–55). New York: Plenum Press.

Leventhal, G. S., Karuza, J., & Fry, W. R. (1980). Beyond fairness: A theory of allocation preferences. In G. Mikula (Ed.), *Justice and social interaction* (pp. 167–218). New York: Springer-Verlag.

Leventhal, G. S., Michaels, J. W., & Sanford, C. (1972). Inequity and interpersonal conflict: Reward allocation and secrecy about reward as methods of preventing conflict. *Journal of Personality and Social Psychology, 23,* 88–102.

Lind, E. A. (1992, April). *The fairness heuristic: Rationality and "relationality" in procedural evaluations.* Paper presented at the Fourth International Conference of the Society for the Advancement of Socio-Economics, Irvine, CA.

Lind, E. A. (1994). *Procedural justice, disputing, and reactions to legal authorities* (ABF Working Paper No. 9403). Chicago: American Bar Foundation.

Lind, E. A. (2001). Fairness heuristic theory: Justice judgments as pivotal cognitions in organizational relations. In J. Greenberg & R. Cropanzano (Eds.), *Advances in organizational justice* (pp. 56–88). Stanford, CA: Stanford University Press.

Lind, E. A., Greenberg, J., Scott, K. S., & Welchans, T. D. (2000). The winding road from employee to complainant: Situational and psychological determinants of wrongful termination claims. *Administrative Science Quarterly, 45,* 557–590.

Lind, E. A., Kanfer, R., & Earley, P. C. (1990). Voice, control, and procedural justice: Instrumental and noninstrumental concerns in fairness judgments. *Journal of Personality and Social Psychology, 59,* 952–959.

Lind, E. A., Kulik, C. T., Ambrose, M., & de Vera Park, M. V. (1993). Individual and corporate dispute resolution: Using procedural fairness as a decision heuristic. *Administrative Science Quarterly, 38,* 224–251.

Lind, E. A., Lissak, R. I., & Conlon, D. E. (1983). Decision control and process control effects on procedural fairness judgments. *Journal of Applied Social Psychology, 13,* 338–350.

Lind, E. A., & Tyler, T. R. (1988). *The social psychology of procedural justice.* New York: Plenum Press.

Lind, E. A., Tyler, T. R., & Huo, Y. J. (1997). Procedural context and culture: Variation in the antecedents of procedural justice judgments. *Journal of Personality and Social Psychology, 73,* 767–780.

Lind, E. A., & Van den Bos, K. (2002). When fairness works: Toward a general theory of uncertainty management. In B. M. Staw & R. M. Kramer (Eds.), *Research in organizational behavior* (Vol. 24, pp. 181–223). Boston: Elsevier.

Locke, J. (1994). *An essay concerning human understanding.* New York: Prometheus. (Original work published 1669)

Lord, R. G., & Hohenfeld, J. A. (1979). Longitudinal field assessment of equity effects on the performance of major league baseball players. *Journal of Applied Psychology 64,* 19–26.

Mannix, E. A., Neale, M. A., & Northcraft, G. B. (1995). Equity, equality, or need? The effects of organizational culture on the allocation of benefits and burdens. *Organizational Behavior and Human Decision Processes, 63,* 276–286.

Mansour-Cole, D. M., & Scott, S. G. (1998). Hearing it through the grapevine: The influence of source, leader-relations, and legitimacy on survivors' fairness perceptions. *Personnel Psychology, 51,* 25–54.

Martin, J. (1981). Relative deprivation: A theory of distributive injustice for an era of shrinking resources. In L. L. Cummings & B. M. Staw (Eds.), *Research in organizational behavior* (Vol. 3, pp. 53–107). Greenwich, CT: JAI Press.

Marx, K. (1978). Critique of the Gotha program. In R. C. Tucker (Ed.), *The Marx-Engels reader* (2nd ed., pp. 42–56). New York: Norton. (Original work published 1875)

Masterson, S. S., Lewis, K., Goldman, B. M., & Taylor, M. S. (2000). Integrating justice and social exchange: The differing effects of fair procedures and treatment on work relationships. *Academy of Management Journal, 43,* 738–748.

McFarlin, D. B., & Sweeney, P. D. (1992). Distributive and procedural justice as predictors of satisfaction with personal and organizational outcomes. *Academy of Management Journal, 35,* 626–637.

Meindl, J. R. (1989). Managing to be fair: An exploration of values, motives, and leadership. *Journal of Applied Psychology, 34,* 252–276.

Merton, R., & Rossi, A. S. (1957). Contributions to the theory of reference group behavior. In R. Merton (Ed.), *Social theory and social structure* (pp. 3–19). New York: Free Press.

Mill, J. S. (1940). *Utilitarianism, liberty, and responsive government.* London: J. M. Dent. (Original work published 1861)

Miner, J. B. (2003). The rated importance, scientific validity, and practical usefulness of organizational behavior theories: A quantitative review. *Academy of Management Learning and Education, 2,* 250–268.

Moorman, R. H. (1991). Relationship between organizational justice and organizational citizenship behaviors: Do fairness perceptions influence employee citizenship? *Journal of Applied Psychology, 76,* 845–855.

Moschetti, G. J. (1979). Calculating equity: Ordinal and ratio criteria. *Social Psychology Quarterly, 42,* 172–176.

Mowday, R. T. (1979). Equity theory predictions of behavior in organizations. In R. M. Steers & L. W. Porter (Eds.), *Motivation and work behavior* (pp. 53–71). New York: Academic Press.

Mowday, R. T., & Colwell, K. A. (2003). Employee reactions to unfair outcomes in the workplace: The contributions of equity theory to understanding work motivation. In L. W. Porter, G. A. Bigley, & R. M. Steers (Eds.), *Motivation and work behavior* (pp. 65–113). Boston: McGraw-Hill Irwin.

Niehoff, B. P., & Moorman, R. H. (1993). Justice as a mediator of the relationship between methods of monitoring and organizational citizenship behavior. *Academy of Management Journal, 36,* 527–556.

Nozick, R. (1974). *Anarchy, state, and utopia.* New York: Basic Books.

Organ, D. W. (1990). The motivational basis of organizational citizenship behavior. In L. L. Cummings & B. M. Staw (Eds.), *Research in organizational behavior* (Vol. 12, pp. 43–72). Greenwich, CT: JAI Press.

Pritchard, R. D. (1969). Equity theory: A review and critique. *Organizational Behavior and Human Decision Processes, 4,* 176–211.

Rawls, J. (1999). *A theory of justice,* revised edition. Cambridge, MA: Harvard University Press.

Rawls, J. (2001). *Justice as fairness: A restatement.* Cambridge, MA: Harvard University Press.

54 COLQUITT, GREENBERG, ZAPATA-PHELAN

Reis, H. T. (1986). Levels of interest in the study of interpersonal justice. In H. W. Bierhoff, R. L. Cohen, & J. Greenberg (Eds.), *Justice in social relations* (pp. 187–226). New York: Plenum.
Romer, D. (1977). Limitations in the equity theory approach: Toward a resolution of the "negative inputs" controversy. *Personality and Social Psychology Bulletin, 3*, 228–231.
Ross, W. D. (1925). *The Oxford translation of Aristotle, Vol. IX, The Nichomachean ethics.* London: Oxford Press.
Rupp, D. E., & Cropanzano, R. (2002). The mediating effects of social exchange relationships in predicting workplace outcomes from multifoci organizational justice. *Organizational Behavior and Human Decision Processes, 89*, 925–946.
Sadker, M., & Sadker, D. (1995). *Failing at fairness: How America's schools cheat girls.* New York: Scribner.
Samuel, W. (1978). Toward a simple but useful equity theory: A comment on the Romer article. *Personality and Social Psychology Bulletin, 4*, 135–138.
Skarlicki, D. P., & Latham, G. P. (1997). Leadership training in organizational justice to increase citizenship behavior within a labor union: A replication. *Personnel Psychology, 50*, 617–633.
Smith, H. J., Tyler, T. R., Huo, Y. J., Ortiz, D. J., & Lind, E. A. (1998). The self-relevant implications of the group-value model: Group membership, self-worth, and treatment quality. *Journal of Experimental Social Psychology, 34*, 470–493.
Sober, E., & Wilson, D. S. (1998). *Unto others: The evolution and psychology of unselfish behavior.* Cambridge, MA: Harvard University Press.
Stouffer, S. A., Suchman, E. A., DeVinney, L. C., Star, S. A., & Williams, R. M., Jr. (1949). *The American soldier: Adjustment during Army life, Volume I.* Clinton, MA: Colonial Press.
Sturman, T. S., & Thibodeau, R. (2001). Performance-undermining effects of baseball free agent contracts. *Journal of Sport and Exercise Psychology, 23*, 23–36.
Sweeney, P. D., & McFarlin, D. B. (1993). Workers' evaluations of the "ends" and the "means": An examination of four models of distributive and procedural justice. *Organizational Behavior and Human Decision Processes, 55*, 23–40.
Thibaut, J., & Walker, L. (1975). *Procedural justice: A psychological analysis.* Hillsdale, NJ: Lawrence Erlbaum Associates.
Thibaut, J., & Walker, L. (1978). A theory of procedure. *California Law Review, 66*, 541–566.
Thibaut, J., Walker, L., LaTour, S., & Houlden, P. (1974). Procedural justice as fairness. *Stanford Law Review, 26*, 1271–1289.
Thibaut, J., Walker, L., & Lind, E. A. (1972). Adversary presentation and bias in legal decision-making. *Harvard Law Review, 86*, 386–401.
Tyler, T. R. (1987). Conditions leading to value-expressive effects in judgments of procedural justice: A test of four models. *Journal of Personality and Social Psychology, 52*, 333–344.
Tyler, T. R. (1989). The psychology of procedural justice: A test of the group-value model. *Journal of Personality and Social Psychology, 57*, 830–838.
Tyler, T. R. (1994). Psychological models of the justice motive: Antecedents of distributive and procedural justice. *Journal of Personality and Social Psychology, 67*, 850–863.
Tyler, T. R. (1997). The psychology of legitimacy: A relational perspective on voluntary deference to authorities. *Personality and Social Psychology Review, 1*, 323–345.

Tyler, T. R., & Bies, R. J. (1990). Beyond formal procedures: The interpersonal context of procedural justice. In J. Carroll (Ed.), *Applied social psychology and organizational settings* (pp. 77–98). Hillsdale, NJ: Lawrence Erlbaum Associates.

Tyler, T. R., & Blader, S. L. (2000). *Cooperation in groups: Procedural justice, social identity, and behavioral engagement.* Philadelphia: Psychology Press.

Tyler, T. R., & Blader, S. L. (2002). Autonomous vs. comparative status: Must we be better than others to feel good about ourselves? *Organizational Behavior and Human Decision Processes, 89,* 813–838.

Tyler, T. R., & Blader, S. L. (2003). The group engagement model: Procedural justice, social identity, and cooperative behavior. *Personality and Social Psychology Review, 7,* 349–361.

Tyler, T. R., & Caine, A. (1981). The influence of outcomes and procedures on satisfaction with formal leaders. *Journal of Personality and Social Psychology, 41,* 642–655.

Tyler, T. R., Degoey, P., & Smith, H. (1996). Understanding why the justice of group procedures matters: A test of the psychological dynamics of the group-value model. *Journal of Personality and Social Psychology, 70,* 913–930.

Tyler, T. R., & Lind, E. A. (1992). A relational model of authority in groups. In M. P. Zanna (Ed.), *Advances in experimental social psychology* (Vol. 25, pp. 115–191). San Diego, CA: Academic Press.

Tyler, T. R., Rasinski, K. A., & Spodick, N. (1985). Influence of voice on satisfaction with leaders: Exploring the meaning of process control. *Journal of Personality and Social Psychology, 48,* 72–81.

Van den Bos, K. (2001a). Fairness heuristic theory: Assessing the information to which people are reacting has a pivotal role in understanding organizational justice. In S. Gilliland, D. Steiner, & D. Skarlicki (Eds.), *Theoretical and cultural perspectives on organizational justice* (pp. 63–84). Greenwich, CT: Information Age.

Van den Bos, K. (2001b). Uncertainty management: The influence of uncertainty salience on reactions to perceived procedural fairness. *Journal of Personality and Social Psychology, 80,* 931–941.

Van den Bos, K., & Lind, E. A. (2002). Uncertainty management by means of fairness judgments. In M. P. Zanna (Ed.), *Advances in experimental social psychology* (Vol. 34, pp. 1–60). Boston: Elsevier.

Van den Bos, K., E. A. Lind, & Wilke, H. A. M. (2001). The psychology of procedural and distributive justice viewed from the perspective of fairness heuristic theory. In R. Cropanzano (Ed.), *Justice in the workplace* (Vol. 2, pp. 49–66). Mahwah, NJ: Lawrence Erlbaum Associates.

Van den Bos, K., & Miedema, J. (2000). Toward understanding why fairness matters: The influence of mortality salience of reactions to procedural fairness. *Interpersonal Relations and Group Processes, 79,* 355–366.

Van den Bos, K., & Van Prooijen, J.-W. (2001). Referent cognitions theory: The role of closeness of reference points in the psychology of voice. *Journal of Personality and Social Psychology, 81,* 616–626.

Van den Bos, K., Vermunt, R., & Wilke, H. A. M. (1997). Procedural and distributive justice: What is fair depends more on what comes first than on what comes next. *Journal of Personality and Social Psychology, 72,* 95–104.

Van den Bos, K., Wilke, H. A. M., & Lind, E. A. (1998). When do we need procedural fairness? The role of trust in authority. *Journal of Personality and Social Psychology, 75,* 1449–1458.

Walker, L., LaTour, S., Lind, E. A., & Thibaut, J. (1974). Reactions of participants and observers to modes of adjudication. *Journal of Applied Social Psychology, 4,* 295–310.

Walker, L., Lind, E. A., & Thibaut, J. (1979). The relation between procedural and distributive justice. *Virginia Law Review, 65,* 1401–1420.

Walster, E., Berscheid, E., & Walster, G. W. (1973). New directions in equity research. *Journal of Personality and Social Psychology, 25,* 151–176.

Walster, E., Walster, G. W., & Berscheid, E. (1978). *Equity: Theory and research.* Boston: Allyn & Bacon.

Weick, K. E. (1966). The concept of equity in the perception of pay. *Administrative Science Quarterly, 11,* 414–439.

II

CONSTRUCT VALIDITY ISSUES

2

Are Procedural Justice and Distributive Justice Conceptually Distinct?

Maureen L. Ambrose
University of Central Florida

Anke Arnaud
University of Central Florida

In this chapter we address the question of whether distributive fairness and procedural fairness are conceptually distinct. We organize the chapter in three parts. First, we argue that the literature supports the conceptual distinction between distributive fairness and procedural fairness. Second, we suggest that underlying the interest in the conceptual status of distributive and procedural fairness is not whether they are conceptually distinct, but how they are related. We suggest that too often researchers ignore the interdependence of these distinct constructs. Finally, we conclude the chapter by suggesting that justice research might be better served by focusing on perceptions of overall fairness and its effect relative to other psychological constructs.

When we were first asked to write this chapter for the *Handbook of Organizational Justice,* one of our first thoughts was, "Hasn't that already been done? (e.g., Cropanzano & Ambrose, 2001). Thus, one of the issues we considered as we undertook this chapter was whether there was a need for another chapter that addresses this issue. Is there anything new to be said about the conceptual distinction between procedural and distributive fairness? As will be clear, we agree with Cropanzano and Ambrose's assessment of the relationship between distributive and procedural fairness. However, our current thinking has been influenced by a variety of recent work. And that work takes us in a new direction.

In this chapter, we take a different approach to this issue than Cropanzano and Ambrose (2001) have, although we concur with their analysis and conclusions and we return to some of their thoughts later in this chapter. However, we begin by considering the conceptual distinctness of distributive and procedural fairness by following the lead of Bobocel and Homvall (2001) in their consideration of the conceptual status of procedural and interactional justice.

FOUR KEY QUESTIONS

Drawing on Schwab's (1980) discussion of construct validity, Bobocel and Homvall identified four questions to guide the assessment of constructs as conceptually distinct: Does theory distinguish between the constructs? Can the constructs be operationalized and measured independently? Do the constructs have different effects? Do the constructs have different antecedents? When researchers can find positive support for each of these questions, the value of distinguishing two constructs becomes meaningful and important. We address each question next.

Does Theory Distinguish Between
Distributive Justice and Procedural Justice?

In considering whether distributive justice and procedural justice are distinct, it is useful to examine the evolution of research on organizational justice. Early justice research examined distributive justice; this work focused on the perceived fairness of outcomes (e.g., Adams, 1963, 1965; Dittrich & Carrell, 1979; Mowday, 1987). In the 1970s and 1980s, research by Thibaut and Walker (1975) and Leventhal (1980; Leventhal, Karuza, & Fry, 1980) changed the way researchers thought about fairness by introducing the procedure as a relevant component in individuals' assessment of fairness. Since that time, researchers have distinguished between distributive and procedural fairness.

Distributive Justice Theories. The dominant theory of distributive justice is Adams's equity theory (1963, 1965). According to equity theory, people compare the ratio of their inputs and outcomes to the ratio of inputs and outcomes of referent others. Distributions are fair to the extent that rewards are proportionally matched to contributions. Equity is an allocation norm—a social rule that specifies the criteria that define certain distributions of rewards and resources as fair and just (Leventhal, 1976a).

Subsequent research on the fairness of outcomes (Deutsch, 1985; Leventhal, 1980) identified three allocation norms: equity (distribute rewards in accordance with contributions), equality (give all recipients the same), and need (give more to recipients with greater need) (Leventhal, 1976a). Distributive fairness was defined as "judgments of fair distribution, irrespective of whether the criterion of justice is based on needs, equality, contributions, or a combination of these factors" (Leventhal, 1980, p. 29).

It is worth noting that early work on equity, equality, and need norms did not focus primarily on fairness. Rather, the work considered the motivational effects of different allocation decisions (cf. Leventhal, 1976a; Mowday, 1987). The focus on allocation rules as a basis for fairness judgments came later (e.g., Leventhal, 1980). Additionally, the research that identified allocation norms generally predates the introduction of procedural justice as a construct. Thus, the distinctness of the definitions of distributive and procedural justice is left to procedural justice theorists.

Procedural Justice Theories. Contemporary research on procedural justice generally has its roots in one of three approaches: Thibaut and Walker's (1975, 1978) theory of procedure, Leventhal's (1976b, 1980) justice judgment theory, or Lind and Tyler's (1988) group value model. For each of these theories, we consider the conceptualization of distributive and procedural justice.

Thibaut and Walker's Theory of Procedure.   Thibaut and Walker's (1975) seminal work focused on methods that might be used to resolve conflicts between individuals and between groups. Their primary interest was in third-party decision making and legal procedures. Walker, Lind, and Thibaut defined procedural fairness as "the belief that the techniques used to resolve a dispute are fair and satisfying in themselves" (1979, p. 1402). Distributive justice is defined as "concerned with identifying the principles by which anything of value (money, goods, services, privileges, and so forth) can be fairly or equitably allocated among persons or groups" (Thibaut & Walker, 1975, p. 3).

Leventhal's Justice Judgment Model.   In his theory of justice judgments, Leventhal (1980) defined procedural fairness as "an individual's perception of the fairness of the procedural components of the social system that regulate the allocative process" (p. 35). Individuals are posited to form procedural justice judgments using six decision rules: consistency, bias suppression, accuracy, correctability, representativeness, and ethicality. Procedures are deemed to be fair to the extent that they exhibit these six characteristics. Leventhal distinguished procedural fairness from distributive fairness, which he defined as "judgments of fair distribution" (1980, p. 29).

The Group-Value Model.   Lind and Tyler (1988; Tyler & Lind, 1992) suggested an alternative theoretical approach to understanding fairness. The group value model (subsequently known as the relational model) suggests individuals care about fairness because of their relationship with the groups to which they belong. Tyler and Lind (1992) identified two types of justice models: distributive and procedural. They noted that distributive justice theories address individuals' concerns about outcome fairness. Procedural justice theories focus on how decisions are made (p. 122).

Although theories of procedural justice may differ in *why* they posit that fair procedures are important (see Cropanzano, Rupp, Mohler, & Schminke, 2001, for a review), all the theories distinguish between the fairness of the procedures and the fairness of outcomes. Thus, the answer to the first question is yes. There are distinct theoretical definitions for distributive and procedural justice.

Can Distributive Justice and Procedural Justice Be Operationalized and Measured Independently?

For this question, we consider two issues: experimental operationalizations of distributive and procedural justice, and questionnaire measures of distributive and procedural justice.

Experimental Manipulations: Distributive Justice. Most research on distributive justice has examined equity. This research operationalizes equity by pairing individual inputs with outcomes. Early studies investigated reactions to pay inequity. In simulated work environments, researchers asked subjects to complete clerical tasks such as proofreading and interviewing (e.g., Garland, 1973; Pritchard, Dunnette, & Jorgenson, 1972). Equity was manipulated either by telling subjects that other equally qualified employees were paid more or less than themselves for doing the same task/job or by manipulating the subjects' perceived qualifications to be hired for the task. Equity research has also considered the effect of organizational rewards other than pay. For example, Greenberg and Ornstein (1983) paired individuals' work responsibility and job title. Greenberg (1988a) operationalized inequity by pairing individuals' position with office size.

Operationalization of equality and need has been somewhat different. Much of this work focuses on cross-cultural differences in reactions to different distribution norms (Chen, 1995; Leung & Bond, 1984). Experimental research has examined both how individuals choose to allocate resources to others as well as how they respond to resource allocations. The two dominant approaches are role-plays and scenarios. For example, research has used role-plays in which participants allocated outcomes to their "subordinates." This research also assessed participants' reactions to the outcomes they received under different distributive rules (Giacobbe-Miller, Miller, & Victorov, 1998; Linkey & Alexander, 1998; Miller & Komorita, 1995). It is also common for participants to respond to scenario descriptions of allocations based on equity, equality, or need (Boldizar, Perry, & Perry, 1988; Drake & Lawrence, 2000; Kashima, Siegal, Tanaka, & Isaka, 1988).

Experimental Manipulations: Procedural Justice. Early work on procedural justice was conducted primarily in experimental settings. Thibaut and Walker's (1975) work on dispute resolution compared procedures that differed with respect to two types of control: (a) disputants' amount of control used to settle grievances (process control) and (b) disputants' amount of control over directly determining outcomes (decision control). Subsequent research frequently operationalized procedural fairness in terms of process control (e.g., Folger, 1977; Kanfer, Sawyer, Earley, & Lind, 1987; Lind, Kurtz, Musante, Walker, & Thibaut, 1980). However, some research has manipulated other attributes of procedures such as consistency (Schminke, Ambrose, & Noel, 1997).

Questionnaire Measures: Distributive Justice. Measures of distributive justice are relatively consistent across studies. As with the experimental work on distributive justice, most have focused on equity.

Equity-based measures of distributive justice include items that refer people to an outcome and ask them to assess the fairness of the particular outcome given their contributions (Colquitt, 2001; Lind et al., 1989; McFarlin & Sweeney, 1992; Moorman, 1991; Price & Meuller, 1986). Measures of equality and need norms have asked respondents to rate the fairness of the allocation (Chiu, 1990; Giacobbe-Miller et al., 1998; Kashima, Siegal, Tanaka, & Isaka, 1988; Wagstaff, Huggins, & Perfect, 1993) or their preference for the distribution (Chen, 1995).

Questionnaire Measures: Procedural Justice.   Measures of procedural justice are more varied and reflect the theoretical traditions from which they flow. Much of the early research on procedural justice stemmed from Thibaut and Walker's (1975) work and focused on the influence of voice on perceptions of fairness. This research assessed process control (the ability to voice opinions during the process) and sometimes decision control (the ability to influence outcomes). These assessments were often manipulation checks in experimental work. Additionally, this research usually assessed individuals' fairness and satisfaction with procedures and outcomes. In early work, fairness and satisfaction items were usually combined and considered a measure of fairness (Kanfer et al., 1987; Lind & Lissak, 1985; Lind, Lissak, & Conlon, 1983). However, recently van den Bos, Wilke, Lind, and Vermunt (1998) demonstrated that fairness and satisfaction are affected differently by process control, suggesting this combination may not be appropriate (see also Colquitt & Shaw, this volume).

Other measures of procedural justice were designed to assess perceptions of fairness based on Leventhal's (1980) procedural rules (Barrett-Howard & Tyler, 1986; Colquitt, 2001; Folger & Konovsky, 1989). Another set of measures is based on the relational theory of justice and includes criteria such as trust in authority, neutrality of decision maker, and standing (Tyler & Lind, 1992).

Although measures of procedural justice differ in how they operationalize procedural justice, research demonstrates that the constructs can be adequately measured. Recent meta-analyses indicate that distributive justice and procedural justice measures can be distinguished from one another (Cohen-Charash & Spector, 2001; Colquitt, Conlon, Wesson, Porter, & Ng, 2001; Hauenstein, McGonigle, & Flinder, 2001). However, there are several issues surrounding the measurement of justice that warrant attention (e.g., direct vs. indirect measures, conceptual overlap in measures, ad hoc measures). (For a comprehensive review of these issues, see Colquitt & Shaw, this volume.) Nonetheless, although distributive and procedural justice may not always be adequately operationalized and measured, it is possible to do so. Moreover, proper

operationalizations demonstrate that the two constructs are distinguishable. The answer to the second question is yes.

Do Distributive Justice and Procedural Justice Have Different Effects?

Distinct constructs should differ in their relationships with relevant criterion variables or link to different criterion variables altogether. One of the most widely accepted propositions in justice research is that procedural justice has especially strong effects on global attitudes whereas distributive justice has strong effects on attitudes about specific outcomes. Lind and Tyler (1988) first suggested this relationship in their seminal work on procedural justice. They concluded, "Procedural justice has especially strong effects on attitudes about institutions or authorities as opposed to attitudes about the specific outcome in question" (p. 179). This approach was designated the *two-factor model*.

Explicit tests of the two-factor model support this conceptualization (Folger & Konovsky, 1989; Sweeney & McFarlin, 1993). Additionally, recent meta-analyses generally support these predictions (Cohen-Charash & Spector, 2001; Colquitt et al., 2001). Distributive justice is more strongly related to specific attitudes (e.g., pay satisfaction, job satisfaction), whereas procedural justice is more strongly related to global attitudes (e.g., organizational commitment, group commitment). (See Conlon, this volume, for a more comprehensive discussion of these differential effects.)

Recently, Cohen-Charash and Spector (2001) suggested the differential effects of distributive justice and procedural justice affect not only attitudes, but behavioral reactions as well. However, the research on behavioral reactions is less clear (Cohen-Charash & Spector, 2001; Colquitt et al., 2001). Justice research that examines withdrawal (including absenteeism, turnover and neglect) generally has not shown differential effects (Colquitt et al., 2001). Findings with regard to the relationship between performance and the two justice concepts have been mixed (Gilliland, 1994; Kanfer et al., 1987; Keller & Dansereau, 1995; Konovsky & Cropanzano, 1991). However, meta-analyses find job performance more closely linked to procedural justice than distributive justice (Cohen-Charash & Spector, 2001; Colquitt et al., 2001).

Research on organizational citizenship behavior (OCB) has focused more on procedural justice than distributive justice, sometimes considering only the former (cf. Moorman, Blakely, & Niehoff, 1998). Early research suggested that OCBs were more strongly related to procedural justice than distributive justice (Ball, Trevino, & Sims, 1994; Moorman, 1991). However, meta-analyses demonstrate this effect only for individually oriented OCBs (Cohen-Charash & Spector, 2001; Colquitt et al., 2001).

Not all research demonstrates clear differences between the outcomes associated with distributive justice and those associated with procedural justice. However, research generally suggests the two differentially affect outcomes in theoretically predictable ways, particularly in relation to attitudes. Thus, the answer to the third question is yes.

Do Distributive Justice and Procedural Justice Have Different Antecedents?

In order for distributive justice and procedural justice to be considered distinct constructs, they need to have unique sets of antecedents. We first consider the antecedents of distributive justice.

Distributive Justice Antecedents. Research has identified a variety of relevant organizational outcomes that affect perceptions of distributive justice: pay, benefits, punishments, security, job complexity, supervision, rewards intrinsic to the job, seniority benefits, fringe benefits, and job status and status symbols (Adams, 1963; Cropanzano & Greenberg, 1997; Oldham, Kulik, Ambrose, Stepina, & Brand, 1986). Of course, from an equity theory perspective, these outcomes must be coupled with an individual's assessment of their relevant inputs (e.g., effort, expertise, organizational tenure, subject knowledge) and compared to the relevant inputs and outcomes of a referent other.

Procedural Justice Antecedents. Research on antecedents of procedural justice demonstrates that the opportunity to provide information (voice) during the decision-making process increases perceptions of procedural justice (Kanfer et al., 1987; Lind, Lissak, & Conlon, 1983). Further, voice positively influences judgments of procedural justice independent of outcome favorability (Lind & Tyler, 1988; see Shapiro, 1993, 2001, for a discussion of the instrumental and non-instrumental value of voice). Additionally, several of Leventhal's principles of fairness, including consistency, bias suppression, accuracy of information, correctability, representativeness, and ethicality, predict people's judgments of procedural justice. Research demonstrates judgments of procedural justice are affected by consistency (Barrett-Howard & Tyler, 1986; Greenberg, 1986b; Singer, 1989), accuracy (Cornelius, 1985; Greenberg, 1986b), correctability (Greenberg, 1986b), bias avoidance, ethicality, and choice of selectors (Singer, 1989).

A problem with the procedural antecedents is that the source and content of justice perceptions are frequently confused—researchers use measures of antecedents (indirect measures) as measures of perceived procedural fairness (direct measures). (For a discussion, see Greenberg,

1990; also see Bobocel & Holmvall, 2001, and Colquitt et al., 2001.) For example, process control and voice are antecedents of the procedural justice construct: Whether employees have the opportunity to express their opinion during a decision-making process affects whether they will perceive processes as fair or not. Nevertheless, frequently procedural judgment measures include items that assess the availability of voice. Similarly, Leventhal's six procedural rules are used to measure procedural judgment, yet these rules represent antecedents of procedural justice.

Despite the measurement limitations, there is empirical evidence that suggests that procedural justice and distributive justice have different antecedents. Thus, the answer to the fourth question is yes.

THE INTERDEPENDENCE OF DISTRIBUTIVE AND PROCEDURAL JUSTICE

If the bulk of the existing justice research suggests that distributive and procedural fairness are conceptually distinct, why then is this an issue worthy of inclusion in the first *Handbook of Organizational Justice*? It seems clear that when individuals are asked specific questions about the fairness of outcomes and the fairness of procedures, they can distinguish between them in systematic and meaningful ways. We believe the real interest is not in how they are different, but in how they are related. In the next section we consider this issue.

The Relationship Between Distributive and Procedural Justice

Most justice researchers accept that distributive justice and procedural justice are distinct constructs. However, they also treat them as though they are completely independent. Herein lies the problem. Although the constructs are distinct, they are not independent. Indeed, justice research indicates that these two constructs are strongly related. Recent meta-analyses indicate a relationship of between .57 and .77 for the two constructs (Cohen-Charash & Spector, 2001; Colquitt et al., 2001; Hauenstein et al., 2001).

These correlations highlight the strong relationship between the two types of fairness; although this relationship is usually ignored in both theoretical and empirical research, some researchers have considered the source of the commonality. Here we identify two theoretical explanations for the observed correlations that have emerged in the literature: (a) Distributive fairness and procedural fairness are functionally the same, and (b) distributive fairness and procedural fairness are functionally different, but substitutable.

Distributive Justice and Procedural Justice Are Functionally the Same.
One school of thought on the relationship between distributive and procedural fairness is captured by Cropanzano and Ambrose (2001). Cropanzano and Ambrose (2001) considered the role of procedural justice in two dominant approaches to fairness: the instrumental (or self-interest model) and the relational (formerly group value model). The instrumental view of procedural justice arises from the early work of Thibaut and Walker (1975). The underlying assumption of this work is that individuals are self-interested and their interest in fairness reflects this self-interest. From this perspective, individuals prefer fair procedures (those that offer the opportunity for control) because in the long run these procedures are most likely to provide favorable (economic) outcomes. Thus, procedures that offer the most favorable future outcomes are evaluated as the most fair (Lind & Tyler, 1988; Greenberg, 1990; Shapiro, 1993). Procedural justice, in the self-interest model, is a way to ensure positive—usually economic—outcomes.

The relational model of procedural justice takes a different perspective on why individuals prefer fair procedures (Tyler & Lind, 1992). The relational model suggests the fair procedures are those that convey to the recipient that he or she is a valued member of the group. This group membership can endow an individual with a sense of worth and dignity. Cropanzano and Ambrose (2001) argued that in the relational model, fair procedures provide positive socioemotional outcomes.

Cropanzano and Ambrose (2001) concluded that "procedural justice and distributive justice could be conceptualized as functionally similar" (p. 125). Both perceptions of distributive fairness and perceptions of procedural fairness are derived from individuals' expectations about outcomes. Distributive fairness generally focuses on economic outcomes, although socioemotional outcomes may also be considered (cf. Foa & Foa, 1974; Markovsky, 1985). In the self-interest model, procedural justice concerns economic outcomes, as procedural justice serves as a proxy for fair and favorable outcomes. In the relational model, procedural justice generally focuses on socioemotional outcomes. Cropanzano and Ambrose (2001) suggest that by explicitly considering these two types of outcomes, the similarity between distributive and procedural fairness becomes more apparent.

Although Cropanzano and Ambrose (2001) provided the most comprehensive discussion of the conceptual similarities between procedural fairness and distributive fairness, it is worth noting that other researchers have noted these similarities as well. For example, Shapiro (2001) noted the *"intertwinement* of noninstrumental (relational) and instrumental feelings" (p. 240). Greenberg (2001) suggested that the motives underlying justice can all be construed as stemming from self-interest. These researchers recognize that there

is benefit to focusing on similarities as well as differences across types of justice.

This "functionally the same" approach, which suggests that distributive justice and procedural justice are both about outcomes, is thus able to account for the high correlation between procedural and distributive fairness in two ways. First, if procedural justice is a surrogate for distributive justice, both constructs tap the same perceptions and are thus related. Second, it is likely that "fair" organizations distribute fair economic outcomes as well as fair socioemotional outcomes (Koys, 1988). Thus, although procedural and distributive justice are sampling from different sets of organizational actions, these actions share a common motivation, which is captured in both assessments. In either case, procedural fairness perceptions and distributive fairness perceptions should be highly correlated.

Distributive Justice and Procedural Justice Are Substitutable. A second approach to understanding the relationship between distributive and procedural justice is outlined by Lind (2001) in his most recent discussion of fairness heuristic theory. Lind suggested that procedural, distributive, and interactional fairness experiences all contribute to the development of a general fairness judgment. This general fairness judgment then guides individuals' interpretation of future justice-relevant events as well as individuals' attitudes and behavior.

What is crucial in Lind's conceptualization is the relationship between the distinct justice experiences and a general fairness judgment. Lind (2001) noted that while "previous work by myself and others has generally viewed different forms of justice judgments as distinct in both their antecedents and their consequences ... the various forms of fairness are far more fungible than one would think from existing work on the organizational and social justice judgments" (p. 69). He suggested that while individuals can clearly distinguish between the sources of their justice experiences when asked, what drives behavior is an overall sense of fairness.

Lind's (2001) fairness heuristic theory suggests a two-stage process: the judgment phase and the use phase. In the judgment phase, individuals rely on their justice experience to form a general fairness judgment. In the use phase, this general fairness judgment drives subsequent fairness judgments as well as other outcomes (e.g., prosocial behavior, trust, identification). Fairness heuristic theory maintains that individuals make this general fairness judgment very quickly. The general fairness judgment is based on the information available—be it procedural, interactional, or distributive—when the initial fairness judgment is made. Once made, the general judgment is resistant to change. (See Lind, 2001, for a thorough discussion of the theory.)

For our purpose, the critical aspect of Lind's (2001) conceptualization is the "substitutability effect." Recall that the general fairness judgment becomes the basis for subsequent justice evaluations. Thus, the different types of justice can substitute for one another through the general fairness judgment. For example, if procedural fairness information is available during the judgment phase, and distributive fairness information is missing, the procedural information is used to form the general fairness judgment. The general fairness judgment then becomes the foundation for subsequent distributive fairness judgments. In essence, procedural information "substitutes" for the distributive information. Recent work by Lind and his colleagues provides empirical support for the substitutability effect (van den Bos, Wilke, Lind & Vermunt, 1997, 1998).

How does the "different but substitutable" approach account for the high correlation between procedural and distributive fairness? As noted earlier, after the general fairness judgment is made, individuals rely on this general justice judgment to make judgments about different types of fairness. Because the foundation for distributive justice perceptions and procedural justice perceptions is the same general fairness judgment, the two will be related.

Can There Be Distributive Justice Without Procedural Justice?

We would like to take a brief side trip at this point to address an issue we think is also related to the conceptual distinction between distributive and procedural justice. Can one have fair outcomes without fair procedures? Early justice researchers differed in their beliefs about this. Leventhal et al. (1980) suggested that outcomes flow from the distribution rules. Consequently, there cannot be fair outcomes without fair procedures. Thibaut and Walker (1975) disagreed. They stated, "Although procedural justice may often lead to and produce distributive justice, it is possible for distributive justice to be achieved without the application of any special procedure, as when all parties spontaneously agree about a fair allocation" (p. 3). In the early stages of work on procedural justice, the answer to this question was not clear. However, now there is sufficient data to address the issue.

It would seem that the easy answer to this question is yes. Clearly, if individuals can distinguish between procedural fairness and distributive fairness, it is possible for there to be one without the other. However, research is not consistent with this conclusion.

We first examine the relationship between procedural justice and distributive justice in field settings. In field settings, it may be difficult to tease apart the relationship between procedural justice and distributive

2. PROCEDURAL AND DISTRIBUTIVE JUSTICE

justice because individuals' responses occur in an uncontrolled context. For example, research identifies elements of fairness as a central attribute of organizational culture (Chatman & Jehn, 1994). This aspect of organizational culture is likely to be reflected both in procedures and in allocations. Additionally, individuals' assessments of a focal procedure are influenced by their experience with other organizational procedures. This previous experience (and their general fairness judgment) influences how they assess both the procedure and the outcome. Thus, the notably strong relationship between procedural and distributive justice is not surprising (weighted $r = .55$, Cohen-Charash & Spector, 2001; $r = .63$, Hauenstein et al., 2001).

The most straightforward test of this proposition comes from laboratory studies. In laboratory experiments, researchers manipulate the fairness of the procedures and the fairness of the outcomes. Two results warrant attention. First, this research demonstrates that both the outcome and the procedure affect individuals' reactions (e.g., Folger, 1977; LaTour, 1978; Lind et al., 1983). Second, and most relevant to our issue, recent meta-analyses indicate that perceptions of procedural justice and distributive justice are strongly correlated in the lab. Cohen-Charash and Spector (2001) reported a weighted correlation for procedural and distributive justice for experimental studies of .62. Hauenstein et al. (2001) report a correlation of .70. Indeed, the relationship between procedural justice and distributive justice is stronger in experimental settings than in nonexperimental settings.

What is most striking about the magnitude of these correlations is that in experimental settings, the attributes of procedures and outcomes that are associated with judgments of fairness can be manipulated such that they are "mismatched." It is less likely that this "mismatch" occurs in nonexperimental settings. However, despite the manipulation of "objective" indicators of fairness, participants respond to the manipulations in a nonorthogonal manner.

In accounting for the relationship between procedural justice and distributive justice, we suggest that two processes deserve attention. First, experimenters and organizations manipulate the "objective" attributes of procedures and outcomes, but these are not identical to the subjective experience of fairness. Leventhal (1980) proposed that procedural rules would be more heavily weighted and procedural systems viewed more positively if they promoted the attainment of favorable outcomes for the perceiver or if they promote fair outcomes for all involved. Consistent with this prediction, perceptions of distributive justice affect perceptions of procedural justice (and vice versa; Folger, 1977; Lind & Tyler, 1988; Thibaut & Walker, 1975; Tornblom & Vermunt, 1999). Thus, perceptions of distributive and procedural justice move together.

Second, one needs to consider the role of perspective in the determination of fairness. In other words, fair according to whom? Consider a jury trial in which all the appropriate precautions, rules, and procedures were followed, yet produced the "wrong" verdict (convicting an innocent person or acquitting a guilty person). Is this an example of a fair procedure leading to an unfair outcome? Certainly, for an innocent individual wrongly convicted the answer would be yes. Similarly, the victims of a guilty person who was acquitted would also see the outcome as unfair. However, the jurors' perspective would likely be quite different. They are likely to believe that both the procedure and the outcome were fair. Moreover, we suspect the individuals who experienced an "unfair" outcome (e.g., wrongly convicted) would not believe that the procedure that produced the "wrong" outcome was fair.

A number of studies have examined the effect of perspective (i.e., whether one is an observer of or a participant in a process) on individuals' reactions to procedures and outcomes. In general, this research demonstrates both similarities and differences between observers and participants. For example, Thibaut and Walker (1975) found observers reported similar preferences for procedures and similar perceptions of procedural fairness. However, observers believed that both favorable and unfavorable outcomes were equally fair, whereas participants found favorable outcomes fairer than unfavorable outcomes. Skarlicki, Ellard, and Kelln (1998) found uninvolved observers perceived the fairness of layoffs similarly to layoff victims and layoff survivors. However, Lind, Kray, and Thompson (1998) found that the injustice experiences of others influenced individuals' perceptions of fairness, but this effect was much smaller than the influence of experiencing injustice oneself (see also Kray & Lind, 2002).

So, can there be fair outcomes without fair procedures? Empirical research suggests that it is exceedingly rare for individuals to perceive procedures and outcomes as unrelated. The high correlations in both experimental and nonexperimental settings suggest individuals *perceive* fair outcomes to come from fair procedures and unfair outcomes to come from unfair procedures. Thus, although it may be possible to manipulate attributes of procedures and outcomes that should (objectively) translate to fair procedures leading to unfair outcomes and fair outcomes coming from unfair procedures, individuals link their experiences of procedures and outcomes, making their justice experiences with each more similar than different.

THE IMPORTANCE OF OVERALL JUSTICE

All of this leads us to wonder about the utility of continuing to focus on the distinction of distributive justice and procedural justice. Perhaps

the time has come to take a step back, take a new look at justice, and consider where we go from here. We believe interest in overall justice represents an important direction for justice research. In the final section of this chapter, we consider the role of overall justice.

Distributive Justice, Procedural Justice, and Overall Justice

In some ways, the recent interest in overall justice reflects a return to earlier conceptualizations of fairness. Leventhal's (1980; Leventhal et al., 1980) seminal work on procedural justice framed *procedural rules* and *distributive rules* as the foundation of (overall) justice judgments. Leventhal (1980) noted that "the perception of fairness is governed by two types of justice rules—distribution rules and procedural rules" (p. 53). Lind and Tyler (1988) also acknowledged the role of overall fairness. They stated that procedural fairness "plays at least as large a role as distributive fairness in determining *overall justice judgments*" (p. 135, emphasis added). However, subsequent research moved from a consideration of how these rules combine to affect overall fairness judgments to a focus on judgments of specific types of fairness. The work in Lind (2001) represents a return to this earlier focus.

Leventhal (1980) and Lind (2001) differ on their conceptualizations of the antecedents of an overall fairness judgment. Leventhal suggested an assessment of procedural and distributive rules that combine to form a fairness judgment. Lind (2001) suggested individuals have different types of justice "experiences" (distributive, procedural, interactional), and these experiences combine to form their overall fairness judgment. Leventhal's conceptualization suggests a more controlled cognitive process than Lind's. Leventhal proposes that specific justice rules are weighted and combined to form a general justice judgment. Lind's fairness heuristic theory suggests a rapid, more automatic process by which available information creates the general fairness judgment. However, regardless of the specific mechanism, both recognize the importance of overall fairness judgments as a basis for individual attitudes and behavior.

Other researchers have called for a greater focus on overall fairness as well. For example, Greenberg (2001) suggested that when individuals form impressions of justice, they are making a "holistic judgment in which they respond to whatever information is both available and salient" (p. 211). Similarly, Shapiro (2001) suggested that victims of injustice are unlikely to worry about whether there are two, three, or four types of justice, reacting instead to their general experience of injustice. Hauenstein et al. (2001) suggested that simpler approaches to justice may be more valid than those that focus on different types of justice. Recently, Tornblom and Vermunt (1999) proposed a model of "total fairness." They suggested, "People conceive the fairness of a situation as a Gestalt ... the

components of fairness—distributive fairness, procedural fairness, and the valence of the outcome to be allocated—are meaningful only in relation to the overall fairness of the situation" (p. 51).

In many ways, it seems surprising that so little attention has been given to overall judgments of fairness. Empirical research demonstrates strong correlations between distributive, procedural, and interactional justice. Other areas that have dealt with similar issues seem comfortable dealing with both specific facet judgments and an overall judgment (e.g., job satisfaction). Why then has so little attention been given to overall fairness judgments?

We believe the primary reason is the focus of justice research: (a) unique variance accounted for by the different types of justice, rather than on the shared (or total) variance, and (b) the differential effects of different types of justice on different types of outcomes. Certainly, these foci have served the field well in many ways, yet these approaches are limiting as well. We next consider the benefits and costs of each.

Focus on Unique Variance.   The dominant approach in organizational justice research is to examine the unique variance accounted for by each type of justice. Historically, this approach made sense, as it demonstrates the usefulness of considering different types of justice. For example, when the concept of procedural justice was first introduced into the literature, researchers were interested in determining whether procedural justice had an independent effect on outcomes (e.g., Folger, 1977; LaTour, 1978; Lind et al., 1983). Demonstrating that procedural justice accounted for a significant amount of variance not accounted for by distributive justice demonstrated the importance of considering procedures as well as outcomes.

A consideration of unique variance also allows researchers to assess the relative importance of one type of justice over another. For example, as we discuss in greater detail in the next section, researchers have been interested in how different types of justice affect different outcomes. The relative influence might affect how organizations shape their policies or where they focus their attention and resources.

One ironic attribute of this type of research is that although justice research typically focuses on unique variance, researchers are often notably lax in terms of controlling for distributive justice when examining the effects of procedural justice (and/or interactional justice) (cf. Lind, Tyler, & Huo, 1997; Masterson, Lewis, Goldman, & Taylor, 2000; Mossholder, Bennett, & Martin, 1998; Rupp & Cropanzano, 2002; Skarlicki et al., 1998; Sweeney, McFarlin, & Cotton, 1993). This oversight is particularly important when one considers the typically large correlation between the different types of justice. By omitting one form of justice from consideration, the other forms of justice "pick up" that variance, which may distort the

strength of the relationship between the focal form of justice and the outcome of interest. (See Hauenstein et al. [2001] for a more comprehensive discussion of the theoretical and methodological concerns associated with not considering the relationship between procedural and distributive justice.)

Benefits and Limitations of Focusing on Unique Variance.   The focus on unique variance has been beneficial, in terms of both establishing the importance of different types of justice and providing some indication of the relative importance of these different forms of justice on outcomes. However, the dominance of this empirical approach comes at a cost. Most notably, the emphasis on difference obscures the similarities of the constructs and the relationships between them.

Examining unique variance is useful, but unique variance focuses us on only one part of the justice question. Consider the simple schematic in Fig. 2.1. In a typical study that examines the effect of procedural and distributive justice on an outcome variable, both procedural justice (PJ) and distributive justice (DJ) are entered simultaneously into a regression equation. Under these circumstances, although the explanatory power of the overlapping, shaded portion (PJ–DJ) is reflected in the overall R^2, the significance of the predictive power of the two nonoverlapping, unshaded (crescent-shaped) portions are reflected in the individual variable t-statistics. It is these t-statistics that are generally interpreted. If they are significant, the predictor is considered significant—if they are not, the predictor is not considered significant. The dilemma is that individually, each predictor may describe only a small portion of variance in the outcome, whereas if one considered the shaded section as well, a greater portion of the variance in the outcome variable would be identified with the general construct that underlies it: in this case, overall justice. Thus, the focus on unique variance may obscure the overall impact of fairness on the outcome variable.

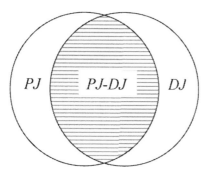

FIG. 2.1.   Unique and overlapping variance between procedural justice (PJ) and distributive justice (DJ).

The crescent approach is useful in understanding how much unique variance procedural justice explains, but it doesn't tell us (as the research is generally interpreted) very much about how much variance "fairness" predicts. Assessing whether a variable predicts "new" variance not already accounted for by a previously known variable is useful, but this is not always the question. If one is interested in distinguishing the impact of justice perceptions relative to other types of predictors, the crescent approach underestimates the importance of fairness.

Differential Effects of Different Types of Justice

Early in the history of organizational justice research, scholars were interested in how different types of justice affected different outcomes. Previously in this chapter we described work on the differential effects of procedural and distributive justice. We noted that empirical work has generally supported Lind and Tyler's (1988) assertion that distributive fairness is related to attitudes about the specific allocation situation (e.g., pay satisfaction) and procedural fairness is related to attitudes about organizations (e.g., organizational commitment; Colquitt et al., 2001; Folger & Konovsky, 1989; Sweeney & McFarlin, 1993).

Recently, a similar examination of differential effects emerged in justice research for procedural and interactional justice. This research suggests that whereas procedural justice affects organizational outcomes, interactional justice affects supervisory outcomes. For example, Malatesta and Byrne (1997) found that procedural justice was the best predictor of organizational commitment and citizenship behaviors that benefited the organization. Interactional justice was the best predictor of supervisory commitment and citizenship behaviors that benefited the supervisor. Masterson et al. (2000) predicted similar effects, although they suggested the procedural justice—organizational outcome relationship and the interactional justice—supervisory outcome relationship are mediated by perceived organizational support and leader member exchange, respectively. The results supported their predictions. Most recently, Rupp and Cropanzano (2002) examined psychological contracts as mediators of the procedural justice—organizational outcome and interactional justice—supervisory outcome relationships. Their results were generally consistent with the previous work.

Benefits and Limitations of Examining Differential Effects

As with the focus on unique variance, focusing on differential effect has benefited the field. First, it allows researchers to refine their understanding of the relationship between different types of justice. The differential effects results have been instrumental in establishing new

types of justice as conceptually distinct (cf. Bobocel & Homvall, 2001; Colquitt, 2001; Colquitt et al., 2001; Cohen-Charash & Spector, 2001; Cropanzano, Byrne, Bobocel, & Rupp, 2001). Moreover, the results of studies examining differential effects may provide guidance for organizations about how to best utilize scarce resources. If interactional justice is primarily associated with supervisory outcomes and procedural justice is associated with organizational outcomes, organizations might choose to invest resources in the development of fair procedures, rather than training supervisors to be fair.

However, there are limitations to the differential effects research as well. First, this approach does not consider the relationship between the justice variables either theoretically or empirically. The theoretical rationale for differential effects usually treats each type of justice as if it were independent of the others. Empirically, as with the focus on unique variance, the interpretation of results does not consider the shared variance.

Additionally, none of this research considers in any serious detail the relationship between relevant outcome variables. For example, in their seminal study on the two-factor model, Sweeney and McFarlin (1993) demonstrated that distributive justice predicted specific attitudes (e.g., pay satisfaction), whereas procedural justice predicted global attitudes (e.g., organizational commitment). However, these two types of attitudes were significantly related. The relationship between the outcome variables—and its implication for the indirect impact of distributive justice on organizational commitment and procedural justice on pay satisfaction—were not explored. Among the four competitive models Sweeney and McFarlin tested, a model in which specific attitudes (pay satisfaction) mediate the relationship between justice and global outcomes was not included.

Recently, Ambrose and Hess (2001) integrated this early work on the two-factor model with contemporary work on justice from the management and the marketing literatures. Of note for this chapter, Ambrose and Hess (2001) found that attitudes associated with specific outcomes (satisfaction with how a customer complaint was handled) fully mediated the relationships between three types of justice (distributive, procedural, and interpersonal) and global attitudes (organizational satisfaction). Only informational justice had a direct effect on global attitudes.

In the most recent work on the differential effects of justice, models continue to ignore the relationships between the "differentiated" outcome variables, even though the correlation among the outcome variables is often large. For example, in Masterson et al. (2000), supervisor directed citizenship behaviors and organization directed citizenship behaviors were correlated .48. In Rupp and Cropanzano (2002), the

correlation was .43. Although some researchers have suggested that one set of outcomes may affect the others (e.g., Cropanzano et al., 2001), there are no empirical tests of these relationships or more complex models.

We suggest that examining differential effects on outcome variables overstates the impact of one form of justice versus the other. Not only are the different types of justice significantly related to one another, the outcome variables are similarly related. A simplified summary of the "differentiation" research is that one type of justice affects one type of outcome exclusively. However, a more comprehensive view suggests that the types of justice affect outcomes in two ways. First, the different forms of justice are related. Therefore, conceptually, one form of justice is embedded in the effect of the other forms. Second, the effects of justice on outcomes may be either direct or indirect. The "differential effects" paradigm ignores the indirect effects.

MOVING FORWARD

As we close this chapter, we are struck by the degree to which justice research has become self-interested. We would characterize the majority of contemporary justice research as focusing on "within justice" questions. That is, the typical justice study includes multiple types of justice as predictors and assesses the effect of these on multiple outcomes or mediating variables. The trend is toward slicing justice more and more finely. We have moved from one type of justice (distributive) to two types (distributive and procedural) to three types (distributive, procedural, and interactional) toward four types (distributive, procedural, interpersonal, and informational). At this point in the evolution of justice research, is this the most useful avenue for our collective efforts? Although the introduction of each type may allow us to account for an additional sliver of variance, this approach may distract researchers from other important questions.

Justice research has had a powerful presence in the organizational literature. However, recent critiques raise concerns that the field is becoming too insular (Shapiro, 2001; Taylor, 2001). We suggest that justice research would benefit from a different perspective. In an effort to establish the importance of different forms of justice, current research has neglected the importance of fairness relative to other constructs.

In his seminal work on procedural justice, Leventhal (1980) stated, "Concern for justice is only one motivational force among many that influence social perception and behavior, and it may often be a weaker force than others" (p. 28). Recent research has also echoed this point. Lind (2001) noted that fairness can be a powerful tool for organizations, but

that fairness cannot do everything. Greenberg (2001) stated, "The suggestion that justice is an omnipresent concern of people in organizations is misleading.... Justice might always be a potential concern, but the potential will only materialize sometimes" (p. 246). Perhaps it is time for justice researchers to investigate Leventhal's assertion and move from a focus that pits one type of justice against another toward a comparison of justice to other variables. To really understand the power of justice, we need to be able to demonstrate that fairness is more important to individuals than other psychological variables. Demonstrating that procedural fairness is more important that distributive fairness in predicting organizational commitment does not accomplish this.

Nearly 40 years after Adams's original work on equity theory, research on organizational justice continues to thrive. Certainly there are still issues to be addressed and questions to be answered that stem from considering the conceptually distinct forms of justice. But we join the other voices in the justice literature that suggest the benefits of considering the role of overall justice judgments. We believe there is much to be gained by focusing less on the differences between justice types, more on how these conceptually distinct forms of justice contribute to an employees' overall sense of organizational fairness, and how this overall sense of fairness "stacks up" to other motivational forces in organizations.

REFERENCES

Adams, J. S. (1963). Toward an understanding of inequity. *Journal of Abnormal and Social Psychology, 67*, 422–436.

Adams, J. S. (1965). Inequity in social exchange. In L. Berkowitz (Ed.), *Advances in experimental social psychology*, (Vol. 2, pp. 267–299). New York: Academic Press.

Ambrose, M. L., & Hess, R. L. (2001, July). *Organizational justice and customer satisfaction*. Paper presented at the International Roundtable on Organizational Justice, Vancouver, Canada.

Ball, G. A., Trevino, L. K., & Sims, H. P. (1994). Just and unjust punishment: influences on subordinate performance and citizenship. *Academy of Management Journal, 37*, 299–323.

Barrett-Howard, E., & Tyler, T. R. (1986). Procedural justice as a criterion in allocation decisions. *Journal of Personality and Social Psychology, 50*, 296–304.

Bobocel, D. R., & Holmvall, C. (2001). Are interactional justice and procedural justice different? Framing the debate. In S. Gilliland, D. Steiner, & D. Skarlicki (Eds.), *Research in social issues in management: Theoretical and cultural perspectives on organizational justice* (pp. 85–110). Greenwich, CT: Information Age.

Boldizar, J. P., Perry, D. G., & Perry, L. C. (1988). Gender and reward distributions: A test of two hypotheses. *Sex Roles, 19*, 569–579.

Chatman, J., & Jehn, K. (1994). Assessing the relationship between industry characteristics and organizational culture: How different can you be? *Academy of Management Journal, 37*, 522–554.

Chen, C. C. (1995). New trends in rewards allocation preferences: A Sino–U.S. comparison. *Academy of Management Journal, 38*, 408–429.

Chiu, C. (1990). Distributive justice among Hong Kong Chinese college students. *Journal of Social Psychology, 130*, 649–657.

Cohen-Charash, Y., & Spector, P. E. (2001). The role of justice in organizations: A meta-analysis. *Organizational Behavior and Human Decision Processes, 86*, 278–321.

Colquitt, J. A. (2001). On the dimensionality of organizational justice: A construct validation of a measure. *Journal of Applied Psychology, 86*, 386–400.

Colquitt, J. A., Conlon, D. E., Wesson, M. J., Porter, C. O. L. H., & Ng, K. Y. (2001). Justice at the millennium: A meta-analytic review of 25 years of organizational justice research. *Journal of Applied Psychology, 86*, 425–445.

Cornelius, G. W. (1985). *Evaluation fairness and work motivation.* Unpublished master's thesis, University of Illinois, Champaign.

Cropanzano, R., & Greenberg, J. (1997). Progress in organizational justice: Tunneling through the maze. In L. T. Robertson & C. L. Cooper (Eds.), *International review of industrial and organizational psychology* (pp. 317–372). New York: John Wiley & Sons.

Cropanzano, R., & Ambrose, M. L. (2001). Procedural and distributive justice are more similar than you think: A monistic perspective and a research agenda. In J. Greenberg & R. Cropanzano (Eds.), *Advances in organizational justice* (pp. 119–151). Stanford, CA: Stanford University Press.

Cropanzano, R., Byrne, Z. S., Bobocel, D. R., & Rupp, D. R. (2001). Moral virtues, fairness heuristics, social entities, and other denizens of organizational justice. *Journal of Vocational Behavior 58*, 164–209.

Cropanzano, R., Rupp, D. E., Mohler, C. J., & Schminke, M. (2001). Three roads to organizational justice. In G. Ferris (Ed.), *Research in personnel and human resources management* (Vol. 20, pp. 1–113). Kidlington, Oxford: Elsevier Science.

Deutsch, M. (1985). *Distributive justice: A social-psychological perspective.* New Haven, CT: Yale University Press.

Dittrich, J. E., & Carrell, M. R. (1979). Organizational equity perceptions, employee satisfaction, and department absence and turnover rates. *Organizational Behavior and Human Performance, 24*, 29–40.

Drake, D. G., & Lawrence, J. A. (2000). Equality and distribution of inheritance in families. *Social Justice Research, 13*, 271–290.

Foa, U. G., & Foa, E. B. (1974). *Societal structures of the mind.* Springfield, IL: C. C. Thomas.

Folger, R. (1977). Distributive and procedural justice: Combined impact of "voice" and improvement on experienced inequity. *Journal of Personality and Social Psychology, 35*, 108–119.

Folger, R., & Konovsky, M. A. (1989). Effects of procedural and distributive justice on reactions to pay raise decisions. *Academy of Management Journal, 32*, 115–130.

Garland, H. (1973). The effects of piece-rate underpayment and overpayment on job performance: A test of equity theory with a new induction procedure. *Journal of Applied Social Psychology, 3*, 325–334.

Giacobbe-Miller, J. K., Miller, D. J., & Victorov, V. I. (1998). A comparison of Russian and U.S. pay allocation decisions, distributive justice judgments, and productivity under different payment conditions. *Personnel Psychology, 51*, 137–164.

Gilliland, S. W. (1994). Effects of procedural and distributive justice on reactions to a selection system. *Journal of Applied Psychology, 79*, 691–701.

Greenberg, J. (1986b). The distributive justice of organizational performance evaluations. In H. W. Bierhoff, R. L. Cohen, & J. Greenberg (Eds.), *Justice in social relations* (pp. 337–351). New York: Plenum.

Greenberg, J. (1988a). Equity and workplace status: A field experiment. *Journal of Applied Psychology, 73,* 606–614.

Greenberg, J. (1990). Organizational justice: Yesterday, today, and tomorrow. *Journal of Management, 16,* 399–432.

Greenberg, J. (2001). Setting the justice agenda: Seven unanswered questions about "what, why, and how." *Journal of Vocational Behavior, 58,* 210–219.

Greenberg, J., & Ornstein, S. (1983). High status job title as compensation for underpayment: A test of equity theory. *Journal of Applied Psychology, 68,* 285–297.

Hauenstein, N. M. T., McGonigle, T., & Flinder, S. W. (2001). A meta-analysis of the relationship between procedural justice and distributive justice: Implications for justice research. *Employee Responsibilities and Rights Journal, 13,* 39–56.

Kanfer, R., Sawyer, J., Earley, P. C., & Lind, E. A. (1987). Participation in task evaluation procedures: The effects of influential opinion expression and knowledge of evaluation criteria on attitudes and performance. *Social Justice Research, 1,* 235–249.

Kashima, Y., Siegal, M., Tanaka, K., & Isaka, H. (1988). Universalism in lay conceptions of distributive justice: A cross-cultural examination. *International Journal of Psychology, 23,* 51–64.

Keller, T., & Dansereau, F. (1995). Leadership and empowerment: A social exchange perspective. *Human Relations, 48,* 127–147.

Konovsky, M., & Cropanzano, R. (1991). The perceived fairness of employee drug testing as a predictor of employee attitudes and job performance. *Journal of Applied Psychology, 76,* 698–707.

Koys, D. J. (1988). Human resource management and a culture of respect: Effects on employees' organizational commitment. *Employee Responsibilities and Rights Journal, 1,* 57–69.

Kray, L. J., & Lind, E. A. (2002). The injustices of others: Social reports and the integration of others' experiences in organizational justice judgments. *Organizational Behavior & Human Decision Processes, 89,* 906–925.

LaTour, S. (1978). Determinants of participant and observer satisfaction with adversary and inquisitorial modes of adjudication. *Journal of Personality and Social Psychology, 36,* 1531–1545

Leung, K., & Bond, M. H. (1984). The impact of cultural collectivism on reward allocation. *Journal of Personality and Social Psychology, 47,* 793–804.

Leventhal, G. S. (1976a). The distribution of rewards and resources in groups and organizations. In L. Berkowitz & E. Walster (Eds.), *Advances in experimental social psychology* (Vol. 9, pp. 91–131). New York: Academic Press.

Leventhal, G. S. (1976b). Fairness is social relationships. In J. W. Thibaut, J. T. Spence, & R. C. Carson (Eds.), *Contemporary topics in social psychology* (pp. 211–239). Morristown, NJ: General Learning Press.

Leventhal, G. S. (1980). What should be done with equity theory? In K. J. Gergen, M. S. Greenberg, & R. H. Willis (Eds.), *Social exchange: Advances in theory and research* (pp. 27–55). New York: Plenum.

Leventhal, G. S., Karuza, J., & Fry, W. R. (1980). Beyond fairness: A theory of allocation preferences. In G. Mikula (Ed.), *Justice and social interaction* (pp. 167–213). New York: Springer-Verlag.

Lind, E. A. (2001). Fairness heuristic theory: Justice judgments as pivotal cognitions in organizational relations. In M. S. Greenberg, & R. Cropanzano (Eds.), *Advances in organizational justice* (pp. 56–88). Stanford, CA: Stanford University Press.

Lind, E. A., Kray, L. J., & Thompson, L. (1998). The social construction of injustice: Fairness judgments in response to own and others' unfair treatment by authorities. *Organizational Behavior and Human Decision Processes, 75,* 1–22.

Lind, E. A., Kray, L. J., & Thompson, L. (2001). Primacy effects in justice judgments: Testing predictions from fairness heuristic theory. *Organizational Behavior and Human Decision Processes, 85,* 189–210.

Lind, E. A., Kurtz, S., Musante, L., Walker, L., & Thibaut, J. (1980). Procedure and outcome effects on reactions to adjudicated resolutions of conflicts of interest. *Journal of Personality and Social Psychology, 39,* 338–350.

Lind, E. A., & Lissak, R. I. (1985). Apparent impropriety and procedural fairness judgments. *Journal of Experimental Social Psychology, 21,* 19–29.

Lind, E. A., Lissak., R. E., & Conlon, A. E. (1983). Decision control and process control effects on procedural justice judgments. *Journal of Applied Social Psychology, 4,* 338–350.

Lind, E. A., MacCoun, R. J., Ebener, P. A., Felstiner, W. L. F., Hensler, D. R., Resnik, J., & Tyler, T. R. (1989). *The perception of justice: Tort litigants' views of trial, court-annexed arbitration, and judicial settlement conferences.* Santa Monica, CA: Rand Corporation.

Lind, E. A., & Tyler, T. R. (1988). *The social psychology of procedural justice.* New York: Plenum.

Lind, E. A., Tyler, T. R., & Huo, Y. L. (1997). Procedural context and culture: Variation in the antecedents of procedural justice judgments. *Journal of Personality and Social Psychology, 10,* 99–114.

Linkey, H. E., & Alexander, S. (1998). Need norm, demographic influence, social role, and justice judgment. *Current Psychology: Developmental, Learning, Personality, Social, 17,* 152–162

Malatesta, R. M., & Byrne, Z. S. (1997, April). *The impact of formal and interactional justice on organizational outcomes.* Poster session presented for the twelfth annual conference of the Society for Industrial and Organizational Psychology, St. Louis, MO.

Markovsky, B. (1985). Toward a multilevel distributive justice theory. *American Sociological Review, 50,* 822–839.

Masterson, S. S., Lewis, K., Goldman, B. M., & Taylor, M. S. (2000). Integrating justice and social exchange: The differing effects of fair procedures and treatment on work relationships. *Academy of Management Journal, 43,* 738–748.

McFarlin, D. B., & Sweeney, P. D. (1992). Distributive and procedural justice as predictors of satisfaction with personal and organizational outcomes. *Academy of Management Journal, 35,* 626–637.

Miller, C. E., & Komorita, S. S. (1995). Reward allocation in task-performing groups. *Journal of Personality and Social Psychology, 69,* 80–91.

Moorman, R. H. (1991). Relationship between organizational fairness and organizational citizenship behaviors: Do fairness perceptions influence employee citizenship? *Journal of Applied Psychology, 76,* 845–855.

Moorman, R. H., Blakely, G. L., & Niehoff, B. P. (1998). Does perceived organizational support mediate the relationship between procedural justice and organizational citizenship behavior? *Academy of Management Journal, 41,* 351–357.

Mossholder, K. W., Bennett, N., & Martin, C. L. (1998). Relationship between bases of power and work reactions: The mediational role of procedural justice. *Journal of Management, 24,* 533–552.

Mowday, R. T. (1987). Equity theory predictions of behavior in organizations. In R. M. Steers & L. W. Porter (Eds.) *Motivation and work* (4th ed., pp. 89–110). New York: McGraw-Hill.

Oldham, G. R., Kulik, C. T., Ambrose, M. L., Stepina, L. P., & Brand, J. F. (1986). Relations between job fact comparisons and employee reactions. *Organizational Behavior and Human Decision Processes, 38,* 28–47.

Price, J. L., & Meuller, C. W. (1986). *Handbook of organizational measurement.* Marshfield, MA: Pitman.

Pritchard, R. A., Dunnette, M. D., & Jorgenson, D. O. (1972). Effects of perceptions of equity and inequity on worker performance and satisfaction. *Journal of Applied Psychology, 56,* 75–94.

Rupp, D. E., & Cropanzano, R. (2002). Integrating psychological contracts and multifocused organizational justice. *Organizational Behavior and Human Decision Processes, 89,* 925–946.

Schminke, M., Ambrose, M. L., & Noel, T. W. (1997). The effect of ethical frameworks on perceptions of organizational justice. *Academy of Management Journal, 40,* 1190–1207.

Schwab, D. P. (1980). Construct validity in organizational behavior. In B. Staw & L. L. Cummings (Eds.), *Research in organizational behavior* (Vol. 2, pp. 3–43). Greenwich, CT: JAI Press.

Shapiro, D. (1993). Reconciling theoretical differences among procedural justice researchers by re-evaluating what it means to have one's view "considered"; Implications for third-party managers. In R. Cropanzano (Ed.), *Justice in the workplace: Approaching fairness in human resource management* (pp. 51–78). Hillsdale, NJ: Lawrence Erlbaum Associates.

Shapiro, D. (2001). The death of justice theory is likely if theorists neglect the "wheels" already invented and the voices of the injustice victims. *Journal of Vocational Behavior, 58,* 235–242.

Singer, M. (1989). Determinants of perceived fairness on selection practices: An organizational justice perspective. *Genetic, Social, and General Psychology Monographs, 116,* 477–495.

Skarlicki, D. P., Ellard, J. H., & Kelln, B. R. C. (1998). Third-party perceptions of a layoff: Procedural, derogation, and retributive aspects of justice. *Journal of Applied Psychology, 83,* 119–127.

Sweeney, P. D., & McFarlin, D. B. (1993). Workers evaluations of the "ends" and the "means": An examination of four models of distributive and procedural justice. *Organizational Behavior and Human Decision Processes, 55,* 23–40.

Sweeney, P. D., Mc Farlin, D. B., & Cotton, J. L. (1993). Locus of control as a moderator of the relationship between perceived influence and procedural justice. *Human Relations, 44,* 333–342.

Taylor, M. (2001). Reflections on fairness: Continuing the progression of justice research and practice. *Journal of Vocational Behavior, 58,* 243–253.

Thibaut, J., & Walker, L. (1975). *Procedural justice: A psychological analysis.* Hillsdale, NJ: Lawrence Erlbaum Associates.

Thibaut, J., & Walker, L. (1978). A theory of procedure. *California Law Review, 66,* 541–566.

Tornblom, K. Y., & Vermunt, R. (1999). An integrative perspective on social justice: Distributive and procedural fairness evaluations of positive and negative outcome allocations. *Social Justice Research, 12,* 39–64.

Tyler, T. R., & Lind, E. A. (1992). A relational model of authority in groups. In M. Zanna (Ed.), *Advances in experimental social psychology* (Vol. 25, pp. 115–191). New York: Academic Press.

Van den Bos, K., Lind, E. A., Vermunt, R., & Wilke, H. A. M. (1997). How do I judge my outcome when I do not know the outcome of others? The psychology of the fair process effect. *Journal of Personality and Social Psychology, 72*, 1034–1072.

Van den Bos, K., Wilke, H. A. M., Lind, E. A., & Vermunt, R. (1998). Evaluating the outcomes by means of the fair process effect: Evidence for different processes in fairness and satisfaction judgments. *Journal of Personality and Social Psychology, 74*, 1493–1503.

Wagstaff, G. F., Huggins, J. P., & Perfect, T. J. (1993). Equity, equality, and need in the adult family. *Journal of Social Psychology, 133*, 439–444.

Walker, L., Lind, E. A., & Thibaut, J. (1979). The relationship between procedural and distributive justice. *Virginia Law Review, 65*, 1401–1420.

3

Are Procedural Justice and Interactional Justice Conceptually Distinct?

Robert J. Bies
Georgetown University

Despite the growing body of empirical evidence that demonstrates interactional justice is a key concern for people in organizations, the construct has also been at the center of a swirling controversy among organizational justice researchers. The core of the controversy is over the distinctiveness and construct validity of interactional justice vis-à-vis procedural justice. More specifically, is interactional justice merely a form of procedural justice? This chapter reviews the empirical evidence that bears on that question, concludes that the answer is "no," and proposes recommendations to guide future research. By embracing interactional justice—or its two components (informational and interpersonal justice) —as legitimate, it is argued that justice concerns must be viewed more broadly in terms of encounters, not just exchanges—a perspective that challenges the fundamental assumptions guiding current organizational justice theory. The implications of the encounter perspective and its possible integration with the exchange perspective are explored.

One of the core values of our corporate culture is justice. For me, what gives meaning to that value is not so much our pay and benefits packages, which are the best in the industry; and it is not so much that upper management seeks our consultation on major and minor matters, which is unique in our industry; no, what gives real meaning to justice for me is how I am treated on a day-to-day basis by my bosses and my peers. To be treated with respect and dignity is what makes this company special to me.   (Senior manager, energy company)

In 1985, I presented at the Research on Negotiations Conference, a paper that summarized empirical findings from my research on individual reactions to corporate recruitment practices. My findings suggested that people were quite concerned with the fairness of the interpersonal treatment they received from corporate recruiters, concerns that I referred to as *interactional justice* (Bies & Moag, 1986). I further elaborated on interactional justice in my chapter in the *Research in Organizational Behavior* series (Bies, 1987). In that chapter, I presented a typology of social accounts—that is, explanations and justifications—that I conceptualized as important to people's concerns about interactional justice. These two chapters became the conceptual "sparks" that have generated growing scholarly interest in interactional justice over the past 15 years.

Stimulated by Bies (1987), there has been one stream of research that has focused on social accounts as a key element of interactional justice. Interactional justice, in the form of social accounts, has been found to

be an important variable for understanding individual reactions to a variety of organizational decisions and actions, including corporate recruitment practices (Bies & Shapiro, 1988), personnel selection (Ployhart, Ryan, & Bennett, 1999), budget allocations (Bies & Shapiro, 1987), conflict management (Bies, Shapiro, & Cummings, 1988; Sitkin & Bies, 1993), "hardball" negotiation tactics (Shapiro & Bies, 1994), deceptive practices (Shapiro, 1991), opportunistic behavior (Bottom, Gibson, Daniels, & Murnighan, 2002), corporate responses to consumer product complaints (Conlon & Murray, 1996), work-site smoking bans (Greenberg, 1994), employee theft (Greenberg 1993a), organizational change initiatives (Daly, 1995), corporate layoffs (Brockner, DeWitt, Grover, & Reed, 1990), and the delivery of bad news (Bies, 2003).

Stimulated by Bies and Moag (1986), another stream of research has focused on interactional justice in the form of respectful and socially sensitive treatment. Scholars have found interactional justice to be an important variable for understanding organizational citizenship behaviors (Maletesta & Byrne, 1997; Moorman, 1991; Rupp & Cropanzano, 2002), job performance (Cropanzano, Prehar, & Chen, 2002), perceptions of systemic justice (Beugre & Baron, 2001), trust in management and organizational commitment (Barling & Phillips, 1993), trust in one's supervisor (Aryee, Budhwar, & Chen, 2002), supervisor legitimacy (Masterson, Lewis-McClear, Goldman, & Taylor, 2000), union participation (Fuller & Hester, 2001), feedback processes (Baron, 1988), radical organizational change (Kickul, Lester, & Finkl, 2002), workplace reconfigurations (Kernan & Hanges, 2002), job layoffs (Bennett, Martin, Bies, & Brockner, 1995; Bies, Martin, & Brockner, 1993; Naumann, Bennett, Bies, & Martin, 1998), occupational stress (Elovainio, Kivimäki, & Helkama, 2001), conflict resolution style and negotiating behaviors (Rahim, Magner, & Shapiro, 2000), abusive bosses (Bies & Tripp, 1999; Tepper, 2000), workplace privacy concerns (Bies, 1996), workplace revenge (Bies & Tripp, 1996), workplace incivility (Andersson & Pearson, 1999l; Cortina, Magley, Williams, & Langhout, 2001), workplace sabotage (Ambrose, Seabright, & Schminke, 2002), organizational retaliatory behaviors (Skarlicki & Folger, 1997; Skarlicki, Folger, & Tesluk, 1999), employee litigation behavior (Bies & Tripp, 1993; Bies & Tyler, 1993), customer service practices (Clemmer, 1993), consumer complaint behavior (Blodgett, Hill, & Tax, 1997), consumer privacy concerns (Culnan & Bies, 2003), marketing channel dynamics (Sindhav, 2001), and citizen encounters with the police and courts (Tyler, 1988).

In addition to the growing number of empirical studies of interactional justice, Bies and Moag (1986) created shifts in the conceptual landscape, as scholars incorporated interpersonal treatment into their models of organizational justice. For example, in the group-value

model of procedural justice (Lind & Tyler, 1988) and the relational model of authority (Tyler & Lind, 1992), a key variable is *standing*, which is equivalent to my construct of interactional justice in terms of treating people with respect and dignity. Conversely, disrespect—a key interactional justice concern—is a central variable in the analysis of the psychology of injustice (Miller, 2001). Finally, in an insightful and generative conceptual analysis that I address in more detail later, Greenberg (1993b) proposed a conceptual framework for analyzing justice, one that explicitly recognized the importance of interpersonal treatment as a key determinant of organizational justice.

Yet despite empirical evidence pointing to interactional justice as a key concern for people in organizations, coupled with the increasing acknowledgment from justice scholars that interpersonal treatment is a key determinant of organizational justice dynamics, there has been a growing controversy surrounding interactional justice. Specifically, the controversy is over the distinctiveness and construct validity of interactional justice vis-à-vis procedural justice. In other words, to reframe the question that is the title of this chapter, are interactional justice and procedural justice "two sides of the same coin" or are they "two different coins" (Bies & Bobocel, 2001)?

The purpose of this chapter is to address the question of whether interactional justice is merely a form of procedural justice—or not. In the next section, I "unpack" the core elements of this controversy. This analysis reviews the empirical evidence that bears on the core elements of the controversy, including recommendations to guide future research on interactional justice. Finally, I discuss the future of interactional justice, including challenges and controversies created by the construct.

INTERACTIONAL JUSTICE VIS-À-VIS PROCEDURAL JUSTICE: THE CONTROVERSY, THE EVIDENCE

"There is no third type of justice" (Senior organizational justice scholar, Research on Negotiations Conference, 1985).

Unbeknownst to me at the time I presented my initial findings in 1985, that "small" paper would create a "large" controversy, and even a few "disputes," across the years, as the preceding quotation hints. At the core of the controversy is a debate over the conceptual distinctiveness and construct validity of interactional justice vis-à-vis procedural justice (Bies, 2001; Bobocel & Holmvall, 2001; Colquitt & Greenberg, 2003; Cropanzano & Greenberg, 1997). I next identify the positions and core issues in this controversy, followed by a review of the empirical evidence that bears on this controversy.

The Core of the Controversy: Construct Discrimination

It is important to recognize that the debate over interactional justice vis-à-vis procedural justice is actually embedded in a larger debate among organizational justice researchers as to whether organizational justice is best conceptualized as one, two, three, or four factors. The traditional view over the years has been that of a "two-factor" theory of organizational justice—distributive justice and procedural justice (Sweeney & McFarlin, 1993). With the introduction of interactional justice, we had the emergence of a three-factor theory (Bies, 1987; Bies & Moag, 1986). Greenberg (1993b) introduced a four-factor theory in which he argued that interactional justice should be separated into two separate constructs that he labeled *informational justice* and *interpersonal justice*. Finally, in what they referred to as a "monistic" perspective, Cropanzano and Ambrose (2001) argued that justice is all about expectations with respect to two kinds of outcomes, economic and socioemotional. Distributive, procedural, and interactional factors each provide information about outcomes, which is the core judgment with respect to evaluating justice. Hence, the "one-factor" theory.

But it is the debate about interactional justice vis-à-vis procedural justice that has proved to be most heated. In this debate, a variety of positions have been taken. As one position staked out, there are those who argue that interactional justice is independent of procedural justice, that it represents a third dimension of organizational justice (Bies, 1987; Bies & Moag, 1986; Folger & Cropanzano, 1998). Those who take this position point to the growing empirical evidence demonstrating the distinctiveness and different correlates of interactional justice relative to procedural justice (Bies, 2001).

By contrast, others have staked out the position that interactional justice is either (a) an interpersonal component of procedural justice (Cropanzano & Randall, 1993; Folger & Bies, 1989; Tyler & Bies, 1990; Tyler & Lind, 1992), (b) a social dimension of both distributive justice and procedural justice (Greenberg, 1993b), or (c) conceptually similar (Tyler & Blader, 2000). Those who take one of these three related positions, share the viewpoint of Cropanzano and Greenberg (1997), who argued that interactional justice

> became increasingly difficult to distinguish from structural procedural justice. For one thing, both the formal procedures and the interpersonal interactions jointly comprise the process that leads to an allocation decision. Additionally, interactional and structural procedural justice had similar consequences and correlates ... [and were] highly related to one another. (p. 330)

To be honest, this controversy and debate are, in part, my own doing. For example, in my initial theorizing (Bies, 1987; Bies & Moag, 1986), I conceptualized interactional justice as a third form of justice, separate from distributive justice and procedural justice. Clearly, my focus was on interpersonal treatment, thus making it separate from procedural justice as then defined in the literature. But because I embedded the analysis of interactional justice in the context of a decision-making process, one could view interactional concerns as another component of procedural justice—thus, the beginning of the confusion.

The confusion was compounded when I later took a position different from my initial one. In Tyler and Bies (1990), I argued that interactional justice could be fruitfully conceptualized as an interpersonal dimension of procedural justice. Indeed, justice scholars often point to my shift in position as "evidence" that interactional justice and procedural justice are conceptually similar.

But a theory is a "living" document, and not set in stone, impervious to change. When new data emerge that challenges existing theory, then new theory is one means of organizing existing data and emerging empirical "anomalies" (Lakatos, 1971). In Bies (2001), I reviewed a growing body of evidence on interactional justice, including studies that compared interactional justice and procedural justice and their effects on different correlates. The results of that analysis led me back to my original position: Interactional justice is independent of procedural justice.

This analysis was motivated, in part, by Greenberg's (1990) not so gentle "nudge" to bring some clarity to the conceptual controversy surrounding interactional justice and procedural justice. For guidance on how to bring clarity to the controversy, Greenberg (1990) outlined a two-stage analysis for determining whether there is a meaningful distinction between different justice constructs. As the first stage, following Greenberg's logic, I examined studies that have empirically differentiated interactional justice and procedural justice. In the second stage, I examined whether there are different classes of dependent variables associated with interactional justice and procedural justice.

First, in assessing the distinction between interactional justice and procedural justice, I established that the distinction between interactional justice and procedural justice is "not simply a theoretical heuristic but rather a real one from the perspective of the worker's phenomenology" (Greenberg, 1990, p. 404), and sought "to determine whether employees are intuitively aware of the distinction" (Greenberg, 1990, p. 405). I reviewed five investigations that addressed this issue (Bies & Tripp, 1996; Clemmer, 1993; Messick, Bloom, Boldizar, & Samuelson, 1985; Mikula, 1986; Mikula, Petri, & Tanzer, 1990). Reviewing the findings from this study led me to conclude that people are aware of both interactional justice and procedural justice (Bies, 2001).

Although the ability of people to distinguish between the different facets of organizational justice is important, it is insufficient evidence to make the case for the distinctiveness of interactional justice. In addition, it must be demonstrated that interactional justice and procedural justice relate to different organizational variables.

As the second step in analysis, I examined studies that tested how interactional justice and procedural justice related to a variety of organizational variables. I identified five investigations that addressed this issue (Barling & Phillips, 1993; Blodgett et al., 1997; Malatesta & Byrne, 1997; Masterson, Lewis-McClear, Goldman, & Taylor, 1997; Moorman, 1991; Skarlicki & Folger, 1997). From the review of the findings from these studies, I found evidence that interactional justice and procedural justice had different correlates. One key finding from my review was that interactional justice perceptions tend to be associated with *direct supervisor evaluations* whereas procedural justice perceptions tend to be associated with *organizational system evaluations*.

Subsequent to my analysis, other studies compared interactional justice with procedural justice. One set of studies followed from the three-factor view of organizational justice—distributive, procedural, and interactional. Another set of studies followed from a four-factor model, which is discussed later. These studies and their relevant findings are detailed next.

Empirical Evidence: Organizational Justice as Three Factors

Cropanzano et al. (2002) argued that interactional justice could be distinguished from procedural justice using social exchange theory. Specifically, they proposed that interactional justice refers to the exchange between employee and supervisor whereas procedural justice refers to the exchange between employee and the organization. Thus, interactional justice should be associated with reactions toward one's supervisor whereas procedural justice should be associated with reactions toward upper management and organizational policies. In a field study of over 100 employees and their supervisors, Cropanzano et al. found general support for their predictions. Of particular relevance to the present analysis, they found interactional justice to be a better predictor of job performance than procedural justice.

In a field study of a steelworkers' union, Fuller and Hester (2001) examined the relationship between process-related justice and union participation as mediated by perceived union support and union commitment. Process-related justice was operationalized as two distinct variables: procedural justice and interactional justice. These researchers found support for a fully mediated model. But, of importance to the present analysis, relative to procedural justice,

interactional justice had a significantly stronger relationship with perceived union support.

Aryee et al. (2002) examined trust (organization, supervisor) as a mediator of the relationship between organizational justice (distributive, procedural, and interactional factors) and worker attitudes (job satisfaction, turnover intentions, organizational commitment) and work outcomes (task performance, organizationally-oriented dimensions of citizenship behavior). Using LISREL to analyze data collected from a study of employees in a public sector organization, Aryee et al. found that although all three factors of organizational justice were related to trust in the organization, only interactional justice was related to trust in the supervisor. Further, trust in the organization only partially mediated the relationship between distributive and procedural justice and worker attitudes and work outcomes, whereas trust in supervisor fully mediated the relationship between interactional justice and worker attitudes and work outcomes.

Ambrose et al. (2002) examined the relationship between injustice and workplace sabotage. These researchers examined the roles of distributive justice, procedural justice, and interactional justice in explaining workplace sabotage. When individuals evaluated accounts of workplace sabotage, perceived injustice was the most common cause of sabotage. Of relevance to the present analysis, interactional injustice was the most likely source of injustice leading people to engage in sabotage. Finally, Ambrose et al. (2002) found that there was an additive effect of distributive justice, procedural justice, and interactional justice on the severity of sabotage.

In an even more definitive study, Cohen-Charash and Spector (2001) conducted a meta-analysis of the role of justice in organizations. These researchers examined the correlates of distributive justice, procedural justice, and interactional justice from the samples of 190 (148 field and 42 laboratory) studies. Using the Rosenthal (1991) approach to conducting meta-analysis, the results led Cohen-Charash and Spector to conclude that distributive justice, procedural justice, and interactional justice, although related, represent distinct constructs, and thus they "supported the need in having separate conceptualizations of justice" (p. 307). As one example, with relevance to the present analysis, leader–member exchange quality was more related to interactional justice (weighted mean $r = .67$) than it was to procedural justice (weighted mean $r = .37$).

In summary, studies following the three-factor perspective yield findings that suggest interactional justice and procedural justice have different correlates. Further, apart from procedural justice, interactional justice provides additional unique variance in predicting worker attitudes and behaviors. I now turn attention to studies that

compare interactional justice with procedural justice that follow from the four-factor perspective.

Empirical Evidence: Organizational Justice as Four Factors

In an insightful and generative conceptual analysis, Greenberg (1993b) proposed a taxonomy "formed by cross cutting two independent dimensions: (a) category of justice—procedural and distributive—and (b) focal determinants—structural and social" (p. 68). This taxonomy created four classes of justice: *systemic justice*, or achieving procedural justice through structural means; *configural justice*, or distributive justice achieved via structural means; *informational justice*, or social determinants of procedural justice (or what had been one aspect of interactional justice—social accounts); and *interpersonal justice*, or social aspects of distributive justice (or what had been the other aspect of interactional justice—respectful and socially sensitive treatment). This taxonomy has guided recent empirical studies of organizational justice, yielding findings that bear directly on the question that motivates this chapter.

Inspired by Greenberg's (1993b) four-factor model, Colquitt (2001) conducted two studies to explore the dimensionality of organizational justice and the construct validation of a measure of organizational justice. Developing items from the seminal works in the study of organizational justice, Colquitt designed a justice measure with the four separate factors of organizational justice (distributive, procedural, informational, and interpersonal factors). Colquitt then conducted two independent studies to test the construct validity of the justice measure, one in a university setting and one in a field setting (e.g., automotive parts company). The results of both studies provided supporting evidence for organizational justice to be conceptualized as a four distinct dimensions—distributive, procedural, informational, and interpersonal. With respect to the comparison of interactional justice and procedural justice, interpersonal justice predicted agent-referenced variables (leader evaluation, helping behavior), whereas procedural justice predicted system-referenced outcomes (rule compliance, group commitment). In addition, informational justice, alone, predicted collective esteem.

Colquitt, Conlon, Wesson, Porter, and Ng (2001) conducted a meta-analytic review of 25 years of organizational justice research. As did Colquitt (2001), Colquitt et al. examined the four factors of organizational justice. Using Hunter and Schmidt's (1990) procedures, Colquitt et al. analyzed a sample of 183 organizational justice studies. The meta-analysis yielded findings relevant to the present analysis. First, Colquitt et al. concluded that procedural, interpersonal, and informational justice are distinct constructs, empirically distinguishable from each other.

Second, the analysis demonstrated that procedural justice, interpersonal justice, and informational justice have different correlates. Although procedural justice, along with distributive justice, was the strongest or second strongest predictor of many key outcomes (e.g., job satisfaction, organizational commitment), informational and interpersonal justice were the strongest contributors to predicting other outcomes (e.g., organizational citizenship behaviors—individual referenced, withdrawal, negative reactions).

Kernan and Hanges (2002) studied survivor reactions to workplace reconfigurations, using multiple predictors and consequences of procedural justice, informational justice, and interpersonal justice. Of relevance to the present analysis, Kernan and Hanges found that the three justice factors had different antecedents: procedural justice (employee input), informational justice (communication quality, implementation), and interpersonal justice (employee input, communication quality, implementation, support for victims). Although procedural justice was strongly related to all four outcome variables—organizational commitment, job satisfaction, turnover intentions, trust in management—informational justice and interpersonal justice each contributed unique variance in the prediction of trust in management.

In summary, studies following the four-factor perspective yielded findings similar to the three-factor perspective. That is, interpersonal and informational justice, the two components of interactional justice, and procedural justice have different correlates. Further, there is some evidence that procedural, informational, and interpersonal justice have different antecedents, again more evidence to support the claim that interactional justice, or its components, are not merely a form of procedural justice.

SUMMARY, PUNCTUATION, AND RECOMMENDATIONS

Is interactional justice merely a form of procedural justice? One answer to that question is provided by Cohen-Charash and Spector (2001), who, after assessing the finding from their meta-analysis, concluded that "distributive, procedural, and interactional justice are strongly related, yet distinct constructs.... Thus, our findings support the need in having separate operationalizations of the construct" (p. 317). A similar answer is provided by Colquitt et al. (2001), who, in assessing the implications of their meta-analytic review, concluded that "the construct discrimination results suggests that procedural, interpersonal, and informational justice are distinct constructs that can be empirically distinguished from one another" (pp. 437–438). To summarize and punctuate, the empirical evidence provides a loud and clear answer to the question of

whether interactional justice is merely a form of procedural justice—and that answer is *"no."*

Given that answer, what should organizational justice researchers do now with respect to interactional justice? The meta-analyses of Cohen-Charash and Spector (2001) and Colquitt et al. (2001), along with my conceptual analysis (Bies, 2001), provide a foundation for responding to that question. That foundation is the basis for the following eight recommendations that are offered as guidance for organizational justice researchers.

As the first recommendation, justice researchers should always *measure interactional justice as a construct separate from procedural justice.* The meta-analysis conducted by Cohen-Charash and Spector (2001) concluded that although procedural justice and interactional justice are strongly correlated, they are also distinct constructs. Further, procedural justice and interactional justice have different relationships with different correlates (Bies, 2001).

In operational terms, this means that researchers should *not* combine procedural and interactional items as part of one umbrella measure of "procedural justice" or "process fairness" (Colquitt et al., 2001). There is little doubt that, in combining procedural and interactional items, one will achieve a high scale reliability as measured by the alpha coefficient. Yet as Cohen-Charash and Spector (2001) and Colquitt et al. (2001) argued, based on their meta-analytic reviews, such a combination only "muddies" the conceptual waters and hides important relationships between the two types of justice and their correlates.

As a second recommendation, not only should researchers measure interactional justice separate from procedural justice, researchers should *measure interactional justice as two separate constructs—informational justice and interpersonal justice.* Based on their meta-analytic review of organizational justice research, Colquitt et al. (2001) found clear evidence supporting Greenberg's (1993b) distinction between informational justice and interpersonal justice. Thus, not only is there a conceptual rationale underlying this recommendation, as provided by Greenberg (1993b), but also empirical support for it, as provided by Colquitt et al. (2001).

In operational terms, Colquitt (2001) provided helpful guidance as to how to measure informational justice and interpersonal justice. He developed and validated scales for these dimensions in two independent studies. Researchers developing similar scales for their specific contexts should be informed and guided by Colquitt (2001). The Kernan and Hanges (2002) study provides a good example of how to follow Colquitt's (2001) lead.

As a third recommendation, researchers need to *fill in gaps in research on interactional justice and its two components.* Both Cohen-Charash and

Spector (2001) and Colquitt et al. (2001) noted there were too few studies of interactional justice, or its two components, represented in their samples for meta-analysis. Although this chapter has documented the burgeoning stream of research on interactional justice, even more empirical studies are needed to more fully understand the dynamics of interactional justice and its two components, which is necessary for organizational justice to develop into an even more mature field of inquiry (Greenberg, 1993b).

Although previous research has identified organizational processes in which interactional justice concerns are salient to people, thus already providing some direction for researchers, there are environmental and technological shifts in the landscape of doing business that can provide additional direction. For example, in terms of the economic environment, organizations are facing increasing competitive pressures and decreasing resources to meet those pressures. As a result of those conditions, processes such as organizational change (and the myriad forms that it might take), conflict management and negotiation, and leadership immediately come to mind as rich contexts to apply an interactional justice perspective. In addition, as economies become even more service driven, interactional justice may be useful for analyzing the dynamics of boundary-spanning roles such as service employees dealing with customers (or health care professionals dealing with patients) in which informational and interpersonal concerns can be so central to the interaction and the experience. Also, given the globalization of business operations, examining cross-cultural similarities and differences with respect to informational and interpersonal concerns is an area in need of exploration. Finally, given the rise of technology and its impact on organizational communications, an interactional justice analysis of the use of e-mails and their impact on senders and receivers is another avenue for fruitful research opportunities. The limited richness of the medium of e-mail may raise informational justice concerns, whereas the impulsiveness of some responses via e-mail (e.g., "flaming") may raise interpersonal justice concerns.

As a fourth recommendation, *multiple justice dimensions should be analyzed in single studies*. As the meta-analytic reviews of Colquitt et al. (2001) and Cohen-Charash and Spector (2001) found, the different justice dimensions—whether it be the three- or four-factor models—have different correlates. By including multiple dimensions, we can discover further differences and interactions between the dimensions of organizational justice.

There are illustrative examples of the importance of analyzing multiple dimensions of organizational justice in one study. For example, Kernan and Hanges (2002) found that although procedural justice was a stronger predictor of outcomes in response to corporate reorganization,

informational justice and interpersonal justice add unique contribution in terms of variance explained. As another example, Ambrose et al. (2002) found additive effects of distributive justice, procedural justice, and interactional justice on workplace sabotage. As a third example, Skarlicki and Folger (1997) found that organizational retaliation behavior was predicted by a three-way interaction of distributive justice, procedural justice, and interactional justice.

As a fifth recommendation, *more research is needed to identify the antecedents of interactional justice and its two components relative to procedural justice.* Bies (2001) suggested that there may be different principles or criteria that people use in judging interactional justice versus procedural justice. But we need to go beyond the conceptual level and identify, at the empirical level, the antecedents that are more closely associated with interactional justice but not procedural justice (Bobocel & Holmvall, 2001).

Supporting the Bobocel and Holmvall thesis, Kernan and Hanges (2002) found different antecedents of procedural justice, informational justice, and interpersonal justice in their study of workplace reconfigurations. Similarly, Moye, Masterson, and Bartol (1997) found that the manipulation of consistency and accuracy significantly influenced perceptions of procedural justice while the manipulation of respect and justification significantly influenced ratings of interactional justice. Further, Moye et al. found no interactions among the manipulations, which again points to different constructs with differential antecedents.

As a sixth recommendation, *more studies with a broader conceptualization of informational justice are needed.* Although social accounts are clearly central to informational justice (Greenberg, 1993b), informational justice is not limited to social accounts (Bies, 2001). Further, as discussed later in this chapter, informational justice concerns should not be limited to the enactment of a specific procedure or the allocation of a specific outcome, as proposed by Greenberg (1993b). Indeed, information sharing about organizational matters—that is, just keeping people "informed"—is often viewed by people as a fairness issue (Bies, 2003).

With this broader conceptualization of informational justice, researchers should begin to examine the effects of different amounts of information sharing, including the frequency of information disclosure, on perceptions of informational justice. For example, to be kept "in the dark" about an impending change in the organization—and particularly if that change affects one directly—can create feelings of anger and unfairness, feelings that may not be mitigated by a social account (Bies, 2003). In terms of the frequency of information disclosure, organizations or leaders that share information more regularly may create a greater sense of informational justice relative to those that don't (Bies, 2003). The timing of information sharing—whether before a decision,

during the announcement of a decision, or after the decision—is another variable relevant to informational justice (Bies et al., 1993). For example, Bies (2003) found that advance warning of impending bad news is a key fairness concern, in addition to information provided during the delivery of bad news. Finally, as mentioned earlier, different media through which information is shared (e.g., face-to-face, e-mail) may also be a key factor shaping people's sense of informational justice.

As a seventh recommendation, *more studies conducted on different facets of interpersonal justice are needed.* Again, as discussed later in this chapter, interpersonal justice concerns should not be limited to the enactment of a specific procedure or the allocation of a specific outcome, as proposed by Greenberg (1993b). In a previous analysis (Bies, 2001), I argued that interpersonal justice is multifaceted and identified four categories of actions that can violate one's sense of interpersonal justice, which can provide guidance for future research.

One category of actions is *derogatory judgments* made about people by others, which, in terms of interpersonal justice, refers to the truthfulness and accuracy of statements and judgments about a person. Let me provide illustrative examples of this category. Accusing another of "stealing ideas" when in fact that was not true would be an example of a derogatory statement (Bies & Tripp, 1996). Similarly, a manager blaming the team for a performance failure, when it was really due to a bad decision by the manager, would be another example of a derogatory statement (Bies & Tripp, 1996). Finally, "bad-mouthing" another person to create an unfavorable image of that person, a common occurrence in organizations (Bies & Tripp, 1996), can violate one's sense of interpersonal justice (Mikula et al., 1990).

A second category of actions involves *deception*, which, in terms of interpersonal justice, refers to the correspondence between one's words and actions. As an example, when people feel "lied" to, it makes them angry and resentful (Bies, 2001). Future research should focus on organizational contexts and processes in which lies and other deceptive practices may be prevalent, such as corporate recruitment (Bies & Moag, 1986), negotiation (Shapiro & Bies, 1994), and leadership (Lewicki, McAllister, & Bies, 1998).

A third category of actions involves *invasion of privacy*, which, in terms of interpersonal justice, refers to the legitimacy of disclosure of personal information about one person to another. An example of one's privacy being invaded would be the disclosure of confidences and secrets by one's boss to another person, which is a common occurrence in the politics and conflict of everyday organizational life (Morrill, 1995), and thus a promising avenue for future research. Also, the unwarranted disclosure of employee information to a third party would be another avenue for future research (Culnan & Bies, 2003).

As the fourth category, people are concerned about a variety of forms of *disrespect*, which, in terms of interpersonal justice, refers to the signs and symbols conveying respect for the intrinsic value or worth of the individual. Among contexts or processes ripe for more research, a focus on any type of bad news (e.g., budget cuts, layoffs, employee terminations) has already demonstrated the usefulness of an interpersonal justice lens of analysis. Two additional directions for future research on interpersonal justice include leadership—particularly abusive bosses (Bies & Tripp, 1999; Hornstein, 1996)—and e-mail communication in which it is often difficult to convey "respect" given the limited "richness" of that medium of communication.

As the final recommendation, *researchers should reexamine previous studies that have combined procedural justice and interactional justice dimensions of organizational justice in their scales or models.* One implication of this recommendation is that, for studies that combined procedural justice and interactional justice items into one scale—and there are several that did so (see Colquitt et al., 2001)—scholars might redo those analyses with separated scales and assess the differential effects of procedural justice and interactional justice.

As another implication, models that have combined procedural justice and interactional justice dimensions, such as the seminal relational model of procedural justice (Lind & Tyler, 1988; Tyler & Lind, 1992), might want to reinterpret the meaning of their findings. The relational model combined procedural elements (e.g., neutrality, trust) and interactional elements (e.g., standing). Assessing the relative influence of those three variables on different consequences would be important for a richer understanding of the relational model. Indeed, given that interactional justice is a better predictor of rating supervisory authority whereas procedural justice is a better predictor of higher organizational authorities (Masterson et al., 2000), there is empirical support underlying this recommendation as well.

WHAT IS THE FUTURE OF INTERACTIONAL JUSTICE? NEW VISTAS ON THE CONCEPTUAL HORIZON

Now that the evidence has been "sifted and sorted," and the question of whether interactional justice is merely a form of procedural justice answered, one might conclude that the controversy surrounding interactional justice is over. However appealing that conclusion might be, it is a conclusion that is not warranted. For, as one question was answered in this chapter, it opens the door to a new question. That being so, what is the future of interactional justice?

One response to that question could be informed by Greenberg's (1993b) groundbreaking taxonomy of justice classes. More specifi-

cally, by separating interactional justice into two separate dimensions—informational justice and interpersonal justice—coupled with
empirical evidence demonstrating the generative theory-building of
that taxonomy (Colquitt, 2001; Kernan & Hanges, 2002), one might
conclude that there is no future for interactional justice. Indeed, one
cannot dispute the empirical evidence pointing to the two components
of interactional justice.

Yet such an answer misses the deeper and more profound implications of interactional justice. In a Lewinian (1935) sense, much of the
controversy about interactional justice versus procedural justice has
been about *phenotyes*—that is, distinguishing the characteristics of one
type of justice relative to another type of justice. Although distinguishing between phenotypes is important, the *genotype* of interactional justice is also important. Genotype refers to the conditional-genetic
properties of the phenomenon (Lewin, 1935). In the case of interactional
justice, people possess a view of the self as "sacred," and a violation of
that sacred self is personal and painful, resulting in an emotionally intense experience (Bies, 2001; Bies & Tripp, 2002).

On one level, it does not matter to me whether interactional justice
is one construct or two (i.e., informational justice, interpersonal justice). But although I make that statement, let me also state for the record that this chapter is a public affirmation that I have come to
"believe" in the two-component view of interactional justice
(Greenberg, 1993b). Moreover, this statement is not meant to diminish
or detract from Greenberg's (1993b) conceptual advancement, which,
again in my judgment, represents the most significant development in
our understanding of organizational justice in the last 10 years.

Again, for me, the deeper significance of interactional justice is in
terms of its genotype. If we take interactional justice seriously, regardless of its one- or two-component form, and examine its underlying psychological dynamics more closely, the construct opens up
new conceptual vistas for organizational justice research. Such an
analysis can provide directions for future theory-building and empirical research.

This section of the chapter is organized around an analysis of three
new conceptual vistas created by interactional justice. First, by embracing interactional justice or its two components as legitimate, it
leads one to view justice concerns more broadly in terms of encounters, not just exchanges. Second, if we take the encounter perspective
seriously, it raises the issue of whether interactional justice is different
from related nonjustice constructs. Finally, research on interactional
justice, which began with injustice is the starting place for analysis,
rather than justice, raises the question of whether injustice and justice
are similar or different constructs.

Justice as Encounter Versus Justice as Exchange

Despite its powerful conceptual insights, Greenberg's (1993b) justice taxonomy is an analysis limited only to the *exchange* context—specific organizational decisions or resource allocations. Unfortunately, the exchange perspective truncates the analysis of important justice concerns raised by people in their everyday *encounters* in organizations (Bies, 2001). Indeed, there are justice concerns directly relevant to Greenberg's (1993b) informational and interpersonal justice constructs that would be excluded from his taxonomy.

As support for this line of reasoning, empirical evidence suggests that advance warning about possible job layoffs is a critical fairness concern for people (Bies, 2003). Conversely, the failure to share information about impending changes or bad news is associated with feelings of anger, resentment, and unfairness (Bies, 2003). Each of these examples is not associated with a specific decision or allocation, but they clearly are informational in nature and associated with justice concerns raised in encounters between organizational authorities and the people in the organization.

As further support, people raise justice concerns about abusive bosses, broken promises, disclosure of confidences and secrets, and coercion—and such concerns often have nothing to do with a specific decision or resource allocation (Bies, 2001). Similarly, justice concerns are raised by the use of insults (Cropanzano & Ambrose, 2001; Miller, 2001) and working environments that are oppressive and inhumane (Bies & Greenberg, 2001). In the eyes of the victim, all of these interpersonal actions are viewed as *harmful* and *wrong*, the bases for feeling unjustly treated (Bies & Tripp, in press). Yet these examples are not currently captured by Greenberg's (1993b) taxonomy.

The argument for the encounter perspective is not new (Bies, 2001; see also Cropanzano, Byrne, Bobocel, & Rupp, 2001). Over a decade ago, Mikula et al. (1990) advanced a similar argument when they analyzed the controversy over status of interactional justice relative to procedural justice. From that analysis, Mikula et al. (1990) concluded that "the results of the present and the Messick et al. (1985) studies suggest a broader concept of interpersonal treatment which goes beyond situations of judgement and decision-making includes all kinds of interactions and encounters" (p. 143). Similarly, in their groundbreaking theory of procedural justice, Lind and Tyler (1988, p. 214) proposed that procedural justice effects might also occur in *routine social interaction* (emphasis added), thus linking procedural justice concerns to encounters.

What are implications of the encounter perspective for Greenberg's (1993b) taxonomy of justice classes? For me, the implications are small but significant. I propose that we follow Folger and Cropanzano (2001),

who separated economic benefits and costs from socioemotional benefits and costs in their analysis of justice. Then, in each of the four justice classes identified by Greenberg, we focus on economic benefits and costs and socioemotional benefits and costs, not just economic benefits and costs that follows from Greenberg's exchange perspective. Then we can extend the scope of Greenberg's analysis to include socioemotional benefits and costs, which are central to the encounter perspective (Bies, 2001), while preserving the taxonomy of justice classes as proposed by Greenberg. The significant implication of this proposal is that justice researchers can now dramatically expand the scope of organizational justice theory and research.

Proposing the encounter perspective brings to the conceptual forefront another controversy. Specifically, proposing the encounter perspective raises questions about the distinctiveness of interactional justice relative to constructs in other literatures (e.g., the leader behavior variable, consideration, from the Ohio State Leadership Studies). More specifically, applying the encounter perspective could lead one to claim that there would be so much overlap with interactional justice and related nonjustice constructs that, as a result, interactional justice is just part of some overarching construct such as consideration (Locke, 2003).

Interactional Justice and Related Nonjustice Constructs

In a recent and provocative analysis, Locke (2003) presented a critique of interactional justice and its construct validity. This analysis apparently was guided by the "good intentions" of bring some rigor to the analysis of organizational justice. Unfortunately, the analysis was filled with misunderstandings, if not misrepresentations, of my work on interactional justice. There are two major flaws in Locke's analysis that warrant attention.

First, in critiquing interactional justice, Locke drew on Piekoff's (1991) normative definition of justice as "the virtue of judging man's character and conduct objectively and or acting accordingly, granting to each man that which he deserves" (Piekoff, 1991, p. 276). From that normative definition, Locke argued that justice is only about the realms of cognition and action, and justice should only be about using reason, not emotion. Further, the only "valid" justice rule, according to Locke, is that of merit.

Although Locke's reasoning is entirely appropriate as part of the realm of a normative analysis of justice, it is not appropriate for the empirical realm. For, the study of organizational justice is about discovering the *psycho*-logic that shapes people's views of justice and fairness in organizations. Just as justice researchers could be legitimately criticized for committing the *naturalistic fallacy*, when they derive normative implica-

tions from empirical data (Greenberg & Bies, 1992), Locke may be committing the more general *definist fallacy* (Audi, 1999), which involves defining what *ought* to be justice in the eyes of people to the exclusion what people *actually* perceive and feel to be fair and just in the workplace.

Second, when Locke reviewed the different categories of violations of interactional justice that I identified in Bies (2001), he asserted that "none of these other categories has anything directly to do with justice, nor can all these elements be described by means of a single concept" (p. 433). Once again, Locke did not do justice to my work. Specifically, in "analyzing" the violations that I identified, Locke provided a "selective" list of violations without providing the critical information that there were meaningful conceptual categories that organized each of the examples (see Bies, 2001). Further, Locke's analysis is not informed by empirical evidence and conclusions from two recent meta-analyses on justice (e.g., Cohen-Charash & Spector, 2001; Colquitt et al., 2001), which makes it clear that interactional justice is a meaningful construct to people in forming judgments about justice in organizations.

But to be fair to Locke, once he departs from the normative perspective, he does raise an important conceptual question that is relevant to the present analysis. That being so, how is interactional justice different from that of the leader behaviors known as "consideration" from the Ohio State Leadership Studies (see Fleishman, 1973, and Bass, 1990, for reviews)? That is an important question, and one that warrants further discussion and analysis.

Summarizing 20 years of research that followed from the groundbreaking research on leader behavior by Halpin, Winer, Hemphill, and others, Fleishman (1973) noted that consideration initially involved "behavior indicating friendship, mutual trust, respect, a certain warmth and rapport between the supervisor and his group. As we continued to do research with these, the emphasis on friendship seemed to drop and the tolerance for two-way communications seemed to become a key feature of this dimension" (p. 8). At first glance, it appears that consideration shares conceptual overlap with interactional justice in that both variables focus on how people are treated. Leader behaviors associated with consideration, such as *integration* (i.e., trying to stop rumors when they occur), is similar to truthfulness and accuracy of statements and judgments about another, one category of interactional justice that I identified in Bies (2001). As another example, *two-way communications,* as another enactment of consideration, is similar to the informational justice construct (Greenberg, 1993b). Similarly, consideration in the form of *helping people with personal problems and finding time to listen to people* is similar to interpersonal justice (Greenberg, 1993b).

But other consideration variables, such as friendship, warmth, and rapport, are not part of interactional justice or its components, although they may be correlates or consequences. Two other categories that I identified as characteristic of interactional justice—correspondence between one's words and actions and respect, and the legitimacy of disclosure of personal information—are not part of how consideration is conceptualized. Thus, although there may be similarities, there are also differences.

Interestingly, when one undertakes a closer examination of several other consideration behaviors, they are similar to other facets of organizational justice. For example, the consideration category of *recognition* is similar to distributive justice (e.g., making sure that workers are rewarded for a job well done). *Encouraging others to express their opinions* and *getting group approval on important decisions*, which are other consideration behaviors, are similar to aspects of voice, which is central to procedural justice.

Following this line of reasoning, the question Locke posed in his analysis about interactional justice may be framed incorrectly. Instead of Locke's question of "how is interactional justice different from consideration?" the question should be, "how is consideration different from interactional justice?" Reframing Locke's question is not merely an exercise in semantics; rather, it raises the issue that justice is the figural element in the analysis of leadership, not some background element embedded in consideration behaviors of leaders.

Now, to be fair, one response to my reframed question is that research on consideration predated that of justice. But such a response would not be the result of an informed analysis. If one went back to the influential writings of French industrialist, Henri Fayol, the so-called "father" of management theory (Kast & Rosenzweig, 1974), one would find organizational justice is central to his conceptualization of management. Based on his experiences as a leader, which were first published in 1916 in France and translated for English-speaking audiences in 1949, Fayol (1949) identified 14 principles of general management. Of particular relevance to the present analysis, Fayol (1949) listed equity as principle 11. More specifically, Fayol argued that "For the personnel to be encouraged to carry out its duties with all the devotion and loyalty of which it is capable it must be treated with kindliness, and equity results from the combination of kindliness and justice ... [the manager] should strive to instill a sense of equity throughout all levels of the scalar chain" (p. 38). Thus, elements of interactional justice (i.e., kindliness in Fayol's terms) and distributive justice (justice in Fayol's terms) are central to the process of leadership and management.

The concern for justice in leadership and management was also a guiding influence on the early human relationists such as Elton Mayo

and those conducting the Hawthorne studies between 1927 and 1932 (Mayo, 1933). Guided by an ideology that Scott (1967) referred to as "industrial humanism," Mayo and others focused on designing a work environment that would restore the human dignity of workers. That focus on human dignity is central to my work on interactional justice.

Why justice is no longer a figural element in the dominant models of leadership and management today emerges as intriguing question from a sociology of knowledge point of view. As Lind and Tyler's (1992) research so compelling demonstrates, justice variables can explain important aspects of leadership, such as trust and support and approval of leaders. One direction for future analysis is to determine how justice got "lost" in the models of leadership, particularly since it was so central to early models of leadership and management.

Injustice Versus Justice: Similar or Different Constructs?

What has distinguished research on interactional justice relative to procedural justice is the starting point of analysis. Specifically, beginning with Bies and Moag (1986), the starting point for analyzing interactional justice dynamics has been the experience of injustice, not justice. In contrast, the starting point for analyzing procedural justice dynamics has been justice, not injustice (Leventhal, 1980; Thibaut & Walker, 1975).

In choosing such a starting point, I was guided by the seminal legal theory of Edmond Cahn (1949) in his book *The Sense of Injustice*. In that book, Cahn asked: "Why do we speak of the 'sense of injustice' rather than the 'sense of justice'?" Cahn answered: "Because 'justice' has been so beclouded by natural-law writings that it almost inevitably brings to mid some ideal relation or static condition or set of perceptual standards, while we are concerned, on the contrary, with what is active, vital, and experiential in the reactions of human beings" (p. 13). Moreover, Cahn argued that justice is "not a state, but a process; not a condition, but an action. 'Justice,' as we shall use the term, means the *active process* of remedying or preventing that which would arouse the sense of injustice" (p. 13). He defined the sense of injustice as "the sympathetic reaction of outrage, horror, shock, resentment, and anger, those affections of the viscera and abnormal secretions of the adrenals that prepare the human animal to resist attack. Nature has thus equipped all men to regard injustice to another as personal aggression" (p. 24). Thus, for Cahn, injustice and justice are related, but different.

That injustice and justice may be different constructs has empirical support. For example, Gilliland, Benson, and Schepers (1998) demonstrated that reactions to unjust acts are more intense than reactions to a just act. In fact, Gilliland et al. (1998) found a threshold at which no amount of just acts can compensate for unjust acts. Moreover, following

Gilliland, Goldman, Tripp, and Beach (2000), justice and injustice are separate constructs that provoke qualitatively different reactions. That is, justice and injustice are two different, although related, constructs.

Similarly, Lewicki et al. (1998) demonstrated that trust is not the opposite of distrust, that they are not two ends of the same construct, because it is possible for a person to simultaneously trust and distrust another party. Similarly, in the study of affectivity, Watson and Clark (Watson & Clark, 1984; Watson, Clark, & Tellegen, 1988) found that negative affectivity is not the opposite of positive affectivity because each consists of different emotions, not different quantities of the same emotions.

This line of reasoning carries important methodological implications for organizational justice researchers. Specifically, when researchers measure interactional justice (or its two components), they might ask such questions that focus on interactional *justice* like, "Were the authorities honest with you?" and "Did the authorities treat you with respect?"—and ask reverse-coded items interactional *injustice* like, "Were you lied to by authorities?" and "Were you treated rudely?" The items are then added and combined into an interactional justice scale, or informational and interpersonal justice scales. The evidence just reviewed suggests that this approach of combining justice and injustice—and treating them as equivalents—may have confounded two different, although related, variables. Future studies should measure the justice and injustice aspects of interactional, informational, and interpersonal justice separately, and not combine them.

CONCLUSION

In reflecting back over the past two decades, a reasonable person could, and perhaps should, conclude that the controversy and dispute over the distinctiveness and independence of interactional justice have been a natural by-product of normal science efforts conducted by organizational justice scholars (Kuhn, 1970). But now, given the growing weight of empirical evidence, one would hope that the question of "is interactional justice merely a form of procedural justice?" becomes an echo of the past, useful for justice researchers to remember as important in the development of field's intellectual maturity. If not, then, like some scholarly "urban legend," the belief that interactional justice is merely a form of procedural justice will still persist.

Although one controversy has been put to rest with this chapter, this chapter also creates a new controversy. Specifically, my advancement of the encounter perspective will likely be viewed as provocative, even subversive, as again I challenge the fundamental assumptions of organizational justice theory. To those who get provoked, even agitated, let me remind them that *it is the data, not me, speaking*. As the field assimi-

lated interactional justice, and, I think it is fair to say is better off for it, my hypothesis is that the same fate will await the encounter perspective. Although history may not repeat itself, it surely does rhyme.

REFERENCES

Ambrose, M. L., Seabright, M. A., & Schminke, M. (2002). Sabotage in the workplace: The role of organizational injustice. *Organizational Behavior and Human Decision Processes, 89*, 947–965.

Andersson, L. M., & Pearson, C. M. (1999). Tit for tat? The spiraling effect of incivility in the workplace. *Academy of Management Review, 24*, 452–471.

Aryee, S., Budhwar, P. S., & Chen, Z. X. (2002). Trust as a mediator of the relationship between organizational justice and work outcomes: Test of a social exchange model. *Journal of Organizational Behavior, 23*, 267–286.

Audi, R. (1999). *The Cambridge dictionary of philosophy* (2nd ed.). Cambridge: Cambridge University Press.

Barling, J., & Phillips, M. (1993). Interactional, formal, and distributive justice in the workplace: An exploratory study. *Journal of Psychology, 127*, 649–656.

Baron, R. A. (1988). Negative effects of destructive criticism: Impact on conflict, self-efficacy, and task performance. *Journal of Applied Psychology, 73*, 199–207.

Bass, B. M. (1990). *Bass and Stogdill's handbook of leadership: Theory, research, and managerial applications.* New York: Free Press.

Bennett, N., Martin, C. L., Bies, R. J., & Brockner, J. (1995). Coping with a layoff: A longitudinal study of victims. *Journal of Management, 21*, 1025–1040.

Beugre, C. D., & Baron, R. A. (2001). Perceptions of systemic justice: The effects of distributive, procedural, and interactional justice. *Journal of Applied Social Psychology, 31*, 324–339.

Bies, R. J. (1987). The predicament of injustice: The management of moral outrage. In L. L. Cummings & B. M. Staw (Eds.), *Research in organizational behavior* (Vol. 9, pp. 289–319). Greenwich, CT: JAI Press.

Bies, R. J. (1996). Beyond the hidden self: Psychological and ethical aspects of privacy in organizations. In D. Messick & A. Tenbrunsel (Ed.), *Codes of conduct: Behavioral research into business ethics* (pp. 104–116). New York: Russell Sage Foundation.

Bies, R. J. (2001). Interactional (in)justice: The sacred and the profane. In J. Greenberg & R. Cropanzano (Eds.), *Advances in organizational justice* (pp. 89–118). Palo Alto: Stanford University Press.

Bies, R. J. (2003). *The manager as intuitive politician: Blame management and the delivery of bad news.* Unpublished manuscript.

Bies, R. J., & Bobocel, D. R. (2001, August). The case of interactional justice v. procedural justice: Concurring and dissenting opinions. Presented at J. Greenberg (Chair), *Controversial Issues in Organizational Justice.* Symposium conducted at the annual meeting of the Academy of Management, Washington, DC.

Bies, R. J., & Greenberg, J. (2001). Justice, culture, and corporate image: The swoosh, the sweatshops, and the sway of public opinion. In M. Gannon & K. Newman (Eds.), *Handbook of cross-cultural management* (pp. 320–334). Oxford, England: Blackwell.

Bies, R. J., Martin, C. L., & Brockner, J. (1993). Just laid off, but still a "good citizen"? Only if the process is fair. *Employee Responsibilities and Rights Journal, 6*, 227–238.

Bies, R. J., & Moag, J. S. (1986). Interactional justice: Communication criteria of fairness. In R. J. Lewicki, B. H. Sheppard, & M. H. Bazerman (Eds.), *Research on negotiation in organizations* (pp. 43–55). Greenwich, CT: JAI Press.

Bies, R. J., & Shapiro, D. L. (1987). Interactional fairness judgments: The influence of causal accounts. *Social Justice Research, 1,* 199–218.

Bies, R. J., & Shapiro, D. L. (1988). Voice and justification: Their influence on procedural fairness judgments. *Academy of Management Journal, 31,* 676–685.

Bies, R. J., Shapiro, D. L., & Cummings, L. L. (1988). Causal accounts and managing organizational conflict: Is it enough to say it's not my fault? *Communication Research, 15,* 381–399.

Bies, R. J., & Tripp, T. M. (1993). Employee-initiated defamation lawsuits: Organizational responses and dilemmas. *Employee Responsibilities and Rights Journal, 6,* 313–324.

Bies, R. J., & Tripp, T. M. (1996). Beyond distrust: "Getting even" and the need for revenge. In R. M. Kramer & T. Tyler (Eds.), *Trust in organizations* (pp. 246–260). Newbury Park, CA: Sage.

Bies, R. J., & Tripp, T. M. (1999). Two faces of the powerless: Coping with tyranny. In R. M. Kramer & M. A. Neale (Eds.), *Power and influence in organizations* (pp. 203–219). Thousand Oaks, CA: Sage.

Bies, R. J., & Tripp, T. M. (2002). Hot flashes, open wounds: Injustice and the tyranny of its emotions. In S. Gilliland, D. Steiner, & D. Skarlicki (Eds.), *Emerging perspectives on managing organizational justice* (pp. 203–223). Greenwich, CT: IAP Press.

Bies, R. J., & Tripp, T. M. (in press). The study of revenge in the workplace: Conceptual, ideological, and empirical issues. In P. Spector & S. Fox (Eds.), *Counterproductive workplace behavior: An integration of both actor and recipient perspectives on causes and consequences.* Washington, DC: American Psychological Association.

Bies, R. J., & Tyler, T. (1993). The "litigation mentality" in organizations: A test of alternative psychological explanations. *Organization Science, 4,* 352–366.

Blodgett, J. G., Hill, D. J., & Tax, S. S. (1997). The effects of distributive, procedural, and interactional justice on postcomplaint behavior. *Journal of Retailing, 73,* 185–210.

Bobocel, D. R., & Holmvall, C. (2001). Are interactional justice and procedural justice different? Framing the debate. In S. Gilliland, D. Steiner, & D. Skarlicki (Eds.), *Research in social issues in management: Theoretical and cultural perspectives on organizational justice* (pp. 85–110). Greenwich, CT: Information Age Publishing.

Bottom, W. P., Gibson, K., Daniels, S. E., & Murnighan, J. K. (2002). When talk is not cheap: Substantive penance and expressions of intent in rebuilding cooperation. *Organization Science, 13,* 497–513.

Brockner, J., DeWitt, R. L., Grover, S., & Reed, T. (1990). When it is especially important to explain why: Factors affecting the relationship between managers' explanations of a layoff and survivors' reactions to the layoff. *Journal of Experimental Social Psychology, 26,* 389–407.

Cahn, E. (1949). *The sense of injustice.* New York: New York University Press.

Clemmer, E. C. (1993). An investigation into the relationship of fairness and customer satisfaction with services. In R. Cropanzano (Ed.), *Justice in the workplace: Approaching fairness in human resource management* (pp. 193–207). Hillsdale, NJ: Lawrence Erlbaum Associates.

Cohen-Charash, Y., & Spector, P. E. (2001). The role of justice in organizations: A meta-analysis. *Organizational Behavior and Human Decision Processes, 86,* 278–324.

Colquitt, J. A. (2001). On the dimensionality of organizational justice: A construct validation of a measure. *Journal of Applied Psychology, 86,* 386–400.

Colquitt, J. A., Conlon, D. E., Wesson, M. J., Porter, C., & Ng, K. Y. (2001). Justice at the millennium: A meta-analytic review of 25 years of organizational justice research. *Journal of Applied Psychology, 86,* 425–445.

Colquitt, J. A., & Greenberg, J. (2003). Organizational justice: A fair assessment of the state of the literature. In J. Greenberg (Ed.), *Organizational behavior: The state of the science* (pp. 165–210). Mahwah, NJ: Lawrence Erlbaum Associates.

Conlon, D. E., & Murray, N. M. (1996). Customer perceptions of corporate responses to product complaints. *Academy of Management Journal, 39,* 1040–1056.

Cortina, L. M., Magley, V. J., Williams, J. H., & Langhout, R. D. (2001). Incivility in the workplace: Incidence and impact. *Journal of Occupational Health Psychology, 6,* 64–80.

Cropanzano, R., & Ambrose, M. L. (2001). Procedural and distributive justice are more similar than you think: A monistic perspective and a research agenda. In J. Greenberg & R. Cropanzano (Eds.), *Advances in organizational justice* (pp. 119–151). Palo Alto, CA: Stanford University Press.

Cropanzano, R., Byrne, Z. S., Bobocel, D. R., & Rupp, D. R. (2001). Moral virtues, fairness heuristics, social entities, and other denizens of organizational justice. *Journal of Vocational Behavior, 58,* 164–209.

Cropanzano, R., & Greenberg, J. (1997). Progress in organizational justice: Tunneling through the maze. In C. L. Cooper & I. T. Robertson (Eds.), *International review of industrial and organizational psychology* (Vol. 12, pp. 317–372). London: Wiley.

Cropanzano, R., Prehar, C. A., & Chen, P. Y. (2002). Using social exchange theory to distinguish procedural from interactional justice. *Group and Organizational Management, 27,* 324–351.

Cropanzano, R., & Randall, M. L. (1993). Injustice and work behavior: A historical review. In R. Cropanzano (Ed.), *Justice in the workplace: Approaching fairness in human resource management* (pp. 1–20). Hillsdale, NJ: Lawrence Erlbaum Associates.

Culnan, M. J., & Bies, R. J. (2003). Consumer privacy: Balancing economic and justice considerations. *Journal of Social Issues, 59,* 323–342.

Daly, J. P. (1995). Explaining changes to employees: The influence of justifications and change outcomes on employees' fairness judgments. *Journal of Applied Behavioral Science, 31,* 415–428.

Elovainio, M., Kivimäki, M., & Helkama, K. (2001). Organizational justice evaluations, job control, and occupational strain. *Journal of Applied Psychology, 86,* 418–424.

Fayol, H. (1949). *General and industrial management* (C. Storrs, Trans.). London: Pittman & Sons.

Fleishman, E. A. (1973). Twenty years of consideration and structure. In E. A. Fleishman & J. G. Hunt (Eds.), *Current developments in the study of leadership* (pp. 1–37). Carbondale, IL: Southern Illinois University Press.

Folger, R., & Bies, R. J. (1989). Managerial responsibilities and procedural justice. *Employee Responsibilities and Rights Journal, 2,* 79–90.

Folger, R., & Cropanzano, R. (1998). *Organizational justice and human resource management.* Beverly Hills, CA: Sage.

Folger, R., & Cropanzano, R. (2001). Fairness theory: Justice as accountability. In J. Greenberg & R. Cropanzano (Eds.), *Advances in organizational justice* (pp. 1–55). Palo Alto, CA: Stanford University Press.

Fuller, J. B., & Hester, K. (2001). A closer look at the relationship between justice perceptions and union participation. *Journal of Applied Psychology, 86*, 1096–1105.

Gilliland, S. W, Benson, L., & Schepers, D. H. (1998). A rejection threshold in justice evaluations: Effect on judgment and decision-making. *Organizational Behavior and Human Decision Processes, 76*, 113–131.

Gilliland, S. W., Goldman, B. M., Tripp, T., & Beach, L. R. (2000, May). *Violating images of justice: A decision to act.* Paper presented at the 7th Behavioral Decision Research in Management Conference, Tucson, AZ.

Greenberg, J. (1990). Organizational justice: Yesterday, today, and tomorrow. *Journal of Management, 16*, 399–432.

Greenberg, J. (1993a). Stealing in the name of justice: Informational and interpersonal moderators of theft reactions to underpayment inequity. *Organizational Behavior and Human Decision Processes, 54*, 81–103.

Greenberg, J. (1993b). The social side of fairness: Interpersonal and informational classes of organizational justice. In R. Cropanzano (Ed.), *Justice in the workplace: Approaching fairness in human resource management* (pp. 79–103). Hillsdale, NJ: Lawrence Erlbaum Associates.

Greenberg, J. (1994). Using socially fair treatment to promote acceptance of a work site smoking ban. *Journal of Applied Psychology, 79*, 288–297.

Greenberg, J. (2001). The seven loose can(n)ons of organizational justice. In J. Greenberg & R. Cropanzano (Eds.), *Advances in organizational justice* (pp. 245–271). Palo Alto, CA: Stanford University Press.

Greenberg, J., & Bies, R. J. (1992). Establishing the role of empirical studies of organizational justice in philosophical inquiries into business ethics. *Journal of Business Ethics, 11*, 97–108.

Hornstein, H. A. (1996). *Brutal bosses and their prey.* New York: Riverhead Books.

Hunter, J. E., & Schmidt, F. L. (1990). *Methods of meta-analysis.* Newbury Park, CA: Sage.

Kast, F. E., & Rosenzweig, J. E. (1974). *Organization and management: A systems approach* (2nd ed.). New York: McGraw-Hill.

Kernan, M. C., & Hanges, P. J. (2002). Survivor reactions to reorganization: Antecedents and consequences of procedural, interpersonal, and informational justice. *Journal of Applied Psychology, 87*, 916–928.

Kickul, J., Lester, S. W., & Finkl, J. (2002). Promise-breaking during radical organizational change: Do justice interventions make a difference? *Journal of Organizational Behavior, 23*, 469–488.

Kuhn, T. (1970). *The structure of scientific revolutions* (2nd ed.). Chicago: University of Chicago Press.

Lakatos, I. (1971). Falsification and the methodology of scientific research programmes. In I. Lakatos & A. Musgrove (Eds.), *Criticism and the growth of knowledge* (pp. 91–196). Cambridge, UK: Cambridge University Press.

Leventhal, G. S. (1980). What should be done with equity theory? New approaches to the study of fairness in social relationships. In K. Gergen, M. Greenberg, & R. Willis (Eds.), *Social exchange: New advances in theory and research* (pp. 27–55). New York: Plenum Press.

Lewicki, R. J., McAllister, D. M., & Bies, R. J. (1998). Trust and distrust: New relationships and realities. *Academy of Management Review, 23*, 438–458.

Lewin, K. (1935). *A dynamic theory of personality.* New York: McGraw-Hill.

Lind, E. A., & Tyler, T. R. (1988). *The social psychology of procedural justice.* New York: Plenum.

Locke, E. A. (2003). Good definitions: The epistemological foundation of scientific progress. In J. Greenberg (Ed.), *Organizational behavior: The state of the science* (pp. 415–444) Mahwah, NJ: Lawrence Erlbaum Associates.

Maletesta, R. M., & Byrne, Z. S. (1997, April). *The impact of formal and interactional justice on organizational outcomes.* Paper presented at the annual conference of the Society for Industrial and Organizational Psychology, St. Louis, MO.

Masterson, S. S., Lewis-McClear, K., Goldman, B. M., & Taylor, M. S. (1997). *Interactional justice revisited: The differential effects of treatment and procedures on work relationships and outcomes.* Unpublished manuscript.

Masterson, S. S., Lewis-McClear, K., Goldman, B. M., & Taylor, M. S. (2000). Integrating justice and social exchange: The differing effects of fair procedures and treatment on work relationships. *Academy of Management Journal, 43,* 738–748.

Mayo, E. (1933). *The human problems of industrial civilization.* New York: Macmillan.

Messick, D. M., Bloom, S., Boldizar, J. P., & Samuelson, C. D. (1985). Why we are fairer than others. *Journal of Experimental Social Psychology, 21,* 480–500.

Mikula, G. (1986). The experience of injustice: Toward a better understanding of its phenomenology. In H. W. Bierhoff, R. L. Cohen, & J. Greenberg (Eds.), *Justice in interpersonal relations* (pp. 103–123). New York: Plenum Press.

Mikula, G., Petri, B., & Tanzer, N. (1990). What people regard as just and unjust: Types and structures of everyday experiences of injustice. *European Journal of Social Psychology, 20,* 133–149.

Miller, D. T. (2001). Disrespect and the experience of injustice. *Annual Review of Psychology, 52,* 527–553.

Morrill, C. (1995). *The executive way: Conflict management in corporations.* Chicago: University of Chicago Press.

Moorman, R. H. (1991). Relationship between organizational justice and organizational citizenship behaviors: Do fairness perceptions influence employee citizenship? *Journal of Applied Psychology, 76,* 845–855.

Moye, N. A., Masterson, S. S., & Bartol, K. M. (1997, August). *Differentiating antecedents and consequences or procedural and interactional justice: Empirical evidence in support of separate constructs.* Paper presented at the Academy of Management Meetings, Boston.

Naumann, S. E., Bennett, N., Bies, R. J., & Martin, C. (1998). Laid off, but still loyal: The influence of perceived justice and organizational support. *International Journal of Conflict Management, 9,* 356–368.

Piekoff, L. (1991). *Objectivism: The philosophy of Ayn Rand.* New York: Dutton.

Ployhart, R. E., Ryan, A. M., & Bennett, M. (1999). Explanations for selection decisions: Applicants' reactions to informational and sensitivity features of explanations. *Journal of Applied Psychology, 84,* 87–106.

Rahim, M. A., Magner, N. R., & Shapiro, D. L. (2000). Do justice perceptions influence styles of handling conflict with the supervisor? What justice perceptions, precisely? *International Journal of Conflict Management, 11,* 9–31.

Rosenthal, R. (1991). *Meta-analytic procedures for social research* (rev. ed.). Thousand Oaks, CA: Sage.

Rupp, D. E., & Cropanzano, R. (2002). The mediating effects of social exchange relationships in predicting workplace outcomes from multifoci organizational justice. *Organizational Behavior and Human Decision Processes, 89,* 925–946.

Scott, W. G. (1967). *Organization theory: A behavioral analysis for management.* Homewood, IL: Richard D. Irwin.

Shapiro, D. L. (1991). The effect of explanations on negative reactions to deceit. *Administrative Science Quarterly, 36*, 614–630.

Shapiro, D. L., & Bies, R. J. (1994). Threats, bluffs, and disclaimers in negotiations. *Organizational Behavior and Human Decision Processes, 60*, 14–35.

Sindhav, B. (2001). The role of organizational justice in managing change within marketing channels. *Journal of Marketing Channels, 9*, 65–91.

Sitkin, S. B., & Bies, R. J. (1993). Social accounts in conflict situations: On using explanations to manage conflict. *Human Relations, 46*, 349–370.

Skarlicki, D. P., & Folger, R. (1997). Retaliation in the workplace: The roles of distributive, procedural, and interactional justice. *Journal of Applied Psychology, 82*, 434–443.

Skarlicki, D. P., Folger, R., & Tesluk, P. (1999). Personality as a moderator in the relationship between fairness and retaliation. *Academy of Management Journal, 42*, 100–108.

Sweeney, P. D., & McFarlin, D. B. (1993). Workers' evaluations of the "ends" and the "means" An examination of four models of distributive and procedural justice. *Organizational Behavior and Human Decision Processes, 55*, 23–40.

Tepper, B. J. (2000). Consequences of abusive supervision. *Academy of Management Journal, 43*, 178–190.

Thibaut, J., & Walker, L. (1975). *Procedural justice: A psychological analysis*. Hillsdale, NJ: Lawrence Erlbaum Associates.

Tyler, T. R. (1988). What is procedural justice? *Law and Society Review, 22*, 301–335.

Tyler, T. R., & Bies, R. J. (1990). Beyond formal procedures: The interpersonal context of procedural justice. In J. . Carroll (Ed.), *Applied social psychology and organizational settings* (pp. 77–98). Hillsdale, NJ: Lawrence Erlbaum Associates.

Tyler, T. R., & Blader, S.L. (2000). *Cooperation in groups: Procedural justice, social identity, behavioral engagement*. Philadelphia, PA: Psychology Press.

Tyler, T. R., & Lind, E. A. (1992). A relational model of authority in groups. In M. P. Zanna (Ed.), *Advances in experimental social psychology* (Vol. 25, pp. 115–191). New York: Academic Press.

Watson, D., & Clark, L. A. (1984). Negative affectivity: The disposition to experience aversive emotional states. *Psychological Bulletin, 96*, 465–490.

Watson, D., Clark, L. A., & Tellegen, A. (1988). Development and validation of brief measures of positive and negative affect: The PANAS scales. *Journal of Personality and Social Psychology, 54*, 1063–1070.

4

How Should Organizational Justice Be Measured?

Jason A. Colquitt
University of Florida

John C. Shaw
Mississippi State University

This chapter reviews the important choices inherent in choosing or de-signing measures for use in organizational justice research. These choices include considering the type of justice (i.e., distributive, proce-dural, interpersonal, informational), the source of justice (human agent vs. formal organization), the context of justice (a specific event or more general context), and the measurement approach (direct "how fair" items or indirect items focusing on justice rules). We describe the construct va-lidity implications of these choices, and conduct a review of key measures from the 1970s to present, with special attention paid to Colquitt's (2001) recently validated scales. We close by describing important ques-tions and controversies that are key to the measurement of justice in the future. These include questions surrounding the appropriateness of spe-cific measurement choices, concerns about intercorrelations among jus-tice types, and the relevance of more general or global justice measures.

Few would disagree with the notion that theory forms the foundation for scientific research. In fact, Kerlinger and Lee (2000) called theory the "basic aim of science" (p. 11). Theories provide the general expla-nations used to explain and predict natural phenomena. They are also used to frame and organize complex events (Bacharach, 1989) and raise people's consciousness of critical concepts and processes (Brief & Dukerich, 1991). It is therefore not surprising that submission infor-mation in top scholarly journals consistently calls for strong theoreti-cal contributions. It is also not surprising that reviewers for top journals are instructed to use theory as a primary means of evaluating submitted manuscripts.

Of course, theories cannot be tested without measurement (Bacharach, 1989). Simply put, measurement is the assignment of numer-als to objects, events, or concepts (Kerlinger & Lee, 2000). Measurement serves to operationalize the constructs in a theory so that they can be sub-jected to empirical testing. Even the most interesting and powerful theo-ries are useless if their component constructs are poorly measured. Indeed, when Campbell (1990) discussed how to improve the flaws pres-ent in industrial and organizational psychology, he concluded that better measurement was every bit as important as better theory.

At one point, the organizational justice literature was hindered by both limited theory development and poor measurement. In their landmark re-view, Lind and Tyler (1988) observed, "In our view, the body of research in procedural justice is, at this time, both too extensive and too limited to per-mit one to advance a broad and specific theory" (p. 221). Lind and Tyler

(1988) also noted that "there is too little attention devoted to constancy of measurement across studies." (p. 245). In the years since Lind and Tyler's (1988) review, theory building in the justice literature has seen a marked increase with the introduction of the relational model (Tyler & Lind, 1992), fairness theory (Folger & Cropanzano, 1998, 2001), and fairness heuristic theory (Lind, 2001a; van den Bos, Lind, & Wilke, 2001).

One key question explored in this chapter is whether advances in measurement have kept pace with advances in theory. In three subsequent reviews, Greenberg (1990, 1993a, 2001) continued to echo Lind and Tyler's (1988) call for better measurement. In particular, Greenberg noted the frequency of one-item measures, the continuing use of ad hoc measures, and the poor construct validity often found in justice research. Similarly, Bobocel and Holmvall (2001) summarized the state of the literature by noting that justice scholars have emphasized predictive validity more than construct validity.

The purpose of our chapter is to review the current state of organizational justice measurement, with the goal of providing recommendations that can be used to guide future research. We begin with a step-by-step decision tree that can be used to summarize the most important choices in measuring justice. We then provide a brief overview of construct validity criteria and how they apply to the measurement of organizational justice. Next we review the most widely used measures of organizational justice and discuss some important questions and controversies worthy of future study.

MEASURING ORGANIZATIONAL JUSTICE: CRITICAL CHOICES

Justice measures come in a variety of shapes and sizes. Scholars new to the literature may be confused when one study assesses "procedural justice" by asking how consistent a process is, a second study asks how much control the process affords, and a third study simply asks how fair it is. The new reader might wonder, "Is this really the same construct?" Such variation is created by a number of choices inherent in the design of the measures. These choices are represented in Fig. 4.1, and discussed in the sections to follow.

The Type of Justice

The most obvious choice in designing a justice measure is the choice of justice dimension. Scales that focus on the fairness of decision outcomes are assessing distributive justice (Adams, 1965; Deutsch, 1975; Leventhal, 1976). Scales that focus on the fairness of decision making

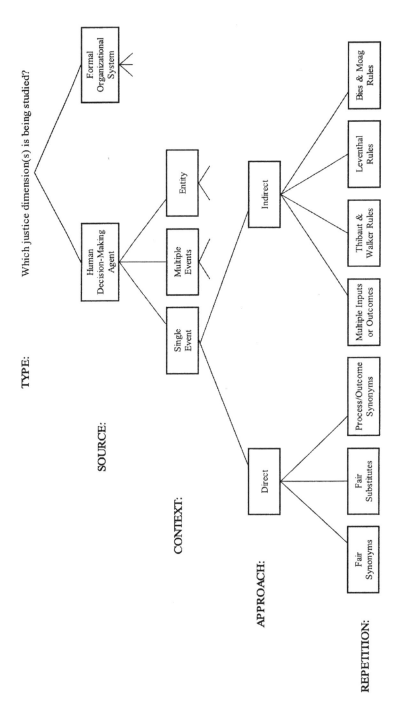

TYPE: Which justice dimension(s) is being studied?

SOURCE:

CONTEXT:

APPROACH:

REPETITION:

FIG. 4.1. Choices inherent in justice measurement.

116

procedures are assessing procedural justice (Leventhal, 1980; Thibaut & Walker, 1975). Scales that focus on the fairness of the treatment received when authorities enact procedures are assessing interactional justice (Bies & Moag, 1986). Greenberg (1993b) and Colquitt (2001) distinguished between two dimensions of interactional justice: the respect and sincerity shown (i.e., interpersonal justice) and the extent to which procedures are honestly and adequately explained (i.e., informational justice).

The choice of justice type is often salient to the researcher because it is usually relevant to the specific hypotheses being tested in the study. For example, the study may be contrasting the effects of distributive and procedural justice on job attitudes (e.g., Folger & Konovsky, 1989) or examining the effects of interpersonal and informational justice on trust (e.g., Kernan & Hanges, 2002). However, other choices may or may not be relevant to specific research questions, and may therefore be made unintentionally or as a function of the specific research context. These include the source of the justice, the context in which it is examined, and the measurement approach used.

The Source of Justice

Choosing a particular justice type focuses the researcher's attention on specific fairness "rules" or "criteria." Table 4.1 provides a summary of the rules that underlie the various justice types, along with the sources that proposed the rules.[1] However, it is important to realize that the rules in Table 4.1 may be judged in reference to multiple sources. That is, formalized organizational policies can build in mechanisms to insure consistency, and human decision-making agents can strive to be consistent in their implementation of those policies. Organizations can utilize job evaluation systems to ground salaries in important employee qualifications, and supervisors can study performance evaluation records to tie raises and bonuses to relevant inputs. Finally, organizations can design newsletters and web sites to frequently release honest, detailed, and respectful explanations about decision-making events, just as bosses can complement such systems with "open-door policies" that foster respectful and honest communication.

These examples illustrate that different types of justice can originate in different sources of justice (Blader & Tyler, 2003; Cobb, Vest, & Hills, 1997; Colquitt, 2001; Rupp & Cropanzano, 2002). Blader and Tyler

---

[1]A recent review by Bies (2001) has articulated more examples of interactional justice criteria, including bad-mouthing, using pejorative labels, breaking promises, disclosing secrets, and public beratement.

TABLE 4.1

Rules Often Referenced in Justice Measures

Type of justice	Rule name	Rule explanation	Source
Distributive justice	Equity	Outcomes should be distributed in proportion to individuals' inputs	Leventhal (1976)
Procedural justice		Procedures should:	Thibaut and Walker (1975); Leventhal (1980)
	Process control	Offer opportunities to express views	
	Decision control	Offer opportunities to influence outcomes	
	Consistency	Be consistent across people and time	
	Bias suppression	Be neutral and free of bias	
	Accuracy	Be based on accurate information	
	Correctability	Include mechanisms for appeals	
	Representativeness	Be representative of all concerns	
	Ethicality	Uphold ethical and moral standards	
Interactional Justice		Implementations of procedures should:	Bies and Moag (1986)
	Respect	Utilize respectful communication	
	Propriety	Refrain from improper comments	
	Justification	Include adequate explanations	
	Truthfulness	Be truthful and candid	

Note. Leventhal (1976) discussed other distributive justice rules, including allocating outcomes equally and in proportion to one's needs (see also Deutsch, 1975). Adams (1965) argued that equity is judged by comparing one's own outcome/input ratios to those of a comparison other. Although each of these conceptualizations is noted, they are not discussed in this chapter because they are rarely incorporated into actual justice measures. With respect to interactional justice, Greenberg (1993b) and Colquitt (2001) distinguished between interpersonal facets (respect and propriety) and informational facets (justification and truthfulness).

(2003) discussed this issue by distinguishing between "formal justice" (organization-originating) and "informal justice" (supervisor-originating). Byrne and Cropanzano (2000) used the term "multi-foci" to refer to the multiple sources from which justice can originate (see also Rupp & Cropanzano, 2002). Of course, this is not an entirely new distinction, given that scholars have long understood that justice was the responsibility of both systems and supervisors (Folger & Bies, 1989; Tyler & Bies, 1990). What is new is the explicit understanding that type and source can be fully crossed—that one does not dictate the other.

The Context of Justice

Regardless of what type of justice is being examined, or from which source that justice originates, a critical question is the context in which fairness is to be judged. For example, the researcher might study the perceived fairness of a performance evaluation rating, the perceived accuracy of the procedure used to arrive at that rating, or the respect and sincerity shown when explaining the rating. Here the context is that of a performance evaluation event (Greenberg, 1986). Other justice scholars have examined the fairness of events in other contexts, including personnel selection (Gilliland, 1993), training (Quinones, 1995), and compensation (Welbourne, Balkin, & Gomez-Mejia, 1995).

Justice investigations that examine justice in the context of one particular event could be termed "context specific." For example, field studies have examined the perceived fairness of corporate relocations (Daly & Geyer, 1994), layoffs (Brockner, Wiesenfeld, Grover, & Martin, 1993) and drug tests (Konovsky & Cropanzano, 1991). Similarly, laboratory studies of justice have tended to bound fairness perceptions in the specific event created by the experimental setting. For example, Colquitt and Chertkoff (2002) examined the perceived fairness of the procedures used to add new members to an experimental group.

A less common approach is to examine fairness across multiple decision-making events. For example, Sweeney and McFarlin (1997) asked a sample of federal employees about the procedural and distributive fairness of a number of events, including performance evaluations, promotions, policy changes, disciplinary actions, and grievances. A related approach explicitly asks employees to consider the fairness of their treatment across all possible decision-making events. Cropanzano, Byrne, Bobocel, and Rupp (2001) refer to such measures as *entity* measures, because they instruct employees to appraise the supervisor or organization as a whole. Such measures essentially sample all of the events experienced by an employee in aggregate, in the form of a more global judgment.

Measure Approach: Direct or Indirect

Regardless of the choices made about justice type, justice source, and justice context, the researcher must also decide whether to employ a "direct" or "indirect" approach to measuring justice. Lind and Tyler (1988) were the first to explicitly draw the distinction between direct and indirect measures of justice. Direct measures explicitly ask "how fair" the outcome, process, or interpersonal treatment was, as the respondent is asked to form a global evaluative judgment. Indirect measures assess the rules that foster a sense of fairness, as the respondent is asked to rate particular characteristics of the event or entity in a more descriptive sense. Thus indirect measures are typically comprised of the rules discussed in Table 4.1.

Lind and Tyler's (1988) Table A-2 provided examples of both direct and indirect items. For example, "How fair are the procedures by which government benefits are distributed?" (Tyler & Caine, 1981) and "How fair are the procedures by which the federal government decides the level of taxes each citizen will pay?" (Tyler, Rasinski, & McGraw, 1985) are two examples of direct items assessing procedural justice. In contrast, "In deciding what national policies to implement do you think that President Reagan usually, sometimes, or seldom considers the views of all sides before making decisions?" is an example of an indirect item (Tyler et al., 1985). It references a descriptive judgment of the characteristics of a decision event, in this case Thibaut and Walker's (1975) process control rule. Similarly, "Is he usually, sometimes, or seldom unbiased and impartial in making policy decisions?" is an indirect item tapping Leventhal's (1980) bias suppression rule (Rasinski & Tyler, 1988).

Measurement Repetition

The final choice to make when measuring justice is the nature of the measurement repetition. How will the multiple items within the scale differ from one another? One method for creating measurement repetition has been to sample multiple decision events, as discussed earlier (Sweeney & McFarlin, 1997). Other methods for creating measurement repetition are dictated by whether a direct or indirect measurement approach is utilized. If the approach is indirect, then measurement repetition is usually created by referencing multiple fairness rules. For example, a four-item indirect procedural justice measure might assess Leventhal's (1980) consistency, accuracy, bias suppression, and correctability rules.

When a direct measure is used, a variety of approaches can be used to create measurement repetition. One possibility is to use synonyms for the

word *fair*. For example, Earley and Lind's (1987) study of the relationships among control and justice used a two-item measure with the words *fair* and *just*. Other approaches to measurement repetition have relied on evaluative endings that might best be described as "substitutes" (rather than synonyms) for *fair* or *just*. For example, Shapiro and Brett (1993) examined the effects of different conflict resolution procedures in a sample of coal miners. In addition to using the word *fair* in connection with the procedure, the authors used substitutes like "angry about," "frustrated with," "felt good about," and "satisfied with." This last substitute has been the most common, as several direct measures of procedural justice have contained "satisfaction" evaluations (e.g., Giacobbe-Miller, 1995; Lind, Lissak, & Conlon, 1983; Lowe & Vodanovich, 1995). Still other approaches have used synonyms for *outcome* or *process* to provide measurement repetition. Daly and Geyer (1994) provide an example of this in their study of the perceived fairness of relocation decisions. Each of the authors' items contained the word *fair*, but used synonyms such as "the way" or "the steps" to refer to decision-making procedures (see also Bies, Shapiro, & Cummings, 1988; Brockner, Siegel, Daly, & Martin, 1997).

CONSTRUCT VALIDITY IN JUSTICE MEASUREMENT

Many of the choices reviewed above have implications for the construct validity of the justice measure. Schwab (1980) defined construct validity as follows:

> *Construct validity is defined as representing the correspondence between a construct (conceptual definition of a variable) and the operational procedure to measure or manipulate that construct.* From this definition it is acceptable to think of construct validity as representing the correlation coefficient between the construct and the measure.... Departures from construct validity coefficients of 1.00 are due to *contamination* (variance in the measure not present in the construct) and/or *deficiency* (variance in the construct not captured by the measure). (pp. 5–6, emphasis in original)

Schwab's definition is depicted in Fig. 4.2, which also includes the effects of unreliability (see Schwab, 1999, p. 38).

Unreliability

Unreliability is that portion of a measure's variance that is random, rather than systematic (Nunnally, 1978). It is generally driven by two factors: the number of measurement repetitions and the correlations among those repetitions. As mentioned earlier, measurement repetition

122

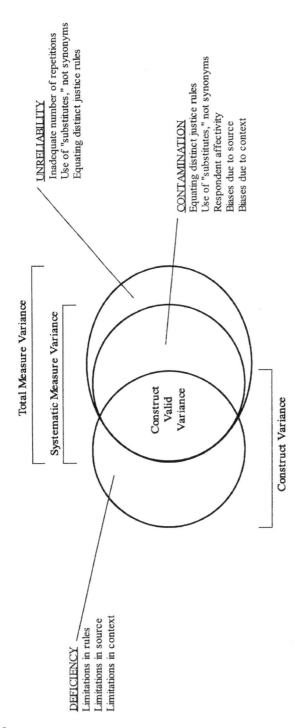

UNRELIABILITY
Inadequate number of repetitions
Use of "substitutes," not synonyms
Equating distinct justice rules

CONTAMINATION
Equating distinct justice rules
Use of "substitutes," not synonyms
Respondent affectivity
Biases due to source
Biases due to context

DEFICIENCY
Limitations in rules
Limitations in source
Limitations in context

Total Measure Variance

Systematic Measure Variance

Construct Valid Variance

Construct Variance

FIG. 4.2.   Construct validity in justice measurement.

may be created by referencing multiple rules from Table 4.1, or by relying on synonyms or substitutes for words like *fair* or *outcome* or *procedure*. The two drivers of reliability offer concrete recommendations for the design of justice measures. With all else equal, reliability will be enhanced by including more items, whether by sampling more justice rules or by employing more synonyms and substitutes.

However, scholars must also consider the expected correlations among those repetitions. In the case of direct measures, inadequate correlations among repetitions could arise from using substitutes rather than synonyms, as the correlation between "fair" and "satisfied" should be lower than the one between "fair" and "just." In the case of indirect measures, inadequate correlations among repetitions could arise from equating distinct justice rules, as the correlation between bias suppression and respect, for example, should be lower than the one between bias suppression and consistency.

Contamination

Of course, we should note that the majority of justice measures do possess adequate reliability. Far more problematic are issues of contamination. The most common cause is equating distinct justice rules, as measures of one justice type contain items that are actually measuring another. Colquitt (2001) referred to this problem as a "cross-pollination" of justice items. For example, Fryxell and Gordon (1989) assessed distributive justice by asking individuals whether they had the ability to express their ideas during grievance procedures—an item capturing the procedural rule of process control. Similarly, Joy and Witt's (1992) distributive justice measure asked about the treatment that respondents received, which may have tapped interactional justice rules.

To illustrate the potential seriousness of the contamination issue, consider the results reported in Colquitt, Conlon, Wesson, Porter, and Ng's (2001) meta-analysis of the justice literature. The authors conducted a meta-analytic regression in which procedural fairness perceptions—a direct measure—was regressed on all conceivable indirect conceptualizations of justice, including process control, Leventhal's (1980) rules, interpersonal justice, and informational justice. Ideally, the indirect criteria would explain 100% of the variance in procedural fairness perceptions, particularly because the meta-analytic procedures removed unreliability from the relationships. Unfortunately, the Colquitt et al. (2001) results showed that the indirect criteria only explained roughly half (53%) of the variance in fairness perceptions.

The key question here concerns the meaning of the remainder—the variance not shared between the direct and indirect conceptualizations. One possibility is that the remainder is evidence of contamination

within the direct measure, as other factors are affecting it besides the justice rules. This may be particularly likely for direct measures that rely on substitutes like "satisfied with" or "angry about." These reference "hot cognitions" that may be more a function of respondent affectivity than actual decision-making procedures. Direct measure items may be more susceptible to such biases because of the morally-charged nature of the word *fair*. Indirect assessments of justice rules are more descriptive and less evaluative, and many (though obviously not all) rules are less value-laden. To some extent, appeals either exist or do not exist; procedures are either consistent or variable; explanations are either given or withheld.

Other contaminants may be a function of the justice source. It seems likely that a form of "halo" error could occur when creating evaluative justice judgments. An outgoing, magnetic supervisor may be deemed more fair than an unassuming or socially anxious one. A successful, well-regarded organization may be deemed more fair than a struggling one in a less popular industry. Similar sorts of "halo" could occur with respect to the event context. The perceived fairness of selection events may be rated more highly by organizational incumbents, given that they were hired by the organization. Alternatively, the perceived fairness of compensation events may be rated less favorably in tough economic times when raises and bonuses are harder to come by.

Deficiency

Returning again to the issue of the remainder from the Colquitt et al. (2001) analysis, the unshared variance may also be evidence of deficiency. This would reflect aspects of justice that are not captured by the specific measures. In most cases, deficiency is a sin of omission. For example, a procedural justice measure might omit important justice rules, such as Thibaut and Walker's (1975) control rules or Leventhal's (1980) correctability rule. A distributive justice measure might omit relevant inputs, such as training and education or job responsibilities (Price & Mueller, 1986). An interactional justice measure might omit propriety and truthfulness, despite assessing respect and justification.

Deficiency may also be a product of limitations in justice source. With a few recent exceptions (Byrne & Cropanzano, 2000; Masterson, Bartol, & Moye, 2000; Tyler & Blader, 2000), justice studies tend to focus on either human decision-making agents or formal organizational systems, but not both. To the extent that both sources drive justice, this represents an aspect of the construct not captured by the measure. On the other hand, many articles limit the source because of their particular research question. For example, Skarlicki and Latham's (1996, 1997) investigations of leader justice training necessarily limited the source to human

decision-making agents. Thus the seriousness of source as an indicator of deficiency depends on the study's research question.

The same discussion applies to limitations with regard to the justice context. Often the research question focuses on how to improve the fairness of one specific procedure, be it performance appraisal, compensation, selection, and so on. In such cases the researcher must necessarily limit the referent to a single procedure, rather than a multiple procedure or entity approach. However, other research questions often require a more general justice assessment, particularly in research where general outcomes like organizational commitment or job performance are being predicted. Here the use of a single procedural context would create deficiency. Thus, as with the source, the seriousness of the context as an indicator of deficiency depends on the study's research question.

JUSTICE MEASUREMENT: A REVIEW

The preceding sections have described the critical choices that must be considered when designing or choosing a justice measure, along with the criteria used to judge the adequacy of that measure (i.e., reliability, contamination, deficiency). We now turn our attention to a brief historical review of the measures used in the justice literature, organized around the aforementioned choices and criteria.

1970s and 1980s

Many of the earliest measures of justice were one-item measures used in laboratory studies. For example, LaTour (1978) examined the effects of various forms of trial procedures on perceptions of procedural and distributive justice among undergraduates. The fairness of the trial procedure was measured with one item on a 9-point scale, as was the fairness of the eventual verdict. Similarly, Folger, Rosenfield, Grove, and Corkran's (1979) classic examination of the "fair process effect" linked the provision of process control to perceptions of fairness among undergraduates. Distributive and procedural justice were both measured with one item, this time using an 11-point scale (1 = *very unfair* to 11 = *very fair*). Similar approaches were used by Tyler and colleagues (e.g., Tyler, Rasinski, & McGraw, 1985, Study 1; Tyler, Rasinski, & Spodick, 1985).

To this point, justice measurement had been focused on outcomes and procedures manipulated in a laboratory environment. No real distinction was made regarding whether these outcomes and procedures were a function of a human decision-making agent (i.e., the experimenter) or some more formal system, because such distinctions are blurred in a laboratory environment. Moreover, the laboratory setting dictated the use of a single event context, as the participants

reacted to the experimental procedures created by the artificial environment. That event context was typically assessed using direct "how fair" measures, as the research question was often geared toward comparing the perceived fairness of multiple types of procedures. Finally, measurement repetition was rarely used, preventing the assessment of reliability.

Multi-item measures became more common in the late 1980s. Consider, for example, Earley and Lind's (1987) study linking process and decision control to fairness perceptions. The authors relied on two items to assess Thibaut and Walker's (1975) control-based conceptualization of procedural justice: "How much influence did you have over the task?" and "Compared to the experimenter, how much control did you have over the task?" (1 = *no influence/control* to 5 = *complete influence/control*). Although this would be considered an indirect approach, the authors also included a direct measure of procedural justice: "How fair was the *way* your task was developed?" and "How just was the *way* that the experimenter decided what task you would work on?" (1 = *not at all fair/just* to 5 = *extremely fair/just*). Here measurement repetition was created by relying on fair synonyms and by describing the process using two different phrases. Note too that the second item explicitly references a human decision-making agent (the experimenter) as the source of the justice.

1980s and 1990s

The preceding examples assessed distributive and procedural justice perceptions in the laboratory. One of the earliest examples of field research on justice was Price and Mueller's (1986) work on absenteeism and turnover among hospital employees. Believing that distributive justice was a key predictor of those outcomes, the authors created the Distributive Justice Index (see Appendix). The measure examines distributive justice in a single event context—compensation. An indirect approach is used by considering whether rewards are consistent with relevant inputs (Adams, 1965; Deutsch, 1975; Leventhal, 1976). Item repetition is created by relying on multiple inputs, including responsibilities, education and training, amount of experience, and so forth. Price and Mueller's (1986) measure has been used by several different researchers since its introduction (e.g., Moorman, 1991; Sweeney & McFarlin, 1993).

One of the first field studies to measure both distributive and procedural justice was Konovsky, Folger, and Cropanzano's (1987) study of manufacturing plant employees. The authors' measures are shown in the Appendix, and are notable on three counts. First, they explicitly reference the justice source as a human decision-making agent (the super-

visor). Second, they explicitly ground the measure in a single event context (a raise). Third, they include both direct and indirect approaches, which the authors refer to as "global" and "component" measures. Only three of the nine indirect procedural justice items are given in the paper, but they are clearly relying on multiple Thibaut and Walker (1975) and Leventhal (1980) rules to create measurement repetition. In contrast, the direct procedural justice measure relies on synonyms for *fair* (i.e., the way you deserve to be treated) and *process* (i.e., practices, procedures). The distributive justice measure is similar, except that it also included an indirect item that compared outcomes (the raise) to inputs (performance).

Two years later, Folger and Konovsky (1989) published a more extensive 26-item indirect procedural measure (their distributive measure was similar to Konovsky et al., 1987). The authors crafted their measure around Thibaut and Walker's (1975) and Leventhal's (1980) rules, along with an empirical test of justice criteria by Greenberg (1986). Greenberg (1986) conducted an open-ended survey of 217 middle managers exploring the determinants of fair performance appraisal procedures. His Q-sort procedure resulted in five determinants, which closely matched Thibaut and Walker's (1975) and Leventhal's (1980) rules. As shown in the Appendix, Folger and Konovsky's (1989) measure again focused on a human decision-making agent and a single event context (a raise).

Folger and Konovsky (1989) factor-analyzed their measure, determining that it consisted of five factors: feedback (items 1–11), planning (items 12–15, 20–21), recourse (items 22–23, 25–26), and observation (item 16). The fifth factor (items 17–19), which may have been an artifact of reverse coding, was not retained. The sheer length of the measure offers both strengths and weaknesses from a construct validity perspective. The measure avoids deficiency by sampling all relevant procedural justice criteria from Table 4.1. However, the measure does include some contamination, as some items tapped concepts that had just recently been introduced by Bies and Moag (1986) as interactional justice criteria. Items 1 and 6 reflect their honesty criterion, items 6 and 11 reflect their justification criterion, and item 17 reflects their propriety rule. Of course, Bies and Moag's (1986) chapter had likely not appeared before Folger and Konovsky (1989) planned their study, and it should be noted that these items did load on the same factors as more procedural concepts.

The influence of Bies and Moag's (1986) and Folger and Konovsky's (1989) work can be seen in a subsequent measure created by Moorman (1991). His examination of justice and organizational citizenship behavior included a measure of both procedural justice (dubbed "formal procedures") and interactional justice (see Appendix). Four facets of Moorman's (1991) measure make it a significant contribution to the literature. First, it was the first to explicitly separate procedural justice

and interactional justice, an idea that had by that point already become controversial (Tyler & Bies, 1990). Second, it was one of the first to reference procedural justice items to a formal decision making system, rather than the behaviors of a supervisor. Third, it was the first measure that was not tied to a specific procedural event, such as a performance appraisal. This makes it an "entity" measure, in the terms of Cropanzano et al. (2001). Fourth, it was the first measure to be subjected to confirmatory factor analysis.

Moorman's (1991) measure was utilized by many justice scholars throughout the remainder of the decade (e.g., Adams-Roy & Barling, 1998; Gellatly, 1995; Mansour-Cole & Scott, 1998; Skarlicki & Latham, 1997). However, this time period was marked by a debate surrounding the distinction between procedural and interactional justice, as some reviews argued that the two were different forms of the same construct (Cropanzano & Greenberg, 1997; Tyler & Bies, 1990). Empirical research utilizing Moorman's (1991) measure often followed suit by combining the procedural and interactional justice items into one variable (e.g., Mansour-Cole & Scott, 1998; Skarlicki & Latham, 1997). One factor that seems to have contributed to this practice is the nature of Moorman's (1991) first and second interactional justice items, which assessed the procedural justice rules of process control and bias suppression.

Although the measures reviewed mostly followed an indirect approach, other field studies have continued to rely on direct assessment of justice. For example, Sweeney and McFarlin (1993) employed a direct measure in their study of justice perceptions among engineers in a public utility company (see Appendix). Their measure is notable in that it is one of the few that explicitly references multiple event contexts (performance evaluation, feedback communication, promotions, salary increases), although all in the broad domain of performance management.

2000 to Present

The most recent indirect measure published in the justice literature was created by Colquitt (2001). Four characteristics of this measure are noteworthy. First, the items are based on a close examination of the construct definitions given in the seminal works in the literature. For example, the interactional justice items follow Bies and Moag's (1986) initial conceptualization, as opposed to managerial sources of procedural justice rules. Second, the respect/propriety and truthfulness/justification aspects of interactional justice are kept separate, based on two separate confirmatory factor analyses. Consistent with an earlier review by Greenberg (1993b), the former are termed "interpersonal justice" whereas the latter are termed "informational justice." This distinction has also received meta-analytic support (Colquitt et al., 2001).

Third, the measure can be tailored to fit any particular event context (performance appraisal, compensation, selection, conflict resolution, etc.) by altering the "[outcome]" part of the instructions. It can also be used to provide a general assessment of justice by inserting multiple types of decisions or more entity-style endings like "outcomes in this organization." It therefore provides the kind of "convertibility" needed to apply standardized measures in different contexts (Greenberg, 1993a). Fourth, and relatedly, the measure can be tailored to examine multiple sources of justice by altering the instructions and/or item stems. Thus the procedural justice items can be referenced to a human authority figure (rather than an organizational system) and the interactional justice items can be referenced to an organizational system (rather than a human authority figure).

Colquitt (2001) conducted two empirical studies validating the measure, one using a student sample and one relying on manufacturing employees. Confirmatory factor analyses were used to contrast the fit of a one-factor "overall organizational justice" factor, a two-factor model combining the procedural and interactional dimensions, and a three-factor distributive–procedural–interactional structure, along with the four-factor structure. The four-factor model provided a significantly better fit than all other models in both samples. The corrected correlations among the factors ranged from .22 to .64 in the student sample (average .46) and .14 to .74 in the field sample (average .44). The reliabilities for the four factors ranged from .78 to .92 in the student sample and .90 to .93 in the field sample.

Due to its recent introduction, Colquitt's (2001) measure has appeared in few published articles. One of the first studies to publish findings with it was conducted by Ambrose and Schminke (2003). The authors explored whether organizational structure moderated the relationship between procedural justice and perceived organizational support, and interactional justice and trust in supervisors (the inter-personal vs. informational distinction was not relevant to the research question, so the two were combined). A study of 506 employees in 68 organizations revealed that procedural justice had stronger effects in mechanistic structures, whereas interactional justice had stronger effects in organic structures. Most relevant to the current discussion, the distributive, procedural, and interactional scales had acceptable reliabilities (.96, .93, and .86, respectively) and the correlations among the factors were reasonable in magnitude (ranging from .40 to .55). The authors also conducted a confirmatory factor analysis to ensure that the three justice dimensions and the trust and support variables loaded on five distinct factors, with the results supportive of that structure.

Of course, one study provides insufficient evidence about the psychometric quality of the Colquitt (2001) measure. To present more

widespread data, we contacted a convenience sample of 25 justice scholars to see if any had collected data using the measure that they would be willing to share. A total of 12 authors contributed 16 independent samples.[2] The samples ranged in size from 99 to 788 with an average of 291, and explored both specific decision-making contexts (employment testing, performance evaluation, product complaints, travel planning, work–family policies, athletic coaching) and more entity-style perceptions in both laboratory and field settings. We merged the data into a single set with 3,646 individual respondents, with 2,332 having complete data on all 20 items in the measure. Missing data at this stage was typically due to a researcher omitting one dimension of justice, or conducting the study in a context where specific justice rules were not applicable.

A confirmatory factor analysis of the merged data set yielded a good fit for the four-factor structure (see Table 4.2). Arbitrary hurdles for good fit typically include an IFI or CFI of .90 or above, an SRMR of .10 or below, and an RMSEA of .08 or below (Browne & Cudeck, 1993; Kline, 1998). Comparisons to alternative models can be conducted by calculating the statistical significance of the difference in c^2, or by comparing the confidence intervals for the RMSEA. In either case, a four-factor model fit the data better than a three-factor model that combines the interactional facets, or a two-factor model that combines all of the procedural and interactional dimensions. The factor loadings for the 20 items were all statistically significant and ranged from .40 to .96, with an average of .77. Seventeen of the 20 loadings were above .70, and 10 were above .80. The two lowest-loading items corresponded to the Thibaut and Walker (1975) process and decision control rules, and may be reflective of study contexts where those concepts are less relevant or generally lacking.

Table 4.3 provides the reliability levels for the four scales, as well as their intercorrelations. All four scales possess acceptable reliabilities, with alphas ranging from .83 to .92. Uncorrected correlations among the dimensions range from a low of .37 (distributive and interpersonal) to a high of .64 (interpersonal and informational). These levels are quite consistent with the Colquitt et al. (2001) meta-analytic review (see their Table 1), with an average absolute difference of .07 across the six correlations. Thus the measure seems to be replicating the typical magnitude of the intercorrelations among the justice dimensions. These findings, together with the factor analysis results, provide some preliminary sup-

---

[2]The authors thank the following scholars (and their coauthors) for graciously agreeing to lend us their data for these analyses: Maureen Ambrose, Bradford Bell, Christopher Bell, Zinta Byrne, Donald Conlon, Ronald Hess, Stephen Humphrey, Timothy Judge, Suzanne Masterson, Soo Phen, Quinetta Roberson, and Warren Whisenant.

TABLE 4.2
Confirmatory Factor Analysis of Colquitt (2001) Measure

Structure	c^2	df	IFI	CFI	SRMR	RMSEA	RMSEA confidence interval
Four-factor	2314.15	164	.94	.94	.058	.075	(.072, .078)
Three-factor	6214.14	167	.82	.82	.109	.125	(.122, .127)
Two-factor	10045.29	169	.70	.70	.117	.158	(.156, .161)
One-factor	14923.50	170	.56	.56	.118	.193	(.190, .196)

Note n = 2,331 individuals from 16 independent samples.

TABLE 4.3
Descriptive Statistics and Correlations for Justice Dimensions
Using Colquitt (2001) Measure

Justice dimension	a	M	SD	(1)	(2)	(3)	(4)
(1) Procedural justice	.83	3.09	.86	—			
(2) Distributive justice	.92	3.20	1.15	.55*	—		
(3) Interpersonal justice	.92	4.07	1.00	.45*	.37*	—	
(4) Informational justice	.88	3.56	1.04	.56*	.50*	.64*	—

Note. n = 2,331 individuals from 16 independent samples. *p < .05.

port for the psychometric qualities of Colquitt's (2001) measure. As with any new measure, however, more published research is needed to test its adequacy across research contexts.

JUSTICE MEASUREMENT: QUESTIONS AND CONTROVERSIES

Having described the choices involved in measuring justice, the impact of those choices on construct validity, and the various measures available for use, we close with some questions and controversies regarding justice measurement. The discussion to follow attempts to predict the most common questions and concerns that a scholar is likely to encounter when planning justice-related research. Some have relatively straightforward answers, while others are more debatable.

Which Should I Use? Direct or Indirect?

As mentioned at the outset, the justice literature can be quite confusing to newcomers in that one scholar might measure "procedural justice" by asking how consistent a procedure was, whereas another might simply ask how fair the process was. Such direct and indirect approaches are typically used interchangeably, yet there are clearly times when one approach is more appropriate than another. Like most measurement choices, the appropriate decision depends on the research question being investigated.

Exogenous or Endogenous?   One important consideration is whether justice is exogenous in the model (an independent variable in the causal system) or endogenous in the model (a mediator or dependent variable in the causal system). The exogenous versus endogenous distinction is often discussed in the justice literature by contrasting "proactive" and "reactive" research (Greenberg, 1987; Greenberg & Wiethoff, 2001). Proactive research questions seek to link characteristics of a decision-making event to assessments of fairness. Reactive research questions seek to link fairness perceptions to attitudinal and behavioral reactions to decision events.

Proactive research often utilizes a direct approach, as fairness perceptions serve as the dependent variable whereas event characteristics serve as the independent variable. This is particularly common in the laboratory. For example, Bartol, Durham, and Poon (2001) examined the impact of the number of performance appraisal categories of an appraisal instrument on procedural and distributive justice. Using a direct measurement approach, the authors found that individuals reported higher levels of procedural and distributive justice when five rating categories were provided than when two rating categories were provided. Similarly, Alge (2001) examined the effects of various electronic monitoring policies on procedural justice. Again using a direct approach, Alge (2001) found that individuals perceived the procedures to be more fair when monitoring applied to work activities rather than break time.

Could an indirect approach have been utilized in these cases? Consider what might have been expected if Bartol et al. (2001) had utilized Colquitt's (2001) procedural justice measure (see Appendix) rather than the direct approach. The number of performance appraisal categories might have been expected to influence the fifth item that pertains to Leventhal's (1980) accuracy rule, with the notion being that more discrete categories results in more precise measurement. However, there is little reason to expect the number of categories to impact any of Leventhal's (1980) other rules, and hence any of the other items in

Colquitt's (2001) measure. Similarly, Alge's (2001) examination of work activity versus break time monitoring might have affected responses to the fifth or seventh item in Colquitt's (2001) measure (the accuracy and ethicality rules), with the notion being that monitoring break time resulted in a less accurate picture of employee withdrawal while breaking fundamental moral tenets about employee rights to privacy. However, there is little reason to expect the variable to impact any other items.

Of course, justice may also be an endogenous variable in correlational field studies. For example, Elovainio, Kivimaki, and Helkama (2001) examined procedural and interactional justice as mediators of the job control-strain relationship. Rather than relying on a direct measurement approach, they utilized Moorman's (1991) measures of the justice dimensions. Consider the significant relationship they uncovered between job control and procedural justice (b = .23 in a structural equation modeling analysis). Clearly, employees who have the ability to make decisions in their everyday jobs might also be given more opportunities for voice and process control, as reflected in Moorman's (1991) "have sides represented," "hear concerns," and "consider viewpoints" items. However, the relevance of job control to the other procedural items is unclear.

Our contention is that proactive research, or research where justice is endogenous in the causal system, should usually utilize a direct measurement approach. One exception to this is when the justice predictors are expected to influence several of the rules included within the justice measure. In such cases the rules embedded within the indirect measure can serve as multiple theoretical explanations for grounding an expected relationship. A second exception is when a partial set of justice rules—limited to those with theoretical relevance—is utilized in the study. For example, Schminke, Ambrose, and Cropanzano (2000) examined the effects of centralization, formalization, and size on procedural justice perceptions. The authors utilized a set of items developed by Tyler and Schuller (1990) that assessed the process control, decision control, and consistency rules. Presumably, items referencing the other rules were omitted because any relationships between the organizational variables and those rules were uncertain.

In contrast, reactive research—where justice is exogenous in the causal system—allows for more discretion in measurement approach. Examples of reactive research include studies linking justice perceptions with satisfaction and commitment (e.g., McFarlin & Sweeney, 1992; Sweeney & McFarlin, 1993) or citizenship and retaliation behaviors (e.g., Moorman, 1991; Skarlicki, Folger, & Tesluk, 1999). Some of these researchers relied on direct measurement in their investigations (McFarlin & Sweeney, 1992; Sweeney & McFarlin, 1993), whereas others relied on indirect measure-

ment (Moorman, 1991; Skarlicki et al., 1999). Two primary criteria could guide the choice of measurement approach in reactive research: predictive validity, and ability to generate managerial implications.

Which measurement approach is most predictive of attitudinal and behavioral outcomes? Answers can be found in the meta-analytic review by Colquitt et al. (2001). In deriving the meta-analytic relationships between justice dimensions and various outcome variables, the authors distinguished between direct measurement (i.e., procedural fairness perceptions) and indirect measurement (i.e., process control, Leventhal's rules, interpersonal justice, and informational justice). The results showed that indirect measures had stronger relationships with many outcomes, but only when a comprehensive set of justice rules were utilized. Specifically, Colquitt et al. (2001) showed that indirect combination measures (which include both procedural and interactional rules) were the strongest predictors of six of the eleven outcomes examined.

Of course, justice scholars often possess a dual responsibility. In addition to predicting outcomes relevant to organizations, they are often asked to distill those results into practical implications for managers. Here indirect measures have a distinct advantage. Consider a case where Leventhal's (1980) rules yield strong relationships with citizenship behaviors, but interpersonal and informational justice do not. The practical implication is to devote more resources to the consistency, accuracy, correctability, and so on of decision-making procedures. A direct measure provides no such information.

What Theory Are You Testing?   Given that the "raison d'être" of a measure is to represent the constructs in a theory (Bacharach, 1989), then the theory being tested must also dictate the measurement approach. Some theories require the use of indirect measurement approaches. For example, the relational model of justice argues that procedural justice is important because it signifies that individuals are valued by their authority figures and the groups to which they belong (Lind & Tyler, 1988; Tyler & Lind, 1992). Tests of the relational model typically employ justice rules similar to Leventhal's (1980) and Bies and Moag's (1986). Tyler (1989) originally proposed three rules relevant to the relational model: neutrality, trust, and standing, which reference content similar to Leventhal's (1980) bias suppression rule and Bies and Moag's (1986) respect rule. As such, they are constructs that must be assessed via indirect measurement.

Other theories require the use of a direct measurement approach. Fairness heuristic theory seeks to explain the process by which individuals form justice judgments (Lind, 2001a; Van den Bos et al., 2001). The theory suggests that individuals are faced with several daily decisions

regarding whether to cooperate with others or act in their own self-interest. Lacking concrete data on how trustworthy other parties are, individuals form "fairness heuristics" as a means of guiding these decisions. Such judgments are formed very quickly, almost unconsciously, using whatever information is available at the time. Importantly, the fairness heuristic is itself a global, evaluative judgment of fairness—essentially a subconscious direct measure. Moreover, the theory explicitly argues that individuals will not consider all of the rules referenced in Table 4.1, because the heuristic is formed quickly using whatever information is first encountered (or is most easily interpreted). This suggests that asking individuals to answer each of the items in Moorman's (1991) or Colquitt's (2001) measure is artificial, as it does not mirror the justice judgment process that occurs in everyday life.

Do I Have to Include Everything?

The full implications of Fig. 4.1 could be intimidating to scholars who are planning a justice study. Assume for a moment that all four justice types were relevant to the research question, and both human and organizational sources were vital to the study context. This has already resulted in eight separate variables, even before considering the context and measurement approach! As with the first question discussed, the research setting may be the driver of what to include. In some organizations, formal organizational systems may be the preeminent driver of justice levels, with clear procedures governing most important decision events. In other organizations that formalization may be lacking, with supervisors having significant discretion in how decision events play out. The need to assess the human decision-making agent as a source of justice would be less critical in the former case, at least for procedural justice. The same issues would occur in the laboratory, where the design of the experimental procedures will likely make one source more relevant than the other.

Just as the setting affects the relevant justice source, so too does the research question affect the relevant justice types. We would echo the call of recent reviews to measure all justice dimensions whenever possible (Colquitt et al., 2001; Colquitt & Greenberg, 2003; Cropanzano et al., 2001). This practice maximizes the variance explained in key outcomes, while also providing more information for designing justice interventions across settings. That said, there are times when a research question does not have any bearing on one or more justice dimensions. For example, Avery and Quinones (2002) attempted to clarify the relationship between "voice" (or process control) and procedural justice perceptions by distinguishing voice opportunity (the opportunity to present one's views), voice behavior (actual presenting those views), and voice in-

strumentality (actual influence). This study had no bearing on the distributive or interactional forms of justice, so they were not included.

Greenberg's proactive versus reactive research distinction is also relevant to this question (Greenberg, 1987; Greenberg & Wiethoff, 2001). Avery and Quinones (2002) would fall into the proactive category because it clarifies the relationship between various conceptualizations of Thibaut and Walker's (1975) justice rules and perceptions of procedural justice. We suspect that proactive research will more often require the omission of one or more justice dimensions, depending on the type of fairness being fostered. In contrast, there are fewer reasons to omit dimensions of justice in reactive research. Consider Tepper, Lockhart, and Hoobler's (2001) study of organizational citizenship and job roles. The authors addressed an important gap in the citizenship literature by showing that role definitions (i.e., the extent to which "extra-role" behaviors are actually viewed as "in-role") moderated the relationship between procedural justice and citizenship behavior. Other justice dimensions were not included, however, despite their significant meta-analytic correlations with citizenship (Colquitt et al., 2001).

The "do I have to include everything?" question also applies to specific justice rules, not just the larger justice types. As noted earlier, Schminke et al. (2000) assessed only the process control, decision control, and consistency rules in their study of centralization, formalization, size, and procedural justice perceptions. The authors may have omitted other rules because they were less likely to be affected by the independent variables. Such omissions are likely to be quite common in the laboratory. Consider a laboratory study that manipulates procedural and interpersonal justice by making a process either biased or unbiased, and treating the participants either respectfully or rudely when implementing that process. Clearly, a measure of justice perceptions should be included in this study, either as a manipulation check or as an intervening mechanism linking the manipulations to some other outcome. However, if an indirect measure like Colquitt's (2001) is used, then omissions of some items would likely be in order as only 5 of the 20 items are relevant to the manipulations. Indeed, designing a laboratory study that tapped all 20 items could require almost 10 individual manipulations!

The question of whether to include everything speaks to a key aspect of measuring justice: the need for convertibility. Compared to other organizational behavior constructs, justice is quite context-specific. The rules referenced in Table 4.1 do not apply to all decision-making events in all organizations, and will not be relevant in all laboratory settings created by researchers. Greenberg (1993a) called for "semistandardized" justice measurement by calling for "a set of general questions that can be adapted to the context in which they are used.... From this list, questions can be added or deleted, or adapted as necessary to fit the sit-

uations within which they are used" (p. 145). Of course, such deletions could occur after data has been collected, and could be based on reliability and factor-analytic tests in addition to the logic of which items are relevant to the context. In any event, we encourage justice scholars to think critically about how the context of their study affects the form of their measurement.

When Are Dimensions Too Highly Correlated?

Most scholars familiar with the justice literature have read numerous articles where multiple justice dimensions have been assessed, whether directly or indirectly, and have been found to be very highly correlated. Consider the analyses presented for Colquitt's (2001) measure in Tables 4.2 and 4.3. On the one hand, the confirmatory factor analysis clearly supports a four-factor structure. On the other hand, interpersonal and informational justice are correlated at .64, procedural and informational justice are correlated at .56, and procedural and distributive justice are correlated at .55. These relationships all fall within the meta-analytic confidence intervals presented in the Colquitt et al. (2001) review. Such strong relationships beg the question, "When are dimensions *too highly* correlated?"

Justice scholars have, from the early stages of the literature, grappled with the high correlations between distributive and procedural justice. Field studies assessing the two dimensions have occasionally shown correlations as high as .70 (Sweeney & McFarlin, 1997; Welbourne et al., 1995). Meta-analytic estimates of the uncorrected correlation range from the high .40s for direct measures to the low .60s for some indirect measures. Few would argue for eschewing the distributive-procedural distinction in the literature. As a result, justice scholars have effectively become "inoculated" against worrying about interdimension correlations in the .50s (and sometimes higher).

How do these correlations compare to the relationships among other constructs' dimensions? Two relevant comparisons can be drawn from the most common dependent variables in justice research: organizational commitment and organizational citizenship behavior. With respect to the former, Allen and Meyer (1990) proposed a three-dimensional structure for commitment: affective (emotion-based), continuance (cost-based), and normative (obligation-based). A recent meta-analytic review derived a corrected correlation of .63 between affective and normative commitment (Meyer, Stanley, Herscovitch, & Topolnytsky, 2002). In discussing this relationship, the authors noted:

> We found that affective and normative commitment are indeed highly correlated. The correlation between the constructs, however, is not unity.

Moreover, although affective and normative commitment show similar patterns of correlations with antecedent, correlate, and consequence variables, the magnitude of the correlations is often quite different. (Meyer et al., 2002, p. 40)

With respect to organizational citizenship behavior, LePine, Erez, and Johnson (2002) conducted a meta-analytic review of the dimensions underlying that construct. Organ (1988) had suggested that citizenship behavior could assume multiple forms, including altruism, civic virtue, conscientiousness, courtesy, and sportsmanship. The LePine et al. (2002) review showed that the corrected correlations among the dimensions ranged from .40 to .87, with an average of .67. The authors concluded:

Organ's (1988) five dimensions should be thought of as somewhat imperfect indicators of the same underlying construct. Consistent with this idea, when OCB is the focal construct of interest, scholars should avoid focusing on the specific dimension of OCB when conducting research and interpreting results. (p. 61)

Thus Meyer et al. (2002) and LePine et al. (2002) both derived correlations among dimensions in the .60s, but interpreted the implications of those relationships quite differently. Meyer et al. (2002) argued that such correlations were low enough to support separation, whereas LePine et al. (2002) argued that they were high enough to support aggregation. Our own view is that correlations in the .50s are typically not worthy of aggregation, whereas correlations in the .70s clearly are. Reasonable scholars can—and obviously have—disagreed about what to do with correlations in the .60 range. Confirmatory factor analyses can provide some guidance, but it must be noted that the fit statistics in those analyses almost always reward a more complex factor structure, even when correlations among the factors are particularly high.

What About Overall Organizational Justice?

One potential solution to the question just raised is to focus more on overall organizational justice. As Ambrose and Anand (this volume) point out, there has been surprisingly little attention devoted to overall justice given its place in early theorizing (Leventhal, 1980) and more recent justice models (Lind, 2001a). However, two separate commentaries on the Cropanzano et al. (2001) narrative review did call for more of a focus on overall justice perceptions (Lind, 2001b; Shapiro, 2001). How might overall organizational justice be conceptualized? We suggest two possibilities: overall justice as a latent construct, and overall justice as a global perception.

Overall Justice as a Latent Construct.   Consider again the correlations among the justice dimensions in Table 4.3, as measured by Colquitt's (2001) scales. If we compute scale scores and enter those scores into a principal axis factor analysis, one factor emerges (explaining 64% of the variance) with loadings ranging from .64 to .84. Moreover, if we use the four scale scores as items in an overall organizational justice scale, then the coefficient alpha is .80. These kinds of results point to the possibility that overall justice could be modeled as a higher order factor that drives scores on the procedural, distributive, interpersonal, and informational dimensions.

A more stringent test of overall justice as a latent construct can be derived from a second-order confirmatory factor analysis to supplement the models tested in Table 4.2. Such a model fit the data from the 16 independent samples reasonably well: c^2 (166) = 2436.74; IFI = .93; CFI = .93; SRMR = .067; RMSEA = .077 (.074, .079). Not surprisingly, these fit statistics are only marginally different than the four-factor model without the higher order factor (see Table 4.2). Factor loadings for the higher order organizational justice factor and the lower order justice dimensions are shown in Fig. 4.3. The justice dimensions loaded on the overall organizational justice factor to a high and statistically significant degree, with loadings ranging from .64 to .86.

These results suggest that overall organizational justice could be modeled as a higher order latent variable that drives responses to the more specific justice factors. However, several cautionary notes must be considered. First, there must be at least three specific factors for a second-order factor model to be identified (Kline, 1998), and Kenny's (1979) standard for number of indicators should also be considered: "Two *might* be fine, three is better, four is best, and anything more is gravy" (p. 143, emphasis in original; see also Kline, 1998). This standard suggests that any study employing this strategy must assess three, if not four, justice dimensions.

Second, modeling overall justice in this way will likely be most appropriate for reactive field studies employing either a multiple event or an entity context. The relationships among the justice dimensions will likely be more modest in magnitude when grounded in a laboratory environment or a specific event context, harming the fit of a second-order model. As an example, Judge and Colquitt (2004) examined the effects of the four justice dimensions on work–family conflict, with the justice items grounded in the specific context of work–family policymaking. The correlations among the four dimensions were much lower than those shown in Table 4.3 (ranging from .21 to .61 with an average of .43), and reanalysis of the data for this manuscript showed that a second-order model did not provide an acceptable fit to the data.

140

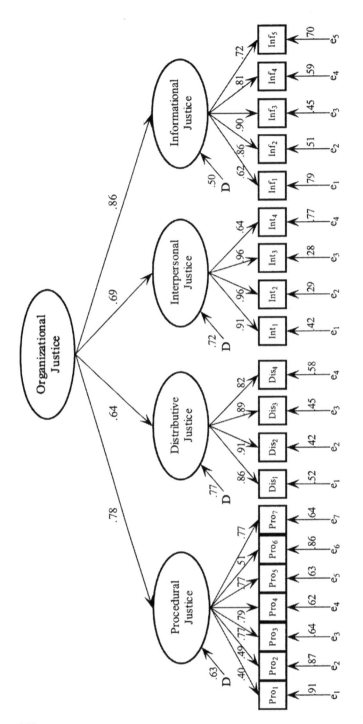

FIG. 4.3. Overall organizational justice as a higher order latent variable.

Overall Justice as a Global Perception.   A second method for operationalizing overall organizational justice is to use a more global direct assessment approach. Consider the following three items, the first of which is taken from the Cropanzano et al. (2001) review:

- My supervisor is a fair person.
- In general, my supervisor is fair.
- Overall, my supervisor does things fairly.

Each of these items captures an overall sense of fairness, which may be dictated by how fair outcome distributions are, how fair decision-making procedures seem, and how fairly those procedures are implemented. This sort of global perception closely mirrors the fairness heuristic discussed in Lind's (2001a) review of fairness heuristic theory.

Like most direct measures, these global items might best be utilized in research where justice is endogenous in the causal system. They could be used in the laboratory to assess the effects of manipulations of multiple justice dimensions on overall fairness, or could be used in the field as mediators of the relationships between indirect assessments and attitudinal and behavioral reactions. The latter affords the researcher a great deal of flexibility. If the global assessment retains much of the explanatory power of the specific dimensions, then variance is explained without the multicollinearity concerns summarized by Ambrose and Anand (this volume). Moreover, practical implications can still be derived by examining which of the justice dimensions is most strongly related to overall fairness. Of course, we should note that the sample items just suggested are only one form that an overall justice scale might take. They could just as easily be referenced to a formal organization (i.e., "My company is a fair one.") or to both human and formal sources.

CONCLUSION

As noted at the outset, theories cannot be tested without adequate measurement (Bacharach, 1989; Campbell, 1990). Lind and Tyler's (1988) landmark review helped trigger a flurry of theory building within the justice literature, as reflected in the relational model (Tyler & Lind, 1992), fairness theory (Folger & Cropanzano, 1998, 2001), and fairness heuristic theory (Lind, 2001a; Van den Bos et al., 2001), among others. If the justice literature is to continue to progress, those advances in theory must be matched by advances in measurement. We hope that this chapter has helped illustrate the key choices inherent in designing or adapting justice measures, as well as the impact of those choices on construct validity. We also hope that the questions and controversies raised in our chapter will

spur further debates and research on alternative approaches to measuring these important constructs.

APPENDIX: MEASURING ORGANIZATIONAL JUSTICE: REPRESENTATIVE EXAMPLES

Price and Mueller (1986)

Type: Distributive; **Source:** Formal system; **Context:** Single event; **Approach**: Indirect; **Repetition:** Multiple inputs.

"Fairness in the following questions means the extent to which a person's contributions to the hospital are related to the rewards received. Money, recognition, and physical facilities are examples of rewards."

1. "To what extent are you fairly rewarded considering the *responsibilities* that you have?"
2. "To what extent are you fairly rewarded taking into account the amount of *education and training* that you have had?"
3. "To what extent are you fairly rewarded in view of the *amount of experience* that you have?"
4. "To what extent are you fairly rewarded for the *amount of effort* that you have put forth?"
5. "To what extent are you fairly rewarded for *work that you have done well?*"
6. "To what extent are you fairly rewarded for the *stresses and strains* of your job?"
   (1 = *rewards are not distributed at all fairly* to 5 = *rewards are very fairly distributed*)

Konovsky, Folger, & Cropanzano (1987)

Type: Procedural; **Source:** Human agent; **Context:** Single event; **Approach:** Indirect; **Repetition:** Thibaut and Walker/Leventhal rules.

Participants rated the extent to which their supervisor …

1. "gave you an opportunity to express your side."
2. "used consistent standards in evaluating performance."
3. "frequently observed your performance."
   (1 = *not at all* to 9 = *very much*)

Type: Procedural; **Source:** Human agent; **Context:** Single event; **Approach:** Direct; **Repetition:** Fair synonyms, process synonyms.

1. "In your opinion, how fair were the practices your supervisor followed in reaching a decision about the size of raise to recommend for you?"
2. "In terms of just the *procedures* your supervisor used to determine your raise, to what extent were you treated the way you deserve to be treated?"
   (1 = *not at all* to 9 = *very much*)

Type: Distributive; **Source:** Human agent; **Context:** Single event; **Approach:** Direct/indirect; **Repetition:** Fair synonyms, multiple approaches.

1. "How fair do you consider the size of your raise to be?"
2. "To what extend did your raise give you the full amount you deserved?"
3. "To what extent was the size of your raise related to your performance?"
   (1 = *not at all* to 9 = *very much*)

Folger & Konovsky (1989)

Type: Procedural (and interactional); **Source:** Human agent; **Context:** Single event; **Approach:** Indirect; **Repetition:** Thibaut and Walker/Leventhal rules (and Bies and Moag).

"Indicate the extent to which your supervisor did each of the following:"

1. "Was honest and ethical in dealing with you."
2. "Gave you an opportunity to express your side."
3. "Used consistent standards in evaluating your performance."
4. "Considered your views regarding your performance."
5. "Gave you feedback that helped you learn how well you were doing."
6. "Was completely candid and frank with you."
7. "Showed a real interest in trying to be fair."
8. "Became thoroughly familiar with your performance."
9. "Took into account factors beyond your control." (R)
10. "Got input from you before a recommendation."
11. "Made clear what was expected of you."
12. "Discussed plans or objectives to improve your performance."

13. "Obtained accurate information about your performance."
14. "Found out how well you thought you were doing your job."
15. "Asked for ideas on what you could do to improve company performance."
16. "Frequently observed your performance."
17. "Behaved in a way you thought was not appropriate." (R)
18. "Allowed personal motives or biases to influence recommendation." (R)
19. "Was influenced by things that should not have been considered." (R)

"Indicate how much of an opportunity existed, AFTER THE LAST RAISE DECISION, for you to do each of the following things:"

20. "Review, with your supervisor, objectives for improvement."
21. "With your supervisor, resolve difficulties about your duties and responsibilities."
22. "Find out why you got the size of raise you did."
23. "Make an appeal about the size of your raise."
24. "Express your feelings to your supervisor about salary decision."
25. "Discuss, with your supervisor, how your performance was evaluated."
26. "Develop, with your supervisor, an action plan for future performance."

Moorman (1991)

Type: Procedural; **Source:** Formal system; **Context:** Entity; **Approach**: Indirect; **Repetition:** Thibaut and Walker/Leventhal rules.

Procedures designed to ...

1. "collect information necessary for making decisions."
2. "provide opportunities to appeal or challenge the decision."
3. "have all sides affected by the decision represented."
4. "generate standards so that decisions could be made with consistency."
5. "hear the concerns of all those affected by the decision."
6. "provide useful feedback regarding the decision and its implementation."
7. "allow for requests for clarification or additional information about the decision."

Type: Interactional; **Source:** Human agent; **Context:** Entity; **Approach:** Indirect; **Repetition:** Bies and Moag Rules.

1. "Your supervisor considered your viewpoint."
2. "Your supervisor was able to suppress personal biases."
3. "Your supervisor provided you with timely feedback about the decision and its implications."
4. "Your supervisor treated you with kindness and consideration."
5. "Your supervisor showed concern for your rights as an employee."
6. "Your supervisor took steps to deal with you in a truthful manner."

Sweeney and McFarlin (1993)

Type: Procedural; **Source:** Formal system; **Context:** Multiple events; **Approach:** Direct; **Repetition:** Multiple events.

1. "How fair or unfair are the *procedures* used to evaluate performance?"
2. "How fair or unfair are the *procedures* used to communicate performance feedback?"
3. "How fair or unfair are the *procedures* used to determine promotions?"
4. "How fair or unfair are the *procedures* used to determine salary increases?"
   (1 = *very unfair* to 5 = *very fair*)

Colquitt (2001)

Type: Procedural; **Source:** Convertible; **Context:** Convertible; **Approach:** Indirect; **Repetition:** Thibaut and Walker/Leventhal rules.

"The following items refer to the procedures used to arrive at your (outcome). To what extent:"

1. "Have you been able to express your views and feelings during those procedures?"
2. "Have you had influence over the (outcome) arrived at by those procedures?"
3. "Have those procedures been applied consistently?"

4. "Have those procedures been free of bias?"
5. "Have those procedures been based on accurate information?"
6. "Have you been able to appeal the outcome arrived at by those procedures?"
7. "Have those procedures upheld ethical and moral standards?"
   (1 = *to a small extent* to 5 = *to a large extent*)

Type: Interpersonal; **Source:** Human agent; **Context:** Convertible; **Approach:** Indirect; **Repetition:** Bies and Moag Criteria.

"The following items refer to (the authority figure who enacted the procedure). To what extent:"

1. "Has (he/she) treated you in a polite manner?"
2. "Has (he/she) treated you with dignity?"
3. "Has (he/she) treated you with respect?"
4. "Has (he/she) refrained from improper remarks or comments?"
   (1 = *to a small extent* to 5 = *to a large extent*)

Type: Informational; **Source:** Human agent; **Context:** Convertible; **Approach:** Indirect; **Repetition:** Bies and Moag Rules.

"The following items refer to (the authority figure who enacted the procedure). To what extent:"

1. "Has (he/she) been candid in (his/her) communications with you?"
2. "Has (he/she) explained the procedures thoroughly?"
3. "Were (his/her) explanations regarding the procedures reasonable?"
4. "Has (he/she) communicated details in a timely manner?"
5. "Has (he/she) seemed to tailor (his/her) communications to individuals' specific needs?"
   (1 = *to a small extent* to 5 = *to a large extent*)

Type: Distributive; **Source:** Convertible; **Context:** Convertible; **Approach:** Indirect; **Repetition:** Multiple inputs.

"The following items refer to your (outcome). To what extent:"

1. "Does your (outcome) reflect the effort you have put into your work?"
2. "Is your (outcome) appropriate for the work you have completed?"

3. "Does your (outcome) reflect what you have contributed to the organization?"
4. "Is your (outcome) justified, given your performance?"
(1 = *to a small extent* to 5 = *to a large extent*)

REFERENCES

Adams, J. S. (1965). Inequity in social exchange. In L. Berkowitz (Ed.), *Advances in experimental social psychology* (Vol. 2, pp. 267–299). New York: Academic Press.

Adams-Roy, J., & Barling, J. (1998). Predicting the decision to confront or report sexual harassment. *Journal of Organizational Behavior, 19,* 329–336.

Alge, B. J. (2001). Effects of computer surveillance on perceptions of privacy and procedural justice. *Journal of Applied Psychology, 86,* 797–804.

Allen, N. J., & Meyer, J. P. (1990). The measurement and antecedents of affective, continuance, and normative commitment to the organization. *Journal of Occupational Psychology, 63,* 1–18.

Ambrose, M. L., & Schminke, M. (2003). Organizational structure as a moderator of the relationship between procedural justice, interactional justice, perceived organizational support, and trust. *Journal of Applied Psychology, 88,* 295–305.

Avery, D. R., & Quinones, M. A. (2002). Disentangling the effects of voice: The incremental roles of opportunity, behavior, and instrumentality in predicting procedural fairness. *Journal of Applied Psychology, 87,* 81–86.

Bacharach, S. B. (1989). Organizational theories: Some criteria for evaluation. *Academy of Management Review, 14,* 496–515.

Bartol, K. M., Durham, C. C., & Poon, J. M. L. (2001). Influence of performance evaluation rating segmentation on motivation and fairness perceptions. *Journal of Applied Psychology, 86,* 1106–1119.

Bies, R. J. (2001). Interactional (in)justice: The sacred and the profane. In J. Greenberg & R. Cropanzano (Eds.), *Advances in organizational justice* (pp. 89–118). Stanford, CA: Stanford University Press.

Bies, R. J., & Moag, J. F. (1986). Interactional justice: Communication criteria of fairness. In R. J. Lewicki, B. H. Sheppard, & M. H. Bazerman (Eds.), *Research on negotiations in organizations* (Vol. 1, pp. 43–55). Greenwich, CT: JAI Press.

Bies, R. J., Shapiro, D. L., & Cummings, L. L. (1988). Causal accounts and managing organizational conflict: Is it enough to say it's not my fault? *Communication Research, 15,* 381–399.

Blader, S. L., & Tyler, T. R. (2003). What constitutes fairness in work settings? A four-component model of procedural justice. *Human Resource Management Review, 13,* 107–126.

Bobocel, D. R., & Holmvall, C. M. (2001). Are interactional justice and procedural justice different? Framing the debate. In S. Gilliland, D. Steiner, & D. Skarlicki (Eds.), *Theoretical and cultural perspectives on organizational justice* (pp. 85–110). Greenwich, CT: Information Age.

Brief, A. P., & Dukerich, J. M. (1991). Theory in organizational behavior: Can it be useful? In B. M. Staw & L. L. Cummings (Eds.), *Research in organizational behavior* (Vol. 13, pp. 327–352). Greenwich, CT: JAI Press.

Brockner, J., Siegel, P. A., Daly, J. P., & Martin, C. (1997). When trust matters: The moderating effect of outcome favorability. *Administrative Science Quarterly, 42*, 558–583.

Brockner, J., Wiesenfeld, B. M., Reed, T., Grover, S., & Martin, C. (1993). Interactive effect of job content and context on reactions of layoff survivors. *Journal of Personality and Social Psychology, 64*, 187–197.

Browne, M. W., & Cudeck, R. (1993). Alternative ways of assessing model fit. In K. A. Bollen & J. S. Long (Eds.), *Testing structural equation models* (pp. 136–162). Thousand Oaks, CA: Sage.

Byrne, Z. S., & Cropanzano, R. S. (2000, April). *To which source do I attribute this fairness? Differential effects of multi-foci justice on organizational work behaviors.* Presented at the 15th Annual Conference of the Society for Industrial & Organizational Psychology. New Orleans, LA.

Campbell, J. P. (1990). The role of theory in industrial and organizational psychology. In M. D. Dunnette and L. M. Hough (Eds.), *Handbook of industrial and organizational psychology* (Vol. 1, pp. 39–74). Palo Alto, CA: Consulting Psychologists Press.

Cobb, A. T., Vest, M., & Hills, F. (1997). Who delivers justice? Source perceptions of procedural fairness. *Journal of Applied Social Psychology, 27*, 1021–1040.

Colquitt, J. A. (2001). On the dimensionality of organizational justice: A construct validation of a measure. *Journal of Applied Psychology, 86*, 386–400.

Colquitt, J. A., & Chertkoff, J. M. (2002). Explaining injustice: The interactive effects of explanation and outcome on fairness perceptions and task motivation. *Journal of Management, 28*, 591–610.

Colquitt, J. A., Conlon, D. E., Wesson, M. J., Porter, C. O. L. H., & Ng, K. Y. (2001). Justice at the millennium: A meta-analysis of 25 years of organizational justice research. *Journal of Applied Psychology, 86*, 425–445.

Colquitt, J. A., & Greenberg, J. (2003). Organizational justice: A fair assessment of the state of the literature. In J. Greenberg (Ed.), *Organizational behavior: The state of the science* (pp. 165–210). Mahwah, NJ: Lawrence Erlbaum Associates.

Cropanzano, R., Byrne, Z. S., Bobocel, D. R., & Rupp, D. E. (2001). Moral virtues, fairness heuristics, social entities, and other denizens of organizational justice. *Journal of Vocational Behavior, 58*, 164–209.

Daly, J. P., & Geyer, P. D. (1994). The role of fairness in implementing large-scale change: Employee evaluations of process and outcome in seven facility relocations. *Journal of Organizational Behavior, 15*, 623–638.

Deutsch, M. (1975). Equity, equality, and need: What determines which value will be used as the basis for distributive justice? *Journal of Social Issues, 31*, 137–149.

Earley, P. C., & Lind, E. A. (1987). Procedural justice and participation in task selection: The role of control in mediating justice judgments. *Journal of Personality and Social Psychology, 52*, 1148–1160.

Elovainio, M., Kivimaki, M., & Helkama, K. (2001). Organizational justice evaluations, job control, and occupational strain. *Journal of Applied Psychology, 86*, 418–424.

Folger, R., & Bies, R. J. (1989). Managerial responsibilities and procedural justice. *Employee Responsibilities and Rights Journal, 2*, 79–89.

Folger, R., & Cropanzano, R. (1998). *Organizational justice and human resource management.* Thousand Oaks, CA: Sage.

Folger, R., & Cropanzano, R. (2001). Fairness theory: Justice as accountability. In J. Greenberg & R. Cropanzano (Eds.), *Advances in organizational justice* (pp. 1–55). Stanford, CA: Stanford University Press.

Folger, R., & Konovsky, M. A. (1989). Effects of procedural and distributive justice on reactions to pay raise decisions. *Academy of Management Journal, 32,* 115–130.

Folger, R., Rosenfield, D., Grove, J., & Corkran, L. (1979). Effects of "voice" and peer opinions on responses to inequity. *Journal of Personality and Social Psychology, 37,* 2253–2261.

Fryxell, G. E., & Gordon, M. E. (1989). Workplace justice and job satisfaction as predictors of satisfaction with union and management. *Academy of Management Journal, 32,* 851–866.

Gellatly, I. R. (1995). Individual and group determinants of employee absenteeism: Test of a causal model. *Journal of Organizational Behavior, 16,* 469–485.

Giacobbe-Miller, J. (1995). A test of the group values and control models of procedural justice from the competing perspectives of labor and management. *Personnel Psychology, 48,* 115–142.

Gilliland, S. W. (1993). The perceived fairness of selection systems: An organizational justice perspective. *Academy of Management Review, 18,* 694–734.

Greenberg, J. (1986). Determinants of perceived fairness of performance evaluation. *Journal of Applied Psychology, 71,* 340–342.

Greenberg, J. (1987). A taxonomy of organizational justice theories. *Academy of Management Review, 12,* 9–22.

Greenberg, J. (1990). Organizational justice: Yesterday, today, and tomorrow. *Journal of Management, 16,* 399–432.

Greenberg, J. (1993a). The intellectual adolescence of organizational justice: You've come a long way, maybe. *Social Justice Research, 6,* 135–148.

Greenberg, J. (1993b). The social side of fairness: Interpersonal and informational classes of organizational justice. In R. Cropanzano (Ed.), *Justice in the workplace: Approaching fairness in human resource management* (pp. 79–103). Hillsdale, NJ: Lawrence Erlbaum Associates.

Greenberg, J. (2001). The seven loose can(n)ons of organizational justice. In J. Greenberg & R. Cropanzano (Eds.), *Advances in organizational justice* (pp. 245–272). Stanford, CA: Stanford University Press.

Greenberg, J., & Wiethoff, C. (2001). Organizational justice as proaction and reaction: Implications for research and application. In R. Cropanzano (Ed.), *Justice in the workplace: From theory to practice* (pp. 271–302). Mahwah, NJ: Lawrence Erlbaum Associates.

Joy, V. L., & Witt, L. A. (1992). Delay of gratification as a moderator of the procedural justice–distributive justice relationship. *Group and Organization Management, 17,* 297–308.

Judge, T. J., & Colquitt, J. A. (2004). Organizational justice and stress: The mediating role of work-family conflict. *Journal of Applied Psychology, 89,* 395–404.

Kenny, D. A. (1979). *Correlation and causality.* New York: Wiley.

Kerlinger, F. N., & Lee, H. B. (2000). *Foundations of behavioral research.* Orlando, FL: Harcourt.

Kernan, M. C., & Hanges, P. J. (2002). Survivor reactions to reorganization: Antecedents and consequences of procedural, interpersonal, and informational justice. *Journal of Applied Psychology, 87,* 916–928.

Kline, R. B. (1998). *Principles and practice of structural equation modeling.* New York: Guilford Press.

Konovsky, M. A., & Cropanzano, R. (1991). Perceived fairness of employee drug testing as a predictor of employee attitudes and job performance. *Journal of Applied Psychology, 76,* 698–707.

Konovsky, M. A., Folger, R., & Cropanzano, R. (1987). Relative effects of procedural and distributive justice on employee attitudes. *Representative Research in Social Psychology, 17,* 15–24.

LaTour, S. (1978). Determinants of participant and observer satisfaction with adversary and inquisitorial modes of adjudication. *Journal of Personality and Social Psychology, 12,* 1531–1545.

LePine, J. A., Erez, A., & Johnson, D. E. (2002). The nature and dimensionality of organizational citizenship behavior: A critical review and meta-analysis. *Journal of Applied Psychology, 87,* 52–65.

Leventhal, G. S. (1976). The distribution of rewards and resources in groups and organizations. In L. Berkowitz & W. Walster (Eds.), *Advances in experimental social psychology* (Vol. 9, pp. 91–131). New York: Academic Press.

Leventhal, G. S. (1980). What should be done with equity theory? New approaches to the study of fairness in social relationships. In K. Gergen, M. Greenberg, & R. Willis (Eds.), *Social exchange: Advances in theory and research* (pp. 27–55). New York: Plenum Press.

Lind, E. A. (2001a). Fairness heuristic theory: Justice judgments as pivotal cognitions in organizational relations. In J. Greenberg & R. Cropanzano (Eds.), *Advances in organizational justice* (pp. 56–88). Stanford, CA: Stanford University Press.

Lind, E. A. (2001b). Thinking critically about justice judgments. *Journal of Vocational Behavior, 58,* 220–226.

Lind, E. A., Lissak, R. I., & Conlon, D. E. (1983). Decision control and process control effects on procedural fairness judgments. *Journal of Applied Social Psychology, 13,* 338–350.

Lind, E. A., & Tyler, T. R. (1988). *The social psychology of procedural justice.* New York: Plenum Press.

Lowe, R. H., & Vodanovich, S. J. (1995). A field study of distributive and procedural justice as predictors of satisfaction and organizational commitment. *Journal of Business and Psychology, 10,* 99–114.

Mansour-Cole, D. M., & Scott, S. G. (1998). Hearing it through the grapevine: The influence of source, leader-relations, and legitimacy on survivors' fairness perceptions. *Personnel Psychology, 51,* 25–54.

Masterson, S. S., Bartol, K. M., & Moye, N. (2000, April). *Interactional and procedural justice: Type versus source of fairness.* Presented at the 15th Annual Conference of the Society for Industrial & Organizational Psychology. New Orleans, LA.

McFarlin, D. B., & Sweeney, P. D. (1992). Distributive and procedural justice as predictors of satisfaction with personal and organizational outcomes. *Academy of Management Journal, 35,* 626–637.

Meyer, J. P., Stanley, D. J., Herscovitch, L., & Topolnytsky, L. (2002). Affective, continuance, and normative commitment to the organization: A meta-analysis of antecedents, correlations, and consequences. *Journal of Vocational Behavior, 61,* 20–52.

Moorman, R. H. (1991). Relationship between organizational justice and organizational citizenship behaviors: Do fairness perceptions influence employee citizenship? *Journal of Applied Psychology, 76,* 845–855.

Nunnally, J. (1978). *Psychometric theory.* New York: McGraw-Hill.

Organ, D. W. (1988). *Organizational citizenship behavior: The good soldier syndrome.* Lexington, MA: Lexington Books.

Price, J. L., & Mueller, C. W. (1986). *Handbook of organizational measurement.* Marshfield, MA: Pitman.

Quinones, M. A. (1995). Pretraining context effects: Training assignment as feedback. *Journal of Applied Psychology, 80,* 226–238.

Rasinski, K. A., & Tyler, T. R. (1988). Fairness and vote choice in the 1986 Presidential election. *American Politics Quarterly, 16,* 5–24.

Rupp, D. E., & Cropanzano, R. (2002). The mediating effects of social exchange relationships in predicting workplace outcomes from multifoci organizational justice. *Organizational Behavior and Human Decision Processes, 89,* 925–946.

Schminke, M., Ambrose, M. L., & Cropanzano, R. S. (2000). The effect of organizational structure on perceptions of procedural fairness. *Journal of Applied Psychology, 85,* 294–304.

Schwab, D. P. (1980). Construct validity in organizational behavior. In L. L. Cummings & B. M. Staw (Eds.), *Research in organizational behavior* (Vol. 2, pp. 3–43). Greenwich, CT: JAI Press.

Schwab, D. P. (1999). *Research methods for organizational studies.* Mahwah, NJ: Lawrence Erlbaum Associates.

Shapiro, D. L. (2001). The death of justice theory is likely if theorists neglect the "wheels" already invented and the voices of the injustice victims. *Journal of Vocational Behavior, 58,* 235–242.

Shapiro, D. L., & Brett, J. M. (1993). Comparing three processes underlying judgments of procedural justice: A field study of mediation and arbitration. *Journal of Personality and Social Psychology, 6,* 1167–1177.

Skarlicki, D. P., Folger, R., & Tesluk, P. (1999). Personality as a moderator in the relationship between fairness and retaliation. *Academy of Management Journal, 42,* 100–108.

Skarlicki, D. P., & Latham, G. P. (1996). Increasing citizenship behavior within a labor union: A test of organizational justice theory. *Journal of Applied Psychology, 81,* 161–169.

Skarlicki, D. P., & Latham, G. P. (1997). Leadership training in organizational justice to increase citizenship behavior within a labor union: A replication. *Personnel Psychology, 50,* 617–633.

Sweeney, P. D., & McFarlin, D. B. (1993). Workers' evaluation of the "ends" and the "means": An examination of four models of distributive and procedural justice. *Organizational Behavior and Human Decision Processes, 55,* 23–40.

Sweeney, P. D., & McFarlin, D. B. (1997). Process and outcome: Gender differences in the assessment of justice. *Journal of Organizational Behavior, 18,* 83–98.

Tepper, B. J., Lockhart, D., & Hoobler, J. (2001). Justice, citizenship, and role definition effects. *Journal of Applied Psychology, 86,* 789–796.

Thibaut, J., & Walker, L. (1975). *Procedural justice: A psychological analysis.* Hillsdale, NJ: Lawrence Erlbaum Associates.

Tyler, T. R. (1989). The psychology of procedural justice: A test of the group-value model. *Journal of Personality and Social Psychology, 57,* 830–838.

Tyler, T. R., & Bies, R. J. (1990). Beyond formal procedures: The interpersonal context of procedural justice. In J. S. Carroll (Ed.), *Applied social psychology and organizational settings* (pp. 77–98). Hillsdale, NJ: Lawrence Erlbaum Associates.

Tyler, T. R., & Blader, S. L. (2000). *Cooperation in groups: Procedural justice, social identity, and behavioral engagement.* Philadelphia, PA: Psychology Press.

Tyler, T. R. & Caine, A. (1981). The influence of outcomes and procedures on satisfaction with formal leaders. *Journal of Personality and Social Psychology, 41,* 642–655.

Tyler, T. R., & Lind, E. A. (1992). A relational model of authority in groups. In M. P. Zanna (Ed.), *Advances in experimental social psychology* (Vol. 25, pp. 115–191). San Diego, CA: Academic Press.

Tyler, T. R., Rasinski, K., & McGraw, K. (1985). The influence of perceived injustice on support for political authorities. *Journal of Applied Social Psychology, 15,* 700–725.

Tyler, T. R., Rasinski, K. A., & Spodick, N. (1985). Influence of voice on satisfaction with leaders: Exploring the meaning of process control. *Journal of Personality and Social Psychology, 48,* 72–81.

Tyler, T. R., & Schuller, R. (1990). *A relational model of authority in work organizations: The psychology of procedural justice.* Unpublished manuscript. Cited in Ambrose and Schminke (2003).

Van den Bos, K., Lind, E. A., & Wilke, H. (2001). The psychology of procedural justice and distributive justice viewed from the perspective of fairness heuristic theory. In R. Cropanzano (Ed.), *Justice in the workplace: Volume II—From theory to practice* (pp. 49–66). Hillsdale, NJ: Lawrence Erlbaum Associates.

Welbourne, T. M., Balkin, D. B., & Gomez-Mejia, L. R. (1995). Gainsharing and mutual monitoring, A combined agency–organizational justice interpretation. *Academy of Management Journal, 38,* 881–899.

III

THE JUSTICE JUDGMENT PROCESS

5

What Is the Role of Control in Organizational Justice?

Debra L. Shapiro
University of Maryland

Jeanne M. Brett
Northwestern University

Since Thibaut and Walker (1975) first proposed their control-oriented theory of procedural justice, there has been much research and theorizing attempting to explain why greater procedural justice is associated with having (rather than lacking) the chance to voice—termed the voice effect (Folger, 1977). In this chapter we review literature on the voice effect and the instrumental and noninstrumental explanations for it. Rather than treat each explanation as separate and independent of the other, we argue that the two are inexorably intertwined in both the structural and interpersonal aspects of judicial and organizational conflict resolution procedures. We also argue the need to test the generalizability of voice effects across cultures since most of the voice effect studies have been conducted in Western cultures. We conclude with the hope that future justice research will recognize the interrelationship of instrumental and noninstrumental voice dynamics so we can better understand when, as well as why, more voice leads to more perceived justice.

The right to express one's views is one of the hallmarks of American culture. It is protected in the Bill of Rights by the 5th and 14th Amendments of the U.S. Constitution regarding free press, free assembly, and individual rights (cf. Sugawara & Huo, 1994). It is institutionalized in the American adversarial judicial system, which, in contrast to the European inquisitorial judicial system, allows claimants and defendants to express their views and prohibits the testimony of experts beholden to the court and independent of the parties. Not surprisingly, this important element of American culture is reflected in the psychology of social interaction. The effect of being able to express one's views has been a major theme of social and organizational psychology since Thibaut and Walker's (1975) seminal study set in the context of judicial disputes. Their research showed that disputants who thought the dispute resolution process was fair were more satisfied with the outcome than those who did not think the process was fair. This finding has been called the *fair process effect* (Folger, Rosenfield, Grove, & Corkran, 1979).

Thibaut and Walker (1975) introduced the terms process control and outcome control to explain their findings. Process control refers to the right to express one's views, and outcome control to the right to determine the outcome. These authors concluded that the fair process effect was due to process control. This effect of process control—disputants' ability to express their views—on perceptions of procedural justice has been called the *voice effect* (Folger, 1977). Thus, control played an early and pivotal role in understanding judgments of justice.

In this chapter we elaborate on the theme of the role of control in organizational justice by first briefly reviewing the research documenting the fair process effect in judicial and organizational settings. We then turn to a discussion of the voice effect and the instrumental and noninstrumental explanations for it. Rather than treat each explanation as separate and independent of the other, we argue that the two are inexorably intertwined in both the structural and interpersonal aspects of judicial and organizational conflict resolution procedures. This observation, in turn, allows us to explain how data interpreted as supporting the noninstrumental perspective may in fact support the instrumental perspective (and vice versa) and thus why both explanations account for the voice effect. We end as we have begun: talking about culture. What we know about the role of control in organizational justice is almost exclusively the result of research in Western cultures. As cross-cultural research in social and organizational psychology blossoms, the role of control in justice perceptions is a promising avenue for future research.

FAIR PROCESS AND THE VOICE EFFECT: CONCEPTUAL BACKGROUND

The fair process effect is the tendency for perceptions of procedural justice to influence perceptions of, and satisfaction with, outcomes (Folger et al., 1979). Subsequent to Thibaut and Walker's (1975) identification of the fair process effect in laboratory research on judicial decision making, it has been identified by organizational scholars in a variety of contexts, including the context of participatory organizational practices (cf. Folger & Greenberg, 1985; Greenberg & Folger, 1983) and the context of actual (not simulated) dispute resolution (cf. Lind, Kulik, Ambrose, & Park, 1993; Shapiro & Brett, 1993). The general principle identified by these studies confirming the fair process effect is that fair procedures enhance the acceptance of outcomes (Greenberg, 2000).

Voice plays a critical role in explaining the fair process effect. To "voice" is to express one's views—for example, when disputants present facts or other evidence to a judge, arbitrator, or mediator, or when an employee confronts a manager over a poor performance review. The voice effect, which is among the most widely documented findings in the organizational justice literature (cf. Colquitt, Conlon, Wesson, Porter, & Ng, 2001), refers to the tendency for people to judge procedures in which they have the opportunity to express their feelings, or voice, as more fair than procedures that withhold this right (Folger, 1977). This discovery came about via a series of studies by Thibaut and Walker (1975) in which they asked participants to imagine that they were dispu-

tants and to evaluate the fairness of various dispute-resolution procedures. In these procedures process control was operationalized as voice
in the context of the *adversarial* or the *inquisitorial* judicial system, in
which disputants could present evidence to a third-party judge or
merely answer questions an authority posed to them, respectively. It
seems likely that Thibaut and Walker used the term *process control* as
they did because they viewed the opportunity versus the restriction of
voice as a structural element of a dispute resolution procedure. That is,
the structure of the procedure provided disputants with more or less
control over the process. Importantly, most of the studies conducted by
Thibaut and Walker had authority figures (rather than the disputants)
making the dispute resolution decisions; thus, disputants typically
lacked "outcome control," or the ability to decide how their dispute
would ultimately be resolved. As a result perhaps of studying procedures in which process (i.e., the chance to present evidence to a third
party) but not outcome control varied, Thibaut and Walker (1975) concluded that the key procedural element essential for judgments of procedural justice was the degree to which the procedure's structure
allowed disputants' control over the process (for an elaboration, see
Shapiro & Brett, 1993).

A question unanswered by judicially oriented justice research is,
"When disputants are allowed control over the process (as is the case in
arbitration or other judicial procedures), *and* the *outcome* regarding their
dispute's resolution (as is the case in mediation), will they perceive such
procedures as more fair?" "Yes," is the answer suggested by the findings reported by Shapiro and Brett (1993) in their field study comparing
the perceptions of procedural justice held by grievants who went to mediation versus arbitration.

However, a different conclusion was reached in a scenario-based
study by Houlden, LaTour, Walker, and Thibaut (1978), as their study
participants generally rated a procedure in which disputants would
have outcome control (i.e., the chance to accept or reject a third party's
recommended outcome) but no process control (i.e., the chance to express their views) as less fair than a procedure in which disputants
would have process but not outcome control. Although Houlden et al.
characterized their comparison as "mediation" versus "arbitration," it
is important to note that the procedural comparison reported by
Houlden et al. differs from the mediation versus arbitration comparison
made by Shapiro and Brett (1993). The procedures contrasted by
Shapiro and Brett involved giving disputants only process control (as
occurs in arbitration and in the adversarial procedure used in much of
the procedural justice research) versus giving disputants *both* forms of
control (i.e., process control and outcome control), as is the case in the
practice of mediation (see Shapiro & Kolb, 1994, for an elaboration on

the mediation process). Instead of contrasting these procedures, Houlden et al. (1978) compared the first procedure with one that gave disputants only outcome control (and no process-control). Cumulatively, these studies suggest that there is something about having both process and outcome control that disputants may value over having only one or the other form of control. This is why Brett (1986) argued for the importance of examining *the relationship between* perceptions of process and outcome control—in particular, the possibility that having voice may lead disputants to feel an indirect sense of outcome control. Articulating, and testing, such a relationship gave rise to competing explanations for why voice mattered at all.

INSTRUMENTAL AND NONINSTRUMENTAL EXPLANATIONS OF THE VOICE EFFECT

The conclusion that voice is the key antecedent to procedural justice inspired a great deal of research and theorizing seeking to explain what it is about voice that causes this effect. Researchers have proposed two explanations for this, one termed instrumental and the other noninstrumental. The main feature distinguishing between the instrumental and noninstrumental explanations for the voice effect regards the importance of giving disputing parties control over the outcome. The instrumental explanation proposes that the voice effect is due to the influence of voice on the decision maker. This is a control perspective. The noninstrumental explanation—the group value model (Tyler, 1987; Tyler & Lind, 1992)—proposes that the voice effect is due to the affirmation of status in the decision maker's social milieu associated with having the right to express one's views. Next, we clarify the differences between the instrumental and the noninstrumental perspectives, and in so doing explain how data interpreted as supporting one or the other perspective may in fact support the other. This clarity, in turn, promises to explain why both explanations can account for the voice effect.

Instrumental Explanations

At the core of the instrumental theory is an assumption and an inference. The assumption is that people engaged in conflict are motivated by self-interest (Tyler & Blader, 2000). The inference from the data demonstrating the voice effect is that self-interested people believe the opportunity to voice will further those interests. Why might people believe that voice will influence their outcomes?

One explanation is based on the tendency for disputants to have self-serving or egocentric biases. People who are in conflict or in a dispute already think they are right and the other party wrong, because other-

wise there would be no dispute in the first place (Felsteiner, Able, & Serat, 1980–1981). Disputants' self-serving, overconfident, egocentric biases lead them to believe that the decision maker, once informed, will see the "rightness" of their claim. Consistent with this, in simulated final arbitration proceedings in which disputing parties submitted a final offer to an arbitrator whose role as third-party was to choose between them, Neale and Bazerman (1985) found that the disputants estimated that their offers were 18% more likely to be accepted than they could possibly be given the structure of the decision context.

Additional data consistent with the view that voice provides outcome control via the opportunity to inform the decision maker come from our study of grievance mediation and arbitration (Shapiro & Brett, 1993). This was not a simulation study; those making judgments in this study were coal miners whose grievances were sent to arbitration (where they had no outcome control) or mediation (where they had outcome control). Both procedures provided opportunities for voice. In the arbitration procedure, voice was provided to disputants in a manner that was consistent with the dispute resolution procedures described in Thibaut and Walker's (1975) studies. The grieving miner was represented by a union representative, and the company was represented by a labor relations manager. In the mediation procedure the same parties were present; however, the mediator was generally a much more active participant than the arbitrator in that he or she engaged the grievants in direct discussion and gave them ultimate say over any resolution the mediator recommended. In this study we fit a model that allowed for direct and indirect effects of voice on procedural justice, controlling for procedure. The results showed an indirect effect of voice on perceptions of procedural justice that was mediated by perceptions of outcome control. This effect occurred controlling for perceptions of the fairness of the third party and procedure. Apparently, then, having the chance to inform the third party (be this a mediator or arbitrator) led grievants to perceive that they had greater outcome control.

Another explanation for why people believe that having voice will influence their outcomes regards the tendency for people to believe, after an authority has asked for their opinion, that their views will be taken into consideration (Barry & Shapiro, 2001; Greenberg, 2000; Shapiro, 1993)[1]—and in turn, the tendency for people to report greater levels of procedural justice when they perceive that authorities gave greater consideration to their expressed views (Tyler, 1987). Similarly, Avery and Quinones (2002) recently found that when study partici-

---

[1]The tendency for people, after authorities ask for their opinions, to perceive that their voice has been considered has been observed even when they had been told that the authority's decision had already been made (cf. Lind, Kanfer, & Earley, 1990).

pants learned that fewer rather than more of their suggested ideas were incorporated in the outcome of the experimenter's decision—that is, when the experimenter apparently gave less rather than more consideration to participants' suggestions—participants' voice behavior was generally associated with lower (rather than higher) levels of perceived procedural justice. Avery and Quinones (2002) explained:

> If individuals see that their voice has had no impact on the outcome, they may deem the situation to be procedurally unfair and wonder, *why did the decision maker ask for my input only to disregard it?* (p. 82, emphasis added)

A decision maker who would behave in the way just described would probably *not* be trusted. There is substantial data by Tyler and Blader (2000) indicating that (a) fair procedures are ones in which the third party is judged to be trustworthy; (b) trust entails believing that the decision maker will try to do what is right for the party, that is, will try to be fair; and (c) one way that decision makers do this is by providing justification and explanations to make it clear that they have listened to and considered the voiced expressions that a disputant (or anyone perceiving injustice) has made. As can be seen in Fig. 5.1 (in which all relationships are positive), voice initiates many of these processes. This is because, consistent with Avery and Quinones (2003) and as illustrated by arrow B in the figure, people tend to perceive those who have requested hearing their views to be more interpersonally caring (why else would they have asked their opinion?) than those who do not make this request. Arrow B reflects this tendency for people whose input is (vs. isn't) sought to perceive their solicitor as more (rather than less) concerned, hence responsive, to their needs. Moreover, as Shapiro and her colleagues (Barry & Shapiro, 2000; Shapiro, 1993) and others (Greenberg, 2000) explained, the belief that one might influence decision makers (hence the hope that decision makers may do the right thing) tends to be stronger when people are given rather than denied the chance to express their views. This tendency for people, after their voice has (rather than hasn't) been solicited, to feel greater potential to influence decision makers is shown via arrow A in the figure. Such hope is often made stronger when listeners seem to be more rather than less interpersonally caring, or responsive, via their exhibiting nonverbal affirmation, empathy, or other sensitive behaviors; arrow C illustrates this tendency. Figure 5.1, which was initially presented by Shapiro (1993), thus visually illustrates that listeners' interpersonal responsiveness can increase feelings of hope about outcomes that, in turn, can heighten perceptions of procedural justice. The latter positive relationship, illustrated in the figure by the positive sign on arrow D, represents a control oriented, hence instrumental, perspective (see Barry & Shapiro, 2000, for an elaboration and empirical support of this view).

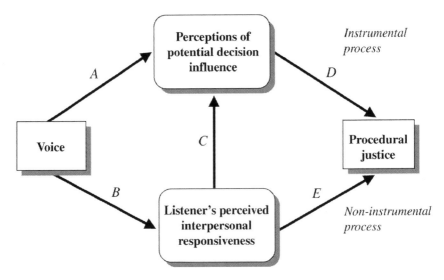

FIG. 5.1.   A revised model of procedural justice. From Shapiro (1993).

Noninstrumental Explanations

There are also an assumption and an inference at the core of the noninstrumental explanation for the voice effect. The assumption is that people engaged in conflict are motivated by factors other than self-interest
(Tyler & Blader, 2000). The inference from data demonstrating the voice
effect is that those other interests are met by voice. What are these other
interests? The group value model (Lind & Tyler, 1988; Tyler, 1987; Tyler,
Degoey, & Smith, 1996) substitutes a relational criterion for evaluating
voice for the rational self-interest criterion assumed by the instrumental
model (Greenberg, 2000). It assumes that people value being members
of groups, such as communities or organizations, and that interactions
with community or organizational authorities either affirm or
disconfirm their status in that group. The group value model proposes
that the opportunity to voice affirms disputants' status with the decision maker and that such status is important to disputants because it acknowledges that they are valued members of the group whom the
decision maker represents. An unstated assumption in the group value
model is that the decision maker asking for others' input genuinely
wants to hear and consider it, because the absence of the latter perception would surely make speakers feel manipulated and disrespected.
Figure 5.1 illustrates this unstated assumption via arrow B by showing

the tendency for voice opportunities to enhance the perception that listeners (at least those who asked to hear one's views) are behaving in interpersonally positive ways that lead those whose input has been sought to feel respected. If, indeed, feelings of respect and status that result from being asked to voice are, more accurately, a result of perceiving those soliciting voice to be interpersonally responsive (e.g., appreciative of one's input), then arrow E in the figure is conceptually consistent with the group value model. This is because it indicates that more justice will be perceived when people perceive others to be acting in more rather than less interpersonally responsive (e.g., respect-giving) ways. This is why this relationship in the model represents the noninstrumental process.

Data supporting the group value model come from studies that show that voice affects procedural justice when controlling for influence over the outcome (Lind et al., 1990; Shapiro & Brett, 1993; Tyler et al., 1996; Tyler, Rasinski, & Spodick, 1985). Importantly, with rare exception (cf. Barry & Shapiro, 2000), the kinds of influence that researchers have used as control variables in past justice research regard grievants' perceptions of their actual, rather than potential, influence. Therefore, the voice effects reported in past studies may have occurred because grievants who were given (rather than denied) voice valued the *potential* that voice gave them to influence their outcomes. To rule out this rival explanation for the voice effect, future justice studies need to include measures of, both, potential and actual influence (cf. Barry & Shapiro, 2000; Shapiro, 1993, 2001).

Fairness Theory Heuristic.   An explanation for the voice effect that takes into account both the instrumental and noninstrumental perspective is Lind's (2001) fairness theory heuristic. Lind pointed out that people feel vulnerable to exploitation (with attendant loss of outcomes) and exclusion (with attendant loss of social identity) by authorities and decision makers. This vulnerability, Lind explained, is why people try to determine whether or not authorities can be trusted. Given scant information about outcomes (which is the normal research paradigm), people base their heuristic judgments on whatever information is available, which Lind said tends to be information about the process, such as the extent to which they have or will have voice (e.g., the chance to appeal an unfavorable decision).[2] This uncertainty reduction explanation for

---

[2]According to Lind and van den Bos (2002), the reverse also is true. That is, when there is scant information about process and greater information about outcomes, people decide whether to trust authorities (such as a potential Supreme Court Judge appointee) on the outcome information available (e.g., the appointee's past voting record). Therefore, whatever information is available will be used to make fairness judgments; hence this substitutability effect can cause fair outcome effects.

the voice effect is instrumental because it argues that procedures have a heuristic value for reducing uncertainty about outcomes. The explanation is noninstrumental because it argues that procedures have a heuristic value for reducing uncertainty about authorities. In simple terms, the fairness theory heuristic explains the voice effect by proposing that disputants find it easier to make sense of outcomes and evaluate authorities when they have more rather than less voice.

RESOLVING COMPETING EXPLANATIONS OF THE VOICE EFFECT

The instrumental versus noninstrumental explanations for the voice effect have resulted in claims that the latter perspective is more powerful than the former (e.g., Tyler, 1987) and vice versa (e.g., Shapiro & Brett, 1993). More recently, justice scholars have pointed out that both explanations for the voice effect provide important insight into the underlying reasons for the fair process effect and have treated these explanations as complementary rather than competing (Barry & Shapiro, 2000; Cropanzano & Greenberg, 1997; Greenberg, 2000; Shapiro, 1993, 2001).

Perhaps the reason for the controversy is that it is difficult to partition pure instrumental from pure noninstrumental effects of voice. What was never easy was only made more difficult as the focus in the procedural justice research shifted away from voice, a structural element of procedure, to the interpersonal treatment of the disputant by the decision maker. (For example, note the relative emphasis placed by both Greenberg [2000] and Tyler and Blader [2000] on interpersonal treatment compared to structural elements and/or the group value model.) Two elements of interpersonal treatment that have received much empirical attention in procedural justice research regard the extent to which decision makers (i.e., typically authority figures) behave in ways that make decision receivers such as disputants, grievants, and employees perceive (a) that their views have been considered, or respected, and (b) that decision-related explanations were communicated in a sensitive and informationally thorough way.

Consideration

Is consideration an instrumental or noninstrumental effect? To treat others with dignity and respect publicly recognizes their status and, as such, would seem unrelated to the outcomes that people receive when they deal with authorities (Tyler & Blader, 2000). This reasoning suggests that the effect of consideration is noninstrumental and status-affirming. Yet decision makers' consideration not only confers status but also raises expectations that decision makers will listen and be influ-

enced (Greenberg, 2000; Shapiro, 1993, 2001). Consistent with this, Barry and Shapiro (2000) found that consideration on the part of decision makers significantly influenced participants' belief that they were respected (a noninstrumental perception) and that their expressed views *might* change the decision maker's thinking (an instrumental perception that Barry and Shapiro referred to as a perception of "*potential influence*"). Thus, these data suggest that authorities' interpersonal actions guide the inferences people make about not only how much they are valued and respected, but how much influence they might have in the organization. In turn, the latter observation suggests that the effect of instrumental and noninstrumental voice-related explanations may be inextricably intertwined (Barry & Shapiro, 2000).

The way perceptions of interpersonal relations are measured may further confound instrumental and noninstrumental effects. For example, the Appendix reproduces the questions used by Tyler and Blader (2000, p. 94) to measure interpersonal relations in their study. All the questions with the exception of number 2 ask the respondent to focus on when decisions are made, and hence to recall past events regarding decisions (as well as process issues). The item in the Appendix that asks "Does your supervisor follow through on the decisions and promises he / she makes?" surely conjures up memories of promised outcomes that were versus were not delivered. Thus, it seems likely that the questions trigger past experiences for which presumably the respondent already knows, and has interpreted for good or bad, the outcomes. Responses inconsistent with experience seem unlikely. For example, if you are dissatisfied with a decision made by your supervisor, it seems highly unlikely that you would strongly agree that the supervisor took your views into account. To do so would require that we assume you are making internal attributions for negative outcomes—"well the outcome is terrible, but the supervisor took my advice!"—a relationship that is highly unlikely as a result of people's aversion to cognitive dissonance (cf. Festinger, 1954).

Informational Justification

The organizational justice literature has studied the effect of informational justification on justice quite thoroughly (Greenberg, 1993a). It refers to the extent to which people believe they have adequate information about the decisions affecting them (Greenberg, 2000). The earliest evidence of the effects of informational justification was in studies that found that layoffs were better accepted by both those leaving and those staying when a sensitive explanation for the layoff was provided (Brockner, DeWitt, Grover, & Reed, 1990). More recently, Greenberg (2000) reviewed three studies that underline the importance of informational justification for procedural justice. In a laboratory

study, retaliation for underpayment was lowest when levels of both social sensitivity and information were high (Greenberg, 1993b). In a field
study of an organization introducing a smoking ban, rejection of the ban
was lowest when it was thoroughly explained and presented in a socially sensitive manner (Greenberg, 1994). In an interview study of unemployed people, the better the explanations that people received
about the reasons for their unemployed status, the more dignity and respect they felt and the better they accepted the termination decision
(Lind, Greenberg, Scott, & Welchans, 2000).

It is important to note that the participants in the latter explanation-
related studies had little opportunity for voice; rather, they merely received (or didn't receive) explanations with varying qualities for authorities' decisions. Can these findings be generalized to the situation in
which voice is available, the situation that is the focus of this chapter? To
evaluate this generalization, it is useful to consider why sensitive explanations enhance procedural justice. Is it their instrumental or their noninstrumental value? Again our answer is probably both.

From an instrumental perspective, just as disputants hope that their
voice will educate third-party authorities about the rightness of their
claim, the motive behind authorities' choice to provide explanations is
often their desire to "appear fair" (Greenberg, 1990). That is, authorities
hope that their explanations will inform recipients about the rightness,
or appropriateness, of a management decision. The likelihood of this
education occurring increases if explanation recipients are enabled to
voice their concerns and ask questions about decision-related explanations they receive. If, indeed, this education occurs, then recipients of
such explanations are likely to revise their initial evaluations regarding
the unfairness or unfavorability of the decision. Such *outcome-related revision* thus suggests that the justice-enhancing effect of explanations is,
at least in part, instrumental.

A second reason why the justice-enhancing effect of explanations
may be instrumental regards the tendency for *sensitive* explanations to
provide a basis for making external attributions for negative outcomes
and thereby enable a bad news recipient to maintain a positive self-concept. Consistent with this, Shapiro, Buttner, and Barry (1994) found that
after receiving an unfavorable decision from an authority (i.e., job rejections or a poor grade), study participants generally evaluated the more
adequate explanations to be those that contained an external rather
than internal attribution. External rather than internal explanations for
unfavorable organizational events may be viewed as more adequate because they relieve recipients of personal responsibility and thus help recipients' maintain a positive self-image.

Of course, if the latter outcome is identified as noninstrumental in nature simply because it is not economically oriented (cf. Tyler & Blader,

2000), then the latter dynamic would suggest that the face-saving nature of sensitive explanations supports the noninstrumental perspective too. Sensitive explanations may enhance procedural justice for noninstrumental reasons also, because such explanations make it easier to accept that a decision was a considered judgment rather than one made without thought (Greenberg & Folger, 1983). A considered judgment confers more status on the recipient than a capricious one; it sends the message that the decision maker respected the recipient sufficiently to "consider" the decision. A considered judgment delivered by the decision maker who is speaking for the organization or community also conveys status—it is not just the decision maker but the social entity that respects the recipient. Decisions, such as layoffs, that are fully within the prerogative of management require no explanation. When an explanation is given, the act of explaining signals that the person merits an explanation even when no explanation is necessary.

Effects of perceived consideration have been linked with perceptions not only of status, but of potential instrumentality, such as the belief that one's expressed view might be reflected in an authority's eventual decision (Barry & Shapiro, 2000; Greenberg, 2000). Therefore, the hope that gets enhanced when explaining to decision recipients that their views will be considered supports an instrumental perspective too. Whether the justice-enhancing effect of providing adequate explanations for unfavorable decisions is due to instrumental or noninstrumental processes is thus arguable; why? Because again each of the latter processes seem intertwined when one considers all of the thoughts and feelings triggered by receiving adequate explanations for upsetting circumstances.

Summary: Psychological Processes Underlying the Voice Effect

In summary, voice appears to affect procedural justice via two theoretical channels, one instrumental and the other noninstrumental. Giving disputants voice raises their expectations, hence hopes, about the outcomes they will receive (Barry & Shapiro, 2000; Greenberg, 2000; Shapiro, 1993). It also conveys status on them (Tyler & Blader, 2000). Decision makers' interpersonal behaviors—providing more or less consideration and informational justification—affects decision receivers' inferences about both how much influence and how much interpersonal responsiveness (e.g., respect or status) they have in their organization. Therefore, any finding regarding "interpersonal effects" may be interpreted as supporting either or both of these voice-related explanations. Figure 5.1, whose relationships we explained earlier, visually shows why positive interpersonal responsiveness on the part of listeners (i.e., decision makers) can sometimes lead to instrumental, and at other times lead to noninstrumental, paths to perceived justice, and

therefore, why it is too simplistic to conclude that "interpersonal effects" in justice studies support only one of these two perspectives. Moreover, because Fig. 5.1 highlights the role that *potential* decision influence may play in determining why the voice effect occurs, this figure also illuminates the need in future research to measure and control for this perception (in addition to perceptions of actual influence as is typically done). Recognizing that noninstrumental and instrumental voice-related dynamics do *not* operate independently from each other—indeed, that they are intertwined—and adopting measures to reflect this recognition promise to resolve a longstanding controversy that justice scholars seem to want ended. More importantly, future theorizing and empirical research that reflects and respects these perspectives' intertwinement promises to strengthen understanding of why voice often leads to greater levels of procedural justice.

LIMITS OF THE VOICE EFFECT

The tendency for voice to enhance perceptions of justice is limited to certain conditions. The voice effect (for reasons attributed to either instrumental or noninstrumental processes) has generally been found when (a) people expect to have the opportunity to express their views to decision makers and value this freedom, and (b) people perceive their listeners to be treating them respectfully. With regard to the latter point, the tendency for voice to enhance perceived justice has generally been observed when the listening authorities appear to be more rather than less sincere in their willingness to listen (see Greenberg, 2000, for a review). When third-party decision makers (e.g., mediators, arbitrators, court judges, and other authorities) seem *not* to be considering grievants' views, the voice effect tends not to occur (cf. Shapiro & Brett, 1993; Tyler, 1987). The importance of authorities showing sincerity and consideration to obtain significant voice effects in these studies probably explains, at least in part, why the procedural justice literature's focus over time has gravitated from structural to interpersonal antecedents (see reviews by Colquitt & Greenberg, 2003; Greenberg, 2000).

The first limiting condition of the voice effect just noted suggests that this phenomenon characterizes people who *want* voice and view this as their right. If this is indeed true, it suggests that the justice literature generally represents those who do (rather than do not) belong to a "culture of voice."

A Culture of Voice?

The literature represented by most of the justice studies performed to date regards situations in which *employees generally believe that they*

have a right to be heard. It is this belief with which we began our chapter: "The right to express one's views is one of the hallmarks of American culture." Our choice to begin our chapter that way, and to return to it now, is due to our wanting to emphasize the cultural context in which the voice effect research has been done; very little of this has occurred in non-Western cultures (Suguwara & Huo, 1994). Recognizing that the justice literature may reflect a "culture of voice" is important because, as Von Glinow, Shapiro, and Brett (2004) highlight, the desire to communicate concerns directly to others in situations involving negative affect (as most of the situations studied by procedural justice scholars do) is a Western bias. The value placed on voice is generally *not* shared by people whose national culture such as Asia tends to prefer indirect (less confrontive, more harmony-preserving) forms of handling conflict (cf. Lind, Huo, & Tyler, 1994). Not surprisingly, then, Lind et al. found that when asked to express preferences for various dispute resolution procedures, the one that gave the greatest opportunity for voice—negotiation—was preferred significantly more by the European Americans rather than Asian Americans in their study.

Differences in how people from various cultures respond to having (vs. not having) voice have also been found by Brockner and his colleagues (Brockner et al., 2001). Brockner et al. compared employees' reactions to situations in which they reported having (or were experimentally manipulated to have) higher versus lower levels of voice in the decisions that their managers made. They found that employees with less rather than more voice tended to report lower levels of organizational commitment when they were from the United States rather than China. Brockner et al. explained their findings to be the result of cultural value differences between the United States and China. Specifically, they noted that U.S. Americans tend to have cultural values that are "egalitarian," or similarly low in "power distance," whereas the reverse pole of each of these values (hierarchy and high power distance, respectively) tends to be characteristic of the Chinese culture (cf. Hofstede, 1980; Schwartz, 1994). These cultural values distinguish intolerance versus tolerance for inequality. In egalitarian cultures, social status is relatively flat and permeable (Brett, 2001), and subordinates actively participate in decision making, hence blurring the distance between authorities and subordinates (Schneider & Barsoux, 1997). In hierarchical cultures, social status is differentiated and subordinates expect authorities to make decisions (Schneider & Barsoux, 1997).

The general conclusion of Brockner et al. is that whether voice affects positive work attitudes and behaviors (e.g., organizational commitment) depends on whether people expect to participate in managers'

decisions; and that people's expectations regarding the appropriateness of voice are culturally guided. *Not* having voice in managers' decisions in a culture where this is expected makes the absence of voice a deprivation (hence an injustice), whereas not having voice in a culture where participation is unexpected makes its absence an insignificant event. The reverse is also true: *Being asked* by a leader for decision making input in a culture where this is *unexpected* and deemed weak makes this request an undesirable one. This explains why Scandura, Von Glinow, and Lowe (1997) found harsher evaluations for participative leaders on the part of employees from Saudi Arabia rather than the United States (where the norm for an autocratic style of leadership is stronger and weaker, respectively). Similarly, this explains why leaders whose request for employee input went beyond the norm were also judged as weak (Peterson, 1999). The critical variable is *expectations*. Similarly, Colquitt and Greenberg (2003, pp. 194–195) suggested that justice expectations regarding norms in general will "[affect] expectations of what justice means and the degree of justice expected" and that "an individual's native culture may influence his or her expectations regarding the qualities that characterize a 'fair procedure.'"

If, indeed, people's expectations regarding justice ultimately determine when they do (or don't) perceive it, and if such expectations are guided by cultural values, then future justice research needs to broaden the (mostly Western) cultural contexts that have generally been within researchers' scope. Failing to do so threatens to make the reported observations and conclusions of justice researchers appear relevant only to a "culture of voice."

A Culture of "Authorities"?

Another characteristic dominating most of the justice literature regards its tendency to focus on situations in which *employees are dealing with authorities* (e.g., receiving decisions from them, receiving explanations from them, expressing views to them, and receiving more or less consideration from them). As a result, we know relatively little about dynamics pertaining to the voice effect in situations where employees are dealing with peers. This is of concern in light of the fact that work assignments are increasingly given to teams that are self-managing, virtual, and/or transnational; thus, employees' decisions are increasingly made by people who are *not* authorities (cf. Von Glinow et al., 2004).

In a recent study of third-party intervention into managerial disputes (Tinsley, Brett, Shapiro, & Okumura, 2003), Chinese third parties who had rather than lacked authority relative to the disputing parties were, compared to U.S. American third parties under these circumstances, more likely to behave in an autocratic manner (i.e., to make the

resolution decision rather than ask disputing parties for their input). This result is consistent with general cultural differences. However, when the Chinese third parties were peers to the disputing parties, they were as unlikely as U.S. American third parties under these circumstances to make the decision; rather, they involved the disputants in determining the resolution. In China, being a peer rather than a boss in the dispute resolution context apparently cued different behaviors, including behaviors that were contrary to the voice-indifferent ways attributed to the Chinese culture (cf. Brockner et al., 2001).

This finding has two important implications. First, it suggests that people have repertoires of behaviors that, despite being culturally guided, become available for use depending on the cues (such as whether one is a boss or a peer) in one's contextual environment (Morris & Gelfand, 2004). Second, the Tinsley et al. (2003) finding suggests that it is not fruitful to use (only) cultural values to predict when dynamics associated with the voice effect will be observed in various cultures. Rather, justice researchers and managers in global affiliates may more effectively predict and manage justice perceptions if they are sensitive to both the cultural values of their employees and the contextual features in the work environment that may heighten or lessen the salience of employees' cultural values. Focusing on the cuing function of both the general cultural and the specific social context of the decision is thus advisable in future cross-cultural justice research (Morris & Gelfand, 2004; Morris & Leung, 2000).

Summary: What Are the Limits of the Voice Effect?

In summary, our knowledge regarding when and why voice tends to enhance perceptions of justice is limited by the contexts typically studied by justice researchers. These contexts primarily involve people who belong to a culture of voice and whose voice-related assessments regard authority–subordinate relationships. Studies representing these contexts have yielded important insights to date, such as the essentiality of respect-giving actions (e.g., asking for others' input, showing consideration) on the part of authorities and the importance of being sincere when engaging in such actions (cf. Greenberg, 2000, for a review). Although the latter view has begun to expand to all possible relationships in organizations (cf. Tyler & Blader, 2000), the measurement issues noted earlier in this chapter suggest that justice scholars will need to modify empirical strategies, and do so systematically (cf. Colquitt et al., 2001), if knowledge building is to occur.

With regard to limiting conditions associated with studying a *culture of voice*, we have deliberately used the latter term to highlight that the contexts in need of comparison by justice scholars are those where there

is likely to be variance regarding the presumed goodness of voice (cf. Von Glinow et al., 2004). Although some of this research has been done (e.g., Brockner et al., 2001; Lind et al., 1994; Suguwara & Huo, 1994), it is still the exception more than the rule.

Importantly, in our discussion of culture as a limiting condition of the voice effect, we noted that its influence was probably due to the differing expectations people have regarding the appropriateness of voice. Although such expectations are culturally guided, we also noted that the salience of cultural values sometimes depends on other factors in one's context. The Tinsley et al. (2003) finding suggests that whether third parties will behave in autocratic versus participative ways that are consistent with their culture's values depends on whether the third parties are bosses or peers relative to the disputing parties. Apparently, expectations regarding how to intervene as a boss versus peer overrided expectations regarding how to intervene as a member of one's national culture. This points to the need to examine various factors that influence expectations; Colquitt and Greenberg (2003) identified this as important for understanding what influences "justice expectations," specifically.

BROADENING KNOWLEDGE ABOUT CONTROL EFFECTS IN JUSTICE RESEARCH

With the limits of the voice effect already noted, actions needed to broaden our understanding regarding when (in what context, in what kinds of relationships) the voice effect will occur are implicitly, if not explicitly, clear. For example, knowledge about the voice effect will be culturally broadened when justice scholars' samples include (as control groups to their typically Western participants) participants from Eastern cultures for whom open talk is generally counter to their cultural values (cf. Von Glinow et al., 2004). Knowledge about the voice effect will be relationally broadened when justice scholars examine team members or peers (in addition to authority–subordinate relationships).

But actions are needed, too, to improve understanding about *how* the voice effect occurs. These dual sets of research and actions promise to enable justice scholars to build better theory (cf. Colquitt & Greenberg, 2003). Our goal in the chapter was to clarify the instrumental and noninstrumental explanations for the voice effect in procedural justice research, and thus to illuminate what we do and don't know about how the voice effect occurs. The instrumental theory focuses on control and how voice or the opportunity to express one's views indirectly or directly leads to expectations of outcome control. The noninstrumental explanation focuses on relational affirmation and how voice signals sta-

tus in organizations and communities responsible for making decisions that affect people's lives. We have argued two fundamental points.

First, instrumental and noninstrumental explanations for the voice effect, although conceptually distinct, are inexorably intertwined from a research perspective. Although it is critical for both theoretical and practical reasons to recognize that there may be two very different theoretical explanations for the voice effect, research methods are unlikely to definitively distinguish them. We discussed measurement issues contributing to the controversy in some detail, but laboratory and field methods have also contributed. In the laboratory, of course, structural and sometimes even relationship elements can be manipulated. However, with manipulations the influence of one mediating variable over another on the dependent variable is not generalizable beyond the manipulation. Field research is also a suspect environment for testing the relative power of mediating variables, because outcomes are known, and unmeasured variables abound. The point is not that instrumental or noninstrumental is more important in producing judgments of procedural justice, but that both surely are, because these processes influence one another.

There are two practical reasons for treating instrumental and noninstrumental explanations for the voice effect equally. The first is the fair process effect: Just procedures lead to acceptance of outcomes. The second is that it may be easier to build instrumental voice into some situations and noninstrumental voice into others. Situations like layoffs, for example, are not conducive to instrumental voice, but have been shown to be highly responsive to noninstrumental voice (Brockner et al., 1990; Lind et al., 2000). In contrast, third-party dispute resolution procedures benefit significantly from instrumental voice.

Our second point was that the voice effects that are considered principles in social psychology (Greenberg, 2000) are nevertheless affected by cultural and contextual factors. Instrumental voice is more consistent with individualistic, egalitarian Western cultural contexts and noninstrumental voice is more consistent with collective, hierarchical East Asian cultural contexts (cf. Lind et al., 1994). And yet, the cultural findings cannot be taken as definitive for two reasons. People in all cultures no doubt value both the instrumental and the noninstrumental elements of voice. Indeed, the noninstrumental theory was initially articulated by Western scholars relying on U.S. data. Furthermore, context matters. Contextual cues unleash behavioral differences that can be interpreted as instrumental or noninstrumental voice.

A review of our chapter's fundamental points suggests that a key action needed to broaden understanding about how the voice effect occurs is for justice studies to include measures of participants' feelings of hope as well as their feelings of respect with regard to having versus

lacking voice. Measuring hope in addition to respect will enable justice scholars to observe how the latter dynamics influence each other, and to empirically determine the extent to which "interpersonal effects" represent noninstrumental versus instrumental voice dynamics. Doing this promises, also, to enable justice scholars to make the theoretical and empirical adjustments necessary to recognize the intertwinement between noninstrumental feelings of being respected by authorities and instrumental feelings of hope that authorities will act in accordance with voiced views. Such a focus promises to unlock new insights and important justice-enhancing interventions that "competing paradigms" and mostly untested assumptions regarding what constitutes evidence of "instrumental" versus "noninstrumental" dynamics in the justice literature may have prevented us from seeing.

APPENDIX: A SAMPLING OF MEASURES IN TYLER AND BLADER'S (2000) STUDY

1. "My rights are respected when decisions are made."

2. "My supervisor respects my rights."

3. "My needs are taken into account when decisions are made."

4. "My supervisor takes account of my needs when making decisions."

5. "My views are considered when decisions are made."

6. "My supervisor considers my views when decisions are made."

7. "Does the organization follow through on the decisions and promises it makes?"

8. "Does your supervisor follow through on the decisions and promises he/she makes?"

REFERENCES

Avery, D. R., & Quinones, M. A. (2002). Disentangling the effects of voice: The incremental roles of opportunity, behavior, and instrumentality in predicting procedural fairness. *Journal of Applied Psychology, 87*(1), 81–86.

Barry, B., & Shapiro, D. L. (2000). When will grievants choose voice?: A test of situational, motivational, and attributional explanations. *International Journal of Conflict Management, 11*(2), 106–134.

Brett, J. M. (1986). Commentary on procedural justice papers. In R. Lewicki, M. Bazerman, & B. Sheppard (Eds.), *Research on negotiation in organizations* (Vol.1, pp. 81–90). Greenwich, CT: JAI Press.

Brett, J. M. (2001). *Negotiating globally: How to negotiate deals, resolve disputes, and make decisions across cultural boundaries.* San Francisco: Jossey-Bass.

Brockner, J., Ackerman, G., Greenberg, J., Gelfand, M. J., Francesco, A. M., Chen, Z. X., Leung, K., Bierbrauer, G., Gómez, C., Kirkman, B. L., Shapiro, D. L. (2001). Culture and procedural justice: The moderating influence of power distance on reactions to voice. *Journal of Experimental Social Psychology, 37*, 300–315.

Brockner, J., DeWitt, R. L., Grover, S., & Reed, T. (1990). When it is especially important to explain why: Factors affecting the relationship between managers' explanations of a layoff and survivors' reactions to the layoff. *Journal of Experimental Social Psychology, 26*, 389–407.

Colquitt, J. A., Conlon, D. E., Wesson, M., Porter, C., & Ng, K. (2001). Justice at the millennium: A meta-analytic review of 25 years of organizational justice research. *Journal of Applied Psychology, 86*, 425–445.

Colquitt, J. A., & Greenberg, J. (2003). Organizational justice: A fair assessment of the state of the literature. In J. Greenberg (Ed.), *Organizational behavior: The state of the science* (2nd ed., pp. 165–210). Mahwah, NJ: Lawrence Erlbaum Associates.

Cropanzano, R., & Greenberg, J. (1997). Progress in organizational justice: Tunneling through the maze. In C. L. Cooper & I. T. Roberson (Eds.), *International review of industrial and organizational psychology* (Vol. 12, pp. 317–372). Chichester, England: Wiley.

Felsteiner, W. L. F., Abel, R. L., & Sarat, A. (1980–1981). The emergence and transformation of disputes: Naming, blaming, and claiming. *Law and Society Review, 15*, 631–654.

Festinger, L. (1954). A theory of social comparison processes. *Human Relations, 7*, 117–140.

Folger, R. (1977). Distributive and procedural justice: Combined impact of "voice" and improvement on experienced inequity. *Journal of Personality and Social Psychology, 35*, 108–119.

Folger, R., & Greenberg, J. (1985). Procedural justice: An interpretive analysis of personnel systems. In K. Rowland & G. Rerris (Eds.), *Research in personnel and human resources management* (Vol. 3, pp. 141–183). Greenwich, CT: JAI.

Folger, R., Rosenfield, D., Grove, J., & Corkran, L. (1979). Effects of "voice" and peer opinions on responses to inequity. *Journal of Personality and Social Psychology, 37*, 2253–2261.

Greenberg, J. (1990). Looking versus being fair: Managing impreesions of organizational justice. In B. M. Staw & L. L. Cummings (eds.), *Research in organizational behavior* (Vol. 12, pp. 111–157). Greenwich, CT: JAI Press.

Greenberg, J. (1993a). The intellectual adolescence of organizational justice: You've come a long way, maybe. *Social Justice Research, 5*, 135–148.

Greenberg, J. (1993b). The social side of fairness: Interpersonal and informational classes of organizational justice. In R. Cropanzano (Ed.), *Justice in the workplace: Approaching fairness in human resource management* (pp. 79–103). Hillsdale, NJ: Lawrence Erlbaum Associates.

Greenberg, J. (1994). Using socially fair treatment to promote acceptance of a work site smoking ban. *Journal of Applied Psychology, 79*, 288–297.

Greenberg, J. (2000). Promote procedural justice to enhance acceptance of work outcomes. In E.A. Locke (Ed.), *A handbook of principles of organizational behavior* (pp. 181–195). Oxford, England: Blackwell.

Greenberg, J., & Folger, R. (1983). Procedural justice, participation, and the fair process effect in groups and organizations. In P. B. Paulus (Ed.), *Basic group processes* (pp. 235–256). New York: Springer-Verlag.

Hofstede, G. (1980). *Culture's consequences: International differences in work-related values*. Beverly Hills, CA: Sage.

Houlden, P., LaTour, S., Walker, L., & Thibaut, J. (1978). Preference for modes of dispute resolution as a function of process and decision control. *Journal of Experimental Social Psychology, 14*, 13–30.

Lind, E. A. (2001). Fairness heuristic theory: Justice judgments as pivotal cognitions in organizational relations. In J. Greenberg & R. Cropanzano (eds.), *Advances in organizational behavior* (pp. 56–88). Stanford, CA: Stanford University Press.

Lind, E. A., Greenberg, J., Scott, K. S., & Welchans, T. D. (2000). The winding road from employees to complainant: Situational and psychological determinants of wrongful termination lawsuits. *Administrative Science Quarterly, 45*, 557–590.

Lind, E. A., Huo, Y. J., & Tyler, T. R. (1994). And justice for all: Ethnicity, gender, and preferences for dispute resolution procedures. *Law and Human Behavior, 18*(3): 269–290.

Lind, E. A., Kanfer, R., & Earley, C. (1990). Voice, control, and procedural justice: Instrumental and noninstrumental concerns in fairness judgments. *Journal of Personality and Social Psychology, 59*, 952–959.

Lind, E. A., Kulik, C., Ambrose, M., & Park, M. (1993). Individual and corporate dispute resolution: Using procedural fairness as a decision heuristic. *Administrative Science Quarterly, 38*, 224–251.

Lind, E. A., & Tyler, T. R. (1988). *The social psychology of procedural justice*. New York: Plenum.

Lind, E. A., & van den Bos, K. (2002). When fairness works: Toward a general theory of uncertainty management. *Research in Organizational Behavior, 24*, 181–223.

Morris, M., & Gelfand, M. J. (2004). Cultural differences in cognitive dynamics: Expanding the cognitive tradition in negotiation. In M. J. Gelfand & J. M. Brett (Eds.), *Handbook of negotiation and culture*. Palo Alto, CA: Stanford University Press.

Morris, M. W., & Leung, K. (2000). Justice for all? Progress in research on cultural variation in the psychology of distributive and procedural justice. *Applied Psychology: An International Review, 49*(1), 100–132.

Neale, M. A., & Bazerman, M. H. (1985). The effects of framing and negotiator overconfidence o bargainer behavior. *Academy of Management Journal, 28*, 34–49.

Peterson, R. S. (1999). Can you have too much of a good thing?: The limits of voice for improving satisfaction with leaders. *Personality and Social Psychology Bulletin, 25*, 313–324.

Scandura, T., Von Glinow, M. A., & Lowe, K. (1998). Effects of leader behavior on job satisfaction and leadership effectiveness in the U.S. and the Middle East. In R. Mobley (Ed.), *Advances in global leadership* (pp. 72–95). Greenwich, CT: JAI Press.

Schneider, S. C., & Barsoux, J. L. (1997). *Managing across cultures*. London: Prentice Hall.

Schwartz, S. (1994). Beyond individualism/collectivism: New cultural dimensions of values. In H. C. Triandis, U. Kim, & G. Yoon (Eds.), *Individualism and collectivism* (pp. 85–117). London: Sage.

Shapiro, D. L. (1993). Reconciling theoretical differences among procedural justice researchers by re-evaluating what it means to have one's views "considered": Implications for third-party managers. In R. Cropanzano (Ed.), *Justice in the workplace: Approaching fairness in human resource management* (pp. 51–78). Hillsdale, NJ: Lawrence Erlbaum Associates.

Shapiro, D. L. (2001). The death of justice theory is likely if theorists neglect the "wheels" already invented and the voices of the injustice victims. *Journal of Vocational Behavior, 58*, 235–242.

Shapiro, D. L., & Brett, J. M. (1993). Comparing three processes underlying judgments of procedural justice: A field study of mediation and arbitration. *Journal of Personality and Social Psychology, 65*, 1167–1177.

Shapiro, D. L., Buttner, H. B., & Barry, B. (1994). Explanations: What factors enhance their perceived adequacy? *Organizational Behavior and Human Decision Processes, 58*, 346–368.

Shapiro, D. L., & Kolb, D. M. (1994). Reducing the "litigious mentality" by increasing employees' desire to communicate grievances. In S. Sitkin & R. J. Bies (Eds.), *The legalistic organization* (pp. 304–326). Newbury Park, CA: Sage.

Sugawara, I., & Huo, Y. J. (1994). Disputes in Japan: A cross-cultural test of the procedural justice model. *Social Justice Research, 7*(2), 129–144.

Thibaut, J., & Walker, L. (1975). *Procedural justice: A psychological analysis*. Hillsdale, NJ: Lawrence Erlbaum Associates.

Tinsley, C. H., Brett, J. M., Shapiro, D. L., & Okumura, T. (2003). *When do cultural values explain cross-cultural phenomena? An introduction and test of cultural complexity theory*. Evanston, IL: DRRC Northwestern University Working Paper 299.

Tyler, T. R. (1987). Conditions leading to value-expressive effects in judgments of procedural justice: A test of four models. *Journal of Personality and Social Psychology, 52*, 333–344.

Tyler, T. R., & Blader, S. L. (2000). *Cooperation in groups*. Philadelphia, PA: Psychology Press.

Tyler, T. R., Degoey, P., & Smith, H. (1996). Understanding why the justice of group procedures matters: A test of the psychological dynamics of the group-value model. *Journal of Personality and Social Psychology, 70*, 913–930.

Tyler, T. R., & Lind, E. A. (1992). A relational model of authority in groups. In M. Zanna (Ed.), *Advances in experimental social psychology* (Vol. 25, pp. 115–191). San Diego, CA: Academic.

Tyler, T. R., Rasinski, K. A., & Spodick, N. (1985). Influence of voice on satisfaction with leaders: Exploring the meaning of process control. *Journal of Personality and Social Psychology, 48*, 72–81.

Von Glinow, M. A., Shapiro, D. L., & Brett, J. M. (2004). Can we *talk*, and should we?: Managing emotional conflict in multicultural teams. *Academy of Management Review, 29*, 578–592.

6

*Are the Goals of Organizational
Justice Self-Interested?*

Jennifer Z. Gillespie
Bowling Green State University

Jerald Greenberg
The Ohio State University

Theorists are divided over the question of whether or not the goals of justice are self-interested. Drawing from the research investigating self-interest, we argue that the self-interest debate is more precisely represented by the question of whether the ultimate goals of organizational justice are self-directed or other-directed. To answer this question, we propose a hierarchy of the goals underlying justice. Based on our proposed hierarchy—and, more specifically, our proposed self-directed ultimate goal of belonging—we argue that the pursuit of justice is self-interested. We further argue that this self-interested perspective does not necessitate personal advantage. That is, although individuals are motivated to pursue fairness because it ultimately serves the self-directed goal of belonging, the consequences of this goal pursuit can be mutually beneficial insofar as it simultaneously serves both one's own interests and the interests of others.

Why do people care about justice? As this is one of the so-called "fundamental questions of justice" (Cropanzano, Byrne, Bobocel, & Rupp, 2001a; Van den Bos & Lind, 2002), it is not surprising that theorists have considered several answers. Three perspectives, in particular, have received the most attention.

- The *group-value approach* (also known as the *relational approach*) suggests that workers care about justice because it enhances an individual's feelings of self-worth and acceptance by others (Lind & Tyler, 1988; Tyler & Lind, 1992).
- The *instrumental approach* suggests that people care about justice because it provides control over outcomes, which can serve to maximize the favorability of outcomes received (Greenberg & Folger, 1983; Tyler, 1987).
- The *moral virtues approach* suggests that people care about justice because it provides basic respect for human dignity and worth (Folger, 1998; Folger, Cropanzano, & Goldman, this volume; Turillo, Folger, Lavelle, Umphress, & Gee, 2002).

Not surprisingly, as one might expect when scientists pose different answers to the same question, spirited discussions result. For example, Greenberg (2001) recently asked whether these three orientations to fairness are merely different forms of self-interest. That is, regardless of whether one behaves in a fair manner because it meets the goal of self-worth, control, or a basic respect for humanity, an individual ulti-

mately values fairness because it serve his or her own interests. Turillo et al. (2002) countered that this approach is misleading insofar as it overlooks people's unique concerns about moral virtues. Adding further to this cacophony, Cropanzano, Byrne, Bobocel, and Rupp (2001a, 2001b) suggested that each of the three models offers a unique perspective that should be incorporated into a multiple needs framework.

We assert that the debate over whether the goals of organizational justice are self-interested best may be conceived as three distinct yet interrelated questions. First, what, precisely, is self-interest? Indeed, as noted by Cropanzano et al. (2001a), there is disagreement in the literature about the essential meaning of self-interest. Second, how many goals of justice are there—only one (e.g., promoting moral virtue) or more than one (e.g., the multiple needs framework)? Currently, there is a lack of consensus about not only what the goals of justice are, but also how they may be interrelated. Third, are the highest level goals of justice self-directed or other-directed? This last question is critical, as its answer will indicate whether the goals of justice are ultimately self-interested or altruistic.

The present chapter is organized around these three issues. First, we demonstrate the benefits to the literature of adopting a scientific (rather than a lay) conceptualization of self-interest. Second, using this scientific conceptualization, we review organizational justice research relevant to the question of whether the goals of justice are self-interested. Third, we use elements of existing research to develop a hierarchy of the goals underlying justice, and in doing so arrive at the conclusion that the goals of justice *are*, in fact, self-interested.

The implications of the self-interest debate are more far-reaching than immediately might be apparent. Although some may be tempted to dismiss this debate on the grounds that it is more about semantics than core issues, we hope to demonstrate otherwise. Specifically, we will show that the task of explicitly identifying the goals of justice and how they relate to one another is a first step toward reconciling various perspectives about fairness motives. We do this by organizing the fruits of the justice literature into a goal hierarchy—an approach that we believe offers an especially parsimonious yet more intricate understanding of fairness. Before doing this, however, we begin by taking a look at the various ways in which the concept of self-interest has been examined.

CONCEPTUALIZING SELF-INTEREST AND ALTRUISM

Scientists use the terms *altruism* and *self-interest* differently than lay people. Even among scientists, there has been considerable disagreement about the meanings of these concepts (e.g., Perloff, 1987). To build

a basis for the analysis that follows, we begin by offering several key conceptual distinctions.

Lay Versus Scientific Definitions

Because they are so different, it is useful to distinguish between the conceptualizations of altruism and self-interest used by social scientists and lay persons. An authoritative source, the *American Heritage Dictionary* (Kleinedler, 2000), defines *self-interest* as, "selfish or excessive regard for one's personal advantage or interest" (p. 1580). Implicit in this definition is the idea that self-interest involves personal (often material) gain at the expense of another. This is consistent with many people's everyday use of the word, where "self-interested" is synonymous with "self-absorbed," and is used to describe someone who is unconcerned about the needs of others. The opposite of self-interest is *altruism*, defined by the same source as "unselfish concern for the welfare of others; selflessness" (p. 54). This definition connotes images of sacrifice, where one seeks to benefit others at the expense of oneself. In fact, the word altruism is synonymous with self-sacrifice, a word associated with especially philanthropic acts and/or particularly virtuous people.

By distinguishing between *evolutionary* and *psychological* approaches to self-interest and altruism, scientists define these constructs more precisely. From an evolutionary perspective, the key distinction between self-interested and altruistic behavior centers on the impact of a behavior instead of the thoughts or feelings, if any, that triggers that behavior. Thus, a behavior is said to be self-interested if it results in a gain to oneself with a loss to another, and altruistic if it involves a loss to oneself with a gain to another. The former is called *evolutionary egoism* and the latter *evolutionary altruism*. The question of whether and how altruism can evolve has received an enormous amount of attention from evolutionary biologists, as it represents the very opposite of Darwin's principle of the "survival of the fittest" (e.g., Sober & Wilson, 1998).

More relevant to the present discussion is the psychological perspective. According to this view, the distinction between self-interest and altruism concerns the motives underlying a particular behavior rather than its effects (Sober & Wilson, 1998, 2000a). From a psychological perspective, a behavior is said to be self-interested when an actor ultimately is motivated to serve himself or herself, and altruistic when an actor ultimately is motivated to serve the other, regardless of the effects of his or her actions (Sober & Wilson, 1998, 2000a). The former is called *psychological egoism*; the latter, *psychological altruism*. So, when presented with individuals who are helping others (perhaps by volunteering their time or donating their money), proponents of the psychological egoism perspective may suggest, for example, that they are doing so because it

serves the self-directed ultimate goal of feeling good. This is in keeping with the sentiments of French moralist Jean de La Bruyère (1688/1963), who said, "The most delicious pleasure is to cause that of [pleasure in] other people" (p. 90). Proponents of psychological altruism, on the other hand, may suggest that people are motivated to help others because it serves the ultimate other-directed goal of increasing others' welfare. This is in line with the writings of French social theorist Auguste Comte, who coined the term *altruism*. More specifically, he said, "To live for others" is the "definitive formula of human morality" (1973, p. 313).

Self-Interest and Altruism
in the Organizational Justice Literature

How do organizational justice researchers conceptualize self-interest and altruism? To answer this question, we compiled a list of definitions used by authors of several recent publications on organizational justice (see Table 6.1). As illustrated by the quotes in Table 6.1, self-interest is used to connote self-centered intentions, personal advantage, or both. In some cases, it is presented as the antithesis of fairness. For example, Tyler, Boeckmann, Smith, and Huo (1997), described individuals as being selfish *or* fair. In similar fashion, Turillo et al. (2002) stated that self-interest is capable of "threatening" fairness (p. 841). Thus, although the use of the term *self-interest* in the organizational justice literature is characterized by disagreement (a point made by Cropanzano et al., 2001a, 2001b), a common theme may be identified—namely, that self-interest involves unfair personal advantage and selfishness.

From a psychological perspective, this association between self-interest and selfishness is not only unnecessarily restrictive; it's inaccurate. This point has been made not only by ethnobiologists and philosophers (e.g., Sober & Wilson, 1998), but also by psychologists. Case in point: Robert Perloff, in his 1985 Presidential Address to the American Psychological Association, identified "several positive and beneficial consequences associated with self-interest" and, proposed that "personal responsibility, in the service of self-interest, is an effective tool for enhancing personal well-being, and hence, for contributing to the public good" (Perloff, 1987, p. 3). In a commentary in which he supported and clarified Perloff's message, Locke (1988) touted the "virtue of selfishness," going so far as to say that "self-interest is profoundly moral" (p. 481). Moreover, Locke stated that egoism makes people "more rather than less benevolent towards others" (p. 481). This set of comments reflects a scientific conceptualization of self-interest—that is, an understanding that being motivated to serve oneself does *not* necessitate (and even may preclude) selfishness and personal advantage.

TABLE 6.1

Overview of References to Self-Interest and Altruism in the Organizational Justice Literature

Source	Quotation
Folger and Cropanzano (1998)	• Acting with blatant disregard for others' feelings, therefore, implies so much unfettered self-interest as to interfere with due consideration of opposing interests and others' well-being (p. 30, emphasis added).
	• We think Greenberg's (1994) study reveals an impressively subtle sophistication about the nature of moral obligation and the nature of concern self-interest versus an interest in others' well-being. Although we perhaps stretch the interpretation, we argue that separate manipulations of explanatory content and sensitivity can help illustrate, at least by analogy, a continuum of moral obligation anchored by self-interest on one end and concern for victim suffering on the other. The least adequate (and also insensitive) forms of accounts fail to indicate a sense of moral obligation toward others, as if only one's own self-interest matters (p. 69, emphasis added).
	• Themes we have emphasized throughout these first two chapters: that agent's actions should imply intentions consistent with sufficient regard for general moral obligation transcending self-interest by giving some weight to the interests of others (p. 72, emphasis added).
Cropanzano, Rupp, Mohler, and Schminke (2001)	• Instrumental models of justice posit that individuals care about fairness as a means to an end. Often, justice researchers view the "instrumental" end as being a personal gain. As we have remarked elsewhere (e.g., Cropanzano, Byrne, Bobocel, & Rupp, 2001a, 2001b), there is some disagreement as to the meaning of "self-interest." … We define self-interest narrowly, referring to generally concrete economic and quasi-economic gains and losses. From this point of view, one is self-interested if he or she is motivated by a pay raise or promotion, but not self-interested if motivated by social inclusion (p. 11, emphasis added).

Source	Quotation
Tyler, Boeckmann, Smith, and Huo (1997)	• The question is, how will people respond to [scarcity and conflict with others]? Will they become self-centered and selfish, or will they continue to care about others and about principles of fairness and justice? (p. 223, emphasis added).
Turillo, Folger, Lavelle, Umphress, & Gee (2002)	• Commitment to an ethical standard can entail self-sacrifice, which is the opposite of self-interest (p. 841, emphasis added).
	• Finally, note that the very notion of fairness itself involves, by definition, an ethical standard conceived independently of self-interest so that it can act as a constraint against an otherwise unfettered self-interest capable of threatening fairness (p. 841, emphasis added).

This association between self-interest and selfishness and/or personal advantage also is present in social justice examinations of the effects of the "norm of self-interest" (e.g., Holmes, Miller, & Lerner, 2002; Miller, 1999; Miller & Ratner, 1996, 1998; Ratner & Miller, 2001). This research suggests that "the theory of self-interest has spawned a norm of self-interest, the consequence of which is that people often act and speak in accordance with their perceived self-interest solely because they believe to do otherwise is to violate a powerful descriptive and prescriptive expectation" (Miller, 1999, p. 1053). There are two components to this argument. The first is that people assume that others are more self-interested than they really are. In support of this idea, Miller and Ratner (1998, Study 4) found that participants overestimated the extent to which being a smoker or a nonsmoker affected people's attitudes toward cigarette taxes and smoking restrictions. The second component of the argument is that this faulty assumption prompts people to act more self-interested than they really are and, conversely, to not act in ways that do not appear self-interested. Consistent with this, Ratner and Miller (2001, Study 1) found that men predicted that they would be evaluated negatively if they were to take action in favor of abortion coverage (a cause for which they have no explicit stake) and thus reported hesitancy to take such actions.

This research intentionally takes the perspective of the layperson, suggesting that to act in accordance with the self-interest norm, "people's actions must conform to, at least crudely, the strictures of neoclassical economic theory," meaning that their interests must appear to be "material ones (e.g., economic profit)" (Miller, 1999, p. 1052). In fact, some authors (e.g., Miller & Ratner, 1998; Ratner & Miller, 2001) use the term *self-interest* interchangeably with *vested interest*, which, according to the *American Heritage Dictionary*, means "a special interest in protecting or promoting that which is to one's own personal advantage" (Kleinedler, 2000, p. 1914). Further, self-interest is operationalized as being "personally affected" (Miller & Ratner, 1998, p. 60). For example, smokers are considered to be "self-interested"—or stated differently, as having a "vested interest" in cigarette taxes and smoking restrictions (Miller & Ratner, 1998, p. 57).

This lay conceptualization of self-interest is generally appropriate, as the purpose of the literature is to determine the effects of the "norm of self-interest" on various outcomes (e.g., propensity to take social action; Miller & Ratner, 1996). The problem arises when this lay conceptualization and operationalization of the construct is used to make claims about "the *actual power* of self-interest" (Miller & Ratner, 1998, p. 59, italics added). We believe that studies using a lay conceptualization and operationalization of self-interest should limit their conclusions to the effects of the *norm* of self-interest (which involves personal advantage)

and refrain from drawing conclusions about the effect of self-interest itself (which does not involve personal advantage).

Summary

The literatures on social and organizational justice have adopted a lay conceptualization of self-interest as opposed to a scientific one. As such, in referring to "self-interest," most organizational justice scholars are referring to "selfishness" and "personal advantage" instead of the ultimate desire to serve one's own interests (which may or may not involve a personal advantage). This distinction is particularly important when addressing the question of whether the goals of justice are self-interested insofar as it necessities a precise understanding of self-interest itself. Thus, in the interest of conceptual and methodological rigor, we recommend that the organizational justice literature adopt the scientific constructs of *psychological egoism* and *psychological altruism*. In so doing comes acknowledgment that self-interest is not synonymous with selfishness and does not necessitate personal advantage.

This more precise conceptualization will clarify the debate about whether the goals of organizational justice are self-interested. Specifically, it makes evident that determining whether the goals of justice are psychologically self-interested involves examining the *intentions* (or perceived intentions) of behavior instead of the *effects* of the behavior and/or some unspecified combination of the two. Moreover, as we intend to demonstrate, by clarifying the role of goals in justice, it is possible to have a more precise conversation about various theories of organizational justice.

THE ROLE OF SELF-INTEREST IN JUSTICE

At this point, a focused review of the literature on psychological egoism and altruism is in order. By presenting this literature, we provide more detail about the scientific conceptualization of self-interest as it relates to the question of whether self-interest is the underlying goal of justice. More specifically, we demonstrate that the self-interest debate is represented more precisely by the egoism and altruism hypotheses (e.g., Batson, 1991; Sober & Wilson, 1998, 2000a, 2000b).

Key Terms

With this in mind, we define some key terms. First, both the egoism and altruism hypotheses involve *goals*, which are "internal representations of desired states, where states are broadly construed as outcomes, events, or processes" (Austin & Vancouver, 1996, p. 338).

Second, both hypotheses involve *ultimate* and *instrumental* goals. The distinction between ultimate and instrumental is based on one simple premise: "Some things we want for their own sakes; other things we want only because we think they are means to some more ultimate end" (Sober & Wilson, 1998, p. 200). Thus, an *ultimate goal* is one that someone holds for reasons that go beyond its ability to contribute instrumentally to the attainment of something else. Put differently, an ultimate goal is something we want for its own sake, an end in itself. An *instrumental goal*, in contrast, is a goal that someone seeks because it is the means to an ultimate goal, a means to an end.

Third, the egoism and altruism hypotheses distinguish between *self-directed* and *other-directed* goals. Self-directed goals are intended for oneself, whereas other-directed goals are intended for someone else. So, for example, if Adam wants the apple, his goal is self-directed. But if Adam wants Eve to have the apple, then his goal is other-directed (Sober & Wilson, 1998).

The Egoism and Altruism Hypotheses

Now that we have laid the necessary groundwork, we can apply the egoism and altruism hypotheses to the study of justice. Essentially, each represents a different view as to whether individuals ever can be psychologically altruistic— that is, whether individuals are motivated ultimately to serve others. The fundamental point on which these hypotheses vary is whether they posit that individuals' ultimate goals are self-directed or other-directed.

The egoism hypothesis maintains that the only ultimate goals that individuals have are self-directed. People desire their own well-being, and nothing else, as an end in itself (Sober & Wilson, 1998). This represents what is more commonly known as self-interest. In contrast, the altruism hypothesis maintains that people sometimes care about the welfare of others as an end in itself. That is, it suggests that people sometimes have other-directed ultimate goals (Sober & Wilson, 1998).

By adopting justice-oriented versions of these hypotheses, we contend that researchers can engage in a clearer and more focused debate about whether the goals of justice are self-interested. Currently, this debate is too imprecise. It consists simply of those who *do not* believe that all the goals of justice are self-interested (e.g., Cropanzano et al., 2001b, p. 262; Folger et al., this volume; Turillo et al., 2002) and those who *do* believe that the goals of justice are self-interested (Greenberg, 2001). However, justice-specific versions of the altruism and egoism hypotheses make each of these positions more precise. Specifically, a justice version of the altruism hypothesis suggests that people sometimes have other-directed fairness as an ultimate goal, whereas a justice version of

the egoism hypothesis suggests that people do not have other-directed fairness as an ultimate goal. This, of course, begs the question of what people *do* hold as ultimate goals, a point to which we return later.

Although the altruism and egoism hypotheses clarify the sides in the self-interest debate, they do not provide us with an immediate resolution. As pointed out by Sober and Wilson (1998), these theories suffer from the same shortcoming—a lack of specificity regarding the content of individuals' instrumental and ultimate goals. This shortcoming is relevant for justice versions of these hypotheses insofar as they collectively reveal the absence of a unified perspective regarding *what* the goals of organizational justice are and *how* they are related to one another.

Researchers have proposed various potential goals of justice—such as self-worth (e.g., Lind & Tyler, 1988), control (e.g., Tyler, 1987), and respect for humanity (e.g., Folger, 1998)—but these usually are presented as "alternative" approaches (e.g., Cropanzano, Rupp, Mohler, & Schminke, 2001; Tyler, Degoey, & Smith, 1996; Turillo et al., 2002) rather than as a collection of interrelated goals. That is, organizational justice researchers present them as competing approaches that have generated debate (Colquitt & Greenberg, 2002), rather than as complementary approaches that collectively can serve to explain more fully the underlying phenomenon. Recently, Cropanzano and his colleagues (2001a) presented these goals in a unified "multiple needs framework," which is based on the proposition that all three explanations share a common form: "Justice matters to the extent that it serves some important psychological need" (p. 175). However, even with this useful addition to the literature, it still is unclear *how* the goals of justice relate to one another. The question remains: Is each of these goals an ultimate goal itself or does each serve some other ultimate goal? Alternatively, is one of these an ultimate goal that is served by the other two? Thus, the proposed specification of the self-interest debate makes it evident that to determine whether the ultimate goals of fairness are self-directed or other-directed, we first must develop a unified perspective as to what the goals of justice are and how they are interrelated.

RELEVANT RESEARCH

We have argued that the self-interest debate is best represented by justice versions of the altruism hypothesis, which suggests that the ultimate goals of fairness are other-directed, and the egoism hypothesis, which suggests that the ultimate goals of fairness are self-directed. Using these hypotheses as a guide, we offer an overview of organizational justice research that is relevant to the question of whether the goals of justice are self-interested.

The Instrumental Orientation

The instrumental orientation suggests that people care about justice because it provides influence, which can serve to maximize resource gains in interactions with others (Tyler, 1987). The desire to acquire resources is certainly understandable. Resources make it possible to attain the goods and services they desire. However, once termed "the self-interest model" (e.g., Austin, 1979), the instrumental orientation often is associated with a lay conceptualization of self-interest—that is, with selfishness and personal advantage. This association between the instrumental orientation and personal advantage may have originated with early work on dispute resolution by Thibaut and Walker (1975), who suggested that disputants preferred having voice in adversary procedures because it allowed each disputant "to bolster his case and dispute his opponent's contentions" (p. 109). This association between the instrumental orientation and personal advantage also is evident in more recent work. Tyler et al. (1996), for example, stated that the instrumental orientation "assumes that people are motivated to maximize their self-interest when they interact with each other" and that, for this reason, they "only reluctantly submit themselves to external control" (p. 913; see also, Tyler, 1994). This general description of the instrumental orientation conjures up images of winning a dispute resolution and of "getting them before they get me."

However, the instrumental orientation does not necessitate such a "cutthroat," zero-sum mentality. Early social exchange models of justice (e.g., Walster, Walster, & Berscheid, 1978) suggest merely that people work with others to create collective group-enforced rules about fair reward allocation (Tyler, 1994). That is, they follow collective rules about what constitutes fair allocations to others and, in turn, what others expect to receive as fair allocations (Leventhal, 1976). In addition, Cropanzano and Ambrose (2001) point out that people sometimes care about favorable resource outcomes because they represent something positive about one's own social or professional status and worth. Thus, although rewards—including nonmonetary outcomes, such as office size (Greenberg, 1988) and job titles (Greenberg & Ornstein, 1983)—may reflect "winning," they also serve as tangible representations of one's group status. In other words, people desire a higher salary and nonmonetary trappings of success, not solely because they want to have more of these things than their coworkers, but also because having them signifies in symbolic fashion one's importance to the company.

Thus, the instrumental orientation is not clearly aligned with the egoism or the altruism hypothesis in that it does not specify *why* individuals strive to maximize rewards. Stated differently, it does not specify the content of the ultimate goal of justice and whether this goal is self-directed or other-directed.

The Group-Value/Relational Orientation

The *group-value/relational* approach suggests that workers care about justice because being treated fairly indicates that one is valued by others, thereby enhancing feelings of self-worth (Lind & Tyler, 1988; Tyler & Lind, 1992). According to Tyler (1994), the basic assumption of the relational model is that people are predisposed to belong to social groups and that they are very attentive to signs and symbols that communicate information about their position within groups. Moreover, Tyler (1994) argued that a key reason for seeking out group membership is that groups provide a source of self-validation. In short, this approach suggests that people derive a sense of self and self-worth from the groups to which they belong, and consequently, they are motivated to act in ways that create and maintain successful group relations (Tyler & Blader, 2002).

The group-value/relational orientation proposes a link between cooperative (helping) behavior and the self-concept (Tyler & Blader, 2002). At first glance, this seems consistent with the altruism hypothesis. In fact, in their recent review, Tyler and Blader (2002) used research on helping and altruism to support this claim, pointing out that helping has been shown to improve the helper's mood and self-evaluations (e.g., Harris, 1977; Williamson & Clark, 1989). However, Turillo et al. (2002) characterized the group-value/relational orientation as one of "self-interest" (p. 841), and we agree. Specifically, insofar as this approach suggests that fair relationships are means to feeling good about one's self and one's relationships with others, we argue that ultimately it benefits the self.

Thus, some view the group-value/relational orientation as being consistent with the altruism hypothesis (e.g., Tyler & Blader, 2002), and others view it as consistent with the egoism hypothesis (e.g., Turillo et al., 2002). These perspectives seem to differ as to whether people engage in cooperative behavior for its own sake or because it serves a higher order goal (e.g., approval). In this sense, the group-value/relational orientation is not clearly aligned with either hypothesis. As was true of the instrumental orientation, it is not clear what the content of the ultimate goal of justice is and whether this goal is self-directed or other-directed.

The Moral Virtues Orientation

The moral virtues orientation suggests that people care about justice because it serves a basic respect for human dignity and worth. This approach, although acknowledged by philosophers for many years (Buchanan & Mathieu, 1986), was incorporated into the organizational

justice literature relatively recently (e.g., Folger, 1998). It has been described in a variety of different ways (see Folger et al., this volume). Cropanzano et al. (2001a) described the moral virtues orientation as one that suggests that justice is partly about morality. That is, "individuals worry about fairness because they want to be virtuous actors in a just world" (Cropanzano et al., 2001a, p. 174). Ambrose (2002) described the moral virtues approach as one that suggests that "individuals care about justice because we have a basic respect for human worth" (p. 806). And, in the first empirical examination of the moral virtues orientation, Turillo and his colleagues (2002) said that it "emphasizes commitment to ethical standards" (p. 841). More specifically, Turillo et al. (2002) proposed that individuals have endogenous "deontic emotions" (from the Greek root *deon*, for obligation or duty), and stated, "We treat the deontic goal of punishing moral transgressions as an ultimate goal" (p. 840). The authors then went on to say that these deontic emotions are elicited simply by perceiving a transgression, and that "the intrinsic, endogenous nature of such reactions is expressed in a common colloquial expression regarding moralistic reactions: 'virtue is its own reward'" (Turillo et al., 2002, p. 840). Thus, in short, the moral virtues approach suggests that we care about justice because doing so is virtuous.

No matter how one describes the moral virtues orientation, one thing is clear: This perspective is "the only one contending that human motives can rise above self-interest" (Turillo et al., 2002, p. 841). In this way, the moral virtues orientation is clearly aligned with the altruism hypothesis. To test the contention that "virtue is its own reward," Turillo et al. (2002) engaged in what they call "reductio" logic, by attempting to strip away "any possible self-interest" by constructing a situation in which third parties enforce (or fail to enforce) fairness with no predictable, tangible effects on the way the victim or the perpetrator subsequently might treat them. They interpreted their results to mean that decision makers will make self-sacrificing allocations even in the absence of any benefits for doing so.

Proponents of the moral virtues orientation (e.g., Folger, 1998; Turillo et al., 2002) align themselves with the altruism hypothesis. That is, they suggest that people sometimes have other-directed fairness as an ultimate goal. Stated differently, they suggest that the virtue of fairness is its own reward. We argue that its proponents have not yet specified (and provided evidence for) an other-directed ultimate goal. Because this point is central to our argument, we now analyze this approach more closely.

Critical Analysis.   Most essential to us is the Turillo et al. (2002) claim that their results "cast doubt on the reasoning that self-interest

(either material or social) is the sole, or even prime, motivator for people to attend to the issue of fairness" (p. 861). The authors noted an anticipated counterargument to this conclusion: Colquitt and Greenberg's (2002) point that virtuous deeds might be performed to protect one's one self-image or to avoid feelings of guilt. Their response to this argument was to attack egoism itself, stating that its use as a "universal explanation for all behavior becomes a definitional tautology incapable of disproof" (Turillo et al., 2002, p. 862).[1] In an effort to further discount the egoism hypothesis, Turillo and his colleagues (2002) went on to say, "A self-interested desire is simply any desire of the person who performs an action" (p. 862; citing Holley, 1999, p. 42).

This statement is untrue; a self-interested desire is *not* simply any desire of the person who performs an action. To clarify what Turillo et al. (2002) meant by "self-interest," note the following statements in their article:

- Citing Holley (1999, p. 29): "According to [the self-interest] view, alternative motivations for behavior, such as concern for the good of others, *do not exist*" (p. 862, italics added).
- "Put another way, commitment to an ethical standard can entail self-sacrifice, which is the *opposite* of self-interest" (p. 841, italics added).
- "In Batson's (1994) terms, retribution is an end in itself rather than the instrumental means to achieving *some other ultimate goal (e.g., self-interest)*" (p. 840, italics added).

We believe that each of these excerpts reveals an inaccurate portrayal of self-interest (i.e., the egoism hypothesis). First, Turillo et al. (2002) imply that self-interest entails an absence of concern for others, when, in fact, the scientific definition of self-interest does allow for the concern for others—just not as the ultimate goal. Second, they imply that self-interest entails an absence of self-sacrifice, when, in fact, the presence or absence self-sacrifice is only relevant for *evolutionary* perspectives on self-interest and altruism. As the reader may recall, evolutionary altruism requires a loss at the gain of another, whereas psychological altruism does not. Instead, psychological altruism requires that an actor ultimately is motivated to serve the other, regardless of the ultimate effects of his or her actions. So the implication that self-interest requires an absence of self-sacrifice is incorrect for the present, psychological, purposes. Finally, Turillo et al. (2002) implied that "self-interest" is a hypothetical ultimate goal, when, in fact, the scientific definition of

---

[1]For a further insight regarding this point, see Montada's (2003) related discussion of the "traps of reductionism" (p. 540).

self-interest does not involve a goal called "self-interest," but rather, a self-directed ultimate goal of any content. Stated differently, proponents of the egoism hypothesis do not suggest that there is a goal called "self-interest" (as Turillo and his colleagues imply), but rather that individuals' ultimate goals (whatever they be) are self-directed (rather than other-directed).

Thus, on several grounds we reject Turillo and his colleagues' (2002) conclusion that their results "cast doubt on the reasoning that self-interest is the sole, or even prime, motivator for people to attend to the issue of fairness" (p. 861). First, they did not provide an explicit and defensible definition of "self-interest." Moreover, they made claims that suggest they are using a lay (versus scientific) conceptualization of the construct. For example, they suggested that self-interest entails an absence of concern for others as well as an absence of self-sacrifice, both of which are true from a lay perspective but false from a scientific one. This in and of itself casts doubt on the inferences they made about their data with respect to the self-interest debate.

Second, they have *not*, as claimed, stripped away "any possible self-interest" (Turillo et al., 2002, p. 842). Although they did construct a situation in which there were ostensibly no effects on the way the *other person* viewed them or treated them, there still remains the possibility that there were effects on the way the actors viewed themselves as well as the way they viewed fellow humankind. So, for example, it is possible that participants wanted to make reparations because they felt guilty about the way their "fellow humanity" was willing to exploit others. This idea is consistent with the research of Doosje, Branscombe, Spears, and Manstead (1998), whose results suggest that individuals who feel that their group's moral integrity is threatened experience "collective guilt" and are motivated to make reparations.

Finally, it is not clear what "ultimate goal" underlies the moral virtues orientation. There appear to be three possibilities: virtue, justice, and duty. If the proposed ultimate goal is virtue, then we argue that the moral virtues orientation actually might be proposing a self-directed (vs. other-directed) goal. We base this suggestion on the fact that the word *virtue* derives from the Greek concept *arête*, which means, "being the best you can be" or "reaching your highest human potential" (Cawley, Martin, & Johnson, 2000; Hooker, 1996). In this way, the moral virtues orientation is consistent with the long history of humanistic psychologists interested in promoting the full growth and development of the individual (e.g., Maslow's 1968 idea of self-actualization, and Rogers's 1961 notion of full functioning). However, from a humanistic perspective, the state of full development is not so much a goal as it is something that happens to you (once you are able to free yourself from lower level motives; Carver & Scheier, 1996, 2003). Thus, although the

notion of virtue as a point of full growth and development strikes us as more self-directed (and thus psychologically egoistic) than other-directed (and thus psychologically altruistic), it is necessary to determine whether this is a goal at all before that can be assessed.

If the proposed ultimate goal is justice, then we argue that the explanatory power of the construct is lost. Our perspective is consistent with Batson (1994), who stated, "The abstractness of general, universal principles of justice ironically facilities the self-interested revision of one's perceptions so that one no longer sees a situation as violating/threatening a principle of justice" (pp. 53–54; see also Batson & Powell, 2003). Our perspective is inconsistent with Montada (2003), who viewed "justice as an end itself" (p. 538). To provide support for this claim, Montada (2003) cited the work of Lerner (1977, 1980), whom he credited with being the first to outline the essential psychological features of the justice motive. Lerner's justice motive is rooted in the "just world" or "deserving hypothesis," which essentially states that people get what they deserve: "The rule-following 'good guys' overcome the bad 'outlaws'" (Lerner, 1977, p. 1). Lerner argued that, to maintain the delusion of a just world, individuals have a "personal contract" or "commitment to deserving-ness," where "People have wants but they design their lives so that they deserve, are entitled to, what they want or modify their desires to fit what they can deserve" (Lerner, 1977, p. 5). In this way, the justice motive "arises quite naturally out of the individual's commitment to and desire to maintain his [or her] personal contract" (Lerner, 1977, p. 8) and thus can be adapted in whatever way necessary to satisfy this contract. Thus, although we acknowledge that individuals may have a need to believe in a just world (Lerner, 1977, 1980), we do *not* believe that this establishes that "justice is an end in itself" (Montada, 2003). Moreover, we suggest that the former theoretically may "undo" the latter insofar as maintaining one's delusion of a just world sometimes involves rationalizing one's "unjust" behavior toward another (e.g., via victim blame; Alicke, 2000).

Finally, if the proposed ultimate goal is the dutiful ("deontic") goal of punishing moral transgressions, then we suggest that this concept requires further elaboration before it can be properly evaluated. As pointed out by Cropanzano et al. (2001a), no one has proposed an explicit need for morality, and thus doing so would be an ambitious undertaking. Moreover, some argue that psychology is not capable of identifying a correct moral position in part because moral pluralism "is an inevitable byproduct of an open society" (Kendler, 2003, p. 206; see also Jackson, 2003; Kendler, 1999). Finally, it is not clear how an ultimate goal of punishing moral transgressions explains the desire to be treated fairly, which is a critical component of any justice theory.

Summary

By adopting the constructs of psychological egoism and psychological altruism, the organizational justice literature better can specify the debate regarding whether the goals of organizational justice are self-interested. Specifically, we have argued that representing the debate with justice versions of the altruism and egoism hypotheses results in the more focused question of whether the ultimate goals of fairness are self-directed or other-directed.

In our view, traditional approaches to the question of why people care about justice—the instrumental orientation, the group-value/relational orientation, and the moral virtues orientation—do not offer an explicit and theoretically defensible answer to the question of whether the ultimate goals of fairness are self-directed or other-directed. More specifically, the instrumental orientation does not identify an ultimate goal at all; there is disagreement as to what the ultimate goal of the group-value/relational orientation is (and thus whether it is self-directed or other-directed). And although discussions of the moral virtues orientation have resulted in a variety of potential ultimate goals (e.g., virtue, justice, and duty), we do not believe that a clear case has been made for the existence of the other-directed (as opposed to the self-directed) nature of these goals.

JUSTICE GOAL HIERARCHIES

By framing the debate about self-interest as a matter of altruism and egoism, we underscore the need to specify what the goals of justice are and how they relate to one another. In this section, we argue that couching what we know about organizational justice in terms of a goal hierarchy is a useful strategy for accomplishing this. As we demonstrate, organizing the goals underlying justice into a hierarchy necessitates stipulating an ultimate goal. This theoretically based specification will make evident that the ultimate goals of justice are self-directed, meaning that the goals underlying justice are psychologically egoistic (i.e. self-interested).

Our approach is similar to Cropanzano and his colleagues' (2001a) multiple needs framework in that we too are suggesting that justice matters to the extent that it serves some important psychological needs. However, we are operating from a goal hierarchy perspective, according to which we view psychological needs as higher order (ultimate) goals that are met by achieving lower order goals. Thus, our approach differs from that of Cropanzano et al. (2001a) insofar as we are specifying multiple goal levels and, in so doing, the process by which fairness appraisals meet psychological needs. Moreover, we are sug-

gesting that one psychological need is most relevant to the study of justice: *belonging*, which is the need "to form and maintain at least a minimum quantity of lasting, positive, and significant interpersonal relationships" (Baumeister & Leary, 1995, p. 497). This is not to say that we view the other psychological needs identified by Cropanzano et al. (2001a, 2001b)—that is, the needs for esteem, control, and meaning—as completely irrelevant, but rather that we view the act of making fairness appraisals as promoting the satisfaction of the criteria of what has been hailed a "fundamental intrapersonal motive": "the occurrence of affectively pleasant interactions in the context of a temporally stable and enduring framework of affective concern for each other's welfare" (Baumeister & Leary, 1995, p. 497).

To prepare the reader for this discourse, we begin by briefly introducing the notion of goal hierarchies (for more comprehensive treatments, see Austin & Vancouver, 1996; Carver & Scheier, 1998, 2003).

The General Nature of Goal Hierarchies

As stated previously, Austin and Vancouver (1996) conceived of goals as internal representations of desired states, such as outcomes, events, or processes. These internally represented states range from objective biological indicators (e.g., body temperature) to complex cognitive depictions (e.g., career success). Moreover, goals can span from the moment to a lifetime, and from the neurological to the interpersonal (Austin & Vancouver, 1996; Gardner, 1987; Izard, 1993). Vital to present purposes is the idea that individual goals cannot be understood when isolated from other goals and from the cognitive, behavioral, and affective responses involved in pursuing them (Austin & Vancouver, 1996). In other words, goals are understood best when we recognize the process by which they are pursued and their relationships to other goals.

An effective way of conveying how goals are interrelated is by differentiating between goals that are *instrumental* and goals that are *ultimate*. As noted earlier, an instrumental goal is something we seek because it is a means to something else, whereas an ultimate goal is something we want for its own sake. So, for example, consider a man with the ultimate goal of "belonging," which as noted earlier refers to the formation of significant interpersonal relationships of a positive nature (Baumeister & Leary, 1995). He might work toward this ultimate goal through the instrumental goal of "being a good neighbor." Here, the instrumental goal of "being a good neighbor" is better understood in terms of the ultimate goal it serves (belonging), and the ultimate goal of belonging is better understood in terms of the means by which he achieves it (being a good neighbor). A limitation of repre-

senting goal relationships in this fashion is that it does not specify the relationships among the potentially infinite number of instrumental goals that exist. Continuing the previous example, there are many instrumental goals toward which one can work to achieve the ultimate goal of belonging, and merely classifying them as "instrumental" or "ultimate" does not specify how they relate to each other.

A richer representation of the interrelationship among goals is offered by the concept of a *goal hierarchy* (Austin & Vancouver, 1996; Carver & Scheier, 1998, 2003; Miller, Galanter, & Pribram, 1960; Powers, 1973). It is important to note that this notion is considerably different from the popular notion of need hierarchy as proposed by Maslow (1968, 1970). The biggest difference concerns the content of the hierarchy. Maslow's analysis was explicitly an analysis of biological and psychological needs, whereas a goal hierarchy focuses on the structure of action and how goals relate to psychological needs (for more on this distinction, see Carver & Scheier, 1996, 2003). That is, with goal hierarchies, complex acts are represented by a network of specific tasks (Cropanzano, James, & Citera, 1993), and these acts are understood as manifestations of higher order needs. Goal hierarchies are the "dominant conceptualization of the structure of goals" across psychological domains (Austin & Vancouver, 1996). Researchers have identified the goal hierarchies underlying such diverse acts as leadership behavior (Bateman, O'Neill, & Kenworthy-U'Ren, 2002) and consumer purchases (Lawson, 1997).

Generally speaking, a goal hierarchy involves broad goals encompassing narrower ones (see Fig. 6.1). The broadest goals are at the top of the hierarchy. Beneath it lie subgoals, which in turn have their own subgoals, eventually cascading down to the level of muscle tensions (Powers, 1973). The goals that are farther up the hierarchy are referred to as *higher order goals*; the ones farther down the hierarchy are referred to as *lower order goals*. Lower order goals convey the details or specifics of an action and thus indicate *how* an action is performed, whereas higher order goals convey a more general understanding of the action, indicating *why* the action is performed, as well as its impact (Vallacher & Wegner, 1985, 1987). Returning briefly to the distinction between ultimate and instrumental goals, the highest order level of the hierarchy represents ultimate goals whereas the remaining levels represent instrumental goals. Further, a goal hierarchy makes evident the idea that there exist lower order and higher order instrumental goals, with the lower order ones serving the higher order ones (a point to which we return shortly).

To illustrate these processes, we offer the following example, summarized in Fig. 6.1. Consider again the man who has the goal of being a good neighbor. This goal may serve the highest order (i.e., ultimate)

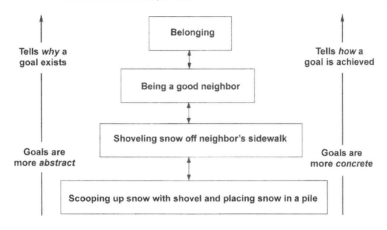

FIG. 6.1.   General example of a goal hierarchy.

goal of belonging and it may be accomplished, for example, by the lower order goal of shoveling snow off his neighbor's sidewalk. And the goal of shoveling his neighbor's sidewalk may be accomplished by the even lower order goals of scooping up the snow with a shovel and then placing the snow in a pile. In this manner, higher order goals inform us as to *why* the man has the goal of being a good neighbor, and lower order goals inform us as to *how* he achieves that goal (Vallacher & Wegner, 1985, 1987).

Drawing on earlier conceptualizations (e.g., Carver & Scheier, 1998; Powers, 1973; Vallacher & Wegner, 1985, 1987), we propose that individuals engage in mental control of action. More specifically, people engage in self-regulation as a process of monitoring what they are doing or want to do—called a *prepotent* (i.e., predominant) goal—and using this goal as a frame of reference for implementing action, make adjustments as necessary to minimize discrepancies between actual and desired states. In what follows, we use the term *discrepancy monitoring* to refer to this general self-regulatory process and the terms *moving up* and *moving down* the hierarchy to refer to the ways that individuals can have a different prepotent goal and thus begin monitoring discrepancies at a different level of the hierarchy. More specifically, moving up the hierarchy refers to the process of attending to an immediately higher order goal and moving down the hierarchy refers to the process of attending to an immediately lower order goal.

Although the prepotent goal, by definition, predominates one's consciousness, this discrepancy monitoring may or may not occur consciously, as attention is not necessary for successful goal pursuit (Bargh, Gollwitzer, Lee-Chai, Barndollar, & Tröetschel, 2001). Generally, indi-

viduals engage in unconscious (i.e., automatic) monitoring until a suffi-ciently large discrepancy triggers effortful and conscious attention (for more on automatic processing, see Bargh & Ferguson, 2000), in which case individuals generally move down the hierarchy so as to concen-trate on the execution of a specific strategy (i.e., the "how"; Vallacher & Wegner, 1987).

The man in our example likely has a variety of life goals and thus it would not be functional to have the goal of being a good neighbor be in-cessantly prepotent. However, he automatically (unconsciously) as-sesses his progress toward the goal of being a good neighbor by periodically comparing his actual state (i.e., his actual relationship with his neighbor) to the desired state (i.e., his desired relationship with his neighbor). If he becomes aware that he is falling short of this goal, per-haps by noting an unfavorable exchange with his neighbor, he will move down the hierarchy and begin to work consciously and actively toward the (now prepotent) lower order goal that serves the higher or-der goal of being a good neighbor (perhaps by retrieving the neighbor's mail while on vacation or by inviting him to dinner). After accomplish-ing one or more of these lower order goals to the point of feeling like he is a good neighbor again, he can move back up the hierarchy and con-tinue to monitor automatically the more abstract (higher order) goal of being a good neighbor.

As stated previously, representing the relationships among goals in a hierarchical fashion does not replace the notion of instrumental versus ultimate goals, but rather it supplements it. Returning to our example, many of the man's goals are instrumental goals (e.g., being a good neighbor, shoveling snow) that serve the ultimate goal of belonging. Thus, simply classifying them as instrumental or ultimate does not rep-resent *how* these goals relate to one another. Representing the goals in a goal hierarchy, however, reveals that the goal of shoveling snow is a means to the goal of being a good neighbor, and that the goal of shovel-ing snow is met by accomplishing the lower order goals of scooping up the snow with a shovel and piling it up out of harm's way. As this illus-trates, the goal level at which the man is operating may be understood best when viewed in relation to the other levels in his hierarchy because it conveys the process by which this goal is pursued and its relation-ships to other goals.

A Goal Hierarchy Approach to Organizational Justice

We propose that fairness goals may be understood best when viewed in the context of a hierarchy that conveys the process by which they are pursued and their relationship to other goals. Moreover, we argue that identifying and organizing the goals underlying justice into a hierarchy

will serve to identify whether the ultimate goals of fairness are self-directed or other-directed. In this manner, we will demonstrate that the goals of justice are self-interested—that is, the ultimate goal of fairness is self-directed (as opposed to other-directed).

Our proposed hierarchy has three levels (see Fig. 6.2). The lowest order goal is to achieve fairness in an event. This goal serves the higher order goal of achieving fair relationship with entities, where entities might be living (e.g., a supervisor) or nonliving (e.g., an organization).[2] The goal of achieving fair relationships with entities serves the highest order goal—the need to belong (Baumeister & Leary, 1995). This highest order goal is met, at least in part, by achieving fair relationships with entities, and each of these fair relationships is accomplished by achieving fairness in events.

Before we describe the hierarchy in more detail, we provide a brief description of our proposed highest order goal—belonging—or what Baumeister and Leary (1995) called the "fundamental interpersonal motive" (p. 497). These theorists suggested that people are motivated to seek positive social interactions and to avoid interactions that are conflicted or laden with negative affect (Baumeister & Leary, 1995). In proposing this, they drew from multiple disciplines to show that belongingness is indeed a fundamental motive. As illustrated in our example about the man wanting to be a good neighbor, there are several goals that are instrumental to the ultimate goal of belonging, but we focus exclusively on those goals relevant to the study of organizational justice.

In Fig. 6.2 we begin with the lowest order goal of achieving fairness in events, to which we refer to as the *event level*. We propose that individu-

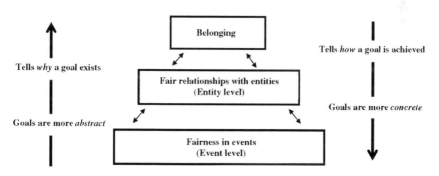

FIG. 6.2. Proposed hierarchy of goals underlying organizational justice.

---

[2]Although previous justice researchers have made a distinction between "person" and "position" (Lerner, 1977) and between "entity" and "source" (e.g., Cropanzano et al., 2001a), we use the broad term *entity* to convey anything having existence, living or nonliving.

als determine whether they are achieving fairness in an event by comparing the event expectations to their event perceptions. The default event expectations are that the rules of justice (e.g., consistency) will be satisfied and that the appropriate rewards (whether instrumental or relational) will be received. If these expectations are met, the event will be perceived as fair—or more specifically, the perceiver will report high levels of distributive, procedural, interpersonal, and/or informational justice (Colquitt, 2001; Colquitt & Greenberg, 2002). If discrepancies are detected, individuals assess the extent to which the relevant source is responsible for the injustice. A specific process by which individuals make this accountability assessment is explained by fairness theory (Folger & Cropanzano, 1998, 2001), which involves cognitive representations of "what might have been." Once individuals have determined whether they have been fairly treated, as well as the source of the (in)justice, they generate a *heuristic* about the general fairness of the source—that is, an impression of the fairness of the source that serves as a guide for future interactions. This heuristic provides a "cognitive shortcut" so that the person does not have to reevaluate the fairness of the source in future events. In this way, the activity at this goal level is similar to the *judgment phase* of fairness heuristic theory (Lind, 2001; Van den Bos, 2001; Van den Bos, Lind, & Wilke, 2001).

Once an individual develops a heuristic about the general fairness of a source, he or she moves up to the next highest goal in the hierarchy, fairness with an entity. At this point, the individual is operating at the *entity level*, which reflects the goal of achieving fair relationships with entities. People at this level attend to discrepancies between the relationship heuristic (i.e., relationship expectations) and their relationship perceptions, much as described in the *use phase* of fairness heuristic theory (Lind, 2001; Van den Bos, this volume). We further propose that this process operates differently depending on the favorability of the heuristic. A favorable heuristic suggests that the individual in question is open to continued contact with an entity. However, an unfavorable heuristic suggests that the person wants to protect himself or herself from future injustices by minimizing contact with the entity.

We propose that discrepancy monitoring at this level will occur largely through unconscious processing, thereby reaping cognitive benefits by not engaging in conscious and deliberate monitoring of the source. In keeping with Van den Bos (this volume), we view heuristics as a reflection of the extent to which a relationship is marked by trust, where trust is defined as "the willingness of a party to be vulnerable to the actions of another party based on the expectations that the other will perform a particular action important to the trustor, irrespective of the ability to monitor control that other party" (Mayer, Davis, & Schoorman, 1995, p. 712; see also Lewicki, Wiethoff, & Tomlinson, this

volume). Thus, if individuals have a favorable entity heuristic—that is, if they trust an entity—then they are willing to grant that entity control over things that are valuable to them (e.g., resources, personal information). Conversely, if individuals have an unfavorable entity heuristic—that is, if they do *not* trust an entity—then they will try to thwart the entity's control over things that are valuable to them. This notion is consistent with the suggestion by Mayer et al. (1995) that risk-taking in a relationship is a behavioral manifestation of trust.

If discrepancies do occur—that is, if the entity does not behave in accordance with expectations—then the individual moves back down to the event level, where he or she consciously assesses the fairness of events and potentially revises the heuristic. Stated differently, discrepancies are signals of a potentially inaccurate heuristic and thus prompt the conscious monitoring of entities in specific situations to generate a revised (i.e., corrected) heuristic. This is in keeping with Van den Bos and Lind's (2002) idea that uncertainty prompts attention to fairness. The process of detecting a discrepancy and moving down to the event level is analogous to *phase shifting* in fairness heuristic theory (Lind, 2001). In the absence of large discrepancies between the expected behavior of the entity (i.e., the fairness heuristic) and the entity's actual behavior, the relationship is, at minimum, conflict free and stable, and potentially marked by both stability and affective concern. So, for example, if an employee does not perceive any large discrepancies between the fairness heuristic he has for his supervisor and the actual behavior of his supervisor, his relationship with this supervisor is at least "not unfavorable" and may even be quite valuable.

In this manner, fair relationships with entities satisfy the criteria for the highest order (ultimate) goal of belonging. Specifically, belonging has two key features. First, belonging is marked by the desire for frequent interpersonal interactions. Ideally, these interactions are pleasant, but primarily they are free from conflict. Second, belonging reflects the desire to view a social bond as marked by stability, affective concern, and continuation into the foreseeable future. Thus, the criteria of belonging are "the occurrence of affectively pleasant interactions in the context of a temporally stable and enduring framework of affective concern for each other's welfare" (Baumeister & Leary, 1995, p. 497).

Again, we are not suggesting that belonging is the *only* high-order goal directing human behavior. Rather, we are arguing that it is most relevant to the study of organizational justice in that it is a fundamental interpersonal (vs. intrapersonal) motive. Baumeister and Leary (1995) provided an abundance of evidence in support of the idea that belonging is a "fundamental interpersonal motive." (p. 497). For example, they

pointed to the spontaneous formation of social attachments (e.g., the "Robbers Cave experiment" by Sherif, Harvey, White, Hood, & Sherif, 1961/1988), and to the way belonging shapes emotion (e.g., love; Sternberg, 1986) and cognition (e.g., the self-serving bias extended to friends; Brown, 1986).

Although there are several mechanisms through which belonging can be achieved, we propose that fair relationships with entities generally serve this goal by being free of conflict and by providing a sense of stability (the two central features of belonging). The fact that higher order goals are more abstract than mid-level goals makes it more difficult to specify the discrepancy–monitoring process, particularly insofar as monitoring at higher levels is largely unconscious (Carver & Scheier, 1998, 2003). However, although it is unclear exactly what is being compared, it is clear—even at this general, abstract level—that discrepancies are meaningful. For example, research suggests that people experience negative consequences, such as feelings of loneliness (e.g., Weiss, 1973), when their belongingness needs are not sufficiently met (Baumeister & Leary, 1995).

The Self-Interest Question

We have proposed that individuals' underlying psychological desires for belonging are served, in part, by fair relationships with entities, given that these relationships are, by definition, free of conflict and provide a sense of stability. Because fair relationships are interpersonal by nature, it follows that they will satisfy the fundamental interpersonal motive to belong. This, combined with the tendency for such fulfillment to promote cooperation (De Cremer, 2002), appears to explain the many positive consequences associated with perceiving justice (e.g., outcome satisfaction; Folger & Konovsky, 1989). The idea that fairness serves the ultimate goal of belonging also is consistent with empirical evidence showing that justice is associated with "pro-group" cognitions and behavior (e.g., organizational commitment, Daly & Geyer, 1995; organizational citizenship behavior, Skarlicki & Latham, 1996; trust, Konovsky & Pugh, 1994) and with why it serves to buffer against "pro-self" cognitions and behavior (e.g., theft, withdrawal; Greenberg & Tomlinson, 2004).

Of greatest importance to the present work is our claim that the proposed ultimate goal of justice (i.e., something that people want for its own sake, an end)—the need for belonging—is self-directed as opposed to other-directed (i.e., it is beneficial for oneself). In support of this claim, Baumeister and Leary (1995) provided evidence for the idea that the need to belong is a fundamental interpersonal motivation that stim-

ulates goal-directed activity designed to satisfy it (such as seeking out and cultivating interpersonal relationships). Thus, based on this claim, we argue that the goals of justice are, in fact, self-interested. Put differently, we argue in support of a justice-directed version of the egoism hypothesis, which maintains that the only ultimate goal(s) of individuals are self-directed (Sober & Wilson, 1998).

Implications

Turillo and his colleagues (2002) represented the self-interest debate in the organizational justice literature as a question of whether humans are "inevitably selfish" (p. 839) or whether they can "rise above self-interest" in pursuit of "moral principle" (p. 841). Framing the debate in this fashion erroneously suggests that the self-interested pursuit of fairness necessitates personal advantage (i.e., wrongdoing toward another). Drawing from the voluminous research investigating self-interest (e.g., Sober & Wilson, 1998), we argue that the self-interest debate is more precisely represented by the question of whether the ultimate goal(s) of organizational justice are self-directed or other-directed. Based on our proposed hierarchy of the goals underlying justice—more specifically, our proposed self-directed ultimate goal of belonging—we have argued that the pursuit of justice *is* self-interested. We also have argued that the self-interested pursuit of fairness does not necessitate personal advantage. That is, although individuals are motivated to pursue fairness because it ultimately serves the self-directed goal of belonging, the consequence of achieving fairness in events and fair relationships with entities is mutually beneficial insofar as it simultaneously serves both one's own interests and the interest of others. This new perspective has three implications for the field of organizational justice.

Self-Interested Fairness Is Moral.   One can engage in actions that serve ultimately their need for belonging while also behaving in accordance with moral principles (e.g., being truthful). So, for example, the act of sharing one's true interpersonal goals within a relationship (Fitzsimons & Bargh, 2003) promotes intrapersonal trust, whereas lying threatens trust (Bok, 1978). As such, the act of being honest simultaneously serves the need for belonging and is in accordance with moral principles. In our proposed hierarchy, we draw from fairness theory (Folger & Cropanzano, 2001) to explain the process by which someone decides whether actions are fair (be they their own or another's), which includes an assessment of whether the behavior meets deontic standards (Turillo et al., 2002; also see Folger et al., this volume). So, for example, breaking a promise made to a coworker (and thus failing to meet

206 GILLESPIE AND GREENBERG

these deontic standards) results in the unpleasant emotional state of guilt, as guilt is one of the "moral emotions that arise from discrepancies between our behavior or characteristics of ourselves and our moral standards" (Tangney, Niedenthal, Covert, & Barlow, 1998, p. 256).[3] In this manner, our proposed hierarchy is consistent with researchers who are emphasizing the interpersonal structure of guilt (e.g., Baumeister, Stillwell, & Heatherton, 1994). From this perspective, guilt serves a relationship-enhancing function given that it signifies a threat to an interpersonal attachment (and thus to one's need to belong), which, in turn, prompts reparative behavior. Thus, being truthful promotes trust, which serves the need to belong and is moral. As such, one's self-directed ultimate goal of belonging can be served by being fair (which includes adhering to moral principles).

Encouraging Self-Interested Fairness Is Beneficial to Organizations. Ryan and Deci (2000) explained that once a psychological need (i.e., an ultimate goal) is identified, it can be targeted to enhance personal thriving in much the same way that the organic needs of plants, once identified, can be targeted to maximize their thriving. We see this in the organizational literature in studies chronicling how individuals suffer from unfair treatment. For example, feelings of underpayment have been reported to lead workers to experience negative emotional reactions, manifesting themselves behaviorally in such adverse reactions as job dissatisfaction (Berkowitz, Fraser, Treasure, & Cochran, 1987; Fields, Pang, & Chiu, 2000), reduced well-being (Tepper, 2001), and emotional exhaustion (Van Dierendonck, Schaufeli, & Buunk, 2001).

Meeting needs (be they psychological or organic in nature) means reaping subsequent benefits. Accordingly, encouraging employees' pursuit of self-interested fairness may be seen as beneficial to organizations in that it serves the ultimate goal of belonging, which, in turn, promotes cooperation (De Cremer, 2002) as well as general health and well-being (Baumeister & Leary, 1995). Typically, we see this in the organizational literature in the negative form.[4] In this way, managers can promote cooperative behavior among their employees by encouraging them to identify and communicate their (self-interested) fairness expectations in organizationally relevant relationships. Stated differently, managers might do well not just to ask employees to give more to the organization, but to ask employees what the organization can do for them (with all do respect to President John F. Kennedy, whose sentiment we corrupted).

---

[3]This broad conception of guilt is different from the concept of inequity distress initially proposed by equity theory (see Greenberg, 1984).

[4]More recently, however, there has been a trend toward also examining the positive side of health and well-being in organizations (e.g., Cameron, Dutton, & Quinn, 2003).

Self-Interested Fairness Decreases Reliance on Material Rewards.
Individuals assess the extent to which they are being treated fairly
within a given event by monitoring whether the rules of justice are
satisfied and whether they have received an appropriate level of rewards (both material and socioemotional). Traditionally, these perceptions have been assessed by measuring one or more of the
dimensions of justice (i.e., distributive, procedural, interpersonal,
and/or informational). And although many researchers have examined these dimensions in isolation (see Colquitt, 2001), some have assessed how they interact with one another (Brockner & Wiesenfeld,
1996, this volume). We refer to this interplay among justice dimensions as "event profiles," in which one recognizes that the relationship between a justice dimension and an outcome may vary across
levels of other justice dimensions. So, for example, Brockner and
Wiesenfeld (1996, this volume) demonstrated that the relationship
between distributive justice and individuals' reactions varies across
levels of procedural justice, and one can propose similar hypotheses
using all four dimensions of justice.

Recognizing the existence of event profiles within a goal hierarchy
underscores that the specific way in which fairness in an event is
achieved is not as important as the satisfaction of the higher order goal it
serves (fair relationships with entities). Thus, understanding the relationship between event profiles and entity heuristics may provide
greater flexibility for organizations, such that there are likely more
ways to earn the trust of an employee than there are ways to satisfy a
specific procedural justice rule in a specific event. For example, individuals might perceive a supervisor who provides them with "high pay"
and "low respect" to be as fair as one who provides them with "medium
pay" and "high respect." Accordingly, although high levels of both outcomes would be best, the higher levels of respect might compensate for
lower levels of pay, still allowing the perceiver to develop a fair entity
heuristic. Viewing fairness in events as a means to the higher order goal
of fair relationships (rather than just as an end in and of itself) highlights
that material rewards are merely one of many ways that this higher order goal can be served.

CONCLUSION

People care about fairness because it provides them with tangible and
interpersonal rewards. However, we propose that, in the end, people
care about justice because it serves the self-directed ultimate goal of belonging. Thus, we have argued that the goals of justice are
self-interested—or, stated more formally, psychologically egoistic. This

is in direct opposition to the notion that people care about justice because "virtue is its own reward" (Turillo et al., 2002; Folger et al., this volume) in that it suggests that belonging, rather than virtue, is the ultimate goal. However, we still contend that engaging in actions that ultimately serve one's need for belonging allows for (and some even may argue, requires) adherence to moral principles.

Saying that the goals of justice are self-interested, such that they serve the self-directed ultimate goal of belong, means recognizing the difference between scientific and lay notions of self-interest (with the latter conveying notions of selfishness and personal advantage). Moreover, it means that it is beneficial for organizations to encourage employees to identify and to reveal their fairness expectations explicitly. Specifically, we argue that open discussion of perceived discrepancies between actual and desired treatment promotes discrepancy resolution, and thus more favorable organizationally relevant entity heuristics (e.g., managers and the organization itself). Ignoring self-interest—that is, avoiding a discrepancy and/or discouraging a conversation about it—does not make it go away. Rather, it prompts individuals privately to note discrepancies, privately to revise entity heuristics in an unfavorable fashion, and privately to behave in ways that indicate that they do not feel they are a part of a fair relationship. And this, we believe, is not in anyone's best interest.

REFERENCES

Alicke, M. D. (2000). Culpable control and the psychology of blame. *Psychological Bulletin, 126*, 556–574.

Ambrose, M. L. (2002). Contemporary justice research: A new look at familiar questions. *Organizational Behavior and Human Decision Processes, 89*, 803–812.

Austin, J. T., & Vancouver, J. B. (1996). Goal constructs in psychology: Structure, process, and content. *Psychological Bulletin, 120*, 338–375.

Austin, W. (1979). Justice, freedom, and self-interest in intergroup conflict. In W. G. Austin & S. Worchel (Eds.), *The social psychology of intergroup relations* (pp. 121–143). Monterey, CA: Brooks/Cole.

Bargh, J. A., & Ferguson, M. J. (2000). Beyond behaviorism: On the automaticity of higher mental processes. *Psychological Bulletin, 126*, 925–945.

Bargh, J. A., Gollwitzer, P. M., Lee-Chai, A., Barndollar, K., & Tröetschel, R. (2001). The automated will: Nonconscious activation and pursuit of behavioral goals. *Journal of Personality and Social Psychology, 81*, 1014–1027.

Bateman, T. S., O'Neill, H., & Kenworthy-U'Ren, A. (2002). A hierarchical taxonomy of top managers' goals. *Journal of Applied Psychology, 87*, 1134–1148.

Batson, C. D. (1991). *The altruism question: Toward a social-psychological answer.* Hillsdale, NJ: Lawrence Erlbaum Associates.

Batson, C. D. (1994). Prosocial motivation: Why do we help others? In A. Tesser (Ed.), *Advanced social psychology* (pp. 333–381). New York: McGraw-Hill.

Batson, C. D., & Powell, A. A. (2003). Altruism and prosocial behavior. In T. Millon & M. J. Lerner (Eds.), *Handbook of psychology: Personality and social psychology* (Vol. 5, pp. 463–484). New York: John Wiley & Sons.

Baumeister, R. F., & Leary, M. R. (1995). The need to belong: Desire for interpersonal attachments as a fundamental human motivation. *Psychological Bulletin, 117*, 497–529.

Baumeister, R. F., Stillwell, A. M., & Heatherton, T. F. (1994). Guilt: An interpersonal approach. *Psychological Bulletin, 115*, 243–267.

Berkowitz, L., Fraser, C., Treasure, F. P., & Cochran, S. (1987). Pay, equity, job gratifications, and comparisons in pay satisfaction. *Journal of Applied Psychology, 72*, 544–551.

Bok, S. (1978). *Lying: Moral choices in public and private life.* New York: Pantheon.

Brockner, J., & Wiesenfeld, B. M. (1996). An integrative framework for explaining reactions to decisions: Interactive effects of outcomes and procedures. *Psychological Bulletin, 120*, 189–208.

Brown, J. D. (1986). Evaluations of self and others: Self-enhancement biases in social judgments. *Social Cognition, 4*, 353–376.

Buchanan, A., & Mathieu, D. (1986). Philosophy and justice. In R. L. Cohen (Ed.), *Justice: Views from the social sciences* (pp. 11–46). New York: Plenum.

Cameron, K. S., Dutton, J. E., & Quinn, R. E. (2003). *Positive organizational scholarship: Foundations of a new discipline.* San Francisco, CA: Berrett-Koehler.

Carver, C. S., & Scheier, M. F. (1996). *Perspectives on personality* (3rd ed.). Boston: Allyn & Bacon.

Carver, C. S., & Scheier, M. F. (1998). *On the self-regulation of behavior.* New York: Cambridge University Press.

Carver, C. S., & Scheier, M. F. (2003). Self-regulatory perspectives on personality. In T. Millon & M. J. Lerner (Eds.), *Handbook of psychology: Personality and social psychology* (Vol. 5, pp. 185–208). New York: John Wiley & Sons.

Cawley, M. J., III, Martin, J. E., & Johnson, J. A. (2000). A virtues approach to personality. *Personality & Individual Differences, 28*, 997–1013.

Colquitt, J. A. (2001). On the dimensionality of organizational justice: A construct validation of a measure. *Journal of Applied Psychology, 86*, 386–400.

Colquitt, J., & Greenberg, J. (2002). Organizational justice: A fair assessment of the state of the literature. In J. Greenberg (Ed.), *Organizational behavior: The state of the science* (pp. 165–210). Mahwah, NJ: Lawrence Erlbaum Associates.

Comte, A. (1973). *The catechism of positive religion* (R. Congreve, Trans.). Clifton, NJ: A. M. Kelley. (Original work published 1883)

Cropanzano, R., & Ambrose, M. L. (2001). Procedural and distributive justice are more similar than you think: A monistic perspective and a research agenda. In J. Greenberg & R. Cropanzano (Eds.), *Advances in organizational justice* (pp. 119–151). Stanford, CA: Stanford University Press.

Cropanzano, R., Byrne, Z. S., Bobocel, D. R., & Rupp, D. E. (2001a). Moral virtues, fairness heuristics, social entities, and other denizens of organizational justice. *Journal of Vocational Behavior, 58*, 164–209.

Cropanzano, R., Byrne, Z. S., Bobocel, D. R., & Rupp, D. E. (2001b). Self-enhancement biases, laboratory experiments, George Wilhelm Friedrich Hegel, and the increasingly crowded world of organizational justice. *Journal of Vocational Behavior, 58*, 260–272.

Cropanzano, R., James, K., & Citera, M. (1993) A goal-hierarchy model of personality, motivation, and leadership. In L. L. Cummings & B. M. Staw (Eds.), *Research in organizational behavior* (pp. 267–322). Greenwich, CT: JAI Press.

Cropanzano, R., Rupp, D. E., Mohler, C. J., & Schminke, M. (2001). Three roads to organizational justice. In J. Ferris (Ed.), *Research in personnel and human resources management* (Vol. 20, pp. 1–113). Greenwich, CT: JAI Press.

Daly, J. P., & Geyer, P. D. (1995). Procedural fairness and organizational commitment under conditions of growth and decline. *Social Justice Research, 8*, 137–151.

De Cremer, D. (2002). The self-relevant implications of distribution rules: When self-esteem and acceptance are influenced by violations of the equity rule. *Social Justice Research, 15*, 327–339.

de la Bruyère, J. (1963). *Characters* (H. van Laun, Trans.). London: Oxford University Press. (Original work published 1688)

Doosje, B., Branscombe, N. R., Spears, R., & Manstead, A. S. (1998). Guilty by association: When one's group has a negative history. *Journal of Personality and Social Psychology, 75*, 872–886.

Fields, D., Pang, M., & Chiu, C. (2000). Distributive and procedural justice as predictors of employee outcomes in Hong Kong. *Journal of Organizational Behavior, 21*, 547–562.

Fitzsimons, G. M., & Bargh, J. A. (2003). Thinking of you: Nonconscious pursuit of interpersonal goals associated with relationship partners. *Journal of Personality & Social Psychology, 84*, 148–163.

Folger, R. (1998). Fairness as a moral virtue. In M. Schminke (Ed.), *Managerial ethics: Moral management of people and processes* (pp. 13–34). Mahwah, NJ: Lawrence Erlbaum Associates.

Folger, R., & Cropanzano, R. (1998). *Organizational justice and human resource management*. Thousand Oaks, CA: Sage.

Folger, R. & Cropanzano, R. (2001). Fairness theory: Justice as accountability. In J. Greenberg & R. Cropanzano (Eds.), *Advances in organization justice* (pp. 1–55). Stanford, CA: Stanford University Press.

Folger, R., & Konovsky, M. A. (1989). Effects of procedural and distributive justice on reactions to pay raise decisions. *Academy of Management Journal, 32*, 115–130.

Gardner, H. (1987). *The mind's new science*. New York: Basic Books.

Greenberg, J. (1984). On the apocryphal nature of inequity distress. In R. Folger (Ed.), *The sense of injustice* (pp. 167–188). New York: Plenum Press.

Greenberg, J. (1988). Equity and workplace status: A field experiment. *Journal of Applied Psychology, 73*, 606–613.

Greenberg, J. (1994). Using socially fair treatment to promote acceptance of a work site smoking ban. *Journal of Applied Psychology, 79*, 288–297.

Greenberg, J. (2001). Setting the justice agenda: Seven unanswered questions about "what, why and how." *Journal of Vocational Behavior, 58*, 210–219.

Greenberg, J., & Folger, R. (1983). Procedural justice, participation, and the fair process effect in groups and organizations. In P. B. Paulus (Ed.), *Basic group processes* (pp. 235–256). New York: Springer-Verlag.

Greenberg, J., & Ornstein, S. (1983). High status job title as compensation for underpayment: A test of equity theory. *Journal of Applied Psychology, 68*, 285–297.

Greenberg. J., & Tomlinson, E. (2004). The methodological evolution of employee theft research: The DATA cycle. In R. Griffin & A. O'Leary-Kelly (Eds.), *The dark side of organizational behavior* (pp. 426–461). San Francisco: Jossey-Bass.

Harris, M. B. (1977). Effects of altruism on mood. *Journal of Social Psychology, 102*, 197–208.

Holley, D. M. (1999). *Self-interest and beyond*. St. Paul, MN: Paragon House.

Holmes, J. G., Miller, D. T., & Lerner, M. J. (2002). Committing altruism under the cloak of self-interest: The exchange fiction. *Journal of Experimental Social Psychology, 38*, 144–151.

Hooker R. 1996. *Areté*. Retrieved 27 April, 2003 from the World Wide Web: http://www.wsu.edu/~dee/glossary/arete.htm.

Izard, C. E. (1993). Four systems for emotion activation: Cognitive and noncognitive processes. *Psychological Review, 100*, 68–90.

Jackson, J. P., Jr. (2003). Facts, values, and policies: A comment on Howard H. Kendler. *History of Psychology, 6*, 195–202.

Kendler, H. H. (1999). The role of value in the world of psychology. *American Psychologist, 54*, 828–835.

Kendler, H. H. (2003). Political goals versus scientific truths: A response to Jackson (2003). *History of Psychology, 6*, 203–207.

Kleinedler, S. (Ed.). (2000). *American heritage dictionary of the English language* (4th ed.). Boston: Houghton Mifflin.

Konovsky, M. A., & Pugh, S. D. (1994). Citizenship behavior and social exchange. *Academy of Management Journal, 37*, 656–669.

Lawson, R. (1997). Consumer decision making within a goal-driven framework. *Psychology & Marketing, 14*, 427–449.

Lerner, M. J. (1977). The justice motive: Some hypotheses as to its origins and forms. *Journal of Personality, 45*, 1–52.

Lerner, M. J. (1980). *The belief in a just world*. New York: Plenum.

Leventhal, G. S. (1976). The distribution of rewards and resources in groups and organizations. In. L. Berkowitz & E. Walster (Eds.), *Advances in experimental social psychology* (Vol. 9, pp. 91–131). New York: Academic.

Lind, E. A. (2001). Fairness heuristic theory: Justice judgments as pivotal cognitions in organizational relations. In J. Greenberg & R. Cropanzano (Eds.), *Advances in organizational justice* (pp. 56–88). Stanford, CA: Stanford University Press.

Lind, E. A., & Tyler, T. R. (1998). *The social psychology of procedural justice*. New York: Plenum.

Locke, E. A. (1988). The virtue of selfishness. *American Psychologist, 43*, 481.

Maslow. A. H. (1968). *Toward a psychology of being* (2nd ed.). New York: Van Nostrand.

Maslow, A. H. (1970). *Motivation and personality* (rev. ed.). New York: Harper & Row.

Mayer, R. C., Davis, J. H., & Schoorman, F. D. (1995). An integrative model of organizational trust. *Academy of Management Review, 20*, 709–734.

Miller, D. T. (1999). The norm of self-interest. *American Psychologist, 54*, 1053–1060.

Miller, G. A., Galanter, E., & Pribram, K. H. (1960). *Plans and the structure of behavior*. Oxford, England: Holt.

Miller, D. T., & Ratner, R. K. (1996). The power of the myth of self-interest. In L. Montada & M. J. Lerner (Eds.), *Current societal issues in justice* (pp. 25–48). New York: Plenum.

Miller, D. T., & Ratner, R. K. (1998). The disparity between the actual and assumed power of self-interest. *Journal of Personality & Social Psychology, 74*, 53–62.

Montada, L. (2003). Justice, equality, and fairness in human relations. In T. Millon & M. J. Lerner (Eds.), *Handbook of psychology: Personality and social psychology* (Vol. 5, pp. 537–568). New York: John Wiley & Sons.

Perloff, R. (1987). Self-interest and personal responsibility redux. *American Psychologist, 42*, 3–11.

Powers, W. T. (1973). *Behavior: The control of perception.* Oxford, England: Aldine.

Ratner, R. K., & Miller, D. T. (2001). The norm of self-interest and its effects on social action. *Journal of Personality & Social Psychology, 81*, 5–16.

Rogers, C. R. (1961). *On becoming a person.* Boston: Houghton Mifflin.

Ryan, R. M., & Deci, E. L. (2000). Self-determination theory and the facilitation of intrinsic motivation, social development, and well-being. *American Psychologist, 55*, 68–78.

Sherif, M., Harvey, O. H., White, B. J., Hood, W. R., & Sherif, C. W. (1988). *The robbers cave experiment: Intergroup conflict and cooperation.* Middletown, CT: Wesleyan University Press. (Original work published 1961)

Skarlicki, D. P., & Latham, G. P. (1996). Increasing citizenship behavior within a labor union: A test of organizational justice theory. *Journal of Applied Psychology, 81*, 161–169.

Sober, E., & Wilson, D. S. (1998). *Unto others: The evolution and psychology of unselfish behavior.* Cambridge, MA: Harvard University Press.

Sober, E., & Wilson, D. S. (2000a). Summary of: "Unto others: The evolution and psychology of unselfish behavior." *Journal of Consciousness Studies, 7*, 185–206.

Sober, E., & Wilson, D. S. (2000b). Morality and "Unto others": Response to commentary discussion. *Journal of Consciousness Studies, 7*, 257–268.

Sternberg, R. J. (1986). A triangular theory of love. *Psychological Review, 93*, 119–135.

Tangney, J. P., Niedenthal, P. M., Covert, M. V., & Barlow, D. H. (1998). Are shame and guilt related to distinct self-discrepancies? A test of Higgins's (1987) hypotheses. Journal *of Personality & Social Psychology, 75*, 256–268.

Tepper, B. J. (2001). Health consequences of organizational injustice: Tests of main and interactive effects. *Organizational Behavior and Human Decision Processes, 86*, 197–215.

Thibaut, J. T., & Walker L. (1975*). Procedural justice: A psychological perspective.* Hillsdale, NJ: Lawrence Erlbaum Associates.

Turillo, C. J., Folger, R., Lavelle, J. J., Umphress, E. E., & Gee, J. O. (2002). Is virtue its own reward? Self-sacrificial decisions for the sake of fairness. *Organizational Behavior & Human Decision Processes, 89*, 839–865.

Tyler, T. R. (1987). Conditions leading to value-expressive effects in judgments of procedural justice: A test of four models. *Journal of Personality & Social Psychology, 52*, 333–344.

Tyler, T. R. (1994). Psychological models of the justice motive: Antecedents of distributive and procedural justice. *Journal of Personality and Social Psychology, 67*, 850–863.

Tyler, T. R., & Blader, S. (2002). The influence of status judgments in hierarchical groups: Comparing autonomous and comparative judgments about status. *Organizational Behavior and Human Decision Processes, 89*, 813–838.

Tyler, T. R., Boeckmann, R., Smith, H. J., & Huo, Y. J. (1997). *Social justice in a diverse society.* Denver, CO: Westview Press.

Tyler, T. R., Degoey, P., & Smith, H. (1996). Understanding why the justice of group procedures matters: A test of the psychological dynamics of the group-value model. *Journal of Personality and Social Psychology, 70*, 913–930.

Tyler, T. R., & Lind, E. A. (1992). A relational model of authority in groups. In M. P. Zanna (Ed.), *Advances in experimental social psychology* (Vol. 25, pp. 115–191). San Diego, CA: Academic Press.

Vallacher, R. R., & Wegner, D. M. (1985). *A theory of action identification.* Hillsdale, NJ: Lawrence Erlbaum Associates.

Vallacher, R. R., & Wegner, D. M. (1987). What do people think they're doing? Action identification and human behavior. *Psychological Review, 94*, 3–15.

Van den Bos, K. (2001). Uncertainty management: The influence of uncertainty salience on reactions to perceived procedural fairness. *Journal of Personality and Social Psychology, 80*, 931–941.

Van den Bos, K., & Lind, E. A. (2002). Uncertainty management by means of fairness judgments. In M. P. Zanna (Ed.), *Advances in experimental social psychology* (Vol. 34, pp. 1–60). San Diego, CA: Academic Press.

Van den Bos, K., Lind, E. A., & Wilke, H. A. M. (2001). The psychology of procedural and distributive justice viewed from the perspective of fairness heuristic theory. In R. Cropanzano (Ed.), *Justice in the workplace: From theory to practice* (Vol. 2, pp. 49–66). Mahwah, NJ: Lawrence Erlbaum Associates.

Van Dierendonck, D., Schaufeli, W. B., & Buunk, B. P. (2001). Burnout and inequity among human service professionals: A longitudinal study. *Journal of Occupational Health Psychology, 6*, 43–52.

Walster, E., Walster, G. W., & Berscheid, E. (1978). *Equity: Theory and research*. Boston: Allyn & Bacon.

Weiss, R. S. (1973). *Loneliness: The experience of emotional and social isolation*. Cambridge, MA: MIT Press.

Williamson, G. M., & Clark, M. S. (1989). Providing help and desired relationship type as determinants of changes in moods and self-evaluations. *Journal of Personality and Social Psychology, 56*, 722–734.

7

What Is the Relationship Between Justice and Morality?

Robert Folger
University of Central Florida

Russell Cropanzano
University of Arizona

Barry Goldman
University of Arizona

This chapter discusses the relationship between injustice and moral accountability. Building on multidisciplinary theory and research, we argue that the sense of fairness is grounded in basic ethical assumptions of normative treatment. The sense of injustice, therefore, often involves holding someone accountable for a deliberate transgression of acceptable conduct. We term this the deontic response. As a result of the close link between injustice and immorality, the deontic response includes strong emotions and behaviors that may at times transcend individuals' short-term economic interests. In order to fully explicate these ideas, we first review the basic antecedents of moral principles and why their violations can evoke powerful but predicable emotional responses. Next, we discuss the five key attributes that define the deontic response. Afterwards, we review fairness theory, a model of justice that specifically incorporates the deontic response. Based on this, we conclude our chapter by considering the implications of the deontic response for interacting individuals.

In this chapter we discuss the relationship of organizational justice to moral emotions. We argue that the sense of justice is largely grounded in basic ethical assumptions as to how other human beings should be treated (Cropanzano & Rupp, 2002; Fehr & Gächter, 2000, 2002; Folger, 1994, 1998, 2001). As we argue, when employees maintain that something is unfair, they are often asserting that this event has transgressed some normative standard of appropriate conduct. As a consequence, the perception that an injustice has occurred can trigger a strong emotional response (Bies & Tripp, 2001, 2002; Bies, Tripp, & Kramer, 1997) and behaviors that are seemingly outside of economic self-interest (Kahneman, Knetsch, & Thaler, 1986). Our term for this reaction is the *deontic response* (from the Greek *deon*, that which is binding or obligatory).[1]

---

[1]The same modifier appears in the term *deontic logic*, referring to the study of permissions and prohibitions and words such as *ought*, *should*, *must*, and *may* as logical operators, and which sometimes deals with moral reasoning by treating it as a special subcase (Von Wright, 1963). We also use *deontic* as a modifier in that generic sense, rather than as a commitment to a particular ethical perspective such as Kantian deontology. Moreover, this chapter tends to place a greater stress on proscriptions than on prescriptions, just as philosophers sometimes distinguish aretaic moral judgments (regarding moral worthiness or positive virtue, such as adhering to prescriptions) from deontic moral judgments (regarding moral obligations, such as proscriptions about what not to do; cf. Lourenco, 2000). Thus it might prove useful to distinguish between pursuing virtue (doing the right thing) and avoiding/condemning vice (not doing the wrong thing).   *(continued)*

The critical link between injustice and morality has only recently begun to receive its due from organizational scientists, and our hope is to continue this promising trend. It offers potential new insights into how and why individuals respond to injustice. With this in mind, we consider the nature of moral standards and opprobrium toward injustice. Our explication of the deontic response will proceed in six parts. First, we consider the importance of moral principles as antecedents to this response. Second, we define the deontic response and describe it in a general way. Third, we articulate five attributes that we see as fundamental to the deontic response. Fourth, we consider some remaining questions about the relationship between justice and morality. Fifth, we consider one example of a deontic model of justice—fairness theory. Finally, we close this chapter by considering deontic responses in an interpsychic context.

DEONTIC RESPONSE ANTECEDENTS: VIOLATED MORAL PRINCIPLES

Ethical principles tell us what's important and how we should treat other human beings (and perhaps animals and nature as well, cf. Singer, 2001). When someone willingly violates these principles, that transgressor has placed him or herself above them as if superior to moral authority. Such actions tend to evoke what we call the deontic response, oriented toward something perceived as wrongful misconduct (e.g., conduct deemed blameworthy according to norms such as fairness; accountability for injustice).

Unfair conditions impose on what's "right" a setback from opposing causal forces. In the realm of social conduct, a perception of wrongdoing associated with unfairness involves attributing the victorious force to a social actor or agent whom we term the *transgressor*. This is a person perceived as exerting willpower in pursuit of self-interest with indifference or even callous disregard both for others' concerns and for dictates known by that person as commonly held moral standards of conduct. Immoral behavior, we show, can be emotionally (and sometimes economically) upending.

Consider the career of the Athenian Solon (c. 638–559 B.C.), described in both Herodotus' *History* and Plutarch's *Lives*. Solon reformed the Athenian government by extending political rights to the poor, forbidding loans guaranteed by a pledge of oneself or one's immediate family,

---

[1](*continued*)   Alternatively, it might be said that both types of moral phenomena involve duties; however, in one the duty is to *not* act while in the other the duty is to act. In this way, they might both be said to comprise parts of deontic justice. For the present chapter, we do not make further distinctions between the two types of moral phenomenon—although, as mentioned, we lean toward emphasis on the violation of prohibitions.

forgiving debts, and repealing harsh penalties for violations of the law.[2] Solon was frequently called on to interpret and/or alter these new laws. Of course, to do so would place Solon above the law, rather than the law above him. At least partially for this reason, Solon voluntarily exiled himself from Athens for a decade. He returned later, ultimately dying in his home *polis*, but Solon never rejoined public life.

Implicitly if not explicitly, Solon would have understood the meaning of our term "moral authority." The word *authority* implies a force or power that has the ability to influence us. As an "authority" that is "moral," rather than some other type, this force is based on ethical principles. Ethical individuals submit to *moral* authority, rather then placing themselves above it. As illustrated by Solon's actions, even someone who creates law should ultimately be subject to it.

Solon's life underscores another aspect of moral authority. Human beings often face the choice of submitting to moral mandates or violating them. When powerful men and women curtail the impulse to pursue self-interest in violation of these moral standards, they exhibit strength of character. This type of moral self-regulation betokens submissiveness to the force of moral authority. To use a loose analogy, we can compare and contrast moral authority with physical forces. We *will* submit to physical forces (i.e., gravity, electromagnetism, the strong atomic force, and the weak atomic force) because we *must*. We *may* submit to moral authority because we *should*.

EMOTION, COGNITION, AND THE DEONTIC RESPONSE

We have argued thus far that people (a) care about moral principles and (b) become upset when other people violate them. Indeed, such a violation is often alarming because it places the transgressor above normative standards whose internalization helps govern social life. As we show, the deontic response includes both unique categorizations of the violation as well as corresponding affective reactions.

What We Think About Moral Authority

When something seems unfair, that also categorizes it as wrong rather than right and bad rather than good. Still, the sense we get from an injustice is unlike our response to, say, a child's claim that "5" is the sum that 2 + 2 produces. An injustice, in contrast to a mere miscalculation, has distinctive qualities. These qualities are common to other constituents of the social domain designated by reference to moral standards—and, in particular, to moral standards for social conduct. In other words, in-

---

[2]Interestingly, many of these heavy-handed punishments came from a prior lawgiver named Draco. From his name comes our modern word "draconian."

justice is not synonymous with all of morality, which includes other precepts, but injustice shares with other moral violations the qualities that make people's reactions to them different from reactions to other categories of social error (e.g., sipping soup through a straw).

Similarly, valuing human life as worth special consideration, or affirming a human right to treatment with dignity and respect, indicates more than merely a matter of personal taste, such as a preference for chocolate rather than vanilla ice cream (and, we suggest, more than a direct implication about straightforward pursuit of personal self-interest). It indicates a regard for some transcendent value or values that go beyond mundane preferences. For this reason, when aware of someone's unfair mistreatment of others, the implications for your impressions of—and possible reactions toward—that person engage moral sentiment. In fact, most of our following discussion is devoted to addressing moral opprobrium.

A subspecialty within philosophy sometimes called *deontics* has distinguished between ordinary modal logic and a deontic variant (cf. footnote 1). Philosophical deontics suggests that individuals conceptualize factual matters in a manner distinct from moral issues (Cropanzano, Goldman, & Folger, 2003). For instance, deductive reasoning involves modal-logic operatives such as "necessary," "possible," and "sufficient," whereas deontic-logic operatives (e.g., "obligation," "permission," and "impermission" or "forbiddance") replace their modal-logic counterparts when people reason in moral terms. Impermission, of course, is also conceptualizable as an obligation *not* to do something (i.e., a prohibition). Moral prohibitions represent the minimalistic core of ethics because, in contrast with a moral obligation that one *must* do some specific thing, prohibitions maximize the liberty to do anything except something specifically forbidden.

We tie unfairness to the deontic notion of morally prohibited social conduct, which includes efforts, intentions, and indications of the willingness to violate such prohibitions. We construe violations of morally prohibited social conduct in dominance-submission terms: Rather than submitting to moral authority as outranking mere self-interest, the transgressor lays claim to a dominant hierarchical status ranked above the status granted others (and their concerns) and even above the status normally accorded to morality as the ultimate source of legitimate authority (cf. "acting above the law").[3]

---

[3]This chapter tends to emphasize the perspective of the victim and/or other observers. Of course, because everyone has a point of view, our analysis begs the obvious question of what the transgressor must think. We suspect that powerful others often feel that they are "above" the "low-brow" moral principles to which others adhere. Instead, they might view themselves as embodying a "different" (and better) morality. Like Nietzsche's "overman," this act of will places the transgressor beyond the normative rules and guidelines by which the rest of us attempt to live our lives.

Human beings are surprisingly good at deontic logic. In fact, evidence suggests that humans fare better at identifying the misbehavior of transgressors than at other sorts of cognitive tasks—for at least two reasons. First, task content influences judgment processes. Cosmides (1989) and Cosmides and Tooby (1987), for example, have shown that individuals are better at solving social problems between people if they involve concrete examples of reciprocity and related aspects of normative transgressions. They are relatively worse at solving abstract problems. Second, evolutionary psychologists note that the mind is not a blank slate (cf. Pinker, 2002). Rather, human cognitive capacities have evolved to solve frequent problems that occurred in our evolutionary environments (Wright, 1994). It is not surprising, therefore, that people are good at detecting "cheaters" (Cosmides & Tooby, 1989; Tooby & Cosmides, 1989).

What We Feel About Moral Authority

Of course, speculating about mechanisms for detecting cheaters and foul play addresses only the beginning of a much longer story. What other emotionally reactive tendencies might also constitute parts of a morally relevant repertoire, given an impression of someone else's conduct as blameworthy for having violated prohibitions against wrongdoing? Posing such a question serves to identify another relatively underexamined feature of justice, namely, that the sense of injustice seems capable of influencing evaluative impressions and emotional reactions in ways that current models would have difficulty explaining. In particular, current approaches focus on when, why, and how you react to unfairness done to you rather than done to others (e.g., tracing a concern about fairness to the negative implications of your being exploited or excluded from a group whose membership is important for your own sense of personal identity and self-esteem).

Our analysis focuses on emotional features of reactions to perceived foul play (unfair conduct as wrongdoing) and on how such features might reflect evolved predispositions of humans as a species rather than the current self-interest of a given individual—one possible explanation of some proneness to react emotionally about unfairness even when it has no direct bearing on you personally. The features to which we draw attention seem consistent with the shaping influence of evolution as a product of natural selection in the human species. Such features point toward the process of natural selection as a distal cause (i.e., one that operated in the ancestral environment of proto-humans to shape the genetically endowed capabilities currently possessed by modern humans, such as components of their emotional makeup).

In contrast, contemporary models of injustice reactions refer much more exclusively to proximal causes—that is, to current concerns about future plans (e.g., "Can I trust this leader not to exploit or exclude me?" "Would future interaction with this other person involve mostly fair dealing, or would foul play predominate?"). We propose that substrates of human emotional equipment predispose people to react consistently with how our ancestors behaved during agonistic encounters. The triggering of this emotional receptivity would not require mental rumination about future self-benefit; instead, it would couple the more instantaneously evaluative encoding of alarm ("this is bad") with physiological arousal and feeling-state accompaniments consistent with preparation for actively engaging an enemy or opponent. We propose that "moral codes" evolved as an adaptive response to otherwise complex (and therefore dangerous if slowly responded to) situations. In essence, we're hardwired for arousal and action in response to injustice.

FIVE ATTRIBUTES OF THE DEONTIC RESPONSE

As noted, people who flaunt the moral principles of others are likely to evoke harsh emotional responses. Moral norms of social conduct represent a set of principles applicable for governing what takes place when humans interact. As a consequence, moral precepts about social conduct serve to differentiate fair play from foul play among competing parties. Rules of fair play and prohibitions against foul play, applicable in at least an implicit sense, help sustain social life and can play an especially useful role when conflicts of interest might otherwise threaten to have a much more detrimental impact.

Nonetheless, violations of mores pertaining to social conduct (e.g., attempts to cheat the system or a specific other) occur commonly enough when individuals seek to have their own self-interest prevail over the legitimate rights of others. This poses a challenge to species whose survival depends heavily on social coordination, such as humans. We suspect that *Homo sapiens* has lasted this long thanks at least in part to mechanisms evolved by natural selection to deal with problems of collective life, such as the potentially deleterious effects of interest conflicts, and that reactions to morally transgressive misconduct reflect ways in which evolution has contributed to the architecture of human neuro-chemistry governing emotional reactivity. For now, we concede that scholars have only made preliminary attempts to explore this issue.

Thus, our present analysis remains a work in progress. Although scholars do not yet know the precise details of every aspect of the deontic response, it is possible to describe such reactions in broad outline. In particular, we consider five attributes of the response: automa-

ticity, short-term irrationality, retribution as its own reward, reconciliation mechanisms, and emotion as the driver of behaviors.

Attribute 1: Automatic Responses to Injustice

Certainly people can think long and hard about injustice (Goldman &
Thatcher, 2002), as numerous philosophical treatises confirm. Although
no one would gainsay the importance of effortful and deliberate thinking about justice, such thorough processing is probably complemented
by a less cognitively demanding system. For one thing, many real-life
situations require quick judgments. A slower and more cautious system
might not be up to that challenge. More directly germane to the present
argument, justice-relevant behaviors appear in small children (Wilson,
1993) and primates (de Waal, 1996). Such beings probably are not deliberating over the philosophical implications of injustice. More than
likely, they are reacting quickly and efficiently, using more basic and
primitive processing (Fukuyama, 1999; Wright, 1994).

   Indeed, research on social judgments shows that attributions regarding others' behavior can be rapid and automatic (Liberman, Gaunt,
Gilbert, & Troupe, 2002). Dijksterhuis and Aarts (2003, p. 14), for example, referred to *automatic evaluation* as an information-processing capability based on natural selection:

> Automatic evaluation refers to the capacity to evaluate incoming stimuli
> automatically. The importance of this capacity is reflected in the lack of its
> boundary conditions. Humans evaluate all stimuli (Bargh, Chaiken, Ray-
> mond, & Hymes, 1996; but see Fazio, Sanbonmatsu, Powell, & Kardes,
> 1986) regardless of an intention to evaluate (Hermans, De Houwer, &
> Eelen, 1994). In addition, evaluation does not require conscious aware-
> ness of the meaning of the stimulus (Bargh, Litt, Pratto, & Spielman, 1989;
> Greenwald, Klinger, & Liu, 1989; Murphy & Zajonc, 1993; see also De
> Houwer, Hermans, & Spruyt, 2001). Automatic evaluation is obviously
> functional. A quick categorization of stimuli allows for the rapid onset of
> appropriate behavior (i.e., approach or avoidance).

The survival value of an ability to detect bad in an even more rapid
fashion than good makes sense on similar evolutionary grounds. As
Dijksterhuis and Aarts (2003, p. 14) put it, "Being a few hundred milli-
seconds late in detecting a lion is extremely dangerous, whereas being a
little late in detecting edible vegetation is not so problematic." In this regard, fairness judgments often work like other social inferences. Considerable evidence suggests that they can occur in an unconscious and
heuristic-like fashion (e.g., Ambrose & Kulik, 2001; Bobocel, McLine, &
Folger, 1997; Cropanzano et al., 2003; Ellard & Skarlicki, 2002; Gilliland,

Benson, & Schepers, 1998; Goldman & Thatcher, 2002; Jones & Skarlicki, 2003; Lind, 2001; Paddock, Goldman, & Gilliland, 2003; Van den Bos, 2001; Van den Bos, Lind, & Wilke, 2001). Later we describe fairness theory, a deontic model of justice that explicitly discusses the role of automatic processing (Cropanzano, Byrne, Bobocel, & Rupp, 2001; Folger & Cropanzano, 1998, 2001).

Attribute 2: The "Irrationality" of Emotional Responses to Injustice

Pinker (2002) noted another feature of emotionally reactive responses to negative events, explicitly addressing moral misconduct. According to Pinker, for social life to run smoothly in the long run, people will sometimes need to behave irrationally with respect to their economic interests (e.g., courts may spend many thousands of dollars prosecuting someone who has stolen only a small sum of money). Pinker provided a compelling illustration. If a man accused of murder attempts to commit suicide, society will do its best to save his life, put him on trial, and perhaps sentence him to death. If death constitutes the same end result in either case, why work so hard to have it occur by one particular means rather than by some other? Undoubtedly several possible rationales might seem to justify following a trial/conviction/execution path rather than allowing accused murderers to kill themselves, including rationales about long-term beneficial effects such as deterrence. People often show a more purely retributive response for its own sake, however, despite the absence of deterrent effects (e.g., Carlsmith, Darley, & Robinson, 2002; Rupp, 2003; Turillo, Folger, Lavelle, Umphress, & Gee, 2002)—the attribute we explore next.

Attribute 3: Retribution as an End in Itself

Moral remedies are desired after the moral motive has been evoked. The moral motive speaks to an intrinsic desire for values such as justice (e.g., Bies, 1987; Cropanzano & Rupp, 2002; Folger, 2001). Some versions of social exchange theory hold that "fairness is a social norm that prescribes just treatment as a moral principle" (Blau, 1986, p. 157). If the moral social norm is violated, the victim might feel exploited and oppressed. In turn, this may lead to a "desire to retaliate ... [which] may well become an end-in-itself in the pursuit of which people ignore other considerations" (Blau, 1986, p. 229). This intrinsic desire for justice can create a motivation to punish the transgressor.

For example, Bies and colleagues (Bies & Tripp, 1995, 2001; Bies, Tripp, & Kramer, 1997) maintained that revenge is common for viola-

tions of rules, norms, or promises and power and status derogation. Cahn (1949) considered justice to be an active process of "remedying or preventing that which would arouse the sense of injustice" (p. 13). The sense of injustice is aroused as a natural response to unfair treatment. Research has shown that self-punishment by the transgressor through feelings of guilt and remorse can also restore justice (O'Malley & Greenberg, 1983) and therefore serve as a moral remedy to injustice. We define a moral remedy as an action taken by the perpetrator in response to perceived injustice that is intended to satisfy the victim's desire for punishment of the perpetrator. Notice that such acts are retribution are not necessarily moral or even legal from the perspective of an outsider. For instance, individuals who experience a workplace injustice may sometimes seek vengeful "payback" through sabotage (Ambrose, Seabright, & Schminke, 2002) or theft (Greenberg, 1993, 2002).

Cropanzano, Rupp, Mohler, and Schminke (2001) argued that research on concern for moral principles is most prevalent in the literature on interactional justice. Bies and Tripp (1995) explicitly discussed the need for revenge after unfair treatment that violates trust. We argue that violations of trust are best considered as instances of interactional injustice because of the untruthfulness involved. Further antecedents of revenge, such as breach of contract, lying, abuse of authority, and public criticisms, involve highly interactionally unfair treatment as well.

One reason why the moral motive should be especially prevalent after interactional injustice is because of the easy identifiability of the perpetrator of the injustice (Folger & Cropanzano, 1998). It is relatively easy to determine the target for moral outrage and possible punishment after an interactionally unfair treatment. It is often much more difficult to assign blame for procedures that are perceived as unfair. The assignment of blame, however, is considered essential to motivate revenge (Aquino, Tripp, & Bies, 2001; Folger & Cropanzano, 1998; Groth, Goldman, Gilliland, & Bies, 2002). Researchers have found that revenge motivation is only present when blame is assigned to a person (Bies & Tripp, 1995). Personalistic attributions of blame are more likely after interpersonally unfair treatment than after procedural injustice. Interpersonal treatment originates with an organization member, whereas organizational procedures often appear to originate with a faceless organizational bureaucracy (Masterson et al., 2000).

The existence of these types of urges suggests the possibility of evolved human mechanisms as distally grounded causes of emotional reactivity that can operate alongside, independently of, or even in place of more proximal causes of action tendencies, such as cognitively con-

scious deliberations about means–ends forecasts concerning the likely effects of pursuing retribution.

Attribute 4: Mechanisms for Reconciliation

An additional feature—bearing on prospects for reconciliation—also speaks to inhibitions that can keep conflict from escalating so much that it dooms any possibility of coordination. Suppose moral outrage went unbridled and unchecked by some other force. Proto-human groups were likely small. It would have been destructive to injure or exclude members of such groups in a willy-nilly fashion. Even today, expelling individuals can create high costs—as evidenced by the diminished reputations of companies that laid off thousands of workers due to the financial chicanery of management (e.g., Enron, Worldcom).

Something should limit and (hopefully) constructively direct our response to injustice. Better yet, this limiting force should afford us the opportunity for rapprochement. Therefore, natural selection must provide some braking mechanism when we believe we have been wronged. Hostile and punitive responses toward offenders should allow for future reconciliation, thereby sustaining grounds for additional interaction sufficient to capitalize on coordinative prospects that the future might hold. When parties formerly in conflict subsequently reconcile, they follow a path less costly—both to themselves and to those around them—than when hostilities continue unabated. Certainly the chances for sustained profit can decline as a function of conflicts that continue to fester within an organization.

Attribute 5: Emotion as the Driver of Behavior

Also consistent with evolutionary influences, all of the features we have already mentioned should function, at least in part, through the impetus of emotion. The obvious reason for this is that morally based retaliation exists in animals that one would assume have less fully developed reasoning capacities than our own species, including the primates mentioned earlier. Assuredly, we do not imply that reason is unimportant in human decision making. When confronting an injustice, individuals often act from self-interested and relational considerations, as well as the moral concerns that are the focus of this chapter (Cropanzano, Byrne, Bobocel, & Rupp, 2001; Cropanzano, Rupp, Mohler, & Schminke, 2001). Our point here is only that the capacity to reason does not operate without the possibility of influence from more primitive sources of anger about injustice and moral transgression (for a discussion of this possibility, see Singer, 1981).

Indeed, the question of emotional responses to injustice has repeatedly been the focus of theoretical speculation (e.g., Bies & Tripp, 2001, 2002; Bies, Tripp, & Kramer, 1997; Cropanzano, Weiss, Suckow, & Grandey, 2001; Krehbiel & Cropanzano, 2000; Weiss, Suckow, & Cropanzano, 1999). For example, Bies (1987) described some injustices as involving "moral outrage" when societal norms of behavior are violated. In turn, he continued, this moral outrage can serve as the basis for acts of retribution. Similarly, anger has been theorized to contribute to the "impulse to sue" (Lieberman, 1981, p. 3). Recently, in a study involving 583 recently unemployed workers, Goldman (2003) found that anger was a response to injustice that predicted legal claiming.

This angry response reflects one way that holding others accountable to standards of moral conduct, and the human capacity for experiencing a sense of injustice, serve as a line of defense against the unfettered exercise of power that would attempt to impose unfair conditions. Similar to how animals respond to attack on themselves or others of their own kind, human anger about injustice can supply a fierce intensity perhaps essential for meeting force with force—the legitimate force of moral authority (right) counterposed against the illegitimacy of imposed dominance (might). Evidence suggests that individuals feel resentment toward those who do violence to the moral order and that such anger can, in turn, cause observers to aggress against wrongdoers (DaGloria & DeRidder, 1977, 1979).

We call this hostile response "deontic anger" (with intensity varying from mild to "deontic fury," and the like) when it is instigated by indications of someone blamed for morally prohibited conduct (cf. Folger, 2001; Solomon, 1990). Deontic anger is a robust phenomenon. Indeed, it can occur even among third-party observers for whom the consequences of an unfair act have no direct bearing (e.g., Ellard & Skarlicki, 2002; Turillo et al., 2002). The key point, though, is that we conceptualize deontic anger as a reaction to the (violated) dictates of moral accountability rather than as the result of a substantive setback to personal self-interest. This response can orient people punitively toward a transgressor even when nothing of (economic) substance accrues from doing so (Bowles & Gintis, 2002; Fehr & Gächter, 2000, 2002).

In research by Kahneman, Knetsch, and Thaler (1986), for example, participants received information about the alleged details of a previous session involving what experimental economists call a "dictator game." Someone assigned the dictator role in such games decides unilaterally how to distribute money between himself or herself (Player A) and an unknown other person (Player B). The participants heard that the earlier session had given dictator-role players a choice between an option designating 90% for themselves ($18, vs. only $2 for the other person, which thereby indicated a very self-serving preference) and an option designat-

ing an even split ($10 for each party). Consistent with details about prior notification of a budgetary constraint, the description of this session further noted that actual payments went only to a small proportion of pairs drawn at random. The participants were also informed that in the current session, they controlled the amount of money set aside for distributions involving themselves and dictator-role players from among the unpaid pairs of the earlier session. One of the two available options indicated a $6 result for them, whereas the other indicated only $5. When the latter (smaller by $1) choice guaranteed that no money at all would go to a prior-session individual who had attempted to get $18 as the maximally self-serving amount, 75% of the respondents picked that option— thereby sacrificing their own potential gain but, at the same time, denying any chance of gains by a person who had exhibited such rampant pursuit of self-benefit at another's expense. This reaction shows that when someone's conduct indicates a willingness to follow courses of action guided by self-interest without regard to others (and, hence, with disregard for moral prohibitions against exploiting others for personal advantage), many of those who learn about the misconduct might feel punitively inclined even at some cost to themselves.

Intuition suggests that people do not endure costs unless they anticipate at least some reasonable prospects of benefit in return. Knowing that 75% of the respondents showed a willingness to endure the (admittedly modest) costliness of a $1 shortfall makes it seem natural to look for some type of compensatory benefit to offset that degree of self-imposed loss. A recent series of experimental investigations by Turillo et al. (2002), however, failed to find effects from any of several manipulations designed to vary the magnitude of beneficial consequences that might constitute extrinsic incentives for punishing unfair conduct. Earlier, for example, we noted that people might support punishment as a function of the extent to which they consider it an effective means for deterring wrongful pursuits such as the willingness to treat others unfairly. Punitive inclinations motivated by the incentive of benefiting from punishment's deterrence-based consequences require at least some means whereby the punishment of present misdeeds reduces the likelihood of future misconduct. When Turillo et al. compared conditions with deterrent consequences made possible or impossible, however, they found no difference in either case from the 75% baseline prevalence of self-sacrificial punishment.

If we commit an injustice, therefore, our peers might punish us in some fashion or another—perhaps even at some cost to themselves— not because it helps them achieve goals they have set themselves (those might come to mind only after having already reacted with an anger that lashes out against you), and not because they feel good about seeing punishment delivered (they might rebuke in sorrow and punish re-

luctantly rather than gleefully), but because ... what? Saying "Because I deserved it" begs the question: Why don't they shrug their shoulders, mutter "Oh well, life's unfair, and it's not my job to make sure that every deed gets its just deserts," or something to that effect?

Our analysis suggests that strongly felt emotions can prompt action tendencies before reasons for acting one way or another get thoroughly considered—or, for that matter, come to mind at all. Holding others accountable for misconduct need not entail deliberating about the degree of one's commitment to that role; rather, our emotional constitution as humans functions like a precommitment device in making some match-ups between emotions and situations more likely than others (i.e., with preset default values). Here we are referring to "anger" generically—it does not just mean blinding rage. In many situations where people act on their *remembered anger*, moreover, this may or may not be exactly the same as actual anger. Nevertheless, remembered anger is often the antecedent for a punitive response (Margalit, 2003).

JUSTICE PERCEPTIONS AND MORAL PRINCIPLES

We argued earlier that a deontic response (a) will often be automatic, (b) may seem economically irrational (at least in the short term), (c) will sometimes be pursued as an end in itself, (d) includes a possibility of reconciliation, and (e) is partially driven by emotions. For all that, some questions remain about the relationship between moral principles and justice perceptions. Although justice plays an important role in morality, "justice" and "moral principles" are not synonymous. Moral principles and justice perceptions perhaps reflect something like overlapping circles in a Ven diagram. As shown in Fig. 7.1, some moral standards have a good deal to do with justice (cf. Rawls, 1971); others do not. The deontic approach applies to the overlapping part of these two circles— that is, to a sense of injustice derived from the violation of ethical precepts. Because the circle representing perceptions of justice only partially overlaps with the circle representing moral principles, there are times when individuals often make judgments of "unfairness" that are quite distinct from their perceptions of "immorality." We develop these ideas next.

When "Moral" Does not Mean "Fair"

Through this chapter we have argued that ethical standards have a special place in judgments of fairness. Many philosophers agree (cf. Rawls, 1971). However, this is not the same thing as saying that one needs to be fair to be seen as moral. In fact, ethicists have shown that fairness is only one of numerous moral principles. For instance, one

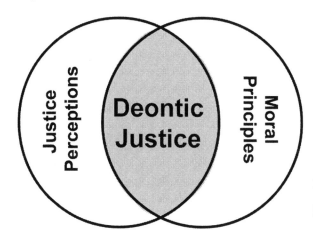

FIG. 7.1. The overlapping relationship between deontic justice and morality.

could derive a coherent sense of ethics from utilitarianism. Loosely, utilitarians argue that a moral action is one that does the greatest good for the greatest number (e.g., Singer, 1979). Another approach emphasizes human rights, which maintain that people are inherently entitled to perform certain actions and/or possess certain benefits (e.g., Ferrell & Fraedrich, 1997; Velasquez, 2001). Each of these philosophical systems provides individuals with a way of ascertaining the "good" or the "right." We are not arguing for one or the other. Rather, our point is that "ethical principles" may or may not be "just," depending on the standards the individual is employing. As shown in Fig. 7.1, fairness includes only one part—albeit an important part—of the larger domain of morality.

When "Fair" Does Not Mean "Moral"

Were we to stop here, we could treat "morality" as a broad construct and "justice" as a narrow one. By this thinking, the former would subsume the latter. Justice would exist within the larger domain, such that all fairness was about morality, but all morality would not be about fairness. However, as shown in Fig. 7.1, the matter appears more complicated than this. There are cases of unfairness that might not seem to fit some connotations associated with particular interpretations of immorality. Let us consider two.

A Continuum of Violations. Gilliland, Benson, and Schepers (1998) and Vermunt and Steensma (2001) argued that individuals distinguish *degrees* of injustice. Something can be very unfair or not that serious. "Immoral" may seem too serious a term for some forms of unfairness

and is best reserved for more serious transgressions. Consider a supervisor who gives an incomplete, "positively spun" explanation for a key decision, versus one who treats a subordinate rudely and disrespectfully. The latter action would likely be viewed as immoral. The former might be a bit sloppy, but "immoral" seems too strong a word.

Lack of Blame.   Both our deontic perspective and moral behavior more broadly are used to describe the conduct of people. However, the word *fairness,* when used more generally, can be viewed as a way of characterizing undeserved misfortune not based on anyone's blameworthy misconduct. Consider a situation in which poor record keeping caused flaws in decisions (making some outcomes unfair). Perhaps this organization had to adopt new software when an older version became obsolete, for example, and the new version still has "bugs" that no one can yet eradicate. Or perhaps a hurricane damaged records that then had to be reconstructed from memory. We can imagine some cases in which certain employees feel "unfairly treated," yet they might not blame any particular person for acting immorally. This reluctance to blame illustrates our distinction between undeserved misfortune as an unfair outcome (not derived from anyone's blameworthy actions) and deontic (and, hence, morally toned) judgments about violations of prohibited conduct. Unfair outcomes—those that differ from what a person deserves—can occur for a variety of reasons other than as the result of someone's morally blameworthy behavior, and such instances might seem to involve unfairness without immorality. Our deontic perspective addresses only blameworthy moral transgressions—which refer to unfair conduct *by* someone in "breaking the rules." Similarly, "you didn't play by the rules" tends to be invoked with respect to deliberate misconduct rather than actions considered accidental, unintentional, and so forth.

Summary: What the Deontic Approach Is Not

As we have seen, the deontic approach represents a way of understanding fairness-related phenomena that points to the key role of morally accountable conduct. Such an approach readily complements various models that also address such phenomena. We believe that extant models have called attention to factors *sufficient* for an impact on justice judgments, whereas a deontic perspective suggests that they have tended to neglect or underplay a key factor *necessary* for judgments to count as bearing on justice and fairness in the first place.

To understand this point, consider the causes of justice emphasized by previous models. Historically, organizational justice researchers have argued that perceived unfairness occurs when one loses control over valuable resources or suffers a loss of interpersonal standing in im-

portant groups (e.g., Cropanzano, Byrne, Bobocel, & Rupp, 2001). Although there is considerable evidence attesting to the importance of these factors, this work shows that instrumental control and group standing are *sufficient* to trigger justice concerns. The evidence has not demonstrated that they are *necessary* for concerns about fairness to arise in the first place. A deontic perspective attempts to pinpoint that necessary ingredient by drawing attention to moral accountability as the domain within which to look for it. In so doing, the deontic approach complements and extends earlier work.

FAIRNESS THEORY

The deontic approach is a conceptual lens for understanding why and how people come to care about injustice. Another way to understand this point is to recognize that the deontic perspective is not currently any *one* theory. In fact, one could envision numerous theories that might feature deontic themes. In principle, these different theories could even be competing, although they would probably share the five attributes we described earlier. At the present time, however, the newness of the deontic perspective has yet to give rise to these different theories. This is unfortunate. A deontic approach might instill more confidence if framed as a scientific theory suitable for empirical testing.

Fortunately, there is one extant model that has explicitly made moral accountability a central feature, namely, fairness theory (Folger & Cropanzano, 1998, 2001). Fairness theory was specifically incorporated with the five deontic attributes in mind. For instance, fairness theory emphasizes ethical transgressions (Folger & Cropanzano, 2000), reconciliation (Cropanzano, Chrobot-Mason, Rupp, & Prehar, 2004), the frequent automatic processing of justice information (Cropanzano, Byrne, Bobocel, & Rupp, 2001), and the centrality of emotions in responding to injustice (Cropanzano, Weiss, Suckow, & Grandey, 2000). In addition, existing empirical tests of fairness theory tend to be supportive (Collie, Bradley, & Sparks, 2002; Colquitt & Chertkoff, 2002; Shaw, Wild, & Colquitt, 2003). Moreover, fairness theory extends Folger's (1987) referent cognitions theory. Both indicate how negative emotional and behavioral reactions stem from interactive combinations of counterfactually deviant outcomes and blameworthy conduct (e.g., use of unfair procedures), and much empirical work testifies to the existence of such interactions (e.g., see review by Brockner & Wiesenfeld, 1996).

Overview of Fairness Theory

Fairness theory attempts to explicate the conditions under which an individual categorizes an action as "unfair." Essentially, the model argues

that three judgments are involved—"would," "could," and "should"—although any or all such aspects of the categorization process might occur only in some implicit fashion. Very loosely speaking, we can think of these judgments as answers to three questions:

- What *would* have happened if the action had not taken place?
- *Could* the actor have taken any alternative steps?
- *Should* the actor have behaved the way he/she did?

As we show, *would* processing can influence the extent to which an event seems disadvantageous relative to better alternatives. *Could* processing indicates who if anyone is preliminarily eligible to be held accountable for the event, by virtue of a presumed ability to have acted otherwise—in ways relevant to what, therefore, *would* have happened instead. Finally, *should* processing pertains to the accountability of conduct by moral standards—whether a (*could*-eligible) person's conduct constituted or contributed to a moral misdeed, for example, as opposed to just an unavoidable misfortune. These ideas are illustrated in Fig. 7.2; next we review them in more detail.

When an individual ascertains what *would* have happened, he or she at least tacitly compares the actual event to some presumably plausible alternative event. The extent to which an event contrasts with better alternatives, for example, can influence the magnitude of that event's perceived harmfulness (i.e., unfavorable deviation from something better, such as disease or infection relative to health). Although individuals sometimes think long and hard about such comparisons, fairness theory maintains that these judgments often can

FIG. 7.2.   Fairness theory.

take place quickly and automatically, thereby in effect (even if not consciously) contrasting actual situations with the counterfactually favorable alternatives that they most readily evoke (Folger & Cropanzano, 1998, 2001). Kahneman and Miller's (1986) norm theory gives a similar account of counterfactual processing, including the possibility of its automaticity. As both theories imply, the more that counterfactual processing makes favorable alternatives readily accessible (whether consciously or not), the more that what *would* have been better will make what did happen seem unfavorable. Not surprisingly, either automatic or more consciously deliberative processing of this kind can be biased by a host of factors that have little do with the merits of the events (cf. Bobocel, McCline, & Folger, 1997).

When an individual ascertains what someone *could* have done, he or she is assessing the extent to which that person had discretion or a reasonable choice when performing an actual behavior. We are less likely to hold someone accountable if we do not believe that he or she could have acted differently. In fact, social accounts indicating that an actor had no realistic choice tend to allay perceptions of injustice (e.g., Bies, 1987, 2001; Tyler & Bies, 1990). Although fairness theory recognizes the importance of such explanations, the model emphasizes that this *could* "judgment" is often made through the automatic processing of information (cf. Roese, 1997; Roese & Olsen, 1995). For example, Bobocel et al. (1997) maintained that the veracity of social accounts is often ascertained through peripheral information, such as the reputation of the speaker. Moreover, various aspects of an implemented procedure, for example, might suggest different ways that such a procedure *could* have been designed or implemented instead. In short, not only the available social accounts but also various actions themselves can have implications about what was seemingly under someone's discretionary control and could have been done differently.

When an individual ascertains what people *should* have done, he or she is attending to the moral implications of their conduct. *Should* refers to what is right or ethically appropriate. A violation of a moral norm is a necessary trigger for the deontic sense of injustice that we are describing in this chapter. As is the case with *would* and *could* information, fairness theory proposes that *should* is often assessed automatically. In other words, individuals take into account salient discrepancies between a given action and a normative standard. Of course, evaluations of interpersonal conduct can occur without addressing moral implications (Folger & Cropanzano, 2001), and fairness theory does not imply that people construe all behavior as calling for a moral judgment. In an insightful chapter, Schminke (1998) argued that attributes of the individual (e.g., their level of moral devel-

opment), the situation (e.g., relevant reinforcement contingencies) and aspects of the issue (e.g., the potential benefits and harms) make employees more or less likely to interpret an event as an ethical issue (for a similar analysis, see Treviño, 1986).

Fairness Theory and Emotion

Fairness theory argues that emotions play an important role in reactions to injustice. According to fairness theory, anger often accompanies blaming someone for a negative event, "when reality is compared with a favored alternative ... which one failed to reach" (Folger, 1987, p. 186, quoting Kahneman and Tversky's 1982 description of counterfactual emotions; cf. Roese, 1997; Roese & Olsen, 1995). For example, anger might occur when a worker believes he or she would not have been terminated if the decision maker had used fairer procedures possible to implement. Resentment of unfair treatment can also combine with behaviors that address the situation in a retributive fashion (e.g., Skarlicki & Folger, 1997; Skarlicki, Folger, & Tesluk, 1999). The following two studies provide illustrations.

Goldman (2003) surveyed 583 terminated workers to investigate the role of state and trait anger in legal-claiming. He reported that state anger (subjective feelings of annoyance, irritation, fury, and rage that relate to a particular set of events) partially mediated the relationship between the three-way interaction of distributive, procedural, and interactional justice (that was predicted by fairness theory) and legal claiming. Moreover, he reported that trait anger (a dispositional trait) moderated the relationship between the three-way interaction and legal claiming. Strictly speaking, Goldman relied on referent cognitions theory (RCT); however, in this regard, the arguments that apply to RCT are just as applicable to fairness theory. In further support of this dispositional approach to emotions and justice, Skarlicki et al. (1999) reported that negativity and agreeableness, dispositional traits, moderate the relationship between perceive fairness and organizational retaliatory behaviors. The data for their study were derived from 188 usable surveys of first-line employees of a manufacturing plant.

INTERPSYCHIC IMPLICATIONS
OF THE DEONTIC RESPONSE

The reader should also note a further implication of our analysis. Often, emotion is understood as an *intra*psychic process that is based on the reactions people have to particular events (cf. Weiss & Cropanzano, 1996). Likewise, scholars as far back as Darwin (1965/1972) have emphasized the value of emotion as a signaling device for conspecifics (e.g., people

who bare their canine teeth can thereby signal anger). We emphasize that emotional communication can also be an *inter*psychic process because one person's emotions predispose a different emotional state in another person.

When humans react to the emotions of others, then emotional displays are serving a social/commutative function (Ekman, 1984, 1992; Katz, 2000; Parkinson, 1996; Tooby & Cosmides, 1990). Facial expressions and body posture can indicate possible motives and likely reactions. Research suggests that emotional displays can elicit feelings in other people (e.g., Kelly & Barsade, 2001; Niedenthal, Halberstadt, & Innes-Ker, 1999; Pugh, 2001). For instance, a display of anger from a powerful person might evoke fear in an observer. Indeed, emotional displays can even elicit physiological responses in observers (Dimberg & Öhman, 1996). Emotions also come with action tendencies (Zajonc, 1998). For instance, someone else's deontic rage might motivate a wrongdoer to rectify harm. The sequence of emotions and action tendencies during the aftermath of perceived wrongdoing can take on the character of something like a wrestling match as a result, with moves and countermoves in response to one another.

To illustrate this process, as well as to document its flexibility, we next discuss some possible sequences. For simplicity, as well as keeping with the purpose of this chapter, each of these begins with deontic anger from a victim or observer in response to perceived wrongdoing by a protagonist. When someone holds another person accountable for wrongdoing, indications of blame and angry condemnation by the former essentially constitute reactions to misconduct as if it were an attacklike activity calling for a counterattack. How might a protagonist who thereby feels accused of a transgression react to signs of anger from other people? An implicit or explicit accusation-as-counterattack can create a situation that a protagonist might find hard to ignore. His or her response in turn will tend to influence what happens next, and so on. The following discussion speculates about certain simplified patterns that might tend to occur as response–counterresponse sequences when observers hold protagonists accountable for wrongdoing. To illustrate, we consider two prototypical sequences and slight variations on them, although obviously these are representative rather than exhaustive.

Sequence 1: Accuser Attacks, Transgressor Experiences Guilt

Given an accusation or awareness of potential blame, the transgressor might experience guilt. Guilt occurs when someone feels accountable for counternormative conduct and accepts some degree of fault or blame but does not substantially alter his or her self-image in the process ("I'm human, and I made a mistake" rather than "I'm a terrible per-

son"). Guilt that arises from misuse of the power to affect others' circumstances does not have to entail self-castigation and can instead focus on the wrongful conduct as having created requirements for remedial action not unlike the obligation to pay a debt (Ashkanasy, Härtel, & Zerbe, 2000; Poulson, 2000). In effect, this characterization of guilt refers to the type of emotion prevalent when people see their misconduct as inappropriate but do not think of themselves as fundamentally bad persons (Tangney & Fischer, 1995). People feeling guilty in this fashion, therefore, tend to admit that they have erred; similarly, they show a tendency to apologize and express remorse (Tangney, 1995). At that point, accusers may accept the apology and drop the matter (Folger, Cropanzano, & Van den Bos, 2002).

The probabilistic and not-guaranteed nature of this sequence raises another important question: What if the accuser fails to follow the convention of forgive-and-forget in the aftermath of apology? In the preceding sequence, we referred to instances in which the transgressor's display of remorse yields a display of accuser forgiveness. A hostile or vindictive accuser might take expressions of contrition and remorse as insincere (e.g., roused by fear rather than self-enforced submissiveness), however, or as inadequate alone to compensate for suffering. Thus, the human accuser might respond to guilt-based displays of submissiveness with heightened anger, unlike the manner in which the behavior of other social animals tends toward relatively more fixed patterns of response to signals regarding dominance and submission. In this circumstance our best guess is that the locus of blame for the transgressor will now tend to move *away* from him- or herself and *toward* the accuser. In other words, the transgressor will now report less remorse and third-party observers might even begin to question the accuser's behavior. We might say that breaking the sequence (to refuse to accept an apology) could be viewed as a moral violation in and of itself.

Sequence 2: Accuser Attacks, Transgressor Experiences Shame

Shame, like guilt, is a self-evaluative emotion, in contrast to anger as an other-evaluative emotion. Shame occurs when a protagonist not only regards his or her conduct as wrongful but also experiences a tendency toward lower self-regard as a result. Shame involves an aversive emotional experience that implies a flaw of the self (Poulson, 2000). The key difference between shame and guilt is that guilt refers to a specific act, whereas shame refers to the self as a whole (Tangney, 1995; Tangney & Fischer, 1995). Ruminations about shame can raise questions that can make one's own moral standing seem problematic (Niedenthal, Tangney, & Gavanski, 1994; Tangney, Miller, Flicker, & Barlow, 1996). The behavioral response associated with shame is typically said to in-

volve hide-or-withdraw tendencies (Keltner & Harker, 1998; Tangney, Wagner, Hill-Barlow, Marshall, & Gramzow, 1996), although a shame–rage combination can also occur when such tendencies include defensiveness—perhaps much as a prey animal seeking to flee a predator might turn and fight if cornered.

A transgressor's shame-based reactions thus make reconciliation of conflict more problematic and, in fact, can actually exacerbate it. As is the case with guilt, sometimes the knowledge of another person's shame might trigger a forgiving response from the accuser. But consider first the shame-based response that is, in effect, equivalent to run and hide. Withdrawal and avoidance make it difficult for the accuser to read the emotion (he or she may not even have the opportunity) and respond accordingly. Indeed, withdrawal might be seen as disinterest or apathy about an important ethical matter. Given this, a transgression that triggers shame might prove especially inimical to the potential for reconciliation.

Next consider that some alleged transgressors might view the deontic anger, and not their own behavior, as unjustified—especially if a shamefully disgraced self-image becomes severe enough to trigger denial. If the initial tendency to internalize blame threatens self-esteem too much, the aggressor might engage rationalizations that instead externalize blame, perhaps even focusing it on victims ("actually, they got what they deserved"). Thus, these transgressors are likely to experience deontic anger of their own! Such anger-to-anger conflicts are likely to spiral out of control, as moral outrage impels both parties to entrench themselves inside their positions. Indeed, this sort of sequence would seem closest to a pure power struggle, whereby each disputant seeks advantage in an attempt to define the moral character of the situation (Bies & Tripp; 2002; Bies, Trip, & Kramer, 1997; Goldman, 2003; Solomon, 1990).

Such a possibility might also arise from a variation in which the accuser begins the sequence with low power relative to the transgressor. In this situation the accuser might simply drop her or his complaint on the grounds that to pursue it further would be deleterious to long-term interests. It may simply be impossible for a low-power person to gain satisfaction. For this reason, an accuser's deontic anger met with anger from the protagonist might cause a low-power accuser (afraid of the protagonist) simply to give up. (How often do we tell ourselves, "It's just not worth fighting"?)

Other possibilities abound—a reason why we have focused on moral accountability as a conceptual domain ripe with unanswered questions worth addressing with future theory and research. Consider, for example, transgressors who react with mere embarrassment. Unlike shame and guilt, embarrassment is usually not associated with a moral viola-

tion. Rather, we feel embarrassment when we make a social error or do something that makes us look foolish (Keltner & Anderson, 2000; Keltner, Young, & Buswell, 1997). The associated behavioral tendency is to hide or cover one's face (Keltner & Buswell, 1997). When we see another individual become embarrassed, our typical response is to assist them in "face-saving" (Goffmann, 1956, 1967; Wagatsuma & Rosett, 1986). For example, we might help the embarrassed person generate an excuse ("she's new and didn't know the rules") or minimize the harm ("he really didn't hurt anyone"). This usual situation does not quite fit the case of deontic anger, however, and it remains an open question how an angry accuser will respond when a transgressor displays mere embarrassment.

For serious violations there is likely to be some negotiation in an attempt to achieve a shared understanding of the event. It could be that the accuser accepts the transgressor's nonmoral understanding of the event. If so, then mutual face-saving should result. It could also be that the transgressor comes to accept the moral understanding. If so, then guilt or shame should result. In either case, the matter could be settled along the lines already explored.

A final possibility could occur when the normative violation is very serious. If the moral harm is especially egregious, the accuser might insist on an acknowledgment of an ethical violation. This would seem most likely when the norm is one that is saturated with important underlying values. In this regard it is also important to consider the public nature of moral transgressions. Seeing a norm flouted, and then not treated as a moral issue, could inspire other acts of rebellion. Consequently, if the transgression is enacted on a public stage where others can understand the implications, it seems more likely that the accuser will insist that issue be treated as an ethical one and might thus work for a harsh punishment.

CONCLUSION

We have devoted this chapter to articulating what we call the deontic response to injustice. As we have discussed, the deontic response occurs when another individual violates normative standards to which we adhere. It is, of course, only one possible reaction to an unfair event. We might also be concerned with our group standing and/or with future economic opportunity (Cropanzano, Byrne, Bobocel, & Rupp, 2001; Cropanzano, Rupp, Mohler, & Schminke, 2001). The uniqueness of the deontic response is based on more than the fact that it is caused by ethical transgressions. In addition, this response has at least five attributes. In particular, the deontic response may be automatically engaged, ex-

hibits short-term economic irrationality, has retribution as an end, possesses mechanisms for reconciliation, and is driven by our emotions. Finally, the deontic response has interpsychic implications. In this regard, we discussed variations on two sequences of relatively lawful dyadic transactions that occur as a result of the deontic response. Of course, much remains for future scholarship. We believe, however, that seeking to understand the deontic response can be a productive domain for future inquiry.

REFERENCES

Ambrose, M. L., & Kulik, C. T. (2001). How do I know that's fair? A cognitive categorization approach to fairness judgments. In S. W. Gilliland, D. D. Steiner, & D. P. Skarlicki (Eds.), *Theoretical and cultural perspectives on organizational justice* (pp. 35–62). Greenwich, CT: Information Age.

Ambrose, M. L., Seabright, M. A., & Schminke, M. (2002). Sabotage in the workplace: The role of organizational justice. *Organizational Behavior and Human Decision Processes, 89,* 947–965.

Aquino, K., Tripp, T. M., & Bies, R. J. (2001). How employees respond to personal offense: The effects of blame attribution, victim status, and offender status on revenge and reconciliation in the workplace. *Journal of Applied Psychology, 86,* 52–59.

Ashkanasy, N., Härtel, C., & Zerbe, W. (2000). Emotions in the workplace: Research, theory, and practice. In N. Ashkanasy, C. Härtel., & W. Zerbe (Eds.), *Emotions in the workplace* (pp. 3–18). Westport, CT: Quorum Books.

Bargh, J. A., Chaiken, S., Raymond, P., & Hymes, C. (1996). The automatic evaluation effect: Unconditional automatic attitude activation with a pronunciation task. *Journal of Experimental Social Psychology, 32,* 104–128.

Bargh, J. A., Litt, J., Pratto, F., & Spielman, L. A. (1989). On the preconscious evaluation of social stimuli. In A. F. Bennett & K. M. McConkey (Eds.), *Cognition in individual and social contexts: Proceedings of the XXV International Congress of Psychology* (pp. 357–370). Amsterdam: Elsevier.

Bies, R. J. (1987). The predicament of injustice: The management of moral outrage. In L. L. Cummings & B. M. Staw (Eds.) *Research in organizational behavior* (Vol. 9, pp. 289–319). Greenwich, CT: JAI Press.

Bies, R. J. (2001). Interactional (in)justice: The sacred and profane. In J. Greenberg & R. Cropanzano (Eds.), *Advances in organizational justice* (pp. 89–118). Stanford, CA: Stanford University Press.

Bies, R. J., & Tripp, T. M. (1995). Beyond distrust: "Getting even" and the need for revenge. In F. Kramer & T. Tyler (Eds.), *Trust in organizations* (pp. 246–260). Thousand Oaks, CA: Sage.

Bies, R. J., & Tripp, T. M. (2001). A passion for justice: The rationality and morality of revenge. In R. Cropanzano (Ed.), *Justice in the workplace* (pp. 197–208). Mahwah, NJ: Lawrence Erlbaum Associates.

Bies, R. J., & Tripp, T. M. (2002). "Hot flashes, open wounds": Injustice and the tyranny of its emotions. In S. W. Gilliland, D. D. Steiner, & D. P. Skarlicki (Eds.), *Emerging perspectives on managing organizational justice* (pp. 203–221). Greenwich, CT: Information Age.

Bies, R. J., Tripp, T. M., & Kramer, R. M. (1997). At the breaking point: Cognitive and social dynamics of revenge in organizations. In R. A. Giacalone & J. Greenberg (Eds.), *Antisocial behavior in organizations* (pp. 18–36). Thousand Oaks, CA: Sage.

Blau, P. M. (1986). *Exchange and power in social life*. New Brunswick, NJ: Transaction.

Bobocel, D., McCline, R., & Folger, R. (1997). Letting them down gently: Conceptual advances in explaining controversial organizational policies. In C. I. Cooper & D. M. Rousseua (Eds.), *Trends in organizational behavior* (Vol. 4, pp. 73–88). Chichester, Sussex: John Wiley & Sons.

Bowles, S., & Gintis, H. (2002). Homo reciprocans. *Nature, 415,* 125–128.

Brockner, J., & Wiesenfeld, B. (1996). An integrative framework for explaining reactions to decisions: Interactive effects of outcomes and procedures. *Psychological Bulletin, 120,* 189–208.

Cahn, E. (1949). *The sense of injustice*. New York: New York University Press.

Carlsmith, K. M., Darley, J. M., & Robinson, P. H. (2002). Why do we punish? Deterrence and just deserts as motives for punishment. *Journal of Personality and Social Psychology, 83,* 284–299.

Collie, T., Bradley, G., & Sparks, B. A. (2002). Fair process revisited: Differential effects of interactional and procedural justice in the presence of social comparison information. *Journal of Experimental Social Psychology, 38,* 545–555.

Colquitt, J. A., & Chertkoff, J. M. (2002). Explaining injustice: The interactive effect of explanation and outcome on fairness perceptions and task motivation. *Journal of Management, 28,* 598–610.

Cosmides, L. (1989). The logic of social exchange: Has natural selection shaped how we reason? *Cognition, 31,* 187–276.

Cosmides, L., & Tooby, J. (1987). From evolution to behavior: Evolutionary psychology as the missing link. In J. Depre (Ed.), *The latest on the best: Essays on evolution and optimality* (pp. 277–306). Cambridge, MA: MIT Press.

Cosmides, L., & Tooby, J. (1989). Evolutionary psychology and the generation of culture, Part II: Case study: A computational model of social exchange. *Ethology and Sociobiology, 10,* 51–98.

Cropanzano, R., Byrne, Z. S., Bobocel, D. R., & Rupp, D. R. (2001). Moral virtues, fairness heuristics, social entities, and other denizens of organizational justice. *Journal of Vocational Behavior, 58,* 164–209.

Cropanzano, R., Chrobot-Mason, D., Rupp, D. E., & Prehar, C. A. (2004). Accountability for corporate injustice. *Human Resource Management Review, 14,* 107–134.

Cropanzano, R., Goldman, B. M., & Folger, R. (2003). Deontic justice: The role of moral principles in workplace fairness. *Journal of Organizational Behavior, 24,* 1019–1024.

Cropanzano, R., & Rupp, D. E. (2002). Some reflections on the morality of organizational justice. In S. W. Gilliland, D. D. Steiner, & D. P. Skarlicki (Eds.), *Emerging perspectives on managing organizational justice* (pp. 225–278). Greenwich, CT: Information Age.

Cropanzano, R., Rupp, D. E., Mohler, C. J., & Schminke, M. (2001). Three roads to organizational justice. In J. Ferris (Ed.), *Research in personnel and human resources management* (Vol. 20, pp. 1–113). Greenwich, CT: JAI Press.

Cropanzano, R., Weiss, H. M., Suckow, K., & Grandey, A. A. (2000). Doing justice to workplace emotions. In N. Ashkanasy, C. Hartel, & W. Zerbe (Eds.), *Emotions at work* (pp. 49–62). Westport, CT: Quorum Books.

DaGloria, J., & DeRidder, R. (1977). Aggression in dyadic interaction. *European Journal of Social Psychology, 7,* 189–219.

DaGloria, J., & DeRidder, R. (1979). Sex differences in aggression: Are current notions misleading? *European Journal of Social Psychology, 9,* 49–66.

Darwin, C. (1972). *The expression of emotions in man and animals.* Chicago: University of Chicago Press. (Original work published 1965)

De Houwer, J., Hermans, D., & Spruyt, A. (2001). Affective priming of pronunciation responses: Effects of target degradation. *Journal of Experimental Social Psychology, 37,* 85–91.

de Waal, F. (1996). *Good natured: The origins of right and wrong in humans and other animals.* Cambridge, MA: Harvard University Press.

Dijksterhuis, A., & Aarts, H. (2003). On wildebeests and humans: The preferential detection of negative stimuli. *Psychological Science, 14,* 14–18.

Dimberg, U., & Öhman, A. (1996). Behold the wrath: Psychophysiological responses to facial stimuli. *Motivation and Emotion, 20,* 149–182.

Ekman, P. (1984). Expression and the nature of emotion. In K. Scherer & P. Ekman (Eds.), *Approaches to emotion* (pp. 319–343). Hillsdale, NJ: Lawrence Erlbaum Associates.

Ekman, P. (1992). An argument for basic emotions. *Cognition and Emotion, 6,* 169–200.

Ellard, J. H., & Skarlicki, D. P. (2002). A third-party observer's reactions to employee mistreatment: Motivational and cognitive processes in deservingness assessments. In S. W. Gilliland, D. D. Steiner, & D. P. Skarlicki (Eds.), *Emerging perspectives on managing organizational justice* (pp. 133–158). Greenwich, CT: Information Age.

Fazio, R. H., Sanbonmatsu, D. W., Powell, M. C., & Kardes, F. R. (1986). On the automatic activation of attitudes. *Journal of Personality and Social Psychology, 50,* 229–238.

Fehr, E., & Gächter, S. (2000). Cooperation and punishment in public goods experiments. *American Economic Review, 90,* 980–994.

Fehr, E., & Gächter, S. (2002). Altruistic punishment in humans. *Nature, 415,* 137–140.

Ferrell, O. C., & Fraedich, J. (1997). *Business ethics: Ethical decision making and cases* (3rd ed.). Boston: Houghton Mifflin.

Folger, R. (1987). Reformulating the preconditions of resentment: A referent cognitions model. In J. C. Masters & W. P. Smith (Eds.), *Social comparison, justice, and relative deprivation: Theoretical, empirical, and policy perspectives* (pp. 183–215). Hillsdale, NJ: Lawrence Erlbaum Associates.

Folger, R. (1994). Workplace justice and employee worth. *Social Justice Research, 7,* 225–241.

Folger, R. (1998). Fairness as a moral virtue. In M. Schminke (Ed.), *Managerial ethics: Moral management of people and processes* (pp. 13–34). Mahwah, NJ: Lawrence Erlbaum Associates.

Folger, R. (2001). Fairness as deonance. In S. W. Gilliland, D. D. Steiner, & D. P. Skarlicki (Eds.), *Research in social issues in management* (Vol. 1, pp. 3–33). New York: Information Age.

Folger, R., & Cropanzano, R. (1998). *Organizational justice and human resource management.* Thousand Oaks, CA: Sage.

Folger, R., & Cropanzano, R. (2001). Fairness theory: Justice as accountability. In J. Greenberg & R. Cropanzano (Eds.), *Advances in organizational justice* (pp. 89–118). Stanford, CA: Stanford University Press.

Folger, R., Cropanzano, R., & Van den Bos, K. (2002). *Moral affect and work motives: "I'm mad as hell and ..."* Unpublished manuscript. University of Central Florida, Orlando.

Fukuyama, F. (1999). *The great disruption: Human nature and the reconstitution of social order*. New York: Free Press.

Gilliland, S. W., Benson, L. III, & Schepers, D. H. (1998). A rejection threshold in justice evaluations: Effects on judgment and decision-making. *Organizational Behavior and Human Decision Processes, 76,* 113–131.

Goffman, E. (1956). Embarrassment and social organization. *American Journal of Sociology, 62,* 264–271.

Goffman, E. (1967). *Interaction ritual: Essays on face-to-face behavior.* Garden City, NY: Anchor.

Goldman, B. (2003). The application of referent cognitions theory to legal-claiming by terminated workers: The role of organizational justice and anger. *Journal of Management, 29,* 705–728.

Goldman, B., & Thatcher, S. M. B. (2002). A social information processing view of organizational justice. In S. W. Gilliland, D. D. Steiner, & D. P. Skarlicki (Eds.), *Emerging perspectives on managing organizational justice* (pp. 103–130). Greenwich, CT: Information Age.

Greenberg, J. (1993). Stealing in the name of justice: Informational and interpersonal moderators of theft reactions to underpayment inequity. *Organizational Behavior and Human Decision Processes, 54,* 81–103.

Greenberg, J. (2002). Who stole the money, and when? Individual and situational determinants of employee theft. *Organizational Behavioral and Human Decision Processes, 89,* 985–1003.

Greenwald, A. G., Klinger, M. R., & Liu, T. J. (1989). Unconscious processing of dichotically masked words. *Memory and Cognition, 17,* 35–47.

Groth, M., Goldman, B., Gilliland, S., & Bies, R. (2002). Commitment to legal-claiming: Influences of attributions, social guidance, and organizational tenure. *Journal of Applied Psychology, 87,* 781–788.

Hermans, D., De Houwer, J., & Eelen, P. (1994). The affective priming of effect: Automatic activation of evaluative information in memory. *Cognition and Emotion, 8,* 515–533.

Jones, D. A., & Skarlicki, D. (2003, April). *Integrating fairness theory with fairness heuristic theory: Reactions to interactional justice.* Manuscript presented at the annual meeting of the Society for Industrial and Organizational Psychology, Orlando, FL.

Kahneman, D., Knetsch, J. L., & Thaler, R. H. (1986). Fairness and the assumptions of economics. *Journal of Business, 59,* 285–300.

Kahneman, D., & Miller, D. T. (1986). Norm theory: Comparing reality to its alternatives. *Psychological Review, 93,* 136–153.

Kahneman, D., & Tversky, A. 1982. Availability and the simulation heuristic. In D. Kahneman, P. Slovic, & A. Tversky (Eds.), *Judgment under uncertainty: Heuristics and biases* (pp. 201–208). New York: Oxford University Press.

Katz, L. D. (Ed.). (2000). *Evolutionary origins of morality: Cross-disciplinary perspectives.* Bowling Green, OH: Imprint Academic.

Kelly, J. R., & Barsade, S. G. (2001). Mood and emotions in small groups and work teams. *Organizational Behavior and Human Decision Processes, 86,* 99–130.

Keltner, D., & Anderson, C. (2000). Saving face for Darwin: The functions and uses of embarrassment. *Current Directions in Psychological Science, 9,* 187–191.

Keltner, D., & Buswell, B. (1997). Embarrassment: Its distinct form and appeasement functions. *Psychological Bulletin, 122,* 250–270.

Keltner, D., & Harker, L. A. (1998). The forms and functions of the nonverbal signal of shame. In P. Gilbert & B. Andrews (Eds), *Shame: Interpersonal behavior, psychopathology, and culture* (pp. 78–98). New York: Oxford University Press.

Keltner, D., Young, R. C., & Buswell, B. N. (1997). Appeasement in human emotion, social practice, and personality. *Aggressive Behavior, 23,* 359–374.

Krehbiel, P. J., & Cropanzano, R. (2000). Procedural justice, outcome favorability, and emotion. *Social Justice Research, 13,* 337–358.

Liberman, M. D., Gaunt, R., Gilbert, D. T., & Trope, Y. (2002). Reflexion and reflection: A social cognitive neuroscience approach to attributional inference. In M. P. Zanna (Ed.), *Advances in experimental social psychology* (Vol. 34, pp. 199–249). New York: Academic Press.

Lieberman, J. K. (1981). *The litigious society.* New York: Basic Books.

Lind, E. A. (2001). Fairness heuristic theory: Justice judgments as pivotal cognitions in organizational relations. In J. Greenberg & R. Cropanzano (Eds.), *Advances in organizational justice* (pp. 56–88). Stanford, CA: Stanford University Press.

Lourenco, O. (2000). The aretaic domain and its relation to the deontic domain in moral reasoning. In M. Laupa (Ed.), *New directions for child and adolescent development: Rights and wrongs: How children and young adults evaluate the world* (pp. 47–61). San Francisco, CA: Jossey-Bass/Pfeiffer.

Margalit, A. (2003). *The ethics of memory.* Cambridge, MA: Harvard University Press.

Masterson, S. S., Lewis, K., Goldman, B. M., & Taylor, M. S. (2000). Integrating justice and social exchange: The differing effects of fair procedures and treatment on work relationships. *Academy of Management Journal, 43,* 738–748.

Murphy, S., & Zajonc, R. (1993). Affect, cognition and awareness: Affective priming with suboptimal and optimal stimuli. *Journal of Personality and Social Psychology, 64,* 723–729.

Niedenthal, P., Halberstadt, J. B., & Innes-Her, A. H. (1999). Emotional response contagion. *Psychological Review, 106,* 337–361.

Niedenthal, P., Tangney, J. P., & Gavanski, I. (1994). "If only I weren't" vs. "If only I hadn't": Distinguishing shame and guilt in counterfactual thinking. *Journal of Personality and Social Psychology, 67,* 585–595.

O'Malley, M. N., & Greenberg, J. (1983). Sex differences in restoring justice. The "down payment effect." *Journal of Research in Personality, 17,* 174–185.

Paddock, E. L., Goldman, B. M., & Gilliland, S. W. (2003, April). *Revisiting the fairness threshold model: Differences in distributive, procedural, and interactional justice.* Manuscript presented at the annual meeting of the Society for Industrial and Organizational Psychology, Orlando, FL.

Parkinson, R. (1996). Emotions are social. *British Journal of Psychology, 87,* 663–683.

Pinker, S. (2002). *The blank slate: The modern denial of human nature.* New York: Viking Press.

Poulson, C., II. (2000). Shame and work. In N. Ashkanasy, C. Härtel., & W. Zerbe (Eds.), *Emotions in the workplace* (pp. 250–271). Westport, CT: Quorum Books.

Pugh, S. D. (2001). Service with a smile: Emotional contagion in the service encounter. *Academy of Management Journal, 44,* 1018–1027.

Rawls, J. (1963). The sense of justice. *Philosophical Review, 72,* 281–305.

Roese, N. J. (1997). Counterfactual thinking. *Psychological Bulletin, 121,* 133–148.

Roese, N. J., & Olsen, J. M. (1995). *What might have been: The social psychology of counterfacutual thinking.* Mahwah, NJ: Lawrence Erlbaum Associates.

Rupp, D. E. (2003, April). *Testing the moral violations component of fairness theory: The moderating role of values preferences.* Manuscript presented at the annual meeting of the Society for Industrial and Organizational Psychology, Orlando, FL.

Schminke, M. (1998). The magic punchbowl: A nonrational model of ethical management. In M. Schmike (Ed.), *Managerial ethics: Moral management of people and processes* (pp. 197–214). Mahwah, NJ: Lawrence Erlbaum Associates.

Shaw, J., Wild, E., & Colquitt, J. (2003). To justify or excuse?: A meta-analytic review or the effects of explanations. *Journal of Applied Psychology, 88,* 444–458.

Singer, P. (1979). *Practical Ethics.* Cambridge, UK: Cambridge University Press.

Singer, P. (2001). *Animal liberation.* New York: HarperCollins.

Skarlicki, D. P., & Folger, R. (1997). Retaliation in the workplace: The roles of distributive, procedural, and interactional justice. *Journal of Applied Psychology, 82,* 434–443.

Skarlicki, D. P., Folger, R., & Tesluck, P. (1999). Personality as a moderator in the relationship between fairness and retaliation. *Academy of Management Journal, 42,* 100–108.

Solomon, R. C. (1990). *A passion for justice: Emotions and the origins of the social contract.* Reading, MA: Addison-Wesley.

Tangney, J. P. (1995). Shame and guilt in interpersonal relationships. In J. P. Tangney & K. W. Fischer (Eds.), *Self-conscious emotions: Shame, guilt, and embarrassment, and pride* (pp. 114–139). New York: John Wiley & Sons.

Tangney, J. P., & Fischer, K. W. (Eds.). (1995). *Self-conscious emotions: Shame, guilt, and embarrassment, and pride.* New York: John Wiley & Sons.

Tangney, J. P., Miller, R. S., Flicker, L., & Barlow, D. H. (1996). Are shame, guilt and embarrassment distinct emotions? *Journal of Personality and Social Psychology, 70,* 1256–1269.

Tangney, J. P., Wagner, P. E., Hill-Barlow, D., Marshall, D. E., & Gramzow, R. (1996). Relation of shame and guilt to constructive versus destructive responses to anger across the lifespan. *Journal of Personality and Social Psychology, 70,* 797–809.

Tooby, J., & Cosmides, L. (1989). Evolutionary psychology and the generation of culture, Part I: Theoretical considerations. *Ethology and Sociobiology, 10,* 29–49.

Tooby, J., & Cosmides, L. (1990). The past explains the present. Emotional adaptations and the structure of ancestral environments. *Ethology and Sociobiology, 11,* 375–424.

Treviño, L. K. (1986). Ethical decision-making in organizations: A person–situation interactionist model. *Academy of Management Review, 11,* 601–627,

Turillo, C. J., Folger, R., Lavelle, J. J., Umphress, E., & Gee, J. (2002). Is virtue its own reward? Self-sacrificial decisions for the sake of fairness. *Organizational Behavior and Human Decision Processes, 89,* 839–865.

Tyler, T. R., & Bies, R. J. (1990). Beyond formal procedures: The interpersonal context of procedural justice. In J. Carroll (Ed.), *Applied social psychology and organizational settings* (pp. 77–98). Hillsdale, NJ: Lawrence Erlbaum Associates.

Van den Bos, K. (2001). Fairness heuristic theory: Assessing the information to which people are reacting has a pivotal role in understanding organizational justice. In S. W. Gilliland, D. D. Steiner, & D. P. Skarlicki (Eds.), *Theoretical and cultural perspectives on organizational justice* (pp. 63–84). Greenwich, CT: Information Age.

Van den Bos, K., Lind, E. A., & Wilke, H. A. M. (2001). The psychology of procedural and distributive justice viewed from the perspective of fairness heuristic theory. In R. Cropanzano (Ed.), *Justice in the workplace (Vol. 2): From theory to practice* (pp. 49–66). Mahwah, NJ: Lawrence Erlbaum Associates.

Velasquez, M. G. (2001). *Business ethics: Concepts and cases* (5th Ed.). Upper Saddle River, NJ: Pearson Education.

Vermunt, R., & Steensma, H. (2001). Stress and justice in organizations: An exploration into justice processes with the aim to find mechanisms to reduce stress. In R. Cropanzano (Ed.), *Justice in the workplace: From theory to practice* (Vol. 2, pp. 27–48). Mahwah, NJ: Lawrence Erlbaum Associates.

Von Wright, G. H. (1963). *Norm and action: A logical enquiry.* London: Routledge & Kegan Paul.

Wagatsuma, H., & Rosett, A. (1986). The implications of apology: law and culture in Japan and the United States. *Law and Society Review, 20*, 461–498.

Weiss, H. M., & Cropanzano, R. (1996). An affective events approach to job satisfaction. In B. M. Staw & L. L. Cummings (Eds.), *Research in organizational behavior* (Vol. 18, pp. 1–74). Greenwich, CT: JAI Press.

Weiss, H. M., Suckow, K., & Cropanzano, R. (1999). Effects of justice conditions on discrete emotions. *Journal of Applied Psychology, 84*, 786–794.

Wilson, J. Q. (1993). *The moral sense.* New York: Free Press.

Wright, R. (1994). *The moral animal: The new science of evolutionary psychology.* New York: Pantheon Books.

Zajonc, R. B. (1998). Emotions. In D. T. Gilbert, S. T. Fiske, & G. Lindzey (Eds.), *Handbook of social psychology* (4th ed., pp. 591–632). Boston: McGraw-Hill.

8

What Is the Role of Trust in Organizational Justice?

Roy J. Lewicki
The Ohio State University

Carolyn Wiethoff
Indiana University—Bloomington

Edward C. Tomlinson
John Carroll University

This chapter reviews the role that trust has played in the organizational justice literature. We review the theory and research already done by justice researchers on the trust–justice interface, dividing that literature into three groups: trust as an outcome of justice (including mediator and moderator relationships), trust as an antecedent of justice, and trust and justice as codeveloping constructs. We then critique the extant work, commenting on ways that the linkages could be strengthened, and also suggesting that justice researchers have not appreciated the complexity of the trust construct. Finally, we introduce selected developments in trust theory, and suggest that our understanding of the trust–justice interrelationship could be strengthened by considering the relational form in which trust and justice co-occur. We conclude with implications for future theory development and empirical investigation.

In the beginning of the 21st century, the United States witnessed an unprecedented wave of corporate fraud, greed, and accounting scandals in companies such as Enron, WorldCom, Tyco, and Adelphia. Numerous stakeholders of these organizations—employees, shareholders, debt holders, and customers—complained loudly about losing their jobs, their investments, and their business relationships, and particularly about being unfairly treated. These stakeholders, and millions of American people who witnessed these events, became less trusting not only of these organizations, but also of all corporations (AFL-CIO, 2001). A significant decline in the stock market was a clear result of this deterioration of trust.

As this example suggests, there is a close relationship between justice, or perceptions of fair treatment from a person or an organization, and resultant trust in that person or organization. Yet in spite of the presumed connections between justice and trust in theory and in practice, the precise association between these constructs has not been fully elaborated. We begin this chapter by describing the current state of the scant literature examining the relationship between trust and justice. We then propose a framework to refine and enhance our understanding of this relationship. This framework is grounded in several principles:

- That two distinct forms of trust—calculus-based and identification-based—can be identified.

- That the relationship between trust and justice can best be understood by examining how these forms of trust are used to evaluate actions within their respective relational contexts.
- That an elaboration of these relational contexts would allow a much richer understanding of how trust and justice are related, and create a research agenda to encourage fuller exploration of their intersection.

PREVIOUS RESEARCH ON THE RELATIONSHIP BETWEEN TRUST AND JUSTICE

Although their review and categorization of the literature did not explicitly address questions of trust, Greenberg and Wiethoff (2001) offered a starting place for a discussion of the relationship between trust and justice. They proposed a sequence of psychological processes likely to be triggered when justice judgments are made. First, an event (stimulus) is perceived by a focal person. This leads to a judgment about the event, categorizing it as "fair" or "unfair," with appropriate subsequent responses. These authors cited considerable empirical evidence indicating that the relative significance of justice judgments is affected by the context in which the events occur, and that primary contextual cues are typically rooted in social interactions. Additionally, they noted that justice perceptions are strongly influenced by the rules and norms established for a particular environment. However, they concluded that the question "How are assessments of justice and injustice affected by the settings in which they occur?" remains an important area for future inquiry (Greenberg & Wiethoff, 2001, p. 280).

We support this call for increased scrutiny of the social/relational context of justice judgments because one of the most clear-cut determinants of a social-emotional context is the trust level between the person perceiving an event and the person or organization responsible for it. This is not a new idea; in fact, a number of researchers have addressed this link. For example, Deutsch (1985) proposed his "crude law of social relationships," stating that "characteristic processes and effects elicited by a given type of social relationship also tend to elicit that type of social relationship" (p. 69), and that trust, fairness, and cooperativeness were closely intertwined.

The Trust–Justice Interrelationship

A number of researchers have tackled the underlying roots of the trust–justice link. Brockner and Siegel (1996) noted that the relationship between the constructs came to the forefront as justice researchers grap-

pled with the complex but consistently occurring correlation between distributive and procedural justice. Our review of this literature reveals three approaches to conceptualizing this correlation. First, trust has been portrayed as a consequence or outcome of justice; second, trust has been viewed as an antecedent of justice, and third, the two constructs have been viewed as closely intertwined and codeveloping. We next explore the literature supporting each of these perspectives.

Trust as an Outcome of Justice.   In their review of 20 field studies, Brockner and Wiesenfeld (1996) affirmed that procedural justice moderated the effect of distributive justice on individuals' reactions to decisions. When procedures were unfair, people responded more favorably when distributive justice was high. When procedures were fair, distributive justice had a smaller effect. Interpreting these results, Brockner and Siegel (1996) proposed that it was not procedural justice per se but the *trust generated by procedurally fair treatment* that governed the interaction. As this review suggests, a number of studies confirm that people's trust in other people and organizations grows as a result of fair treatment. In fact, the majority of research investigating the link between justice and trust falls into this category (e.g., Hartman, Yrle, & Galle, 1998). Trust has been identified as an outcome of distributive (Alexander, Sinclair & Tetrick, 1995), procedural (Konovsky & Cropanzano, 1991; Korsgaard, Brodt, & Whitener, 2002; Korsgaard, Schweiger, & Sapienza, 1995; Mayer, Davis, & Schoorman, 1995), and interactional (Becerra & Gupta, 2003) justice.

Thus, the procedural fairness of an exchange influences perceivers' trust in the exchange partner. Trust, in turn, influences the perceiver's judgment of the time frame and currency of exchange in ways that lead to an interactive effect of trust and outcome favorability on the perceiver's support for decisions, for decision makers, or for organizations (see Whitener, 1997, for application of this relationship to aspects of human resource management). Two sets of studies have shown the robustness of this relationship:

1. Trust as a *mediator* of the relationship between procedural fairness and outcome favorability. Studies by Brockner and colleagues (Brockner, Siegel, Daly, Tyler, & Martin, 1997; Brockner & Wiesenfeld, 1996), Konovsky and Pugh (1994), and Van den Bos, Wilke and Lind (1998) show that people use information about procedural fairness to determine trust in the other party. More recently, Kwok and Leung (2002) found that this relationship was robust only when the focal relationship was important to the actor. Similarly, Aryee, Budhwar, and Chen (2002) demonstrated that trust partially mediated the relationship between distributive/procedural justice and work attitudes

such as job satisfaction, turnover intentions, and organizational commitment, but fully mediated the relationship between interactional justice and these work attitudes.

2. Trust as a *moderator* of the interactive relationship, suggesting that if parties believe the other can be trusted, they are more likely to engage in a sensemaking process about procedural fairness that minimizes the effect of outcome favorability. Studies that explore the ways that cultural differences affect the construal and sensemaking process (e.g., Markus & Kitayama, 1991) support this relationship.

Trust as an Antecedent of Justice. Other researchers contend that trust in the short-term is necessary for just outcomes to be valued, such that trust becomes a prerequisite for justice. Two complementary perspectives have emerged. First, the *self-interest model* argues that people are motivated to maximize their personal outcomes—particularly those that are tangible and concrete. However, because tangible and concrete outcomes are not always immediately obtainable, people depend on social exchange relationships that entail more intangible, unspecified future obligations and rewards (Blau, 1964). Simply put, people trust others in exchange relationships, and this strengthens their belief that fairness will eventually be delivered in the long term (Konovsky & Pugh, 1994). To the extent that they trust that the procedures providing their outcomes are fair, people are willing to trust that desired outcomes will be delivered over time. Thus, "trust in the process" allows relationships to continue even when they may not deliver fairness in the short-term.

Similarly, Lind and Tyler (1988) proposed the *group value* (or *relational*) model. This model contends that people value relationships with individuals, groups, and organizations because they develop identity and self-worth through social relationships (Tajfel & Turner, 1979). Being treated fairly in their social relationships satisfies individuals' needs for self-esteem and positive self-identity (Lind & Tyler, 1988). The more fairly individuals are treated by their social groups, the more valued they come to view themselves as members of those groups (Brockner, Tyler, & Cooper-Schneider, 1992). Thus, people maintain memberships only in those groups or organizations that they trust will treat them in a fair and positive way.

As these models have evolved, the operationalization of trust used by these researchers has also transformed. Early studies started out talking about trust as a characteristic of the perceiver, but more recent authors shifted to talking about *trustworthiness* (a characteristic of the receiver; Tyler, 1994) or *benevolence* (Lind, Tyler, & Huo, 1997). This "erosion" away from more commonly accepted definitions of trust is indicative of the imprecision complicating our understanding of the trust–justice relationship.

Trust and Justice Codevelop.   Brockner and Siegel (1996) extensively explored the shared antecedents of justice and trust. This work
suggests that one particular determinant of the development of both
trust and justice is the other party's *stability*—that is, whether the past
is a good predictor of the other party's behavior in the future. Inferences about stability are drawn by examining both structural and interpersonal components of the relationship. Structural components
(e.g., organizational settings, rules, mechanisms, or practices) tend to
be relatively stable over time. Thus, both trust and justice perceptions
are developed when decisions are grounded in rules, practices, and
mechanisms that are unlikely to change suddenly or capriciously. In
contrast, interpersonal contexts reflect how one has been treated by
another in the recent past. The other's previous behavior and
dispositional tendencies are likely to shape someone's expectations of
how he or she will be treated by the other in the future. These components can be relatively unstable in the short term, but as one grows to
know and understand the other, trust and justice perceptions become
more stable as expectations for treatment are consistently confirmed.
Brockner and colleagues (Brockner, 2002; Brockner & Wiesenfeld,
1996; Brockner et al., 1997) elaborately explored these variables in subsequent work.

Additionally, in a seminal paper furthering our understanding of the
justice–trust relationship, Lind (2001) argued that judgments of interpersonal fairness are a proxy (heuristic) for trust in decisions about
whether or not to cooperate with others. Fairness heuristic theory
(Lind, 2001; see also Kelley, 1966) first recognizes a fundamental tension
between individual and social action: People can attain better results by
affiliating with others, but such affiliation carries risks of exploitation
and restriction. Efforts to resolve this "fundamental social dilemma"
suggest that people search for proxies, or heuristics, to make decisions
about joining a group. For example, one common heuristic is to determine whether the time and energy one will invest will yield sufficient
rewards and gains. Another is to determine how much someone values
the identity established as a result of the roles, relationships, or organizations represented by the group. Judgments about whether one is receiving fair treatment or not, Lind argued, serve as a surrogate for
interpersonal trust. To quote Lind (2001):

> People use fairness judgments in much the same way that they would re-
> fer to feelings of trust—if they had an independent basis for forming
> trust—to decide how to react to demands in a long-standing personal re-
> lationship. We come to use our impressions of fairness as a guide and to
> regulate our investment and involvement in various relationships to
> match the level of fairness that we experience. (pp. 65–66)

Lind and colleagues (Lind & Van den Bos, 2002; Van den Bos & Lind, 2002) extended fairness heuristic theory to suggest that the ultimate reason people care about unfairness is to contend with uncertainty. Under conditions of uncertainty, when individuals are unaware of specific reasons to trust another, they will use procedural fairness information as the critical heuristic in the decision to trust. Van den Bos and colleagues (1998) claimed support for this view through a laboratory experiment in which the prior reputation of an authority figure for trustworthiness was manipulated. These authors found that procedural fairness information was not as necessary when subjects were informed of the authority figure's trustworthy reputation. On the other hand, procedural information was heavily relied on when no reputational information was provided.

Critique of This Work

The volume of both theoretical and empirical work over the last 15 years clearly points to a strong relationship between trust and justice, particularly procedural justice. However, our analysis suggests that when the relationship between trust and justice has been predominantly been explored from the "justice side," many of the finer distinctions about trust, such as components and contributors to trust itself, or trust versus trustworthiness, have been ignored. We see at least four major ways that this perspective limits our understanding of the trust–justice relationship:

1. The argument that fairness is a heuristic or *substitute* for trust (Lind, 2001) implies that trust is really "all about fairness"—that is, that the fairness heuristic adequately explains everything we need to know about trust. This argument ignores the richness of the trust construct. Moreover, the empirical literature validating the trust heuristic reflects a relationship that is not as compelling as has been asserted. For example, Van den Bos and colleagues (1998) operationalized trust only as "reputation," ignoring many of its other facets. In addition, in this study, the manipulation of procedural fairness was to allow subjects the opportunity for voice. But voice is not a "clean" justice manipulation; opportunities for voice can be considered an act of benevolence by the superior, and benevolence is often included as a key component of trust (Mayer et al., 1995). And, as previously noted, Tyler (1994) and other researchers allowed the construct of trust to evolve into merely "benevolence." Finally, although procedural justice may lead to trust, this does not lead to the conclusion that procedural fairness is a heuristic for trust. The trust literature clearly suggests that the use of fair procedures facilitates the development of trust, but that does not mean procedural justice is a substitute for trust.

2. The rich and diverse literature on trust suggests that there are many other ways to understand and account for it. Certainly, fairness has been cited in both theoretical (Whitener, 1997) and empirical (Brockner et al., 1997) works as being a strong contributor to trust, as supported by the research showing justice is an antecedent of trust. However, many other factors enhance the development of trust and trustworthiness in relationships (Bews & Rossouw, 2002). These include openness (willingness to be open and transparent in one's actions and intentions), integrity (adherence to principles and willingness to follow through on commitments), benevolence (the desire to do good toward the other), competency (having skills and capabilities in a key relationship context), and the past history of interaction between the parties (past trust begets expectations of present and future trust), just to name a few (see also Mayer et al., 1995). Existing justice research tends to treat trust as an outcome or code-terminant fully or significantly explained by justice, and this is too simplistic for a complete conceptualization of trust.

3. Other elements commonly associated with procedural justice are also contributors to the development of trust. For example, Leventhal (1980) argued that consistency and ethicality are components of justice perceptions, but these qualities are subsumed under Mayer and colleagues' definition of "integrity" as a key trust component. Although other research can be brought to bear in support of this critique, we argue that much justice research has not attended to the complexity of trust, and efforts to empirically support the trust–justice relationship are confounded by manipulations that oversimplify trust and measures that do not cleanly separate trust-inducing from justice-inducing processes.

4. Finally, no assessments of the trust–justice link in the justice literature provide a fine-grained understanding or analysis of the rich trust literature. None explore the emerging research suggesting multiple forms of trust (Lewicki & Bunker, 1995, 1996; McAllister, 1995), nor do they suggest that trust varies as a function of the relational form in which it exists (Fiske, 1991; Sheppard & Tuchinsky, 1996).

Trust Researchers' Treatment of Justice

Although we have argued that justice researchers have inadequately understood the complexity and component elements of trust, in "fairness," we also should examine how trust researchers have tried to understand and use the fine grained distinctions made by justice researchers. The results are mixed. Some trust researchers include justice in their discussion of constructs, but only casually. Mayer, Davis, and Schoorman (1995), who defined integrity as one core component

of trust, indicated that integrity includes "a belief that the trustee has a strong sense of justice" (p. 719), but also indicated a number of other component parts of integrity, such as credibility, consistency, value congruence, and so on. Similarly, Butler (1991) indicated that fairness is a component of trust in one's manager, but provided no further discussion of fairness. A second group of researchers dealt with issues that are very conceptually similar to those raised in justice research, but did not explicitly draw that connection. McAllister (1995) indicated that affect-based trust is grounded in a strong sense of interpersonal care and concern, suggesting a linkage to interactional justice, but did not elaborate further. Similarly, Bies and Tripp (1996) discussed different types of trust violations that could be connected to different types of justice violations, including distributive, procedural, and interactional justice, but did not explicitly draw the links. Finally, a third group of trust researchers more explicitly juxtaposed justice and trust. Korsgaard and colleagues (Korsgaard et al., 1995; Sapienza & Korsgaard, 1996) explored the relationship between trust and procedural justice. Whitener (1997) explored a number of ways managers can engineer the trust of their subordinates, specifically referring to managing justice processes, including "sharing and delegation of control" (increased procedural justice) and "demonstration of concern" (interactional justice). Finally, Bottom, Gibson, Daniels, and Murnighan (2002) posited that "cheap talk" restores cooperation and positive attitudinal/emotional reactions, an argument that is clearly grounded in the interactional justice literature.

Summary of Previous Research on the Trust–Justice Link

Thus far, we have reviewed theory and research that explored the trust–justice linkage. The justice literature represents three related views: trust as a consequence of justice, trust as an antecedent of justice, and trust and justice as coevolving perceptions. As others read this work, we hope they recognize—as we do—that the distinction between these views is often narrow and slippery. It is difficult to robustly sustain either the causality or the codetermination arguments. Moreover, although we have indicted justice researchers for being "too simple on trust," we find evidence that the reverse is also true. Both situations make the problem of disentangling the trust–justice linkage more difficult.

In the remaining sections, we hope to enrich understanding of the trust–justice interface by elaborating the complexity of that interface, rather than simply trying to track causality through past work. Our thesis is that the trust–justice relationship can be better understood by expanding the narrow construal of trust used in past work, particularly by examining justice judgments more precisely within the context of dif-

ferent relational forms. In the next section, we explore how the two most commonly accepted kinds of trust—calculus-based and identification-based (Lewicki & Bunker, 1995, 1996; Lewicki & Wiethoff, 2001)—develop and operate within specific relational contexts.

THE TRUST CONSTRUCT

Trust has been of interest to behavioral scientists for almost half a century (Deutsch, 1958, 1960, 1962). In the 1960s and 1970s, trust received attention as social scientists examined the structure of interdependence and the relationship between trust and cooperation at the interpersonal (Deutsch, 1962) and organizational (Arrow, 1974; Barnard, 1938; Sitkin, 1995) levels. Our review primarily focuses on trust at the interpersonal level, because this is the primary arena in which trust has been analyzed in work contexts.

There are numerous definitions of trust (cf. Bigley & Pearce, 1998; Kramer, 1999; Kramer & Tyler, 1996; Rousseau, Sitkin, Burt, & Camerer, 1998). One commonly used definition suggests that trust is "a belief in, and willingness to act on the basis of, the words, actions and decisions of another" (Lewicki, McAllister, & Bies, 1998, p. 440; McAllister, 1995). Based on a comprehensive review of many scholarly perspectives, Rousseau et al. (1998) derived a similar definition: "Trust is a psychological state comprising the intention to accept vulnerability based upon positive expectations of the intentions or behavior of another" (p. 395).

Although there has been emerging consensus on a common definition of trust, some other important distinctions about trust are less well integrated with one another. Although this chapter cannot perform that integrative task, it is important for justice researchers to understand some additional parameters.

There Are Several Forms of Trust

Many early researchers spoke about trust as having a single form (e.g., Deutsch, 1960, 1962). Yet most contemporary trust researchers argue that trust takes qualitatively different forms based on the degree to which it has been cultivated within an interpersonal relationship. For example, Lewicki and Bunker (1995, 1996) proposed a model of trust development that has become widely used in the current literature. They suggested two[1] fundamental forms of trust:

---

[1]Earlier theoretical work (Lewicki & Bunker, 1995, 1996; Shapiro, Sheppard, & Cheraskin, 1992) also proposed a third form: knowledge-based trust, grounded in the trustor's knowledge of the trustee. However, further elaboration of that model suggested that knowledge was more likely a dimension of the relationship between the parties rather than a dimension of trust. Hence we have deleted knowledge-based trust from this discussion.

Calculus-based trust (CBT) is a market-oriented calculation in which people decide to trust based on the belief that trust will not be violated because the rewards of being trusting (or trustworthy), coupled with the potential losses in reputation and punishment for being untrustworthy, outweigh any benefits of violating that trust (Lewicki & Bunker, 1996). This form of trust relies on the perceiver accurately recognizing and understanding the deterrents to trust violations, in addition to the benefits derived from trustworthy behavior.

Identification-based trust (IBT) develops as people come to understand that they share basic values, needs, choices, and preferences. When identification-based trust exists, the parties can act as agents for one another because of their confidence that the other person shares their fundamental values and will protect their interests.

Trust Changes as Relationships Develop

Lewicki and colleagues (Lewicki & Bunker, 1995, 1996; Lewicki & Wiethoff, 2001) also suggested that complex interpersonal trust builds sequentially through these types. Thus, interpersonal relationships normally begin with the most elementary form, CBT. As relationships develop and the parties get to know each other well, they may develop an emotional attachment and recognize strong commonality in interests, attitudes, background or values. Here, IBT can develop to further strengthen the relationship. In a similar vein, Kramer (1999) described the process of trust development as one of initial calibration and subsequent updating based on the degree to which progressively developed expectations are confirmed. As expectations of trustworthy behavior continue to be confirmed by subsequent acts of cooperation, trust is developed at "higher" and "deeper" levels.

Trust Has Both Cognitive and Affective Elements

A third commonly accepted distinction is that trust has both cognitive and affective components. Early definitions of trust described it almost exclusively in cognitive terms. Economists suggested that trust was a form of implicit contracting (Arrow, 1974). Cognitive social and organizational psychologists generally tracked the economic perspective, suggesting that trust was the expectation of how another party would behave in a given transaction (Pearce, Branyiczki, & Bigley, 2000), or confidence in the face of risk (Lewis & Weigert, 1985), or "reliance upon information received from another person about uncertain environmental states and their accompanying outcomes in a risky situation" (Schlenker, Helm, & Tedeschi, 1973). Similarly, psychologists described trust as "the generalized expectation of an individual that the promise

or statement of another individual can be consistently relied upon" (Rotter, 1971, p. 1).

More recent definitions of trust have moved away from the cognitive view to incorporate affective components. Although early definitions acknowledged the emotional component of trust (e.g., Lewis & Weigert, 1985), affect has only recently been regularly introduced into conceptual definitions (McAllister, 1995). Trustworthiness dimensions emphasizing affective elements in addition to cognitive assessment include benevolence-based and value-based trust (Mayer et al., 1995; Sitkin, 1995), identification-based trust (Shapiro, Sheppard, & Cheraskin, 1992; Lewicki & Bunker, 1995), faith (Rempel, Holmes, & Zanna, 1985), emotional trust (Lewis & Weigert, 1985) and liking, or affect-based trust (McAllister, 1995).

Returning to the distinction between CBT and IBT, it would appear that CBT is more of a cognitive form of trust, and IBT is grounded more in affect, identification, and perceived value congruence. Yet it has been argued that CBT can arouse affect, particularly when it is violated (Lewicki & Wiethoff, 2000), and that IBT must contain cognitive components as well. The role of affective components in each form of trust has yet to be clearly stated conceptually, or empirically tested. Moreover, as relationships develop from CBT to IBT, it can be speculated (but has yet to be confirmed) that trust will have a stronger affective component (Robinson, 1996).

The Form of Trust Ties to a Broader Relational Form

In their important synthesis of the trust research literature, Rousseau and colleagues (1998) presented a broader description of CBT and IBT. They described trust as having calculative (CBT) and relational (IBT) forms. Calculus-based trust is "based on rational choice—characteristic of interactions based on economic exchange," whereas relational trust "derives from repeated interactions over time between trustor and trustee," and "information available from within the relationship itself forms the basis of relational trust" (Rousseau et al., 1998, p. 399; see also Kramer, 1999).

A growing body of trust research has moved beyond conceptions of trust as only calculus or deterrence based, in which people are thought to act trustworthily as a result of a rational calculation of the costs of doing so versus the benefits of trust violations. This more modern perspective clearly views trust as a relational dynamic. For example, Mayer and colleagues (1995) explicitly referred to the trustor–trustee relationship and the boundary conditions that define it as critical to understanding trust dynamics. Rousseau and colleagues (1998) described relational trust as interpersonal caring, concern, and value congruence between

exchange partners. Lewicki and Bunker (1995, 1996) defined IBT as a deep mutual understanding of the other, perceived congruity of principles and values, and attraction to the other party. Finally, Dirks and McLean Parks (2002), in their recent review of conflict management research, noted that most current definitions of trust specify both the content of trust (trust on what dimension—implying a transactional view) and a particular referent (trust in whom—implying a relational view).

The Rousseau et al. (1998) distinction is an important one. It suggests that trust not only has different forms containing various combinations of cognition and affect, but that these "forms" of trust may dominate in different forms of relationships (cf. Fiske, 1991; Sheppard & Sherman, 1998; Sheppard & Tuchinsky, 1996). We return to elaborate on this point in the remainder of this chapter.

The Need for Integration

These complex distinctions about trust (identifying different types of trust, tracking its development over time, incorporating various mixtures of cognition and emotion, and invoking different relationship forms as the relationship context changes) are becoming well accepted in the trust literature. Although these perspectives have yet to be fully integrated by trust researchers, bringing them all together will significantly strengthen both trust and justice theorizing.

We argue that the acknowledgment of different forms of trust (broadly categorized as CBT and IBT) that have a basis in different relational forms is critical to a full understanding of the trust–justice interface. We now explore those implications a bit more fully.

TRUST, JUSTICE, AND RELATIONAL FORM: A POSSIBLE AVENUE FOR ENLIGHTENMENT

Our effort in this final section is to "unpack" the relationships between two generalized forms of trust (loosely, CBT and IBT), and the relationship forms in which they dominantly exist, vis-à-vis justice perceptions developed within each relational form. Specifically, we maintain that the relational forms characterized by each kind of trust suggest different standards for justice, such that justice violations would be viewed differently within the context of the two types of relationships.

Relational Forms

In recent years, researchers have moved beyond studying dynamic processes within relationships to understanding the nature of relationships themselves. Relationships can be characterized in numerous ways (cf.

Berscheid & Reis, 1998; Greenhalgh & Chapman, 1996). One important contribution to the organizational literature is the insight that there are dominant forms or types of relationships (Fiske, 1991; Sheppard & Tuchinsky, 1995). Although the social-psychological and organizational literature has often tended to characterize relationships in transactional, economic terms (e.g., Homans, 1961; Jensen & Meckling, 1976; Thibaut & Kelley, 1959; Williamson, 1985) or hierarchical, authority terms (Barnard, 1938), relationship theorists have increasingly stressed that other relational forms—such as "equality matching" or "communal sharing" (Fiske, 1991)—are often commonly found in organizational contexts.

We propose that the power of introducing different relational forms into the trust–justice linkage has the potential to enhance our understanding of how these two relationship variables affect each other. In the remaining subsections, we briefly explore how relational form may help to further untangle this linkage. We confine our examination to the calculative (market) and relational (communal sharing) forms described by Rousseau et al. (1998) and Fiske (1991). Within each relational form, we revisit the definition of trust, explain how trust operates, explore the standards for making judgments within the relational form, define the dominant justice dynamics that occur, and comment briefly on how violations are interpreted within the relational form.

Calculus-Based Trust, Justice, and Market Relationships

Calculus-based trust (CBT) is predicated on a transactional, market-oriented exchange grounded in an actor's (a) judgment of the trustee's reliability and dependability and (b) assessments of the costs and benefits of trusting and acting in a trustworthy way. Trust exists at this level because the trustee is expected to do what he or she says he or she will do. CBT is most common in calculative, market relationships. The focus is the exchange, and the expected consequence of trust at this level is the receipt of some specific, tangible benefit. Due to the transactional focus of this type of trust and the mental calculations involved, CBT is largely cognitive in nature.

The standard for creating and maintaining CBT is for the trustee to demonstrate reliability, consistency, and predictability in delivering valued outcomes to the trustor. Sheppard, Lewicki, and Minton (1992) suggested that such judgments were based on "balance" standards— that is, based on a comparison of an action to other actions in similar situations, similar to putting those actions on a simple balance weighing scale. When the scales balance, the actions being compared are judged

as equal or fair; when they do not balance, they are judged as unequal or unfair (cf. also theories of social comparison, relative deprivation, referent cognitions, and fairness theory for comparable descriptions).

Within this relational form, therefore, justice judgments are largely framed in terms of distributive justice, and the self-interest form of procedural justice. These judgments focus on the distributive (outcome) fairness of the transactions, or the rules and procedures that generate those outcomes. Violations are usually cognitively processed, rather than affectively experienced (although we acknowledge that there may be a strong affective reaction as well). Violations of trust and justice are seen as upsetting the "balance" of investments and returns expected in the transaction, hence challenging one's expectations of the appropriate effort to expend toward such investments. Reactions to these violations may be short-term in nature, reflected in immediate employee reductions in trust, or protests for greater returns on one's investments to sustain the trust.

Following a violation, trustors are often faced with reparative choices: to seek ways to repair the relationship with the other, to shift the balance of outcomes such that a perceived distribution is resolved (e.g., through employee theft; e.g., Greenberg, 1990), or to sever that relationship and find alternative ways to meet their needs in the marketplace. Trust repair may require a number of actions by the violator to effectively restore that trust. Trust repair will be more difficult if the magnitude of the violation has been large, if the past relationship between the parties has been marred by other violations, and if there is a strong likelihood of future violations. In contrast, appropriate and sincere apologies, and efforts to restore balance soon after the violation, are likely to be more effective (Tomlinson, Dineen, & Lewicki, 2004). In contrast, efforts at "relationship repair" that focus on healing relational wounds will not heal the damage in a calculative, market relationship. In the vernacular, if the other is angry over significant losses of money or property as a result of a trust breach, a hug, an apology, and a reaffirmation of common values will not fix the problem.

Identity-Based Trust, Justice, and "Communal" Relationships

Identification-based trust (IBT) is grounded in a perceived compatibility of interests, needs, values, and definitions of identity between self and other. This type of trust exists when the parties effectively (and often intuitively) understand and appreciate each other's wants and needs, to the point that each can effectively act for the other. Relationships characterized by identification based trust are ones in which

each party can serve as the other's agent, and substitute for the other in interpersonal transactions (Deutsch, 1949). Parties understand what is required to sustain and enhance the trust of the other, and often create a collective identity, joint products and goals, and a commitment to common values to strengthen their relationship (Lewicki & Bunker, 1995, 1996). Because IBT relationships are grounded in shared goals, values, and close emotional attachment, it is not so much the proximal *behavior* of the other or the transactions per se that produces valued outcomes, but rather the trustee's inferred *motives and intentions* that are more salient in determining trust judgments. The context is the parties' own self-defined relationship, which supersedes any particular transactional exchange. IBT-communal relationships take considerable time and emotional investment to cultivate, and are largely idiosyncratic.

The standard for evaluating and maintaining IBT is grounded in what the parties determine is correct for that relationship (Lewicki et al., 1992). Because relationships across people differ significantly in the dimensions on which parties determine their compatibilities, as well as the strength of attachment between parties in those areas, standards for what is correct in any communal relationship are likely to be much more idiosyncratically derived and maintained. These standards are formed as individuals interact and develop their complex dependencies and interdependencies (Sheppard & Sherman, 1998), through both implicit and explicit normative exploration, discussion, and determination of what is "right" and "appropriate" for them. "Fairness" in these relationships might be judged on the basis of traditionally defined calculative (distributive) rules, but the parties are more likely to develop their own idiosyncratic standards that work for them. Hence, correctness standards resemble the rules and norms for procedural justice suggested by Leventhal (1980) or the rules for interactional justice suggested by Bies and Moag (1986).

Within communal relationships, justice judgments are largely framed in terms of the dynamics of interactional justice (Bies & Moag, 1986) and the group value model of procedural justice (Lind & Tyler, 1988). Rather than weighing inputs and outputs to determine the appropriate course of action in the short term, trustors weigh others' actions through the lens of the existing social cues and norms that set standards for what are "correct" behaviors within the relationship (Lamertz, 2002). Fairness is calibrated by norms specific to the relationship context that has been co-constructed with the other parties. There is a significant amount of research supporting the relationship between communal relational forms and relationally grounded fairness judgments. For example, Scandura (1999), in a study of the effect of leader–member exchange (LMX) and organizational justice, found that em-

ployees' placement in either the leader's in-group or out-group had a strong influence on the norms of justice used to evaluate the leader's actions. Our interpretation of this result is that those in the out-group reacted to perceived injustice from the parameters of a CBT relationship, seeking equity/parity in a way that signified their relative lack of social interaction with the leader. On the other hand, those in the in-group used a more idiosyncratic standard based on established norms for interpersonal behavior within their relationship with that supervisor. Similarly, Deluga (1994) found that employees have higher trust in their supervisor when they feel that (a) the supervisor treats them fairly, and (b) they have a high-quality relationship with the supervisor. Another study indicated that people within the supervisor's in-group were more likely to perform organizational citizenship behaviors because of the indirect effect of a trusting relationship with the supervisor (Pillai, Schriesheim, & Williams, 1999).

When trust is violated in a CBT context, significant work is required to repair that trust. But because correctness judgments focus on what is uniquely appropriate for the relationship, IBT may resiliently weather disruptions from events that would permanently damage a CBT relationship. As long as the trustee is perceived to share the common identity and common values, the relationship endures, and as long as these affective bonds are strong, calculus-based judgments have little place in the relationship. They are simply irrelevant, unimportant, peripheral occurrences that require little or nothing in the way of reparations.

However, communal relationships are subject to their own patterns of violations and implications for relationship repair. Unlike the equity/balance perspective of the CBT relational form, violations in an IBT-communal relationship occur when the other does something highly unanticipated, inappropriate or incorrect. Moreover, the violation is often seen as a threat to the victim's identity: "I thought I knew you, and that we stood for the same things—and now you have cheated on me!" IBT violations cause the victim to primarily focus on the *intent* of the other's actions. Additionally, IBT violations cause the victim to question his or her own judgment because the victim believes he or she so badly misjudged the other, and cannot understand what has motivated the other to act in a way that is alien and strange to him or her. The victim's immediate question is "why?," and efforts at trust repair will need to be concentrated on restoring the benevolent intentions of the actor. To rebuild IBT, it is necessary to convey a sincere apology, restore the trustor's perceptions that the other's intentions are honorable, work through the emotions of anger and rejection, and reassert shared values (Lewicki & Wiethoff, 2000). Given the complexity of this heavy interpersonal and emotional labor, it is not surprising that many breaches of IBT can never be repaired.

CONCLUSION

We believe there are many implications that can be drawn from our analysis. We briefly suggest a few:

1. Justice researchers need to study the trust literature more closely, and approach it with a more finely grained perspective. We believe that the evolution of the "fairness heuristic" (as it relates to trust) is an important and insightful step forward in justice research, but its current links to trust are grounded in a far-too-primitive understanding of the complexities of trust. We encourage those justice researchers interested in pursuing the trust–justice interface to understand the different types of trust and the developing body of research on each type's antecedents and consequences, and to more extensively integrate that work into their own thinking. Similarly, we encourage trust researchers to incorporate justice constructs into their own research more fully, such that further testing of the causal or coevolving relationship between the constructs can be explored.

2. While the relationship between trust and justice is complex as the multifaceted nature of each construct is considered, we suggest that consideration of the relational context in which these dynamics occur offers fertile ground for exploring the interrelationship. One key difference across these relational forms is the standards by which judgments are made. Appropriately applied, these relational forms can enrich our understanding of how people interpret fairness and respond to violations. We have tried to sketch out some of the preliminary implications of considering relational form in understanding the trust–justice interrelationship.

3. Efforts to understand why procedural fairness contributes to trust were grounded in two possible models: the self-interest model and the group-value model. Explanations of the relationship between trust and justice in each of these models make far more sense when we consider different forms of trust—calculus-based and identification-based—and the different relational forms in which they may operate. Evaluations based in self-interest model resemble already-established descriptions of the development of calculus-based trust in market relationships, and evaluations based on the group-value model resemble already-established descriptions of the development of identification-based trust in communal relationships. Research in each paradigm, carefully controlling for relational form, would enlighten both the trust and justice literatures.

4. We see our efforts here as only a beginning. In spite of our attempts to tease out the complex relationship between trust and jus-

tice in this chapter, the two constructs remain quite complexly intertwined. Continued efforts to tease apart the two constructs and understand the nature of their connectedness will require a great deal of careful conceptual thinking and linguistic precision, no less the challenges of actually calibrating these relationships through empirical research. We believe we have only started that initiative in this chapter.

We therefore wish to conclude this chapter with two sets of challenges: one to trust researchers, the other to justice researchers. The challenge to trust researchers is severalfold. First, although CBT has been studied quite extensively to date, IBT has received far less attention. Further studies of trust development, justice calibrations, trust violations, and trust repair in IBT relationships are needed. Second, a richer understanding of the cognitive and affective components of trust is required. Third, because both trust building and trust repair are dynamic processes, further examination of these relationships should occur in studies that intentionally explore time as a key element in how the standards develop, how they evolve, and how they are employed when making trust judgments. Finally, as we have encouraged the justice researchers to embrace a richer understanding of trust, so we encourage trust researchers to incorporate complex measures of fairness and justice into their work. Without a significantly larger database and accumulation of multiple studies that have carefully and explicitly measured both constructs, our speculations about their interrelationship are likely to be just that—speculations.

A comparable agenda can be created for justice researchers. First, we encourage justice researchers to understand the sophisticated work that has been done in the trust literature over the last decade. This will require them to define trust more explicitly, to understand the different forms of trust, and to explore the processes by which trust develops and transforms over time, such that "arm's length" transactional trust may be quite different from "up close and personal" relational trust. Second, we encourage justice researchers to begin to explore the standards by which people make fairness judgments, and to consider how different standards are used in different relational forms. Far more work is needed to understand fairness standards and dynamics within different relational forms, and how standards evolve. Doing so may allow justice researchers to explore justice violations that currently are unnoticed because relational norms confound their studies. For example, leader–member exchange theory indicates that some subordinates have closer personal relationships with their superiors than others; this suggests that intragroup perceptions of fair treatment from that supervisor would vary significantly. If justice re-

searchers fail to take relationships into account, they may miss or misreport workers' perceptions of fairness. Finally, although we believe that fairness heuristic theory offers an important and useful breakthrough in justice research, its structure and presentation are that fairness leads to trust. We would like to see this theory developed to account for the likelihood of the reverse relationship—that trust leads to fairness—and to incorporate the myriad of other interpersonal factors, such as cooperation (Deutsch, 1985) that shape these judgments.

Of course, to truly explore the complex relationship between trust and justice, it would be ideal for trust and justice researchers to jointly plan and execute such ventures. We have learned a lot about the relationship between these constructs by performing this evaluation, but much work remains to be done. The intersection of the trust and justice literatures is an exciting place for research, and we encourage scholars in both arenas to seek cooperative ventures.

ACKNOWLEDGMENT

The authors acknowledge the helpful suggestions of Morton Deutsch, Blair Sheppard, and the editors of this volume for their helpful comments in the preparation of this chapter.

REFERENCES

AFL-CIO. (2001). Workers' rights in America: What employees think about their jobs and employers. Survey by Peter D. Hart Research Associates.

Alexander, S., Sinclair, R. R., & Tetrick, L. E. (1995). The role of organizational justice in defining and maintaining the employment relationship. In L. E. Tetrick & J. Barling (Eds.), *Changing employment relations: Behavioral and social perspectives* (pp. 61–89). Washington, DC: American Psychological Association.

Arrow, K. (1974). *The limits of organization.* New York: Norton.

Aryee, S., Budhwar, P. S., & Chen, Z. X. (2002). Trust as a mediator of the relationship between organizational justice and work outcomes: Test of a social exchange model. *Journal of Organizational Behavior, 23,* 267–285.

Barnard, C. (1938). *The functions of the executive.* Cambridge, MA: Harvard University Press.

Becerra, M., & Gupta, A. K. (2003). Perceived trustworthiness within the organization: The moderating impact of communication frequency on trustor and trustee effects. *Organization Science, 14,* 32–44.

Berscheid, E., & Reis, H. T. (1998). Attraction and close relationships. In D. T. Gilbert, S. T. Fiske, & G. Lindzey (Eds.), *The handbook of social psychology* (4th ed., pp. 193–281). New York: McGraw-Hill.

Bews, N. F., & Rossouw, G. J. (2002). A role for business ethics in facilitating trustworthiness. *Journal of Business Ethics, 39,* 377–390.

Bies, R. J., & Moag, J. S. (1986). Interactional justice: Communication criteria of fairness. In R. J. Lewicki, B. H. Sheppard, & M. H. Bazerman (Eds.), *Research on negotiation in organizations* (Vol. 1, pp. 43–55). Greenwich, CT: JAI.

Bies, R. J., & Tripp, T. M. (1996). Beyond distrust: "Getting even" and the need for revenge. In R. M. Kramer & T. R. Tyler (Eds.), *Trust in organizations: Frontiers of theory and research* (pp. 246–260). Thousand Oaks, CA: Sage.

Bigley, G. A., & Pearce, J. L. (1998). Straining for shared meaning in organizational science: Problems of trust and distrust. *Academy of Management Review, 23,* 405–421.

Blau, P. M. (1964). *Exchange and power in social life.* New York: Wiley.

Bottom, W. P., Gibson, K., Daniels, S., & Murnighan, J. K. (2002). When talk is not cheap: Substantive penance and expressions of intent in the reestablishment of cooperation. *Organization Science, 13, 497–513.*

Brockner, J. (2002). Making sense of procedural fairness: How high procedural fairness can reduce or heighten the influence of outcome favorability. *Academy of Management Review, 27,* 58–76.

Brockner, J., & Siegel, P. (1996). Understanding the interaction between procedural and distributive justice: The role of trust. In R. Kramer. & T. Tyler (Eds.), *Trust in organizations: Frontiers of theory and research* (pp. 390–413). Thousand Oaks, CA: Sage.

Brockner, J., Siegel, P. A., Daly, J., Tyler, T., & Martin C. (1997). When trust matters: The moderating effect of outcome favorability. *Administrative Science Quarterly, 42,* 558–583.

Brockner, J., Tyler, T. R., & Cooper-Schneider, R. (1992). The influence of prior commitment to an institution on reactions to perceived unfairness: The higher they are, the harder they fall. *Administrative Science Quarterly, 37,* 241–261.

Brockner, J., & Wiesenfeld, B. M. (1996). An integrative framework for explaining reactions to decisions: The interactive effects of outcomes and procedures. *Psychological Bulletin, 120,* 189–208.

Butler, J. K. (1991). Toward understanding and measuring conditions of trust: Evaluation of a conditions of trust inventory. *Journal of Management, 17,* 643–663.

Deluga, R. J. (1994). Supervisor trust building, leader-member exchange, and organizational citizenship behavior. *Journal of Occupational and Organizational Psychology, 67,* 315–326.

Deutsch, M. (1949). A theory of cooperation and competition. *Human Relations, 2,* 129–151.

Deutsch, M. (1958). Trust and suspicion. *Journal of Conflict Resolution, 2,* 265–279.

Deutsch, M. (1960). The effect of motivational orientation upon trust and suspicion. *Human Relations, 13,* 123–139.

Deutsch, M. (1962). Cooperation and trust: Some theoretical notes. In M. Jones (Ed.), *Nebraska symposium on motivation* (pp. 275–320). Lincoln: University of Nebraska Press.

Deutsch, M. (1985). *Distributive justice: A social psychological perspective.* New Haven, CT: Yale University Press.

Dirks, K., & McLean Parks, J. (2002). Conflicting stories: The state of the science of conflict. In J. Greenberg (Ed.), *Organizational behavior: The state of the science* (pp. 283–324). Mahwah, NJ: Lawrence Erlbaum Associates.

Fiske, A. P. (1991). *Structures of social life.* New York: Free Press.

Greenberg, J. (1990). Employee theft as a reaction to underpayment inequity: The hidden cost of pay cuts. *Journal of Applied Psychology, 75,* 561–568.

Greenberg, J., & Wiethoff, C. (2001). Organizational justice as proaction and reaction: Implications for research and application. In R. Cropanzano (Ed.), *Justice in the workplace, Vol. 2: From theory to practice* (pp. 271–301). Mahwah, NJ: Lawrence Erlbaum Associates.

Greenhalgh, L., & Chapman, D. (1996). Relationships between disputants: Analysis of their characteristics and impact. In S. Gleason (Ed.), *Frontiers in dispute resolution and human resources* (pp. 203–228). East Lansing, MI: Michigan State University Press.

Hartman, S. J., Yrle, A. C., & Galle, W. P., Jr. (1998). Equity in a university setting: Examining procedural and distributive justice. *International Journal of Management, 15,* 3–14.

Heuer, L., Penrod, S., Hafer, C. L., & Cohn, I. (2002). The role of resource and relational concerns for procedural justice. *Personality and Social Psychology Bulletin, 28,* 1468–1482.

Homans, G. C. (1961). *Social behavior: Its elementary forms.* New York: Harcourt, Brace and World.

Jensen, M. C., & Meckling, W. H. (1976). Theory of the firm: Managerial behavior, agency costs and ownership structure. *Journal of Financial Economics, 3,* 306–360.

Kelley, H. H. (1966). A classroom study of the dilemmas in interpersonal negotiation. In K. Archibald (Ed.), *Strategic interaction and conflict: Original papers and discussion* (pp. 49–73). Berkeley, CA: Institute of International Studies.

Konovsky, M. A., & Cropanzano, R. (1991). Perceived fairness of employee drug testing as a predictor of employee attitudes and job performance. *Journal of Applied Psychology, 76,* 698–709.

Konovsky, M. A., & Pugh, S. D. (1994). Citizenship behavior and social exchange. *Academy of Management Journal, 37,* 656–669.

Korsgaard, M. A., Brodt, S. E., & Whitener, E. M. (2002). Trust in the face of conflict: The role of managerial trustworthy behavior and organizational context. *Journal of Applied Psychology, 87,* 312–319.

Korsgaard, M. A., Schewiger, D. M., & Sapienza, H. J. (1995). Building commitment, attachment, and trust in strategic decision-making teams: The role of procedural justice. *Academy of Management Journal, 38,* 60–84.

Kramer, R. M. (1999). Trust and distrust in organizations: Emerging perspectives, enduring questions. *Annual Review of Psychology, 50,* 569–598.

Kramer, R. M., & Tyler, T. (Eds.). (1996). *Trust in organizations: Frontiers of theory and research.* Thousand Oaks, CA: Sage.

Kwok, J. Y. Y., & Leung, K. (2002). A moderator of the interaction effect of procedural justice and outcome favorability: Importance of the relationship. *Organizational Behavior and Human Decision Processes, 87,* 278–299.

Lamertz, K. (2002). The social construction of fairness: Social influence and sense making in organizations. *Journal of Organizational Behavior, 23,* 19–37.

Leventhal, G. (1980). What should be done with equity theory? In K. J. Gergen, M. S. Greenberg, & R. H. Willis (Eds.), *Social exchange: Advances in theory and research* (pp. 27–55). New York: Plenum.

Lewicki, R. J., & Bunker, B. B. (1995). Trust in relationships: A model of trust development and decline. In B. B. Bunker & J. Z. Rubin (Eds.), *Conflict, cooperation and justice* (pp. 133–174). San Francisco: Jossey-Bass.

Lewicki, R. J., & Bunker, B. B. (1996). Developing and maintaining trust in work relationships. In R. M. Kramer & T. R. Tyler (Eds.), *Trust in organizations: Frontiers of theory and research* (pp. 114–139). Thousand Oaks, CA: Sage.

Lewicki, R. J., McAllister, D., & Bies, R. (1998). Trust and distrust: New relationships and realities. *Academy of Management Review, 23*, 3, 438–458.
Lewicki, R. J., Weiss, S. E., & Lewin, D. (1992). Models of conflict, negotiation, and 3rd party intervention—A review and synthesis. *Journal of Organizational Behavior, 13*, 209–252.
Lewicki, R. J., & Wiethoff, C. (2000). Trust, trust development and trust repair. In M. Deutsch & P. Coleman (Eds.), *Theory and practice of conflict resolution* (pp. 86–107). San Francisco: Jossey-Bass.
Lewis, J. D., & Weigert, A. J. (1985). Trust as a social reality. *Social Forces, 63*, 967–985,
Lind, E. A. (2001). Fairness heuristic theory: Justice judgments as pivotal cognitions in organizational relations. In J. Greenberg & R. Cropanzano (Eds.), *Advances in organizational justice* (pp. 56–88). Stanford, CA: Stanford University Press.
Lind, E. A., & Tyler, T. (1988). *The social psychology of procedural justice.* New York: Plenum.
Lind, E. A., Tyler, T. R., & Huo, Y. J. (1997). Procedural context and culture: Variation in the antecedents of procedural justice judgments. *Journal of Personality and Social Psychology, 73*, 767–780.
Lind, E. A., & Van den Bos, K. (2002). When fairness works: Toward a general management theory of uncertainty management. In B. Staw & R. M. Kramer, *Research in organizational behavior* (Vol. 24, pp. 181–223). Greenwich, CT: JAI Press.
Markus, H. R., & Kitayama, S. (1991). Culture and the self: Implications for cognition, emotion, and motivation. *Psychological Review, 98*, 224–253.
Mayer, R., Davis, J. H., & Schoorman, F. D. (1995). An integrative model of organizational trust. *Academy of Management Review, 20*, 709–734.
McAllister, D. (1995). Affect- and cognition-based trust as foundations for interpersonal cooperation in organizations. *Academy of Management Journal, 38*, 24–59.
Pearce, J. L., Bigley, G. A., & Branyiczki, I. (1998). Procedural justice as modernism: Placing industrial/organisational psychology in context. *Applied Psychology: An International Review, 47*(3), 371–396.
Pearce, J. L., Branyiczki, I., & Bigley, G. A. (2000). Insufficient bureaucracy: Trust and commitment in particularistic organizations. *Organization Science, 11*, 148–162.
Pillai, R., Schriesheim, C. A., & Williams, E. S. (1999). Fairness perceptions and trust as mediators for transformational and transactional leadership. *Journal of Management, 25*, 897–933.
Rempel, J. K., Holmes, J. G., & Zanna, M. P. (1985). Trust in close relationships. *Journal of Personality and Social Psychology, 49*, 95–112.
Robinson, S. (1996). Trust and breach of the psychological contract. *Administrative Science Quarterly, 41*, 574–599.
Rotter, J. (1971). Generalized expectancies for interpersonal trust. *American Psychologist, 26*, 443–452.
Rousseau, D, Sitkin, S., Burt, R., & Camerer, C. (1998). Not so different after all: A cross-discipline view of trust. *Academy of Management Review, 23*, 393–404.
Sapienza, H. J., & Korsgaard, M. A. (1996). Procedural justice in entrepreneur–investor relations. *Academy of Management Journal, 39*(3), 544–574.
Scandura, T. A. (1999). Rethinking leader–member exchange: An organizational justice perspective. *Leadership Quarterly, 10*, 25–40.
Schlenker, B. R., Helm, B., & Tedeschi, J. T. (1973). The effects of personality and situational variables on behavioral trust. *Journal of Personality and Social Psychology, 25*(3), 419–427.

Shapiro, D., Sheppard, B. H., & Cheraskin, L. (1992). Business on a handshake. *Negotiation Journal, 8*(4), 365–377.

Sheppard, B. H., Lewicki, R., & Minton, J. (1992). *Organizational justice: The search for fairness in the workplace.* Boston: Lexington Books.

Sheppard, B. H., & Sherman, D. M. (1998). The grammars of trust: A model and general implications. *Academy of Management Review, 23*(3), 422–437.

Sheppard, B. H., & Tuchinsky, M. (1996). Interfirm relations: A grammar of pairs. In B. M. Staw & L. L. Cummings (Eds.), *Research on organizational behavior* (Vol. 18, pp. 331–373). Greenwich, CT: JAI Press.

Sitkin, S. (1995). On the positive effect of legalization on trust. In R. J. Bies, R. J. Lewicki, & B. H. Sheppard (Eds.), *Research on negotiation in organizations* (Vol. 5, pp. 187–217). Greenwich, CT: JAI.

Tajfel, H., & Turner, J. (1979). An integrative theory of intergroup conflict. In W. G. Austin & S. Worchel (Eds.), *The social psychology of intergroup relations* (pp. 33–47). Pacific Grove, CA: Lawrence Erlbaum Associates.

Thibaut, J., & Kelley, H. (1959). *The social psychology of groups.* New York: John Wiley.

Tomlinson, E. C., Dineen, B. R., & Lewicki, R. J. (2004). The road to reconciliation: Antecedents of victim willingness to reconcile following a broken promise. *Journal of Management, 30,* 165–187.

Tyler, T. R. (1994). Psychological models of the justice motive: Antecedents of distributive and procedural justice. *Journal of Personality and Social Psychology, 67,* 850–863.

Van den Bos, K., & Lind, E. A. (2002) Uncertainty management by means of fairness judgments. In M. P. Zanna (Ed.), *Advances in experimental social psychology* (Vol. 34, pp. 1–60). New York: Academic Press.

Van den Bos, K., Wilke, H. A. M., & Lind, E. A. (1998). When do we need procedural fairness? The role of trust in authority. *Journal of Personality and Social Psychology, 75,* 1449–1458.

Whitener, E. M. (1997). The impact of human resource activities on employee trust. *Human Resource Management Review, 7,* 389–404.

Williamson, O. E. (1985). *The economic institutions of capitalism.* New York: Free Press.

IV

JUSTICE EFFECTS

9

What Is Responsible
for the Fair Process Effect?

Kees van den Bos
Utrecht University

The present chapter discusses the psychology of the fair process effect, the positive effect that people's fairness perceptions have on their subsequent reactions. After an overview of instances where the effect has been found, definition issues are discussed. These include that the effect can be found on outcome judgments and on other important variables that follow fair and unfair procedures. Furthermore, the effect refers to people's reactions that follow the experience of fair and unfair procedures, and not to the process with which fairness judgments themselves are formed. Moreover, the term fair process should be used in organizational justice to refer to the informal way in which people are treated in decision-making processes, and not to formal procedures. The main part of the chapter discusses psychological explanations of the effect. These include instrumental, social influence, referent cognition, relational, and uncertainty explanations. The chapter concludes with future directions for the study of the fair process effect.

This chapter is about the fair process effect, the positive effect that people's procedural fairness perceptions have on their subsequent reactions (such as satisfaction with outcomes received, acceptance of decisions made by supervisors, protest behavior, and many other important dependent variables). The fair process effect is arguably the most replicated and robust finding in the literature on organizational justice and one of the most frequently observed phenomena and among the basic principles in the organizational behavior and management literature (Greenberg, 2000). Thus, insight into the fair process effect is relevant for all people interested in organizations and organizational behavior and not just for those of us who have specialized in organizational justice. Therefore, this chapter is dedicated solely to this effect. After a short overview of instances where the effect has been found, some definition issues and conceptual problems are identified and dealt with. This is followed by the main part of the chapter, which discusses psychological explanations that have been proposed to explain the effect and its robustness. I conclude with a discussion of future directions that researchers may want to take in studying the fair process effect.

INSTANCES OF THE FAIR PROCESS EFFECT

In their 1979 article, Folger and his coauthors were the first to coin the term "the fair process effect" (Folger, Rosenfield, Grove, & Corkran,

1979). Using a modified version of Hirschman's (1970) conception of voice, Folger et al. reframed the first procedural justice findings reported by Thibaut, Walker, and their colleagues, to suggest that getting the opportunity to present evidence supporting one's own case in a court trial has a strong positive effect on the defendant's reactions toward the verdict (Thibaut & Walker, 1975, 1978; Walker, LaTour, Lind, & Thibaut, 1974).

Of the many studies by the Thibaut and Walker group, the experiment conducted by Walker et al. (1974) is widely recognized to be the first procedural justice study that revealed a strong and interesting fair process effect. This experiment set out to investigate the effects of adversary and inquisitorial procedures on the reactions of disputants toward either a favorable or an unfavorable verdict in a simulated court trial. Adversary and inquisitorial procedures may differ on multiple dimensions, but the key distinction that Thibaut and Walker were interested in is that adversary procedures allow people involved in court trials greater levels of control over the process used in the court trial than inquisitorial procedures do. Findings of the Walker et al. study showed that defendants judged the way in which they had been treated to be more fair when they had experienced the adversary procedure than when they had been subjected to the inquisitorial procedure, presumably because the former procedure allowed them greater levels of process control (Thibaut & Walker, 1975, 1978) and opportunities to voice their opinion (Folger et al., 1979). More important for the current purposes is that the findings also revealed a fair process effect such that participants judged their verdict to be more fair and were more satisfied with the verdict in case of the fair (adversary) procedure as opposed to the unfair (inquisitorial) procedure.

Folger et al. (1979) found a similar fair process effect on overall satisfaction ratings. Folger et al. manipulated, among other things, whether participants in experimental setups either received or did not receive an opportunity to voice their opinions about how the experimenter should divide lottery tickets between participants themselves and the other participants. The most important fair process effect presented in this study was that voice procedures resulted in higher ratings of overall satisfaction than no-voice procedures.

Since these first demonstrations of the fair process effect, many studies have reported comparable effects in many different contexts using different research methods. The effect has been observed most often within the organizational context (Lind & Van den Bos, 2002) but has frequently been found elsewhere as well (e.g., Paternoster, Brame, Bachman, & Sherman, 1997; Vermunt, Wit, Van den Bos, & Lind, 1996). Furthermore, as has been argued by Lind and Tyler (1988), an exciting aspect of research on the effects of procedural fairness perceptions is

that effects of these perceptions have been found on very different human reactions. This is important because it suggests that fair process studies may have substantial implications for a multitude of domains of human and organizational behavior (Greenberg, 2000).

In organizations, it has been shown that when people feel they have been treated fairly this frequently leads to a variety of positive responses, such as higher commitment to organizations and institutions (Folger & Konovsky, 1989; Korsgaard, Schweiger, & Sapienza, 1995; McFarlin & Sweeney, 1992; Moorman, 1991), more extra-role citizenship behavior (Konovsky & Folger, 1991; Podsakoff & MacKenzie, 1993), greater likelihood of conflict prevention and resolution (Bobocel, Agar, Meyer, & Irving, 1998), better job performance (Lind, Kanfer, & Earley, 1990), more widespread acceptance of company policy (Greenberg, 1994; Lind, 1990) and supervisor directives (Huo, Smith, Tyler, & Lind, 1996), higher levels of job satisfaction (Folger & Cropanzano, 1998), more positive emotional feelings (Weiss, Suckow, & Cropanzano, 1999), and increased positive affect and decreased negative affect (Van den Bos, 2001a). People who experience unfair treatment, on the other hand, are more likely to leave their jobs (Alexander & Ruderman, 1987), are less likely to cooperate (Lind, 2001), show lower levels of morale and higher levels of work stress and overt and covert disobedience (Huo et al., 1996), are more likely to initiate lawsuits (Lind, Greenberg, Scott, & Welchans, 2000), and may even start behaving in antisocial ways (Greenberg, 1993, 1997; Greenberg & Lind, 2000).

In contexts other than organizations the fair process effect is similarly overwhelming. For example, the belief that one has been treated fairly by judges, the police, or other social authorities enhances acceptance of legal decisions (Lind, Kulik, Ambrose, & De Vera Park, 1993), obedience to laws (Tyler, 1990), and evaluations of public policies (Lind, 1990; Tyler, Rasinski, & McGraw, 1985), whereas the belief that one has been treated unfairly has been shown to prompt protest behavior (Vermunt et al., 1996) and recidivism among spouse abuse defendants (Paternoster et al., 1997).

Fair process effects have been found in laboratory experiments (Folger et al., 1979; Folger, Rosenfield, & Robinson, 1983; Greenberg, 1987a, 1987b, 1993; Kanfer, Sawyer, Earley, & Lind, 1987; Lind et al., 1990; Lind, Kurtz, Musante, Walker, & Thibaut, 1980; Van den Bos, Lind, Vermunt, & Wilke, 1997; Van den Bos, Vermunt, & Wilke, 1997; Walker et al., 1974) and in survey studies with respondents involved in settings such as organizations (Folger & Konovsky, 1989), court trials (Lind et al., 1993; Tyler, 1984), police–citizen encounters (Tyler & Folger, 1980), and political situations (Tyler & Caine, 1981, Studies 2 and 4; Tyler & DeGoey, 1995; Tyler et al., 1985).

Because fair procedures enhance so many important cognitions, feelings, attitudes, and behaviors, insight into what is responsible for the fair

process effect is crucial for understanding how people think, feel, and behave in their social and organizational environments (Cropanzano &
Folger, 1989, 1991; Cropanzano & Greenberg, 1997; Greenberg, 2000;
Folger & Konovsky, 1989; Greenberg, 1990, 1993; Lind & Tyler, 1988; Tyler & Lind, 1992). To this end, this chapter focuses on the psychology of
the fair process effect.

One could well say that the review just presented of the fair process
effect suggests that in the organizational justice literature the issue
nowadays is not so much whether fair process effects can be found (because the answer is definitely "yes") and not even whether it can be
found in a new organizational setting or on a new dependent variable
(as research from the 1970s till the new millennium clearly suggests
that the answer to this question will be "yes" as well). No, the issue
now is, or should be, what is responsible for the fair process effect. Two
things are important for this. First, we have to be clear what it is we are
talking about when we talk about the fair process effect. Second, in the
organizational justice literature it is now time that we start asking and
investigating fundamental questions as to the psychology of the effect
(Van den Bos, 2001b). This latter issue is the main topic of the current
chapter. Before I discuss that subject, a closer look at some important
definition and conceptual problems that revolve around the organizational justice literature in general and the fair process effect in particular is in order.

TOWARD CONCEPTUAL CLARITY

In the organizational justice literature there tends to be some misunder-
standing and ambiguity as to how important terms should be understood (cf. Colquitt & Shaw, this volume). This also applies to the fair
process effect and issues that are related to this concept. With respect to
the fair process effect, the definition that is used in this chapter is that it
refers to the positive effect of people's procedural fairness perceptions
on their subsequent reactions.

The studies by Walker et al. (1974) and Folger et al. (1979) became
known as showing fair process effects on people's outcome fairness
judgments, decision acceptance tendencies, and general satisfaction.
These dependent variables obviously are very important. However,
this does not imply that fair process effects cannot be found on other human reactions as well. Indeed, what makes the fair process effect so important, and why it is exciting to study the psychology of the effect, is
that it has been shown on a huge variety of human responses (Lind & Tyler, 1988). It would be unwise, therefore, to restrict the label "the fair
process effect" only to operationalizations that happen to have been
used in the first fair process studies (outcome fairness and satisfaction

ratings and decision acceptance) and to neglect other important dependent variables.

A precondition before fair process effects can occur is that the experience of a particular procedure leads to the perception of a certain level of procedural fairness. It is this procedural fairness perception that may positively influence the person's later reactions and in this way creates a fair process effect. Thus, for example, when an individual, let's call him Rob, gets an opportunity to voice his opinion about the way in which office space should be allocated in his department, Rob may perceive the way in which he has been treated to be fair. This perception of procedural fairness may then lead Rob to be more satisfied with the final decision of exactly how office space is to be distributed among the staff members. Thus, as is illustrated in Fig. 9.1, the label "the voice effect" should be reserved for the enhancement of procedural fairness when a procedure allows people a chance to express themselves and "the fair process effect" is the enhancement of people's evaluations, attitudes, behaviors, and so on following this procedural fairness perception. Thus, in contrast with what sometimes is done in the literature, a voice effect should not be equated with a fair process effect (Folger et al., 1979). Rather the experience of voice, or encountering an accurate, a consistent, or any other particular procedure (cf. Leventhal, 1980; Van den Bos, Vermunt, & Wilke, 1996, 1997) will lead to fairness perceptions, and these perceptions should be treated as a prerequisite before fair process effects can be found (see Fig. 9.1). Furthermore, it should be noted here that it is not uncommon to find voice effects that are different (e.g., differentially affected by the experimental manipulations used in the study) from the fair process effects found in the same study (for details, see, e.g., Van den Bos, 2001a; Van den Bos, Maas, Waldring, & Semin, 2003; Van den Bos & Miedema, 2000). This suggests that at least sometimes different psychological processes are instigating the two effects.

The previous paragraphs highlighted the importance of *perceptions* of *procedural fairness,* and it should be clear what we mean with each of these concepts. The first issue is the role of *perceptions* in the fair process effect. Numerous authors have stressed that fairness and justice are really in the eye of the beholder (e.g., Adams, 1965; Lind et al., 1990; Mikula & Wenzel, 2000; Tyler, Boeckmann, Smith, & Huo, 1997; Van den Bos & Lind, 2002). It is important to emphasize this once again because there is some tendency in the literature to treat fairness and justice as objective concepts about which there is or may be some objective truth (cf. Hare, 1981; Jasso, 1994, 1999; Rawls, 1971; Sabbagh, Dar, & Resh, 1994). Rationalist conceptions of fairness and justice are normative and often—but not always (see Haidt, 2001)—philosophical in nature and conceive of justice as predominantly a principle that can be defined in reference to objective standards of right and wrong (Hare, 1981). An ex-

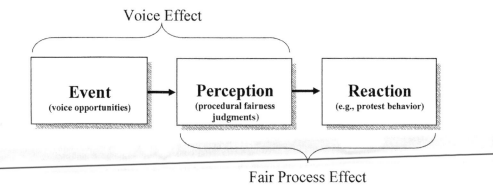

FIG. 9.1. Disentangling the voice effect and the fair process effect.

ample is the work by Jasso (1994, 1999) and Sabbagh et al. (1994), who constructed theories in which justice judgments are studied from articulated rational-normative ideas of justice evaluations and justice functions. Although it might be possible to derive rational-normative principles of procedural justice and there hence is the possibility of an objective fair process effect, we should realize that the fair process effect in essence is a *psychological* effect, constructed in the head of the recipient of the procedure. Thus, psychology of organizational justice and particularly research on the fair process effect should be treated with strong weight to the subjectivity of fairness and justice judgments. This implies that objective conditions that researchers, organizational behaviorists, and employers think are fair or unfair do not have to viewed that way by employees and other lay people.

The second subject is the *fairness* concept. Compared to the related notions of justice and morality, fairness better connotes the subjective, ready judgment that is and has long been the true topic of psychological study (Van den Bos & Lind, 2002). Participants and respondents in research studies find it easier and more relevant to provide judgments of fairness than judgments of justice or morality. This is the reason that most psychologists in our field usually ask people to rate fairness rather than to rate justice or morality (cf. Tyler & Lind, 1992), and this is the rationale for why the central topic of consideration of this chapter is called "the fair process effect" and not "the just process effect" or "the moral process effect." The former simply reflects better both common research practices and the core belief under study. Thus, notwithstanding the fact that organizational psychologists usually call this

area "organizational justice," we are in effect referring to fairness perceptions as the major antecedent of the effects we are interested in (Lind & Van den Bos, 2002).

Related to this is the concern of whether what usually is called the fair process effect should be really conceived of as a *fair* process effect or that it would it be more accurate to start talking about an *unfair* process effect instead (cf. Greenberg & Folger, 1983, p. 243). Although the former perspective is in line with how the effect generally is known, the latter view corresponds with notions that have been ventilated (Folger, 1984; see also Brockner & Wiesenfeld, 1996; Van den Bos & Spruijt, 2002; Van den Bos & Van Prooijen, 2001; Van den Bos, Vermunt, & Wilke, 1997) that we scientists tend to think and talk about the psychology of fairness and justice, whereas unfair events affect lay people's cognitions and reactions stronger than fair events. This finding is probably caused by the important role that people's expectations have in the psychology of fairness judgments (e.g., Van den Bos et al., 1996) and the fact that unfair events may strongly violate these expectations (Van den Bos & Van Prooijen, 2001). The psychological mechanism behind this finding may well be an instance of the more general negativity effect that indicates that negative things typically have a bigger impact on psychological processes than positive things (see, e.g., Baumeister, Bratslavsky, Finkenauer, & Vohs, 2001; Fiske & Taylor, 1991; Peeters & Czapinski, 1990). All this suggests that *un*fairness plays a more prominent role and that it might be better to talk about the psychology of *in*justice as opposed to justice (Folger & Cropanzano, 1998). Furthermore, it is noteworthy that different theories tend to focus on one of the two effects and in their empirical studies tend to use different dependent variables that are best suited to tap either the fair or the unfair process effect. For example, research studies by the Lind and Tyler group are inclined to focus on the influence perceived procedural fairness may have on people's satisfaction and acceptance of authorities (Lind & Tyler, 1988; Tyler & Lind, 1992), whereas Folger and colleagues tend to explore the darker side of the fairness dimension by concentrating on the effects that unfairness may have on resentment and retaliation (e.g., Folger, 1987, 1993; Folger & Baron, 1996; Folger & Skarlicki, 1998). In this chapter, I use the traditional term "the fair process effect," with the understanding that, unless explicitly stated otherwise, this may involve the effects of both fair and unfair procedures on people's reactions.

The final issue that I want to put forward here is what we mean with *procedure*. The name is derived from the law literature and especially from the title of the 1975 book by social psychologist John Thibaut and law professor Lawrence Walker. These authors and their associates were inspired by the psychological differences they saw between different legal procedures, and in their pioneering procedural justice experi-

ments they took these differences as starting point for their investigation of participants' reactions toward procedures that varied the amount of process control that participants experienced in simulated court trials. Thus, Thibaut and Walker combined their mutual interests in social psychology and law and as a result they placed their studies under the heading of "procedural justice" research. However, this should not be taken too literally, because these authors clearly saw their experiments as a first step toward understanding the psychology involved in fairness and justice issues (Thibaut & Walker, 1978) and were intrigued by the implication of their findings that how people are treated in courts of law can have strong impact on their reactions to judges' verdicts (Walker et al., 1974).

Following this pioneering research, scientists have deepened our understanding of the psychological processes hinted at in the Thibaut and Walker work (e.g., Folger et al., 1979; Folger, 1986; Greenberg, 2000; Greenberg & Folger, 1983; Lind & Tyler, 1988; Tyler & Lind, 1992; Van den Bos & Lind, 2002) and rightfully noted that the psychological processes involved in the Thibaut and Walker simulations could be adequately expanded to incorporate how people react to fairness and justice in other contexts than legal settings. Most notably, the role of procedural justice in the workplace was recognized to be very important (Colquitt, Conlon, Wesson, Porter, & Ng, 2001; Greenberg, 2000; Greenberg & Folger, 1983; Lind & Tyler, 1988) and, in fact, nowadays the organizational context is the setting in which the fair process effect has been most widely studied. Furthermore, during the 1975–1985 advancement of research and theory on procedural justice it became clear that what by then had became known as procedural justice effects were really effects of how fairly people felt they had been treated in the particular context under investigation (for an overview, see, e.g., Lind & Tyler, 1988).

In correspondence with this, the fair process effect research that is reviewed in this chapter is about the effect of the fairness of the way in which people feel they have been treated in the workplace or elsewhere. Thus, procedural fairness and justice as they are being used here, and as I think that John Thibaut really intended them to be, refer to the way people are treated. So, in essence, fair or unfair treatment in interpersonal and social interactions is the issue here.

It is important to note that this conception of procedural justice overlaps closely (but see Bies, this volume) with a notion that was developed later in the organizational justice literature, the concept of "interactional justice" (see Bies & Moag, 1986; Bies & Shapiro, 1987). One could argue that a danger of using the procedural justice label is that it may be a bit of a misnomer and that people may wrongfully misinterpret the concept to mean to refer to formal, lawlike procedures. The interactional justice label has as an advantage that it clearly refers to the

justice and fairness aspects of social interactions that are so important in understanding the majority of the fairness effects reported in the psychological literature. Its main disadvantage, however, is that when, in addition to the two earlier developed notions of distributive and procedural justice, researchers start using this concept they have to redefine the concept of procedural justice. That is, because of the obvious overlap of interactional justice with informal procedural justice (Tyler & Bies, 1990; but see Bies, this volume), introducing the concept of interactional justice forces researchers to start redefining procedural justice in terms of *formal* decision-making procedures. In the modern organizational justice literature there is a strong tendency to do this. However, as mentioned before, this formal aspect was never meant to be important in the work by the founders of procedural justice. On the contrary, they were really referring to the more informal way in which people were treated in decision-making processes. It is this latter conception, the fairness of informal treatment, that I think the literature should focus on (for a similar argument, see Tyler & Bies, 1990), and I refer to this by means of the notions that were originally developed for these effects: procedural justice (Thibaut & Walker, 1975) and the fair process effect (Folger et al., 1979). Treating these concepts in a formal, as opposed to an informal, way would be a major error.

ON THE PSYCHOLOGY OF THE FAIR PROCESS EFFECT

Now that we have reviewed studies that have shown the fair process effect and have defined the central topics of this chapter, it is time to start exploring the psychology of the effect. It should be noted here that I discuss some explanations that were developed, and review research studies that were conducted to understand not only the fair process effect but other fairness issues as well. The fair process implications of these accounts are reviewed here, with broader implications of the research studies mentioned when appropriate. For fairness theories that are important to understand the procedural justice concept but that are less directly related to the psychology of the fair process effect, the reader is referred to other chapters of this handbook (see especially the chapter by Brockner and the chapter by Cropanzano & Ambrose). Furthermore, it is important to note here that whether fair process effects have been reported on outcome judgments, satisfaction ratings, stealing behavior, or whatever other dependent variable was used in a particular fair process study does not bother us so much in this chapter as does the psychology of what these effects have in common. For discussion of the effects of perceived procedural fairness on specific dependent variables, please see the chapters by Conlon, Tyler, Moorman, and Vermunt and Steensma in this volume.

I start by reviewing the oldest explanations of the fair process effect first. After having discussed theories that have been developed later, I note some future avenues research on the psychology of the effect may want to take in the conclusion section that follows this discussion of the psychology of the fair process effect.

Instrumental Explanation

Thibaut and Walker (1978; Walker, Lind, & Thibaut, 1979) were the first to construct a general theory of procedural fairness, with special attention to the fairness of disputes dealt with in the legal process. Their theory of procedure applied theories and methods of social psychology to examine and compare various procedural systems incorporated in the legal process and attempted to explain what is responsible for the effects of perceived procedural fairness on human reactions to these procedures and their outcomes.

These authors' analysis of the findings of the Walker et al. (1974) experiment and related studies emphasizes the amount of control allocated to disputants (cf. Shapiro, this volume). Thibaut, Walker, and their colleagues postulated that the distribution of control among disputants involved in a legal process is the most significant factor in characterizing a procedural system and that all changes in procedure may be measured according to their effects on this central control relationship. Two types of control were distinguished: control over the decision and control over the process. A disputant's amount of decision control is the degree to which the disputant may unilaterally determine the outcome of the dispute. Control over the process refers to control over the development and selection of information that will constitute the basis for resolving the dispute. The allocation of process and decision control determines the overall distribution of control among the disputants involved and it therefore, according to Thibaut and Walker (1978), determines the essential character of procedures. Because adversary and inquisitorial procedures differ in the amount of process control given to disputants, with adversary procedures yielding higher levels of process control, this explained, according to Thibaut and Walker (1975, 1978), why their participants judged the former type of procedure to be more fair and reacted more favorably toward the verdict resulting from the procedure.

Thibaut and Walker's working hypothesis was that legal conflicts are predominantly disagreements about the apportoinment of outcomes, such as conflicts of interests and disputes about inconsistent claims to the division of assets or losses, and that these arguments about the division of outcomes are hence best resolved with the aim of achieving distributive justice. These authors, therefore, saw the appropriate goal of

legal procedures to be the achievement of distributive justice (Thibaut & Walker, 1978). The Thibaut and Walker theory thus suggested that people want to have control over the decision or over the processes that lead to the outcome decision so that they can make sure that the ultimate outcome is fair. This instrumental focus implied that they proposed that people attach more weight toward decision control than process control and that their explanation of the fair process effect is more focused on outcome considerations of fairness judgments than later developed accounts are. It is important to note here, however, that an important aspect of the Thibaut and Walker (1975, 1978) model was the focus on whether people received *fair* outcomes and not so much on how *favorable* outcomes were to people (Van den Bos & Lind, 2002). It is therefore more appropriate to label these authors' theory as the "instrumental model," and I think it is wrong to call this the "self-interest model," as is often done in the literature. Using the latter label would easily lead one to conclude, as one sometimes sees in the literature, that Thibaut and Walker conceived of human beings as utterly self-centered and selfish creatures, which I think is an overstatement and is not how these authors conceived of people.

Social Influence Explanation

Greenberg and Folger (1983) were the first to explicitly position the fair process effect in organizational contexts and were also the first to review different explanations of the psychology of the effect. To this end they noted that what is responsible for findings by Thibaut and Walker (1975; Walker et al., 1974) could be either more positive human reactions because of the experience of a fair process (i.e., a fair process effect) or more negative reactions when the freedom to exercise voice has been denied or when other unfair procedures have been experienced (i.e., an unfair process effect). Greenberg and Folger explained the occurrence of these fair and unfair process effects by pointing to the role of effectance (White, 1959) and reactance (Brehm, 1966) motives, respectively. Because effectance is relevant only to positive effects of perceived procedural fairness and reactance is restricted to unfair process effects, both effectance and reactance accounts are limited in their ability to explain the effects of reactions to variations in procedural fairness (Greenberg & Folger, 1983).

A third explanation by Greenberg and Folger (1983), and this is probably their best known account of the fair process effect, points at social influence processes as an important psychological mechanism. This explanation holds that the fair process effect can be explained in terms of people being susceptible to influence via social comparison of others' opinions about whether certain outcome distributions are equitable or

inequitable. Evidence for this line of reasoning was reported by Folger et al. (1979), who predicted and found that the exercise of voice should lead to more positive responses when people do not receive explicit feedback from others supporting their own opinion that the decision was unfair. However, when people receive information from others that confirm their beliefs and indicates that the final decision was inequitable, then voice opportunities may not lead to a fair process effect. The experiments conducted by Folger et al. (1979) and the line of reasoning put forward in Greenberg and Folger (1983) thus suggest that an important psychological mechanism germane to the fair process effect is a social influence explanation.

Referent Cognition Explanation

Referent cognitions theory, another line of work instigated by Rob Folger, constitutes a different explanation of the fair process effect. In the course of time, different versions of the framework have been developed (for overviews, see Cropanzano & Folger, 1989; Folger, 1986, 1987, 1993; see also Folger & Cropanzano, 1998), but these versions all share an important core principle as to the psychology of fairness issues. With respect to the fair process effect, the theory argues that people's reactions to procedural justice depend largely on their counterfactual thoughts (Kahneman & Tversky, 1982). In essence, referent cognitions theory reasons that when a procedural rule is broken people's thinking becomes inherently referential: People use a frame of reference for evaluating what happened that consists of a mental comparison to what might have happened instead (see also Van den Bos et al., 1996; Van den Bos, Lind, Vermunt, & Wilke, 1997).

In classic referent cognitions studies (Cropanzano & Folger, 1989; Folger & Martin, 1986; Folger et al., 1983), all participants failed to obtain a bonus of extra course credit. Participants in the high referent outcome conditions were led to believe that there was an alternative situation in which they would have received the bonus. Participants in the low referent outcome conditions were informed that they would not have obtained the bonus in either case. The manipulation of procedure in the studies by Folger and Martin (1986) and Folger et al. (1983) varied whether participants were given good reasons (high-justification conditions) or poor reasons (low-justification conditions) why they failed to obtain the bonus. The procedure manipulation in the experiment by Cropanzano and Folger (1989) was such that participants got (participant-decision condition) versus did not get (experimenter-decision condition) to decide which of two types of tasks would be the task with which—depending on their performance on the task—they would have an opportunity to obtain the bonus. Findings of these studies indicated

that participants showed the highest levels resentment and discontent when high referent outcomes were combined with bad procedures.

Van den Bos and Van Prooijen (2001) recently resolved some important methodological problems in the earlier referent cognitions studies and showed that people react more strongly to voice versus no-voice procedures when reference points are close as opposed to distant. Participants in one of the Van den Bos and Van Prooijen experiments read and responded to stimulus information manipulated by means of scenarios. In these scenarios, participants were asked to imagine that they were a member of a group of people (the blue team). Participants in the voice condition were informed that members of the blue team received an opportunity to voice their opinions about a decision that had to be made, and participants in the no-voice condition were told that members of the blue team did not receive such an opportunity. By means of the reference point manipulation, we made it easier for participants in the close reference point condition to imagine that something else could have happened than for those in the distant reference point condition: In the close reference point condition, we informed participants that they had until recently been a member of a different group (the red team). In the distant reference point condition, participants were not told that they had been a member of a different team. Following the line of reasoning already presented, we argued that when a clear alternative situation is available (still being a member of the red team) it would be easier for participants to imagine that something else could have happened (if only they would still have been a member of the red team) than in the distant reference point condition (where there is no alternative previous group membership). As a consequence, following referent cognitions theory, we predicted that stronger fair process effects would be found in the close reference point condition than in the distant reference point condition.

Results indeed showed that when it was easier for participants to imagine that something else could have happened (because they had until recently been a member of a different group), their reactions indicated stronger fair process effects than when it was less easy to imagine something else could have happened (because there was no previous group). In other words, when people are confronted with a close reference point their reactions show stronger fair process effects than participants who have been subjected to a distant reference point.

These findings provide supportive evidence for the explanation that referent cognitions play a crucial role in understanding the psychology of the fair process effect. Furthermore, because the referent cognitions explanation argues that particularly when a fairness rule is broken people's thinking becomes inherently referential, and because counterfactual thinking is stronger when people have received nega-

tive as opposed to positive information (e.g., Landman, 1987; Zeelenberg, Van den Bos, Van Dijk, & Pieters, 2002), we reasoned that especially in the no-voice conditions participants' reactions would be affected by their referent cognitions. The findings reported in the Van den Bos and Van Prooijen (2001) article are in correspondence with this in that effects of closeness of reference points on people's reactions were predominantly found in the no-voice conditions and not in the voice conditions. This result suggests that referent cognitions are affecting human reactions more strongly following the experience of unfair procedures, and this may well imply that the referent cognitions explanation is particularly well suited to account for the psychology of the *un*fair process effect.

Relational Explanation

The relational model of authority (Tyler & Lind, 1992) and the associated group-value model (Lind & Tyler, 1988) are broad models of procedural justice and attempt to explain more than only the fair process effect. The core message is that "what makes people tick," what makes them respond so strongly toward perceptions of fair and unfair procedure, is the fact that people are primarily concerned about their long-term relationship to the authorities, institutions, or groups that employ the procedures. Reactions toward fair and unfair treatment by authorities and others therefore depend on the implications of the relational treatment for feelings of self-worth and for the belief that the group is functioning properly and fairly.

The relational explanation of the fair process effect argues that, in comparison with an outcome, a procedure reveals more relational information about what an authority thinks about the recipient of the procedure: Does the authority trust me, am I treated in a neutral manner, am I accorded the appropriate standing, and am I included in the group, organization, or society in question? The relational account thus states that people often think procedural information is especially diagnostic with respect to their inclusion in the group or organization, and they reciprocate this message of belongingness by being more accepting of less than ideal outcomes.

Several research studies have been carried out to test implications of the relational explanation (see, e.g., Smith & Tyler, 1997; Smith, Tyler, Huo, Ortiz, & Lind, 1998; Tyler, 1990, 1991, 1994, 1997; Tyler & DeGoey, 1995; Tyler, DeGoey, & Smith, 1996; Tyler & Lind, 1990). Research by Huo et al. (1996) shows that, as the explanation predicts, procedure treatment evaluations have a greater impact on distributive fairness judgments in intragroup settings, where inclusion is presumably a more potent consideration, than in intergroup settings.

Building on the relational model, Van Prooijen, Van den Bos, and Wilke (2002) recently focused on the role of status as antecedent of fair process effects. Their analysis of the relational explanation led these authors to propose that salience of the general concept status should lead people be more attentive to procedural fairness information and that, as a result, their reactions should show stronger fair process effects. Findings of two experiments indeed showed more compelling fair process effects in status-salient than in status-nonsalient conditions. Further evidence for the relational explanation was found by means of a word-fragment completion task in which participants were presented with uncompleted words that could either be completed as fairness-related or non-fairness-related words. Results of the cognitive activation data thus obtained showed that status salience led to increased accessibility of fairness concerns. In line with the relational explanation, this suggests that following salience of important relational elements, such as status issues, people start becoming more attentive to fairness information and that as a consequence their reactions are more strongly affected by perceived procedural fairness

The relational explanation postulates a value-expressive component to underlie the fair process effects that follow from getting voice, and, in accordance with this perspective, research findings by Lind et al. (1990) indeed reveal that, when given an opportunity to voice their opinions after outcome decisions have been made, perceived procedural fairness may positively affects people's reactions, presumably because of the value-expressive and not a self-interest component. In further correspondence with the relational explanation, Tyler (1987) shows that a key precondition for value-expressive effects to occur are individuals' beliefs that the authorities involved have considered their views. This effect of due consideration is supportive for Tyler and Lind's hypothesis that fairness of relational treatment is what is responsible for the fair process effect. What is noteworthy, I think, is that the strong emphasis on relational treatment issues in the relational model overlaps closely with the concept of interactional justice (Bies & Moag, 1986; Bies & Shapiro, 1987), suggesting that the relational explanation and work on interactional justice are more similar than is often thought. (For an alternative perspective on this issue, please see Bies, this volume.)

Uncertainty Explanation

The final explanation that I would like to review here states that uncertainty is playing a major role in the psychology of the fair process effect (Van den Bos, 2001a; Van den Bos & Lind, 2002). Although the earlier reviewed explanations (Folger, 1986; Greenberg & Folger, 1983; Thibaut & Walker, 1978; Tyler & Lind, 1992) all acknowledged at some point that

uncertainty may be important, the uncertainty explanation discusses this more explicitly and thoroughly.

The uncertainty explanation developed out of research that was conducted following the fairness heuristic framework (see Lind, 2001; Van den Bos, 2001c; Van den Bos, Lind, & Wilke, 2001) at the end of the 1990s and the beginning of the new millennium. By then, strong fair process effects had been found so frequently in research studies that the effect was probably the most important factor that led a number of procedural justice researchers to conclude that the formation of overall fairness judgments is more strongly affected by procedures than by outcomes (see, e.g., Lind & Tyler, 1988, p. 1). This led to the situation that procedural justice research tended to focus on one aspect of the psychological process leading to fairness perceptions and subsequent reactions: procedures. Distributive justice researchers, on the other hand, also were inclined to focus on one aspect of the fairness judgment process: outcomes. Some distributive researchers even suggested that outcomes may be more important for understanding fairness judgments and human reactions than procedures (e.g., Lerner & Whitehead, 1980; Rutte & Messick, 1995). Thus, both procedural and distributive justice research tended to focus on only one aspect of the fairness judgment process, at the expense of other important concepts. As several authors noted at that time, it was time to integrate the procedural and distributive justice domains (Brockner & Wiesenfeld, 1996; Cropanzano & Folger, 1991; Folger, 1984; Greenberg, 1986, 1990; Sweeney & McFarlin, 1993; Tyler, 1994; Van den Bos, Vermunt, & Wilke, 1997).

To this end, my colleagues and I started exploring the psychology of the classical case of the fair process effect, the occurrence of the effect on outcome fairness judgments, and we began wondering how people in effect form evaluations of outcome fairness (Van den Bos, Lind, Vermunt, & Wilke, 1997). We noted that probably the most well-known and the most widely accepted answer to the question of how people decide whether their outcome is fair or unfair has been provided by equity theory (e.g., Adams, 1965; Walster, Berscheid, & Walster, 1973; Walster, Walster, & Berscheid, 1978). In essence, equity theory proposes that people judge an outcome as fair when their own outcome-to-input ratio equals some comparative or referent outcome-to-input ratio. This process is often driven by social comparison with other people's outcomes and inputs such that people judge their outcome as fair when the ratio of their own inputs and outcomes equals the ratio of inputs and outcomes of comparison others (Messick & Sentis, 1983). Equity theory and other related conceptions of justice—such as relative deprivation theory (Crosby, 1976; Stouffer, Suchman, DeVinney, Star, & Williams, 1949) and the distributive justice conceptions of Blau (1964), Deutsch (1975, 1985), and Homans (1961)—all emphasize the importance of social compari-

son information in the process of evaluating outcomes. As Messick and Sentis (1983) noted, a central theme in the literature on outcome fairness is that the comparison of a person's outcome with those of comparison others influences the person's beliefs about the fairness or justice of his or her own outcome.

Equity theory has received wide support in social and organizational studies and has been very influential. But as we noted in the 1997 paper, one of its basic propositions is that, in order to judge whether an outcome is fair, people have to know what outcomes comparison others have received. The Van den Bos, Lind, Vermunt, and Wilke (1997) article began by asking whether people always know the outcomes of others, as most theorizing on equity theory assumes they do. We argued that they frequently do not. For instance, in everyday life we often do not know the salaries of the people with whom we work, and even if we do, we may not have a good idea of their contributions. If, as we believed, social comparison information about outcomes frequently is not available, then in everyday life the issue of how people form judgments of outcome fairness is more complicated than equity theory suggests.

Using this reasoning led us to predict fair process effects on people's outcome judgments: We proposed that when information about outcomes of others is not available, people would start using other fairness-relevant information that is available. But what information is available? We suggested that procedural information is frequently present, even in situations where others' outcomes or contributions are unknown. Thus, in many situations people may turn to the fairness of procedures to determine how to judge their outcome, using procedural fairness as a heuristic substitute to judge the fairness of their outcome. Therefore, in situations where a person only knows his or her own outcome but not other equity-relevant information, we predicted a fair process effect: People would judge their outcome to be more fair following a fair rather than an unfair procedure.

However, we also reasoned that when a person does have enough information to form an equity judgment—when, for example, information is available about the outcome of a comparable other person—the person making the fairness judgment will use this social comparison information as a basis for forming outcome fairness judgments. Therefore, we expected less strong fair process effects in situations where a person knows what outcome the referent other received. When people had social comparison information about outcomes there would be less need for procedural fairness to serve as a heuristic substitute in the process of forming judgments of outcome fairness.

The results of Van den Bos, Lind, Vermunt, and Wilke (1997) strongly support this line of reasoning and suggest that when people are uncertain about outcomes of social comparison others they indeed use proce-

dural fairness—as a heuristic substitute—to assess how to react to their own outcome (yielding fair process effects on people's judgments of outcome fairness). But people rely less on procedure information when they are certain about the outcome received by comparison others (resulting in weak or nonsignificant fair process effects). This shows that, to understand the fairness process effect, it is important to take into account conditions of information certainty or uncertainty.

The uncertainty explanation suggests an interesting implication of the fact that fair process effects on outcome fairness evaluations have been so frequently found: Apparently people are very often uncertain about how to evaluate the fairness of the outcomes they have received, and it is under these conditions of uncertainty about outcome fairness that procedural fairness perceptions start kicking in on people's evaluations of outcome, yielding strong fair process effects on their outcome judgments (Van den Bos, 2001a; Van den Bos et al., 2001). This suggests that the fair process effect is so omnipresent and profound because often, perhaps typically, people are reacting in the way they do because they are uncertain about the things they are reacting to.

In a later paper (Van den Bos, Wilke, Lind, & Vermunt, 1998) we expanded on the 1997 findings and showed that fair process effects occur not just when perceivers lack strong social comparison information of the sort present in the other-outcome-known conditions of the Van den Bos, Lind, Vermunt, and Wilke (1997) studies: In other situations where it is reasonable to suppose that perceivers are uncertain about important elements needed to judge outcome fairness, they rely more strongly on procedure information in the process of judging outcome fairness, and hence their outcome fairness judgments are more strongly affected by procedure information (see Van den Bos, Wilke, Lind, & Vermunt, 1998).

Skitka (2002) also reported similar findings as the Van den Bos, Lind, Vermunt, and Wilke (1997) study using a different operationalization of outcome certainty. In the Van den Bos, Lind, Vermunt, and Wilke experiments, certainty about outcome fairness was manipulated by giving participants either complete or incomplete information about social comparison-based equity. Skitka has found comparable effects by making a distinction between situations in which people have a very clear a priori sense of fair outcomes (a moral mandate) and situations in which they do not have a strong moral mandate. Her findings showed stronger fair process effects on outcome evaluations among respondents who did not have a clear a priori sense of what outcomes are fair or unfair than among those who did have strong moral mandates.

At the beginning of the new millennium, the earlier fairness heuristic studies were expanded to a more broader uncertainty management framework (Van den Bos, 2001a; Van den Bos & Lind, 2002). We argued that heuristic processes are a special case of how people deal with un-

certainty and we argued more explicitly that uncertainty is a crucial assumption in the psychology of the fair process effect in organizations (Lind & Van den Bos, 2002) and elsewhere (Van den Bos & Lind, 2002). Reason for this expansion were research findings that showed strong fair process effects when people were uncertain about authority's trustworthiness in controlled settings (Van den Bos, Wilke, & Lind, 1998) or in organizational contexts (Van den Bos, Van Schie, & Colenberg, 2002) or when issues related to uncertainty (Van den Bos, 2001d; Van den Bos & Miedema, 2000) or general self-related uncertainty were salient (Van den Bos, 2001a). All these findings converge on the same point that strong fair process effects are more likely to be found in uncertain circumstances and that people have a greater interest in fairness in uncertain as opposed to certain situations.

An ironic implication of the uncertainty explanation should be noted here: After having discovered the first instances of the fair process effect, organizational researchers set out to test the effect in what was thought of then as especially difficult circumstances for the effect to occur: The effect was tested in settings where respondents were laid off, where reorganization processes were going on, and so on (for an overview, see Lind & Tyler, 1988; see also Brockner, 1990, 1994; Brockner, Grover, Reed, DeWitt, & O'Malley, 1987). Organizational justice researchers were quite pleased to find strong fair process effects under these harsh conditions. The uncertainty explanation, however, points out that it is not so surprising to find the effects there, but that fair process effects are especially likely to be found in these kind of uncertain situations.

Another reason why the uncertainty explanation may be important for organizational researchers is that it contradicts economic perspectives on organizational behavior and managerial practice, which tend to think of organizational justice as some luxurious good, to be awarded to employees in quite times. The uncertainty analysis, however, suggests that it is especially in times of turmoil that organizational justice is important (Lind & Van den Bos, 2002; Van den Bos, Heuven, Burger, & Fernández van Veldhuizen, in press).

FUTURE RESEARCH DIRECTIONS

Future research may want to investigate the psychological mechanisms proposed by these explanations more thoroughly and deeply than has done before and possibly may want to explore the relative explanatory power of these mechanisms. I hasten to note here that because the fair process effect involves such a wide variety of specific procedures, contexts, and types of human reactions, it could well be that it would turn out to be a wrong and an inefficient research strategy to try to set up a

crucial experiment, aimed at proving that one mechanism can provide a complete explanation (Greenberg & Folger, 1983). The different explanations of the fair process effect that have been put forward in the literature may suggest that various important motives and processes are underlying the effect (cf. Van den Bos, 2002; Van Prooijen, Van den Bos, & Wilke, in press), and it may well be that it turns out to be better and wiser to start investigating the specifics of the psychological mechanisms proposed in the literature and to begin focusing on the differences between the various procedures, conditions, and dependent variables (see, e.g., Folger & Konovsky, 1992; Sweeney & McFarlin, 1993).

In developing new research, organizational psychologists may want to realize that the field is now waiting for answers to fundamental questions and hence that it is now time to start conducting fundamental research on the psychology of the fair process effect and other organizational justice phenomena. Going back to the roots from which research on the fair process effect has developed (Folger et al., 1979; Walker et al., 1974) may be extremely conducive in this respect, as using the basic theories, thorough research methods, and ingenious process measures of social psychology (see, e.g., Hafer, 2000; Steiner, Guirard, & Baccino, 1999; Van den Bos & Van Prooijen, 2001; Van Prooijen et al., 2002) may make it possible to understand the fundamentals of organizational justice issues. It is my hope that this chapter may contribute to these and other future avenues of research on the psychology of the fair process effect in the workplace and elsewhere.

CONCLUSIONS

In this chapter we have seen that the fair process effect is alive and well and that several explanations of the psychology of the effect have been put forward. What I personally find interesting, at the risk of blowing my own horn, is that in all explanations reviewed here uncertainty plays an important role, perhaps suggesting that the uncertainty explanation is best able to integrate the different explanations and may provide the broadest and most accurate explanation of the fair process effect in most (but in all likelihood not all) instances. What we further have seen in this chapter is that the fair process effect, and the varying perspectives on the effect that have been reviewed here, may well serve as a common thread for organizing key contributions to the literature on organizational justice. This implies that the fair process effect may nicely be used as an organizational schema that ties together many seemingly disparate approaches to the justice field. This alone makes the fair process effect very important and exciting to study.

ACKNOWLEDGMENT

I thank Jerry Greenberg for his comments on a previous version of this chapter.

REFERENCES

Adams, J. S. (1965). Inequity in social exchange. In L. Berkowitz (Ed.), *Advances in experimental social psychology* (Vol. 2, pp. 267–299). New York: Academic Press.

Alexander, S., & Ruderman, M. (1987). The role of procedural and distributive justice in organizational behavior. *Social Justice Research, 1*, 117–198.

Baumeister, R. F., Bratslavsky, E., Finkenauer, C., & Vohs, K. D. (2001). Bad is stronger than good. *Review of General Psychology, 5*, 323–370.

Bies, R. J., & Moag, J. S. (1986). Interactional justice: Communication criteria of fairness. In R. Lewicki, B. H. Sheppard, & M. H. Bazerman (Eds.), *Research on negotiation in organizations* (pp. 43–55). Greenwich, CT: JAI.

Bies, R. J., & Shapiro, D. L. (1987). Interactional fairness judgments: The influence of causal accounts. *Social Justice Research, 1*, 199–218.

Blau, P. M. (1964). *Exchange and power in social life*. New York: Wiley.

Bobocel, D. R., Agar, S. E., Meyer, J. P., & Irving, P. G. (1998). Managerial accounts and fairness perceptions in conflict resolution: Differentiating the effects of minimizing responsibility and providing justification. *Basic and Applied Social Psychology, 20*, 133–143.

Brehm, J. W. (1966). *A theory of psychological reactance*. New York: Academic Press.

Brockner, J. (1990). Scope of justice in the workplace: How survivors react to coworker layoffs. *Journal of Social Issues, 46*, 95–106.

Brockner, J. (1994). Perceived fairness and survivors' reactions to layoffs, or how downsizing organizations can do well by doing good. *Social Justice Research, 7*, 345–363.

Brockner, J., Grover, S., Reed, T., DeWitt, R., & O'Malley, M. (1987). Survivors' reactions to layoffs: We get by with a little help from our friends. *Administrative Science Quarterly, 32*, 526–541.

Brockner, J., & Wiesenfeld, B. M. (1996). An integrative framework for explaining reactions to decisions: Interactive effects of outcomes and procedures. *Psychological Bulletin, 120*, 189–208.

Colquitt, J. A., Conlon, D. E., Wesson, M. W., Porter, C. O. L. H., & Ng, K. Y. (2001). Justice at the millennium: A meta-analytic review of 25 years of organizational justice research. *Journal of Applied Psychology, 86*, 425–445.

Cropanzano, R., & Folger, R. (1989). Referent cognitions and task decision autonomy: Beyond equity theory. *Journal of Applied Psychology, 74*, 293–299.

Cropanzano, R., & Folger, R. (1991). Procedural justice and worker motivation. In R. M. Steers & L. W. Porter (Eds.), *Motivation and work behavior* (Vol. 5, pp. 131–143). New York: McGraw-Hill.

Cropanzano, R., & Greenberg, J. (1997). Progress in organizational justice: Tunneling through the maze. In C. L. Cooper & I. T. Robertson (Eds.), *International review of industrial and organizational psychology* (pp. 317–372). New York: Wiley.

Crosby, F. (1976). A model of egoistical relative deprivation. *Psychological Review, 83*, 85–112.

Deutsch, M. (1975). Equity, equality, or need? What determines which value will be used as the basis of distributive justice? *Journal of Social Issues, 31*, 137–149.

Deutsch, M. (1985). *Distributive justice: A social psychological perspective.* New Haven, CT: Yale University Press.

Fiske, S. T., & Taylor, S. E. (1991). *Social cognition* (2nd ed.). New York: McGraw-Hill.

Folger, R. (1984). Preface. In R. Folger (Ed.), *The sense of injustice: Social psychological perspectives* (pp. ix–x). New York: Plenum.

Folger, R. (1986). Rethinking equity theory: A referent cognitions model. In H. M. Bierhoff, R. L. Cohen, & J. Greenberg (Eds.), *Justice in social relations* (pp. 145–162). New York: Plenum.

Folger, R. (1987). Reformulating the preconditions of resentment: A referent cognitions model. In J. C. Masters & W. P. Smith (Eds.), *Social comparison, social justice, and relative deprivation: Theoretical, empirical, and policy perspectives* (pp. 183–215). Hillsdale, NJ: Lawrence Erlbaum Associates.

Folger, R. (1993). Reactions to mistreatment at work. In K. Murnigham (Ed.), *Social psychology in organizations: Advances in theory and research* (pp. 161–183). Stanford, CA: Stanford University Press.

Folger, R., & Baron, R. A. (1996). Violence and hostility at work: A model of reactions to perceived injustice. In G. R. VandenBos & E. Q. Bulatao (Eds.), *Violence on the job: Identifying risks and developing solutions* (pp. 51–85). Washington, DC: American Psychological Association.

Folger, R., & Cropanzano, R. (1998). *Organizational justice and human resource management.* Thousand Oaks, CA: Sage.

Folger, R., & Konovsky, M. (1989). Effects of procedural and distributive justice on reactions to pay raise decisions. *Academy of Management Journal, 32*, 115–130.

Folger, R., & Martin, C. (1986). Relative deprivation and referent cognitions: Distributive and procedural justice effects. *Journal of Experimental Social Psychology, 22*, 531–546.

Folger, R., Rosenfield, D., Grove, J., & Corkran, L. (1979). Effects of "voice" and peer opinions on responses to inequity. *Journal of Personality and Social Psychology, 37*, 2253–2261.

Folger, R., Rosenfield, D., & Robinson, T. (1983). Relative deprivation and procedural justifications. *Journal of Personality and Social Psychology, 45*, 268–273.

Folger, R., & Skarlicki, D. P. (1998). A popcorn metaphor for employee aggression. In R. Griffin, A. O'Leary-Kelly, & J. Collins (Eds.), *Dysfunctional behavior in organizations: Volume 1. Violent behavior in organizations* (pp. 43–82). Greenwich, CT: JAI Press.

Greenberg, J. (1986). Determinants of perceived fairness of performance evaluations. *Journal of Applied Psychology, 71*, 340–342.

Greenberg, J. (1987a). Reactions to procedural injustice in payment distributions: Do the ends justify the means? *Journal of Applied Psychology, 72*, 55–61.

Greenberg, J. (1987b). Using diaries to promote procedural justice in performance appraisals. *Social Justice Research, 1*, 219–234.

Greenberg, J. (1990). Organizational justice: Yesterday, today, and tomorrow. *Journal of Management, 16*, 399–432.

Greenberg, J. (1993). Stealing in the name of justice: Informational and interpersonal moderators of theft reactions to underpayment inequity. *Organizational Behavior and Human Decision Processes, 54*, 81–103.

Greenberg, J. (1994). Using socially fair treatment to promote acceptance of a work site smoking ban. *Journal of Applied Psychology, 79*, 288–297.

Greenberg, J. (1997). A social influence model of employee theft: Beyond the fraud triangle. In R. J. Lewicki, R. J. Bies, & B. H. Sheppard (Eds.), *Research on negotiation in organizations* (Vol. 6, pp. 29–52). Greenwich, CT: JAI Press.

Greenberg, J. (2000). Promote procedural justice to enhance acceptance of work outcomes. In E. A. Locke (Ed.), *A handbook of principles of organizational behavior* (pp. 181–195). Oxford, England: Blackwell.

Greenberg, J., & Folger, R. (1983). Procedural justice, participation, and the fair process effect in groups and organizations. In P. B. Paulus (Ed.), *Basic group processes* (pp. 235–256). New York: Springer-Verlag.

Greenberg, J., & Lind, E. A. (2000). The pursuit of organizational justice: From conceptualization to implication to application. In C. L. Cooper & E. A. Locke (Eds.), *I/O psychology: What we know about theory and practice* (pp. 72–105). Oxford, England: Blackwell.

Hafer, C. L. (2000). Do innocent victims threaten the belief in a just world? Evidence from a modified Stroop task. *Journal of Personality and Social Psychology, 79,* 165–173.

Haidt, J. (2001). The emotional dog and its rational tail: A social intuitionist approach to moral judgment. *Psychological Review, 108,* 814–834.

Hare, R. M. (1981). *Moral thinking: Its levels, method, and point.* Oxford: Clarendon Press.

Hirschman, A. O. (1970). *Exit, voice and loyalty: Responses to declines in firms, organizations, and states.* Cambridge, MA: Harvard University Press.

Homans, G. C. (1961). *Social behavior: Its elementary forms.* New York: Harcourt, Brace, & World.

Huo, Y. J., Smith, H. J., Tyler, T. R., & Lind, E. A. (1996). Superordinate identification, subgroup identification, and justice concerns: Is separatism the problem; is assimilation the answer? *Psychological Science, 7,* 40–45.

Jasso, G. (1994). Assessing individual and group differences in the sense of justice: Framework and application to gender differences in the justice of earnings. *Social Science Research, 23,* 368–406.

Jasso, G. (1999). How much injustice is there in the world? Two new justice indexes. *American Sociological Review, 64,* 133–168.

Kahneman, D., & Tversky, A. (1982). The simulation heuristic. In D. Kahneman, P. Slovic, & A. Tversky (Eds.), *Judgment under uncertainty: Heuristics and biases* (pp. 201–208). New York: Cambridge University Press.

Kanfer, R., Sawyer, J., Earley, P. C., & Lind, E. A. (1987). Fairness and participation in evaluation procedures: Effects on task attitudes and performance. *Social Justice Research, 1,* 235–249.

Konovsky, M., & Folger, R. (1991, August). *The effects of procedural and distributive justice on organizational citizenship behavior.* Paper presented at the annual meeting of the Academy of Management, Miami Beach, FL.

Korsgaard, M. A., Schweiger, D. M., & Sapienza, H. J. (1995). Building commitment, attachment, and trust in strategic decision-making teams: The role of procedural justice. *Academy of Management Journal, 38,* 60–84.

Landman, J. (1987). Regret and elation following action and inaction: Affective reactions to positive versus negative outcomes. *Personality and Social Psychology Bulletin, 13,* 524–536.

Lerner, M. J., & Whitehead, L. A. (1980). Procedural justice viewed in the context of justice motive theory. In G. Mikula (Ed.), *Justice and social interaction: Experimental and theoretical contributions from psychological research* (pp. 219–256). Bern, Austria: Huber.

Leventhal, G. S. (1980). What should be done with equity theory? New approaches to the study of fairness in social relationships. In K. J. Gergen, M. S. Greenberg, & R. H. Willis (Eds.), *Social exchange: Advances in theory and research* (pp. 27–54). New York: Plenum.

Lind, E. A. (1990). *Arbitrating high-stakes cases: An evaluation of court-annexed arbitration in a United States district court.* Santa Monica, CA: Rand Corporation.

Lind, E. A. (2001). Fairness heuristic theory: Justice judgments as pivotal cognitions in organizational relations. In J. Greenberg & R. Cropanzano (Eds.), *Advances in organizational behavior* (pp. 56–88). Stanford, CA: Stanford University Press.

Lind, E. A., Greenberg, J., Scott, K. S., & Welchans, T. D. (2000). The winding road from employee to complainant: Situational and psychological determinants of wrongful termination claims. *Administrative Science Quarterly, 45,* 557–590.

Lind, E. A., Kanfer, R., & Earley, P. C. (1990). Voice, control, and procedural justice: Instrumental and noninstrumental concerns in fairness judgments. *Journal of Personality and Social Psychology, 59,* 952–959.

Lind, E. A., Kulik, C. T., Ambrose, M., & de Vera Park, M. V. (1993). Individual and corporate dispute resolution: Using procedural fairness as a decision heuristic. *Administrative Science Quarterly, 38,* 224–251.

Lind, E. A., Kurtz, S., Musante, L., Walker L., & Thibaut, J. (1980). Procedure and outcome effects on reactions to adjudicated resolution of conflicts of interest. *Journal of Personality and Social Psychology, 39,* 643–653.

Lind, E. A., & Tyler, T. R. (1988). *The social psychology of procedural justice.* New York: Plenum.

Lind, E. A., & Van den Bos, K. (2002). When fairness works: Toward a general theory of uncertainty management. In B. M. Staw & R. M. Kramer (Eds.), *Research in organizational behavior* (Vol. 24, pp. 181–223). Greenwich, CT: JAI Press.

McFarlin, D. B., & Sweeney, P. D. (1992). Distributive and procedural justice as predictors of satisfaction with personal and organizational outcomes. *Academy of Management Journal, 35,* 626–637.

Messick, D. M., & Sentis, K. (1983). Fairness, preference, and fairness biases. In D. M. Messick & K. S. Cook (Eds.), *Equity theory: Psychological and sociological perspectives* (pp. 61–94). New York: Praeger.

Mikula, G., & Wenzel, M. (2000). Justice and social conflict. *International Journal of Psychology, 35,* 126–135.

Moorman, R. H. (1991). Relationship between organizational justice and organizational citizenship behaviors: Do fairness perceptions influence employee citizenship? *Journal of Applied Psychology, 76,* 845–855.

Paternoster, R., Brame, R., Bachman, R., & Sherman, L. W. (1997). Do fair procedures matter? The effect of procedural justice on spouse assault. *Law and Society Review, 31,* 163–204.

Peeters, G., & Czapinski, J. (1990). Positive-negative asymmetry in evaluations: The distinction between affective and information negativity effects. In W. Stroebe & M. Hewstone (Eds.), *European review of social psychology* (Vol. 1, pp. 33–60). Chichester, UK: Wiley.

Podsakoff, P. M., & MacKenzie, S. B. (1993). Citizenship behavior and fairness in organizations: Issues and directions for future research. *Employee Responsibilities and Rights Journal, 6,* 235–247.

Rawls, J. (1971). *A theory of justice.* Oxford: Oxford University Press.

Rutte, C. G., & Messick, D. M. (1995). An integrated model of perceived unfairness in organizations. *Social Justice Research, 8,* 239–261.

Sabbagh, C., Dar, Y., & Resh, N. (1994). The structure of social justice judgments: A facet approach. *Social Psychology Quarterly, 57*, 244–261.

Skitka, L. J. (2002). Do the means always justify the ends, or do the ends sometimes justify the means? A value protection model of justice. *Personality and Social Psychology Bulletin, 28*, 588–597.

Smith, H. J., & Tyler, T. R. (1997). Choosing the right pond: The impact of group membership on self-esteem and group-oriented behavior. *Journal of Experimental Social Psychology, 33*, 146–170.

Smith, H. J., Tyler, T. R., Huo, Y. J., Ortiz, D. J., & Lind, E. A. (1998). The self-relevant implications of the group-value model: Group-membership, self-worth and treatment quality. *Journal of Experimental Social Psychology, 34*, 470–493.

Steiner, D. D., Guirard, S., & Baccino, T. (1999, May). *Cognitive processing of procedural justice information: Application of the oculometer.* Paper presented at the Annual Conference of the Society for Industrial/Organizational Psychology, Atlanta, GA.

Stouffer, S. A., Suchman, E. A., DeVinney, L. C., Star, S. A., & Williams, R. M. (1949). *The American soldier: Adjustment during Army life* (Vol. 1). Princeton, NJ: Princeton University Press.

Sweeney, P. D., & McFarlin, D. B. (1993). Workers' evaluations of the "ends" and the "means": An examination of four models of distributive and procedural justice. *Organizational Behavior and Human Decision Processes, 54*, 23–40.

Thibaut, J., & Walker, L. (1975). *Procedural justice: A psychological analysis.* Hillsdale, NJ: Lawrence Erlbaum Associates.

Thibaut, J., & Walker, L. (1978). A theory of procedure. *California Law Review, 66*, 541–566.

Tyler, T. R. (1984). The role of perceived injustice in defendants' evaluations of their courtroom experience. *Law and Society Review, 18*, 51–74.

Tyler, T. R. (1987). Conditions leading to value-expressive effects in judgments of procedural justice: A test of four models. *Journal of Personality and Social Psychology, 52*, 333–344.

Tyler, T. R. (1990). *Why do people obey the law? Procedural justice, legitimacy, and compliance.* New Haven, CT: Yale University Press.

Tyler, T. R. (1991). Using procedures to justify outcomes: Testing the viability of a procedural justice strategy for managing conflict and allocating resources in organizations. *Basic and Applied Psychology, 12*, 259–279.

Tyler, T. R. (1994). Psychological models of the justice motive: Antecedents of distributive and procedural justice. *Journal of Personality and Social Psychology, 67*, 850–863.

Tyler, T. R. (1997). The psychology of legitimacy: A relational perspective on voluntary deference to authorities. *Personality and Social Psychology Review, 1*, 323–345.

Tyler, T. R., & Bies, R. J. (1990). Beyond formal procedures: The interpersonal context of procedural justice. In J. S. Caroll (Ed.), *Applied social psychology and organizational settings* (pp. 77–98). Hillsdale, NJ: Lawrence Erlbaum Associates.

Tyler, T. R., Boeckmann, R. J., Smith, H. J., & Huo, Y. J. (1997). *Social justice in a diverse society.* Boulder, CO: Westview.

Tyler, T. R., & Caine, A. (1981). The influence of outcomes and procedures on satisfaction with formal leaders. *Journal of Personality and Social Psychology, 41*, 642–655.

Tyler, T. R., & DeGoey, P. (1995). Collective restraint in social dilemmas: Procedural justice and social identification effects on support for authorities. *Journal of Personality and Social Psychology, 69*, 482–497.

Tyler, T. R., DeGoey, P., & Smith, H. J. (1996). Understanding why the justice of group procedures matters: A test of the psychological dynamics of the group-value model. *Journal of Personality and Social Psychology, 70,* 913–930.

Tyler, T. R., & Folger, R. (1980). Distributional and procedural aspects of satisfaction with citizen-police encounters. *Basic and Applied Social Psychology, 1,* 281–292.

Tyler, T. R., & Lind, E. A. (1990). Intrinsic versus community-based justice models: When does group membership matter? *Journal of Social Issues, 46,* 83–94.

Tyler, T. R., & Lind, E. A. (1992). A relational model of authority in groups. In M. P. Zanna (Ed.), *Advances in experimental social psychology* (Vol. 25, pp. 115–191). San Diego, CA: Academic Press.

Tyler, T. R., Rasinski, K. A., & McGraw, K. M. (1985). The influence of perceived injustice on the endorsement of political leaders. *Journal of Applied Social Psychology, 15,* 700–725.

Van den Bos, K. (2001a). Uncertainty management: The influence of uncertainty salience on reactions to perceived procedural fairness. *Journal of Personality and Social Psychology, 80,* 931–941.

Van den Bos, K. (2001b). Fundamental research by means of laboratory experiments is essential for a better understanding of organizational justice. *Journal of Vocational Behavior, 58,* 254–259.

Van den Bos, K. (2001c). Fairness heuristic theory: Assessing the information to which people are reacting has a pivotal role in understanding organizational justice. In S. W. Gilliland, D. D. Steiner, & D. P. Skarlicki (Eds.), *Theoretical and cultural perspectives on organizational justice* (pp. 63–84). Greenwich, CT: Information Age.

Van den Bos, K. (2001d). Reactions to perceived fairness: The impact of mortality salience and self-esteem on ratings of negative affect. *Social Justice Research, 14,* 1–23.

Van den Bos, K. (2003). On the subjective quality of social justice: The role of affect as information in the psychology of justice judgments. *Journal of Personality and Social Psychology, 85,* 482–498.

Van den Bos, K., Heuven, E., Burger, E., & Fernández van Veldhuizen, M. (in press). Uncertainty management after reorganizations: The ameliorative effect of outcome fairness on job uncertainty. *International Review of Social Psychology.*

Van den Bos, K., & Lind, E. A. (2002). Uncertainty management by means of fairness judgments. In M. P. Zanna (Ed.), *Advances in experimental social psychology* (Vol. 34, pp. 1–60). San Diego, CA: Academic Press.

Van den Bos, K., Lind, E. A., Vermunt, R., & Wilke, H. A. M. (1997). How do I judge my outcome when I do not know the outcome of others? The psychology of the fair process effect. *Journal of Personality and Social Psychology, 72,* 1034–1046.

Van den Bos, K., Lind, E. A., & Wilke, H. A. M. (2001). The psychology of procedural and distributive justice viewed from the perspective of fairness heuristic theory. In R. Cropanzano (Ed.), *Justice in the workplace: Volume 2—From theory to practice* (pp. 49–66). Mahwah, NJ: Lawrence Erlbaum Associates.

Van den Bos, K., Maas, M., Waldring, I. E., & Semin, G. R. (2003). Toward understanding the psychology of reactions to perceived fairness: The role of affect intensity. *Social Justice Research, 16,* 151–168.

Van den Bos, K., & Miedema, J. (2000). Toward understanding why fairness matters: The influence of mortality salience on reactions to procedural fairness. *Journal of Personality and Social Psychology, 79,* 355–366.

Van den Bos, K., & Spruijt, N. (2002). Appropriateness of decisions as a moderator of the psychology of voice. *European Journal of Social Psychology, 32,* 57–72.

Van den Bos, K., & Van Prooijen, J.-W. (2001). Referent cognitions theory: The role of closeness of reference points in the psychology of voice. *Journal of Personality and Social Psychology, 81,* 616–626.

Van den Bos, K., Van Schie, E. C. M., & Colenberg, S. E. (2002). Parents' reactions to child day care organizations: The influence of perceptions of procedures and the role of organizations' trustworthiness. *Social Justice Research, 15,* 53–62.

Van den Bos, K., Vermunt, R., & Wilke, H. A. M. (1996). The consistency rule and the voice effect: The influence of expectations on procedural fairness judgements and performance. *European Journal of Social Psychology, 26,* 411–428.

Van den Bos, K., Vermunt, R., & Wilke, H. A. M. (1997). Procedural and distributive justice: What is fair depends more on what comes first than on what comes next. *Journal of Personality and Social Psychology, 72,* 95–104.

Van den Bos, K., Wilke, H. A. M., & Lind, E. A. (1998). When do we need procedural fairness? The role of trust in authority. *Journal of Personality and Social Psychology, 75,* 1449–1458.

Van den Bos, K., Wilke, H. A. M., Lind, E. A., & Vermunt, R. (1998). Evaluating outcomes by means of the fair process effect: Evidence for different processes in fairness and satisfaction judgments. *Journal of Personality and Social Psychology, 74,* 1493–1503.

Van Prooijen, J.-W., Van den Bos, K., & Wilke, H. A. M. (2002). Procedural justice and status: Status salience as antecedent of the fair process effect. *Journal of Personality and Social Psychology, 83,* 1353–1361.

Van Prooijen, J.-W., Van den Bos, K., & Wilke, H. A. M. (in press). The role of standing in the psychology of procedural justice: Toward theoretical integration. In W. Stroebe & M. Hewstone (Eds.), *European Review of Social Psychology, 14.* Hove, UK: Psychology Press.

Vermunt, R., Wit, A., Van den Bos, K., & Lind, A. (1996). The effect of inaccurate procedure on protest: The mediating role of perceived unfairness and situational self-esteem. *Social Justice Research, 9,* 109–119.

Walker, L., LaTour, S., Lind, E. A., & Thibaut, J. (1974). Reactions of participants and observers to modes of adjudication. *Journal of Applied Social Psychology, 4,* 295–310.

Walker, L., Lind, E. A., & Thibaut, J. (1979). The relation between procedural and distributive justice. *Virginia Law Review, 65,* 1401–1420.

Walster, E., Berscheid, E., & Walster, G. W. (1973). New directions in equity research. *Journal of Personality and Social Psychology, 25,* 151–176.

Walster, E., Walster, G. W., & Berscheid, E. (1978). *Equity: Theory and research.* Boston: Allyn & Bacon.

Weiss, H. M., Suckow, K., & Cropanzano, R. (1999). Effects of justice conditions on discrete emotions. *Journal of Applied Psychology, 84,* 786–794.

White, R. W. (1959). Motivation reconsidered: The concept of competence. *Psychological Review, 66,* 297–333.

Zeelenberg, M., Van den Bos, K., Van Dijk, E., & Pieters, R. G. M. (2002). The inaction effect in the psychology of regret. *Journal of Personality and Social Psychology, 82,* 314–327.

10

How Does Organizational Justice Affect Performance, Withdrawal, and Counterproductive Behavior?

Donald E. Conlon
Michigan State University

Christopher J. Meyer
Michigan State University

Jaclyn M. Nowakowski
Michigan State University

In this chapter we focus on key organizational outcomes resulting from justice in the workplace. We review the literature and apply a four-factor structure of organizational justice (Colquitt, 2001) to understand "the good, the bad, and the ugly" behavioral outcomes arising from fair interactions or a breach of fairness in organizational relationships. In the section focusing on good outcomes we examine previous work on task performance and compliance. In the section focusing on bad outcomes, we classify turnover, absenteeism, and employee silence as withdrawal behaviors stemming from unfairness. In discussing the ugly outcomes, we apply the framework as developed by Robinson and Bennett (1995) to understand major or minor instances of counterproductive behavior against organizations or individuals. Finally we address the challenges of operationalization, application, and accessibility inherent in studying justice and organizational outcomes and offer recommendations for future research in this field.

This is a most opportune time to be studying the impact of justice on organizational outcomes, for at least two reasons. First, there seems to be considerable interest in justice and the power it holds to explain employee attitudes and behaviors. Evidence in support of this assertion can be found in the large number of empirical studies, narrative reviews, and books published in the last ten years pertaining to organizational justice.

Second, calendar year 2001 saw the publication of two large meta-analytic reviews, which provide a quantitative summary of the relationships that have been documented between justice and a variety of outcomes. The first one, published in June, summarized the results of 242 independent samples found in 183 articles published between 1976 and 2001 (Colquitt, Conlon, Wesson, Porter, & Ng, 2001). The second, published in November, summarized the results of 190 samples found in 153 articles published between 1979 and 2001 (Cohen-Charash & Spector, 2001; see also Cohen-Charash & Spector, 2002).

Although the two studies rely on many of the same articles in their analyses, the structures of the two meta-analyses differ. For example, Colquitt et al. (2001) conceptualized organizational justice in terms of four constructs: distributive justice, procedural justice, interpersonal justice, and informational justice. Cohen-Charash and Spector (2001) construed organizational justice in terms of three constructs. In addition to distributive and procedural justice, they used the single construct of interactional justice rather than the separate constructs of interpersonal

and informational justice. The two studies also deal with organizational outcomes differently. Colquitt et al. (2001) employ fairly broad categories and collapse organizational outcomes into eleven categories. For example, in the category "withdrawal behaviors," Colquitt et al. included "behaviors and behavioral intentions such as absenteeism, turnover, and neglect"(2001, p. 430). Cohen-Charash and Spector (2001), on the other hand, conceptually described fewer areas (eight) in their introduction and discussion but presented their data at a more micro level, providing data on 30 specific organizational outcomes. Thus, the Colquitt et al. study offers more specificity on the justice side, whereas the Cohen-Charash study offers more specificity on the organizational outcomes side.

In this chapter, we attempt to build on these recent summaries of the justice literature and provide some additional insights as to what types of justice relate most strongly to key organizational outcomes. We begin by defining what we mean by both "justice" and "key organizational outcomes." The first task is fairly easy. We define *justice* in terms of four constructs, distributive, procedural, interpersonal, and informational justice, following the lead of scholars (and book editors!) such as Colquitt and Greenberg. We leave the discussion of whether there are really two, three, or four forms of justice to other authors (and other chapters).

The definition of *key organizational outcomes,* on the other hand is more complex. In defining our turf, we begin by discarding organizational outcomes covered by other authors in this book. Thus we are not considering the effects justice has on topics such as cooperation or organizational citizenship behavior. We further bound our investigation by focusing on behavioral outcomes rather than attitudes. We rely on a Clint Eastwood "spaghetti Western" movie as a heuristic and organize our set of key organizational outcomes into three categories: the good (performance and compliance), the bad (withdrawal behaviors such as turnover and absenteeism), and the ugly (violence and other counterproductive work behaviors). As Fig. 10.1 documents, we examine the utility of organizational justice in predicting three categories of behaviors in organizations. After this review, we highlight three challenges that we see as necessary for the justice literature to become even more helpful in explaining behavioral outcomes in organizations.

THE GOOD: TASK PERFORMANCE AND EMPLOYEE COMPLIANCE

Task Performance

Early studies of the relationship between procedural justice and performance often focused on participation as a key antecedent to procedural

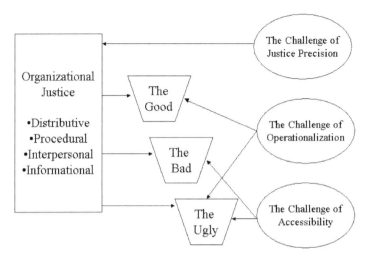

FIG. 10.1.   A model depicting the challenges faced in using organizational
justice to predict key organizational outcomes.

justice. Although the participation–procedural justice relationship was
typically strong, the connection to performance was more tenuous. On
the positive side, Earley (1984) integrated procedural justice and goal-
setting theory and found in both a field and a lab study that allowing
workers greater amounts of voice in setting goals led to higher performance. A later study by Earley and Lind (1987) allowed workers control
over how tasks were assigned to see whether providing such process
control would enhance procedural justice judgments and, ultimately,
performance. They found that providing workers with this form of participation enhanced procedural justice and performance in the lab
study, but not the field study. On the negative side, a study by Kanfer,
Sawyer, Earley, and Lind (1987) found a negative relationship between
procedural justice and performance. In this study, the authors manipulated the amount of voice participants had in a performance appraisal
opportunity.

Lind and Tyler (1988, pp. 190–191) summarized the relationship between procedural justice and performance by discounting the importance of the relationship: "We believe that, notwithstanding the
importance of performance in organizational settings, the great practical value of procedural justice lies in its capacity to enhance the quality
of work life and in its value as a source of both satisfaction and positive
evaluations of the organization." However, some recent studies might
suggest that Lind and Tyler were too pessimistic. Douthitt and Aiello

(2001) examined the impact of participation (input or no input regarding aspects of the work task and reward structure to be used) and control over monitoring (continuous computer monitoring, worker ability to turn computer monitoring on/off, or no monitoring at all) on procedural justice judgments and performance on a computer-based judgment task. Their results showed that the participation manipulation, but not the monitoring manipulation, influenced procedural justice, and that procedural justice (measured in terms of the fairness of the performance evaluation method) was positively correlated ($r = .20$) with performance. The procedural justice–performance link in this study can be viewed as more typical, as Colquitt et al. (2001) reported only modest relationships for procedural justice and performance (corrected correlations ranging from .10 to .36 between procedural justice and performance, depending on how procedural justice was measured).

On the other hand, more recent work might argue that the concepts of interpersonal and informational justice might influence performance. For example, Masterson, Lewis, Goldman, and Taylor (2000) examined the influence of both procedural and interactional justice (the latter measure actually combining items that tap procedural, interpersonal, and informational justice elements) on the performance of university clerical and staff employees. Procedural justice was, as in the Kanfer et al. (1987) study, measured in reference to the performance appraisal procedure used in the organization (in this case, a university). Their results revealed a nonsignificant relationship ($r = -.05$) between procedural justice and performance (measured via supervisor performance ratings). However, performance was positively correlated with the interactional justice measure ($r = .19$).

Unfortunately, there have not been a large number of studies where one can compare the effects of multiple forms of justice on performance. This is particularly true in reference to distributive justice, as many studies examining distributive justice and performance were done without incorporating procedural justice arguments or manipulations. One exception is a study by Robbins, Summers, Miller, and Hendrix (2000), who measured the unique effects of distributive justice, procedural justice (labeled as "instrumental procedural justice"), and interpersonal justice (labeled as "noninstrumental procedural justice") on two measures of employee performance (supervisor ratings and employee self reports of group performance) at a textile products company. Robbins et al. (2000) found that the measure relating to interpersonal justice was the only justice variable to explain unique variance in both supervisor ratings and employee perceptions of workgroup performance. (This study is also noteworthy for being one of the only studies that documents relationships between organizational justice concepts and group performance.)

Another exception is Weaver and Conlon (2003) who conducted a lab study where workers had to work on an interesting task (involving cartoons) or a boring task (involving mathematical logic). Participants were told they would get to work on the task of their choice, and all workers were asked to provide their choice (a very strong form of voice). However, when it came time to do the task half were made to do the boring task (the task they did not choose). Weaver and Conlon (2003) measured distributive, procedural, and interactional justice (the latter a measure containing both interpersonal and informational justice items) and found that distributive justice was the only justice measure significantly correlated with performance, and it was only with the "speed" dimension of performance (number of pages completed), and not the "accuracy" of performance (number of errors).

Compliance

Compliance is a multifaceted concept that can mean many different things depending on the context. We focus on two forms of compliance. The first represents situations where parties accept rather than reject decisions or outcomes made by others that are often not in one's favor. However, we also examine compliance in terms of the continuance of a line of behavior (e.g., choosing to interact in the future with the same person or service provider rather than with someone else).

Decision Acceptance. To the extent that organizations must manage employees in an era of shrinking resources or more restrictive work environments, determining how to "make do" with fewer privileges and fewer resources is an important question to address. Recent studies suggest that interpersonal and informational justice may be key levers by which to make employees more accepting of difficult decisions or outcomes that affect them. For example, Greenberg (1994) manipulated several justice factors in a field experiment designed to test how information thoroughness, social sensitivity, and outcome severity would influence reactions to the imposition of a work site smoking ban. Greenberg found that worker compliance with the smoking ban at work was influenced by manipulations that conveyed both interpersonal justice and informational justice. Moreover, the heaviest smokers, those most impacted by the ban, were the ones whose reactions improved most dramatically through communicating information about the smoking ban in an interpersonally and informationally sensitive manner.

Another study investigating compliance was conducted by Lind, Kulik, Ambrose, and de Vera Park (1993), who proposed that positive procedural justice judgments would increase the likelihood of accept-

ing an authority's decision (in this case, acceptance rather than rejection of arbitration awards) because procedural fairness judgments have a large impact on whether not a person decides to obey an authority. If the individual feels that the authority figure is fair and legitimate, the person is more likely to believe that the authority's decision is fair and legitimate. This "fairness heuristic" suggests that people use their evaluations of the process and outcome to decide whether the authority is fair, and then subsequently to decide if the authority should be obeyed. This hypothesized relationship was supported.

Another operationalization of compliance can be created by examining choices to litigate employee termination decisions. In this case, deciding not to file a wrongful termination claim would be seen as evidence of compliance. Dunford and Devine theorized a link between the context of the termination decision, perceptions of organizational justice, and the act of filing a lawsuit for wrongful dismissal. The authors predicted that employment at-will situations create the potential for employee discharge procedures that could be implemented too hastily or with insufficient attention to justification of the termination decision. If the discharge happens too quickly the employee could perceive that there was an inadequate explanation for the discharge. Similarly, if the discharge is poorly planned it may create more opportunities for mistakes that involve heated arguments and insults during the social exchange. The authors used the framework provided by Bies and Moag, and referred to this as *interactional justice*. Dunford and Devine (1998) argued that the lower levels of justice that would stem from these encounters will negatively influence compliance behavior—and therefore, greater instances of lawsuits.

In a study that provided empirical evidence for the claims just described, Lind, Greenberg, Scott, and Welchans (2000) interviewed hundreds of employees who had recently lost their jobs due to being fired or being laid off. Lind et al. (2000) were interested in the extent to which a variety of factors would influence decisions by workers to file wrongful termination claims. Perceptions of interpersonal justice, both on the job and particularly at the time of termination, were strong predictors of decisions to file a claim.

Relationship Maintenance. As mentioned earlier, compliance can also be thought of in terms of relationship maintenance, as by continuing a relationship with people or institutions, one acknowledges one's willingness to comply with the behaviors performed by this party. For example, in dispute resolution settings, one can view willingness to reuse an arbitrator on a future case as a measure of compliance. In a survey of labor and management representatives, Posthuma, Dworkin, and Swift (2000) found that distributive justice, procedural justice, and interact-

ional justice all explained unique and significant amounts of variance in decision-maker willingness to use an arbitrator in the future.

Customer service environments also present a context in which to study compliance. A critical element of the customer and service-provider relationship is repatronage, or the willingness of the customer to purchase from the vendor in the future (Conlon & Murray, 1996). In a series of laboratory experiments, Humphrey and colleagues (Ellis, Conlon, Tinsley, & Humphrey, 2003; Humphrey, Ellis, Conlon, & Tinsley, 2003) examined customer reactions to using an online service similar to priceline.com in order to get a hotel room. Humphrey et al. (2003) posited that justice judgments would mediate relationships between characteristics of the online transaction (such as whether one is asked to rebid, or how long one waited for a response) and customer willingness to use the service for a second hotel purchase (repatronage). Humphrey et al. (2003) found that perceptions of distributive justice and informational justice mediated the relationships between structural elements of the bid process and repatronage. Procedural and interpersonal justice did not influence repatronage behavior.

In a follow-up study, Ellis et al. (2003) discovered that attempts to enhance informational justice by providing thorough explanations were not always helpful. Again, the design involved a study of customer reactions to having bids accepted or rejected on an online travel system. They found that providing thorough explanations for how the system worked or for why bids were accepted or rejected enhanced repatronage levels only for those whose offers were rejected (adversely affected). For those not adversely affected (whose offers were accepted) providing thorough explanations actually decreased repatronage behavior. Apparently, those who were successful at bidding did not want information about the task, perhaps preferring to bask in their success without hearing other information that might make them less able to take responsibility for it.

A final variation on our theme of relationship maintenance as compliance comes from the strategic management literature. In a study of strategy implementation in multinational corporations, Kim and Mauborgne (1993) found that both procedural justice and outcome fairness (loosely, distributive justice) had a direct effect on subsidiary managers compliance with corporate strategies. The authors used a 5-item scale based on the Leventhal (1980) criteria to measure procedural justice. The context of this study is interesting in that the individuals that were included in the study were top managers of subsidiaries or business units within multinational corporations. The justice measures referred to the process of implementing key strategy decisions made at the head offices of the various corporations. The authors found that pro-

cedures that were perceived as fair were more likely to engender compliance with the decisions from the head office.

THE BAD: WITHDRAWAL BEHAVIORS

The job withdrawal literature (in particular, with respect to the withdrawal behaviors of turnover and absenteeism) has been studied extensively for two reasons. First, there are the obvious problems that absenteeism and turnover present to the efficient functioning of organizations. The second reason is that both variables are usually quite visible and are often tracked by organizations. However, our review of studies investigating justice and turnover was discouraging, as we found no studies where actual turnover behavior was measured in connection with organizational justice. Rather, turnover intentions are measured as a precursor to the actual behavior of turnover (Futrell & Parasuraman, 1984; Roberts, Coulson, & Chonko, 1999). Although this is not as strong a measure as actual turnover it is a reasonable proxy. We discuss three forms of withdrawal: turnover, absenteeism, and employee silence.

Turnover Intentions

The relationship between organizational justice and turnover intentions has produced mixed results. Dailey and Kirk (1992) conducted a field study examining the relationships between justice, job satisfaction, and intent to turnover. The authors measured distributive justice using the scale developed by Greenberg (1986a). The scale for procedural justice was adapted from Folger and Konovsky (1989) and measured two aspects of procedural justice—feedback and planning. No formal measures of interpersonal or informational justice were administered; however, those dimensions were largely picked up by the procedural justice measures related to feedback and planning, respectively. Dailey and Kirk (1992) found that as perceptions of procedural justice in delivering feedback (or what we would call interpersonal justice) diminished, employees were more likely to consider leaving their organization. Lower perceptions of procedural justice in job planning (loosely, informational justice) also predicted intent to turnover. Distributive justice was related to job satisfaction, and job satisfaction was related to intent to turnover. The authors found evidence that employees work attitudes and intent to turnover are sensitive both to rewards and the fairness of the organizational system. Perhaps most interestingly, Dailey and Kirk (1992) found justice to be a stronger predictor of intent to turnover than core work attitudes (such as job satisfaction).

Aryee and Chay (2001) examined the effects of distributive and procedural justice on intent to turnover in a unionized setting. The authors measured the perceptions of justice using the scale from Fryxell and Gordon (1989). The scales developed by Fryxell and Gordon measure distributive and procedural justice as it relates specifically to a unionized setting. No measures of informational or interpersonal justice were procured in this study. Only procedural justice was negatively related to the intent to leave the union. In addition, this relationship was partially mediated by the instrumentality of the union. That is, if the employee felt the union was doing a good job representing and protecting that person, the strength of the injustice–turnover relationship was weakened.

Konovsky and Cropanzano (1991) examined justice–turnover relationships within the context of drug testing procedures and found that procedures (procedural justice) and explanations (informational justice) were strongly related to turnover intentions. Outcomes (distributive justice) were also related to intent to turnover, although not as strongly as the two other forms of justice. In a similar finding, Schaubroeck, May, and Brown (1994) found that an explanation (informational justice) mitigated turnover intentions, such that individuals who received the explanation were much less likely to consider leaving than those who did not receive the explanation.

Although most studies measuring multiple forms of justice find distributive justice to be a weaker predictor of turnover intentions, there are counter-examples. For instance, in a study of salespersons' intent to turnover (Roberts et al., 1999), distributive justice was a better predictor of turnover intentions than procedural justice. The authors developed scales of both internal (referent others within the same organization) and external (referent others outside the organization) distributive justice and internal procedural justice. External procedural justice was not measured, as the organization has no control over the procedures that may be enacted in the environment. Although both distributive and procedural justice were found to predict intent to turnover, the authors found a stronger relationship between internal distributive justice and intent to turnover than internal procedural justice. Although the results are different from the previous studies, they may be influenced by both the sample and the measures. Salespersons are more likely to be focused on an outcome measure due to the typical compensation scheme under which they operate than the samples from Aryee and Chay (2001)—union workers—and Dailey and Kirk (1992)—employees in an R&D laboratory and an engineering design company.

Absenteeism

Job withdrawal can also come in the form of absenteeism. Although not all absenteeism is a job withdrawal behavior, the overall occurrence of

absenteeism is more easily measured. Procedural justice climate (Mossholder, Bennett, & Martin, 1998; Naumann & Bennett, 2000), measured by averaging the perceptions of procedural justice across team members, has been found to be a significant predictor of absenteeism (Colquitt, Noe, & Jackson, 2002). Absenteeism (measured in hours of absence per team member) was measured over a 3-month period in a manufacturing plant. Procedural justice was measured using the scale validated by Colquitt (2001). Procedural justice climate level was calculated by averaging across team member perceptions. Climate strength moderated the relationship between procedural justice climate and absenteeism, such that climate level was more strongly related to absenteeism in teams with greater climate strength.

In a study of U.S. and Hong Kong bank tellers, Lam, Schaubroeck, and Aryee (2002) linked both procedural and distributive justice to absenteeism. They found that the cultural dimension of power distance displayed moderating effects in this relationship. Individuals with a high power distance orientation (i.e., who are more accepting of hierarchical structures) were more likely to accept violations of organizational justice, whereas those with low power distance (those who more strongly endorse more egalitarian structures) were less likely to accept violations of justice and more likely to respond with an absence from work.

Interactional justice has also been linked to absenteeism (Gellatly, 1995). Interactional justice was operationalized as "employees' beliefs regarding the manner in which policies and procedures are explained and enacted by management" and measured with the scale developed by Moorman (1991), which captures both informational and interpersonal justice. Their study of nursing and food-service units within a hospital found that individuals who perceived their supervisors as unfair or inconsiderate were more likely to be absent than individuals who perceived their supervisors as fair.

Employee Silence

A final form of withdrawal behavior we consider may be a precursor to absenteeism or turnover. It is sometimes the case that saying nothing is a form of withdrawal. Pinder and Harlos (2001), in a review of employee silence, noted that a culture of injustice in organizations, be it distributive, procedural, or interactional (what we would call interpersonal), can lead to employee silence. That is, if the organizational norm is an unjust environment such as one that is characterized by intense supervisory control, suppression of conflict, ambiguous reporting structures, and poorly conducted performance reviews, employees will choose not to exercise voice and will therefore not receive the benefits available to those that do express opinions and ideas. This could lead to an escalat-

ing level of dissatisfaction, which manifests itself in absenteeism and turnover and perhaps other undesired behaviors.

The concept of silence or inaction can also be found in the conflict management literature. Rahim, Magner, and Shapiro (2000) measured the extent to which distributive, procedural, and interactional justice (what we would call interpersonal justice) predicted the five conflict management styles of integrating, obliging, compromising, dominating, and avoiding (the last one being similar to our concept of silence). The authors identified the first three management styles as cooperative; the remaining two styles—avoiding and dominating—can be seen as negative behaviors. Using a sample of undergraduate students reporting about relationships with their past supervisors, the authors found that perceptions of interactional justice led to a reliance on integrating behavior in managing conflicts with supervisors. However, distributive justice was related to the use of avoiding behavior, suggesting that perceptions that one's rewards from the organization were fair leads employees to engage in silence and not address perceived conflicts with their managers. Procedural justice had no direct effects. Although it is interesting that perceiving distributive justice led to use of avoiding or silence even when a conflict was perceived, this may also have to do with the fact that subordinates were being asked about conflicts with their superiors (i.e., a low power context). Silence may be a rational response to some forms of unfairness when in a low power position.

THE UGLY: COUNTERPRODUCTIVE WORK BEHAVIOR

The four forms of justice that we consider in this chapter have been important in the prediction of many counterproductive work behaviors. Anecdotally, we might think of someone acting counterproductively when the person wastes time at work, yet these behaviors encompass a much broader set of domains. Counterproductive work behaviors include theft, white-collar crime, tardiness, drug and alcohol abuse, disciplinary problems, accidents, sabotage, sexual harassment, and verbal and physical abuse (Ones, 2002). Our awareness of these behaviors, and in fact the frequency of such behaviors, may be on the rise (Andersson & Pearson, 1999); however, the behaviors in this category are underexamined and the causes are not well understood. In fact, very few of these behaviors have been studied in relation to organizational justice, which is somewhat puzzling as acting in a counterproductive manner could very well stem from feelings of injustice.

In approaching this literature, we borrow an organizing framework developed by Robinson and Bennett (1995). They used multidimensional scaling techniques to empirically derive a two-dimensional

classification system that we use to organize our review of counterproductive behaviors. One dimension reflects the extent to which the counterproductive behavior is targeted toward individuals in the organization or toward the organization itself (which we refer to as interpersonal versus organizational). The second dimension focuses on the severity of the behavior, ranging from minor to serious counterproductive behavior.

The interpersonal–organizational dimension is nicely captured in a study of "deviant behaviors" by Aquino, Lewis, and Bradfield (1999). Aquino et al. (1999) defined deviance as voluntary behavior that violates organizational norms, or threatens the well-being of the organization or its members. They then differentiated between organizational deviance (acts that are aimed at the organization, such as arriving late, ignoring a supervisor's instructions, or using company property in an unauthorized manner) and interpersonal deviance (acts directed at some individual within the organization, such as teasing a coworker, gossiping about a supervisor, making obscene comments or gestures at a coworker, or making ethnic, racial, or religious slurs). These authors proposed a model linking procedural, distributive, and interactional justice perceptions to both forms of deviance. Specifically, the authors predicted that procedural justice perceptions would predict organizational deviance, distributive justice perceptions would predict interpersonal deviance, and interactional justice would predict both types of deviance.

The two forms of deviance were measured using 35 retrospective (self-report) behavioral items. The authors used a stratified random sample of government employees and employees from a private manufacturing concern. Distributive justice was operationalized using the scale adopted from Niehoff and Moorman. Procedural justice and interactional justice were also measured using published scales by McFarlin and Sweeney (1992) and Moorman (1991), respectively. As predicted, distributive justice was significantly related to interpersonal deviance, and interactional justice was significantly related to both organizational deviance and interpersonal deviance. However, contrary to their expectations, Aquino et al. (1999) found no significant relationship between procedural justice and organizational deviance, in spite of the fact that the procedural justice scale focused on the organization's role in creating fair procedures.

In another study looking at organizational and interpersonal sets of behaviors, Fox, Spector, and Miles (2001) surveyed both student and non-student employees in a variety of organizations (manufacturing, financial, utility, entertainment, academic organizations). These authors found a significant relationship between distributive injustice and organizationally directed counterproductive behavior (e.g., behav-

ior that directly affects organizational functioning or property). They also found a significant relationship between procedural injustice and both organizational and interpersonal counterproductive behavior (e.g., behavior that affects employees by hurting them in a way that will reduce their effectiveness).

Although the pair of studies just described examined the dimension of interpersonal-organizational dimension as described by Robinson and Bennett (1995), some other studies examine variation across the severity dimension. For instance, Skarlicki and Folger (1997) examined what they referred to as "organizational retaliatory behaviors" (ORBs), described as actions intended to strike back against some organizational injustice. Possible behaviors include damaging equipment on purpose, wasting company materials, calling in sick when not ill, and disobeying a supervisor's instructions. In a sample of first-line employees in a manufacturing plant, the three-way interaction between distributive, procedural, and interactional justice (which we would label interpersonal justice) predicted ORBs. If procedural justice was high, the effect of the interaction between distributive and interactional justice was not significant. This would suggest that fair procedures mitigated the negative effects of unjust distributive outcomes and unjust interpersonal interactions. In an extension of this work, using the same employee sample as the preceding study, the individual differences of agreeableness and negative affectivity were found to moderate the relationship between organizational justice and ORBs (Skarlicki, Folger, & Tesluk, 1999).

Robinson and Bennett (1995) used the two dimensions they developed to produce a four-quadrant model that provides an efficient way to categorize this literature. We now provide some examples of research on counterproductive behaviors that can be classified using this approach. Each of the studies below can fit into one of the quadrants suggested by Robinson and Bennett. We label these quadrants as minor organizational, minor interpersonal, major organizational, and major interpersonal.

Minor Organizational Counterproductive Behaviors

Blader, Chang, and Tyler (2001) examined the relationship between procedural justice and what they referred to as "organizational retaliatory behaviors" in a sample of U.S. and Taiwanese employees. The retaliatory behaviors included such things as submitting work that is not the employee's best because the employee is angry with the boss, taking office supplies for personal use, and using sick leave when not sick (in other words, all measures collected referred to relatively minor counterproductive behaviors). The authors found that the relationship be-

tween procedural justice and these behaviors was mediated by organizational identity (measured as one's identification, pride, and respect for the organization), although the mediating effect of identity was stronger in a Taiwanese sample than in the U.S. sample.

Another interesting example of counterproductive behavior stemming from the integration of information technology into many jobs would be "cyberloafing," defined as unauthorized personal Internet surfing and non-work-related e-mailing. Lim (2002) hypothesized a relationship between perceptions of organizational justice and personal use of the computer and/or Internet during work hours. Three forms of justice were measured using scales developed by Moorman (1991). The survey was posted on Internet web sites in Singapore and publicized in that country by various online means such as chat rooms and newsgroups. Thus, their sample was comprised of people who found the survey and completed it online. The results suggest that organizations whose employees experience greater levels of injustice—measured as procedural, distributive, and interactional justice—incur more cyberloafing. These authors theorized that individuals who were treated in a manner perceived as unjust went through a process of neutralization, a justificatory process whereby they rationalized their cyberloafing as an acceptable response to the treatment they received.

Minor Interpersonal Counterproductive Behaviors

Gossiping and blaming coworkers are listed by Robinson and Bennett (1995) as examples of less severe counterproductive behaviors directed at individuals. To this list we would add events such as negative emotional displays or anger. Such behaviors are possible outcomes when authority figures or the organization as a whole violate the conditions of the four dimensions of justice. Using a sample of full-time employees residing in a Midwestern city, Tepper (2000) found that abusive supervision, which was defined as the subordinate's perceptions of the extent to which the supervisor engaged in hostile verbal and nonverbal behaviors, produced a number of dysfunctional consequences. Among these consequences were anxiety, emotional exhaustion, and depression. The relationship between the abusive supervision and negative consequences was mediated by distributive justice, procedural justice, and interactional justice (which we would label as interpersonal justice). These aspects of justice also predicted conflict in the home and conflict at work.

Anger has been found to be associated with distributive injustice. In a sample of undergraduates participating in a team competition, Weiss, Suckow, and Cropanzano (1999) examined the relationship between positive and negative outcomes and procedural fairness. Participants

were angrier about their outcome if they were told they lost the competition (distributive justice) and that the procedure used to determine the outcome was biased against the individual or team (procedural justice). Interestingly, Weiss et al. (1999) found that the negative outcome of guilt could be expected when the distributive outcome was positive and the procedure was biased in favor of the individual.

Conlon and Shapiro (2002) analyzed the comments that employees posted to an electronic mail server developed to address worker concerns about upcoming downsizings in their company. These authors coded the tone of each employee statement as "angry" or "neutral" and noted that angry employee comments were related to the type of injustice experienced (distributive, procedural, or interactional—the last category collapsing interpersonal and informational). Employee comments reflecting interactional justice (81%) were more often written in an angry tone than were comments reflecting distributive justice (68%) or procedural justice (66%). Moreover, if employee comments reflected multiple types of injustice, the likelihood of the message being angry was even higher.

Major Organizational Counterproductive Behaviors

Corporate theft and sabotage are two exemplars of serious organizational counterproductive behavior noted by Robinson and Bennett (1995). It has also been a topic examined in relation to organizational justice. In a field study looking at the effects of a pay cut on employees, Greenberg (1990) found that employees who received an inadequate explanation for the pay cut reported greater perceptions of pay inequity (e.g., "How fairly paid do you feel you currently are on your job"), and stole more from the organization during the duration of the pay cut than those employees who were given an adequate explanation for why their pay was decreased. This finding is in line with past research on the acceptance of outcomes and procedures when decision makers communicate their ideas honestly (Bies, 1986) and when the decision is carefully justified based on adequate information (Shapiro & Buttner, 1988).

In a lab study looking at equitable payment and theft, Greenberg (1993) varied the validity of information in an explanation for equitable or inequitable payment and the degree of interpersonal sensitivity displayed to participants to see if these conditions would encourage certain groups of participants to steal. He found that participants who were underpaid for their participation (low distributive justice), who were given low-validity information for their underpayment (low procedural justice), and who were treated with a low degree of interpersonal fairness (measured by interactional justice) took significantly more money than the $3 they were due. Explanation validity and inter-

personal fairness did not affect the payment of participants who were in the equitable pay condition, as those individuals did not take more money than the $5 promised to them.

In a review of first-person accounts of sabotage in the workplace from the book *Sabotage in the American Workplace: Anecdotes of Dissatisfaction, Mischief, and Revenge* (Sprouse, 1992), Ambrose, Seabright, and Schminke (2002) found that individuals who felt distributive injustice would engage in sabotage behavior meant to restore equity, or increase the levels of reward received in order to make up for what the individual felt he or she deserved. Individuals who felt interpersonal injustice (which Ambrose et al., 2002, label interactional justice) were more likely to engage in sabotage behavior meant to retaliate against, or harm, the organization.

Major Interpersonal Counterproductive Behaviors

Stealing from coworkers, sexual harassment, and violence toward colleagues (i.e., endangering coworkers) were all identified by Robinson and Bennett (1995) as exemplars in this category. With regard to theft, the nascent literature linking justice and theft suggests that, even when motivated by perceived injustice, this form of theft may be infrequent. Greenberg (2002) examined the behavior of customer service representatives when faced with a situation where they were underpaid. He found that justice perceptions, the employee's level of moral development, and the source of payment influenced whether or not the employee stole. Employees who had reached Kohlberg's conventional level of moral development and who worked in an office with an ethics program in place stole less than employees who were not as morally evolved, despite the distributive injustice in underpayment. Likewise, employees who thought that the source of payment was from a group of managers, rather than from the organization, stole almost nothing, regardless of their level of moral development. This finding parallels previous research showing that people are more hesitant to take resources from other individuals than they are from organizations (e.g., Greenberg, 1986b), perhaps because the customer service representatives knew that they would be stealing from their colleagues with whom they may have closer personal ties (Greenberg, 2002).

The relationship between sexual harassment and justice was also studied by Adams-Roy and Barling (1998). In a study looking at the predictors of women's decisions to confront or report sexual harassment in the workplace, women who anticipated that their organization's procedures for handling sexual harassment complaints were procedurally fair were more likely to use the formal organizational channels to handle their complaint. However, those who ultimately used their organi-

zation's procedures for handling their harassment complaint actually reported lower levels of interpersonal justice (which is reported as interactional justice) than did women who chose to do nothing or who chose to directly confront their harasser. Adams-Roy and Barling explained this latter pattern by noting that all justice perceptions were measured after the company response to the harassment claim had occurred. It may well be that the lower level of interpersonal justice stems from the victim believing that the supervisor was not responsive to the complaint or that the parties involved in the formal process did not treat the victim with the kindness, respect, or the consideration that was deserved.

The above study is of concern to organizations when combined with the results of a recent study by Hogler, Frame, and Thornton (2002). These authors conducted a scenario study on a female sample of college students and full-time employees. The scenarios presented the women with a situation in which they had been sexually harassed at work, and the primary dependent variable was the likelihood that they would file a lawsuit against the company for which they worked. Women who responded to scenarios indicating that their company had a procedurally and interpersonally fair process for handling their complaint were less likely to file a lawsuit despite having been (hypothetically) sexually harassed.

Violence is the final behavior we cover in this section. Although the number of homicides annually at work in the United States has declined over the past 10 years (from 1,044 in 1992 to 677 in 2000, the most recent year available, according to the Bureau of Labor Statistics), such violence is still shocking. In addition, roughly 1 million assaults occur each year at work (McGovern et al., 2000). In trying to better understand what causes an employee to be violent, justice issues can be taken into account. Antecedents of homicide and assault have been studied much less than the more benign concepts of absenteeism or intent to turnover. Greenberg and Barling (1999) examined relationships between justice and violence. They differentiated between violence—an act that has the intent of physical harm—and aggression—a noxious stimulus to another person, such as verbal abuse. Aggression was measured against coworkers, subordinates, and supervisors in a sample of male non-faculty members at a Canadian university. In using an all-male sample, the authors hoped to increase the probability of finding aggressive behaviors, because past research has shown that men tend to be more aggressive than women in a variety of contexts. Neither procedural (actually a combined scale of procedural and interactional justice items) nor distributive justice predicted aggression against coworkers or subordinates. However, procedural justice did predict aggression against supervisors. If an individual feels that the organization does not imple-

ment fair procedures, the individual retaliates against a supervisor, the proxy for the organization.

CHALLENGES AND RECOMMENDATIONS

One of the conclusions reached by the Colquitt et al. (2001) meta-analysis was that organizational justice concepts appear to do a better job of predicting attitudes than behaviors. Our review of the literature in this chapter suggests at least three avenues researchers may want to pursue to improve the ability of justice concepts to explain key organizational outcomes. One approach focuses on how the behaviors reviewed in this chapter are measured, a second focuses on how justice concepts are measured, and the last focuses on gaining access to environments where better data can be obtained. These three challenges are also presented in Fig. 10.1, with arrows linking these challenges to the area where they would appear to have the most utility.

The Challenge of Operationalization

One of the challenges in linking justice to the kinds of behaviors reviewed in this chapter relates to the variety of different operationalizations that are used to measure the same constructs. This is particularly true when we view the behaviors we described as "good" or "ugly," which is why we have arrows in Fig. 10.1 linking the challenge of operationalization only to these two types of behaviors. For example, consider the tasks reviewed that have been used as measures of performance. The list includes proofreading tasks (Weaver & Conlon, 2003), advertising brainstorming tasks (Kanfer et al., 1987), technical/ clerical work in university settings (Masterson et al., 2000), and computer-based judgment tasks (Douthitt & Aiello, 2001). Certainly, characteristics of work can mitigate the ability of justice concepts to affect performance. For example, we might expect the justice–performance link to be weaker for employees whose work is controlled by automated systems (e.g., people who work on an assembly line) or whose work is highly interdependent with others (to the extent that these others do not feel injustice, they may continue to work at a high level, thereby forcing the employee who feels injustice to continue to perform at high levels).

Compliance has also been operationalized in a variety of ways. Many studies of compliance have examined contexts related to legal decision making, such as employee decisions to litigate (Lind et al., 2000), decisions to accept or reject arbitration awards (Lind et al., 1993), or decisions to reuse a particular third party in dispute resolu-

tion (Posthuma et al., 2000). Studies in other contexts have investigated compliance measured in terms of repatronage of a service provider (e.g., Humphrey et al., 2002) or, within organizations, endorsement of top management strategic directives (Kim & Mauborgne, 1993). Although it can be useful to aggregate these different operationalizations to a higher order construct to look for general patterns, doing so presents the risk of missing important, unique aspects of context that may affect the predictive ability of the different justice constructs.

Two problems plague much of the literature on counterproductive behaviors. First, the literature in this area creates a problem by using a host of different names for similar counterproductive behaviors, leading to considerable construct redundancy. Monikers used to describe the different behaviors in this section include organizational retaliatory behaviors, retributive recompense behaviors, organizational deviance, and interpersonal deviance, to name a few, in addition to the overarching title we give to all of these behaviors. A second problem relates to how accurately measures in this literature map onto desired constructs, instead of other constructs. For instance, it is common for scales measuring counterproductive behavior to include items that may fit better with other constructs such as performance, withdrawal, or citizenship behavior. For example, a measure of counterproductive behavior used by Bennett and Robinson (2000) includes the item "put little effort into your work"—an item perhaps better suited to measuring task performance. Similarly, an item used by Fox and Spector (1999), "Daydreamed rather than did your work," may reflect job withdrawal rather than counterproductive behavior. To the degree that similar items might appear in different scales measuring different constructs, correlations across different outcomes become inflated, and the effects of justice (or other variables) on one outcome are confounded with the effects on another.

Thus, one key challenge for the field is to develop more precise classifications for the behaviors of interest. Relying on a categorization scheme such as Robinson and Bennett's (1995) typology for counterproductive behavior would be useful for those studying counterproductive behavior. Perhaps a similar classification scheme could be used to categorize task performance (e.g., using dimensions such as independent-interdependent and cognitive versus behavioral might be a useful way to classify task performance) or compliance. Upon reflection, it seems to us that operationalizations of performance, compliance, and counterproductive behaviors vary much more than the operationalizations used to measure withdrawal behaviors, or constructs such as job satisfaction or organizational commitment, which are often assessed with fairly standardized sets of attitudinal measures.

The Challenge of Applying Precise Justice Concepts

A common problem we noted in our review is that we often found two studies, purportedly measuring the same thing, reaching different conclusions. Although some of the blame may lie with different operationalizations of constructs, the problem may also lie with the lack of consistency in applying as precise an approach to measuring justice as is possible. For example, consider the results for the Aquino et al. (1999) and Fox et al. (2001) studies, both of which examined organizational and interpersonal deviance. Most of the results of the Fox et al. (2001) study run counter to the results of the Aquino et al. (1999) study (although not counter to the original hypotheses advanced by Aquino et al.), particularly with respect to procedural justice. To summarize, across two studies arguably investigating the same kinds of behaviors, we find that justice matters, but which forms of justice influence which forms of counterproductive behaviors is rarely consistent. We think this is an example of how the fourfold conception of justice might have lead to clearer results. For example, had Aquino et al. (1999) measured the relationship between informational justice and organizational deviance, they might have found a relationship because informational justice would reveal participants' feelings on the more structural aspects of the process; that is, if workers thought the explanations for why procedures were implemented in a certain way were unfair, then they may have blamed the organization and felt a need to display some of the organizationally deviant behaviors.

Certainly, one of the recommendations we can make to those interested in the study of justice and performance is to measure multiple forms of justice simultaneously. Had measures of interpersonal and informational justice been prevalent years ago, perhaps the results of many earlier studies would be interpreted differently. Consider the findings of a classic field experiment by Greenberg (1988) that demonstrated the power of equity theory and distributive justice to influence performance. Greenberg capitalized on an office refurbishment project to examine how employee performance was impacted by a temporary move to an office of higher, lower, or similar status (a higher status office was one that had more space, a larger desk, and privacy). Greenberg theorized that the move to higher status offices would be interpreted by employees as an increase in their received outcomes, and in order to keep their equity ratio constant, they should respond by increasing their inputs via higher performance (their efficiency at processing applications for life insurance).

Results showed that compared to employees who moved to offices of equal status (whose performance did not change), those who moved to higher status offices performed at a higher level during their tenure in

the nicer offices, whereas those who moved to lower status office performed at a lower level during their tenure in the less pleasant offices. Not surprisingly, the magnitude of increase in performance in the "overpayment" conditions (people who moved to higher status offices) was smaller than the magnitude of decrease in performance in the underpayment conditions (people who moved to lower status offices), suggesting a strong relationship between distributive injustice judgments and lowered performance. This study, however, did not measure other justice concepts. It seems likely that if the concept of interpersonal justice had been around (and measured) at this time, it might have accounted for the effects in this study as the move appeared to impact workers' perceptions of their status and dignity.

The Challenge of Accessibility

The "bad" behaviors of job withdrawal also present challenges to the justice literature. Although voluntary turnover can have a significant impact on organizations, it remains for most organizations a somewhat rare event. Nevertheless, it would be highly beneficial to find a context with enough turnover to allow for a strong test of whether justice constructs predict actual turnover and not merely turnover intentions. Clearly, there are work environments where turnover is quite high (e.g., fast food restaurants), and there are some large organizations that could potentially provide a reasonable size sample of employee turnover for researchers to investigate. We recommend that future research on job turnover try to employ a longitudinal design to measure the actual behavior. Several measures of intent could also be collected during the course of the study to determine if intent does in fact predict actual behavior or if the behavior is more a factor of context. It also seems plausible that a clever laboratory study could also be designed to measure turnover. For instance, a researcher could design a task and manipulate different types of justice in part one of a study, and then give participants a chance to continue with the current study or move to a new study. Those who leave the current study to partake in the subsequent study might be construed as turnover participants.

Turning to the "ugly" behaviors, we note that the repugnancy of such behaviors produces a challenge to researchers wishing to study these behaviors. Organizations may be hesitant to provide information about employees who display counterproductive behaviors because they are afraid of the potential negative ramifications related to their organizational image or their viability in the market. For example, if the public discovered that at a particular firm a high percentage of employees engaged in counterproductive behavior such as drinking while at work or harassing coworkers, it would likely create some backlash in the com-

munity and business for that firm would suffer. This creates a dilemma for those interested in measuring counterproductive behavior. In pursuit of such data, the researcher is often forced to rely on a self-report measure, a whistleblower, or a proxy measure. None of these is an attractive option. As a result, counterproductive behavior in the organization has been studied much less often than the more popular withdrawal behaviors such as absenteeism and turnover.

Clearly, there remains much work to be done on articulating the connections between justice and "ugly" behaviors such as those described in this section of our chapter. Moreover, it would seem that the uglier the behavior, the fewer the studies that have been conducted. However, by studying these behaviors and applying the fourfold model of justice, we may learn insights to prevent such behaviors from happening in the future. Consider the case of Michael McDermott, who in 2000 shot and killed coworkers at an internet company in Massachusetts. In the murder trial against McDermott, prosecutors successfully argued that McDermott, who was unhappy about his employer's plan to take a portion of his wages to pay back taxes, gunned down his coworkers in an attempt to get back at the organization (Naraine, 2002). One can easily imagine that such wage garnishments created both distributive and interpersonal injustice in the mind of this employee. In other words, both distributive and interpersonal injustice may be important antecedents predicting the most severe negative behaviors. Perhaps by insuring that interpersonal justice is maintained at a high level, such terrible outcomes can be averted even if distributive injustice (in the eyes of the perpetrator) remains. In summary, it appears that the challenge of accessibility primarily occurs in attempts to study the behaviors we have labeled as "bad" or "ugly"; hence, we have arrows in our figure only to these two sets of behaviors and not to the "good" behaviors.

Much as was the case with identifying contexts in which to study actual turnover behavior, it would be nice to identify more environments in which justice, counterproductive behavior, and violence can be studied longitudinally. Alternatively, perhaps some investigators can try unusual methods (e.g., interviewing people in jails who have been convicted of assault or homicide in the workplace) in order to shed light on this issue. Acting on these recommendations can help us fully leverage the power of justice to explain behavior—good, bad, or ugly—in organizations.

REFERENCES

Adams-Roy, J., & Barling, J. (1998). Predicting the decision to confront or report sexual harassment. *Journal of Organizational Behavior, 19,* 329–336.

Ambrose, M. L., Seabright, M. A., & Schminke, M. (2002). Sabotage in the workplace: The role of organizational injustice. *Organizational Behavior and Human Decision Processes, 89*, 947–965.

Andersson, L. M., & Pearson, C. M. (1999). Tit for tat? The spiraling effect of incivility in the workplace. *Academy of Management Review, 24*, 452–471.

Aquino, K., Lewis, M. U., & Bradfield, M. (1999). Justice constructs, negative affectivity, and employee deviance: A proposed model and empirical test. *Journal of Organizational Behavior, 20*, 1073–1091.

Aryee, S., & Chay, Y. W. (2001). Workplace justice, citizenship behavior, and turnover intentions in a union context: Examining the mediating role of perceived union support and union instrumentality. *Journal of Applied Psychology, 86*, 154–160.

Bies, R. J. (1986, August). *Identifying principles of interactional justice: The case of corporate recruiting.* Symposium conducted at the annual meeting of the Academy of Management, Chicago.

Bies, R. J., & Moag, J. F. (1986). Interactional justice: Communication criteria of fairness. In B. H. S. R. J. Lewicki, & M. H. Bazerman (Ed.), *Research on negotiations in organizations* (Vol. 1, pp. 43–55). Greenwich, CT: JAI Press.

Blader, S. L., Chang, C., & Tyler, T. R. (2001). Procedural justice and retaliation in organizations: Comparing cross-nationally the importance of fair group processes. *International Journal of Conflict Management, 12*, 295–311.

Cohen-Charash, Y., & Spector, P. (2001). The role of justice in organizations: A meta analysis. *Organizational Behavior and Human Decision Processes, 86*, 278–321.

Cohen-Charash, Y., & Spector, P. (2002). Erratum to "The role of justice in organizations: A meta analysis" [*Organizational Behavior and Human Decision Processes, 86*(2001), 278–321]. *Organizational Behavior and Human Decision Processes, 89*, 1215.

Colquitt, J. A. (2001). On the dimensionality of organizational justice: A construct validation of a measure. *Journal of Applied Psychology, 86*, 386–400.

Colquitt, J. A., Conlon, D. E., Wesson, M., Porter, C., & Ng, K. Y. (2001). Justice at the millennium: A meta-analytic review of 25 years of organizational justice research. *Journal of Applied Psychology, 86*: 425–445.

Colquitt, J. A., Noe, R. A., & Jackson, C. L. (2002). Justice in teams: Antecedents and consequences of procedural justice climate. *Personnel Psychology, 55*, 83–109.

Conlon, D. E., & Murray, N. M. (1996). Customer perceptions of corporate responses to product complaints: The role of explanations. *Academy of Management Journal, 39*, 1040–1056.

Conlon, D. E., & Shapiro, D. L. (2002). Employee postings and company responses to downsizing inquiries: Implications for managing and reacting to organizational change. *Advances in Qualitative Organizational Research, 4*, 39–67.

Dailey, R. C., & Kirk, D. J. (1992). Distributive and procedural justice as antecedents of job dissatisfaction and intent to turnover. *Human Relations, 45*, 305–316.

Douthitt, E. A., & Aiello, J. R. (2001). The role of participation and control in the effects of computer monitoring on fairness perceptions, task satisfaction, and performance. *Journal of Applied Psychology, 86*, 867–874.

Dunford, B. B., & Devine, D. J. (1998). Employment at-will and employee discharge: A justice perspective on legal action following termination. *Personnel Psychology, 51*, 903–934.

Earley, P. C. (1984). *Informational mechanisms of participation influencing goal acceptance, satisfaction, and performance.* Unpublished doctoral dissertation, University of Illinois, Champaign.

Earley, P. C., & Lind, E. A. (1987). Procedural justice and participation in task selection: The role of control in mediating justice judgments. *Journal of Personality and Social Psychology, 52*, 1148–1160.

Ellis, A. P., Conlon, D. E., Tinsley, C. H., & Humphrey, S. E. (2003, June). *Informational justice and brokered ultimatums: When more information is not necessarily more fair.* Paper presented at the 16th conference of the International Association for Conflict Management, Melbourne, Australia.

Folger, R., & Konovsky, M. A. (1989). Effects of procedural and distributive justice on reactions to pay raise decisions. *Academy of Management Journal, 32*, 115–130.

Fox, S., & Spector, P. E. (1999). A model of work frustration-aggression. *Journal of Organizational Behavior, 20*, 915–931.

Fox, S., Spector, P. E., & Miles, D. (2001). Counterproductive work behavior (CWB) in response to job stressors and organizational justice: Some mediator and moderator tests for autonomy and emotions. *Journal of Vocational Behavior, 59*, 291–309.

Fryxell, G., & Gordon, M. (1989). Workplace justice and job satisfaction as predictors of satisfaction with union and management. *Academy of Management Journal, 32*, 851–866.

Futrell, C. M., & Parasuraman, A. (1984). The relationship of satisfaction and performance of sales force turnover. *Journal of Marketing, 48*, 33–40.

Gellatly, I. R. (1995). Individual and group determinants of employee absenteeism: Test of a causal model. *Journal of Organizational Behavior, 16*, 469–485.

Greenberg, J. (1986a). Determinants of perceived fairness of performance evaluations. *Journal of Applied Psychology, 71*, 340–342.

Greenberg, J. (1986b). Differential intolerance for inequity from organizational and individual agents. *Journal of Applied Social Psychology, 16*, 191–196.

Greenberg, J. (1988). Equity and workplace status: A field experiment. *Journal of Applied Psychology, 73*, 606–613.

Greenberg, J. (1990). Employee theft as a reaction to underpayment inequity: The hidden cost of pay cuts. *Journal of Applied Psychology, 75*, 561–568.

Greenberg, J. (1993). Stealing in the name of justice: Informational and interpersonal moderators of theft reactions to underpayment inequity. *Organizational Behavior and Human Decision Processes, 54*, 81–103.

Greenberg, J. (1994). Using socially fair treatment to promote acceptance of a work site smoking ban. *Journal of Applied Psychology, 79*, 288–297.

Greenberg, J. (2002). Who stole the money, and when? Individual and situational determinants of employee theft. *Organizational Behavior and Human Decision Processes, 89*, 985–1003.

Greenberg, L., & Barling, J. (1999). Predicting employee aggression against coworkers, subordinates and supervisors: The roles of person behaviors and perceived workplace factors. *Journal of Organizational Behavior, 20*, 897–913.

Hogler, R. L., Frame, J. H., & Thornton, G. (2002). Workplace sexual harassment law: An empirical analysis of organizational justice and legal policy. *Journal of Managerial Issues, 14*, 234–250.

Humphrey, S. E., Ellis, A. P., Conlon, D. E., & Tinsley, C. H. (2004). Understanding customer reactions to brokered ultimatums: Applying negotiation and justice theory. *Journal of Applied Psychology, 89*, 466–482.

Kanfer, R., Sawyer, J., Earley, P. C., & Lind, E. A. (1987). Participation in task evaluation procedures: The effects of influential opinion expression and knowledge of evaluative criteria on attitudes and performance. *Social Justice Research, 1*, 235–249.

Kim, W. C., & Mauborgne, R. A. (1993). Procedural justice, attitudes, and subsidiary top management compliance with multinationals' corporate strategic decisions. *Academy of Management Journal, 36*, 502–526.

Konovsky, M. A., & Cropanzano, R. (1991). Perceived fairness of employee drug testing as a predictor of employee attitudes and job performance. *Journal of Applied Psychology, 76*, 698–707.

Lam, S. S. K., Schaubroeck, J., & Aryee, S. (2002). Relationship between organizational justice and employee work outcomes: a cross-national study. *Journal of Organizational Behavior, 23*, 1–18.

Leventhal, G. S. (1980). What should be done with equity theory? New approaches to the study of fairness in social relationships. In M. G. K. Gergen & R. Willis (Eds.), *Social exchange: Advances in theory and research* (pp. 27–55). New York: Plenum Press.

Lim, V. K. G. (2002). The IT way of loafing on the job: Cyberloafing, neutralizing, and organizational justice. *Journal of Organizational Behavior, 23*, 675–694.

Lind, E. A., Greenberg, J., Scott, K. S., & Welchans, D. (2000). The winding road from employee to complainant: Situational and psychological determinants of wrongful termination claims. *Administrative Science Quarterly, 45*, 557–590.

Lind, E. A., Kulik, C. T, Ambrose, M., & de Vera Park, M. V. (1993). Individual and corporate dispute resolution: Using procedural fairness as a decision heuristic. *Administrative Science Quarterly, 38*, 224–251.

Lind, E. A., & Tyler, T. R. (1988). *The social psychology of procedural justice.* New York: Plenum Press.

Masterson, S. S., Lewis, K., Goldman, B. M., & Taylor, M. S. (2000). Integrating justice and social exchange: The differing effects of fair procedures and treatment on work relationships. *Academy of Management Journal, 43*, 738–748

McFarlin, D. B., & Sweeney, P. D. (1992). Distributive and procedural justice as predictors of satisfaction with personal and organizational outcomes. *Academy of Management Journal, 35*, 626–637.

McGovern, P., Kochevar, L., Lohman, W., Zaidman, B., Gerberich, S., Nyman, J., & Findorff-Dennis, M. (2000). The cost of work-related physical assaults in Minnesota. *Health Services Research, 35*, 663–686.

Moorman, R. H, (1991). Relationship between organizational justice and organizational citizenship behaviors: Do fairness perceptions influence employee citizenship? *Journal of Applied Psychology, 76*, 845–855.

Mossholder, K. W., Bennett, N., & Martin, C. L. (1998). A multilevel analysis of procedural justice context. *Journal of Organizational Behavior, 19*, 131–141.

Naraine, R. (2002). *Murder conviction for Edgewater killer.* http://www.internetnews.com/bus-news/article.php/3_1015741

Naumann, S. E., & Bennett, N. (2000). A case for procedural justice climate: Development and test of a multilevel model. *Academy of Management Journal, 43*, 881–889.

Niehoff, B. P., & Moorman, R. H. (1993). Justice as a mediator of the relationship between methods of monitoring and organizational citizenship behavior. *Academy of Management Journal, 36*, 527–556.

Ones, D. S. (2002). Introduction to the special issue on counterproductive behaviors at work. *International Journal of Selection and Assessment, 10*, 1–4.

Pinder, C. C., & Harlos, K. P. (2001). Employee silence: Quiescence and acquiescence as responses to perceived injustice. *Research in Personnel and Human Resources Management, 20*, 331–369.

Posthuma, R. A., Dworkin, J. B., & Swift, M. S. (2000). Arbitrator acceptability: Does justice matter? *Industrial Relations, 39*, 313–335.

Rahim, M. A., Magner, N. R., & Shapiro, D. L., (2000). Do justice perceptions influence styles of handling conflict with supervisors?: What justice perceptions, precisely? *International Journal of Conflict Management, 11*, 9–31.

Robbins, T. L, Summers, T. P., Miller, J. L., & Hendrix, W. H. (2000). Using the group-value model to explain the role of noninstrumental justice in distinguishing the effects of distributive and procedural justice. *Journal of Occupational and Organizational Psychology, 73*, 511–518.

Roberts, J. A., Colson, K. R., & Chonko, L. B. (1999, Winter). Salesperson perceptions of equity and justice and their impact on organizational commitment and intent to turnover. *Journal of Marketing Theory and Practice*, pp. 1–16.

Robinson, S. L., & Bennett, R. J. (1995). A typology of deviant workplace behaviors: A multidimensional scaling study. *Academy of Management Journal, 38*, 555–572.

Schaubroeck, J., May, D. R., & Brown, F. W. (1994). Procedural justice explanations and employee reactions to economic hardship: A field experiment. *Journal of Applied Psychology, 79*, 455–460.

Shapiro, D. L., & Buttner, E. H. (1988, August). *Adequate explanations: What are they, and do they enhance procedural justice under severe outcome circumstances?* Paper presented at the annual meeting of the Academy of Management, Anaheim, CA.

Skarlicki, D. P., & Folger, R. (1997). Retaliation in the workplace: The roles of distributive, procedural, and interactional justice. *Journal of Applied Psychology, 82*, 434–443.

Skarlicki, D. P., Folger, R., & Tesluk, P. (1999). Personality as a moderator in the relationship between fairness and retaliation. *Academy of Management Journal, 42*, 100–108.

Sprouse, M. (1992). *Sabotage in the American workplace: Anecdotes of dissatisfaction, mischief, and revenge.* San Francisco, CA: Pressure Drop Press.

Tepper, B. J. (2000). Consequences of abusive supervision. *Academy of Management Journal, 43*, 178–190.

Weaver, G. R., & Conlon, D. E. (2003). Explaining facades of choice: Timing, justice effects, and behavioral outcomes. *Journal of Applied Social Psychology, 33*, 2217–2243.

Weiss, H. M., Suckow, K., & Cropanzano, R. (1999). Effects of justice conditions on discrete emotions. *Journal of Applied Psychology, 84*, 786–794.

11

How Can Theories of Organizational
Justice Explain the Effects of Fairness?

Steven L. Blader
New York Universtiy

Tom R. Tyler
New York University

Although organizational justice research has produced compelling evidence that employee perceptions of justice matter, there has been relatively less progress in understanding the psychological processes that underlie the effects of justice. This shortcoming presents obstacles to researchers trying to advance our understanding of organizational justice and to practitioners hoping to develop successful justice-based strategies for eliciting employee engagement in work organizations. This chapter directly addresses the issue of why employees react to their fairness perceptions by considering several major theoretical frameworks that help explain those reactions. The major propositions of these various theories are reviewed, evidence supporting each is discussed, and linkages between the theories are proposed. Overall, the goal of the chapter is to stimulate greater thinking among justice researchers about conceptual frameworks for why employees react to their fairness perceptions, and for predicting when, where, and for whom justice will matter most.

Employee perceptions of the fairness of their work organizations have a vital impact on their attitudes and behaviors in those organizations. The robust nature of the relationship between fairness and employee cooperation—and the extensive number of journal articles, book chapters, and volumes dedicated to highlighting it—has rendered this phenomenon self-evident to those who regularly follow the organizational research literature (see Conlon, Meyer, & Nowakowski, this volume; Moorman & Byrne, this volume; or Tyler & Blader, 2000, for reviews). This self-evident quality has been reinforced by supportive justice findings in the areas of law, politics, education and interpersonal relations (Tyler, Boeckmann, Smith, & Huo, 1997; Tyler & Smith, 1997).

It is likely that readers of this current volume—a handbook of organizational justice—are intimately aware of the finding that justice matters, and that it (often) matters more than other types of employee evaluations, such as evaluations of the favorability of their pay and opportunities for promotion. Therefore, in this chapter we extend the discussion about justice from a focus on its importance to a consideration of theoretical frameworks that can help us better understand the impact of fairness on employee attitudes and behavior.

Clearly, the surge of research interest and activity in organizational (and, in particular, procedural) justice over the last 20 years is inextricably linked to the impact justice has on employee attitudes and behaviors, and to the possibilities it presents for shaping these attitudes and behaviors. Organizational justice research first addressed the "so

what?" question, and consequently the importance of studying justice in organizational settings has not faced serious or significant challenge. As might be expected, this starting point has also influenced the trajectory of subsequent research. Specifically, the traditional emphasis in organizational justice work has been on new demonstrations of the basic justice phenomena, with a significant amount of work dedicated to identifying new organizational variables linked to justice and various factors that moderate the link between justice and employee engagement.

We argue that this approach—although important—has detracted from a focus on more conceptual issues. That is, we claim that the phenomena-based roots of justice research have not encouraged the adequate development of comprehensive conceptual, theoretically driven frameworks. This neglect stymies the progress of justice research and the implementation of that research. In particular, it prevents justice researchers from being able to understand why employees react to justice. It also prevents them from predicting when, where, and for whom justice will matter most.

In this chapter, we go beyond the repeated recognition of the strength and resilience of the justice phenomenon and address *how* and *why* justice fosters cooperation in organizations. Our focus is on procedural justice, or evaluations of the fairness of organizational decision making and treatment of employees. We adopt a broad perspective on what procedural justice encompasses, and our use of the term subsumes both traditional definitions of procedural justice and the related concept of interactional justice (discussed as informational and interpersonal justice by some researchers; for a fuller discussion on the meaning of procedural justice, see Blader & Tyler, 2003a, 2003b). We emphasize procedural justice work because recent advances in the justice arena have primarily been focused on this class of justice effects (for more on this emphasis, see Tyler & Blader, 2003b). Where relevant, however, we also consider evaluations of the fairness of outcomes (pay, benefits, etc.), or distributive justice.

We review major justice theories and research in our effort to consider why (procedural) justice has such a potent impact on employee attitudes and behavior. We hope to make a contribution to justice research by bringing the discussion of these theories together and, where possible, by comparing and integrating them. By doing so, we hope to spur deeper thinking about the reasons that researchers detect an impact of employee perceptions of fairness and about the psychological underpinnings of these effects.

We often refer to the concept of employee cooperation. By *cooperation*, we refer to the various ways in which employees support (or, conversely,

undermine) their work organizations. Although cooperation can certainly include holding positive attitudes toward the organization and its authorities, our use of the term cooperation is primarily targeted toward a discussion of the various behaviors that employees may engage in that help their organization.

HOW DOES JUSTICE FOSTER COOPERATION IN ORGANIZATIONS?

As we noted in the introduction, justice research has been dominated by the goal of linking employees' justice perceptions to an ever-expanding range of employee attitudes and behaviors. This is not meant to imply, however, that no research has considered the psychological dynamics underlying these effects. Some significant strides have been made in developing an understanding of how justice fosters cooperation in groups, and in particular in the workplace. That said, relatively less work has been conducted on this question—as compared to work demonstrating the influence of justice on employees—and consensus among justice researchers about how justice fosters cooperation remains elusive.

We can reframe the issue of how justice fosters cooperation by posing the question: Why do employees care about fairness and why do they demonstrate such potent reactions to it? In other words, what are the thoughts and psychological drives that mediate the link between justice and cooperation? Various theories propose explanations for why people react so strongly to perceived justice. Each adopts a different viewpoint about why people care about justice—and/or how they evaluate justice—and thus each implicitly invokes different psychological concerns and drives to explain reactions to processes. We next review each of these theories. We note in advance, however, that although these theories all contribute to the discourse on why people care about fairness, they have not all been explicitly involved in efforts to link justice to cooperation. We adopt the perspective that the reasons that people care about fairness may mediate the link between justice and cooperation, and thus include in our review some theories that have not explicitly considered the issue of employee cooperation but from which we can infer a psychological dynamic that might explain that link.

Before reviewing these theories, it is important to stress that these multiple explanations for why people react to justice are not all necessarily mutually exclusive of one another. Some may be true under certain conditions, whereas others may be true under alternate conditions. Furthermore, even under the same set of circumstances, there may be multiple psychological motives at play, each of which makes a unique contribution to the link between justice and coopera-

tion. After we review each of the theories, we elaborate on the interrelationships among them. Consistent with the relative dearth of research on how and why justice fosters cooperation, little empirical work has worked toward an *integration* of these various theories. Because many of these theories are in relatively early stages of their development, most efforts have been focused on demonstrating their validity. Understandably, integration can only be accomplished once the validity of the models has been confirmed.

Instrumental Models of Justice

One important class of theories about why employees care about and react to their justice perceptions focuses on the resource- and exchange-based concerns that employees have in their relationships with their organizations. According to these theories, procedural justice is valued because it is part of the process by which employees garner valued outcomes from their work organizations. Although the theories differ in the role in which they place procedural justice in this process, common to them is the emphasis that people's reactions to procedural justice are linked to their desire to attain valued outcomes from the organization. The accrual of desirable outcomes, thus, is the primary underlying drive emphasized by these theories.

Control Model. The classic instrumental procedural justice theory is the seminal work by Thibaut and Walker (1975), which is regarded by many as the original effort that delineated the concept of procedural justice. According to Thibaut and Walker's (1975) control model of procedural justice, people regard procedures as fair to the extent that procedures allow them input into decision making processes (i.e., voice, termed *process control* by Thibaut and Walker). Because people ultimately lack complete control over the outcomes they receive from decision makers, Thibaut and Walker reasoned that people value process control because input provides them with the next best opportunity to influence the outcomes they receive. That is, in their theory input is valued because people do not ultimately have complete control over their outcomes; thus, input to the decision provides the next best alternative in their attempts to impact their outcomes. Procedural justice—embodied in the level of input that processes allow—is therefore valued because it is seen as instrumental to trying to achieve outcomes that are desirable. Thibaut and Walker conceptualized desirable outcomes as those that were perceived as distributively fair, thereby linking the two primary forms of justice.

Original development of the control model was primarily conducted in legal settings, where the concern was whether allowing input in court

proceedings affected people's willingness to accept judgments and decisions. Organizational contexts are a rather different domain, however, where the key concern is to understand employee behavior and less the issue of decision acceptance. Although linkages between process control and decision acceptance seem natural—because the link between input into decision making and decision acceptance is direct—it is less clear how the theory could be extended to understand employee cooperation (cf. Tyler, 1989). Although it is possible that input affects behavior through decision acceptance (i.e., that input increases decision acceptance—such as pay or promotion satisfaction—which in turn influences behavior), little research has made an attempt to empirically test this proposition.

Alternatively, procedural justice may foster cooperation because people infer that it is an antecedent of fair outcomes. In line with this suggestion, justice research typically shows strong correlations between procedural and distributive justice, and some work directly suggests that procedural fairness may be an important factor in distributive justice evaluations (Tornblom & Vermunt, 1999; Van den Bos, Lind, Vermunt, & Wilke, 1997). This approach would suggest that outcome evaluations (specifically, evaluations of outcome fairness) mediate the effects of procedural justice on cooperation. Research is needed to directly test this mediational relationship (cf. Sweeney & McFarlin, 1993).

According to both of these potential explanations for how the control model might explain justice effects on cooperation, fair processes are valued because they are regarded as instrumental in achieving desired economic and material outcomes, typically defined as fair outcomes. The receipt of fair outcomes is therefore regarded as a fundamental goal, which may in and of itself lead to employee cooperation.

We can consider the insights of the control model through an organizational example. For instance, employees do not have complete control over whether they are promoted or over the amount of their raises. However, performance review processes that provide them with voice do permit them the opportunity to let decision makers know how they evaluate their own performance and provide them with a chance to make the case for the raise or promotion that they feel is just. Providing input into such organizational processes thus represents a way that employees can at least try to impact the outcomes they experience. However, this input should only impact cooperation to the extent that employees perceive the outcomes that are associated with the provision of voice and input as fair; research indicates that this pattern of results may not always be the case (e.g., Lind, Kanfer, & Earley, 1990).

Social Exchange Theories. Social exchange theory represents another type of instrumental explanation for why people cooperate in

groups (Foa & Foa, 1974; Kelly & Thibaut, 1978; Rusbult & Van Lange, 1996), and has been adopted in several recent studies to help understand the link between perceived procedural justice and cooperation (Cropanzano & Prehar, 2001; Konovsky & Pugh, 1994; Masterson, Lewis, Goldman, & Taylor, 2000; Moorman, Blakely, & Niehoff, 1998; Rupp & Cropanzano, 2002). This approach argues that the impact of justice perceptions on employee cooperation is mediated by social exchange variables, such as leader–member exchange and perceived organizational support (e.g., Masterson et al., 2000). These social exchange variables emphasize the reciprocal obligations between two parties to a relationship; in the employment context, those parties can be the employee and their supervisor or the organization. According to these theories, the medium of the exchange can be, but need not necessarily be, economic in nature (for a discussion of this issue, see Montada, 1996; Tyler & Blader, 2000, p. 199). Regardless of the medium, social exchange theory focuses on the mutual give-and-take relationship that operates between the employee and either the supervisor or the organization. It emphasizes that that give-and-take represents the glue that binds the parties of the exchange together.

Social exchange explanations for justice effects adopt the view that employees regard fairness as a benefit deserving of reciprocation. Therefore, the experience of justice begets an obligation on the part of employees to reciprocate and thus fosters the development and maintenance of a social exchange relationship, with the expectation that such a relationship will lead to the exchange of valued benefits between the parties. Employee reciprocation for justice may take the form of positive attitudes or cooperation with the organization or one's supervisor. Employees will be hesitant to risk nonreciprocation of perceived fairness from the organization, because that may interrupt the cycle of exchanging valued benefits with the other party. Studies testing the social exchange approach demonstrate that the relationship between justice and cooperation is mediated by perceptions of the quality of the social exchange between the parties, and thus focus on the role that justice plays in determining the perceived quality of that exchange.

Social exchange theories share the perspective of the control model that people react to procedural justice because fairness is part of a process in which they accrue and maintain valued benefits. The control model regards procedural fairness as a factor in expectations or perceptions of desired outcomes, whereas the social exchange approach regards procedural justice as part of the exchange of benefits. Although the underlying dynamic postulated by each is rather different, both regard procedural justice as instrumental to employees garnering valued outcomes or benefits from their organizations. In both cases employees' reactions to their justice perceptions are rooted in their desire to gain re-

sources and other types of desired benefits. Further, social exchange theory makes the explicit link to cooperation and argues that cooperation is driven by the desire to maintain the reciprocal exchange of valued benefits between the parties.

Relational Models of Justice

A different research stream focuses on employees' reactions to procedures and the identity implications that process fairness evaluations have for how employees construe their social identities vis-à-vis their work organizations. This approach, originally developed in the group-value model (Lind & Tyler, 1998) and the relational model of authority (Tyler & Lind, 1992), has recently been extended into an integrative framework of how procedural justice fosters cooperation in groups (the "group engagement model"; Tyler & Blader, 2000, 2001, 2003a, 2003c). The relational models argue that important inferences about the self as a member of the work organization flow from employees' procedural justice judgments, and thus they emphasize the relational inferences and implications of process fairness perceptions. From this perspective, employees make evaluations about their identities as members of their work organization based on the procedural justice that they experience in that organization. Procedural fairness communicates a positive message about their membership, while procedural unfairness communicates a negative message. In either case, people are drawing conclusions about themselves as members of the organization based on their process fairness evaluations.

The primary insights of the group-value and relational models are that noninstrumental (and, in particular, relational) criteria will affect procedural justice judgments, and that procedural justice is closely linked to group-related identity concerns. The group engagement model extends this idea and directly argues that these justice-based social identity inferences mediate the impact of justice on employee cooperation (Tyler & Blader, 2000, 2003a, 2003c). In other words, the model establishes how justice can be linked to understanding the issue of employee cooperation. It does so by emphasizing that group-related identity judgments are shaped by perceived procedural justice, and that identity judgments in turn influence and determine employee cooperation. The group engagement model is presented in Fig. 11.1.

The group engagement model highlights three important identity-related variables that are linked to procedural justice (Tyler & Blader, 2000, 2003; Tyler, Degoey, & Smith, 1996; Tyler & Smith, 1999): perceptions of the status or standing of the group (pride), perceptions of one's status or standing within the group (respect), and the extent to which employees define themselves as members of the group (identifi-

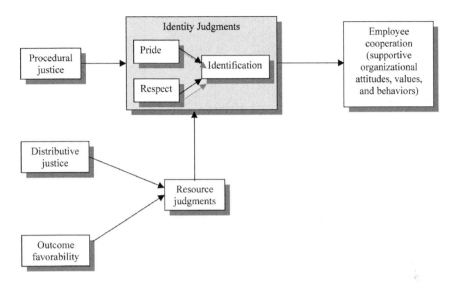

FIG. 11.1.   The group engagement model.

cation—i.e., the extent to which they cognitively intermingle their concepts of themselves and their group). Pride and respect represent evaluative judgments, while identification embodies the extent to which cognitive representations of self and group overlap. Each of these identity judgments addresses an issue with regard to how employees think of themselves as members of their work organizations. Pride addresses the intergroup issue of the status or standing of the organization, and respect addresses the intragroup issue of whether employees feel included and respected by the organization. Identification represents the extent to which employees think of themselves as members of the organization.

When employees view their work organizations as operating and treating them in procedurally fair ways, they infer that the organization is one that they can be proud of (i.e., that has high status) and that they are respected members of the organization. When they view the organization as procedurally unfair, they evaluate their inter- and intraorganizational standing in negative terms. These two evaluations about the standing of the organization and their place in it, in turn, are hypothesized to influence their level of identification with the organization (Tyler & Blader, 2001, 2003). More specifically, positive evaluations about these two standing or status judgments will in part lead employees to be strongly identified with their work organization, be-

cause the organization presents an opportunity for them to develop a positive social identity. Negative evaluations about these two standing or status judgments are predicted to have the opposite effect on identification, leading the employee to a weak intermingling of the self and the organization.

Thus, procedural fairness is related to each of these identity-related judgments, insofar as perceived fairness is positively associated with greater perceived pride, respect, and ultimately identification with the organization. This suggests that employees care about justice because it is a cue that they use to make important relational evaluations. Employees look to procedural justice when they are evaluating their relationships with their work organizations, and they make positive inferences about those relationships when they see the organization's procedures as fair.

Of greatest relevance to the central question addressed in this chapter, the group engagement model argues that identity variables mediate the link between justice and cooperation (e.g., Tyler & Blader, 2000). That is, the potent influence that justice has on cooperation can primarily be accounted for by the implications of procedural justice on how employees construct their identities with regard to their work organizations. When they are highly identified with their work organization— and when they have pride in the organization and a sense that they are respected members of the organization—they become intrinsically motivated to see the organization succeed (Tyler & Blader, 2000, 2003b). They hold positive attitudes toward the organization and want to work on its behalf, because they care about it and because it is part of their self-concept. This framework emphasizes that procedural justice fosters cooperation in organizations by directly addressing employees' needs for affiliation and belonging (Baumeister & Leary, 1995; Deci & Ryan, 2000) and by leading them to determine that their need to develop and maintain a positive social identity (Tajfel & Turner, 1986) will be satisfied through their association with the work organization.

In contrast to instrumental theories of justice, the group engagement model emphasizes that employees become intrinsically motivated to cooperate and work on the organization's behalf; they work for the organization's success because they want to, not for the personal benefits that may accrue from such cooperation. Once they are strongly identified with the organization, its success becomes tantamount to their own success, and they are internally motivated to cooperate. Thus, cooperation is not linked to the exchange of desired benefits or to the anticipation that the organization will be providing them with valued outcomes (material or otherwise) as a function of their cooperation. Although such outcomes may be associated with cooperation, according to the group engagement model they are not the

primary force driving cooperation and thus are not the primary motivational impetus to cooperation (cf. Batson, 1991). Employees may indeed receive valued benefits because of their cooperation, and they may even enjoy receiving those benefits. The point is that those benefits do not drive their behavior and do not determine their justice-based reactions; they are incidental to cooperation, not determinants of it. The group engagement model asserts that people do not engage in the calculus that social exchange processes presuppose. Instead, it has as its basis people's drive to affiliate with groups.

Relational justice models argue for a rather different understanding of what employees seek from their affiliations with their work organizations, as compared to instrumental models. They assert that a primary goal people have for joining and working on behalf of groups is to develop and maintain a positive identity, and to fulfill their affiliation and belongingness needs. Therefore employees focus on procedural justice—and not on other types of information—because it is directly linked to these identity and affiliation-related goals. Social exchange models provide a less direct explanation for why people focus on fairness information in particular, as opposed to one of the multitudes of other types of information available to them.

Fairness Heuristic Theory

Fairness heuristic theory (for reviews, see Lind, 2001; Van den Bos & Lind, 2002)—with the related uncertainty management model of justice (Van den Bos, 2001; Van den Bos & Lind, 2002)—is focused on exploring the cognitive processing of fairness information. The underlying premise of these theories is that group contexts are naturally imbued with uncertainty that people need to manage. That uncertainty relates to people's fear of exploitation by group authorities and to their fear of rejection (Lind, 2001), and thus group members search for signals in the environment about whether authorities can be trusted and whether they are included in the group. Integrating this perspective to organizational contexts, it can be argued that being an employee of a work organization is a risky undertaking, because employees face the possibility that organizational authorities will exploit and/or reject them. Consequently, they search for cues that can inform them whether they can safely associate themselves with the organization and its authorities. Procedural justice is regarded as one of these cues. That is, process fairness evaluations are a heuristic for determining whether organizational authorities can be trusted.

An impressive series of experimental studies supports many of the assertions of fairness heuristic theory (e.g., Van den Bos, Lind, Vermunt, &

Wilke, 1997; Van den Bos, Vermunt, & Wilke, 1997; Van den Bos, Wilke, Lind, & Vermunt, 1998). This work demonstrates that procedural justice evaluations are most potent when other types of information are not available, confirming that process fairness may have important heuristic value. Additional work has directly linked process fairness to the concerns raised by uncertainty, by showing that the effects of procedural fairness are heightened when uncertainty concerns are brought to the foreground (Van den Bos, 2001; Van den Bos & Miedema, 2000).

What can we infer about how fairness fosters employee cooperation, based on the insights of fairness heuristic theory? Based on the theory, we can infer that fairness fosters cooperation by reassuring employees that they need not fear exploitation or rejection by the organization. With the alleviation of those fears, employees may feel free to approach their relationship with their organization in a less defensive manner (Lind, 2002). In other words, the sense of security that fairness fosters may lead employees to feel that their cooperation and prosocial behaviors on behalf of the organization are not open to exploitation. This pattern may be dependent, however, on what other types of information are available to employees (Van den Bos, Lind, & Wilke, 2001). That is, if other types of information are available that also provide reassurance about issues such as trust and rejection, then the theory would predict that we should see the influence of justice attenuated.

It is important to note that—unlike the instrumental theories and group engagement model outlined above—fairness heuristic theory does not explicitly test or indicate *why* people would choose to cooperate in reaction to justice. The theory's goal is to understand why people react to perceived justice, but not necessarily to explain why cooperation in particular emanates from justice. Thus, it does not focus on why (or how) cooperation would flow from fairness evaluations. It leaves open the question of why increased security in the nature of the employee/organization relationship should promote cooperation in particular.

Consistent with its emphasis, several realities of the research on fairness heuristic theory limit its current utility for understanding employee cooperation. First, research on fairness heuristic theory has primarily been experimental in nature, and relatively little work has tested the theory and its assumptions in field settings. Second, procedural justice is typically operationalized in these experiments as the provision of voice, to the relative neglect of many other characteristics and dimensions of procedural justice (Blader & Tyler, 2003a, 2003b; Colquitt, 2001; Rupp & Cropanzano, 2002; Tyler, 1994). This limits the generalizability of the results to contexts such as work organizations, where procedural justice information is more varied and multi-faceted.

These limitations notwithstanding, fairness heuristic theory provides a valuable perspective into the issue of why justice matters. It highlights the predicament that employees find themselves in as they enter into relationships with organizations, and posits an important role for procedural justice in how employees negotiate that predicament. Although it does not directly address the issue of how justice fosters cooperation in groups, it does put forth an important proposition for why people care about fairness.

Fairness Theory

Another justice theory currently gaining increased prominence is fairness theory (Folger & Cropanzano, 2001), an update to these theorists' earlier work on referent cognitions theory (e.g., Folger, 1987). The primary emphasis in fairness theory is the explanation of what people mean when they say that an experience was fair or unfair. In other words, what are the factors that determine whether individuals perceive fairness or not?

Fairness theory differentiates itself from other justice theories insofar as it highlights the important role of accountability judgments. The theory emphasizes counterfactual thinking (Roese, 1997) as a fundamental cognitive procedure in the evaluation of accountability and thus fairness. In particular, three types of counterfactual thoughts are emphasized: would judgments (has injury to one's state of being occurred?), could judgments (could a target person have behaved differently; was an alternative action feasible?), and should judgments (do particular referent standards suggest that things should have been different than they were?). All three elements are needed in order to evaluate an experience as unfair: People need to infer that injury has occurred, that it could have been prevented, and that it violated some moral or other standard that dictates what "should" have happened. When a person judges that injury *has* occurred, that the target causing the injury *could* have acted differently, and that according to some standard the target *should* have acted differently, injustice will be perceived.

Fairness theory makes an interesting contribution to the literature on how people evaluate fairness, because it brings to the foreground several facets of accountability, most of which have been lacking from previous work in this area. The contribution of the theory to understanding how or why justice influences cooperation, however, is less evident, because that was not the primary goal of the theory. Although fairness theory develops an elaborate model of the circumstances and preconditions that precede judgments of (un)fairness, it is less explicit on why and how these fairness judgments, once made, would result in cooperative behavior. Although some researchers have used its predic-

tions to examine outcomes other than fairness, such as customer satisfaction (Collie, Bradley, & Sparks, 2002), the model itself does not explicitly present a psychological rationale for why justice impacts cooperation in organizations.

Perhaps the foremost obstacle to fairness theory explaining the justice–cooperation relationship is that the processes highlighted by the theory tend to focus on the evaluation of unfairness, as opposed to fairness. That is, counterfactual thoughts are primarily generated in the face of aversive outcomes or situations (Roese, 1997; Roese & Hur, 1997; Roese & Olson, 1996). Although it has been argued that fairness theory could be extended to positive events or conditions (Folger & Cropanzano, 2001, p. 47), research evidence on counterfactual thinking suggests that such an extension is not likely to be a robust one because counterfactual thoughts are not typically generated in reaction to positive events.

These restrictions to primarily negative events and evaluations of injustice present obvious limitations for the theory's applicability to cooperation. Negative events and evaluations of injustice may likely result in uncooperative, or retaliatory, behavior against the organization (e.g., Greenberg, 1990; Skarlicki & Folger, 1997), but are unlikely to contribute to our understanding of more positive, prosocial organizational behaviors.

Other Theories

Several other justice theories also address why people care about justice, and thus may also lend insight into how justice fosters cooperation in organizations. For instance, Folger (1998) proposed that people's concern about justice is linked to a basic human drive to respect human dignity and worth, termed the moral virtues model of justice (Cropanzano, Byrne, Bobocel, & Rupp, 2001). Justice and fairness convey respect for human dignity, and thus people are drawn to it and motivated to react to it. The moral virtues model describes why people value justice, but one can imagine how it can be extended to help develop an understanding of the justice–cooperation link. For instance, if employees regard justice as a moral issue (i.e., as a "moral virtue"), they will be inclined to be a part of (and to work on behalf of) organizations that they see as respecting this moral imperative. Similarly, employees will want to disassociate themselves from (and thus not cooperate with) those organizations that do not demonstrate a concern for issues central to the their sense of morality. Thus, the moral virtues model can be adapted to explain the justice–cooperation link as a reaction to perceptions that the organization holds the same moral perspectives as the individual. Organizational research has shown that such perceived congruence be-

tween employees and their work organizations in related constructs, such as values, can be an important predictor of cooperation (O'Reilly & Chatman, 1986; Tyler & Blader, 2003a). Of course, the moral virtues model may even more directly predict cooperative behavior in response to perceived fair treatment, because such fairness by the organization toward the employee is likely to fulfill that employee's drive to feel a sense of self-worth.

A different approach to the issue of why people react to procedural justice focuses on the role that procedural justice plays in causal attribution processes (e.g., Gilliland, 1994; Ployhart & Ryan, 1997; Schroth & Shah, 2000; Van den Bos, Bruins, Wilke, & Dronkert, 1999). This work, which can be labeled the "attributional model" of procedural justice, builds from the observation that fair procedures imply that the outcomes that are associated with procedure are deserved. In other words, fair procedures are tantamount to internal causal attributions (and unfair procedures tantamount to external causal attributions) for outcomes, because decision-making characteristics such as neutrality and attempts to be accurate tend to foster distributions that reflect people's inputs (and thus the outcomes received are reflections of each individual's input). Note that the attributional function of procedures is primarily in operation when equity is the distributive rule; when need or equality are the active distributive rules, the attributional function of procedures is not relevant. Because equity is the normative distribution rule in organizational settings, the attributional model of procedural justice has high relevance to our discussion of justice in organizations.

In a demonstration of this approach, Gilliland (1994) found that self-efficacy was higher among those receiving a negative outcome through an unfair process as compared to those receiving the same outcome through a fair process. Schroth and Shah (2000) found across three studies that self-esteem was negatively affected when negative outcomes were matched with fair procedures or when positive outcomes were matched with unfair procedures. Van den Bos and colleagues (1999) also found that the experience of negative outcomes spurs attributional processes, and that inferring fairness in such situations can have deleterious consequences. When people receive unfair or unfavorable outcomes, it may be more psychologically comforting for them to think that such negative outcomes were due to error, sloppiness, and even to group-level issues such as race, age, or gender prejudice (Major, Quinton, and McCoy, 2002), as opposed to thinking that they were due to something about themselves. These studies all show that procedural fairness inferences may be related to causal attributions for outcomes.

These results suggest that people react to procedural fairness because it is informative for understanding their role in the outcomes that they experience. Note the similarity between this approach and fairness theory,

which was reviewed earlier. Both involve assessments of responsibility for events or outcomes. However, the theories differ in their emphasis and in the phenomena they are attempting to explain. Fairness theory has as its goal understanding whether people perceive fairness or not. It focuses on judging how accountable target individuals are for (negative) shifts in one's state of well-being, and thus it is primarily relevant when outcomes are negative. In contrast, attributional models focus on issues of outcome deservedness. They address the implications of a given process fairness judgment on how people react to outcomes.

From the attributional perspective, two possibilities arise for how procedural justice may foster cooperation. First, people may value procedural fairness (and react to it) because it allows them to make self-serving causal attributions for their outcomes (i.e., internal attributions for positive outcomes, external attributions for negative outcomes). Such self-serving attributions may serve two important functions: (a) It satisfies their distributive justice motives, by allowing them to feel that positive outcomes are deserved and negative outcomes are undeserved, and (b) it operates in the service of their self esteem, by allowing them to take credit for positive outcomes and to disassociate themselves from negative outcomes. Indeed, research shows that people may make procedural fairness judgments in self-serving ways, at least when information about the actual procedures used is sufficiently lacking (making self-serving attributions plausible) and when alternative motives do not interfere with outcome-based preferences (Blader, 2002).

The self-serving attribution function of procedures, however, would predict that outcomes interact with procedures in predicting cooperation, such that fair procedures would have to be matched with positive outcomes in order to elicit cooperation. Cooperation may result as people are motivated to continue to engage in behaviors that may perpetuate the receipt of positive outcomes, which they believe are internally caused. Fair procedures that are matched with negative outcomes would not satisfy the person's drive for self-serving attributions, and although unfair procedures matched with negative outcomes may preclude negative internal attributions, there is little basis to think that this would lead to cooperation. However, procedural justice research typically finds a different interaction effect between outcomes and procedures, whereby procedures have their largest impact when outcomes are negative (Brockner & Wiesenfeld, 1996). This suggests that this explanation for the attributional model of procedural justice cannot describe how justice fosters cooperation.

A second explanation may be that procedural fairness enables people to feel high levels of control (Langer, 1975; Rotter, 1966) since it suggests internal causality. Fulfilling people's need for control may satisfy a fun-

damental psychological drive that is unrelated to outcomes, and in turn may elicit cooperation because people value relationships with groups that allow them to satisfy that need. Importantly, control in this sense refers to a basic psychological drive and not to control over outcomes as described in the control model by Thibaut and Walker (1975). The provision of control itself can be motivating to employees, as has been shown in the research on empowerment.

INTEGRATING THE THEORIES

We have outlined several prominent theories about why people care about justice, and inferred from each some of the dynamics that may prompt justice evaluations to foster cooperation in organizations. They are the instrumental (control and social exchange) theories, the relational theories, fairness heuristic theory, fairness theory, the moral virtues model, and the attributional model of procedural justice. This begs the question, which one is right? As with all complex issues, there is no single answer to this question. The theories are not all mutually exclusive from one another, and furthermore multiple motives may be at work within the same judgmental context. With that in mind, we next consider some of the linkages among these theories, and discuss available evidence supporting one or another of the theories.

It is important to note up front that fairness heuristic theory, fairness theory, the moral virtues model, and the attributional model of justice do not explicitly link justice to cooperation. Although many of these theories propose an explanation for why people may care about perceived justice (or the factors they use to evaluate justice), they are less explicit about what drives the link between justice and cooperation in particular. We have attempted to derive some predictions for that relationship based on these theories, but feel compelled to add the caveat that many of these predictions were derived by us, not by the theorists themselves.

With that in mind, we observe that these theories are not necessarily incompatible with one another. Each theory posits a psychological reaction to justice that may coexist with the reactions posited by the other theories. In fact, in some cases the theories may complement one another. For instance, fairness theory's emphasis on accountability may make an important contribution to determining leaders' trustworthiness and their likelihood of exploiting group members. Finding leaders accountable for aversive actions should heighten group members' vigilance about the potential for exploitation, whereas lack of accountability may reduce the fear of exploitation even when outcomes are not desirable. So accountability judgments (the focus of fairness theory) may help address fears of exploitation and rejection (the focus of fairness heuristic theory),

which in turn may help group members feel the sense of security in their relationship with the organization that frees them up to cooperate. Other important linkages between attributional models of justice, fairness theory, and fairness heuristic theory may also exist, centered around their common focus on issues of causality and intention.

The explanations proposed by some of these theories for why people care about justice may also complement the identity effects of justice posited by the relational models. For instance, the reduction in fears of rejection (and exploitation) that result from perceived procedural fairness, posited by fairness heuristic theory, may allow employees to feel a sense of identity security (Tyler & Blader, 2003b). Identity security is the sense that identification with the group, and drawing one's sense of self from the group, can be pursued with little risk of negative psychological consequences. Identity security frees people up to reap the psychological benefits of group membership.

Similarly, a belief that one's organization shares one's value for human dignity and worth, which according to the moral virtues model is communicated by justice, may contribute to the sense that the organization is one from which people will want to draw their sense of self. Therefore, the moral virtues model may also be compatible with the relational theories, insofar as the perceived congruence in morality (or incongruence, as the case may be) between the employee and the organization may influence the extent to which employees are willing to let the organization define who they are and how they feel about themselves. That is, the level of congruence in moral values between the organization and the person may shape their level of identification with the organization, which in turn prompts cooperation and links the moral virtues and group engagement models. Other factors associated with process fairness, such as an increased sense of control (related to the attributional model), may likewise prompt increased identification with the organization, and in turn may prompt employee cooperation.

More generally, the point to emphasize is that the various reasons proposed by these theories for why people care about justice may be compatible with a relational understanding of justice effects (Tyler & Blader, 2000; Tyler & Huo, 2002). Each explanation provides a reasonable basis for employees wanting to define themselves as members of the organization and for seeing their intra- and interorganizational status in positive ways. Of course, future research is needed to empirically determine whether these theories actually fuse with relational and identity concerns to shape cooperation. Little work has been done to date on integrating these theories (although some recent work in this vein has begun to integrate fairness heuristic theory and the relational models; Van Prooijen, Van den Bos, & Wilke, 2004).

On the other hand, with the exception of fairness heuristic theory, it is harder to determine how these theories can be aligned with the instrumental justice theories. Moral evaluations are inherently distinct from outcome and exchange concerns, and thus employee reactions to justice as an intrinsic moral right are incompatible with cooperation that is linked to outcome evaluations. Likewise, people's need to feel a sense of control over their lives is regarded as a fundamental human drive. People do not only or primarily value a strong sense of control because of the positive implications it may have on their accrual of resources, but rather because feelings of autonomy fulfill a fundamental drive. On the other hand, reduced feelings of exploitation may be valued and reacted to because of the instrumental or economic benefits that come with not being exploited; employees may view resources more favorably if they believe that they are coming from authorities that are not exploitative. So to the extent that justice allays fears of exploitation, the insights of fairness heuristic theory may complement instrumental models of justice. In particular, fairness heuristic theory may contribute to an understanding of why procedural justice is regarded as instrumentally beneficial, insofar as it is a cue that conveys that organizational authorities will provide reasonable levels of resources and benefits. Additional research is needed to investigate this prediction.

Perhaps the strongest contrast between the theories lies in the distinction between the instrumental and relational models. Both models are supported by empirical research that specifically links justice to cooperation, and both explicitly posit different variables that should mediate the link between justice and cooperation. More fundamentally, though, the instrumental and relational models make very different arguments about what employees primarily care about and what motivates them. Instrumental theories argue that employees' essential concerns are over resources, whereas relational theories assert that employees' primary concerns relate to the construction and maintenance of their social identities.

In our research on the group engagement model (Tyler & Blader, 2000), we directly compare the relative impact of the instrumental and relational models, to determine which best accounts for the process by which justice influences cooperation. We have extensively reviewed our comparison of these models elsewhere (Tyler & Blader, 2000, 2001, 2003a, 2003c), but we will briefly review those results here. First, when we investigate the types of variables that procedural justice most strongly impacts, we find that process fairness evaluations are most strongly linked to the identity-related variables that we outlined earlier, and that they have a much weaker association with the types of outcome-oriented variables emphasized by the instrumental approaches. In other words, employees' perceptions of procedural justice have a

greater influence on their identities (e.g., on their identification with the organization and on their evaluations of inter- and intraorganization status) than they do on their evaluations of the outcomes they are receiving from the organization (e.g., outcome fairness, outcome favorability, expectations of future outcomes, etc.). Thus, when we compare the influence of procedural justice on instrumental and relational variables, we find that the influence on relational variables is greater. These relational evaluations are more strongly impacted by procedural justice than are the instrumental judgments.

Although this finding specifies the types of judgments most closely linked to procedural justice, it does not explain which ones lead justice to influence cooperation. Thus, we have also investigated which class of variables (instrumental, relational) are the strongest mediators of the link between justice and cooperation. We find that the relational variables account for the effects of procedural justice on cooperation, but that instrumental variables do not (Tyler & Blader, 2000, 2003). When we account for the influence of the relational variables on cooperation, we generally find little to no influence for the instrumental judgments. Furthermore, we find that relational variables fully explain the impact of procedural justice on cooperation, and that no independent influence of procedural fairness remains. Thus, research on our group engagement model directly indicates that the effects of justice on cooperation can be explained by the ideas of the relational theories of justice.

What do these results tell us about the importance of instrumental judgments? In our work, we find that instrumental judgments do have an impact on cooperation, but that that impact is mediated by relational concerns (Tyler & Blader, 2000). That is, instrumental judgments influence the identity constructs we have outlined here—identification, pride, and respect. To some extent, when employees regard their organizations as fulfilling their instrumental goals, they view their intra- and interorganization status more positively and they may more strongly identify with their organization. It is through this impact that instrumental judgments influence cooperation; no direct paths from instrumental judgments to cooperation remain when we account for relational judgments. It is in this way that the relational and instrumental models can be intermingled in an inclusive model of the justice–cooperation link.

Earlier, we cited a set of research theories and results that indicated that instrumental judgments, such as social exchange variables, mediate the link between justice and cooperation. Our results lead us to predict that these studies would have found a different pattern of results if they had included relational variables as well. Of course, additional work is needed to corroborate these emerging results. It is also important for future research to flesh out how the various explanations of why people care about procedural justice, such as those outlined here, can be

integrated with each other and with the relational and instrumental models. Such integration has the potential to foster more unified models of why people care about justice and how justice fosters cooperation in groups. These unified models are essential for designing the most effective justice-based strategies to gain employee cooperation in work organizations.

In addition to highlighting points of similarity and difference between the various justice theories, and positing ways in which they can be combined in a cohesive model of justice and cooperation, we hope to emphasize in this discussion the importance of addressing these issues from a theoretical perspective. We have tried to move beyond the mere observation of associated phenomena, and have focused the discussion on underlying psychological processes and dynamics. By doing so, we were able to identify those theories and explanations that are compatible and those that are incompatible. This approach facilitates the development of insights not just of justice but also more broadly of employee motivation. It brings the discussion of how justice fosters cooperation into the more extensive discourse on organizational behavior.

FRAMEWORKS FOR THE CONSEQUENCES OF JUSTICE

Thus far, we purposely have avoided explicit reference to particular employee reactions to justice, referring instead to the concept of "employee cooperation." Our vagueness on this issue reflects an intentional effort to defer addressing the specific types of reactions that have been linked to procedural justice, since the range and diversity of those dependent variables is so extensive and striking (Brockner & Wiesenfeld, 1996). Consistent with the phenomena-oriented approach by which procedural justice literature has developed, there have been few efforts at theoretically distinguishing the types of dependent variables associated with procedural justice. This shortcoming precludes theoretically based prediction of the variables that should be most strongly linked to procedural justice. Furthermore, it harms the credibility of procedural justice research, because it seems to imply the point of view that procedural justice is related to *every* employee attitude and behavior, while providing no insight into where or when justice should be most important. Finally, it neglects the important opportunity to test various hypotheses about how justice fosters cooperation, because different explanations for how justice fosters cooperation should predict different forms of cooperation that would be most strongly linked to justice.

A notable effort that addresses this issue is that by Conlon, Meyer, and Nowakowski (this volume), who distinguish between three different employee reactions to justice: performance and compliance ("the good"), withdrawal ("the bad"), and counterproductive behav-

ior ("the ugly"). We have also developed a different approach to organizing the components of cooperation, one that uses conceptual
distinctions to identify the various forms of what Conlon, Meyer and
Nowakowski refer to as "the good" (Tyler & Blader, 2000). Our model
identifies two important dimensions for classifying the various behaviors that constitute "the good": the function of a behavior (i.e., the goal
orientation of the behavior; is the behavior proactive in the way in
which it promotes the success of the organization, or is the behavior
one that limits the occurrence of negative consequences for the organization?) and the source or origin of the behavior (i.e., is it mandatory
behavior that is stipulated by the organization [in-role behavior], or is
it discretionary behavior that originates with the employee themselves [extra-role behavior]?).

Regardless of which model of cooperative behavior one adopts, the
point to emphasize is that distinguishing the forms that cooperation
may take fosters theoretically driven analysis and prediction of when
and what justice will impact. For instance, within the issue of employee
performance (i.e., "the good"), an important distinction exists between
in-role and extra-role behavior (i.e., performance vs. citizenship behavior). Relational models of justice should be relatively more applicable to
predicting extra-role behavior, because linking one's identity to their
organization may make people especially committed to ensuring the
success of the organization and thus to developing ways to help beyond
those stipulated by the organization itself. On the other hand, instrumental models of justice may be relatively more applicable to predicting in-role behavior, because prescribed behaviors are more likely to be
linked to organizational reward systems and are less reliant on intrinsic
motivational forces that may be rooted in strong relational and identity
bonds with the organization. Preliminary evidence from our own work
(Tyler & Blader, 2003) confirms an especially strong influence of procedural justice on discretionary cooperation (cf. Colquitt, Conlon,
Wesson, Porter, & Ng, 2001).

Future research should investigate the role that relational and instrumental mediators play in this pattern of results, and more generally should explore how various models of why justice influences
cooperation may be more or less relevant for different forms or aspects
of cooperation. Such exploration increases the depth of our understanding of when and how justice fosters cooperation and provides a
forum for testing theoretically based hypotheses that flow from the
various justice models discussed in this chapter. Perhaps most importantly, the results of such an investigation further help refine the development and implementation of justice-based strategies to attaining
employee cooperation.

CONCLUSION

The power and importance of justice findings speak for themselves: employees care about justice, and it shapes their thoughts, feelings, and behaviors in groups and organizations. Our goal in this chapter is to delve deeper and encourage research on theoretical frameworks that help give meaning to these findings by identifying the processes by which justice fosters cooperation.

We have pursued this goal by reviewing justice research that may help shed light on this issue and by discussing commonalities and potential linkages between these various theories. In particular, our review highlights the value of relational and identity models of procedural justice (and our "group engagement model" [Tyler & Blader, 2000] in particular), because empirical research findings indicate that this approach provides the most compelling explanation for justice effects on cooperation. People use procedural justice as a key cue when making judgments about the identity implications of organizational rules and practices, and they react to their identity inferences through their level of cooperation with the organization.

More generally, we believe that the field of social justice in general, and organizational justice in particular, can be advanced by going beyond merely identifying justice effects and instead developing strong conceptual frameworks within which to study justice issues. Procedural justice has been brought to visibility by the many compelling and counterintuitive demonstrations that justice matters. What is needed in the future are theoretical frameworks to help us to better understand the motivations that lead people to react to procedural justice and the various forms that those reactions may take.

REFERENCES

Batson, C. D. (1991). *The altruism question.* Hillsdale, NJ: Lawrence Erlbaum Associates.

Baumeister, R. F., & Leary, M. R. (1995). The need to belong: Desire for interpersonal attachments as a fundamental human motive. *Psychology Bulletin, 117,* 497–529.

Blader, S. L. (2002). *Justice is in the eye of the beholder: Motivated reasoning and procedural fairness evaluations.* Unpublished doctoral dissertation: New York University.

Blader, S. L., & Tyler, T. R. (2003a). What constitutes fairness in work settings? A four-component model of procedural justice. *Human Resource Management Review, 13,* 107–126.

Blader, S. L., & Tyler, T. R. (2003b). A four component model of procedural justice: Defining the meaning of a "fair" process. *Personality & Social Psychology Bulletin, 29,* 747–758.

Brockner, J., & Wiesenfeld, B. M. (1996). An integrative framework for explaining reactions to decisions: Interactive effects of outcomes and procedures. *Psychological Bulletin, 120,* 189–208.

Colquitt, J. (2001). On the dimensionality of organizational justice: A construct validation of a measure. *Journal of Applied Psychology, 86,* 386–400.

Colquitt, J. A., Conlon, D. E., Wesson, M. J., Porter, C. O. L. H., & Ng., K. Y. (2001). Justice at the millennium: A meta-analytic review of 25 years of organizational justice research. *Journal of Applied Psychology, 86,* 425–445.

Collie, T., Bradley, G., & Sparks, B. A. (2002). Fair process revisited: Differential effects of interactional and procedural justice in the presence of social comparison information. *Journal of Experimental Social Psychology, 38,* 545–555.

Cropanzano, R., Byrne, Z. S., Bobocel, D. R., & Rupp, D. E. (2001). Moral virtues, fairness heuristics, social entities and other denizens of organizational justice. *Journal of Vocational Behavior, 58,* 164–209.

Cropanzano, R., & Prehar, C. A. (2001). Emerging justice concerns in an area of changing psychological contracts. In R. Cropanzano (Ed.), *Justice in the workplace (Vol. II): From theory to practice* (pp. 245–265). Mahwah, NJ: Lawrence Erlbaum Associates.

Deci, E. L., & Ryan, R. M. (2000). The what and why of goal pursuits: Human needs and the self-determination of behavior. *Psychological Inquiry, 11,* 227–268.

Foa, U. G., & Foa, E. B. (1974). *Societal structures of the mind.* Springfield, IL: Charles C. Thomas.

Folger, R. (1987). Reformulating the preconditions of resentment: A referent cognitions model. In J. C. Masters & W. P. Smith (Eds.), *Social comparison, justice, and relative deprivation: Theoretical, empirical, and policy perspectives* (pp. 183–215). Hillsdale, NJ: Lawrence Erlbaum Associates.

Folger, R. (1998). Fairness as a moral virtue. In M. Schminke (Ed.), *Managerial ethics: Moral management of people and processes* (pp. 13–34). Mahwah, NJ: Lawrence Erlbaum Associates.

Folger, R. & Cropanzano, R. (2001). Fairness theory: Justice as accountability. In J. Greenberg & R. Cropanzano, *Advances in organizational justice* (pp. 1–55). Stanford, CA: Stanford University Press.

Gilliland, S. W. (1994). Effects of procedural and distributive justice on reactions to a selection system. *Journal of Applied Psychology, 9,* 691–701.

Greenberg, J. (1990). Employee theft as a reaction to underpayment inequity. *Journal of Applied Psychology, 75,* 561–568.

Kelley, H. H., & Thibaut, J. (1978). *The social psychology of groups.* New York: Wiley.

Konovsky, M. A., & Pugh, S. D. (1994). Citizenship behavior and social exchange. *Academy of Management Journal, 37,* 656–669

Langer, E. J. (1975). The illusion of control. *Journal of Personality and Social Psychology, 32,* 311–328.

Lind, E. A. (2001). Fairness heuristic theory: Justice judgments as pivotal cognitions in organizational relations. In J. Greenberg & R. Cropanzano (Eds.), *Advances in organizational behavior* (pp. 56–88). Stanford, CA: Stanford University Press.

Lind, E. A., Kanfer, R., & Earley, P. C. (1990). Voice, control, and procedural justice: Instrumental and noninstrumental concerns in fairness judgments. *Journal of Personality and Social Psychology, 59,* 952–959.

Lind, E. A., & Tyler, T. R. (1988). *The social psychology of procedural justice.* New York: Plenum Press.

Major, B., Quinton, W. J., & McCoy, S. K. (2002). Antecedents and consequences of attributions to discrimination: Theoretical and empirical advances. In M. Zanna (Ed.), *Advances in experimental social psychology* (Vol. 34, pp. 251–304). San Diego, CA: Academic Press.

Masterson, S. S., Lewis, K., Goldman, B. M., & Taylor, M. S. (2000). Integrating justice and social exchange: The differing effects of fair procedures and treatment on work relationships. *Academy of Management Journal, 43,* 738–748.

Montada, L. (1996). Tradeoffs between justice and self interest. In L. Montada & M. J. Lerner (Eds.), *Current societal concerns about justice* (pp. 259–275). New York: Plenum Press.

Moorman, R. H., Blakely, G. L., & Niehoff, B. P. (1998). Does perceived organizational support mediate the relationship between procedural justice and organizational citizenship behavior? *Academy of Management Journal, 41,* 351–357.

O'Reilly, C. A., & Chatman, J. A. (1986). Organizational commitment and psychological attachment: The effects of compliance, identification, and internalization on prosocial behavior. *Journal of Applied Psychology, 71,* 492–499.

Ployhart, R. E., & Ryan, A. M. (1997). Toward an explanation of applicant reactions: An examination of organizational justice and attribution frameworks. *Organizational Behavior & Human Decision Processes, 72,* 308–335.

Roese, N. J. (1997). Counterfactual thinking. *Psychological Bulletin, 121,* 133–148.

Roese, N. J. & Hur, T. (1997). Affective determinants of counterfactual thinking. *Social Cognition, 15,* 274–290.

Roese, N. J., & Olson, J. M. (1996). Counterfactuals, causal attributions, and the hindsight bias: A conceptual integration. *Journal of Experimental Social Psychology, 32,* 197–227.

Rotter, J. B. (1966). Generalized expectancies for internal versus external control of reinforcement. *Psychological Monographs: General and Applied, 80,* 1–27.

Rusbult, C., & Van Lange, P. (1996). Interdependence processes. In E. T. Higgins & A. W. Kruglanski (Eds.), *Social psychology* (pp. 564–596). New York: Guilford.

Rupp, D. E., & Cropanzano, R. (2002). The mediating effects of social exchange relationships in predicting workplace outcomes from multifoci organizational justice. *Organizational Behavior and Human Decision Processes, 89,* 925–946.

Schroth, H. A., & Shah, P. P. (2000). Procedures: Do we really want to know them? An examination of the effects or procedural justice on self-esteem. *Journal of Applied Psychology, 85,* 462–471.

Skarlicki, D. P., & Folger, R. (1997). Retaliation in the workplace. *Journal of Applied Psychology, 82,* 434–443.

Sweeney, P. D., & McFarlin, D. B. (1993). Workers' evaluations of the "ends" and the "means": An examination of four models of distributive and procedural justice. *Organizational Behavior and Human Decision Processes, 55,* 23–40.

Tajfel, H., & Turner, J. C. (1986). The social identity of intergroup behavior. In S. Horchel & H. G. Austin (Eds.), *Psychology of intergroup relations* (pp. 7–24). Chicago: Nelson Hall.

Thibaut, J., & Walker, L. (1975). *Procedural justice.* Hillsdale, NJ: Lawrence Erlbaum Associates.

Tornblom, K. Y., & Vermunt, R. (1999). An integrative perspective on social justice: Distributive and procedural fairness evaluations of positive and negative outcome allocations. *Social Justice Research, 12,* 39–64.

Tyler, T. R. (1989). The psychology of procedural justice: A test of the group-value model. *Journal of Personality and Social Psychology, 57,* 830–838.

Tyler, T. R. (1994). Psychological models of the justice motive. *Journal of Personality and Social Psychology, 67,* 850–863.

Tyler, T. R., & Blader, S. L. (2000). *Cooperation in groups: Procedural justice, social identity and behavioral engagement.* Philadelphia, PA: Psychology Press.

Tyler, T. R., & Blader, S. L. (2001). Identity and cooperative behavior in groups. *Group Processes & Intergroup Relations, 4,* 207–226.

Tyler, T. R., & Blader, S. L. (2003a). *Intrinsic motivation and cooperation in groups: A test of the group engagement model.* Unpublished manuscript, New York University.

Tyler, T. R., & Blader, S. L. (2003b). The group engagement model: Procedural justice, social identity, and cooperative behavior. *Personality and Social Psychology Review, 7,* 349–361.

Tyler, T. R., & Blader, S. L. (2003c). Social identity and fairness judgments. In S. Gilliland, D. Steiner, & D. Skarlicki (Eds.), *Social issues in management, 3,* 67–96. Greenwich, CT: Information Age Publishing.

Tyler, T. R., Boeckmann, R. J., Smith, H. J., & Huo, Y. J. (1997). *Social justice in a diverse society.* Boulder, CO: Westview.

Tyler, T. R., Degoey, P., & Smith, H. J. (1996). Understanding why the justice of group procedures matters. *Journal of Personality and Social Psychology, 70,* 913–930.

Tyler, T. R., & Huo, Y. J. (2002). *Trust in the law: Encouraging cooperation with the police and courts.* New York: Russell-Sage Foundation.

Tyler, T. R., & Lind, E. A. (1992). A relational model of authority in groups. M. Zanna (Ed.), *Advances in experimental social psychology* (Vol. 25, pp. 115–191). New York: Academic.

Tyler, T. R., & Smith, H. J. (1997). Social justice and social movements. In D. Gilbert, S. Fiske, & G. Lindzey (Eds.), *Handbook of social psychology* (4th ed., Vol. 2, pp. 595–629). New York: McGraw-Hill.

Tyler, T. R., & Smith, H. J. (1999). Justice, social identity, and group processes. In T. R. Tyler, R. M. Kramer, & O. P. John (Eds.), *The psychology of the social self* (pp. 223–264). Mahwah, NJ: Lawrence Erlbaum Associates.

Van den Bos, K. (2001). Uncertainty management: The influence of human uncertainty on reactions to perceived fairness. *Journal of Personality and Social Psychology, 80,* 931–941.

Van den Bos, K., Bruins, J., Wilke, H. A. M., & Dronkert, E. (1999). Sometimes unfair procedures have nice aspects: On the psychology of the fair process effect. *Journal of Personality and Social Psychology, 77,* 324–366.

Van den Bos, K., & Lind, E. A. (2002). Uncertainty management by means of fairness judgments. In M. P. Zanna (Ed.), *Advances in experimental social psychology* (Vol. 34, pp. 1–60). San Diego, CA: Academic Press.

Van den Bos, K., Lind, E. A., Vermunt, R., & Wilke, H. A. M. (1997). How do I judge my outcome when I do not know the outcome of others? The psychology of the fair process effect. *Journal of Personality and Social Psychology, 72,* 1034–1046.

Van den Bos, K., Lind, E. A., & Wilke, H. A. M. (2001). The psychology of procedural and distributive justice viewed from the perspective of fairness heuristic theory. In R. Cropanzano, *Justice in the workplace* (Vol. 2, pp. 49–66), Mahwah, NJ: Lawrence Erlbaum Associates.

Van den Bos, K., & Miedema, J. (2000). Towards understanding why fairness matters: The influence of mortality salience on reactions to procedural fairness. *Journal of Personality and Social Psychology, 79,* 355–366.

Van den Bos, K., Vermunt, R., & Wilke, H. A. M. (1997). Procedural and distributive justice: What is fair depends more on what comes first than on what comes next. *Journal of Personality and Social Psychology, 72,* 95–104.

Van den Bos, K., Wilke, H. A. M., Lind, E. A., & Vermunt, R. (1998). Evaluating outcomes by means of the fair process effect: Evidence for different processes in fairness and satisfaction judgments. *Journal of Personality and Social Psychology, 74,* 1493–1503.

Van Prooijen, J. W., Van den Bos, K., & Wilke, H. A. M. (2004). Group belongingness and procedural justice: Social inclusion and exclusion by peers affects the psychology of voice. *Journal of Personality and Social Psychology, 87,* 66–79.

12

How Does Organizational Justice Affect Organizational Citizenship Behavior?

Robert H. Moorman
Creighton University

Zinta S. Byrne
Colorado State University

*Our purpose is to move beyond simply reporting significant relation-
ships between perceived fairness and organizational citizenship behaviors (OCB) and, instead, seek to clarify the underlying psychological
processes that may explain why they relate. We first review two general
explanations—a social exchange explanation, where employees perform
OCB to reciprocate fair treatment, processes, and outcomes, and a social
identity-based explanation, where employees perform OCB to support a
group in which they feel they belong and to which they feel closely connected. After describing the basic mechanisms that link fairness perceptions and OCB for both explanations, we discuss potential mediators that
may represent those mechanisms. Examples of such mediators include
perceived organizational support, trust, affective organizational commitment, group pride, and respect received from the group. Finally, we
discuss potential moderators, like exchange ideology and group
connectedness, that may serve to enrich both explanations and potentially serve as possible avenues for their integration.*

When he first proposed the type of job performance called organizational citizenship behavior, Dennis Organ's intention was very similar
to the intention of every chapter in this handbook. He was trying to provide an answer to a compelling, yet elusive question. His question of interest was whether job satisfaction is related to job performance (Organ,
1977, 1988b). His answer was that researchers were defining job performance too narrowly and that may be a reason why researchers were
having difficulty finding support for the conventional wisdom that a
satisfied worker is more productive. Drawing on the work of Katz and
Kahn (1966), Organ (1977) distinguished between dependable role performance and "spontaneous and innovative behavior." This latter category was labeled "organizational citizenship behaviors," or OCB
(Smith, Organ, & Near, 1983), which he defined as "individual behavior
that is discretionary, not directly or explicitly recognized by the formal
reward system, and that in the aggregate promotes the effective functioning of the organization" (Organ, 1988a, p. 4).

Organ's original point was that discretionary forms of job performance, like OCB, are relatively unconstrained by situational forces
and thus can be affected by an individual employee's job attitudes.
In-role behavior, because it is more clearly linked to job descriptions,
work rules, and reward contingencies, is less likely to be affected by
job attitudes alone.

Interestingly, even though Organ and colleagues reported some support for his hypothesis that OCB would more likely be related to job attitudes than in-role behavior (Smith et al., 1983) recent meta-analyses reanalyzing the magnitude of the job satisfaction—job performance relationship suggest that both OCB and more traditional measures of job performance may be related to job satisfaction to the same degree. For example, Judge, Thoreson, Bono, and Patten (2001) performed a meta-analysis on job satisfaction–job performance studies and estimated that the uncorrected mean correlation between overall job satisfaction and job performance is .18 and the mean true correlation is .30. Similarly, LePine, Erez, and Johnson's (2002) meta-analytic results showed an uncorrected mean correlation of .20 and .24 corrected. These results compare favorably to Organ and Ryan's (1995) report of uncorrected mean correlations between job satisfaction and two OCB dimensions of .22 and .24. Thus, Organ's initial reasons that justified the creation of OCB may no longer be well supported. OCB may be related to job satisfaction, but no more or less so than other measures of job performance.

Even so, research since Organ's first efforts to describe OCB has offered a great deal of evidence of the value of OCB to the organizational behavior literature beyond its relationship to job satisfaction. OCB has emerged as a construct that plays a significant role as both a consequence of employee attitudes and personalities and as an antecedent of positive organizational outcomes.

OCB AND PERCEPTIONS OF JUSTICE

The success of research in the 1980s that supported a consistently significant relationship between job satisfaction and OCB (Bateman & Organ, 1983; Smith et. al. 1983) opened the door for the examination of possible relationships between other job attitudes and OCB performance (see Organ & Ryan, 1995, or Podsakoff, MacKenzie, Paine, & Bachrach, 2000, for a review). One job attitude that emerged from Organ's efforts to explain the job satisfaction to performance relationship was perceived job fairness. Indeed, Organ's (1988a) first efforts to describe a relationship between perceptions of fairness and OCB grew from the overlap between measures of job satisfaction and measures of fairness. Organ (1988a) suggested that it might be more accurate to reinterpret the cognitive, evaluative portion of the job satisfaction measures as cognitions of job fairness or workplace justice. Moorman (1991) examined the relative contribution of job satisfaction and job fairness in predicting OCB performance and found that when the relationship between fairness and OCB was controlled, job satisfaction failed to predict any additional variance in OCB.

The relationship between justice perceptions and OCB performance has been studied extensively in the literature and the results appear to support a relatively robust relationship (e.g., Farh, Podsakoff, & Organ, 1990; Konovsky & Organ, 1996; Moorman, 1991; Moorman, Niehoff, & Organ, 1993; Niehoff & Moorman, 1993). Recent meta-analyses examining the relationship suggest correlations in the range of .2 to above .4 between different dimensions of justice and various OCB dimensions (Colquitt, Conlon, Wesson, Porter, & Ng, 2001; Cohen-Charash & Spector, 2001; LePine et al., 2002; Organ & Ryan, 1995; Podsakoff et al., 2000). Much like the relationship between OCB and job satisfaction, these recent meta-analyses also suggest that perceptions of justice are related to other measures of job performance to about the same degree.

Given this support for the relationship between justice and OCB, the issue for this chapter is not whether justice is related to OCB. As Greenberg (1993) first stated, the general relationship between justice and OCB is based on the easily accepted belief that "people will behave altruistically toward the organization in which they work if they believe they have been fairly treated by that organization" (p. 250) and we thus do not really need more arguments for this point. Our issue of interest is to move beyond simply reporting significant relationships between perceived fairness and OCB and, instead, seek to explain the processes through which they are related. To that end, we first review two general explanations—a social exchange explanation and a relational model of authority or social identity-based explanation. For both explanations, we describe the basic processes that link fairness perceptions and OCB and then describe the potential mediators that may represent those processes. Finally, we discuss potential moderators that may serve to enrich both explanations and even serve as possible avenues to integrate them.

THE SOCIAL EXCHANGE EXPLANATION FOR THE RELATIONSHIP BETWEEN JUSTICE AND OCB

In order to explain why justice perceptions might be related to OCB, Organ (1988a, 1990) first proposed a social exchange interpretation. Organ suggested that social exchange theories, like those proposed by Homans (1961, 1974), Gergen (1969), Malinowski (1926), Adams (1963, 1965), Blau (1964), and Foa and Foa (1980), would be helpful in understanding a relationship between fairness and OCB because those theories describe how social relationships are based on the exchange of benefits between parties (for a review of social exchange explanations for the effects of fairness perceptions see Cropanzano & Byrne, 2000, and Cropanzano, Rupp, Mohler, & Schminke, 2001). If we consider fair treatment on the part of the organization as a perceived benefit for em-

ployees, social exchange theories suggest that employees will be motivated to reciprocate that benefit. Organ (1990) has suggested that this reciprocation could include OCB. This interpretation has been extensively studied over the last decade (e.g., Cropanzano, Prehar, & Chen, 2002; Greenberg, 1993; Konovsky & Pugh, 1994; Masterson, Lewis, Goldman, & Taylor, 2000b; Moorman, 1991; Moorman, Blakely, & Niehoff, 1998; Niehoff & Moorman, 1993; Settoon, Bennett, & Liden, 1996; Shore & Wayne, 1993; Wayne, Shore, & Liden, 1997; Wayne, Shore, Bommer, & Tetrick, 2002), and the results of those studies tend to support the utility of the social exchange approach.

The Norm of Reciprocity

Why would a party within an exchange relationship be motivated to offer types of job performance? A first reason is the norm of reciprocity (Gouldner, 1960). The norm of reciprocity suggests that people act to help others who have helped them because reciprocating the receipt of benefits is proper and appropriate for the continued health of the relationships between people. Gouldner proposed that this norm is universally held. He wrote, "The norm of reciprocity may be conceived of as a dimension to be found in all value systems and ... as one among *a number* [italics in original] of 'Principle Components' universally present in moral codes" (p. 171).

Reciprocity can be used to explain the motivation of all forms of job performance. For in-role performance, the reward system provides motivation to reciprocate job performance and may often do so independent of an employee's evaluation of the job or of his/her treatment in that job. However, for extra-role performance, the motivation to reciprocate may come from aspects of work beyond the formal pay system. Therefore, OCB performance may more likely be related to socioemotional outcomes received (like fair treatment, trust, support, respect, etc.) rather than formal economic outcomes (Foa & Foa, 1980).

A second reason why social exchange theory predicts performance is not necessarily tied to a reciprocation norm, although it is related. Blau (1964) disagreed with Gouldner (1960) that the norm of reciprocity is the fundamental mechanism driving all patterns of exchange. Blau instead suggested that each party's self-interest in continuing to receive benefits ultimately motivates the exchange of performance for benefits. Blau accepted an obligation to repay benefits received, but the mechanism that underlies this obligation is not a norm of reciprocity ("we should repay"), but rather the self-interest to continue to receive benefits. In other words, if we fail to repay we may be violating the reciprocity norm, but more importantly, we would be stopping the processes that resulted in our receiving benefits in the first place.

Although it might appear contradictory to suggest a role for self-interest in the motivation of OCB, Organ (1990) has always suggested that self-interest is an important part of a person's motivation to perform OCB. However, he was not ready to rely entirely on it as the only motivator because he believed OCB is motivated in ways different from in-role performance. Self-interest and some relation to future benefits contribute to the motivation of OCB. However, such motivation is also a measure different from the strict quid pro quo calculations that drive in-role performance.

Economic and Social Exchange Relationships[1]

Although reciprocation that occurs in exchange relationships may be a fundamental mechanism explaining OCB performance, it is important to recognize that different exchange relationships can differ in their propensity to evoke OCB. Blau's (1964) social exchange theory introduced two types of exchange relationships. The first is an economic exchange, where the respective parties agree in terms of a specific exchange of benefits that are articulated with an exact time frame and terms that are enforceable by third parties.

However, Blau (1964) also suggested a second type of exchange relationship because he acknowledged that not all exchanges are prescribed and based on clearly articulated contractual relationships or legal forms. To capture this other form of relationship, Blau (1964) described social exchange relationships, which consist of diffuse, nonspecified, informal agreements between the two parties. There is a general expectation of some future return, thus the processes within social exchange do not ignore self-interest. However, the exact nature of the obligation is not agreed upon in advance.

The reason why this distinction between economic and social exchange relationships is so important is that in only one of the two exchanges is a relationship between perceptions of fairness (and other indicators of positive organizational treatment) and OCB performance likely. If economic exchange is the only type of exchange relationship that could exist between parties in organizations, employees would only perform OCB if they considered them as a way to fulfill the obligations of their performance contract. Although there is evidence that employees and employers take OCB performance into account when evaluating job

---

[1]Cropanzano et al. (2001) discussed the problematic overuse of terms like social exchange. Their conclusions and the ones we follow here differentiate between social exchange theories and social exchange relationships. Social exchange theories are those that acknowledge and explain the nature of exchanges between parties. Within social exchange theories, Blau (1964) described two relationships. The first is an economic exchange relationship and the second is a social exchange relationship.

performance and determining performance-based raises (Kiker & Motowidlo, 1999; Rotundo & Sackett, 2002; Werner, 1994), no one has argued for the primacy of OCB over more specific, job-related behaviors.

Hence, the real value of Blau's (1964) identification of a second form of exchange relationship is that he identified a relationship in which it is possible to see OCB performance as a form of reciprocation. Thus, if employees view their exchange relationship as social, they will (a) hold an obligation to reciprocate received benefits and (b) have the opportunity to reciprocate by performing OCB.

The Role of Justice Perceptions in Social Exchange

How then do perceptions of justice relate to the development of a social exchange relationship and the reciprocation of OCB? First, the most obvious way is that fair treatment could be considered a benefit to be reciprocated (Greenberg & Cohen, 1982; Malatesta & Byrne, 1997; Masterson, Bartol, & Moye, 2000). Perceptions of fair treatment from an organization or supervisor could represent an accounting of benefits received. Fair treatment may then invoke an obligation to reciprocate.

Second, perceptions of fairness, to the degree they reflect fair treatment, can offer employees evidence that it is appropriate to be in a social exchange relationship with the supervisor or organization. The emergence of a social exchange relationship to complement an economic exchange relationship requires that employees appraise the quality and nature of their present relationship with the other party. They must believe they can offer contributions and seek benefits safely without needing legal or formal assurances. Social exchange relationships are such that each party will participate without the safety net of a formal agreement. There is a threat that one could be taken advantage of, but the relationship is perceived to be of such high quality that there is essentially little risk.

Perceptions of fair treatment may be a key source of information about the quality of the present relationship. If employees believe they are treated fairly, they have a sense that even without legal protection, their interests will still be, at least generally, supported. When employees perceive the existence of fair procedures and are treated fairly, they will develop trust that their extra-role behavior will be reciprocated (e.g., Folger & Konovsky, 1989). Greenberg (1993) suggested that the display of trust in others is effective for building relationships that are perceived as fair. As Organ and Moorman (1993) noted, if the work environment is construed as fair, an "individual will have the basis for taking a longer-run view that permits sacrifice of immediate self-interest" (p. 8). Such a sacrifice is often at the root of a person's motivation to perform OCB.

It might be even clearer to view this from the perspective of perceived unfairness (Greenberg & Scott, 1996). If employees perceive they are treated unfairly, they will see substantial evidence that they need legal and formal safeguards built into any agreement with the other party. In essence, fair treatment may nudge parties into social exchange relationships where OCB performance could likely occur, whereas unfair treatment will shove them back into an economic exchange relationship and under the protection of a formal contract where OCB performance is much less likely.

SOCIAL IDENTITY EXPLANATION
FOR THE RELATIONSHIP BETWEEN JUSTICE AND OCB

A second explanation for the relationship between justice perceptions and OCB is a social identity-based explanation (Tyler, 1999; Tyler & Blader, 2000), which builds on the relational model of authority first proposed by Tyler and Lind (1992). The social identity-based explanation employs a different mechanism to account for how fairness perceptions relate to OCB, and thus it may provide additional information toward our understanding of OCB.

The relational model of authority, originally proposed as the group-value model (Lind & Tyler, 1988), is rooted in social identity theory (Tajfel & Turner, 1986). The relational model says that procedural justice is based on an individual's concern about his or her status as a member of a group, and procedural justice conveys information about that status. Procedural justice judgments, therefore, are based on a concern about the quality of relationships with authorities and group members and a procedure is seen as fair if it indicates a positive, full-status relationship with the authority figure (e.g., supervisor). Lind (1995) stated that perceptions of procedural justice are influenced by three factors, termed relational factors: (a) status recognition, which is based on the quality of interpersonal treatment (e.g., with dignity and respect) an individual receives from the authority; (b) benevolence, which is perceived when the authority gives the impression of real consideration of an individual's views and attempts to "do the right thing" (Lind, 1995, p. 87); and (c) the neutrality of the authority's decision-making process.

Tyler and Blader (2000) recently clarified the relational model by stating that individuals care more about concerns of identity than concerns of exchange. Thus when individuals receive treatment that communicates a sense of identification with the group, they contribute to the viability of the group (e.g., demonstrate OCB). Tyler and Blader suggested that people draw inferences about the reason why authorities behave as they do and it is those inferences that shape individuals' responses. Therefore, the degree to which the authority behaves in accordance

with concern and caring behavior determines how others respond. The more the authority figure shows that individuals are "members" of the group, the more individuals will respond with beneficial behaviors such as OCB.

Tyler and Blader (2000) presented a newer version of the relational model of authority, which they called the social identity-based model, to explain why people might demonstrate these cooperative or beneficial behaviors towards the group. They argued that when people feel positive about the group (e.g., pride) to which they identify, they expend energy to maintain that favorable identification with the group by working harder for the group's success. People may see the group's status and effectiveness as a source of their positive self-identity and will be motivated to maintain and even enhance the group's status as a way to maintain and even enhance their own. They are hence motivated to aid the welfare of the group and support its continued success by conforming to group rules, remaining active within the group, and engaging in extra-role behaviors (like OCB). Greenberg (1993) offered a similar explanation for how justice would affect OCB, although from the perspective of injustice. He stated, "Employees who believe they have been unfairly treated may *dissociate* (emphasis added) themselves from the organization that has wronged them" (p. 251).

Stated otherwise, Tyler and Blader (2000) seem to suggest that individuals will demonstrate more OCB in order to maintain their favorable identification with the group, which has been conveyed to them via fair procedures and treatment. This perspective is different from social exchange theory in that the social exchange model of fairness is simply an instrumental one, in which the primary objective of the relationship is to exchange resources. According to their social identity-based model, individuals do not necessarily seek resources from their relationships, but rather seek information about their identity and value within that relationship.

As explained here, both the social exchange and social identity-based explanations rely on mechanisms where justice perceptions evoke positive impressions of the other party. However, we, along with Tyler and his colleagues, believe there is an important difference to note. Using the social exchange explanation, employees perform OCB to reciprocate fair treatment and believe such reciprocation will increase the likelihood that such fair treatment will continue. Using the social identity-based explanation, employees perform OCB because such behavior supports the welfare of the group to which they closely identify and these behaviors support their own relative status within that group. OCB is not necessarily offered as one link in the chain of offered and reciprocated benefits, but is extended as a means to support the prosperity of a collective to which the employees may closely identify.

Admittedly, we believe self-interest may play a role in both explanations, although the role is more pronounced in the social exchange explanation and, in contrast, tends to be played down in the social identity-based explanation. In the social identity-based explanation, even though our actions to support the group and its welfare may prompt us to subordinate our immediate self-interest, our longer term self-interest would be enhanced by our close identification with and improved standing in the group. As Tyler and Blader (2000) noted, "Because group status reflects on the person, people want their groups to be successful and to have high status so that high status will reflect favorably on them" (p. 144).

Tyler (1999) reported two studies designed to assess the relative contribution of the social identity-based model and the social exchange model for cooperative behavior. These tests compared the relative explanatory power of judgments about member status (pride with and status in the group) with judgments about the nature and quality of resources received. Tyler (1999) found that when compared in a usefulness analysis judgments of status explained 19% of the variance in behavior beyond that explained by judgments about resources received, whereas those resource judgments could only explain about 1% of the variance beyond that explained by status. Tyler and Blader (2000) used these results to conclude, "Cooperative actions to help the group generally were shaped more by status assessments than by evaluations of the quality of resources people received" (p. 153). They further state, "identity concerns often are more influential than are judgments about the favorability of the resources obtained from the group" (p. 148).

However, it may be noted that Tyler and Blader (2000) maintained a distinction between "respect received from a group" and other resources that may also be conferred by a group. Unlike monetary rewards or job opportunities, they did not consider respect received as a resource that group members might be motivated to reciprocate. Tyler and Blader (2000) noted that social exchange relies on the exchange of "desired material resources" (p. 147). A more broad reading of what would constitute a resource might go beyond only material resources and include less tangible resources like respect (Foa & Foa, 1980). Thus, their results for the effect of respect received from the group on cooperative behaviors may include some element of reciprocation.

REFINING THE SOCIAL EXCHANGE AND SOCIAL IDENTITY-BASED EXPLANATIONS

The general processes described in both the social exchange explanation and the social identity-based explanation provide a good starting point in our understanding of the relationship between fairness and

OCB and help to explain how and why justice leads to OCB. We can obviously benefit, however, from examining in detail the dynamics that occur within that relationship. This is the proverbial "black box" problem—we have justice perceptions entering the box from the left and OCB emerging from the right, but the key issue is what goes on inside the black box to transform fair treatment by one party into OCB performance from the other. In this section, we review possible mediators of the justice/OCB relationship and discuss how these mediators may fit into either of the two explanations described within this chapter.

Mediators Based on the Social Exchange-Based Explanation

To summarize our discussion, the social exchange explanation suggests that, like other forms of job performance, employees perform OCB to reciprocate benefits received from the organization. Based on this discussion, the first step in filling in the black box is to recognize the central importance of reciprocity. In social exchange, employees perform to reciprocate receiving benefits. Therefore, any mediators that could explain the relationship between fairness and OCB must offer some indication that benefits have been received that deserve reciprocation.

The centrality of the obligation to reciprocate can be represented by a construct studied in social psychology called "felt obligation" (Eisenberger, Armeli, Rexwinkel, Lynch, & Rhoades, 2001). Felt obligation is defined as a descriptive belief regarding whether one should care about the organization's well-being and should help the organization reach its goals. Sample items from the Eisenberger, et al. (2001) measure of felt obligation include, "I have an obligation to the company to ensure that I produce high quality work," "I feel a personal obligation to do whatever I can to help the company achieve its goals," and "I would feel an obligation to take time from my personal schedule to help the company if it needed my help." These and the other items in their scale all assess a perceived obligation to act in the company's behalf. Such obligation is fundamental to the social exchange explanation for the relationship between justice and OCB because it represents employees' judgment that they should act given their current circumstances. Actually acting to repay that obligation is the logical next step.

Felt obligation can be considered part of Rousseau's (1995) conception of a psychological contract. A psychological contract represents the expectations or beliefs held by an employee about the reciprocal obligations that comprise an employee–organization exchange relationship. Employees hold a certain set of expectations about the benefits that they should receive as part of their employment relationship (what the organization owes them), and they hold a certain set of expectations about how they should act in response to those benefits (what they owe the or-

ganization). The mutual promissory nature of the psychological contract, therefore, includes the Eisenberger et al. (2001) definition of felt obligation as the belief of what the employee owes the organization, yet also entails what the employee believes the organization owes him or her (the organization's felt obligation).

Eisenberger et al. (2001) showed support for the central role played by felt obligation. In a study of relationships between perceived organizational support (POS), felt obligation, affective commitment, organizational spontaneity (which is a form of extra-role behavior similar to OCB), in-role performance, and withdrawal behavior, felt obligation fully mediated the relationship between POS and organizational spontaneity and between POS and in-role behavior.

We next discuss variables that capture the reasons why perceptions of fairness would create felt obligations. Researchers have explored the efficacy of other job attitudes and relational constructs that may mediate the relationship between perceived fairness and OCB. Results of these studies tend to support significant relationships among these variables and OCB, and, more importantly, some studies support a mediating role for these variables in the relationship between justice and OCB.

Trust.   Among the many different definitions that exist, trust has been defined as the extent to which one can have "confidence in the words and actions of other people" and "be willing to ascribe good intentions to" their actions (Cook & Wall, 1980, p. 39). Mayer, Davis, and Schoorman (1995) discussed two forms of trust, one from the view of the person doing the trusting (i.e., trustor), and the other from the view of the trustee (person being trusted). Mayer et al. (1995) suggested that the person who trusts someone else must be willing to be vulnerable to the actions of the person whom they are trusting. The trustee must possess the quality of trustworthiness in order to be trusted. Trustworthiness is the quality of fulfilling obligations or beneficial tasks, benevolence or the desire to want to help the trustor, and integrity or adhering to principles of ethical behavior. The notions of trustworthiness and benevolence have been incorporated into the works of Lind and Tyler (Lind & Tyler, 1988; Tyler & Degoey, 1996; Tyler, DeGoey, & Smith, 1996; Tyler & Lind, 1992).

Konovsky and Pugh (1994) proposed that trust serves as an important precondition for the emergence of a social exchange relationship and is essential for its continuation. They also suggested that perceptions of procedural justice serve as a source of trust because they "demonstrate an authority's respect for the rights and dignity of individual employees" (p. 658). They found support for a model where trust in the supervisor fully mediated the relationship between procedural justice and OCB. Pillai, Schriesheim, and Williams (1999) also examined trust

as a mediator of the justice to OCB relationship. In their study assessing relationships among leadership behaviors, perceptions of justice, trust, and OCB, they reported significant paths between procedural justice and trust and between trust and OCB. Finally, Aryee, Budhwar, and Chen (2002) assessed how trust in both supervisors and in the organization may mediate relationships between three dimensions of justice and both work attitudes and work performance. Their results suggest that only trust in the supervisor played a mediating role between interactional justice and OCB.

Although these studies have shown support for trust as a mediator, the ability to ascertain which view of trust served as the mediator is lacking. We suggest that both views of trust as defined by Mayer et al. (1985), qualities of the trustor and qualities of the trustee, be considered as mediators.

Perceived Organizational Support and Leader–Member Exchange. Two additional relational constructs that have been studied extensively as they pertain to both justice and OCB are perceived organizational support and leader–member exchange (LMX). Perceived organizational support represents an assessment of the social exchange relationship between an employee and the organization (Rhoades & Eisenberger, 2002). Employees determine the organization's readiness to participate in a social exchange relationship by forming "a general perception concerning the extent to which the organization values their contributions and cares about their well-being" (Eisenberger, Fasolo, & Davis-LaMastro, 1990, p. 51).

On the other hand, LMX assesses the nature of the relationship that may exist between leader and follower. Two types of leader–follower relationships are described—a low-quality relationship where contributions offered by both the leader and the follower only rise to the level of that required in the job, and a high-quality relationship where leaders seek to offer followers influence and support beyond what is called for in the employment contract (Graen & Cashman, 1975).

Studies have, in general, supported the relationship between LMX, POS, and OCB performance. For example, Eisenberger et al. (1990), Shore and Wayne (1993), Randall, Cropanzano, Bormann, and Birjulin (1999), Settoon et al. (1996), and Wayne, Shore, and Liden (1997) together suggested that both POS and LMX are related to various measures of OCB. More germane to our topic, recent studies have generally supported a mediating role for both POS and LMX in the relationship between justice and OCB. Moorman et al. (1998) assessed the degree to which POS alone mediated the relationship between procedural justice and OCB. Their results suggest that procedural justice affects citizenship behavior because such judgements may influence the degree an

employee perceives organizational support and this perception of support prompts the reciprocation of citizenship behavior. Aryee and Chay (2001) reported similar results. They found that perceived union support mediated a relationship between justice and OCB directed toward union members.

Masterson, Lewis, Goldman, and Taylor (2000) explored whether justice perceptions were related directly to OCB performance or whether the relationship was indirect through relationships with both POS and LMX. They found that LMX mediated the relationship between interactional justice and OCB beneficial to the supervisor and that POS mediated the relationship between procedural justice and OCB beneficial to the organization.

Wayne et al. (2002) also assessed whether both POS and LMX would mediate the relationship between perceptions of procedural and distributive justice (among other potential antecedents) and OCB. They found that both procedural and distributive justice were related to POS, but neither was related to LMX. Also, they found that while POS was related to OCB, LMX was not. We must note that Wayne et al. (2002) did not replicate the distinction between supervisor and organization-directed OCB present in Masterson, Lewis, Goldman, and Taylor (2000), and this difference may account for their different results.

The research just cited argues for a certain causal direction for the relationships among perceptions of justice, POS, LMX, and OCB. Given the relatively high intercorrelations among respondents' perceptions about their work and work context, other causal directions may be plausible. However, our search of the justice, POS, and LMX literature reveals no studies yet that support alternative causal directions (e.g., justice mediates the POS, LMX, and OCB relationships). Exploring the contribution of such models is clearly an issue for future research.

Mediators Based on the Social Identity-Based Explanation

The mechanism employed by the social identity-based explanation suggests a second set of potential mediators. Instead of reciprocity, the social identity model suggests that identification with the group and the subsequent motivation to work for the group's benefit explains why justice is related to OCB.

Affective Organizational Commitment.   One mediator previously recognized as an indicator of identification is affective organizational commitment. For example, Meyer and Allen's (1984) affective commitment scale includes items that ask "I feel a strong sense of belonging to the organization," and "I feel emotionally attached to the organization." In addition, O'Reilly and Chatman (1986) labeled "identification

with the group" as one component of affective organizational commitment. Affective organizational commitment may also relate separately to both perceptions of fairness and OCB. In Organ and Ryan's (1995) meta-analytic review of the antecedents of OCB, they reported evidence for a relationship between affective organizational commitment and both altruism and conscientiousness. Schappe (1998) found that affective organizational commitment was related to fairness perceptions and also accounted for unique variance in OCB performance.

Group Pride and Respect From the Group. Tyler et al. (1996) identified two additional mediators. They suggested that relational judgments of authority (neutrality, trustworthiness, and status recognition), which relate to procedural justice, affect group-oriented behaviors through perceptions of (a) group pride and (b) perceived respect within the group. Those who feel greater pride in the group and perceive that they are highly respected by the group will be more likely to closely identify with the group and perform OCB. Tyler et al. (1996) examined the potential mediating role of group pride and respect and found that both mediated the relationship between relational judgements of authority and extra-role behavior directed at groups.

Legitimacy of Authorities. A final potential mediator to consider in the social-identity-based framework is *legitimacy of authority* and rule-following behavior. Tyler and Blader (2000, p. 57) stated that "legitimacy and obligation are intertwined with the realm of morality and involve people's feelings of responsibility and obligation to others." According to these authors, employees may develop a sense of obligation and responsibility for following rules that are presented by a legitimate organizational authority. Employees will accept decisions and seem obligated to follow procedures when they are made by an authority perceived to be legitimate (Tyler & Blader, 2000). Tyler (2001, p. 416) suggested that "the roots of legitimacy lie in people's assessments of the fairness of the decision-making procedures used by authorities" indicating that individual's judge the legitimacy of an authority by his/her procedural fairness. Given this, we suggest that if individuals perceive the authority to be fair, they'll rate the authority as legitimate and develop a sense of obligation toward the authority, perhaps responding with OCB.

Which Mediator With Which Model?

The preceding discussion identified seven relational variables that may, based on either the social exchange explanation or the social identity-based explanation, mediate the relationship between perceptions of jus-

tice and OCB. To varying degrees, research results suggest that these seven capture the psychological processes that move someone from their evaluations of fair treatment to their OCB performance. Additionally, we believe that there is room for each to contribute to both models of mediation suggested above. For example, trust may affect OCB because of how it indicates one party's identification with the other, as well as how it represents a resource to be reciprocated in a social exchange process. However, for the sake of theoretical elegance, we next speculate which of the seven may be most useful in capturing the processes in each of our two explanations.

In the social exchange explanation, the most likely mediators may be those that clearly evaluate the benefits received from the exchange partner. In essence, the mediators of the social exchange explanation must assess beliefs about what has been received from the exchange partner, be it tangible resources or less tangible benefits. Mediators that may assess benefits received include perceived organizational support, leader–member exchange, and trust. Perceptions of support received from the organization and from a supervisor could prompt one to feel an obligation to reciprocate with OCB performance. In addition, trust established between exchange partners may represent a resource that employees may believe should be reciprocated (i.e., "I will respond favorably to those I trust and to those who show trust in me").

One additional mediator that may also assess beliefs about what has been received is respect from the group. Even though Tyler suggested this mediator as part of the social identity-based explanation, we believe respect from the group may be similar to perceived organizational support and also may capture a perception of a benefit received from that group. Indeed, other than the use of either the group or the organization as the source, the measure of respect received reported by Tyler and Blader (2000) includes items that are similar to the measure of perceived organization support included in the social exchange explanation. For example, items like "Others in the work setting value what you contribute at work" and "Others in the work setting value you as a member of your work group" included in the respect scale are similar to items like "The organization values my contributions to its well-being" and "The organization takes pride in my accomplishments" that are in the POS scale used by Eisenberger et al. (2001).

In the social identity-based explanation, the key process tying justice to OCB is the perceived connection and identification with the group. Thus, the most likely mediators are those that assess the degree of connection felt by the employees. The mediators of choice for this model include affective organizational commitment, group pride, legitimacy of authorities, and even trust in the group. Even though Konovsky and Pugh (1994) suggested trust primarily as a mediator in a social exchange

framework, trust may also be critical in describing a connection with the group. Greater trust may yield a closer identification.

Of course, all the potential mediators described here are highly intercorrelated and overlap both theoretically and operationally. For example, employees are more likely to hold positive attitudes and feelings of connection with the organization if the organization provides them with benefits. Also, variables like trust, POS, and LMX may prompt a felt obligation to reciprocate, but they may also affect the degree of affective commitment felt and increase one's connection with the group. Our objective is not to argue clean and complete divisions between the potential mediators and the potential models. Our intent is to try to capture two related but overlapping mechanisms explaining the relationship between justice and OCB. These relationships are illustrated in Fig. 12.1.

POTENTIAL MODERATORS OF THE RELATIONSHIP BETWEEN JUSTICE AND OCB

Beyond efforts to understand potential mediators of the justice to OCB relationship, a complete picture should also include some discussion of potential moderators of the relationships in each explanation. Because the focus of this chapter is on the relationship between justice and OCB, a discussion of mediators seems more appropriate because of the central role played by mediators in explaining how this relationship may occur. However, for completeness, we included some discussion of moderators because moderators may strengthen or weaken the justice to OCB relationship.

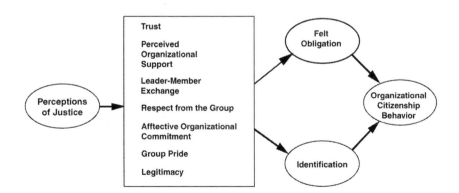

FIG. 12.1. Mediators based on the social exchange and social identity explanations for the relationship between perceptions of justice and OCB.

Recognizing the value of understanding the conditions that could affect how justice is related to OCB, researchers have been studying the role of potential moderators for some time and several recent candidates have emerged, described next.

Exchange Ideology

Exchange ideology refers to the degree to which the norm of reciprocity may appeal to certain persons (Eisenberger, Cotterell, & Marvel, 1987). Granted, Gouldner (1960) suggested that the norm of reciprocity is universal, but he did not suggest that it is unconditional and he listed a number of examples for how the obligation of repayment may depend on characteristics of the benefit received and the person receiving it. Exchange ideology simply assesses the degree to which employees believe a norm of reciprocation is appropriate and whether it is always useful to apply the reciprocity norm to their relationship with the work organization.

The effect of differences in exchange ideology on OCB is relatively straightforward. Those with a "strong" exchange ideology will reciprocate benefits with behaviors like OCB, whereas those with a "weak" ideology will perform or not perform OCB regardless of whether they have received benefits. Research results tend to support the moderating effect of exchange ideology. For example, Witt (1991) found that exchange ideology moderates the relationships between ratings of OCB and perceived organizational support. Eisenberger et al. (2001) similarly found that the relationship between POS and felt obligation increased with the acceptance of the reciprocity norm in work organizations. Finally, Ladd and Henry (2000) found that organizational exchange ideology moderated the relationship between perceived organizational support and OCB directed toward the organization.

Role Definition

A second potential moderator of the relationship between justice and OCB is the degree employees define OCB as extra-role or in-role. Tepper, Lockhart, and Hoobler (2001) described two competing models assessing the effect of role definition on the relationship between justice perceptions and OCB. The first model describes a role enlargement effect that examines whether role definitions mediate the relationship between justice and OCB. Following Morrison (1994), Tepper et al. (2001) tested whether procedural justice perceptions would prompt subjects to view their job tasks as more in-role and whether this redefinition would increase their performance of those tasks. The second model was a role discretion model that suggested that role definitions moderated

the relationship between justice perceptions and OCB. In this model, Tepper et al. (2001) argued that defining OCB as in-role may impact its performance, but it may also reduce the influence that justice perceptions may have on its performance. Tepper et al. (2001) found more support for the role discretion effect where role definitions moderated the relationship between justice and OCB and less support for role definitions mediating the relationship between justice and OCB. Tepper and Taylor (2003) replicated those results when they found that the effect of procedural justice on OCB performance was more pronounced when employees defined OCB as extra-role rather than in-role. A similar result for role definition as a moderator was reported by Hofmann, Morgeson, and Gerras (2003). Thus, any attempt to understand why justice perceptions may relate to OCB should take into account the ways in which employees define their own contributions. Such definitions might influence the form and magnitude of the effect of justice on OCB.

Connectedness

One final moderator may serve as one means to integrate the two explanations discussed here. Byrne (2001) proposed a new conceptual model for predicting the nature of the relationship between justice and a sense of connectedness, and subsequent predictions for relevant organizational outcomes. Her study examined whether connection (which she called identification in her study) moderated the relationship between justice perceptions and relational variables, such as support, and whether support was expected to fully mediate the relationship between fairness (interacting with connectedness) and supervisory and coworker oriented outcomes. This model thus employed the variables from the social exchange explanation (justice to perceived support to OCB), but it included a concept from the social identity-based explanation—the notion of connection with others—as a moderator.

Byrne (2001) found support for this integrated model at the coworker level. Specifically, she found that connectedness with coworkers moderated the relationship between interactional fairness and support from coworkers, and that the relationship between interactional fairness (moderated by connectedness) and satisfaction in coworkers was fully mediated by support from coworkers. In other words, a sense of connection and acceptance with the team strengthened the effect of perceptions of interactional justice from team members on perceptions of team member support, and support led to satisfaction in coworkers. Unfortunately, Byrne (2001) failed to measure OCB from the perspective of team members and therefore was unable to effectively test the integrated model using OCB as an outcome. We believe that further research might show additional support for this integrated model. Thus, we propose

that the moderators that may influence the strength and form of the relationship between perceptions of fairness and OCB (e.g., exchange ideology, role definition, connectedness) are illustrated in Fig. 12.2.

REFINING THE EXPLANATIONS USING DISTINCT
SOURCES OF JUSTICE, JOB ATTITUDES, AND OCB

If we take the examination of the details of the dynamics of the justice to
OCB relationship one step further and with a little more specificity, we
can utilize both social exchange and social identity-based explanations
and yet also keep in mind recent research that suggests that justice comes from sources (Colquitt, 2001, calls this the agent–system model)
and that these sources play a role in the level of the outcome variable.
Specifically, justice perceived as coming from the organization best predicts organizational-level outcomes, justice perceived as coming from
the supervisor best predicts supervisory-level outcomes, and justice
perceived as coming from coworkers predicts coworker-level outcomes
(Blader & Tyler, 2000; Byrne, 1999, 2001; Byrne & Cropanzano, 2000;
Colquitt et al., 2001; Colquitt, Noe, & Jackson, 2002; Masterson, Bartol,
& Moye, 2000; Rupp & Cropanzano, 2002). We therefore suggest that
perceptions of justice from the organization will predict perceived organizational support, trust in the organization, affective organizational
commitment, and organizational pride, which in turn will influence felt
obligation with the organization, ultimately resulting in OCB beneficial
to the organization; perceptions of justice from the supervisor will predict perceived supervisory support, LMX, and respect with the supervisor, which in turn will predict felt obligation with the supervisor,

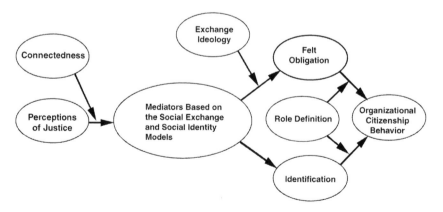

FIG. 12.2.   Potential moderators of the relationship between perceptions of
justice and OCB.

resulting in OCB beneficial to the supervisor; and finally, perceptions of justice from coworkers will predict perceived coworker support, which in turn will predict felt obligation with coworkers, resulting in OCB beneficial to coworkers.

Similarly, identification or connectedness (with the supervisor, organization, coworker) will moderate complimentary-level variables. For example, connection with the supervisor will moderate perceptions of fairness from the supervisor and perceived supervisory support (PSS), exchange ideology with the supervisory will moderate the PSS to felt obligations with the supervisor relationship, and role discrepancy will moderate felt obligations with the supervisor and OCB beneficial to the supervisor relationship; likewise for the organization and coworker as sources.

CONCLUSION

Our examination of the social exchange explanation and the social identity-based explanation bring us to two general themes to explain the relationship between justice and OCB. First, justice affects OCB because fairness perceptions are instrumental in developing a social exchange relationship where OCB could occur and because fair treatment is a benefit that employees may wish to reciprocate following the norm of reciprocity. The mediators of this relationship, such as POS, LMX, trust, and respect from the group or supervisor, capture whether subjects have received benefits and believe they should be reciprocated. Second, justice affects OCB because fairness perceptions communicate information about employees' social connection and relative standing within the group or with the supervisor, or the legitimacy of the authority. Such information helps employees identify with the group and work to supports its goals and future success. Mediators of this relationship, such as affective commitment, legitimacy, and group pride, capture whether individuals identify with the group and would seek to perform on its behalf.

Beyond the mediators that serve to explain the social exchange and social identity-based explanations of OCB, potential moderators of the justice to OCB relationship may include exchange ideology, role discretion, and connectedness. The potential contributions of these and other possible moderators clearly indicate the obvious complexity of the relationship between justice and OCB. Our intention was to offer a more focused discussion of this complexity and to attempt to refine our understanding of how justice perceptions may relate to OCB performance.

We began this chapter with the objective of clarifying the processes through which justice and OCB are related. To that end, we first reviewed two general explanations—a social exchange explanation and a relational model of authority or social identity-based explanation. For both

explanations, we described the basic processes that link fairness perceptions and OCB and then described the potential mediators that may represent those processes. Finally, we discussed potential moderators that may serve to enrich both explanations and even serve as possible avenues to integrate them. It is our hope that this detailed examination provided insight into the justice–OCB relationship and sparks ideas for future research that further extends our understanding of what role justice plays in promoting organizational citizenship behaviors.

REFERENCES

Adams, J. S. (1963). Toward an understanding of inequity. *Journal of Abnormal and Social Psychology, 47*, 422–436.

Adams, J. S. (1965). Inequity in social exchange. In L. Berkowitz (Ed.), *Advances in experimental social psychology* (Vol. 2, pp. 267–299). New York: Academic.

Aryee, S., & Chay, Y. W. (2001). Workplace justice, citizenship behavior, and turnover intentions in a union context: Examining the mediating role of perceived union support and union instrumentality. *Journal of Applied Psychology, 86*, 154–160.

Aryee, S., Budhwar, P. S., & Chen, Z. X. (2002). Trust as a mediator of the relationship between organizational justice and work outcomes: Test of a social exchange model. *Journal of Organizational Behavior, 23*, 267–285.

Bateman, T. S., & Organ, D. W. (1983). Job satisfaction and the good soldier: The relationship between affect and employee "citizenship." *Academy of Management Journal, 26*, 587–595.

Blau, P. M. (1964). *Exchange and power in social life.* New York: John Wiley & Sons.

Blader, S. L., & Tyler, T. R. (2000, August). *A four-component model of procedural justice: What makes a process fair in work settings?* Paper presented at the annual meeting of the Academy of Management, Toronto, Canada.

Byrne, Z. S. (1999, April). *How do procedural and interactional justice influence multiple levels of organizational outcomes?* Paper presented at the annual meeting of the Society of Industrial and Organizational Psychology, Atlanta, GA.

Byrne, Z. S. (2001). *Effects of perceptions of organizational justice, identification, and support on outcomes within work teams.* Unpublished doctoral dissertation. Colorado State University, Colorado.

Byrne, Z. S., & Cropanzano, R. S. (2000, April). *To which do I attribute this fairness? Differential effects of multi-foci justice on organizational work behaviors.* Paper presented at the annual meeting of the Society for Industrial and Organizational Psychology, New Orleans, LA.

Cohen-Charash, Y., & Spector, P. E. (2001). The role of justice in organizations: A meta-analysis. *Organizational Behavior and Human Decision Processes, 86*, 278–321.

Colquitt, J. A. (2001). On the dimensionality of organizational justice: A construct validation of a measure. *Journal of Applied Psychology, 86*, 386–400.

Colquitt, J. A., Conlon, D. E., Wesson, M. J., Porter, C. O. L. H., & Ng, K. Y. (2001). Justice at the millennium: A meta-analytic review of 25 years of organizational justice research. *Journal of Applied Psychology, 86*, 425–445.

Colquitt, J. A., Noe, R. A., & Jackson, C. L. (2002). Justice in teams: Antecedents and consequences of procedural justice climate. *Personnel Psychology, 55*, 83–109.

Cook, J., & Wall, T. (1980). New work attitude measures of trust, organizational commitment, and personal need non-fulfillment. *Journal of Occupational Psychology, 53*, 39–52.

Cropanzano, R., & Byrne, Z. S. (2000). Workplace justice and the dilemma of organizational citizenship. In M. VanVugt, T. Tyler, & A. Biel (Eds.), *Collective problems in modern society: Dilemmas and solutions* (pp. 142–161). London: Routledge.

Cropanzano, R., Prehar, C. A., & Chen, P. Y. (2002). Using social exchange theory to distinguish procedural from interactional justice. *Group & Organization Management, 27*, 324–351.

Cropanzano, R., Rupp, D. E., Mohler, C. J., & Schminke, M. (2001). Three roads to organizational justice. In G. Ferris (Ed.), *Research in personnel and human resources management* (Vol. 20, pp. 1–113). Greenwich, CT: JAI.

Eisenberger, R., Armeli, S., Rexwinkel, B., Lynch, P. D., & Rhoades, L. (2001). Reciprocation of perceived organizational support. *Journal of Applied Psychology, 86*, 42–51.

Eisenberger, R., Cotterell, N., & Marvel, J. (1987). Reciprocation ideology. *Journal of Personality and Social Psychology, 53*, 743–750.

Eisenberger, R., Fasolo, P., & Davis-LaMastro, V. (1990). Perceived organizational support and employee diligence, commitment, and innovation. *Journal of Applied Psychology, 75*, 51–59.

Farh, J.-L., Podsakoff, P. M., & Organ, D. W. (1990). Accounting for organizational citizenship behavior: Leader fairness and task scope versus satisfaction. *Journal of Management, 16*, 705–721.

Foa, E. B., & Foa, U. G. (1980). Resource theory: Interpersonal behavior as exchange. In K. J. Gergen, M. S. Greenberg, & R. H. Willis (Eds.), *Social exchange: Advances in theory and research* (pp. 77–94). New York: Plenum.

Folger, R., & Konovsky, M. A. (1989). Effects of procedural and distributive justice on reactions to pay raise decisions. *Academy of Management Journal, 32*, 115–130.

Gergen, K. J. (1969). *The psychology of behavioral exchange.* Reading, MA: Addison-Wesley.

Gouldner, A. W. (1960). The norm of reciprocity: A preliminary statement. *American Sociological Review, 25*, 161–178.

Graen, G., & Cashman, J. (1975). A role-making model of leadership in formal organizations: A developmental approach. In J. G. Hunt & L. L. Larson (Eds.), *Leadership Frontiers* (pp. 143–166). Kent, OH: Kent State University Press.

Greenberg, J. (1993). Justice and organizational citizenship: A commentary on the state of the science. *Employee Responsibilities and Rights Journal, 6*, 249–256.

Greenberg, J., & Cohen, R. L. (1982). Why justice? Normative and instrumental interpretations. In J. Greenberg & R. L. Cohen (Eds.), *Equity and Justice in Social Behavior* (pp. 437–469). New York: Academic Press.

Greenberg, J., & Scott, K. S. (1996). Why do workers bite the hands that feed them? Employee theft as a social exchange process. In B. M. Staw & L. L. Cummings (Eds.), *Research in organizational behavior* (Vol. 18, pp. 111–156). Greenwich, CT: JAI.

Hofmann, D. A., Morgeson, F. P., & Gerras, S. J. (2003). Climate as a moderator of the relationship between leader-member exchange and content specific citizenship behavior: Safety climate as an exemplar. *Journal of Applied Psychology, 88*, 170–178.

Homans, G. C. (1961). *Social behavior: Its elementary forms.* New York: Harcourt Brace Jovanovich.

Homans, G. C. (1974). *Social behavior: Its elementary forms* (rev. ed.). New York: Harcourt Brace Jovanovich.

Judge, T. A., Thoresen, C. J., Bono, J. E., & Patton, G. K. (2001). The job satisfaction–job performance relationship: A qualitative and quantitative review. *Psychological Bulletin, 127,* 376–407.

Katz, D., & Kahn, R. L. (1966). *The social psychology of organizations.* New York: Wiley.

Kiker, D. S., & Motowidlo, S. J. (1999). Main and interaction effects of task and contextual performance on supervisory reward decisions. *Journal of Applied Psychology, 84,* 602–609.

Konovsky, M. A., & Pugh, S. D. (1994). Citizenship behavior and social exchange. *Academy of Management Journal, 37,* 656–669.

Konovsky, M. A., & Organ, D. W. (1996). Dispositional and contextual determinants of organizational citizenship behavior. *Journal of Organizational Behavior, 17,* 253–266.

Ladd, D., & Henry, R. A. (2000). Helping coworkers and helping the organization: The role of support perceptions, exchange ideology, and conscientiousness. *Journal of Applied Social Psychology, 30,* 2028–2049.

LePine, J. A., Erez, A., & Johnson, D. E. (2002). The nature and dimensionality of organizational citizenship behavior: A critical review and meta-analysis. *Journal of Applied Psychology, 87,* 52–65.

Lind, E. A. (1995). Justice and authority relations in organizations. In R. Cropanzano & M. K. Kacmar (Eds.), *Organizational politics, justice, and support: Managing the social climate of the workplace* (pp. 83–96). Westport, CT: Quorum Books.

Lind, E. A., & Tyler, T. R. (1988). *The social psychology of procedural justice.* New York: Plenum Press.

Malatesta, R. M., & Byrne, Z. S. (1997, April). *The impact of formal and interactional procedures on organizational outcomes.* Paper presented at the 12th annual conference of the Society for Industrial and Organizational Psychology, St. Louis, MO.

Malinowski, B. (1926). *Crime and custom in savage society.* New York: Harcourt Brace Jovanovich.

Masterson, S. S., Bartol, K. M., & Moye, N. (2000, April). *Interactional and procedural justice: Type versus source of fairness.* Paper presented at the annual meeting of the Society of Industrial and Organizational Psychology, New Orleans, LA.

Masterson, S. S., Lewis, K., Goldman, B. M., & Taylor, M. S. (2000). Integrating Justice and Social Exchange: The Differing Effects of Fair Procedures and Treatments on Work Relationships. *Academy of Management Journal, 43,* 738–748.

Mayer, R. C., Davis, J. H., & Schoorman, F. D. (1995). An integrative model of organizational trust. *Academy of Management Review, 20,* 709–734.

Meyer, J. P., & Allen, N. J. (1984). Testing the "side-bet theory" of organizational commitment: Some methodological considerations. *Journal of Applied Psychology, 75,* 710–720.

Moorman, R. H. (1991). Relationship between organizational fairness and organizational citizenship behaviors: Do fairness perceptions influence employee citizenship? *Journal of Applied Psychology, 76,* 845–855.

Moorman, R. H., Blakely, G. L., & Niehoff, B. P. (1998). Does perceived organizational support mediate the relationship between procedural justice and organizational citizenship behavior? *Academy of Management Journal, 41,* 351–357.

Moorman, R. H., Niehoff, B. P., & Organ, D. W. (1993). Treating employees fairly and organizational citizenship behaviors: Sorting the effects of job satisfaction, organizational commitment, and procedural justice. *Employee Responsibilities and Rights Journal, 6,* 209–225.

Morrison, E. W. (1994). Role definitions and organizational citizenship behavior: The importance of the employee's perspective. *Academy of Management Journal, 37*, 1543–1567.

Niehoff, B. P., & Moorman, R. H. (1993). Justice as a mediator of the relationship between methods of monitoring and organizational citizenship behaviors. *Academy of Management Journal, 36*, 527–556.

O'Reilly, C., & Chatman, J. (1986). Organizational commitment and psychological attachment: The effects of compliance, identification, and internalization on prosocial behavior. *Journal of Applied Psychology, 71*, 492–499.

Organ, D. W. (1977). A reappraisal and reinterpretation of the satisfaction– causes– performance hypothesis. *Academy of Management Review, 2*, 46–53.

Organ, D. W. (1988a). *Organizational citizenship behavior: The good soldier syndrome.* Lexington, MA: Lexington Books.

Organ, D. W. (1988b). A restatement of the satisfaction-performance hypothesis. *Journal of Management, 14*, 547–557.

Organ, D. W. (1990). The motivational basis of organizational citizenship behavior. In B. M. Staw & L. L. Cummings (Eds.), *Research in Organizational Behavior* (Vol. 12, pp. 43–72). Greenwich, CT: JAI Press.

Organ, D. W., & Moorman, R. H. (1993). Fairness and organizational citizenship behavior: What are the connections? *Social Justice Research, 6*, 5–18.

Organ, D. W., & Ryan, K. (1995). A meta-analytic review of attitudinal and dispositional predictors of organizational citizenship behavior. *Personnel Psychology, 48*, 775–802.

Podsakoff, P. M., MacKenzie, S. B., Paine, J. B., & Bachrach, D. G. (2000). Organizational citizenship behaviors: A critical review of the theoretical and empirical literature and suggestions for future research. *Journal of Management, 26*, 513–563.

Pillai, R., Schriesheim, C. A., & Williams, E. S. (1999). Fairness perceptions and trust as mediators for transformational and transactional leadership: A two-sample study. *Journal of Management, 25*, 897–933.

Randall, M. L., Cropanzano, R., Bormann, C. A., & Birjulin, A. (1999). Organizational politics and organizational support as predictors of work attitudes, job performance, and organizational citizenship behavior. *Journal of Organizational Behavior, 20*, 159–170.

Rhoades, L., & Eisenberger, R. (2002). Perceived organizational support: A review of the literature. *Journal of Applied Psychology, 87*, 698–714.

Rotundo, M., & Sackett, P. R. (2002). The relative important of task, citizenship, and counterproductive performance to global ratings of job performance: A policy-capturing approach. *Journal of Applied Psychology, 87*, 66–80.

Rousseau, D. M. (1995). *Psychological contracts in organizations: Understanding written and unwritten agreements.* Thousand Oaks, CA: Sage.

Rupp, D. E., & Cropanzano, R. (2002). The mediating effects of social exchange relationships in predicting workplace outcomes from multifoci organizational justice. *Organizational Behavior and Human Decision Processes, 89*, 925–946.

Schappe, S. P. (1998). The influence of job satisfaction, organizational commitment, and fairness perceptions on organizational citizenship behavior. *Journal of Psychology, 132*, 277–290.

Settoon, R. P., Bennett, N., & Liden, R. C. (1996). Social exchange in organizations: Perceived organizational support, leader-member exchange, and employee reciprocity. *Journal of Applied Psychology, 81*, 219–227.

Shore, L. M., & Wayne, S. J. (1993). Commitment and employee behavior: Comparison of affective commitment and continuance commitment with perceived organizational support. *Journal of Applied Psychology, 78,* 774–780.

Smith, C. A., Organ, D. W., & Near, J. P. (1983). Organizational citizenship behavior: Its nature and antecedents. *Journal of Applied Psychology, 68,* 653–663.

Tajfel, H., & Turner, J. C. (1986). The social identity of intergroup behavior. In S. Worchel & W. G. Austin (Eds.), *Psychology of intergroup relations* (pp. 7–24). Chicago: Nelson Hall.

Tepper, B. J., Lockhart, D., & Hoobler, J. (2001). Justice, citizenship, and role definition effects. *Journal of Applied Psychology, 86,* 789–796.

Tepper, B. J., & Taylor, E. C. (2003). Relationships among supervisors' and subordinates' procedural justice perceptions and organizational citizenship behaviors. *Academy of Management Journal, 46,* 97–105.

Tyler, T. R. (1999). Why people cooperate with organizations: An identity-based perspective. In B. M. Staw & R. Sutton (Eds.), *Research in organizational behavior* (Vol. 21, 201–246). Greenwich, CT: JAI Press.

Tyler, T. R. (2001). A psychological perspective on the legitimacy of institutions and authorities. In J. T. Jost & B. Major (Eds.), *The psychology of legitimacy: Emerging perspectives on ideology, justice, and intergroup relations* (pp. 416–436). Cambridge, UK: Cambridge University Press.

Tyler, T. R., & Blader, S. L. (2000). *Cooperation in groups: Procedural justice, social identity, and behavioral engagement.* Philadelphia, PA: Psychology Press.

Tyler, T. R., & Degoey, P. (1996). Trust in organizational authorities: The influence of motive attributions on willingness to accept decisions. In R. Kramer & T. R. Tyler (Eds.), *Trust in organizations: Frontiers of theory and research* (pp. 331–356). Thousand Oaks, CA: Sage.

Tyler, T., Degoey, P., & Smith, H. (1996). Understanding why the justice of group procedures matters: A test of the psychological dynamics of the group-value model. *Journal of Personality and Social Psychology, 70,* 913–930.

Tyler, T. R., & Lind, E. A. (1992). A relational model of authority in groups. In M. P. Zanna (Ed.), *Advances in experimental social psychology* (Vol. 25, pp. 115–191). San Diego, CA: Academic Press.

Wayne, S. J., Shore, L. M., & Liden, R. C. (1997). Perceived organizational support and leader–member exchange: A social exchange perspective. *Academy of Management Journal, 40,* 82–111.

Wayne, S. J., Shore, L. M., Bommer, W. H., & Tetrick, L. E. (2002). The role of fair treatment and rewards in perceptions of organizational support and leader-member exchange. *Journal of Applied Psychology, 87,* 590–598.

Werner, J. M. (1994). Dimensions that make a difference: Examining the impact of in-role and extra-role behaviors on supervisory ratings. *Journal of Applied Psychology, 79,* 98–107.

Witt, L. A. (1991). Exchange ideology as a moderator of job attitudes–organizational citizenship behaviors relationships. *Journal of Applied Social Psychology, 21,* 1490–1501.

V

JUSTICE APPLICATIONS

13

How Can Justice Be Used to Manage Stress in Organizations?

Riël Vermunt
Leiden University

Herman Steensma
Leiden University

This chapter describes the relationship between justice and stress in order to find justice-based ways to reduce or prevent job stress. The discrepancy approach that lies at the core of both injustice experiences and stress experiences is described first. The following part of the chapter links types of injustices to types of stressors and presents empirical evidence of the relationship between distributive justice and stress, and between procedural justice and stress. Next, four justice-related methods are described that can be used to reduce stress in an organizational context: Stress that is caused by distributive injustice may be reduced by a fair procedure or by another fair distribution; stress that is caused by procedural injustice may be reduced by a fair distribution or by another fair procedure. Finally, conclusions are drawn about further theorizing and research to improve our understanding of justice-based stress reduction.

Many employees experience stress at work. The prevalence of this so-called job stress is high. A survey among European employees showed that 29% considered that their work affected their health (Paoli, 1997). The costs of stress to organizations, for instance, in the United States, for absenteeism, reduced productivity, compensation claims, health insurance, and direct medical expenses, has been estimated at approximately $150 billion per year (Cartwright & Cooper, 1996). It is therefore not surprising that much research is initiated to find the main causes of stress as well as the best ways to reduce stress. In this chapter a justice-based stress approach is outlined to shed some new light on causes of stress and on stress reduction.

Job stress may arise from different sources. Some employees are stressed because their job is boring, lacks autonomy, or is monotonous. More common, however, is stress that is caused by work overload. Employees experience stress because of insufficient material working conditions, such as working in noise, dirt, and toxic environment. Organizational relations may cause stress as well, as they arise from conflicts over domains of work control between supervisor and subordinates. Moreover, employees may experience stress because of primary and secondary working conditions, such as salary, promotion, working hours, and spread of holidays (see also Allegro, Kruidenier, & Steensma, 1991). Recently, attention has been paid to a special source of stress: violence in the workplace (Steensma, 2002).

Because of the many negative consequences of job stress, attempts were made to reduce stress. Clinical and organizational psychologists have developed instruments to measure stress and have developed

therapies and training sessions to let employees cope better with stress. Moreover, instruments to improve organizational effectiveness have often led, as a by-product, to the reduction of stress (Le Blanc, de Jonge, & Schaufeli, 2000; Steensma, Allegro, & Knip, 1999–2000). Cartwright and Cooper (1997) described in detail strategies to deal with stressful situations at work, such as dealing with difficult people, dealing with sexual harassment, and coping with unethical behavior in the workplace. Current theories of stress emphasize the strategies people apply and learn to apply in dealing with job stress. The focus of most of the theories is on the individual employee and the way he or she copes with stressful job events. The justice-based approach to stress described in this chapter emphasizes the fair behavior of the authority (supervisors, managers) in preventing and reducing job stress.

Since the 1960s, researchers have focused on injustice and stress. As part of his research on equity theory, John Stacy Adams investigated negative responses to inequitable rewards (Adams, 1963). Adams labeled these reactions *psychological distress*, the emotional reaction to a decision that is experienced as unfair, and studied reactions to unfairness, such as reduction of task effort. Reactions to unfair allocations can be viewed as reactions to cope with a stressful situation (Greenberg, 1984; Siegrist, 1996).

In this chapter we describe the relationship between justice and stress in more detail in order to find justice-based ways to reduce or prevent job stress. The first section starts with the definition of stress and describes the discrepancy approach to stress and justice. The next section links injustices to stressors and presents empirical evidence of the relationship between distributive justice and stress, and between procedural justice and stress. Following that section, four justice-related methods are described that can be used to reduce stress in an organizational context. In the final section, conclusions are drawn about further theorizing and research to improve our understanding of justice-based stress.

JUSTICE[1] AND STRESS AS EXPERIENCED DISCREPANCY

Justice

Justice is the evaluation of an event in which an authority allocates resources to recipients. An authority is a person, role person, or entity (organization, board) having resources at his or her disposal and making decisions about allocation of resources between recipients. In some situations the authority allocates resources between him- or herself and

---

[1]In this text the terms *justice* and *fairness* are used interchangeably.

other(s), in which case the authority is a recipient as well. However, in the work situation, the focus is on the manager, superior, or supervisor, the authority, who allocates resources between subordinates, the recipients. In this chapter the focus is on situations in which the authority allocates resources between recipients.

An allocation event consists of a distribution and a procedure. The *distribution* is the part recipients get from the allocated resource, whereas the *procedure* refers to the rules the authority uses to allocate a resource between recipients. The distribution as well as the procedure can be evaluated in terms of fairness. The fairness evaluation of the distribution of the resource allocation event is labeled *distributive fairness,* whereas the fairness evaluation of the procedure is labeled *procedural fairness.*

The observation that individuals evaluate distribution and procedure in terms of justice can be traced back to childhood, when children learned to delay the satisfaction of an immediate gratification in order to receive a bigger gratification later on. This personal contract between the growing child and its social environment teaches the child that good deeds are followed by positive rewards and bad deeds by negative rewards. The development of the justice motive makes the growing child sensitive to the gratifying aspects of high effort and high performance and the punishing aspects of laziness and low performance: One will get what one deserves (Lerner, 1980; Vermunt, 2002a). Equity theory (Adams, 1965), for example, may be viewed as the result of the operation of the justice motive: The higher the input, the more output one thinks one deserves. The justice motive is also the basis for the attribution process, in which individuals have a tendency to attribute a positive evaluation to positive actions or characteristics of oneself or others and a negative evaluation to negative actions or characteristics of oneself or others. This so-called "belief in a just world" (Lerner, 1980; Rubin & Peplau, 1976) affects people's view of events and actions. People with a strong belief in a just world have a strong tendency to overlook the injustices in the world and attribute unfairness to negative characteristics of the participants in the event. Well known in this respect is derogation of innocent victims of crime or accidents (Montada & Lerner, 1998). However, Dalbert (1998) has called attention to the beneficial effects of a strong belief in a just world: Personal belief in a just world may predict subjective well-being and self-esteem (see also Tomaka & Blascovich, 1994).

A distribution or a procedure is evaluated as unfair if a discrepancy between what one deserves and what one gets is experienced. When a subordinate receives insufficient time to do a task properly, the subordinate may experience an injustice. Or when a subordinate gets inadequate equipment to do the job properly, the subordinate may experience

an injustice. According to fairness theory (Folger & Cropanzano, 1998), the resources one receives are attributed to the decision of the authority (supervisor), making the authority accountable for the allocation.

Stress

Most social scientists adhere to a stress model in which a distinction is made between stressors, stress, and strains. Stressors are the objective and/or perceived environmental characteristics (stimuli, demands; for example, workload, role ambiguity). If these demands tax or exceed the adaptive resources of the individual, an unpleasant state called stress will be experienced. The stress leads to strains, that is, behavioral, physiological, or psychological responses (for example, alcohol consumption, higher blood pressure, job dissatisfaction). In the long run, strains can cause sickness. Relations between stressors and strains, and between strains and long-term effects, may be affected by moderator variables such as personality differences and social support by colleagues or supervisors (although sometimes lack of social support is seen as a direct stressor, too). This stress model, the "Michigan model," integrates earlier models developed by Kahn (1970) and French and Caplan (1972). In a refined version of this model known as the person–environment (P-E) fit model, work stress is defined as a "misfit" between environmental factors and resources, and individual needs and abilities (French, Rogers, & Cobb, 1981).

The Justice-Based Approach to Stress

The definition of injustice as the discrepancy between what one deserves and what one gets comes very close to the definition of stress. Stress is defined as the experienced discrepancy between demands of the environment (stressors) and capacities of the individual (Carver, 1995). Demands from the work environment—the potential stressors—are, in our view, part of an allocation event in which resources (tasks, equipment, time) are allocated by the organization (supervision and management). For example, employees get a task assignment and receive equipment and time to complete the task well. The demand is to complete the task with this equipment and in this time period. If employees experience that type of task and/or quality of equipment and/or amount of time does not meet their standards of what they think they deserve, employees will evaluate the allocated task, equipment, and time as unfair (the stressor). Stress will be experienced if the unfair allocation blocks the employee's goal attainment.

One of the most salient characteristics of stress is that individuals' capacities are not transient or statelike entities, such as low effort that can

easily be repaired or over which one has more or less control. On the contrary, capacities are stable, traitlike entities over which one has hardly any or no control at all. When a subject in the Adams (1963) experiments experienced an unfair and unfavorable payment, the subject may lower his or her effort to restore justice. With regard to capacities, restoring of justice is not that easy, because the person has hardly any control over, for instance, intelligence, skills, or bodily condition. The experience of a discrepancy between one's capacities and the demands from the environment thus makes the accountability (Folger & Cropanzano, 1998) of the authority prominent and the unfairness strong, making unfairness a stressor.

The justice-based approach to stress fits well into Lazarus and Folkman's (1978) model, which views stress as the product of appraisal of an event. According to the appraisal model, stress is a result of the interaction between organism and environment: When a pressure is exerted, the organism's reaction will depend on the evaluation of the event and the resources the organism has to its disposal. Lazarus and Folkman distinguished between a primary appraisal process and a secondary appraisal process. The primary appraisal is intended to assess the threat value of an event, whereas the secondary appraisal is intended to evaluate the options for coping with the presumed threat.

Resources and Stressors

Resources can be very diverse. A resource is "any property of an individual which he makes available to persons in his environment as a means for their positive or negative need-satisfaction" (Levinger, 1959, p. 84). Foa and Foa (1974) distinguished six types of resources: love, status, information, money, goods, and services. Love is described in terms of accepting and liking the other; status is described in terms of esteem and regard for the other; information is described as being familiar with a subject or with facts; money is salary or payment; goods are merchandise or a certain product; services can be seen as being available to do some work, doing an errand, doing a favor. The six types of resources can be differentiated between material resources like money and goods and to a lesser extent services and immaterial resources like love, status, and information. Resources can be given to the other, or can be taken away from the other. A supervisor can promote a subordinate or can take away responsibility (status) from a subordinate. A resource can have a positive valence or a negative one. Salary is a positive material resource, whereas a fine is a negative material resource (see Törnblom & Vermunt, 1999)

Stressors can be derived from several sources. Table 13.1, adapted from Le Blanc, de Jonge, and Schaufeli (2000), shows categories of

job-related stressors. As shown in Table 13.1, the stressors are subsumed under four categories: job content, working conditions, employment conditions, and social relations at work. Job content can be described as the kind of tasks one is doing in one's job, such as doing monotonous work; working conditions can be described as the environmental characteristics of the job, such as working in a noisy environment; employment conditions have to do with the status of the job, such as getting low pay; and social relations at work have to do with the amount of influence one has in the job, that is, participation in decision making.

The stressors can at face value be related to Foa and Foa's (1974) types of resources people may receive. In the work situation, love may de defined as maintaining good relationships; status as confidence in the other person's abilities and effort; information as experience and knowledge exchange; money as pay and bonuses; goods as equipment and working conditions; and services as social support. We can also look at this the other way around: Job content stressors can be defined

TABLE 13.1

Categories of Job-Related Stressors and Types of Resources

Stressor	Type of resources
Job content	Information/goods
Work over-/underload, complex work	
Monotonous work, too much responsibility	
Dangerous work, conflicting/ambiguous demands	
Working conditions	Goods
Toxic substances, poor conditions (noise)	
Work posture, physically demanding work	
Dangerous situations, lack of hygiene	
Lack of protective devices	
Employment conditions	Money/status
Shift work, low pay, poor career prospects	
Flexible labor contract, job insecurity	
Social relations at work	Services/love
Poor leadership, low social support	
Low participation in decision-making	
Liberties, discrimination	

in terms of (negative; lack of) goods and (insufficient; lack of) information; working conditions stressors can be defined in terms of (negative) goods; employment conditions stressors can be defined in terms of (negative; lack of) money and (low; lack of) status; and negative social relations at work can be viewed in terms of (negative; lack of) services and (negative; lack of) love (see Table 13.1). Some stressors can be related to distributions, such as low pay, and others to procedures, such as participation in decision making. For some stressors it is not easy to decide whether they may be subsumed under distributions or under procedures. For instance, poor leadership can be defined as a distribution: Poor leadership is a negative service or lack of service and as such a distribution; some workers are allocated good leaders whereas other workers have to do with poor leaders. A poor leader, however, can be described as someone who applies unfair procedures, such as being inconsistent or being rude; poor leadership then reflects application of unfair procedures. Discrimination can be an outcome in that one worker, as a member of a specific group, receives lesser outcomes than another worker. Discrimination also reflects application of a procedure because it shows a lack of respect for the worker. The situation and the person involved determine whether a stressor will be conceived of as a distribution or as a procedure (see also Cropanzano & Ambrose, 2001). For instance, when workers have no formal or informal opportunity to participate in decision making and they think they deserve it, participation is probably viewed as a distribution and not as a procedure. When employers decide the number of working hours, workers' participation or voice is a procedure and not an outcome or distribution.

Justice-based stress theory emphasizes the authority (supervisor, manager) as the crucial factor in the stress process, because the authority is assumed to be accountable for the occurrence of the stressor. Distributions of resources and the procedures that are applied in the allocation event are part of the decision power of the authority. Research shows that fair distributions and fair outcomes are related to decision acceptance and positive attitudes toward the authority (see Tyler & Lind, 1992), whereas unfair distributions and unfair procedures give rise to negative attitudes. It is correct to conclude therefore that employees attribute unfair distributions and unfair procedures as potential stressors to the decision behavior of the supervisor or manager. With regard to the causes of stressors the justice-based stress approach must be distinguished from other stress approaches. These approaches view stressors as part of the job with which employees have to cope with or that are the subject matter of organizational change such as job or task restructuring, but view stressors not exclusively as related to authority's allocation decisions.

EMPIRICAL SUPPORT FOR THE RELATIONSHIP BETWEEN JUSTICE AND STRESS

The Interview Study

To find out whether the proposed relation between stress and justice is a valid one, we conducted a qualitative study with 10 employees who were sent into the disability regulations program because of enduring and serious stress symptoms (Vermunt, Oskam, & Steensma, 1998). All employees were interviewed individually, with each interview lasting about 1 hour. The main part of the interview consisted of letting the respondent describe stressful events in his or her work situation. The respondent could mention freely all relevant events. After the respondent had spontaneously mentioned stressful events, the respondent was asked whether he or she as subordinate recognized one or more of the following behaviors of the supervisor: rude behavior, withholding relevant information, lack of consideration with one's opinion, or emphasizing status difference. If the respondent recognized one or more of these behaviors, he or she was asked to give concrete examples of the behavior, as well as the frequency of occurrence of the behavior.

More than three respondents spontaneously mentioned the following stressors:

1. Lack of trust. One of the respondents mentioned that her supervisor was not willing to delegate responsibilities. "Endlessly, the supervisor revised the letter I was working on. I am convinced that the supervisor most likely did the job himself."

2. Emphasis on hierarchical relations. Respondents were irritated by the supervisors' sick jokes intended to assess his or her authority, "As if he has to strengthen his power."

3. Lack of consideration. A male worker who could not do evening shifts, but offered instead to work in the weekends, was told that his wife had to look for another job so that she could care for the children.

4. Lack of a pat on the shoulder after a good performance. Respondents complained that supervisors did not reward good performance.

5. Incorrect reprimand. Respondents reported that if supervisors were making a reprimand, they did so in an incorrect way.

These behaviors corresponded fairly well with respondents' recognition of the list of stress causing behaviors, especially lack of consideration of the opinion and well-being of the subordinate, and emphasis on hierarchical relations. Many respondents recognized inadequate communication as well. Respondents' reactions to the stressful events were

a lack of effort in carrying out the job and low motivation to seek personal contact with the supervisor. Several respondents mentioned dissatisfaction, fatigue, having problems relaxing, uncertainty, feelings of being powerless, and sick leave. Van Meer (1997), a Dutch psychiatrist, expert in treating supervisor-related stress, described many examples of negative consequences for the subordinate of supervisors' behavior. The reactions of our respondents correspond well with Van Meer's description of symptoms. We may conclude that respondents' reactions were highly similar to Van Meer's descriptions. Reflecting on supervisors' behaviors, one may conclude that most of the behaviors can be conceived as behaviors related to the allocation of resources and the procedures applied in the allocation event that several authors (Bies & Moag, 1986; Leventhal, 1980; Tyler & Lind, 1992) have mentioned. Lack of a pat on the shoulder and an incorrect reprimand may be classified as negative immaterial resources, while lack of trust, lack of consideration, and inadequate communication of information can be classified as procedures applied in the allocation event. Some of the behaviors at first sight may be difficult to subsume under the resources mentioned, such as emphasis on hierarchical relations. But if one considers emphasis on hierarchical relations as a type of humiliation, one can subsume this behavior as a lack of respect for the subordinate.

From the analysis of the answers of employees who were under great strain as a consequence of their relation with their supervisor, we may conclude that many of the supervisors' behaviors are justice related; that is, supervisors' behaviors have to do with the allocation of material and immaterial resources. From this modest interview study, we may conclude that unfair behavior of the supervisor and stress reactions are related in a rather direct way.

Some Additional Remarks About the Relationship Between Justice and Stress

Stress is the consequence of experiencing a discrepancy between one's own capacities and demands from the environment. According to Tomaka and Blascovich (1994), this experience may end in a threat appraisal or a challenge appraisal. A threat appraisal is likely when one experiences that the demands exceed one's own capacities. Because one's capacities are less easy to accommodate to the situation at hand, individuals may experience feelings of helplessness or anger: helplessness when they attribute stress to one's own shortcomings, and anger when they attribute stress to the decisions and behaviors of others. Initially, the behavior of the self-blamers and other-blamers is different. Self-blamers will try to escape from the situation by being absent, or by trying to get another job. Other-blamers will first try to get even, to take re-

venge (Bies & Tripp, 2001), or will try to retaliate (Greenberg, 1990, 1993; Modde & Vermunt, 1995; Skarlicki & Folger, 1997). The blame can be attributed to the other as a person (Bies & Tripp, 1996) or to the other as role player. Bies and Tripp (1996) identified selfishness and malevolence as personalistic attributions. Attribution of injustice of the personalistic type gives rise to reactions to get even with the harm doer. Often, revenge may take the form of norm-violating behavior. The question is whether norm-violating behavior as response to injustice does alter the situation and reduces stress. Probably not; it may even increase stress, because norm violation may cause an extra burden in that the relationship with the organization and the supervisor deteriorates. One may conclude therefore that injustices as stressors may result in ineffective norm-violating behavior.

The role-player type of attribution is not directed at the person of the harm doer, but to his or her role in the organization. A major role player in organizations is the supervisor. Most supervisors are subordinate as well and have therefore a dual position in the organization. Vermunt (2002b) argued that middle-range supervisors are caught between two different types of demands. One demand comes from the higher levels of the organization and require the supervisor to carry out the organization's mission, to produce as much as possible against the lowest costs. The other demand is the well-being of the subordinates. In other words, the supervisor is caught between norms of efficiency and justice. The supervisor's dual position may end in unfair outcomes and/or unfair procedures for subordinates. Vermunt assumed that because of the structurally liable position of the boss, these injustices are inevitable. It was assumed, further, that the injustices can be decreased or even prevented by interpersonal fair behavior of the supervisor's superior.

As already noted, the perceived discrepancy between capacities and demands from the environment may cause injustices that, in the end, may result in stress. The observation might be made that experiences of injustice are derived not from processes, such as described by Folger (1987) and Folger and Cropanzano (1998) in referent cognitions theory, or fairness theory, or relative deprivation theory (Crosby, 1976), or reference-group theory (Hyman & Singer, 1968). These theories state that the magnitude of felt injustice depends, among other things, on the comparison standard that is used, such as the outcomes others have received, or the outcomes one has received at an earlier point in time. Individuals can "play" with comparison standards and arrive at different amounts of felt injustice. However, individuals can hardly "play" with discrepancies experienced between one's capacities and demands from the environment. Stress is not experienced as less intense by thinking of a more stressful situation in the past. The kind of standard one applies does not alter the experienced stress.

For stressed individuals, it is therefore very difficult to apply cognitive distortion to cope with injustice. It is hard to say, "Oh, my blood pressure of 190 is not an important indication of my well-being." It is cognitively difficult to take another comparison level or comparison standard in order to feel better or to come to terms with the stress. Cognitive distortion of inputs and outcomes, as suggested by Adams (1965), is difficult to achieve. Moreover, improving one's capacities is not the same as increasing one's efforts. Improving one's capacities takes time and will in the short term perhaps even increase stress, because of extra effort to learn to improve skills and capacities. The individual, conceived in this way, is rather helpless to cope with stress effectively. Support form the organization is therefore necessary. Consistent with Maslach, Schaufeli, and Leiter (2001), we argue that the organization, and specifically the direct supervisor, is the best source for remedying against stress.

INJUSTICES AS STRESSORS

The discrepancy approach to explain feelings of injustice as well as to explain stress symptoms and the identification of stressors in terms of resources show that stress and injustice have structural properties as well as substantive properties in common. Empirical evidence makes the relationship between stress and justice even more evident. However, the relationship between stress and justice is more intricate than can be concluded from the foregoing analysis. The justice literature makes a distinction between distributive justice and procedural justice. Employees apply norms of distributive justice when they evaluate the allocation of negative resources, the eventual stressors. But how are procedural justice and the combination of distributive justice and procedural justice related to the evaluation of stressors? Although the literature describing the relationship between stress and justice is rather recent, some ideas have been developed to relate stress theory to justice theory. In this section, the most important approaches and findings will be discussed.

Distributive Injustice and Stress: Empirical Evidence

Rutte and Messick (1995) described an integrated model of perceived unfairness in organizations. The authors' intentions were to understand and to predict the psychological and behavioral reactions of employees being unfairly treated by their superior. The fairness model they described consists of three components. The first component consists of the antecedents of the evaluation process: evaluation of the out-

come of the allocation decision process. The second component is the psychological process of distress, and the third component is the reaction to the distress. Outcome evaluation is the product of the evaluation itself and the frame of reference applied. Egocentric distortions may affect outcome evaluations: Applying a frame of reference may depend on the aims one has for the comparison. The authors stated that distress may be determined by (a) the valence of the outcome, (b) the importance of the outcome for the person, (c) the unexpectedness of the outcome, and (d) the discrepancy of received and expected outcome. According to the authors, people form justice evaluations by receiving an answer to three questions:

1. Is the outcome fair or not?
2. Who is responsible for the outcome?
3. What does the outcome signify for a person's status position in the organization?

Reactions to unfairness may be differentiated between cognitive reactions and behavioral reactions. Adams (1965) formulated three types of behavioral reactions to distress: (a) increase or decrease one's effort, (b) increase or decrease one's outcomes, (c) leave the situation. Others have added: (d) decreasing performance, (e) retaliation, (f) insubordination, (g) protest, (h) absenteeism, and other behaviors. Rutte and Messick (1995) stated that employees make a cost-benefit calculation to determine what kind of reaction to distress they will employ.

Markovsky (1988) designed an experiment closely after Adams's overpayment and underpayment experiments. Participants were asked to perform a task for which they were promised a certain amount of money. One group of participants got the promised amount of money (equitable group), another group received less than was promised, and a third group got more money than was promised before. Markovsky showed that overpayment as well as underpayment resulted in strong emotional arousal, as indicated by an increase in participants' skin conductance, where underpayment resulted in stronger emotional arousal than overpayment.

Based on the distributive justice model, Taris, Schreurs, Peeters, Le Blanc and Schaufeli (2001) carried out an extensive study under teachers about the relationship between unfairness, and stress and burnout. Stress was assessed measuring how much respondents felt upset by the following aspects of the job: relationship with students, colleagues, and organization. The hypothesis that the more people experience an unbalance between investments and rewards in their relationships the more stress will be experienced, was confirmed. In addition, frame of reference had an effect on stress as well. Student stressors, unbalanced ex-

change relationship between teacher and student, had a stronger effect on stress than colleague stressors and organization-stressors.

Another study among 228 teachers (Willemsen, Steensma, & Van der Vlist, 2002) measured distributive organizational injustice of seven behaviors. As predicted, injustice correlated positively with intention to report sick (a significant predictor of actual sickness absenteeism), with general health complaints, with health complaints due to work, and with emotional exhaustion as measured by the Dutch version of the Maslach Burnout Inventory (Schaufeli & Van Dierendonck, 1994).

Individual Moderators.   Tomaka and Blascovich (1994) made a specific interpretation of the relationship between distributive justice and stress. They state that individuals with a high belief in a just world—the belief that people get what they deserve—perceive stressful tasks as challenging, whereas individuals with a low belief in a just world perceive stressful tasks as threatening. Seeing the world as a fair place protects individuals who adhere to these beliefs from damaging appraisals, resulting in more benign appraisals of the tasks. High and low believers in a just world were asked to perform a mentally stressful task while psychophysiological responses as indicators of stress were measured. Subjective stress was measured by asking participants how stressful the task they just completed was. High believers in a just world had physiological responses that were consistent with challenge, and high-belief individuals rated the tasks as less stressful.

Another important moderator between injustice and stress could be personality factors as brought forward by the five-factor model of personality (Goldberg, 1990), which distinguishes neuroticism, extraversion, openness to experience, agreeableness, and conscientiousness as the five central dimensions of personality. A study by one of the authors found that scores on some "big five" dimensions correlated with adherence to and experience of distributive and procedural justice norms (Ramakers, Steensma, & Vijlbrief, 2003). Because we assume that some dimensions of the "big five" will also co-vary with stress, one or more of the five central dimensions of personality will be a possible moderator of the relationship between injustice and stress.

Procedural Injustice and Stress: Empirical Evidence

Elovianio, Kivimaki, and Vahtera (2002) conducted a study investigating the effects of procedural and interactional justice on health. In a survey of male and female employees in Finnish hospitals, Elovainio and coworkers asked respondents to fill out the Moorman scale of procedural and interactional justice and self-report questions about absenteeism as a response to stress. Medical reports of absent employees were

used as well. Results showed that procedural and interactional justice were related to self-report absenteeism and medical reports of absenteeism. In another Finnish study, Elovainio, Kivimaki, and Helkama (2001) showed that organizational injustice (procedural justice and interactional justice) was correlated with stress. Stress was measured with items measuring nervousness, depression, and experienced difficulty on concentrating. Moreover, it could be shown that organizational justice mediated between job control evaluation and stress: High job control correlated negatively with stress only when respondents evaluated the procedure and interaction as fair. Job control data correlated positively with procedural fairness evaluations.

Zohar (1995) investigated the effects of role justice, "the perceived fairness of role senders when the subordinate is under conflict, ambiguity, overload, or restricted latitude" (p. 487), on stress. Stress was not directly measured. The author used two scales of role strain: a general health questionnaire, and a scale to measure intentions to leave. The study was conducted under a group of nurses known to have high levels of job stress. The results showed that role injustice constitutes an additional source of stress next to overload, conflict, ambiguity, and latitude of responsibility, suggesting that role injustice has an additive and not an interactive effect on stress.

Distributive and Procedural Injustice and Stress: Empirical Evidence

In the literature two models have appeared that deal with the issue how distributive justice and procedural justice combine to affect subsequent attitudes and behavior. One is a model proposed by Tepper (2001); the other model is proposed by Vermunt and Steensma (2001). In a recent study, Tepper paid attention to the integration of stress and coping theory with justice theory. The stress model used is the one developed by Lazarus and Folkman (1984). These authors noted that individuals constantly monitor the stream of events they encounter. In this appraisal process, individuals classify events as a threat or challenge, or as benign or irrelevant. Events are appraised as threatening "if they violate our beliefs about the world or block our ability to carry out our commitments in life" (Lovallo, 1997, p. 76). A benign or irrelevant event is safely ignored requiring no special adaptive responses. An event that is evaluated as a threat or a challenge triggers a secondary appraisal process. The secondary appraisal motivates the individual to carry out further behavioral and psychological responses along with physiological activation. Individuals then evaluate their coping responses and the effectiveness of them at reducing the threat. Beliefs and commitments are the standard on which our evaluation of an event as a threat is based. Indi-

viduals with high commitments may evaluate an event as a threat, whereas the same event for individuals with low commitments is not evaluated as a threat. The appraisal process makes it plausible that individual differences can be accounted for.

Tepper (2001) assumed that unfair outcomes are evaluated as a threat (harm/losses) by the primary appraisal process. Because distributive unfairness also negatively affects self-esteem and self-efficacy, the secondary appraisal process evaluates distributive unfairness as a threat to self-esteem. Both threats, triggered by distributive injustice, will be regarded as stressors, producing psychological stress. In addition, Tepper assumed a relationship between procedural justice and the primary and secondary appraisal process. The author made the distinction between the instrumental component of procedural justice and the noninstrumental component (Tyler, 1994). The instrumental component of procedural justice indicates that a fair procedure is valued because a fair procedure is more likely to produce favorable outcomes. The noninstrumental component of procedural justice indicates that a fair procedure is valued because a fair procedure gives an indication of ones status in the group or in relation to others. According to Tepper (2001), unfair procedure "robs the employee of two vital coping resources—a social support system and a sense of self-efficacy" (p. 200).

Distributive justice and procedural justice not only have effects on subsequent psychological responses and behavioral responses independently of each other, but their effects on psychological and behavioral responses depend also on their interaction. Koper, Van Knippenberg, Bouhuys, Vermunt, and Wilke (1993) found, for instance, that a decrease in self-esteem by applying an unfair procedure was visible when the outcome was unfair, but the decrease was not visible when the outcome was evaluated as fair. Tepper viewed distributive justice as a moderator of the relationship between procedural justice and stress. He suggested that the relationship between procedural justice and attitudinal responses is stronger when distributive justice is lower. The hypotheses about the effects of distributive justice, procedural justice, and the moderator effect of distributive justice on the relation between procedural justice and psychological distress (depression, anxiety, emotional exhaustion) were tested in two two-wave surveys in which respondents answered justice related questions in wave 1 and questions about psychological distress in wave 2. Stress responses were measured with a depression subscale (Derogatis, 1993): the Brief Symptom Inventory. The hypotheses about the main effects of distributive justice, procedural justice, and their interaction were confirmed in both studies. For instance, depression was higher when procedural justice was lower, but this relationship was only significant when distributive justice was low and not when distributive justice was high.

Vermunt and Steensma offered another approach to the relationship between distributive and procedural justice and stress (Vermunt, 2002b; Vermunt & Steensma, 2001). They also applied the Lazarus and Folkman model of psychological stress. They argued that a distributive injustice or a procedural injustice will be evaluated as a threat only if additional information gives reason to it. Otherwise, it will be evaluated as a challenge or as irrelevant or even as benign. If the combined injustice is evaluated as a threat, the second appraisal process will be triggered, in which the available resources and options are evaluated to cope as effectively as possible with the threat. For instance, when employees perceive distributive injustice, the injustice will be evaluated as a threat, as the information is available that the procedure with which the decision to cut their salary is experienced as unjust as well, ending in a stressful situation. An effective coping behavior would be to protest against the applied procedure. When, however, the employee experiences that the applied procedure was just, the injustice will hardly be evaluated as a threat but more as a challenge. An effective coping strategy would be to put more effort in the job, and if that will not work in the short run, the employee may become stressed. Not only an unfair distribution but also a fair distribution may trigger an appraisal process in which information about the fairness of the procedure is sought. As a consequence, a fair distribution may end up in psychological distress as well: when employees discover that their salary increase was accomplished by an unfair procedure. It must be added, however, that this stress is less high than stress caused by an unfair distribution and an unfair procedure. In many situations individuals receive distributive information and procedural information at the same time. They process both types of information online, and online processing is most likely when interactional justice is involved (Vermunt & Steensma, 2001). In online processing it is most likely that the information about procedure and distribution are combined to form a primary appraisal.

Evidence From a Scenario Study. To investigate how distributive injustice and procedural injustice combine to result in stress, a study was conducted to find out how respondents would evaluate a fictitious situation in a controlled scenario study (Vermunt, Oskam, & Steensma, 1998). The aim of the study was to show that in addition to high workload (distributive injustice), unfair treatment is an important stress-increasing factor. Participants were presented with a short story in which a supervisor in a small firm allocated to a subordinate a sufficient amount of time to finish a task or an insufficient amount of time to finish the task. The supervisor treated the subordinate in a fair way or in an unfair way. In this 2 (workload: high vs. medium) × 2 (treatment: fair vs. unfair) design, the dependent variable was the amount of stress that is

experienced by the subordinate. Stress was measured by asking participants how stressed they would be in the described situation. It was predicted that participants in the high-workload condition would perceive more stress than those in the medium-workload condition. It was predicted further that participants in the unfair-treatment condition would perceive more stress than in the fair-treatment condition.

Eighty participants, employed, older than 18 years, and from the social environment of the five experimenters who carried out the study were asked to fill out a questionnaire about experiences at work. Participants were assigned to one of the four conditions, resulting in 20 participants in each condition. Participants were asked to read the story and to answer the questions. Each scenario started with a description of the work situation, followed by the description of workload and procedural fairness (Vermunt et al., 1998). The dependent variable, imagined subjective stress, was measured with the question, "Would you, in such a situation, experience stress?" ($1 = no\ stress$, to $5 = very\ much\ stress$). The results showed that highest stress was reported in the high-workload and unfair-procedure condition. Lowest stress was reported in the medium-workload and fair-procedure condition. The results suggest an additive effect of workload and procedural fairness on imagined stress.

Experimental Evidence

In another study (see Vermunt & Steensma, 2003), stress and fairness were induced experimentally. The dependent variables were the physiological responses heart action and blood pressure. Social science student participants performed an arithmetic task that was rather difficult for them. Half of the participants got ample time to perform the task; the other half of the participants got hardly enough time to perform the task. It was communicated to the participants that task performance was a good predictor of academic success. After participants had performed the task, they were treated fairly (participants got the opportunity to give arguments why their performance was as it was) or unfairly (participants did not receive that opportunity). Before, during, and after the task and manipulations, the physiological responses were measured. Results showed that participants in the high-stress conditions as well as in the low-stress conditions showed significant decreases in heart action as a consequence of fair treatment, whereas these effects were absent in the unfair-treatment conditions. Table 13.2 shows all the mean heart actions.

As can be inferred from the mean heart actions, the effects of fair treatment were stronger in the high-stress conditions than in the low-stress conditions. This two-way interaction was qualified by a three-way interaction in which it was shown that this pattern was present for female par-

TABLE 13.2

**Average Heart Actions of Participants in Pretest and Posttest
for Mental Load and Treatment**

Mental load	Treatment	Test period		Difference
		Pretest	Posttest	
High	Fair	73.9	70.3	–3.6
	Unfair	70.6	72.1	1.5
Low	Fair	72.9	70.8	–2.1
	Unfair	69.7	68.5	–1.1

ticipants only. For female participants in the high- as well as in the low-stress conditions a fair treatment led to a significant decrease in heart action. In the no-voice conditions the decrease was less strong and not significant. For male participants none of the effects were significant. We may conclude that the additive model we predicted has received some but not full support. We predicted a main effect of mental load, but the results showed that this effect is not significant. Moreover, the predicted additive pattern was shown only for female subjects and not for male subjects: The two-way interaction reached not the usual levels of significance, although the paired t-tests showed significant results.

We may conclude from these findings that participants are able to recognize and experience stressful situations and that workload and mental load (distributive injustice) as well as treatment (procedural justice) have effects on the perception and experience of stress. More important, the two studies give some support to the additive model of the relationship between justice and stress.

USING JUSTICE TO MANAGE STRESS

In an overview of the history and development of research on stress and burnout, Maslach, Schaufeli, and Leiter (2001) differentiated interventions to decrease stress between interventions on the individual level and those on the organizational level. According to the authors, interventions on the individual level are intended to improve the coping behavior of employees. Interventions on the organizational level are intended to remove the stressors causing stress. Their conclusion is that interventions on the individual level show mixed results with regard to their effectiveness. Some studies do show a decrease in stress symptoms, whereas others do not. They make a strong argument for interven-

tions on the organizational level. The main reason is that employees have hardly any influence on stressors because these operate on the group or organizational level. Interventions on the individual level are therefore less effective than interventions on the organizational level. The authors draw a direct relationship between justice and stress and how justice-based interventions can be very effective in decreasing stress. The examples the authors give of a successful intervention are the weekly sessions of employees on how to decrease perceived injustices in their work situation.

How Distributive Justice May Be Used to Manage Stress

Taris et al. (2001) focused on the effects of distributive injustice on stress. They asked attention for the inequalities in investments and rewards between exchange partners in a work relationship. Employees experiencing that their investments or rewards are higher or respectively lower than those of others in the work relationship may experience stress and, in the long run, symptoms of burnout. The authors argued that a more equitable allocation of investments and rewards in a work relationship may decrease stress. Individual intervention would focus on how to bring back one's own investments, for instance, by exerting less effort, or by improving the communication skills and request more input from the other. Organizational-based interventions would focus on how to overcome ego depletion of teachers, for instance, by organizing regular meetings in which teachers can tell their story and in which they get support form colleagues and supervisors. The organization can help teachers by appointing experts to help students with their (personal) problems.

Injustice may concern the outcome of the allocation decision process or the procedure. A supervisor may not be able for financial reasons to promote a subordinate, although he or she deserves promotion. The supervisor may—after consultation with the subordinate—decide to give the subordinate more responsibility or more challenging and interesting tasks. The supervisor compensates in this case for the unfairness of the initial outcome: not to promote the subordinate. Vermunt and Steensma (2001) called restoring distributive justice by another fair allocation *compensation*. Compensation is a widespread phenomenon in the daily practice of companies and institutions. For example, in a large company a high-ranking human resources manager was not given a position on the board of management, although he believed he deserved it. He was then offered a nice position with high decision latitude and a higher salary. Maybe the compensation would not fully restore justice, but the negative effects of the unfairness would be less strong than when the compensation was not offered. If the compensation was not al-

lowed, the manager could easily subside in lethargy and get stressed because of tasks that are not attractive and challenging anymore.

In many work situations employees may feel that the procedure with which resources are allocated is unfair. For example, Van den Bos, Vermunt, and Wilke (1997) investigated the valence of procedural fairness judgments followed by a favorable outcome versus the valence of procedural fairness judgments followed by an unfavorable outcome. In the study, participants were instructed that they would perform an estimation task. After completing the estimation task, with which they could earn a bonus if they successfully passed the task, the manipulations were induced. In the condition where participants were informed about the procedure before they received information about the outcome, first information about the procedure that was used to assess the outcome of the task was offered. In the unfair (inaccurate) procedure condition, participants were informed that the experimenter graded only part of the tasks. Thereafter, the participants were informed about the outcome of the task: In the favorable-outcome condition, the experimenter informed the participants that they had succeeded in doing the estimation task. In the unfavorable outcome condition, participants were informed that they had not succeeded in passing the estimation task. The results showed among other things that procedural fairness judgments were more positive when an unfair procedure was followed by a favorable outcome than when the unfair procedure was followed by an unfavorable outcome. Vermunt and Steensma (2001) labeled this process of restoring procedural fairness by outcome fairness *appreciation*.

How Procedural Justice May Be Used to Manage Stress

To escape from the situation in which employees become increasingly helpless because of the inadequacies of coping with unfairness stress on an individual basis, an organization—in our case, the supervisor— has to follow other ways of reducing or preventing employee stress. Greenberg and Wiethoff (2001) developed a framework in which the sequence of action and reaction to decisions that influence employees' fairness conceptions is described: Perceptions of injustice as a reaction to decisions are followed by reactions to perceived injustice, feedback by the organization, the enactment of actions to restore justice, and the evaluation of it. Implicit in this framework is the assumption that decisions taken by management and supervisors will affect (some) employees and that management and supervisors should be alert to eventually felt injustices. Sometimes initial injustices cannot be avoided, but by repairing the injustices, demotivation, sickness, and absenteeism may be diminished or even prevented (Vermunt, 2002b).

Vermunt and Steensma (2001) developed two ways to restore justice in situations of initial injustices. The initial outcome unfairness may be followed by a fair procedure. In a study by Van den Bos et al. (1997), half of the participants, after having performed an estimation task, received information about the outcome, after which they were informed about the applied procedure. In the favorable outcome condition, the participants were informed that they had succeeded in passing the estimation task. After outcome information was given, these participants were informed about the procedure that was used to assess the outcome of the estimation task. In the fair-procedure condition, participants were informed that the experimenter had graded all estimation tasks, whereas participants in the unfair-procedure condition were informed that the experimenter had graded only a part of the estimation tasks. The findings showed that outcome judgments were more positive when the unfavorable outcome was followed by a fair procedure than when followed by an unfair procedure.

Most important in restoring justice is that trust between authority (supervisor, management) and recipient (subordinate) that has been diminished temporarily will be repaired. A way to overcome outcome injustice is to enact fair procedures, which is labeled, after Folger (1987), *justification*. Many studies show the justification phenomenon. Folger and Cropanzano (1998) gave examples when discussing the results of performance appraisal studies. According to the authors, the studies showed positive effects of the following policies: Appraise subordinates on the appropriate criteria, have knowledgeable appraisals, apply fair rating formats, maintain interpersonal fairness in the performance appraisal interview, and train subordinates to participate. Justification is measured in terms of giving arguments for a certain decision, but also in terms of the length of accounts, as Folger, Rosenfield, Grove, and Corkran (1979) did. In their study, participants expect to have high chances to get a bonus, but a change in procedure lowered this chance. Participants who got a lengthy account of why the experimenter had changed the procedure were more satisfied than participants with a short account. Justification is also used in situations where voice is given, in a situation when their opinion could not have any influence on the decision of the authority: postdecisional voice (Lind, Kanfer, & Earley, 1990). Procedures are often used as justifications. When a supervisor has to take decisions that may trigger fairness perceptions, he or she may apply fair procedures in order to meet possible negative reactions of insubordinates.

In everyday working life, supervisors apply procedures to allocate tasks and equipment to subordinates. Those procedures may be evalu-

ated as not fair. A supervisor may be in a position in which his or her superior have a strong preference for efficiency. The supervisor is then more or less forced to adopt less fair procedures. These unfair procedures may have detrimental effects on subordinates' health and on subjective well-being. The supervisor might wish to overcome the unfairness by applying a fair alternative procedure, that is, by applying fair interpersonal treatment, so as to restore trust in the relationship with the subordinates. The supervisor may try to soften the blow for the subordinates and will establish good relationship with them, for example, by treating them politely and by demonstrating respect for them. Restoring justice in this way is labeled *mitigation* (Vermunt & Steensma, 2001).

The already mentioned ways to restore justice are the result of a combination of two types of past injustices and one type of handling them. In everyday life, supervisors will not confine themselves to only one type of restoration. It is often more effective to apply a combination of restoring activities. It is most effective to repair an unfair outcome with a combination of a fair procedure with another but fair outcome. A supervisor withholding from a subordinate a deserved promotion may try to reduce the subordinate's feelings of injustice by giving the subordinate voice (justification) in the selection of interesting tasks (compensation).

We conclude this section with the following observation. Strategies to repair justice—compensation, appreciation, justification, and mitigation—will be implemented only by supervisors who are both willing and able to strive for justice. Unfortunately, not all supervisors meet these conditions. For instance, it has been shown time and again that supervisors bully subordinates in the workplace (Hubert, Furda, & Steensma, 2001). In such cases, other methods should be used. Recently, a research program has been started to develop these methods.

CONCLUSION FROM FIELD AND EXPERIMENTAL RESEARCH

The scarce studies devoted to the relationship between justice and stress have mainly focused on the detrimental effects of injustice on health of employees. Inequitable reward increases stress and burnout (Taris et al., 2001). Unfair procedures and unfair treatment lead to stress reactions (Elovainio et al., 2001, 2002; Zohar, 1995; Tepper, 2001). Moreover, these studies are all correlation studies, and it is difficult to draw definitive conclusions about causal relationships between justice and stress. So, it is possible that the relationship between justice and stress is the reverse of that predicted in the studies presented: Employees who

experience stress may evaluate the outcome or/and the procedure of the allocation decision process as more unfair than employees who experience less stress. There are only a few studies so far that have investigated the beneficial effects of justice in a more strict way. Tomaka and Blascovich (1994) showed that participants high on belief in a just world (BJW) cope better with stressful situations than participants low on BJW, as shown by psychophysiological indices and self-reports. Vermunt and Steensma (2003) showed that fair procedures have a beneficial effect on experienced stress, as concluded from the participants' psychophysiological responses. Taking the findings of all the studies together, there is a strong case to conclude that injustice increases stress, whereas justice decreases stress.

Future Research

More studies are necessary to find out more precisely:

1. What kind of inequity affects stress most. Although it is known that underpayment causes more distress then overpayment (Adams, 1963; Markovsky, 1988), information about the effects of other types of resources on distress is necessary.

2. Which kind of procedures and treatments affects stress most. Vermunt and Steensma (2003) showed that giving participants opportunity to reflect on their test results has positive effects on several physiological responses, but information about the effects of other procedures and interactional behaviors is highly welcome.

3. How the combination of outcomes and procedures affects stress most. Brockner and Wiesenfeld (1996) showed that the interaction effects of distributive justice and procedural justice on self-esteem are rather intricate. In studies by Brockner et al. (2003) it was shown that procedural justice after outcome injustice affected self-esteem negatively when performance was involved but positively when commitment was involved.

4. How the relationship between justice and stress is affected by (a) person(ality) characteristics of employees—Tomaka and Blascovich (1994) and Vermunt and Steensma (2003) showed that belief in a just world and sex of participants moderate the effects of injustice on stress; the effects of other characteristics like age, self- esteem, and status position on the relationship between injustice and stress should be investigated as well—(b) the valence of the resource; and (c) the way it is distributed (Törnblom & Vermunt, 1999).

Another line of research could focus on stress as a mediator between justice and counterproductive behavior. The relationship between jus-

tice and counterproductive behavior is strongly confirmed by empirical evidence (see, e.g., Folger & Skarlacki, 1998; Greenberg, 1990; Modde, Vermunt & Wiegman, 1995). We assume that stress mediates the relationship between justice and counterproductive behavior because "productive" responses to injustice are most likely when the person has control over his or her responses, such as giving more effort. Capacities are less easy to handle, and a discrepancy between demands from the environment and individuals' capacities will probably lead to alternative types of responses.

ACKNOWLEDGMENT

We thank Jason A. Colquitt for his valuable comments on a previous version of this chapter.

REFERENCES

Adams, J. S. (1963). Toward an understanding of inequity. *Journal of Abnormal and Social Psychology, 67*, 422-436.

Adams, J. S. (1965). Inequity in social exchange. In L. Berkowitz (Ed.), *Advances in experimental social psychology* (Vol. 2, pp. 267–299). New York: Academic Press.

Allegro, J., Kruidenier, H., & Steensma, H. (1991). Aspects of distributive and procedural justice in quality of working life. In H. Steensma & R. Vermunt (Eds.), *Social justice in human relations, Vol. 2: Societal and psychological consequences of justice and injustice* (pp. 99–116). New York: Plenum Press.

Bies, R. J., & Moag, J. S. (1986). Interactional justice: Communication criteria for justice. In B. Sheppard (Ed.), *Research on negotiation in organizations.* (Vol. 1, pp. 43–55). Greenwich, CT: JAI.

Bies, R. J., & Tripp, T. M. (1996). Beyond distrust: "Getting even" and the need for revenge. In R. M. Kramer & T. Tyler (Eds.), *Trust in organizations* (pp. 246–260). Newbury Park, CA: Sage.

Bies, R. J., & Tripp, T. M. (2001). A passion for justice: The rationality and morality of revenge. In R. Cropanzano (Ed.), *Justice in the workplace: From theory to practice* (pp. 56–80). Mahwah, NJ: Lawrence Erlbaum Associates.

Brockner, J., Heuer, L., Magner, N., Folger, R., Umphress, E., Van den Bos, K., Vermunt, R., Magner, M., & Siegel, P. (2003). The interactive effect of outcome favorability and procedural fairness on self-evaluations: The pleasure and pain of fair procedures. *Organizational Behavior and Human Decision Processes, 91*, 51–68.

Brockner, J., & Wiesenfeld, B. M. (1996). An integrated framework for explaining reactions to decisions: The interactive effects of outcomes and procedures. *Psychological Bulletin, 120*, 189–208.

Cartwright, S., & Cooper, G. L. (1996). Public policy and occupational health psychology in Europe. *Journal of Occupational Health Psychology, 1*, 349–361.

Cartwright, S., & Cooper, C. L. (1997). *Managing workplace stress.* London: Sage.

Carver, C. S. (1995). Stress and coping. In A. S. Manstead & M. Hewstone (Eds.), *The Blackwell encyclopedia of social psychology* (pp. 635–639). Oxford, England: Blackwell.

Cropanzano, R., & Ambrose, M. L. (2001). Procedural and distributive justice are more similar than you think: A monistic perspective and a research agenda. In J. Greenberg & R. Cropanzano (Eds.), *Advances in organizational justice* (pp. 119–151). Stanford, CA: Stanford University Press.

Crosby, F. (1976). A model of egoistical relative deprivation. *Psychological Review*, 83–112.

Dalbert, C. (1998). Belief in a just world, well-being, and coping with an unjust fate. In L. Montada & M. J. Lerner (Eds.), *Responses to victimizations and belief in a just world* (pp. 87–106). New York: Plenum.

Derogatis, L. R. (1993). *Brief sympton inventory: Administration, scoring, and procedures manual*. Minneapolis, MN: National Computer Systems.

Elovainio, M., Kivimaki, M., & Helkama, K. (2001). Organizational justice evaluations, job control and occupational strain. *Journal of Applied Psychology, 86*, 418–424.

Elovainio, M., Kivimaki, M., & Vahtera, J. (2002). Organizational justice: Evidence of a new psychosocial predictor of health. *American Journal of Public Health, 92*, 105–108.

Foa, U. G., & Foa, E. B. (1974). *Societal structures of the mind*. Springfield, IL: Charles C. Thomas.

Folger, R. (1987). Reformulating the preconditions of resentment: A referent cognitions model. In J. Masters & W. Smith (Eds.), *Social comparison, social justice, and relative deprivation: Theoretical, empirical, and policy perspectives* (pp. 183–215). Hillsdale, NJ: Lawrence Erlbaum Associates.

Folger, R., & Cropanzano, R. (1998). *Organizational justice and human resource management*. London: Sage.

Folger, R., Rosenfield, D., Grove, J., & Corkran, L. (1979). Effects of "voice" and peer opinions on responses to inequity. *Journal of Personality and Social Psychology, 37*, 2253–2261.

Folger, R., & Skarlicki, D. P. (1998). A popcorn metaphor for employee aggression. In R. W. Griffin & A. O'Leary-Kelley (Eds.), *Dysfunctional behavior in organizations: Violent and deviant behavior* (pp. 43–82). Greenwich, CT: JAI Press.

French, J. R. P., & Caplan, R. D. (1972). Organizational stress and individual strain. In A. J. Marrow (Ed.), *The failure of success* (pp. 30–67). New York: Amacom.

French, J. R. P., Rogers, W., & Cobb, S. (1981). A model of person-environment fit. In L. Levi (Ed.), *Society, stress and disease* (Vol. 4, pp. 39–44). New York: Oxford University Press.

Goldberg, L. R. (1990). An alternative "description of personality": The big-five factor structure. *Journal of Personality and Social Psychology, 59*, 1216–1229.

Greenberg, J. (1984). On the apocryphal nature of inequity distress. In R. Folger (Ed.), *The sense of injustice: Social psychological perspectives* (pp. 167–186). New York: Plenum.

Greenberg, J. (1990). Employee theft as a reaction to underpayment inequity. *Journal of Applied Psychology, 75*, 561–568.

Greenberg, J. (1993). Stealing in the name of justice: Informational and interpersonal moderators of theft reactions to underpayment inequity. *Organizational Behavior and Human Decision Processes, 54*, 81–103.

Greenberg, J., & Wiethoff, C. (2001). Organizational justice as proaction and reaction: Implications for research and application. In R. Cropanzano (Ed.), *Justice in the workplace: From theory to practice* (pp. 271–301). Mahwah, NJ: Lawrence Erlbaum Associates.

Hubert, A., Furda, J., & Steensma, H. (2001). Mobbing, systematisch pestgedrag in organisaties. Twee studies naar antecedenten en gevolgen voor de gezondheid

[Mobbing in organisations: Two studies towards antecedents and effects for health]. *Gedrag en Organisatie, 14,* 378–396.

Hyman, H. H., & Singer, E. (1968). *Readings in reference group theory and research.* New York: Free Press.

Kahn, L. (1970). Some propositions towards a researchable conceptualization of stress. In J. W. McGrath (Ed.), *Social and psychological factors of stress* (pp. 97–104). New York: Holt, Rinehart, & Winston.

Koper, G., Van Knippenberg, D., Bouhuys, F., Vermunt, R., & Wilke, H. (1993). Procedural fairness and self-esteem. *European Journal of Social Psychology, 26,* 313–325.

Lazarus, R. S., & Folkman, S. (1984). *Stress, appraisal and coping.* New York: Springer-Verlag.

Le Blanc, P., de Jonge, J., & Schaufeli, W. B. (2000). Job stress and health. In N. Chmiel (Ed.), *Work and organizational psychology* (pp. 148–177). Oxford, England: Blackwell.

Lerner, M. J. (1980). *Belief in a just world: A fundamental delusion.* New York: Plenum Press.

Leventhal, G. S. (1980). What should be done with equity theory? New approaches to the fairness in social relationships. In K. Gergen, M. Greenberg, & R. Willis (Eds.), *Social exchange theory* (pp. 27–55). New York: Plenum.

Levinger, G. (1959). The development of perceptions and behavior in newly formed social power relationships. In D. Cartwright (Ed.), *Studies in social power* (pp. 26–44). Ann Arbor: University of Michigan.

Lind, E. A., Kanfer, R., & Earley, P. C. (1990). Voice, control, and procedural justice: Instrumental and noninstrumental concerns in fairness judgments. *Journal of Personality and Social Psychology, 59,* 952–959.

Lovallo, W. R. (1997). *Stress and health. Biological and psychological interactions.* London: Sage.

Markovsky, B. (1988). Injustice and arousal. *Social Justice Research, 2,* 223–233.

Maslach, C., Schaufeli, W. B., & Leiter, M. P. (2001). Job burnout. *Annual Review of Psychology, 52,* 397–422.

Modde, J., Vermunt, R., & Wiegman, O. (1995). Procedurele rechtvaardigheid en normovertredend gedrag. *Fundamentele Sociale Psychologie, 9,* 107–117.

Montada, L., & Lerner, M. J. (1998). *Responses to victimizations and belief in a just world.* New York: Plenum Press.

Paoli, P. (1997). *Second European survey on the work environment: 1995.* Dublin, Ireland: European Foundation for the Improvement of Living and Working Conditions.

Ramakers, K., Steensma, H., & Vijlbrief, H. (2003, May). *Relationship between personality factors, distributive justice, procedural justice, and just world belief.* Paper presented at the eleventh annual meeting of the European Association of Work and Organizational Psychology, Lisbon, Portugal.

Rubin, Z., & Peplau, L. A. (1975). Who believes in a just world? *Journal of Social Issues, 31,* 65–89.

Rutte, C. G., & Messick, D. M. (1995). An integrated model of perceived unfairness in organizations. *Social Justice Research, 8,* 239–262.

Schaufeli, W., & Van Dierendonck, D. (1994). Burnout, een begrip gemeten. De Nederlandse versie van de Maslach Burnout Inventory. *Gedrag en Gezondheid, 22,* 153–172.

Siegrist, J. (1996). Adverse health effects of high effort/low reward conditions. *Journal of Occupational Health Psychology, 1,* 27–41.

Skarlicki, D., & Folger, R. (1997). Retaliation for perceived unfair treatment: Examining the role of procedural and interactional justice. *Journal of Applied Psychology, 82,* 434–443.

Steensma, H. (2002). Violence in the workplace: The explanatory strength of social (in)justice theories. In M. Ross & D. T. Miller (Eds.), *The justice motive in everyday life* (pp. 149–167). New York: Cambridge University Press.

Steensma, H., Allegro, J., & Knip, J. (1999–2000). Procedural justice and organizational change in a municipal organization. *Journal of Individual Employment Rights, 8*, 307–323.

Taris, T. W., Schreurs, P. J. G., Peeters, M. C. W., Le Blanc, P. M., & Schaufeli, W. B. (2001). From inequity to burnout: The role of job stress. *Journal of Occupational Health Psychology, 6*, 303–323.

Tepper, B. J. (2001). Health consequences of organizational injustice: Tests of main and interactive effects. *Organizational Behavior and Human Decision Processes, 86*, 197–215.

Tomaka, J., & Blascovich, J. (1994). Effects of justice beliefs on cognitive appraisal of and subjective, physiological, and behavioral responses to potential stress. *Journal of Personality and Social Psychology, 67*, 732–740.

Törnblom, K., & Vermunt, R. (1999). An integrative perspective on social justice: Distributive and procedural fairness evaluations of positive and negative outcome allocations. *Social Justice Research, 12*, 39–64.

Tyler, T. R. (1994). Psychological models of the justice motive: Antecedents of distributive and procedural justice. *Journal of Personality and Social Psychology, 67*, 850–863.

Tyler, T. R., & Lind, E. A. (1992). A relational model of authority in groups. In M. Zanna (Ed.), *Advances in experimental social psychology* (Vol. 25, pp. 115–191). San Diego, CA: Academic Press.

Van den Bos, K., Vermunt, R., & Wilke, H. A. M. (1997). Procedural and distributive justice: What is fair depends more on what comes first than on what comes next. *Journal of Personality and Social Psychology, 72*, 95–104.

Van Meer, R. (1997). *Overspannen door je baas: Ziekmakende stress en wat er aan te doen is [Stress through your boss: Sick making stress and what to do about it].* Utrecht, the Netherlands: Kosmos Uitgevers.

Vermunt, R. (2002a). The justice motive in perspective. In M. Ross & D. Miller (Eds.), *The justice motive in everyday life* (pp. 63–79). New York: Cambridge University Press.

Vermunt, R. (2002b). The dual position of the boss, injustice and stress. In D. Steiner, S. Gilliland, & D. Skarlacki (Eds.), *Research in social issues in management* (Vol. 2, pp. 159–176). Greenwich, CT: Information Age.

Vermunt, R., Oskam, M., & Steensma, H. (1998). Van baas tot bazig: Stress door onrechtvaardig gedrag van de baas [From boss to bossy. Stress through superiors' unfair treatment]. *Gedrag en Organisatie, 11*, 354–372.

Vermunt, R., & Steensma, H. (2001). Stress and justice in organisations: An exploration into justice processes with the aim to find mechanisms to reduce stress. In R. Cropanzano (Ed.), *Justice in the workplace* (Vol. 2, pp 27–48). Mahwah, NJ: Lawrence Erlbaum Associates.

Vermunt, R., & Steensma, H. (2003). Physiological relaxation: Stress reduction through fair treatment. *Social Justice Research, 16*, 135–149.

Willemsen, M., Steensma, H., & Van der Vlist, R. (2002). *Organizational justice and employee absenteeism.* Manuscript submitted for publication.

Zohar, D. (1995). The justice perspective of job stress. *Journal of Organizational Behavior, 16*, 487–495.

14

How Can Justice Be Used to Improve Employee Selection Practices?

Stephen W. Gilliland
University of Arizona

Jeff M. S. Hale
University of Arizona

The 10 years since the publication of Gilliland's (1993) organizational justice model of employee selection have witnessed the development of a large body of research on applicants' perceptions of justice. We review this literature by considering three stages of the employee selection process: recruiting and initial communication, screening and selection, and decision making and communication. Although the preponderance of research has considered the second stage, existing research suggests that interpersonal and informational justice are salient at all stages, whereas procedural justice is most salient during screening and selection, and distributive justice is most salient during decision making and communication. We suggest that researchers should consider the dynamic nature of justice reactions, with the primary determinants of fairness perceptions changing over the course of the hiring process. We also argue that in focusing solely on applicants' reactions, research has failed to examine how employees might perceive justice in selection processes and decisions.

There's not a shortage of people ... but there is a shortage of great people. The competition for the best of the best is incredible. If you want to hire the next Michael Jordon, you have to recruit that person differently, evaluate him or her differently, and offer him or her a job differently. (Sullivan, 1998, p. 214)

A substantial body of research on organizational justice has demonstrated that justice and fairness are important concerns for employees. As summarized in other chapters in this handbook, employees respond positively to fair treatment through increased cooperation (Blader & Tyler, chap. 11, this volume) and organizational citizenship behavior (Moorman & Byrne, chap. 12, this volume). Employees also are more likely respond negatively and in a retaliatory manner when they perceive they have been subject to unfair treatment (Greenberg, 1990, 1993; Skarlicki & Folger, 1997). However, employees are not the only organizational stakeholders concerned about justice. As the introductory quote suggests, job applicants are also concerned about justice. A decade ago, Gilliland (1993) outlined a number of dimensions along which justice can be managed in the selection process and suggested a variety of consequences of managing the applicant selection process fairly. Subsequent research has demonstrated that applicants indeed respond to justice in the selection and hiring process (for reviews, see Gilliland & Steiner, 2001; Ryan & Ployhart, 2000; Truxillo, Steiner, & Gilliland, 2001).

Applicants' fairness perceptions have been related to satisfaction with the selection process (Macan, Avedon, Paese, & Smith, 1994), orga-

nizational attractiveness (Bauer et al., 2001), and intentions to recommend the organization to others (Smither, Reilly, Millsap, Pearlman, & Stoffey, 1993). Research has also demonstrated that these effects persist beyond the receipt of feedback on the hiring decision (Bauer, Maertz, Dolen, & Campion, 1998). Conversely, unfairness in the selection process can have negative consequences. Bauer et al. (2001) demonstrated that after controlling for outcome favorability (pass/fail), the perceived fairness of a selection process was negatively related to perceived litigation likelihood. Although most of the research on outcomes of applicants' perceptions of fairness has addressed attitudinal, perceptual, or intentional outcomes, some research has also demonstrated effects of fair treatment on behavior. Gilliland and colleagues (2001, Study 2) influenced perceptions of fairness by providing explanations to rejected job applicants. The researchers found that applicants who were provided a more thorough explanation judged procedures and interpersonal treatment to be more fair than applicants who received a standard rejection letter. Significantly, job applicants who received the more thorough explanation were more than twice as likely to reapply for a future position with the organization.

The research on consequences of applicant fairness perceptions clearly demonstrates that managing organizational justice in the selection process is an important concern. However, it is also useful to acknowledge the limits on the impact of justice in employee selection. Research that examined the influence of fairness perceptions on applicant withdrawal from a selection process failed to demonstrate significant relationships (Ryan, Sacco, McFarland, & Kriska, 2000). Similarly, suggestions made by Gilliland (1993) that the justice of selection practices can influence post-hire attitudes have generally not been supported (Cunningham-Snell, Anderson, & Fletcher, 1999).

As recent reviews have thoroughly addressed issues of consequences of applicants' perceptions of fairness (e.g., Cropanzano & Wright, 2003; Gilliland & Steiner, 2001; Truxillo et al., 2001), we have chosen to focus this chapter on the question: "How do theories of organizational justice inform fair employee selection practices?" That is, we focus on the *antecedents* of fair employee selection practices, rather than the consequences.

Our chapter begins with a presentation of employee selection as a process with a series of stages. We then review research that has examined determinants of justice at each of these stages. This research demonstrates that different aspects of organizational justice are more relevant or salient than others at different stages in the selection process. As a result of the differential salience, justice perceptions change throughout the process. Although the focus of this chapter is predominantly retrospective, in that we review research that has been conducted over the past 10 years, we also look forward and suggest major directions for future re-

search. One direction we highlight is the need to consider a broader group of stakeholders of selection practices than have generally been studied. In particular, we urge researchers to consider the effects of co-workers' perceptions of justice in selection processes and decisions. Much as Gilliland (1993) argued that organizational justice theories apply to job applicants as well as employees, we argue that organizational justice in employee selection practices impact existing employees as well as applicants. Although researchers have conducted a plethora of studies on applicant reactions since Gilliland's foundational article, the impact of justice in selection procedures on existing employees has not received attention.

STAGES OF EMPLOYEE SELECTION

The introductory quote to this chapter suggests organizations should be concerned with justice in the way prospective employees are recruited, evaluated, and offered jobs. This insight highlights the fact that selection is not an isolated event, but rather a series of stages or interactions between applicants and the hiring organization. In a traditional staffing perspective, these stages are often parsed into recruiting activities, selection processes, and decision making (e.g., Heneman, Judge, & Heneman, 2000). Further, research into these three areas is conceptually and empirically very distinct, with little overlap and integration. However, when considered from an organizational justice perspective, these stages appear both related and ready for integration. Fairness perceptions, although influenced by the actions at each stage, are continual and can provide researchers with a unifying framework for the selection process. Indeed, when Gilliland (1993) presented his initial model of justice in the applicant selection process, he did not distinguish between these stages.

We believe there may be value in considering organizational justice reactions at each of the stages of selection. By viewing fairness perceptions at different points in the selection process, it might be possible to examine how these perceptions vary over time. More importantly, there are likely different dimensions of organizational justice that influence applicants at different stages of the selection process. A stage-specific, organizational justice perspective also has an advantage over the more traditional organizational staffing perspective because it allows researchers to carefully compare and contrast recommendations for selection practices. Gilliland (1993) contrasted the psychometric concerns of reliability and validity with the organizational justice concerns of perceived fairness. However, Gilliland's framework becomes richer when justice in employee selection is expanded to include recruiting and decision making stages. Then it is possible to link organizational justice

principles with results from research on recruiting, cut score decision making (banding), and utility estimation procedures. For these reasons we adopt a stage-specific framework when considering the justice of employee selection practices.

The first stage in the selection process is *recruiting and initial communication*. This stage encompasses activities involved in generating an applicant pool, including formal and informal recruiting and collecting applications. We also include in this stage the initial communication to applicants acknowledging their entry into the selection process. The next stage is *screening and selection processes* and involves evaluating the viability and potential of job applicants. In this stage, applicants may experience screening procedures, selection tests, and interviews. Most of the research on applicants' perceptions of fairness has focused on the screening and selection stage. The final stage is *decision making and communication*. Both how the hiring decision is ultimately made and how this decision is communicated have important effects on applicants' perceptions of fairness. As this is the final stage, it is possible that perceptions at this stage last longest and influence subsequent decisions and actions.

As indicated earlier, although these stages serve as a useful heuristic for evaluating the selection process in its entirety, our clear distinctions between the stages are somewhat artificial. For example, initial screening may take place in the application process and prior to any direct communication from the organization. Similarly, decision making can occur throughout the screening and selection process such that the hiring decision is a culmination of a series of decisions (e.g., Macan et al., 1994; Ployhart, McFarland, & Ryan, 2002; Ryan et al., 2000). Finally, justice perceptions at one stage might influence reactions at a subsequent stage. For example, Gilliland (1994) found that applicants' expectations regarding their likelihood of being hired, which can be shaped through recruiting materials and initial communication, significantly influenced perceptions of fairness associated with the hiring decision.

Organizing Framework

We next examine organizational justice at each of these stages in the selection process. As Colquitt, Conlon, Wesson, Porter, and Ng (2001) suggested, and as echoed throughout this volume, organizational justice can be categorized into four types—interpersonal justice, informational justice, procedural justice, and distributive justice. Following these authors, we separate justice dimensions into (a) *interpersonal* justice, which refers to how respectfully one is treated; (b) *informational* justice, or the quality and quantity of relevant information provided; (c) *procedural* justice, which refers the structural aspects of the decision making

process; and (d) *distributive* justice, or the perceived fairness of outcomes. Gilliland (1993) presented different principles or rules of justice associated with interpersonal, informational, and procedural categories. Subsequent research (e.g., Bauer et al., 2001) has validated and refined this set of principles. Comparatively less attention has been paid to the distributive justice principles that Gilliland discussed. In our review, we consider which procedural, interpersonal, informational, and distributive justice principles are salient in the recruiting and initial communication, screening and selection processes, and decision-making and communication stages of employee selection.

We organize our review in a three by four matrix that combines the three stages of selection delineated above with the four dimensions of justice (see Table 14.1). We review the research relevant to each cell of this matrix. Throughout our analyses we evaluate the support for Gilliland's (1993) justice rules, highlight gaps that await researchers' attention, and offer suggestions for future research. We first examine empirical findings that show how justice can inform recruiting and initial communication. We then explore how justice judgments are affected by dimensions of the screening and selection process. Next we highlight employee justice perceptions during decision making and feedback. We conclude the section with a discussion of how justice perceptions fluctuate throughout the hiring process.

RECRUITING AND INITIAL COMMUNICATION

Drawing from several leading recruiting scholars (Barber, 1998; Gatewood & Field, 1998; Taylor & Bergmann, 1987), we define recruiting as organizations' efforts to attract applicants who will fulfill their needs. Organizations often attempt to fulfill a variety of organizational goals with their recruiting efforts. Possible goals include increasing the overall number of employees, employee diversity, and retention.

Researchers have learned that recruiting variables affect applicants' perceptions of organizations (Breaugh & Starke, 2000; Rynes, Bretz, & Gerhart, 1991; Scheu, Ryan, & Nona, 1999). However, the recruiting process has received less attention from organizational justice researchers (Anderson, Born, & Cunningham-Snell, 2001). Nonetheless, it seems likely that early interactions affect applicant fairness perceptions in some cases. For example, imagine that a potential applicant calls a company to inquire about a job opening and is treated rudely by the receptionist. Suppose the receptionist puts the potential applicant on hold for 20 minutes, tells the applicant there might or might not be a job opening, and refuses to transfer the potential applicant. This interaction would certainly have a negative impact on the potential applicant's justice perceptions. Similarly, Gilliland (1995) found that applicants reported

TABLE 14.1
Principles for Justice in Selection

Selection stage	Justice Type			
	Interpersonal	Informational	Procedural	Distributive
Recruiting and initial communication	• Interpersonal effectiveness	• Timeliness • Selection information • Honesty	• Widespread use • Propriety	[Not applicable]
Screening and selection processes	• Interpersonal effectiveness • Two-way communication	• Timeliness • Selection information • Honesty	• Job relatedness • Consistency • Propriety • Invasiveness • Opportunity to perform • Ease of faking answers • Reconsideration opportunity • Widespread use	• Equity • Need
Decision making and communication	• Interpersonal effectiveness	• Timeliness • Selection information • Honesty	[Not applicable]	• Equity • Equality

417

418 GILLILAND AND HALE

"blatantly biased and potentially illegal" behaviors with some frequency (p. 17).

In this section we review what researchers have learned about the effects of recruiting and initial communication on justice perceptions. We include any interactions between organizations and applicants or potential applicants prior to substantial screening and selection processes.

Interpersonal Justice

Interpersonal Effectiveness. Recruiters' respect (or lack of respect) for candidates is clearly important for perceptions of justice. In their seminal research on interactional justice, Bies and Moag (1986) demonstrated that issues of respect and, conversely, rudeness were central to recruits' descriptions of fair and unfair treatment. Similarly, recruiting research demonstrated that recruiters' personalities and behaviors are important determinants of reactions to recruiting (Rynes, 1993). Unfortunately, little subsequent research has systematically examined the extent to which recruiters' interpersonal effectiveness influences perceptions of justice and fairness.

Informational Justice

Timeliness. Communication with hiring staff (e.g., to set up interviews) that is delayed is likely to decrease perceptions of fairness. This proposal is based on research showing delays are perceived negatively throughout the selection process (Rynes et al., 1991). However, researchers should isolate delays before selection procedures have begun and examine their impact on applicants' fairness perceptions.

Selection Information. Researchers have found that advance notice of procedures is related to perceptions of their fairness. Bauer et al. (1998) found applicants for an entry-level accounting job perceived the testing process more fairly when they had more information about the test. Conversely, Gilliland (1995) found that lack of selection information prior to the selection process was a source of perceptions of unfairness with the process. Given that selection information can be presented prior to, during, or after the selection process, it may be fruitful for future research to examine how timing of presentation of selection information influences perceptions of fairness.

Honesty. Applicants require accurate information about the upcoming selection procedures and the organization, or else they are likely to see the organization as unfair (Bies & Moag, 1986). Generally, research suggests that dishonesty diminishes trust and subsequently

increases perceptions of unfairness (Lind & Tyler, 1988; Tyler & Lind, 1992). Unfortunately, honest and dishonesty have not received much attention in selection justice literature.

Procedural Justice

Widespread Use. Widely used procedures in recruiting and initial communication are likely to be related to perceptions of fairness. For example, before tests or interviews take place, many organizations require that applicants submit a resumé. Steiner and Gilliland (1996) found that the use of resumés was seen as fair in both France and the United States. Resumés might be seen as fair because applicants expect them to be solicited—their use is seen as normal and part of the job application script. Researchers have suggested that one reason some hiring practices are seen as fair (e.g., unstructured interviews) is because they are expected. However, this proposal awaits empirical testing.

Propriety. Improper questions or statements in recruiting and initial communication are likely to result in perceptions of unfairness. Saks, Leck, and Saunders (1995) found that their student sample reacted negatively to common discriminatory questions. Saks et al. provided students with an application bank that contained items "generally considered to be inappropriate" (p. 419)—questions that inquired about gender, marital status, age, ethnic/cultural/racial group, and disabilities—to one group of participants, and did not ask the other group inappropriate questions. Although the discriminatory questions negatively influenced participants' perceptions, we cannot pinpoint which individual questions led to this result. Future research should isolate which types of questions are perceived to be most improper by different groups of applicants.

Distributive Justice

Because distributive justice refers to evaluations of the fairness of outcomes, and outcomes are not allocated at this stage of the process, we do not believe distributive justice is a salient concern in the recruiting and initial communication process.

Summary

Many aspects of applicants' perceptions of the fairness in recruiting and initial communication await further study. We echo the call of other scholars for further theoretical development on the effects of recruitment on applicant reactions (e.g., Anderson et al., 2001; Breaugh & Starke,

2000). Given the research on fairness heuristic theory (see chap. 3) that demonstrates how early information has a greater influence on fairness perceptions than later information (Van den Bos, Vermunt, & Wilke, 1997), applicants' fairness perceptions that are formed during the recruiting and initial communication stage may be particularly important in shaping final fairness perceptions.

SCREENING AND SELECTION PROCESSES

This stage consists of interactions between applicants and the hiring organization in which applicants engage in selection procedures and are evaluated by hiring personnel (e.g., tests, work samples, interviews). In this stage we include all interactions that occur before an organization makes its decision of who to hire for a position. Most of the research that has examined applicants' perceptions of fairness has been oriented around processes associated with screening and selection.

Interpersonal Justice

Interpersonal Effectiveness. Hiring personnel's interpersonal skills are especially important for applicants' perceptions of the common unstructured interview (Singer, 1990). In a study of recent and current job applicants Gilliland (1995) found that interpersonal effectiveness was a commonly cited determinant of fairness. Likewise, Bies and Moag (1986) reported the results of a study in which many (23%) of job applicants felt they were the victims of unfairness when treated rudely by potential employers. Clearly, research demonstrates that effective interpersonal treatment is important for applicant fairness perceptions.

Two-Way Communication. Two-way communication is a determinant of fairness perceptions, particularly with interviews (Gilliland, 1995). Although unstructured interviews might be perceived fairly for a variety of reasons (Kohn & Dipboye, 1998), the opportunity for two-way communication is likely to be a substantial reason (Gilliland, 1993). This is one of the few times in the selection process that applicants can learn about the organization by asking questions of interviewers. Although organizations might be tempted to move from unstructured interviews to structured interviews because of validity concerns (Folger & Cropanzano, 1998), this problem could be resolved by separating interviews into structured and unstructured segments (Kohn & Dipboye, 1998). Applicants would benefit from the unstructured segment through the opportunity to assess how well they fit with the organization, and organizations would benefit from the structured segment by assessing how well applicants fit with their needs using a mecha-

nism with reasonable predictive validity (Barber, 1998; Folger & Cropanzano, 1998; Kohn & Dipboye, 1998; Werbel & Gilliland, 1999).

Informational Justice

Timeliness.   Applicants want timely feedback of their performance in a multiple hurdle process, and react negatively to delays (Rynes et al., 1991). However, explanations for feedback delays might attenuate negative feelings (Rynes et al., 1991, p. 507). Indeed, Truxillo, Bauer, Campion, and Paronto (2002) conducted a quasi-experiment with applicants in a multiple-hurdle selection process for a police officer position. Applicants who were provided a warning of the extensive time required to score a test perceived the process more fairly than applicants not provided this additional information. However, job-relevant information was also given with the time required to score the test, so these results cannot be interpreted unambiguously. Nonetheless, it is worth noting that applicants reported higher satisfaction with the timeliness of feedback when warned of the time required to score a test.

Selection Information.   Fairness perceptions are affected by explanations for procedures in the hiring process. Truxillo et al. (2002) provided one cohort of applicants in a multiple-hurdle selection process with explanations of the time it would take to score tests, the consistency in scoring, the procedures' predictive validity, the procedures' opportunity to perform, and the procedures' job-related face validity. Compared to a cohort without these explanations, the applicants in the information condition saw the process as more fair at the time of the test and a month later when given feedback.

Honesty.   Research shows that individuals feel unfairly treated when lied to in organizational settings. Singer's (1990) study of professionals and students in New Zealand found that "clear, honest, two-way communication in interviews for a realistic picture of [the] job" was very important to applicants' fairness perceptions (p. 485). Similarly, a study presented by Bies and Moag (1986), demonstrated that MBA job candidates' perceptions of unfairness were most likely to result from deception by selection personnel.

Procedural Justice

Job relatedness.   Procedures that are highly face valid, meaning they appear to measure what they purport to measure, are seen as more fair than less face valid procedures (Gilliland, 1994). Steiner and Gilliland (1996) found the job-related face validity of procedures was extremely

important for favorable reactions in students' evaluations of selection procedures. This finding helps account for the high perceived fairness of procedures that approximate actual job tasks, such as work samples (Kravitz, Stinson, & Chavez, 1996) and assessment centers (Macan et al., 1994). Ryan, Gregarus, and Ployhart (1996) also found that the perceived job relatedness of physical ability tests for firefighters correlated with their fairness perceptions. Likewise, Chan, Schmitt, Jennings, Clause, and Delbridge (1998) found that perceived job relevance of tests influenced fairness perceptions for applicants for a state police trooper position. Interestingly, job relatedness appears to be more important to fairness in employment tests than interview situations. In a scenario study, Kohn and Dipboye (1998) found that an organization was seen more favorably in interviews when the interviewer asked questions low in job relevance than when the interviewer asked questions high in job relevance. This result might have been found because other justice principles that influence fairness (e.g., two-way communication) overwhelmed the desire for job relatedness in an employment interview.

In addition to job-related face validity, perceived predictive validity —how well a procedure predicts future performance (Gatewood & Field, 1998)—is related to perceived fairness of selection procedures (Bauer et al., 2001; Smither et al., 1993). In their development of the selection procedural justice scale (SPJS), Bauer et al. found that job-related face validity and predictive validity were distinct dimensions of selection fairness. Substantiating evidence comes from a study by Ryan and Chan (1999). These researchers found that test takers' perceptions of job-related face validity and predictive validity were differentiable and highly correlated with perceptions of procedural fairness. Truxillo, Bauer, and Sanchez (2001) found similar results in a study of applicant reactions to tests for a police officer position. Thus, we encourage researchers to separate perception of job-related face validity and predictive validity and in their studies.

Consistency.   Researchers have found that applicants perceive consistently administered test procedures to be linked to perceptions of fairness. In particular, consistency in time allowed for test taking has been shown to be important to perceptions of fairness for both actual job applicants performing a physical ability test (Ryan et al., 1996) and for students in lab studies performing a cognitive ability test (Ployhart & Ryan, 1998). Singer (1990) found that professionals and students in New Zealand reported that giving every applicant the same selection procedure was very important to fairness perceptions. Organizations that clearly demonstrate that all applicants are treated similarly are likely to be seen more fairly than organizations with less transparent selection procedures.

Propriety. The propriety of questions and statements are important to applicants' fairness perceptions. Ten percent of the MBA job candidates in the study discussed in Bies and Moag (1986) reported being asked improper questions during their recruitment. Ten percent of the sample also reported selection personnel made prejudicial statements to them. Both factors were cited as leading to perceived unfair treatment.

Invasiveness. In general, research suggests that invasive procedures are seen as unfair. Kravitz, Stinson, and Chavez (1996), in research with a student sample, found that descriptions of honesty, personality and drug tests were seen as relatively invasive. The researchers also found that perceptions of invasiveness and fairness were substantially correlated ($r = -.4$). Because drug tests are seen as invasive (Stone, Stone-Romero, & Hyatt, 1994), organizations must follow other justice rules to mitigate perceptions of unfairness. For example, Cropanzano and Konovsky (1995) found that the more employees at an organization perceived sufficient advance notice, voice in the process, opportunity to appeal, and justification for the use of drug tests, the more fairly the process was seen. Murphy, Thorton, and Reynolds (1990) found that drug testing was viewed as more appropriate for jobs when the safety of other people was a concern. Although the aforementioned studies were conducted with employees, we expect the results to generalize to job applicants.

Opportunity to Perform. Research suggests that job applicants' fairness perceptions are tied to the presence of procedures that allow them the opportunity to demonstrate their skills and abilities. Singer (1990) found that two items that tap opportunity to perform: "chance for applicant to make a case for himself/herself in the selection process" and "sufficient time for interviews" were rated to be important determinants of perceived fairness (p. 485). Similarly, Truxillo, Bauer, and Sanchez (2001) found opportunity to perform to be important for fairness perceptions. Steiner and Gilliland (2001) also reported that opportunity to perform is seen as important across cultures.

Research suggests that one way organizations can increase applicants' fairness perceptions while retaining procedures not generally seen as fair (e.g. personality tests) is by adding other procedures that increase applicants' opportunity to perform (Cropanzano & Wright, 2003). This solution is one way to resolve the *justice dilemma*, or the phenomena of negative applicant reactions to some valid procedures (Cropanzano & Wright, 2003; Folger & Cropanzano, 1998). Certain combinations of assessment procedures (e.g., biodata, cognitive ability test, and work sample) might increase fairness perceptions through increased opportunity

to perform. Rosse, Miller, and Stecher (1994) conducted a field experiment in which all applicants filled out an application and underwent an interview and reference checks. One group of applicants underwent no additional procedures, another group also took a personality test containing job-related questions, and the third group took personality and cognitive ability tests. Rosse et al. found that when a cognitive ability test was given in conjunction with a personality test, the test procedures were seen more favorably than when the personality test was absent. Although these findings are suggestive of the importance of opportunity to perform, this variable was not measured. Future research should assess the extent to which opportunity to perform drives fairness perceptions, as proposed by Gilliland (1993).

Ease of Faking Answers. If applicants want to have the opportunity to perform, it is reasonable to expect that they want their performance to be judged accurately. Consequently, it is not surprising that researchers have found that applicants perceive procedures that provide opportunities to fake answers to be unfair. Ease of faking answers is a large concern for biodata, integrity tests, and personality tests where applicants can try to guess the desired answer and misrepresent the truth. Gilliland (1995) found that integrity and personality tests that appeared easy to fake created perceptions of unfairness in job applicants. Honesty tests, a type of integrity test, were seen as one of the most unfavorable selection procedures across cultures (Steiner & Gilliland, 2001). Interestingly, although students in Ryan and Sackett's (1987) study were able to improve their scores on an integrity test when instructed to try to do so, they also judged the test to be appropriate for use. Faking on a biodata inventory, which is seen as easier than a faking on a cognitive ability test (Kluger & Rothstein, 1993), can be decreased by requiring that respondents elaborate on their answers (Schmitt & Kunce, 2002). For a discussion of the complicated morass of faking and perceived socially desirable responding, see Levin and Zickar (2002). In sum, although more research is needed on how perceived opportunities for faking and socially desirable responding relate to fairness perceptions (Ryan & Ployhart, 2000; Rynes, 1993), it appears that easy to fake procedures are perceived to be unfair.

Reconsideration Opportunity. It is unclear whether a second chance on a similar test after falling below an organization's cutoff point leads to higher perceptions of justice. Although Arvey and Sackett (1993) and Gilliland (1993) argued that reconsideration opportunity is likely to be important for justice perceptions, the empirical results are inconclusive. In a police officer selection context, Truxillo, Bauer, and Sanchez (2001) found that reconsideration opportunity was

related to fairness perceptions for a multiple choice test, but not when applicants underwent a video-based test in which their oral answers were scored by a team of experts.

Widespread Use. Researchers have found that use of highly unusual procedures (e.g., graphology) is perceived negatively. Ployhart, Erhart, and Hayes (2001) found that perceptions of wide use of procedures were related to fairness perceptions in both a lab study and a field study. Similarly, Steiner and Gilliland (1996) found that a selection procedure's perceived ubiquity correlated with favorable reactions to it. This effect was found to be stronger with a U.S. student sample than a French student sample. It is important to note that cultural differences might lead to one procedure being perceived as normal in some cultures but unusual in others (Steiner & Gilliland, 2001). The effects of new technologies on recruitment and selection await study, as they have since Schmitt and Gilliland (1992) drew attention to them a decade ago. One of the reasons that the use of new technologies might be seen as unfair (Truxillo, Steiner, & Gilliland, 2001) is their perceived abnormality.

It is interesting to note that the procedural dimension widespread use has not been identified in other justice contexts. It is possible that rather than representing a justice dimension in itself, widespread use is related to fairness perceptions because it suggests consistency or some other justice principle. We believe that future research should examine the ways in which procedures may be seen as fair simply because they are common.

Distributive Justice

If applicants must undergo multiple selection procedures before hiring (e.g. tests, then interviews) and the field of candidates is narrowed along the way, then whether an applicant advances to the next hurdle or is dropped from the field is an outcome (Gilliland, 1993; cf. Cropanzano & Ambrose, 2001). A number of studies have demonstrated that performance on a selection test can influence perceptions of fairness (e.g., Truxillo, Steiner, & Gilliland, 2001). Consequently, distributive justice concerns can arise during the selection and screening stage.

Equity. Organizations that make their decisions using an equity principle are most likely to be seen as fair in most organizational contexts (Bierhof, Buck, & Klein, 1986; Deutsch, 1975). We expect this finding to generalize to the outcomes of screening and selection processes. That is, applicants are likely to view test results as fair if their outcome is consistent with self-perceived input, relative to comparison others. Chan and colleagues (1998) found that actual test performance was re-

lated to perceived test performance, which in turn predicted perceived job relatedness and fairness perceptions. Unfortunately, this study did not specifically examine equity perceptions. In many assessment situations, applicants are likely to have incomplete and/or inaccurate information of their own inputs (e.g., knowledge, skills, and abilities) and the inputs of others. As a result, equity perceptions may not reflect true equity-based evaluations. Further research should examine this proposition.

Need.   The distributive justice rule of need might also arise in test situations. For example, test score banding can be seen as decision procedure that follows a need-based principle. Banding is a method of acknowledging error of measurement and selecting from among similar scores to increase the hiring of minority applicants. Truxillo and Bauer (1999) found that applicants' race interacted with their beliefs that banding is associated with affirmative action; Blacks who perceived banding to be related to affirmative action saw the process as most fair. Truxillo and Bauer suggested that highlighting the psychometric justification for banding might improve the fairness perceptions of applicants who do not benefit from the practice.

Summary

By far, most research on applicants' perceptions of selection justice has addressed screening and selection processes. Considerable research has identified a number of dimensions of procedural justice that are salient in selection processes. However, even with this body of research, we see many unanswered questions. In particular, although research has considered the influence to test performance on perceptions of fairness, little research has considered test performance from an equity perspective.

DECISION MAKING AND COMMUNICATION

After selection personnel have gathered selection information from applicants, they must decide who to hire and communicate hiring outcomes to applicants. This final stage has been the focus of some justice research, particularly studies that examine informational justice dimensions.

Interpersonal Justice

Interpersonal Effectiveness.   Research suggests that organizations should treat applicants with empathy and respect when communicating job offers or rejections (Bies & Moag, 1986). This treatment entails

communicating thorough and specific information in an honest manner. Because these dimensions are primarily informational concerns, we discuss them in the following section.

Informational Justice

Timeliness. As with feedback during procedures, timely feedback after applicant complete procedures is important for their fairness perceptions. Rynes et al. (1991) found that feedback delays throughout the hiring process were judged very negatively. Similarly, Gilliland (1995) found that delays in feedback were a major cause of applicant perceptions of unfairness.

Selection Information. Ployhart, Ryan, and Bennett (1999), in two within-subjects scenario studies, found that the content of selection decision explanations affected perceptions of the fairness of procedures and perceptions of the hypothetical organization. Other researchers have found that thorough explanations are seen as fair (Singer, 1990). Similarly, Gilliland et al. (2001, study 2) found that thorough justifications (thought to reduce the ease of calling to mind more positive alternative outcomes) reduced unfairness perceptions and increased reapplication for a position. Horvath, Ryan, and Stierwalt (2000) found that reactions to tests showed complex interactions between types of explanation, fairness perceptions, and self-efficacy. It is also worth noting that Shaw, Wild, and Colquitt (2003) conducted a meta-analysis of the effects of explanations on justice perceptions in a variety of organizational contexts. The analysis revealed that although explanations were generally related to fairness perceptions and a variety of outcomes, explanations had less impact in selection contexts than in other settings.

Honesty. Based on the evidence presented in a study discussed by Bies and Moag (1986), we propose that misleading applicants into thinking that positions will be filled when they will not be filled are likely to lead to perceptions of unfairness. Similarly, we expect that when organizations rescind offers or intimate that offers are imminent and then fail to make them, candidates are likely to feel that they were treated unfairly. Substantive justifications (e.g., our hiring program was cut midway through the hiring process due to lack of funds) and apologies have been found to decrease perceptions of injustice (Bies & Shapiro, 1988).

Procedural Justice

Procedural dimensions are not applicable after selection procedures have ceased and therefore do not apply during the decision making and communication stage.

Distributive Justice

Gilliland (1993) explained how three rules of distributive justice—equity, equality, and need—are likely to be important to applicants' perceptions of justice. However, since Gilliland's article, researchers have largely ignored distributive fairness concerns and instead focused on interpersonal, informational, and procedural dimensions of applicant fairness. Studies that have considered outcome effects have shown that hiring decision have a main effect on fairness perceptions (e.g., Ployhart et al., 1999), but most studies have not considered the distributive justice that underlies this main effect. We echo other researchers' calls for more attention to the importance of outcomes and distributive rules on applicants' reactions (Ryan & Ployhart, 2000; Schmitt & Chan, 1997).

Equity. Gilliland (1993) suggested that equity would be important in a hiring situation through an evaluation of the extent to which the selection decision matched expectations for being hired. Consistent with this suggestion, Gilliland (1994) found that hiring expectations and selection decision interacted to determine fairness perceptions such that the outcome was viewed as most fair when individuals had high expectations of being selected and were actually selected, and the outcome was viewed as least fair when individuals had high expectations of being selected and were not actually selected.

Given a matching of expectations to determine equity, one relevant dimension from an equity perspective is the selection ratio. Presumably, applicants will have the highest expectation of being selected when most applicants are selected and lower expectations as the selection ratio decreases. Consequently, it should seem more equitable and fair to be rejected when few applicants are selected than when many are selected. Contrary to this hypothesis, Thorsteinson and Ryan (1997) did not find support for the influence of selection ratio on fairness perceptions in a lab simulation.

Equality. Equality of treatment is related to the procedural justice rule of nonbiased evaluation. However, when discussing equality in decision making and communication, we are not referring to an aspect of the process such as an equal amount of time to take a test, but rather to the feelings of equal treatment after an outcome. Singer (1990) found that both professionals and students rated avoidance of nepotism and equality of opportunity to be highly important determinants of perceived fairness. A disregard for an equality principle by favoring an applicant based on personal connections leads to negative fairness perceptions in many cultures (Steiner & Gilliland, 2001). Nonetheless, the effects of the salience of equality rules on perceptions of fairness have not been systematically examined by researchers.

Summary

Clearly, informational and distributive justice are salient concerns in the decision-making and communication stage of selection. However, more research needs to consider the precise nature of these concerns and the way in which they shape fairness perceptions. Further, researchers must examine the extent to which fairness perceptions are influenced and shaped over time. The selection process is dynamic; reactions at one stage can influence fairness perceptions at subsequent stages. We now discuss how applicants' justice perceptions might change over the course of the selection process.

JUSTICE OF THE DYNAMIC PROCESS

A reexamination of Table 14.1 in light of the preceding discussion demonstrates that different types of justice are salient at different stages in the selection process. During the recruiting and initial communication stage it appears that informational justice could be the primary concern. Then, during screening and selection many different principles of procedural justice are salient. Finally, during decision making and communication both informational and distributive justice principles are salient. Interpersonal justice is salient in all three stages. In spite of this overall pattern in the extant research, we know of no studies that examine how interpersonal, informational, procedural, and distributive justice reactions change over the course of the selection process, especially in terms of their relative influence on overall fairness perceptions. We believe this area is ripe for future research.

In addition to changes in the salience of different types of justice over the course of selection, it would be useful to examine how fairness perceptions at one stage influence perceptions at subsequent stages. As suggested earlier, fairness heuristic theory argues that earlier information is more important in forming fairness impressions of another individual (Lind, 2001). Does this foundational hypothesis of fairness heuristic theory hold in the selection context? As an alternative hypothesis, fairness theory (Folger & Cropanzano, 1998, 2001), might suggest that perceptions formed after the decision is communicated are most important because they will lead to the strongest counterfactual reasoning (i.e., interpreting and explaining negative results in light of what would, could, and should have happened).

More generally, researchers have not yet asked the question, "When is justice most important to job applicants?" Reviews that have examined consequences of applicants' justice perceptions have asked if justice is important (e.g., Truxillo, Steiner, & Gilliland, 2001), but not *when* it is most important. It is possible that justice concerns are most salient

when applicants are in the midst of the screening and selection process. After the decision has been made, the selection justice context ends and justice might become less important. If applicants are hired, then they become employees and their treatment during socialization and management processes is likely more critical than events that occurred during selection. If applicants are not hired, then in most cases their relationship with the organization ends. Do applicants invest energy in justice evaluations at that point, or do they move on to other selection situations with different companies? Although it might appear simplistic, asking the question "When is justice most important?" could open new paths for justice researchers to explore.

A natural extension of the timing question is to ask, "To whom is selection justice most important?" Our discussion to this point has focused on justice from an applicant's perspective. We now turn our attention to coworkers as another stakeholder in the selection process.

COWORKERS' PERCEPTIONS OF JUSTICE IN EMPLOYEE SELECTION

Stakeholders are groups of people substantially affected by an organization. Several stakeholders are affected by an organization's selection process, including applicants, managers, coworkers, and customers (Gilliland & Cherry, 2000). Ryan and Ployhart (2000) suggested that the reactions of multiple stakeholders could influence organizational outcomes related to the selection process (p. 600). It is possible to consider many different stakeholders of the selection process. However, next to applicants, employees are probably the most important stakeholder group to consider from an organizational justice perspective.

Traditionally, organizational justice research has focused on employees' justice perceptions. However, in certain situations researchers have created employee subcategories within the general employee stakeholder group. For example, in the layoff literature, Brockner and others (e.g., Brockner, Grover, Reed, DeWitt, & O'Malley, 1987; Konovsky & Brockner, 1993) distinguished between survivor and victim reactions to layoffs. This research demonstrated that both groups respond to procedural and informational justice in the layoff process. Although their employment status is not directly impacted by layoff decisions, survivors are emotionally impacted by the layoff (e.g., through increased job insecurity) and could see their work situation change as a result of the layoff (e.g., increased job duties).

Similar to layoff survivors, employees are directly and indirectly influenced by selection decisions and therefore have reason to be concerned with the selection process. Most directly, employees might work with hired applicants, and therefore experience the results of the selec-

tion decision firsthand. Thus, the distributive justice of the hiring decision could be a relevant concern for employees. Because of their stake in the hiring decision, employees might also feel a need to take part in the hiring process. Their involvement in this process (or lack thereof) can lead to perceptions of interpersonal, informational, and procedural justice. In this section we speculate on the salience of the different types of justice for employees. Table 14.2 summarizes these proposed dimensions of justice.

Procedural Justice

Organizational justice researchers have long demonstrated that input or voice is a critical dimension of procedural justice (Thibaut & Walker, 1975). In a performance appraisal context, research demonstrated that both instrumental voice (i.e., input that has direct or indirect influence on a decision outcome) and noninstrumental voice (i.e., the ability to express an opinion regardless of the impact on the ultimate decision) are related to satisfaction with the performance appraisal (Korsgaard & Roberson, 1995). Similarly, we would expect employees to want a voice in the hiring of coworkers. This opportunity for voice serves a functional role for employees and demonstrates that they are valued and respected members of the organization.

It is important to note that even noninstrumental voice must be heard in a timely and appropriate manner. We recently witnessed dissatisfaction and anger among a group of coworkers who were asked to interview applicants but were not asked for their input based on these interviews prior to the hiring decision. In this case, voice that was

TABLE 14.2
Salient Selection Justice Dimensions for Employees

Justice type	Salient justice dimensions

Procedural	• Voice (instrumental and non-instrumental)
	• Instrumental influences of:
	  —Job relatedness
	  —Consistency
	  —Ease of faking

Informational	• Timely information • Accurate information • Explanation for decisions
Interpersonal	• Respectful treatment
Distributive	• Equity in hiring decision

never heard was much more destructive than if involvement had never been solicited.

We would expect that the perceived need for voice would be greater when there is more interaction and interdependence among coworkers. For example, in a team work environment, coworkers have a significant interest in the selection of new members of their team and would likely perceive considerable injustice if they did not have a voice in this selection process. It would be interesting to compare the importance of voice (both instrumental and noninstrumental) for coworkers in a team environment with employees who do not work in teams.

It is less clear how other dimensions of procedural justice might influence employees' reactions to selection decisions. It is possible that job relatedness, ease of faking, and consistency in selection procedures are salient concerns in that all are procedural dimensions that could affect the quality of the hiring decision. That is, job relatedness and other dimensions of procedural justice are valued for their instrumental function in the selection of applicants who are most likely to be high-quality employees. If instrumentality is a causal antecedent of justice concerns, then it should be possible to demonstrate that the impact of these dimensions of procedural justice on overall fairness reactions is mediated by perceived distributive justice.

Informational Justice

To the extent that employees view themselves as stakeholders in selection decisions, they are likely to want timely and accurate information on the status of the selection process. Violations of these justice dimensions (their absence) are likely to be more salient to employees than the presence of these dimensions. That is, employees will complain when they are not "kept in the loop" in a hiring decision, but might not praise the organization for keeping them informed. Being kept in the loop might be the expectation.

Another dimension of informational justice is the explanation or justification that is offered for the hiring decision. Employees are likely to view a decision with a greater sense of fairness if they understand the factors that went into the decision. Just as explanations are important for employees in layoff contexts (Konovsky & Brockner, 1993), we expect that explanations are important for employees in hiring contexts.

Interpersonal Justice

Bies and Moag (1986) demonstrated that recruits are particularly sensitive to being treated with respect in the recruiting process. We believe the same need for respectful treatment can be found in employees in-

volved in the hiring process. Interpersonal justice associated with respectful treatment might mediate the influence of noninstrumental voice on fairness perceptions. That is, employees might value voice in the hiring process, in part, because it demonstrates that the organization respects their opinions.

Distributive Justice

From a distributive justice perspective, employees are likely to seek equity in the hiring decision. That is, the hiring decision should be reflect applicants that are most qualified for the position. To the extent that employees believe the hired applicant was not the best candidate, they will view the hiring decision as inappropriate and unfair. As suggested with regard to voice in the selection process, concerns for equity and distributive justice are likely to be most salient in work environments with high levels of employee interdependence. When employees have the most to gain or lose through a successful or unsuccessful hire, they are likely to be most concerned about distributive justice.

Summary

In this section we have argued that employees' perceptions of fairness associated with selection are an important and overlooked aspect of the selection process. We identified procedural, informational, interpersonal, and distributive dimensions of justice that are likely to be salient for employees. Clearly, all of these proposed justice dimensions need to be examined empirically. We also suggested that some dimensions of procedural justice are valued for instrumental and noninstrumental reasons. It is possible that all dimensions of selection justice for employees can be categorized into instrumental issues, for which an accurate decision (distributive justice) is the central focus, and noninstrumental issues, for which respectful treatment is the central focus. It might also be the case that employees care about justice in the selection decision because justice is valued in itself (Folger, 2001; Turillo, Folger, Lavelle, Umphress, & Gee, 2002). Researchers should develop and test a model in which distributive justice and interpersonal justice mediate the instrumental and noninstrumental influences of procedural and informational justice on employees' reactions to hiring decisions.

CONCLUSION

It has been more than 10 years since Gilliland (1993) proposed an organizational justice model of applicant reactions to personnel selection. Since that article, many studies have examined how different dimen-

sions of organizational justice are influenced by various aspects of the selection process. Our review indicates that much of this attention has focused on the screening and selection processes and far less has been devoted to recruiting and decision making. We believe that these stages are important components of the selection process that would benefit from additional attention from organizational justice researchers. We also note that more research should consider the dynamic nature of applicants' fairness perceptions. Some research has examined the extent to which the hiring decision changes perceptions of the hiring process, but it would be useful to consider a broader set of justice dimensions that might alter justice perceptions over time.

Gilliland (1993) argued that organizational justice constructs apply not only to organization members but also to job applicants. Research has supported this extension of organizational justice. We now draw attention to the fact the applicants are not the only relevant stakeholders in selection decisions. In this chapter we have suggested a number of ways in which employees might perceive organizational justice in selection decisions. We believe that examination of employees' perceptions of selection fairness will provide new insights and inform selection practices.

REFERENCES

Anderson, N., Born, M., & Cunningham-Snell, N. (2001). Recruitment and selection: Applicant perspectives and outcomes. In N. Anderson, D. S. Ones, H. K. Sinangil, & C. Viswesvaran (Eds.), *Handbook of industrial, work and organizational psychology* (Vol. 1, pp. 200–217). Thousand Oaks, CA: Sage.

Arvey, R. D., & Sackett, P. R. (1993). Fairness in selection: Current developments and perspectives. In N. Schmitt & W. C. Barman & Associates (Eds.), *Personnel selection in organizations* (pp. 171–202). San Francisco, CA: Jossey-Bass.

Barber, A. E. (1998). *Recruiting employees*. Thousand Oaks, CA: Sage.

Bauer, T. N., Maertz, C. P., Jr., Dolen, M. R., & Campion, M. A. (1998). Longitudinal assessment of applicant reactions to employment testing and test outcome feedback. *Journal of Applied Psychology, 83*, 892–903.

Bauer, T. N., Truxillo, D. M., Sanchez, R. J., Craig, J., Ferrara, P., & Campion, M. A. (2001). Applicant reactions to selection: Development of the selection procedural justice scale (SPJS). *Personnel Psychology, 54*, 387–419.

Bierhoff, H. W., Buck, E., & Klein, R. (1986). Social context and perceived justice. In H. W. Bierhoff, R. L. Cohen, & J. Greenberg (Eds.), *Justice in social relations* (pp. 165–186). New York: Plenum Press.

Bies, R. J., & Moag, J. S. (1986). Interactional justice: Communication criteria for fairness. In B. Sheppard (Ed.), *Research on negotiation in organizations* (Vol. 1, pp. 43–55). Greenwich, CT: JAI.

Bies, R. J., & Shapiro, D. L. (1988). Voice and justification: Their influence on procedural fairness judgments. *Academy of Management Journal, 31*, 676–685.

Breaugh, J., & Starke, M. (2000). Research on employee recruitment: So many studies so many remaining questions. *Journal of Management, 26*, 405–434.

Brockner, J., Grover, S., Reed, T., DeWitt, R., & O'Malley, M. (1987). Survivors' reactions to layoffs: We get by with a little help for our friends. *Administrative Science Quarterly, 32,* 526–541.

Chan, D., Schmitt, N., Jennings, D., Clause, C. S., & Delbridge, K. (1998). Applicant perceptions of test fairness: integrating justice and self-serving bias perspectives. *International Journal of Selection and Assessment, 6,* 232–239.

Colquitt, J. A., Conlon, D. E., Wesson, M. J., Porter, C. O. L. H., & Ng, K. Y. (2001). Justice at the millennium: A meta-analytic review of 25 years of organizational justice research. *Journal of Applied Psychology, 86,* 425–445.

Cropanzano, R., & Ambrose, M. L. (2001). Procedural and distributive justice are more similar than you think: A monistic perspective and a research agenda. In J. Greenberg & R. Cropanzano (Eds.), *Advances in organizational justice* (pp. 119–151). Stanford, CA: Stanford University Press.

Cropanzano, R., & Konovsky, M. A. (1995). Resolving the justice dilemma by improving the outcomes: The case of employee drug screening. *Journal of Business and Psychology, 10,* 221–243.

Cropanzano, R., & Wright, T. A. (2003). Procedural justice and organizational staffing: A tale of two paradigms. *Human Resource Management Review 13,* 7–39.

Cunningham-Snell, N., Anderson, N., & Fletcher, C. (1999, June). *A longitudinal analysis of procedural justice at an assessment centre: The immediate, intermediate and long-term impact.* Paper presented at the International Round Table on Innovations in Organizational Justice, Nice, France.

Deutsch, M. (1975). Equity, equality, and need: What determines which value will be used as the basis of distributive justice? *Journal of Social Issues, 31,* 137–149.

Folger, R. (2001). Fairness as deonance. In S. Gilliland, K. Steiner, & D. Skarlicki (Eds.), *Theoretical and cultural perspectives on organizational justice* (pp. 3–33). Greenwich, CT: Information Age.

Folger, R., & Cropanzano, R. (1998). *Organizational justice and human resource management.* Thousand Oaks, CA: Sage.

Folger, R., & Cropanzano, R. (2001). Fairness theory: Justice as accountability. In J. Greenberg & R. Cropanzano (Eds.), *Advances in organizational justice* (pp. 1–55). Stanford, CA: Stanford University Press.

Gatewood, R. D., & Field, H. S. (1998). *Human resource selection* (4th ed.). Fort Worth, TX: Harcourt Brace.

Gilliland, S. W. (1993). The perceived fairness of selection systems: An organizational justice perspective. *Academy of Management Review, 18,* 694–734.

Gilliland, S. W. (1994). Effects of procedural and distributive justice on reactions to a selection system. *Journal of Applied Psychology, 79,* 691–701.

Gilliland, S. W. (1995). Fairness from the applicant's perspective: Reactions to employee selection procedures. *International Journal of Selection and Assessment, 3,* 11–19.

Gilliland, S. W., & Cherry, B. (2000). Managing "customers" of selection processes. In J. F. Kehoe (Ed.), *Managing selection in organizations* (pp. 158–196). San Francisco, CA: Jossey-Bass.

Gilliland, S. W. & Steiner, D. D. (2001). Causes and consequences of applicant fairness. In R. Cropanzano (Ed.), *Justice in the workplace* (Vol. 2, pp. 175–195). Mahwah, NJ: Lawrence Erlbaum Associates.

Gilliland, S. W., Groth, M., Baker, B., Dew, A. F., Polly, L., & Langdon, J. (2001). Improving applicants' reactions to rejection letters: An application of fairness theory. *Personnel Psychology, 54,* 669–703.

Greenberg, J. (1990). Employee thefts as a reaction to underpayment inequity: The hidden cost of pay cuts. *Journal of Applied Psychology, 75,* 561–568.

Greenberg, J. (1993). Stealing in the name of justice: Informational and interpersonal moderators of theft reactions to underpayment inequity. *Organizational Behavior and Human Decision Processes, 54,* 81–103.

Heneman, H. G., III Judge, T. A., & Heneman, R. L. (2000). *Staffing organizations.* Middleton, WI: Irwin McGraw-Hill.

Horvath, M., Ryan, A. M., & Stierwalt, S. L. (2000). The influence of explanations for selection test use, outcome favorability, and self-efficacy on test-taker perceptions. *Organizational Behavior and Human Decision Processes, 83,* 310–330.

Kluger, A. N., & Rothstein, H. R. (1993). The influence of selection test type on applicant reactions to employment testing. *Journal of Business and Psychology, 8,* 3–25.

Kohn, L. S., & Dipboye, R. L. (1998). The effects of interview structure on recruiting outcomes. *Journal of Applied Social Psychology, 28,* 821–843.

Konovsky, M. A., & Brockner, J. (1993). Managing victim and survivor layoff reactions: A procedural justice perspective. In R. Cropanzano (Ed.), *Justice in the workplace: Approaching fairness in human resource management* (pp. 133–153). Hillsdale, NJ: Lawrence Erlbaum Associates.

Korsgaard, M. A., & Roberson, L. (1995). Procedural justice in performance evaluation: The role of instrumental and non-instrumental voice in performance appraisal discussions. *Journal of Management, 21,* 657–669.

Kravitz, D. A., Stinson, V., & Chavez, T. L. (1996). Evaluations of tests used for making selection and promotion decisions. *International Journal of Selection and Assessment, 4,* 24–34.

Levin, R. A., & Zickar, M. J. (2002). Investigating self-presentation, lies, and bullshit: Understanding faking and its effects on selection decisions using theory, field research and simulation. In C. L. Hulin, J. M. Brett, & F. Drasgow (Eds.), *The psychology of work: Theoretically based empirical research* (pp. 253–276). Mahwah, NJ: Lawrence Erlbaum Associates.

Lind, E. A. (2001). Fairness heuristic theory: Justice judgments as pivotal cognitions in organizational relations. In J. Greenberg & R. Cropanzano (Eds.), *Advances in organizational justice* (pp. 56–88). Stanford, CA: Stanford University Press.

Lind, E. A., & Tyler, T. R. (1988). *The social psychology of procedural justice.* New York: Plenum Press.

Macan, T. H., Avedon, M. J., Paese, M., & Smith, D. E. (1994). The effects of applicants' reactions to cognitive ability tests and an assessment center. *Personnel Psychology, 47,* 715–738.

Murphy, K. R., Thornton, G. C., & Reynolds, D. H. (1990). College students' attitudes toward employee drug testing programs. *Personnel Psychology, 43,* 615–631.

Ployhart, R. E., Ehrhart, K. H., & Hayes, S. C. (2001, April). *Using attributions to understand the effects of explanation on applicant reactions: Are reactions consistent with the covariation principle?* Paper presented at the annual meeting of the Society for Industrial and Organizational Psychology, San Diego, CA.

Ployhart, R. E., McFarland, L. A., & Ryan, A. M. (2002). Examining applicants' attributions for withdrawal from a selection procedure. *Journal of Applied Social Psychology, 32,* 2228–2252.

Ployhart, R. E., & Ryan, A. M. (1998). Applicants' reactions to the fairness of selection procedures: The effects of positive rule violation and time of measurement. *Journal of Applied Psychology, 83,* 3–16.

Ployhart, R. E., Ryan, A. M., & Bennett, M. (1999). Explanations for selection decisions: Applicants' reactions to information and sensitivity features of explanations. *Journal of Applied Psychology, 84*, 87–106.

Rosse, J. G., Miller, J. L., & Stecher, M. D. (1994). A field study of job applicants' reactions to personality and cognitive ability testing. *Journal of Applied Psychology, 79*, 987–992.

Ryan, A. M., & Chan, D. (1999). Perceptions of the EPPP: How do licensure candidates view the process? *Professional Psychology, 30*, 519–530.

Ryan, A. M., Greguras, G. J., & Ployhart, R. E. (1996). Perceived job relatedness of physical ability testing for firefighters: Exploring variations in reactions. *Human Performance, 9*, 219–240.

Ryan, A. M., & Ployhart, R. E. (2000). Applicants' perceptions of selection procedures and decisions: A critical review and agenda for the future. *Journal of Management, 26*, 565–606.

Ryan, A. M., Sacco, J. M., McFarland, L. A., & Kriska, S. D. (2000). Applicant self-selection: Correlates of withdrawal from a multiple hurdle process. *Journal of Applied Psychology, 85*, 163–179.

Ryan, A. M., & Sackett, P. R. (1987). Pre-employment honesty testing: Fakeability, reactions of test takers, and company image. *Journal of Business and Psychology, 1*, 248–256.

Rynes, S. L. (1993). Who's selecting whom? Effects of selection practices on applicant attitudes and behavior. In N. Schmitt & W. C. Borman (Eds.), *Personnel selection in organizations* (pp. 240–274). San Francisco: Jossey-Bass.

Rynes, S. L., Bretz, R. D., & Gerhart, B. (1991). The importance of recruitment on job choice: A different way of looking. *Personnel Psychology, 33*, 529–542.

Saks, A. M., Leck, J. D., & Saunders, D. M. (1995). Effects of application blanks and employment equity on applicant reactions and job pursuit intentions. *Journal of Organizational Behavior, 16*, 415–430.

Scheu, C., Ryan, A. M., & Nona, F. (1999, April). *Company web-sites as a recruiting mechanism: What influences applicant impressions?* Paper presented at the 14th Annual Conference for the Society of Industrial and Organizational Psychology, Atlanta, GA.

Schmitt, N., & Chan, D. (1997). *Personnel selection: A theoretical approach.* Thousand Oaks, CA: Sage.

Schmitt, N., & Gilliland, S. W. (1992). Beyond differential prediction: Fairness in selection. In D. M. Saunders (Ed.), *New approaches to employee management: Fairness in employee selection* (Vol. 1, pp. 21–46). Greenwich, CT: JAI.

Schmitt, N., & Kunce, C. (2002). *The effects of required elaboration of answers to biodata questions.* Unpublished manuscript, Michigan State University.

Shaw, J. C., Wild, E., & Colquitt, J. A. (2003). To justify or excuse? A meta-analytic review of the effects of explanations. *Journal of Applied Psychology, 88*, 444–458.

Singer, M. (1990). Determinants of perceived fairness in selection practices: An organizational justice perspective. *Genetic, Social and General Psychology Monographs, 116*, 477–494.

Skarlicki, D. P., & Folger, R. (1997). Retaliation in the workplace: The roles of distributive, procedural, and interactional justice. *Journal of Applied Psychology, 82*, 434–443.

Smither, J. W., Reilly, R. R., Millsap, R. E., Pearlman, K., & Stoffey, R. W. (1993). Applicant reactions to selection procedures. *Personnel Psychology, 46*, 49–77.

Steiner, D., & Gilliland, S. W. (1996). Fairness reactions to personnel selection techniques in France and the United States. *Journal of Applied Psychology, 81*, 134–141.

Steiner, D. D., & Gilliland, S. W. (2001). Procedural justice in personnel selection: International and cross-cultural perspectives. *International Journal of Selection and Assessment, 9*(1–2), 124–137.

Stone, D. L., Stone-Romero, E. F., & Hyatt, D. E. (1994, April). *Some potential determinants of individuals' reactions to personnel selection procedures.* Paper presented at the Meeting of the Society for Industrial and Organizational Psychology, Nashville, TN.

Sullivan, J. (1998, December). How to hire the next Michael Jordon. *Fast Company,* pp. 212–219.

Taylor, M. S., & Bergmann, T. J. (1987). Organizational recruitment activities and applicants' reactions at different stages of the recruitment process. *Personnel Psychology, 40,* 261–285.

Thibaut, J., & Walker, L. (1975). *Procedural justice: A psychological analysis.* Hillsdale, NJ: Lawrence Erlbaum Associates.

Thorsteinson, T. J., & Ryan, A. M. (1997). The effect of selection ratio on perceptions of the fairness of a selection test battery. *International Journal of Selection and Assessment, 5,* 159–168.

Truxillo, D. M., & Bauer, T. N. (1999). Applicant reactions to test score banding in entry-level and promotional contexts. *Journal of Applied Psychology, 84,* 322–339.

Truxillo, D. M., Bauer, T. N., Campion, M. A., & Paronto, M. E. (2002). Selection fairness information and applicant reactions: A longitudinal field study. *Journal of Applied Psychology, 87,* 1020–1031.

Truxillo, D. M., Bauer, T. N., & Sanchez, R. J. (2001). Multiple dimensions of procedural justice: Longitudinal effects on selection system fairness and test-taking self-efficacy. *International Journal of Selection and Assessment, 9,* 330–349.

Truxillo, D. M., Steiner, D. D., & Gilliland, S. W. (2001, June). *A critical examination of selection justice: Does it really matter?* Paper presented at the 2nd International Round Table on Innovations in Organizational Justice, Vancouver, Canada.

Turillo, C. J., Folger, R., Lavelle, J. J., Umphress, E. E., & Gee, J. O. (2002). Is virtue its own reward? Self-sacrificial decisions for the sake of fairness. *Organizational Behavior and Human Decision Processes, 89,* 839–865.

Tyler, T. R., & Lind, E. A. (1992). A relational model of authority in groups. In M. P. Zanna (Ed.), *Advances in experimental social psychology* (Vol. 25, pp. 115–191). San Diego, CA: Academic.

Van den Bos, K., Vermunt, R., & Wilke, H. A. M. (1997). Procedural and distributive justice: What is fair depends more on what comes first than on what comes next. *Journal of Personality and Social Psychology, 72,* 95–104.

Werbel, J. D., & Gilliland, S. W. (1999). Person–environment fit in the selection process. In G. Ferris (Ed.), *Research in personnel and human resources management* (Vol. 17, pp. 209–243). Greenwich, CT: JAI.

15

How Do Organizational Justice Concepts
Relate to Discrimination and Prejudice?

Eugene F. Stone-Romero
University of Central Florida

Dianna L. Stone
University of Central Florida

Research shows a long history of injustice toward members of various out-groups in the United States (e.g., African Americans, American Indians, Jews, individuals with disabilities, unattractive individuals). In addition, there is abundant evidence of unfairness in the treatment of members of many out-groups in organizations in the United States. To explain these problems, we present a group-based differential justice model (GBDJM) that is based on social-psychological theories having to do with justice and social identity. It links the in-group versus out-group status of individuals to a number of outcomes, including differential levels of distributive, procedural, and interactional justice accorded to members of in-groups and out-groups. In addition to presenting the GBDJM and supporting research, we suggest strategies for reducing the unjust treatment of out-group members and the plethora of problems caused by such treatment.

In an 1833 address to the Congress of the United States, President Andrew Jackson stated that "[Cherokee Indians] have neither the intelligence, the industry, the moral habits, nor the desire for improvement which are essential to any favorable change in their condition. Established in the midst of another and a superior race, and without appreciating the causes of their inferiority or seeking to control them, they must necessarily yield to the force of circumstances and ere long disappear" (Jackson, 1833/2004). In an 1861 speech, President Andrew Johnson said, "We hold that it is upon the intelligent free white people of the country that all Government should rest, and by them all government should be controlled" (Johnson, 1861/2000). And in a 1911 letter to his future wife, President Harry S. Truman wrote: "I think one man is just as good as another as long as he's honest and decent and not a nigger or a Chinaman.... I am strongly of the opinion that negros [sic] ought to be in Africa, yellow men in Asia and white men in Europe and America" (Truman, 1911/1991). Regrettably, the sentiments conveyed by the pronouncements of these presidents of the United States are still shared by many people in the nation. In addition, they appear to be quite consistent with what Myrdal (1944) considered to be "the great American dilemma," that is, the general endorsement of democratic values by Whites in the United States, juxtaposed against the widespread belief in and practice of racial discrimination by them.

Unfortunately, the practice of unfair discrimination is still widespread in the United States. Moreover, unfair discrimination extends to large numbers of individuals who are members of various social out-

groups (Allport, 1954; Ashmore & DelBoca, 1976; Deutscher, 1966, 1973; Dovidio & Gaertner, 1986; Myrdal, 1944; Stone, Stone, & Dipboye, 1992). More specifically, it is practiced against individuals who are stigmatized or marked by virtue of their status on such variables as age, physical attractiveness, physical ability, race, sexual orientation, religious beliefs, mental illness, nationality, and socioeconomic status (Goffman, 1963; Herman, Zanna, & Higgins, 1986; Jones, Farina, Hastorf, Markus, Miller, & Scott, 1984; Katz, 1981; Stone & Colella, 1996; Stone et al., 1992; Stone-Romero, 2004).

INTRODUCTION

Notes on Terminology

We generally refer to unfair discrimination against others as *bias* in the treatment of out-group members (i.e., members of social groups other than one's own group) by in-group members (i.e., members of one's own group who have a sense of solidarity and a set of common interests vis-à-vis members of other groups). Bias is present under several conditions, two of which are of central importance to the purposes of this chapter. First, bias exists when individuals are treated in a *prejudicial* manner—that is, when their treatment is based on inaccurate data regarding their characteristics. This occurs, for example, when their treatment is based on stereotypes (e.g., group-based) that are applied to them, rather than on valid information about their characteristics. Second, bias is a problem when individuals are the targets of *unfair discrimination*—that is, when decisions about them (e.g., hiring, promotion) are based on factors that are unrelated or poorly related to the criteria of interest (e.g., job aptitude, job performance). This occurs, for instance, when hiring decisions for managerial jobs are based on the race, sex, or physical attractiveness of applicants, rather than their ability to do managerial work.

Note also that in this chapter, we define *in-group members* as male, White, Anglo-Saxon Protestants (MWASPs). Compared to non-MWASPs, MWASPs are generally the dominant group in many organizations in the United States. Relative to many other groups, they typically hold most positions of power, both within and outside of organizations (Kerbo, 1983). In addition, they tend to be of higher socioeconomic status than members of many other out-groups (Kerbo, 1983). Thus, MWASPs generally determine how resources of various types (e.g., jobs, educational opportunities, pay levels, access to medical treatment) are allocated to others in various contexts (e.g., educational institutions, work organizations). Moreover, they set up legislation, policies, and procedures that serve to protect or en-

hance their power, ensuring that they will have the ongoing ability to maximize their own outcomes in the same contexts (Kerbo, 1983). For example,
in the political arena, U.S. White males denied voting rights to Blacks and
women for several centuries. In addition, in work organizations,
MWASPS typically have the capacity to dictate both the types and levels of
criteria used in assessing performance.

Finally, note that hereinafter we refer to the individual who has control over the allocation of outcomes and/or the promulgation of allocation procedures as the *allocator* or *allocation agent*. In addition, we refer
to the individual who is the object of allocations (i.e., the recipient) as
the *target*.

Discrimination and Prejudice in the United States

Targets of Injustice.   Members of numerous social groups have been
the targets of biased treatment by MWASPs in the United States. Most
notable perhaps are members of various race-, sex-, and ethnicity-based
minority groups (e.g., African Americans, Asian Americans, Native
Americans or American Indians, Jews, women; see, for example,
Crosby, Bromley, & Saxe, 1980; Dovidio, & Gaertner, 1986; Harding,
Proshansky, Kutner, & Chein, 1969; Heller, 1987; Katz, 1981; Katz &
Braly, 1933; Kerbo, 1983; Kinder, 1986; Myrdal, 1944; Plous & Williams,
1995; Stone et al., 1992; Wilson, 1973). However, as we noted, members
of numerous other social groups and categories also have experienced
biased treatment by MWASPs.

Nature of Bias.   There is a long and clear history of overt discrimination and prejudice in the United States. Among the numerous examples of this are (a) the enslavement of African Americans and Native
Americans by Whites (Acrey, 1992; Lomawaima, 1994; Macleod, 1928;
Parish, 1990; Sando, 1992), (b) the segregation of schools and residential
areas (e.g., McEneaney, 1996; U.S. Commission on Civil Rights, 1979),
(c) the ongoing practice of such environmental racist practices as locat-
ing toxic waste storage or dump sites near minority communities (e.g.,
Weaver, 1996; Westra & Wenz, 1995), (d) the denial of voting rights and
reproductive rights to women (e.g., Dusky, 1996; Hull, 2001), and (e) the
marginalization, imprisonment, institutionalization, lynching, and
genocide of members of out-groups who were perceived to represent a
threat to the supremacy of MWASPs (e.g., Acrey, 1992; Blalock, 1967;
Brown, 1970; Churchill, 1997; Heller, 1987; Lomawaima, 1994; Perry,
1991; Sniderman & Hagen, 1985; Wilson, 1973), and the involuntary
sterilization of Native American women (e.g., Churchill, 1997; Hoxie,
1996; Reilly, 1991).

Expression of Bias. For decades, MWASPs were open in expressing their negative views of members of various out-groups. For example, until the mid 1960s it was common to hear Whites use such highly offensive epithets as "nigger," "chink," "gook," "kike," and "redskin" to describe members of several minority groups. Today, however, bias against out-group members typically works through more indirect means, one of which is modern or symbolic racism (Crosby et al., 1980; Deutscher, 1966, 1973; Kinder, 1986; Kinder & Sears, 1981; McConahay & Hough, 1976). Rather then expressing overt dislike and hostility toward various minorities, MWASPs rationalize their treatment of such individuals by appealing to "traditional American values," such as achievement, freedom, individualism, competition, and, most notably, *fairness* (Kinder, 1986). Moreover, the same values also are used to justify the biased treatment of members of various out-groups (e.g., women, people with disabilities, homosexuals).

Treatment Implications of Bias

Bias has clear implications for the way that out-group members are treated in various settings. In the interest of brevity, in the paragraphs that follow, we generally limit our discussion to issues that arise in work organizations. In this setting, bias takes on two basic forms, access discrimination and treatment discrimination.

Access Discrimination. Individuals suffer *access discrimination* when they are denied access to jobs. For instance, for many decades it was a common practice not to hire (or even to consider seriously the hiring of) members of many minority groups. This was especially true for managerial and professional jobs (e.g., Kanter, 1977; Kelley & Streeter, 1992). Until the mid 1960s, want ads specified the desired skin color and sex of applicants, and job postings on windows of businesses clearly indicated the type of people who should and should not apply for openings.

Treatment Discrimination. Employees experience *treatment discrimination* when, as result of their belonging to an out-group, they are provided with lower levels of various outcomes (e.g., mentoring, pay) or opportunities (e.g., promotion, training) than in-group members (Kelley & Streeter, 1992; Stone & Colella, 1996; Stone et al., 1992).

Justice Implications

Both of the forms of bias just described may lead to the perception of unfair treatment on the part of the target. Interestingly, however, the allocator may see no problem whatsoever with either the allocation or the

procedures used in determining allocation levels. In fact, for reasons that are detailed later, the allocator will generally have a well-conceived rationale for the allocation of outcomes to others, the procedures used in the allocation process, and the interpersonal treatment accorded to others (Kerbo, 1983).

Purpose of this Chapter

Surprisingly, the literature on social justice in organizations has not made a clear connection between bias against out-group members and various forms of justice (e.g., distributive, procedural, interactional). Therefore, the major purpose of this chapter is to provide a link between these concepts. Toward that end, in the paragraphs that follow we (a) provide a very brief review of several justice notions, (b) summarize major arguments associated with social identity theory, (c) present a model that describes the process through which out-group status leads to the biased treatment of out-group members in organizations, (d) consider research that is needed to test the model, and (e) offer several recommendations for reducing bias in the treatment of out-group members.

SOCIAL JUSTICE

A basic premise of this chapter is that MWASPs treat members of out-groups in a biased fashion. Their capacity to do so is a function of the fact that they are typically the individuals who (a) hold positions of power in organizations, (b) allocate outcomes (e.g., rewards, punishments) to others in organizations and other contexts (Kerbo, 1983; Leventhal, 1976a), and (c) establish the procedures used in allocating such outcomes.

Justice Types

The literature on organizational justice is concerned with three major types of justice: distributive, procedural, and interactional. *Distributive justice* has to do with the fairness of the outcomes allocated to individuals vis-à-vis their inputs or contributions (e.g., Adams, 1963, 1965; Homans, 1961; Leventhal, 1976a, 1980). *Procedural justice* is concerned with the fairness of the procedures used in allocating the outcomes (e.g., Leventhal, 1980; Folger & Greenberg, 1985; Lind & Tyler, 1988). *Interactional justice* deals with the fairness of interpersonal treatment accorded to targets by the allocator (e.g., Bies & Moag, 1986; Greenberg, 1993). In the interest of brevity, we do not offer detailed explanations of these three justice perspectives. Moreover, such explanations appear elsewhere in this book (e.g., chap. 1).

Major Premises of Organizational Justice

Among the major premises of this chapter are the following: (a) Relative to out-group members, allocators generally view in-group members as having greater inputs and as being more deserving of positive outcomes; (b) allocation procedures, including the setting of evaluation criteria, are generally established so as to favor in-group members; and (c) allocators provide more considerate interpersonal treatment to in-group members than to out-group members. In the next section we consider the social psychological underpinnings of these premises. Thereafter, we present a model (GBDJM) that specifies how distributive, procedural, and interactional justice are influenced by the group memberships of allocators and targets.

SOCIAL IDENTITY THEORY

There is clear evidence that in-group members have a propensity to treat out-group members in a biased fashion (Tajfel, 1981, 1982; Turner, 1982). *Social identity theory* (Tajfel, 1970, 1974, 1978, 1981, 1982; Tajfel & Turner, 1979; Turner, 1987) provides a compelling explanation of why in-group members behave in this manner. The theory is based on several core assumptions, one of which is that individuals have social identities that are based on the social groups (or categories) with which they identify and to which they belong or are viewed as belonging.

The Social Identity Notion

A person's *social identity* is a function of all of the social identifications that a person uses to define (identify, classify) himself or herself or that others use to define him or her. These identifications stem from a host of factors, including a person's genetic endowment, nationality, education, and socialization. They lead to identifications that are based on social groups defined in terms of such factors as ethnicity, sex, occupation, social class, religious beliefs, and age. Thus, for example, a person may define herself as a female, Native American physician who works for the welfare of members of her tribe, and subscribes to the traditional *Diné* (Navajo) values of *k'é* (kinship, love, kindness, generosity, and peacefulness) and *hózhó* (harmony, happiness, universal beauty) (Witherspoon, 1977).

Major Premises of Social Identity Theory

Some other important premises of social identity theory are as follows. First, it is assumed that individuals have a desire to maintain and en-

hance their self-esteem. Second, the groups to which individuals belong constitute an important basis for their self-definition. Third, membership in in-groups provides individuals with a basis for maintaining and/or enhancing their self-esteem. Fourth, individuals tend to view out-groups in ways that lead them to emphasize differences between their in-group(s) and various out-groups. Fifth, esteem is maintained and/or enhanced by viewing members of in-groups in a more positive manner than members of out-groups. Sixth, and finally, in many situations, social identities are a more important determinant of individuals' attitudes, beliefs, and actions than are their personal identities.

It deserves adding that the desire to maintain a positive social identity is considered to be a relatively widespread value (Tajfel, 1981, 1982; Wetherell, 1982). However, there are cultural differences in the way that such an identity is achieved (Markus & Kitayama, 1991; Wetherell, 1982). We comment on this issue later.

A GROUP-BASED DIFFERENTIAL JUSTICE MODEL

Figure 15.1 provides a model of the factors that lead to the biased treatment of members. Hereinafter we refer to this as the group-based differential justice model (GBDJM). It is grounded in the just-considered social-psychological theory and research.

The overall purpose of the GBDJM is to explain how group membership influences the distributive, procedural, and interpersonal justice that in-group members accord to members of in-groups and out-groups. We now describe the elements in the model and the linkages between them. In the process, we also show the relevance of social-psychological theory and research for explaining the treatment of out-group members by in-group members.

Recognition and Categorization of Target

Our GBDJM is concerned primarily with the way in which allocators behave in organizational contexts and the impact of this behavior on in-group versus out-group targets. Accordingly, our general focus in on the behavior of the allocator, as opposed to the target.

The process of dealing with a target begins with the allocator's identification of him or her. In work organizations the target typically is a job applicant or job incumbent. Having identified the target, the allocator then categorizes him or her on the basis of readily available information about one or more of his or her salient attributes ($A_1, A_2, A_3, \ldots, A_j$), including skin color, sex, body size, physical fitness, and accents. It deserves adding that the social categorization process results in the social world being divided into discontinuous classes ($C_1, C_2, C_3, \ldots, C_k$) or cat-

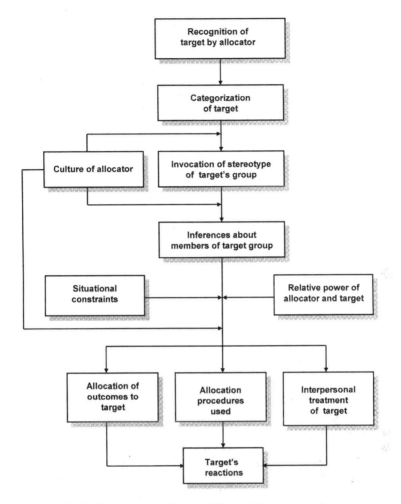

FIG. 15.1.   A group-based differential justice model.

egories (Tajfel, 1981, 1982). Thus, for example, an allocator may categorize a job applicant as being in the distinctive class of Black, female,
middle-class, middle-aged, certified public accountants.

There is considerable evidence that categorization takes place in social systems (Higgins & Bargh, 1987; Schneider, 1991; Tajfel, 1981, 1982;
Turner, 1982). A key reason for it is that "one of the major cognitive tasks
humans face [in life] is placing things, events, and people into categories" (Schneider, 1991, p. 533). In fact, the categorization of others is one
of the major means through which individuals are able to deal with the
complexity of the social milieus within which they find themselves
(Allport, 1954; Schneider, 1991).

Invocation of Stereotype

Categorization has both deductive and inductive aspects (Doise, 1978; Tajfel, 1959; Turner, 1982). The *inductive* aspect of categorization has to do with the assignment of a person to a given category. Thus, for example, on the basis of a target's standing on one or more attributes an allocator induces that the target is a member of a given social category.

Having categorized the target, the allocator then retrieves the relevant stereotype about him or her from memory (Hamilton, 1976, 1981a, 1981b). This is the *deductive* aspect of categorization. Thus, for example, having categorized a target as a member of a specific category (e.g., Mexican American), the individual then deduces the target's standing on such attributes as intelligence, trustworthiness, aggressiveness, and motivation to work (Doise, 1978; Tajfel, 1959; Turner, 1982).

The categorization process is fairly automatic and serves a number of functions for the allocator. For example, it minimizes the cognitive demands that he or she faces in dealing with various targets (Allport, 1954; Schneider, 1991).

It merits adding that work on social representation (e.g., Doise, 1978) has shown that stereotypes are influenced by group membership. *Social representations* are systems of beliefs that members of a group have about their own group and other groups. These representations vary as a function of such factors as the nature of relations between groups. In addition, they are developed and maintained in such a way as to protect and/or enhance the esteem of the in-group. Moreover, as a considerable amount of evidence from experimental research has shown, the mere act of categorizing individuals into groups (e.g., in-group vs. out-group) leads to bias against out-group members (Ng, 1982; Tajfel, 1970, 1978; Turner, 1982). For example, assuming that the in-group has power over the allocation of outcomes to in-group and out-group members, an out-group member will be allocated lower levels of desirable outcomes than an in-group member.

Another important consequence of the categorization of targets is the evocation of emotional reactions to them. In the case of many out-group members, these may be quite negative (Bodenhausen, 1993; Crosby et al., 1980; Goffman, 1963; Hosoda, Stone-Romero, & Stone, 1999, 2004; Stone & Colella, 1996; Stone et al., 1992). Moreover, the same reactions may serve to enhance the degree of bias shown toward out-group members.

Inferences About Group Members

As we noted, the category-based stereotype of the target serves as the basis for a set of deductively derived beliefs about his or her characteristics. Typically, these are based on beliefs about the characteristics of the prototype for the group to which the target is assumed to belong (e.g.,

Black, male, Vietnam war veteran). These stereotypical beliefs may involve such factors as the personality, abilities, aptitudes, motivation, and morality of the prototype for the group.

Research has shown that stereotypes of various out-groups often are quite negative (Herman et al., 1986; Katz, 1981; Katz & Braly, 1933; Plous & Williams, 1995; Stone-Romero, Stone, & Hartman, 2002). For example, Plous and Williams's (1995) survey of 1,490 Connecticut residents revealed that most respondents endorsed such views as "Whites have greater abstract thinking ability than Blacks" and "Blacks have thicker skulls than Whites." In addition, research by Stone-Romero et al. (2002) showed that relative to Anglo Americans, African Americans and Mexican Americans were perceived to have lower levels of cognitive ability, emotional adjustment, performance capability, social skills, integrity, status, leadership ability, and dependability.

Expectancies About Target. Not only does the allocator generate beliefs about the target's attributes, but he or she uses category membership as a basis for making inferences about the behaviors that are likely to be exhibited by the target (Rosenthal & Jacobson, 1968; Miller & Turnbull, 1986). More specifically, inferences that are generated about the typical member of the group serve as the basis for a host of *expectancies* about the target. These inferences are typically made on a *prospective* basis. For example, in advance of having information about the actual motivation of a job applicant, an MWASP interviewer may reason that job applicants who are members of various minority groups have neither the ability nor the motivation needed to succeed on jobs for which they have applied.

Attributions About Target. Not only do allocators make *prospective* inferences about a target on the basis of his or her category membership, but they use stereotypes as a basis for making *retrospective* inferences (i.e., attributions) about the reasons for the target's behavior (e.g., job performance, preemployment test performance). *Attributions* are inferences about the factors responsible for the target's behavior, and typically have to do with the locus of the behavior and its stability (Jones, Kanouse, Kelley, Valins, & Weiner, 1972; Kelley, 1967, 1972, 1973; Weiner, 1985a, 1985b, 1986).

With respect to *locus*, the attribution can be either internal or external to the person. In the case of internal or dispositional attributions, the inference is that the person is responsible for the observed behavior. In the case of external or situational attributions, factors in the person's environment are viewed as the cause of the behavior. With regard to *stability*, attributions can be to stable or unstable causes. Stable causes are those that are relatively invariant across time. In contrast, unstable causes are those that fluctuate from one period to the next.

Considering both of these dimensions simultaneously leads to four basic types of attributions about the target: ability (internal, stable), motivation (internal, unstable), task difficulty (external, stable), and luck or chance (external, unstable).

Attributions also are known to have an *egocentric bias*. More specifically, individuals have a tendency to infer that (a) they (as opposed to others) are the causes of events that result in positive outcomes, and (b) others (as opposed to themselves) are the causes of events that lead to negative outcomes (Kelley, 1973). In addition, attributions are influenced by group membership; that is, the attributions made by an observer are likely to vary as a function of the group to which the target belongs. More specifically, the same sorts of egocentric biases that affect individuals' attributions operate in instances of intergroup attributions (i.e., those involving group-based inferences about the causes of events; Hewstone & Jaspars, 1982). For example, research has shown that when the target is an in-group (as opposed to an out-group) member, the allocator is more likely to attribute good performance to stable internal factors (e.g., high ability) and poor performance to unstable external factors (e.g., bad luck). In addition, the research shows that when the target is an out-group (as opposed to an in-group) member, the allocator is more likely to attribute good performance to unstable external factors (e.g., good luck) and poor performance to stable internal factors (i.e., low ability) (Hewstone & Jaspars, 1982; Tajfel, 1982). In short, the biases in attributions that are found at the individual level also are found at the group level (Hewstone & Jaspars, 1982).

Organizational Justice Implications

The just-considered literature is both relevant and important in terms of understanding organizational justice issues. More specifically, as detailed next, it has implications for distributive justice, procedural justice, and interactional justice.

Distributive Justice Implications. In making allocation decisions, an allocator considers the inputs of targets (Adams, 1963, 1965). Because of category-based beliefs and attributions, relative to out-group members, members of in-groups generally will be viewed as having greater inputs and thus as more deserving of positive outcomes and less deserving of negative outcomes (Turner, 1982). In addition, out-group members will be seen as providing lesser inputs and therefore being less deserving of positive outcomes and/or more deserving of negative outcomes. For example, in the case of an MWASP allocator making judgments about the relative inputs of workers in a work group having

members of various races, in-group members will be regarded as having contributed more to the performance of the group than out-group members. Consistent with these arguments, Greenberg and McCarty (1990) argued that allocators often base their evaluations of workers' inputs on the basis of gender, viewing males as more "worthy" (i.e., deserving higher wage levels) than females.

Moreover, the allocator will use these views about the inputs of various targets as the basis for making inferences about the levels of various outcomes (positive and negative) that they deserve. Thus, in terms of the preceding example, the MWASP allocator will conclude that in-group members are more deserving of positive outcomes and/or less deserving of negative outcomes than out-group members. Similarly, the allocator will conclude that out-group members are less deserving of positive outcomes and/or more deserving of negative outcomes than in-group members.

In the United States, the equity norm, which has generally guided the behavior of allocators (e.g., managers), specifies that an allocator *should* distribute outcomes (rewards, punishments) in proportion to a target's (recipient's) contributions (Adams, 1963, 1965; Homans, 1961; Leventhal, 1976a, 1980). It deserves adding, however, that other norms (e.g., equality, need, reciprocity) may be used in making allocation decisions (Deutsch, 1975; Leventhal, 1976a).

In determining what is fair, we believe that allocators will consider group membership in making decisions about the allocation of outcomes to members of in-groups and out-groups. Thus, for example, MWASP allocators will consider such "inputs" as the race, age, ethnicity, and sex of their subordinates in making decisions about the allocation of outcomes to them. The consideration of these and other factors that have no direct connection to work performance opens the door to the biased distribution of outcomes by the allocator. For example, to the degree that allocators believe that out-group members have lower levels of inputs that in-group members, they can rationalize the allocation of lower levels of outcomes to out-group members than to in-group members. One way that this can occur is through the *recognition* (Adams, 1963, 1965) of inputs by allocators. For example, an MWSAP allocator may view the "Whiteness" of workers as a valued input in making allocation decisions. Another way is through allocators' beliefs about the *relevance* (Adams, 1963, 1965) of inputs. For example, an MWASP allocator may consider an individual's ascribed status (resulting from such factors as ancestry, membership in country clubs, and presence on social registers) as a relevant input. Thus, in the absence of any other constraints (two of which are described later), the allocator will distribute available rewards and punishments to individuals in accordance with his or her views of deservedness.

Recent research on intergroup relations suggests that the favorable treatment that is typically accorded to in-group members may stem more from a liking of them than from disliking out-group members (Brewer, 1999). If this is true, then the differential allocation of outcomes to in-group and out-group members may stem more from the desire to overreward in-group members than to underreward out-group members. However, it is critical to recognize that whatever the *motives* of the allocator, the *effect* on the target is the same; that is, relative to the in-group member, the out-group member receives a lower level of outcomes. Thus, for the purpose of the present analysis, the motives of the allocator are irrelevant.

Procedural Justice Implications.   The GBDJM posits that in-group versus out-group status is a determinant of the allocation procedures used by an allocator in dealing with a target. This takes place in several ways. First, in-group members set up allocation procedures in such a way as to favor other in-group members. For example, in the now famous *Griggs v Duke Power Company* (1971) case, the Whites in the organization set up procedures that barred Blacks from being selected for certain jobs by requiring them to pass two aptitude tests and have a high school diploma. Whites who were already in such jobs did not have to meet the same requirements. This is a clear instance of procedural injustice attributable to violations of several justice rules. More specifically, Duke Power Company's blocking of Blacks from filling such jobs violated the ethicality rule, the bias suppression rule, the accuracy rule, the representativeness rule, and the consistency rule (Leventhal, 1980; Thibaut & Walker, 1975).

Second, in-group members work to insure ongoing control over allocation procedures (Lind & Tyler, 1988; Tyler, 1989). One way of doing so is by insuring that only in-group members are selected to fill positions involving the setting of policies and the establishment of procedures. For example, MWASPs may set up rules that restrict incumbency in upper level managerial positions to MWASPs, thus assuring that organizational policies and procedures will generally work to their benefit.

Interpersonal Justice Implications.   Not only will allocators apportion outcomes of various types on the basis of beliefs about the deservedness of targets, but the same beliefs will serve as the basis for the type of interpersonal treatment accorded to targets. For example, because of the effects of similarity on interpersonal attraction, MWASP allocators will be more likely to form friendships with in-group members than with members of out-groups (e.g., Byrne, 1971). The resulting friendship patterns are likely to influence both the role expectations formed about targets and the ways in which such expectations are communicated to

targets (Graen, 1976; Katz & Kahn, 1978; Stone & Stone-Romero, 2004; Stone-Romero, Stone, & Salas, 2003).

Schneider's (1987) attraction–selection–attrition (ASA) model is quite informative about the way in which members of in-groups and out-groups are treated in organizational contexts. More specifically, it argues that existing members of an organization (i.e, the in-group) behave so as to (a) *attract* individuals who are similar to themselves to the organization (e.g., through focused recruiting efforts), (b) *select* individuals for jobs based, at least in part, on their similarity to extant members of the organization, and (c) encourage the *attrition* of individuals who are hired but who don't seem to "fit" in the organization (i.e., out-group members). One important way of accomplishing these objectives is to accord in-group members more favorable interpersonal treatment than out-group members in all of their dealings with an organization.

Graen's work on leader–member exchange and role-making (e.g., Graen, 1976; Graen & Wakabayashi, 1994) is also highly relevant to interactional justice notions. More specifically, his research shows that the greater is the similarity between a supervisor and a subordinate, the more harmonious will be their interpersonal relationship. Thus, for example, MWASPs will accord better interpersonal treatment to in-group members than they will to out-group members. In addition, the better the leader–member exchange, the more positive will be the supervisor's treatment of the subordinate with respect to such outcomes as performance ratings, mentoring, and advancement opportunities (Graen, 1976; Graen & Wakabayashi, 1994; Stone & Stone-Romero, 2004; Stone-Romero et al., 2003).

The Just World Phenomenon. Note also that views about fairness are influenced by beliefs in a just world (Lerner, 1980). Thus, for example, allocators are likely to believe that the outcomes experienced by a target are fair in the sense that good people (i.e., in-group members) experience positive outcomes and that bad people (i.e., out-group members) experience negative outcomes. Regrettably, just world-based thinking may often serve as a post hoc rationalization for out-group members getting lower levels of outcomes than in-group members, thereby contributing to the ongoing biased treatment of out-group members.

Some Moderating Effects

As shown in Fig. 15.1, there are three important moderators of relationships in the GBDJM. We now briefly comment on these.

Culture of Allocator. Individual differences stemming from the cultural background of allocators are likely to moderate three relation-

ships. First, they influence the stereotypes and resultant inferences that are generated about targets. Individuals from different cultures are likely to have different culture-based values and beliefs about members of various social groups. As a result, they are likely to generate different stereotypes and stereotype-based inferences about any given target (e.g., Bobocel, Hing, Davey, Stanley, & Zanna, 1998; Chen, Brockner, & Katz, 1998; Jackson, Sullivan, & Hodge, 1993; Markus & Kitayama, 1991; Menon, Morris, Chiu, & Hong, 1999; Norenzayan, Choi, & Nisbett, 1999). Research by Jackson et al. (1993) showed that the relationships between (a) race of a target (Black vs. White) and (b) inferences made about the target were moderated by the degree to which individuals subscribed to humanitarian values. Markus and Kitayama (1991) reviewed evidence showing that people who are socialized so as to have interdependent (as opposed) to independent views of themselves are more likely to be modest, view others in more positive terms, and treat others in such a way as to promote harmony and goodwill. Plous and Williams's (1995) research on stereotypes of ethnic groups showed that the lower the educational level of the respondents, the more likely they were to hold negative views about Blacks. Finally, research by Bobocel et al. (1998) showed that the greater the degree to which individuals were prone to prejudice, the greater was their resistance to Affirmative Action programs.

Second, we predict that the cultural background of the allocator will moderate the relationship between the stereotype of group members and the inferences made about the target. For example, if the allocator is a product of a collective culture (e.g., Japanese), as opposed to an individualistic culture (e.g., Anglo American), he or she is more likely to infer that a target's performance resulted from situational factors than from dispositional factors.

Third, we posit that the culture of the allocator will influence the way in which outcomes are allocated. The reason for this is that culture will influence beliefs about the deservedness of the target. For example, research reviewed by Wetherell (1982) showed that individuals from collective cultures are more likely to allocate outcomes in terms of an egalitarian norm than an equity (proportionality) norm. Moreover, although both Polynesian children and European children demonstrated an in-group bias in their allocation of outcomes, the Polynesians were more generous in their allocation of outcomes to out-group members than were European children. The behavior of the Polynesians appeared to be based on cultural norms that stress generosity, cooperation, and maximization of the collective good. Thus, for Polynesians and other collective people, a positive social identity is achieved through different means than it is for people who subscribe to individualistic values (Kitayama, Markus, Matsumoto, & Norasakkunkit, 1997; Markus & Kitayama, 1991).

Situational Constraints. As shown in Fig. 15.1, situational variables also are hypothesized to moderate the relationship between inferences about deservedness and the allocation of outcomes to targets. We comment on two ways in which such constraints may operate. First, allocations can be affected by the type of data considered in making decisions about allocations. In some organizations, decisions about the allocation of various outcomes (e.g., merit increases, promotions) are based on "soft data" (e.g., the subjective judgments of allocators), whereas in other organizations such decisions are based on "hard" data (e.g., objective records of production quantity and quality). We hypothesize that the capacity of allocators to bias allocations on the basis of their inferences about deservedness will be much greater in situations in which decisions are based on soft data than on hard data.

Second, organizations vary in terms of the extent to which the allocator has discretion over the allocation of outcomes. At one extreme is the situation in which the allocator does nothing more than use existing rules, policies, and procedures to determine how outcomes will be allocated, and has no discretion over the amounts distributed to various targets. An example of this is the allocation of salary increases on an across-the-board basis. At the other extreme is the situation in which organizations give the allocator complete control over such factors as (a) the bases that are used in determining the deservedness of targets, (b) the measurement of the inputs of the targets, and (c) the allocation of outcomes to the targets.

Relative Power of Allocator and Target. We hypothesize that the relative power of the groups to which the allocator and the target belong will moderate three relationships. More specifically, the greater the power of the allocator, the greater the degree to which he or she will be able to unilaterally dictate (a) the allocation of outcomes to the target, (b) the procedures used in allocating outcomes, and (c) the interpersonal treatment accorded to the target. More specifically, the allocator can act with impunity when the target has little or no power (Ng, 1982). As Ng (1982) noted, "Outgroup discrimination is confined to situations where the power relations are functionally capable of sustaining discrimination" (p. 189); that is, it is limited to situations in which the in-group allocator has power over members of out-groups. An extreme, organizationally relevant illustration of this may be seen in the way that allocators (e.g., correctional officers, guards, hospital workers) deal with inmates in such total institutions as prisons, concentration camps, and mental hospitals (Goffman, 1961). In such situations, the allocator has almost complete control over the allocation procedures used, the levels of outcomes allocated to targets, and the nature of the interpersonal treatment experienced by targets. One reason for this is that the targets have little or no capacity to "leave the field" as a means of at-

tempting to achieve a more acceptable level of outcomes, better inter-personal treatment, or greater control over allocation procedures. (Adams, 1963, 1965). Thus, the allocator has fate control over the targets (Thibaut & Kelley, 1959).

A far less extreme example of the effects of power on the way out-comes are distributed is evidenced by the way rewards are allocated in organizations that have different levels of unionization. We hypothe-size that allocators (e.g., MWASP managers) will be far less likely to al-locate outcomes in a biased or capricious manner in instances in which out-group members (e.g., minority employees) are represented by pow-erful unions than when they lack such representation. In addition, as Mechanic (1962) noted years ago, in many organizations, "lower partic-ipants" have considerable power. This tends to be informal and stems from such bases as specialized expertise, extra effort devoted to work, personality, location in organizational space, membership in coalitions, and the strategic use of organizational rules. In cases where workers can retaliate against the allocator for perceived injustice in experienced out-comes (e.g., file grievances, go on strike, sabotage operations), alloca-tors must be circumspect in allocating outcomes. Thus, in such situations, allocators are less likely to use in-group favoritism as a basis for outcome allocation. Nevertheless, they may express in-group favor-itism in a number of subtle as opposed to direct ways.

The Target's Reactions

The final element in the GBDJM has to do with the target's reactions to levels of perceived justice. Because our chapter has dealt with the bi-ased treatment of out-group members, our focus here is on reactions to perceived injustice. There is a substantial literature on individuals' re-actions to injustice. However, a thorough review of it is beyond the scope of this chapter. Thus, in this subsection we provide a brief sum-mary of common reactions to perceived injustice. The summary consid-ers cognitive, attitudinal, and behavioral reactions (see, e.g., Adams, 1965; Alexander & Ruderman, 1987; Folger & Cropanzano, 1998; Gilliland & Steiner, 2001; Greenberg, 1987, 1988, 1989, 1990; Greenberg & McCarty, 1990; Stone & Colella, 1996; Stone & Stone, 1990; Stone-Romero, Stone, & Hyatt, 2003).

Cognitive Reactions. In terms of distributive justice, when targets perceive that relative to in-group members (e.g., MWASPs) they are be-ing treated inequitably, they can cope with it by such cognitive means as believing that (a) their inputs are not as valuable as those of in-group members (e.g., Greenberg & McCarty, 1990), and/or (b) their outcomes

are as great as those of in-group members (Adams, 1965). With respect to interactional justice, the target can cope with unfair treatment by believing that there is nothing of value to be gained through good interpersonal relations with in-group members; in fact, being treated considerately by them may be a sign that one has "sold out." Finally, the experience of procedural injustice can be dealt with through such beliefs as "that's all one can expect from them" (i.e., in-group members).

Attitudinal Reactions.   Among the many attitudinal responses to perceived injustice of various types are (a) increased feelings of anger, resentment, alienation, powerlessness, and rejection, (b) decreased satisfaction with such facets as the job in general, the organization, supervision, coworkers, organizational policies and procedures, pay, and promotion opportunities, (c) decreased organizational commitment, job involvement, and motivation to perform, and (d) increased intentions to quit one's job.

Behavioral Reactions.   When out-group members experience distributive injustice, several behavioral responses are likely. First, out-group members can attempt to decrease their own inputs or work to get members of the in-group to increase their inputs. Unfortunately, neither of these strategies is likely to prove successful in either the short or the long run. The reason for this is that in-group members typically control the procedures used in making allocations. Thus, attempts to restrict inputs will typically result in out-group members experiencing even more negative outcomes (e.g., disciplinary actions, job loss). Second, distributive injustice can be addressed through behaviors designed to "even the score," including theft or sabotage of company property. Third, out-group members can exhibit lower levels of organizational citizenship behavior. Fourth, and finally, the out-group members can communicate negative views of the organization, its managers, and its products or services to friends and acquaintances.

In response to experienced injustice of the procedural variety, out-group members can use a number of strategies aimed at making procedures fairer. Among the possibilities are: (a) forming unions to improve their capacity to deal collectively with in-group members, (b) instituting legal action against the organization or its representatives, (c) working for the passage of legislation aimed at insuring the fairness of organizational procedures, (d) forming action groups to change stereotypes of out-group members, and (e) working collectively to challenge and change extant organizational policies and procedures. Regrettably, many such actions are met with considerable resistance by in-group members. One of the many examples of this is individual and organizational resistance to complying with the letter and the spirit of such laws

as the Age Discrimination in Employment Act of 1967, the Civil Rights
Act of 1964, the Civil Rights Act of 1991, the Equal Pay Act of 1963, and
the Americans With Disabilities Act of 1990.

RESEARCH NEEDS

Our GBDJM has roots in social-psychological theory and research. The
relevant research provides considerable *indirect* support for the predictions associated with the model. Nevertheless, at this point in time there
is no research that provides a comprehensive test of the whole model.
Thus, research is needed that deals with this issue.

Because of the need to test for moderating effects, the same research will
need to be conducted either (a) within a single organization in which there
is considerable variance in the hypothesized moderators (i.e., situational
constraints, and relative power of allocator), or (b) across two or more organizations in which there is variance in the same moderators. Assuming
the same research uses a sufficiently large sample and well-validated measures, the complete GBDJM can be tested by using data from a nonexperimental study and structural equation modeling procedures.

Although not as appealing as a comprehensive test of the GBDJM, research that tests one or more of its linkages also would be useful. For example, a study might examine the link between the invocation of
stereotypes about members of the target's group and inferences about
the target (e.g., motivation, ability, deservedness). Although research
on stereotypes is quite useful in this regard, such research is generally
silent about issues of deservedness.

IMPLICATIONS

As already noted, there is considerable evidence that members of various out-groups (e.g., racial minorities, people with disabilities, older individuals) have long experienced lower levels of positively valent
outcomes than members of in-groups. Regrettably, the outcomes experienced by out-group members often are unrelated or weakly related to
their potential or actual contributions (inputs). Thus, in objective terms,
they have been treated quite unfairly vis-à-vis the equity norm. What's
more, members of the same groups have both recognized the injustice
and worked toward its reduction or elimination. Regrettably, relatively
little progress has been made in achieving this goal (Heller, 1987; Kerbo,
1983; Stone et al., 1992).

Prognosis for the Foreseeable Future

Unfortunately, it appears that the biased allocation of outcomes to
out-group members will not diminish greatly in the foreseeable future.
There are several reasons for this.

Social Identity-Based Motives.   Theory and research on social identity theory both indicate that group identity sets up powerful motives in individuals to view one's group positively (Tajfel, 1970, 1974, 1978, 1982; Tajfel & Turner, 1979; Turner, 1987). By implication, other groups will be viewed less positively.

Although the desire to perceive the in-group more favorably than out-groups appears to be a relatively robust phenomenon, there are cultural differences in the paths that are pursued to achieve a positive social identity (Kitayama et al., 1997; Markus & Kitayama, 1991). In the case of individualists, it is achieved by the maximization of either one's own good or that of one's group (Kitayama et al., 1997; Markus & Kitayama, 1991). However, for collectivists it is achieved by behaving in a way that is more consistent with promoting the welfare of both the in-group and the out-group, thus working toward the collective good (Kitayama et al., 1997; Markus & Kitayama, 1991).

Maintenance of Status Quo.   A second factor leading to the biased allocation of outcomes to out-group members is the desire on the part of allocators to maintain their positions of power and prestige in various contexts, including organizations. As Tajfel (1981) noted, "People may be prejudiced and discriminating against certain out-groups because they feel that these outgroups threaten their interests or their way of life" (p. 249). One of the major justifications for maintaining the status quo is to insure that one's in-group is evaluated more favorably then various out-groups. When individuals are "presented with information about ingroup and out-group members, they engage in effortful and creative cognitive activities that allow them to form, maintain, and justify self-serving beliefs" (Schaller, 1992, p. 62).

The motive to maintain the status quo seems especially strong among MWASPs in the United States who subscribe to the value of individualism (Hofstede, 1980, 1991; McClelland, 1961; Spence, 1985). Not only does this value orientation stress the importance of maximizing the current level of outcomes, but it also stresses the value of gaining control over the means used in the allocation of outcomes, thus insuring that positions of power and prestige will be maintained (Heller, 1987; Kerbo, 1983; Ng, 1982; Weber, 1958). Thus, for example, in work organizations MWASPs set up performance standards and methods for measuring performance that favor in-group members.

Reflecting the just-noted views, a well-regarded Black poet, Langston Hughes (1994), wrote:

I am the Negro bearing slavery's scars.
I am the Red man driven from the land.
I am the immigrant clutching the hope I seek—

and finding only the same old stupid plan
of dog eat dog, of mighty crush the weak.

Implications for Organizations

In view of the preceding discussion, we believe that a number of actions
are needed to promote the fair treatment of out-group members in organizational settings. Two are especially noteworthy.

Broaden Set of Individuals Who Make Allocation Decisions.   One
strategy for decreasing in-group-based biases in allocation decisions is
to increase the number of out-group members who have power over
such decisions. For example, rather than allowing a single in-group
member to make allocation decisions, such decisions can be made by
groups composed of representatives from not only the in-group but also
various out-groups. Decision making by groups that are diverse should
tend to reduce undue influence by the in-group.

Modify Organizational Policies and Procedures.   Another strategy
for reducing biases in allocation decisions is to set up policies and procedures that constrain the ability of the allocator to introduce his or her
personal biases in making allocation decisions. In this regard, it also is
critical that both the data on which allocation decisions are based (e.g.,
preemployment test data, scores on outcome measures in training programs, performance evaluation data) be as valid as possible. Unless
they are, the resulting decisions will reflect biases that are present in the
information.

Implications for Legislation

At present, that are several laws aimed at reducing the degree of bias in
the treatment of out-group members (e.g., Age Discrimination in Employment Act of 1967, Americans with Disabilities Act of 1990, Civil
Rights Act of 1964, Civil Rights Act of 1991, Equal Pay Act of 1963). Regrettably, the existence of the same laws has not eliminated the biased
treatment of racial minorities, older workers, workers with disabilities,
or members of various other out-groups. Moreover, the same legislation
affords no protection to members of many social groups. For example,
there are no federal laws that provide protection for individuals who
are unattractive, are gay or lesbian, or who have personalities that differ
from those of the individuals who have the power to make various per-
sonnel-related decisions (e.g., hiring, promotion, job assignment, fir-
ing, layoff). Thus, legislation is needed that considers a broader set of
factors than those considered by existing laws.

In addition, it is vital that government agencies take immediate and decisive action to remedy instances of unfair treatment in organizational contexts. Regrettably, government agencies (e.g., the EEOC) often lack the resources needed to pursue legal action against many organizations that engage in ongoing patterns of unfair discrimination against individuals who are members of various out-groups. Moreover, the social and political philosophies of those in power often militate against government efforts aimed at enabling the disadvantaged from improving their plight. However, in the absence of government action it seems highly likely that members of many out-groups will continue to experience distributive, procedural, and interactional injustice in organizational contexts.

A FINAL WORD

In order to reduce the level of injustice experienced by members of various out-groups, it is vital that we develop a sound understanding of the mechanisms through which bias against out-group members is translated to their unfair treatment. In this regard, we believe that our GBDJM should prove useful to both researchers and practitioners. Researchers can study the mechanisms suggested by the model. In addition, practitioners can establish policies and procedures that lessen the degree to which members of in-groups and out-groups are treated differentially in organizations.

ACKNOWLEDGMENTS

We thank Laticia Bowens and Mark Hartman for assistance with library research. We also thank the editors, Jerald Greenberg and Jason Colquitt, for helpful comments on an earlier version of this chapter.

REFERENCES

Acrey, B. P. (1992). *Navajo history: The land and the people.* Shiprock, NM: Department of Curriculum Materials Development, Central Consolidated School District N. 22, 1978.

Adams, J. S. (1963). Toward an understanding of inequity. *Journal of Abnormal Social Psychology, 67,* 422–436.

Adams, J. S. (1965). Inequity in social exchanges. In L. Berkowitz (Ed.), *Advances in experimental social psychology* (Vol. 2, pp. 267–299). New York: Academic Press.

Age Discrimination in Employment Act of 1967. 29 U.S.C. § 623.

Alexander, S., & Ruderman, M. (1987). The role of procedural and distributive justice in organizational behavior. *Social Justice Research, 1,* 177–198.

Allport, G. W. (1954). *The nature of prejudice.* Cambridge, MA: Addison-Wesley.

Americans With Disabilities Act of 1990. Public Law No. 101-336, 104 Stat. 328 (1990). 42 U.S.C.A. § 12101 *et seq.*

Ashmore, R. D., & Del Boca, F. K. (1976). Psychological approaches to understanding intergroup conflicts. In P. A. Katz (Ed.), *Towards the elimination of racism* (pp. 73–123). New York: Pergamon.

Bies, R. J., & Moag, J. S. (1986). Interactional justice: Communication criteria of fairness. In R. J. Lewicki, B. H. Sheppard, & M. H. Bazerman (Eds.), *Research on negotiation in organizations* (Vol. 1, pp. 43–55). Greenwich, CT: JAI.

Blalock, H. M. (1967). *Toward a theory of minority-group relations.* New York: Wiley.

Bobocel, D. R., Hing, L. S. S., Davey, L. M., Stanley, D. J., & Zanna, M.P. (1998). Justice-based opposition to social policies: Is it genuine? *Journal of Personality and Social Psychology, 75*, 653–669.

Bodenhausen, G. V. (1993). Emotions, arousal, and stereotypic judgements: A heuristic model of affect and stereotyping. In D. M. Mackie & D. L. Hamilton (Eds.), *Affect, cognition, and stereotyping: Interactive processes in group perception* (pp. 13–37). San Diego: Academic Press.

Brewer, M. B. (1999). The psychology of prejudice: Ingroup love or outgroup hate. *Journal of Social Issues, 55*, 429–444.

Brown, D. (1970). *Bury my heart at Wounded Knee.* New York: Henry Holt.

Byrne, D. (1971). *The attraction paradigm.* New York: Academic Press.

Chen, Y., Brockner, J., & Katz, T. (1998). Toward an explanation of cultural differences in in-group favoritism: The role of individual versus collective primacy. *Journal of Personality and Social Psychology, 75*, 1490–1502.

Churchill, W. (1997). *A little matter of genocide: Holocaust and denial in the Americas, 1492 to the present.* San Francisco, CA: City Light Books.

Civil Rights Act of 1964 as amended by the Equal Opportunity Act of 1972. Public Law No. 92–261.

Civil Rights Act of 1991. Public Law No. 102-166, 105 Stat. 1071 (1991). 42 U.S.C. § 1681, 2000 *et seq.*

Crosby, F., Bromley, S., & Saxe, L. (1980). Recent unobtrusive studies of black and white discrimination and prejudice: A literature review. *Psychological Bulletin, 87*, 546–563.

Deutsch, M. (1975). Equity, equality, and need: What determines which value will be used as the basis of distributive justice? *Journal of Social Issues, 31*, 137–149.

Deutscher, I. (1966). Words and deeds. *Social problems, 13*, 235–254.

Deutscher, I. (1973). *What we say/What we do: Sentiments and acts.* Glenview, IL: Scott, Foresman.

Doise, W. (1978). *Groups and individuals: Explanations in social psychology.* Cambridge: Cambridge University Press.

Dovidio, J. F., & Gaertner, S. L. (Eds.). (1986). *Prejudice, discrimination, and racism.* San Diego, CA: Academic.

Dusky, L. (1996). *Still unequal: The shameful truth about women and justice in America.* New York: Crown.

Equal Pay Act of 1963. 29 U.S.C. § 206(d).

Folger, R., & Cropanzano, R. (1998). *Organizational justice and human resource management.* Thousand Oaks, CA: Sage.

Folger, R., & Greenberg, J. (1985). Procedural justice: An interpretive analysis of personnel systems. In G. R. Ferris & K. M. Rowland (Eds.), *Research in personnel and human resources management* (Vol. 3, pp. 141–183). Greenwich, CT: JAI.

Gilliland, S. W., & Steiner, D. D. (2001). Causes and consequences of applicant perceptions of unfairness. In R. Cropanzano (Ed.), *Justice in the workplace: From theory to practice* (Vol. 2, pp. 175–195). Mahwah, NJ: Lawrence Erlbaum Associates.

Goffman, E. (1961). *Asylums: Essays on the social situation of mental patients and other inmates.* Chicago: Aldine.

Goffman, E. (1963). *Stigma: Notes on the management of spoiled identity.* Englewood Cliffs. NJ: Prentice Hall.

Graen, G. B. (1976). Role making processes within complex organizations. In M. D. Dunnette (Ed.), *Handbook of industrial and organizational psychology* (pp. 1201–1245). Chicago: Rand McNally.

Graen, G. B., & Wakabayashi, M. (1994). Cross-cultural leadership making: Bridging American and Japanese diversity for team advantage. In H. C. Triandis, M. D. Dunnette, & L. Hough (Eds.), *Handbook of industrial and organizational psychology,* (2nd ed., Vol. 4, pp. 415–446). Palo Alto, CA: Consulting Psychologists Press.

Greenberg, J. (1987). Reactions to procedural injustice in payment distributions: Do the means justify the ends? *Journal of Applied Psychology, 72,* 55–61.

Greenberg, J. (1988). Equity and workplace status: A field experiment. *Journal of Applied Psychology, 73,* 606–613.

Greenberg, J. (1989). Cognitive re-evaluation of outcomes in response to underpayment inequity. *Academy of Management Journal, 32,* 174–178.

Greenberg, J. (1990). Organizational justice: Yesterday, today, and tomorrow. *Journal of Management, 16,* 399–432.

Greenberg, J. (1993). The social side of fairness: Interpersonal and informational classes of organizational justice. In R. Cropanzano (Ed.), *Justice in the workplace: Approaching fairness in human resource management* (pp. 79–103). Hillsdale, NJ: Lawrence Erlbaum Associates.

Greenberg, J., & McCarty, C. L. (1990). Comparable worth: A matter of justice. In G. R. Ferris & K. M. Rowland (Eds.), *Research in personnel and human resources management* (Vol. 8, pp. 265–301). Greenwich, CT: JAI Press.

Griggs v. Duke Power Company. (1971). 401 U.S. 424.

Hamilton, D. L. (1976). Cognitive biases in the perception of social groups. In J. S. Carroll & J. W. Payne (Eds.), *Cognition and social behavior* (pp. 81–93). Hillsdale, NJ: Lawrence Erlbaum Associates.

Hamilton, D. L. (1981a). *Cognitive processes in stereotyping and intergroup behavior.* Hillsdale, NJ: Lawrence Erlbaum Associates.

Hamilton, D. L. (1981b). Illusory correlation as a basis for stereotyping. In D. L. Hamilton (Ed.), *Cognitive processes in stereotyping and intergroup behavior* (pp. 115–144). Hillsdale, NJ: Lawrence Erlbaum Associates.

Harding, J., Proshansky, H., Kutner, B., & Chein, I. (1969). Prejudice and ethnic relations. In G. Lindzey & E. Aronson (Eds.), *Handbook of social psychology* (2nd ed., Vol. 5, pp. 1–76). Reading, MA: Addison-Wesley.

Heller, C. S. (1987). *Structured social inequality: A reader in comparative social stratification* (2nd ed.). New York: Macmillan.

Herman, C. P., Zanna, M. P., & Higgins, E. T. (Eds.). (1986). *Physical appearance, stigma, and social behavior: The Ontario symposium* (Vol. 3, pp. 144–172). Hillsdale, NJ: Lawrence Erlbaum Associates.

Hewstone, M., & Jaspars, J. M. F. (1982). Intergroup relations and attribution processes. In H. Tajfel (Ed.), *Social identity and intergroup relations* (pp. 99–133). Cambridge, England: Cambridge University Press.

Higgins, E. T., & Bargh, J. A. (1987). Social cognition and social perception. *Annual Review of Psychology, 38,* 369–425.

Hofstede, G. (1980). *Culture's consequences: International differences in work-related values.* Beverly Hills, CA: Sage.

Hofstede, G. (1991). *Cultures and organizations: Software of the mind*. London: McGraw-Hill.

Homans, G. C. (1961). *Social behavior: Its elementary forms*. New York: Harcourt, Brace.

Hosoda, M., Stone-Romero, E. F., & Stone, D. L. (1999, May). *The effects of co-worker race and cognitive demand of a task on white Americans' reactions to African-American co-workers and several task-related outcomes*. Paper presented at the meeting of the Society for Industrial and Organizational Psychology, Atlanta, GA.

Hosoda, M., Stone-Romero, E. F., & Stone, D. L. (2004). Effects of coworker race and task demand on task-related outcomes as mediated by evoked affect. *Journal of Applied Social Psychology, 34*, 1–27.

Hoxie, F. E. (Ed.). (1996). *Encyclopedia of North American Indians*. Boston: Houghton Mifflin.

Hughes, L. (1994). *The collected poems of Langston Hughes*. New York: Knopf.

Hull, N. E. H. (2001). *Roe v. Wade: The abortion rights controversy in American history*. Lawrence: University Press of Kansas.

Jackson, A. (2004). Fifth annual message. In J. D. Richardson (Ed.), *A compilation of the messages and papers of the presidents, 1789–1897* (Vol. 3, p. 33). New York: Bureau of National Literature and Art. (Original work published 1833)

Jackson, L. A., Sullivan, L. A., & Hodge, C. N. (1993). Stereotype effects on attributions, predictions, and evaluations: No two social judgments are quite alike. *Journal of Personality and Social Psychology, 65*, 69–84.

Johnson, A. (2000). *Speeches of Andrew Johnson, President of the United States* (F. Moore, Ed., p. 368). Boston: Little, Brown. (Original work published 1861)

Jones, E. E., Farina, A., Hastorf, A. H., Markus, H., Miller, D. T., & Scott, R. A. (1984). *Social stigma: The psychology of marked relationships*. San Francisco, CA: W. H. Freeman.

Jones, E. E., Kanouse, D. E., Kelley, H. H., Valins, S., & Weiner, B. (1972). *Attribution: Perceiving the causes of behavior*. Morristown, NJ: General Learning Press.

Kanter, R. M. (1977). *Men and women of the corporation*. New York: Basic Books.

Katz, D., & Braly, K. N. (1933). Verbal stereotypes and racial prejudice. *Journal of Abnormal and Social Psychology, 133*, 280–290.

Katz, D., & Kahn, R. L. (1978). *The social psychology of organizations* (2nd ed.). New York: Wiley.

Katz, I. (1981). *Stigma: A social psychological analysis*. Hillsdale, NJ: Lawrence Erlbaum Associates.

Kelley, H. H. (1967). Attribution theory in social psychology. *Nebraska Symposium on Motivation, 14*, 192–240.

Kelley, H. H. (1972). *Causal schemata and the attribution process*. Morristown, NJ: General Learning Press.

Kelley, H. H. (1973). The process of causal attribution. *American Psychologist, 28*, 107–128.

Kelley, K., & Streeter, D. (1992). The roles of gender in organizations. In K. Kelley (Ed.), *Issues, theory, and research in industrial/organizational psychology* (pp. 285–337). Amsterdam: Elsevier Science.

Kerbo, H. R. (1983). *Social stratification and inequality: Class conflict in the United States*. New York: McGraw-Hill.

Kinder, D. R. (1986). The continuing American dilemma: White resistance to racial change 40 years after Myrdal. *Journal of Social Issues, 42*, 151–171.

Kinder, D. R., & Sears, D. O. (1981). Prejudice and politics: Symbolic racism versus racial threats to the good life. *Journal of Social Issues, 40*, 414–431.

Kitayama, S., Markus, H. R., Matsumoto, H., & Norasakkunkit, V. (1997). Individual and collective processes in the construction of the self: Self-enhancement in the

United States and self-criticism in Japan. *Journal of Personality and Social Psychology, 72,* 1245–1267.

Lerner, M. J. (1980). *The belief in a just world: A fundamental delusion.* New York: Plenum Press.

Leventhal, G. S. (1976a). The distribution of rewards and resources in groups and organizations. In L. Berkowitz & E. Walster (Eds.), *Advances in experimental social psychology* (Vol. 9, pp. 91–131). New York: Academic.

Leventhal, G. S. (1976b). Fairness in social relationships. In J. W. Thibaut, J. T. Spence, & R. C. Carson (Eds.), *Contemporary topics in social psychology* (pp. 211–240). Morristown, NJ: General Learning Press.

Leventhal, G. S. (1980). What should be done with equity theory?: New approaches to studying fairness in social relationships. In K. J. Gergen, M. S. Greenberg, & H. Willis (Eds.), *Social exchange: Advances in theory and research* (pp. 27–55). New York: Plenum Press.

Lind, E. A., & Tyler, T. R. (1988). *The social psychology of procedural justice.* New York: Plenum Press.

Lomawaima, K. T. (1994). *They called it prairie light.* Lincoln: University of Nebraska Press.

Macleod, W. D. (1928). Economic aspects of indigenous American slavery. *American Anthropologist, 30,* 632–650.

Markus, H. R., & Kitayama, S. (1991). Culture and the self: Implications for cognition, emotion, and motivation. *Psychological Review, 98,* 224–253.

McClelland, D. C. (1961). *The achieving society.* New York: Free Press.

McConahay, J. B., & Hough, J. C. (1976). Symbolic racism. *Journal of Social Issues, 32,* 23–46.

McEneaney, E. H. (1996). Poverty, segregation, and race riots: 1960 to 1993. *American Sociological Review, 61,* 590–613.

Mechanic, D. (1962). Sources of power of lower participants in complex organizations. *Administrative Science Quarterly, 7,* 349–364.

Menon, T., Morris, M. W., Chiu, C., & Hong, Y. (1999). Culture and the construal of agency: Attribution to individual versus group dispositions. *Journal of Personality and Social Psychology, 76,* 701–717.

Miller, D. T., & Turnbull, W. (1986). Expectancies and interpersonal processes. In M. R. Rosenzweig & L. W. Porter (Eds.), *Annual review of psychology* (Vol 37, pp. 233–256). Palo Alto, CA: Annual Reviews.

Myrdal, G. (1944). *An American dilemma: The Negro problem and American democracy.* New York: Harper.

Ng, S. H. (1982). Power and intergroup discrimination. In H. Tajfel (Ed.) *Social identity and intergroup relations* (pp. 179–206). Cambridge, England: Cambridge University Press.

Noernzayan, A., Choi, I., & Nisbett, R. E. (1999). Eastern and western perceptions of causality for social behavior: Lay theories about personalities and situations. In D. Prentice & D. T. Miller (Eds.), *Cultural divides: Understanding and overcoming group conflict* (pp. 239–272). New York: Russell Sage Foundation.

Parish, P. J. (1989). *Slavery: History and historians.* New York: Harper & Row.

Perry, R. J. (1991). *Western Apache heritage.* Austin: University of Texas Press.

Plous, S., & Williams, T. (1995). Racial stereotypes from the days of American slavery: A continuing legacy. *Journal of Applied Social Psychology, 25,* 795–817.

Reilly, P. (1991). *The surgical solution: A history of involuntary sterilization in the United States.* Baltimore, MD: Johns Hopkins University Press.

Rosenthal, R., & Jacobson, L. (1968). *Pygmalion in the classroom.* New York: Holt, Rinehart & Winston.

Sando, J. S. (1992). *Pueblo nations: Eight centuries of Pueblo Indian history.* San Francisco, CA: City Lights.

Schaller, M. (1992). In-group favoritism and statistical reasoning in social inference: Implications for the formation and maintenance of group stereotypes. *Journal of Personality and Social Psychology, 63,* 61–74.

Schneider, B. (1987). The people make the place. *Personnel Psychology, 40,* 437–453.

Schneider, D. J. (1991). Social cognition. *Annual Review of Psychology, 42,* 527–561.

Sniderman, P. M., & Hagen, M. G. (1985). *Race and inequality: A study in American values.* Chatham, NJ: Chatham House.

Spence, J. T. (1985). Achievement American style: The rewards and costs of individualism. *American Psychologist, 40,* 1285–1295.

Stone, D. L., & Colella, A. (1996). A model of factors affecting the treatment of disabled individuals in organizations. *Academy of Management Review, 21,* 352–401.

Stone, D. L., & Stone-Romero, E. F. (2004). The influence of culture on role-taking in culturally diverse organizations. In M. S. Stockdale & F. J. Crosby (Eds.), *The psychology and management of workplace diversity* (pp. 103–140). Malden, MA: Blackwell.

Stone, E. F., & Stone, D. L. (1990). Privacy in organizations: Theoretical issues, research findings, and protection strategies. In G. R. Ferris & K. M. Rowland (Eds.), *Research in personnel and human resources management* (Vol. 8, pp. 349–411). Greenwich, CT: JAI.

Stone, E. F., Stone, D. L., & Dipboye, R. L. (1992). Stigmas in organizations: Race, handicaps, and physical attractiveness. In K. Kelley (Ed.), *Issues, theory, and research in industrial/organizational psychology* (pp. 385–457). Amsterdam: Elsevier Science.

Stone-Romero, E. (2004). Personality-based stigmas and unfair discrimination in work organizations. In R. L. Dipboye & A. Colella (Eds.), *Discrimination at work: The psycological and organizational bases* (pp. 255–280). Mahwah, NJ: Lawrence Erlbaum Associates.

Stone-Romero, E. F., Stone, D. L., & Hyatt, D. (2003). Personnel selection procedures and invasion of privacy. *Journal of Social Issues, 59,* 343–368.

Stone-Romero, E. F., Stone, D. L., & Hartman, M. (2002, April). *Stereotypes of ethnic groups: Own views versus assumed views of others.* Paper presented at the meeting of the Society for Industrial and Organizational Psychology. Toronto, Canada.

Stone-Romero, E. F., Stone, E. F., & Salas, E. (2003). The influence of culture on role conceptions and role behavior in organizations. *Applied Psychology: An International Review, 52,* 328–362.

Tajfel, H. (1959). Quantitative judgment in social perception. *British Journal of Psychology, 50,* 16–29.

Tajfel, H. (1970). Experiments in intergroup discrimination. *Scientific American, 223,* 96–102.

Tajfel, H. (1974). Social identity and intergroup behavior: *Social Science Information, 13,* 65–93.

Tajfel, H. (Ed.). (1978). *Differentiation between social groups: Studies in the social psychology of intergroup relations.* London: Academic.

Tajfel, H. (1981). *Human groups and social categories.* Cambridge, England: Cambridge University Press.

Tajfel, H. (Ed.). (1982). *Social identity and intergroup relations.* Cambridge, England: Cambridge University Press.

Tajfel, H., & Turner, J. C. (1979). An integrative theory of intergroup conflict. In W. Austin & S. Worchel (Eds.), *The social psychology of intergroup relations* (pp. 33–47). Monterey, CA: Brooks/Cole.

Thibaut, J. W., & Kelley, H. H. (1959). *The social psychology of groups.* New York: John Wiley & Sons.

Thibaut, J. W., & Walker, L. (1975). *Procedural justice: A psychological analysis.* Hillsdale, NJ: Lawrence Erlbaum Associates.

Truman, H. S. (1991). The conversion of Harry Truman. In W. E. Leuchtenberg (Ed.), *American heritage* (pp. 56–57). New York: Oxford University Press. (Original work published 1911)

Turner, J. C. (1982). Towards a cognitive redefinition of the social group. In H. Tajfel (Ed.), *Social identity and intergroup relations* (pp. 15–39). Cambridge, England: Cambridge University Press.

Turner, J. C. (1987). *Rediscovering the social group: A self-categorization theory.* Oxford, England: Basil Blackwell.

Tyler, T. R. (1989). The psychology of procedural justice: A test of the group value model. *Journal of Personality and Social Psychology, 57,* 830–838.

U.S. Commission on Civil Rights. (1979). *Desegregation of the nation's public schools: A status report.* Washington, DC: U.S. Government Printing Office.

Weaver, J. (1996). *Defending mother earth: Native American perspectives on environmental justice.* Maryknoll, NY: Orbis Books.

Weber, M. (1958). *The Protestant ethic and the spirit of capitalism* (T. Parsons, Trans.). New York: Charles Scribner's Sons. (Original work published 1904–1905)

Weiner, B. (1985a). Spontaneous causal thinking. *Psychological Bulletin, 97,* 74–84.

Weiner, B. (1985b). An attribution theory of achievement motivation and emotion. *Psychological Review, 92,* 548–573.

Weiner, B. (1986). *An attributional theory of motivation and emotion.* New York: Springer-Verlag.

Westra, L., & Wenz, P. S. (Eds.). (1995). *Faces of environmental racism: Confronting issues of global justice.* Lanham, MD: Rown & Littlefield.

Wetherell, M. (1982). Cross-cultural studies of minimal groups: Implications for the social identity theory of intergroup relations. In H. Tajfel (Ed.), *Social identity and intergroup relations* (pp. 207–239). Cambridge, England: Cambridge University Press.

Wilson, W. J. (1973). *Power, racism, and privilege.* New York: Macmillan.

Witherspoon, G. (1977). *Language and art in the Navajo universe.* Ann Arbor: University of Michigan Press.

16

How Can Explanations Be Used to Foster Organizational Justice?

D. Ramona Bobocel
University of Waterloo

Agnes Zdaniuk
University of Waterloo

Since the early 1980s, justice researchers have been interested in the role that explanations play in the perception of workplace fairness. Our primary goal in the present chapter is to provide an overview of where research on explanations in the organizational context has been, and where it is going. To do so, we develop a framework to organize the past research, and we review the pertinent findings. We begin by presenting a brief historical overview of research that identifies the major ways that actors account for their own or others' actions. We then address five issues: the effects of explanations on recipient reactions; factors that influence the efficacy of explanations; potential drawbacks to using explanations; when it is most important to explain; and factors that influence how people explain. Along the way, we address seven emerging themes that set the agenda for future research.

Imagine an employee who receives a performance rating that falls short of what he or she expected. Without a convincing reason for this discrepancy, the employee may be apt to perceive the situation as unfair. In general, employees want to understand organizational decisions or events that affect them and their coworkers, in particular when those events are unanticipated or undesired. In fact, there are strong normative expectations among employees, as well as other constituents, such as customers and the general public, for organizational leaders to explain controversial actions (e.g., Bies, 1987).

For the past two decades, justice researchers have been keenly interested in the role that explanations play in the perception of workplace fairness. Initial interest in explanations was stimulated by a then emerging body of research on procedural justice, which demonstrated that people are generally more accepting of decision *outcomes* to the extent that they perceive decision-making *procedures* as fair (e.g., Leventhal, 1980; Thibaut & Walker, 1975). Explanations were conceptualized as one element in the interpersonal enactment of decision-making procedures (Bies, 1987; Bies & Moag, 1986; Lind & Tyler, 1988; Tyler & Bies, 1990). Given that employees often have little direct knowledge of the procedures by which organizational decisions are made, researchers suggested that explanations offered by leaders may be the central—if not sometimes the sole—basis on which employees decide whether a situation is fair or unfair (Bies & Moag, 1986; Tyler & Bies, 1990).[1]

---

[1] Following the work of Bies and Moag (1986), some researchers conceptualize explanations as a determinant of interactional justice perceptions; following Lind and Tyler's work (1988; also see Tyler & Lind, 1992; Tyler & Blader, 2000),   *(continued)*

After two decades of study, what has research revealed about the role of explanations in the perception of fairness? In this chapter, we address this question by reviewing past research on explanations as it pertains to the study of organizational justice. Figure 16.1 provides an organizing framework. As illustrated at the top, explaining comprises at least two interrelated processes: account giving (boxes 1, 4, and 6) and account receiving (boxes 2, 3, 4, and 5). As shown in box 1, actors use a variety of explanations, typically following unfavorable or unanticipated events. Ultimately, explanations influence how receivers respond to the event (box 3). The nature of the response—that is, whether it is positive or negative—is influenced by the receiver's evaluation of the explanation and intentions of the account giver along a number of dimensions (box 2). As indicated in box 4, many factors influence the efficacy of explanations. We have categorized these factors as characteristics of the message, the actor, the receiver, and the situation, with the situation including the social context. Explanations have a greater potential to shape receiver responses in certain conditions (box 5). Finally, as shown in box 6, researchers have recently moved upstream in the account-giving process to uncover factors that influence how managers explain their own or others' actions. Again, we have classified these factors as characteristics of the message, the actor, the receiver, and the situation.

In the following sections, we elaborate on each of the components in Fig. 16.1. We first set the stage by presenting a brief historical overview of research in psychology and sociology that identifies the major ways that actors account for their own or others' actions (box 1). The remainder of the chapter is organized around five questions revealed by our review as characterizing much of the research enterprise to date:

- What are the effects of explanations on recipient reactions? (boxes 2 and 3)
- What factors influence the efficacy of explanations? (box 4)
- Are there potential drawbacks to using remedial explanations? (box 3)
- When is it most important to explain? (box 5)
- What factors influence how people explain? (box 6)

Given its breadth, by necessity our review is not exhaustive. Our goal is to provide a clear overview of where research on explanations in the

---

[1] (*continued*)   others conceptualize explanations as a determinant of procedural justice perceptions. Following Greenberg (1993a), still others view explanations as a determinant of informational justice perceptions. The validity of the various conceptualizations is discussed elsewhere in this volume, so, for simplicity, we do not distinguish among them in the present review (see Bobocel & Holmvall, 2001, for a critique of the distinction between the concepts of procedural and interactional justice).

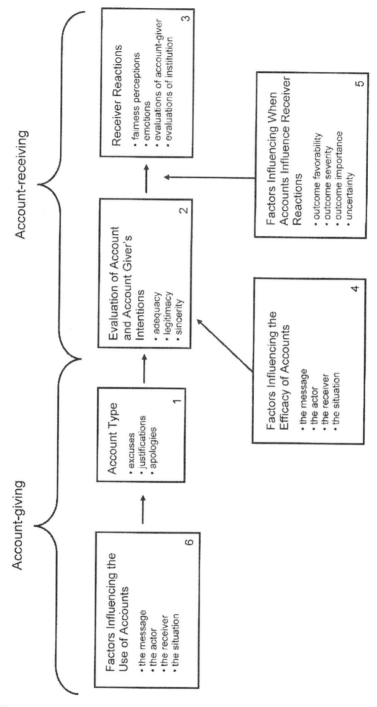

FIG. 16.1. A framework for the study of explanations.

472

organizational context has been, and where it is going. In conducting our review, seven themes emerged, themes that set the agenda for future research. These are summarized in Table 16.1.

A HISTORICAL OVERVIEW: HOW DO PEOPLE ACCOUNT FOR THEIR OWN OR OTHERS' ACTIONS?

Psychologists and sociologists have long recognized that people attempt to account for questionable actions in a variety of ways, and that the accounts offered can have profound implications for interpersonal relations. In a now classic paper, sociologists Scott and Lyman (1968) defined an account as a "statement made by a social actor to explain unanticipated or untoward behavior—whether that behavior is his own or that of others" (p. 46).[2] Scott and Lyman argued that accounts are a crucial element of interpersonal relations because they prevent

TABLE 16.1

Summary of Seven Themes for Future Research

1. Explore the effects of apologies in the organizational context more systematically, and conduct more research into the relative effects of different forms of explanations.

2. Conduct process-oriented research to discover the psychological mechanisms through which explanations exert their effects.

3. Continue research into characteristics of the receiver and the social context that influence how people construe explanations. Investigate the possible interactive effects of various factors that influence the efficacy of explanations.

4. Investigate more systematically the potential downsides of excuses, and when negative effects are likely to occur. Also, examine how managers can offset the potentially negative side effects of "good" explanations on receiver self-evaluations.

5. Examine the moderating role of person variables that might influence receivers' proclivity to ask why.

6. Continue to identify factors that influence how managers explain their own or others' actions.

7. Examine both the potential benefits and the potential downsides of account-giving for the actor in terms of his or her emotions, private evaluations of the self, and task performance.

---

[2]Although Scott and Lyman (1968) distinguished between accounts and explanations (reserving the former for statements pertaining to untoward action or events), this distinction has not been upheld consistently in the contemporary psychological literature. Therefore, we use the terms synonymously in the present review.

conflict from arising by "verbally bridging the gap between action and expectation" (p. 46).

In the decades that followed Scott and Lyman's (1968) article, researchers identified several types of accounts that actors use to remove themselves from social predicaments—referred to by Schlenker (1985) as remedial accounts—and specified the many forms that the different types can take. A comprehensive review of this literature is beyond the scope of the chapter (for excellent reviews, see Cody & McLaughlin, 1990; Schlenker, 1980, 1985; Schönbach, 1990; Scott & Lyman, 1968; Tedeschi & Reiss, 1981). In two seminal review papers, Bies (1987) and Greenberg (1990) highlighted the potential relevance of theory and research on social accounts for the study of organizational justice.

Most of the research in social and organizational psychology has focused on the study of three forms of social accounts: excuses, justifications, and, to a lesser extent, apologies. As is discussed later, however, many organizational studies have not distinguished the type of explanation. Although theorists have defined these categories in slightly different ways, impression management researchers have traditionally distinguished them along two dimensions: whether the actor admits that the event or its consequences are negative, and whether the actor accepts personal responsibility for the event or its consequences (e.g., Schlenker, 1980).

An excuse, which Bies (1987) labeled a causal account, is an explanation in which the actor admits that the event is negative but denies personal responsibility for it. According to Schlenker, an effective excuse is one that convinces the audience that the negative event is not the fault of the actor or, to the extent that the actor is at fault, that it is due to less central aspects of the self, such as forgetfulness rather than incompetence (e.g., Schlenker, Pontari, & Christopher, 2001). Excuses can take many forms, including attempts to convince the audience that the event or its consequences were unforeseeable, and references to extenuating circumstances that influenced the actor's behavior or its consequences.

In contrast to excuses, a justification is an explanation in which the actor admits personal responsibility for the action, but minimizes or denies its severity as perceived by the audience (Scott & Lyman, 1968). Bies (1987) highlighted two forms of justification: In one form, which Bies labeled an ideological account, the actor attempts to reframe the event or its consequences by appealing to superordinate values and goals, or by relabeling the action in positive value-laden terms. In another form, which Bies labeled a referential account, the actor attempts to reduce the severity of the event or its consequences by providing a more favorable standard by which to evaluate the situation.

In contrast to excuses and justifications, an apology (or concession) is a statement in which the actor accepts personal responsibility for the event or it consequences and makes no attempt to reduce the negativity as perceived by the audience. Through an apology, the account giver is hoping to convince the victim that his or her actions were an isolated event, and not representative of what he or she is like as a person (Schlenker, 1980). According to Bies (1987), actors provide apologies, or what he labeled penitential accounts, in an attempt to express regret and seek forgiveness from victims of wrongdoing.

As noted earlier, several other account forms have been proposed. For example, actors may use denials (or refusals) rather than excuses as a means of minimizing personal responsibility (Schlenker, 1980). Denials are more extreme than excuses in that the actor attempts to completely dissociate himself or herself from the alleged event by showing that the actor had nothing to do with it or by denying that it occurred.

In the psychological study of interpersonal relations, researchers have distinguished the four preceding account types—apologies/concessions, excuses, justifications, and denials/refusals—along a continuum in terms of their potential to mitigate or aggravate (respectively) interpersonal conflict following a transgression (e.g., McLaughlin, Cody, & O'Hair, 1983). Mitigating accounts attempt to reduce the tension and conflict created by the event or action by acknowledging the victim's interpretation of it and expressing regret; in contrast, aggravating accounts tend to increase the tension created by the event or action and escalate conflict by challenging the victim's interpretation of the event or their right to question it (e.g., Gonzales, Manning, & Haugen, 1992; Gonzales, Pederson, Manning, & Wetter, 1990). Accordingly, apologies are considered the most mitigating account, followed by excuses. Justifications, then denials are considered the most aggravating accounts. The mitigating–aggravating continuum provides one promising means by which to distinguish among the major account types, and recently justice researchers have begun to explore its implications for the study of accounts in organizations (e.g., Folger & Skarlicki, 2001; Tata, 1998).

With this background on the major ways in which people account for their own or others' actions, we now address our five central questions in turn.

WHAT IS THE EFFECT OF EXPLANATIONS ON FAIRNESS PERCEPTIONS?

In the mid 1980s, Bies and his colleagues published as series of articles that focused on the role of explanations in the study of organizational justice (Bies, 1987; Bies & Moag, 1986; Bies & Shapiro, 1987, 1988; Bies,

Shapiro, & Cummings, 1988). In an initial set of empirical studies, Bies and Shapiro (1987) asked MBA students to evaluate several cases describing a manager's questionable conduct. Half of the participants were provided with an excuse for the manager's conduct; the other half received no such information. Participants perceived the manager as more fair and endorsed him to a greater extent when they received the excuse as compared to when they did not. In a follow-up study, the researchers asked MBA students to recount a time when a request was denied by their boss and to respond to various questions with the event in mind. Again, participants perceived their boss as more fair, and reported less anger and resentment, when they rated their bosses' explanation for the refusal as more adequate. In prior laboratory research, Folger and his colleagues also examined the role of excuses and justifications in mitigating perceived injustice. In a series of classic experiments designed to test referent cognitions theory (e.g., Folger & Martin, 1986; Folger, Rosenfield, & Robinson, 1983), the researchers found that the provision of a credible explanation assuaged participants' anger and resentment following a negative outcome, when they could mentally simulate having received a better outcome had the experimenter used different procedures.

Since the 1980s, there have been numerous investigations into the effect of managerial explanations on receiver reactions. In reviewing this literature, we made five general observations. First, the dominant trend has been to focus on explanations as a potential mechanism by which leaders might enhance perceived fairness and minimize interpersonal conflict in organizations. Second, two types of "receiver" have been examined: In the majority of studies, the receiver comprises people who are personally affected by the event being explained, such as in the case of layoff victims or survivors (e.g., Brockner, DeWitt, Grover, & Reed, 1990; Brockner et al., 1994). In other studies, the receiver comprises third-party observers, who are not directly affected by the event being explained, such as in the case of members of the general public who read about a layoff at a company with which they have no direct association (e.g., Bobocel & Debeyer, 1996; Skarlicki, Ellard, & Kelln, 1998).

Third, much of the experimental research has examined the effects of providing an explanation—typically operationalized as an excuse or a justification—relative to a control condition in which no explanation is provided (e.g., Bies & Shapiro, 1986; Folger & Martin, 1986). Recently, researchers have begun experimental work that compares the relative effectiveness of different types of explanations (e.g., Conlon & Murray, 1996; Shapiro, 1991), a trend that promises to enrich the literature substantially. In field-based correlational research, investigators typically do not measure employees' perceptions of account types, but rather

their perceptions that the event in question was adequately explained (e.g., Wanberg, Bunce, & Gavin, 1999) (for some exceptions, see Konovsky & Folger, 1991; Mellor, 1992).

Fourth, researchers have examined explanations for a wide range of actions or workplace events. Many studies have focused on explanations for a specific decision, such as a selection or layoff decision, or a pay cut (e.g., Brockner et al., 1990; Gilliland, 1994; Greenberg, 1990; Ployhart, Ryan, & Bennett, 1999). Other studies have examined explanations for a superior's questionable conduct, such as denying a subordinate's request for resources, or taking credit for a subordinate's ideas (e.g., Bies & Shapiro, 1987; Bobocel, Agar, Meyer, & Irving, 1998; Davidson & Friedman, 1998; Tata, 2000). Still other studies have examined explanations in the context of protracted organizational change initiatives and the introduction of new organizational policies, such as drug testing (e.g., Conlon & Ross, 1997; Daly, 1995; Greenberg, 1994; Konovsky & Cropanzano, 1991; Rousseau & Tijoriwala, 1999; Schweiger & DeNisi, 1991).

Finally, although many studies have examined effects, few have investigated the psychological processes underlying the effects. Given that explanations have been conceptualized as one element of fair process, researchers typically draw on existing theories of procedural justice to make predictions about, or to interpret, the effects of explanations. Credible explanations have been said to be valued by employees for at least two reasons: the respect that they convey from authorities, and the information that they provide about why and how decisions are made (Bies & Moag, 1986; Greenberg, 1993a; Lind & Tyler, 1988; Tyler & Bies, 1990; Tyler & Lind, 1992). Several specific justice theories have been applied successfully to the study of explanations. As discussed elsewhere in this volume, the effects are often interpreted within the framework of Folger's referent cognitions theory (Folger, 1986, 1993), recently revised and relabeled fairness theory (Folger & Cropanzano, 2001; for two recent illustrations, see Gilliland et al. 2001, and Shaw, Wild, & Colquitt, 2003).

Although there are exceptions, the majority of studies since the 1980s have corroborated the early findings. In general, when controversial, unexpected, or negative events are perceived to be adequately and sincerely explained by organizational authorities, recipients react more favorably toward the event, the account giver, and the institution in which the event occurs than when such events are not explained or are perceived as being inadequately explained. In a recent meta-analytic review of 54 independent samples, Shaw et al. (2003) examined the relation between explanations—operationalized as excuses, justifications, or unspecified type—and four categories of response: justice judgments (e.g., procedural and distributive justice), cooperative responses (e.g.,

task motivation, performance, and organizational citizenship behaviors), retaliation responses (e.g, theft, complaints, anger, blame, and stress), and withdrawal responses (e.g., turnover, absenteeism, intentions to engage in future business with the organization). The researchers found significant relations between explanations and justice judgments as well as the other response variables, such that both justifications and excuses were associated with more positive responses. Shaw et al. also reasoned, from fairness theory (Folger & Cropanzano, 2001), that excuses would be more effective in alleviating negative responses than would justifications. As predicted, the relations between explanations and positive responses were significantly stronger for excuses than for justifications.

Our review revealed that apologies have been relatively understudied in the organizational context compared to excuses and justifications (and apologies were not included in the Shaw et al. meta-analysis). Moreover, the results to date are mixed. For example, in an early series of experiments, Wood and Mitchell (1981) examined the effect of subordinates' use of apologies, following a poor performance, on the appraisals of nursing supervisors. In one study, the researchers found that supervisors were less punitive following subordinates' apologies, but this effect was not replicated in a second study. Clearer support for the role of apologies comes from two studies by Baron (1990). In an initial laboratory study, participants were provided with criticism followed by several interventions. Baron found that an apology was successful in mitigating the negative feelings (e.g., perceived injustice) produced by the destructive criticism. In a second field survey, Baron found that employees (both those in management and those in nonmanagement positions) reported that apologies would be an effective means to counter the negative effects of being severely criticized by another member of the organization. Recently, several researchers have examined the relative effectiveness of apologies compared to other types of explanations. In an investigation of company responses to customer complaints, Conlon and Murray (1996) found that explanations that assumed responsibility for a problem (e.g., apologies and justifications) led to more favorable reactions than did explanations that denied responsibility (e.g., excuses or avoiding the issue). However, in at least two other studies, researchers found that an apology was less effective than a justification in reducing perceived injustice (e.g., Conlon & Ross, 1997; Tata, 2000).

In summary, the results of the Shaw et al. (2003) meta-analysis are consistent with the idea that excuses and justifications can enhance perceived fairness, as well as minimizing other conflict-inducing responses. Further, their research revealed that excuses are particularly effective. From basic research in social psychology (e.g., Ohbuchi,

Kameda, & Agaries, 1989; Weiner, Graham, Peter, & Zmuidinas, 1991) and several organizational studies, there is good reason to think that apologies can also have beneficial effects. Given the mixed evidence on apologies to date, one direction for future research will be to explore their effects in the organizational context more systematically. Research into the relative effects of different forms of explanations promises to illuminate the process of account receiving considerably by elucidating when and for whom particular types of explanations are more effective. It will also be important to conduct more process-oriented research to determine the psychological mechanisms through which explanations exert their effects. At present, the effects of explanations can be accounted for by several theories (e.g., fairness theory, attribution theory, group-value theory, fairness heuristic theory); thus, research on process is necessary to adjudicate the various theoretical perspectives.

A Caveat: The Effect of Explanations on Fairness Perceptions Is Indirect

In light of the evidence just described, most researchers agree that explanations have the *potential* to enhance perceived fairness and assuage other negative reactions, but that they do not necessarily always do so. Almost as soon as justice researchers began the systematic study of managerial explanations, it was clear that the mere provision of an account is itself not sufficient. Consistent with early sociological work on the honoring of social accounts (e.g., Blumstein et al., 1974), the data suggested that for explanations to have beneficial effects they must meet certain requirements. For example, in their initial investigations, Bies and his colleagues demonstrated that managerial accounts were effective only when they were perceived as adequate and sincere (see Bies & Shapiro, 1987, 1988; Bies et al., 1988). The roles of perceived adequacy and sincerity have been replicated in numerous studies over the years (e.g., Bobocel & Farrell, 1996; Greenberg, 1990; Shapiro, 1991). Relatedly, researchers have demonstrated that employees' beliefs about the legitimacy of an organization's account shape their reactions to it (e.g., Manscour-Cole & Scott, 1998; Mellor, 1992).

On the basis of such findings, there is now consensus that managerial explanations do not influence fairness perceptions and other recipient responses directly. Therefore, concepts such as account adequacy and communicator sincerity have been accorded status as mediators. Although the precise nature of the intervening variables needs to be more fully explicated, there is general agreement with the fundamental idea that recipients' responses to an explanation are indirectly determined

by their evaluation of the validity of the explanation and by their assessment of the account givers' intentions (e.g., Sitkin & Bies, 1993).[3]

The early findings pertaining to account adequacy and sincerity were theoretically significant in that they clearly indicated that employees are not passive recipients of explanations, but rather play an active role in their interpretation and, ultimately, in the efficacy of explanations as a conflict-minimizing mechanism. On this basis, from the beginning, justice researchers cautioned organizational leaders against interpreting the evidence demonstrating beneficial effects of accounts to suggest that any explanation will do and—more importantly—not to believe that deceptions can be covered merely by providing an account (e.g., Bies, 1987; Bies et al., 1988; Greenberg 1990; Shapiro, 1991; Sitkin & Bies, 1993; Tyler & Bies, 1990).

WHAT FACTORS CONTRIBUTE TO THE EFFICACY OF EXPLANATIONS?

With early findings indicating that explanations themselves are not always effective, justice researchers soon turned to the systematic investigation of factors that influence their efficacy. Efficacy is operationalized in different ways: Some researchers have examined factors that enhance perceived account adequacy or communicator sincerity (e.g., Shapiro, Buttner, & Barry, 1994); others have examined factors that lead to more favorable responses downstream, such as greater perceived fairness and organizational commitment (e.g., Greenberg, 1994).

Characteristics of the Message and the Actor

To date, much of the research has examined characteristics of the message and characteristics of the account-giver that influence efficacy. In a series of experiments conducted in both laboratory and field settings, Greenberg (1990, 1993b, 1994) demonstrated that explanations are more effective (a) when they contain detailed and thorough information as to why and how the decision was reached as compared to when they are less thorough, and (b) when the communicator displays greater rather than less social sensitivity and concern for the recipient. Moreover, Greenberg (1993b, 1994)

---

[3]It is worth noting that people's perceptions of account adequacy and sender sincerity will likely be somewhat related in natural settings. Factors that induce one to perceive an account as adequate—such as cogent and thorough information—are likely to enhance perceptions of the message sender as sincere and truthful. Similarly, factors that contribute to perceived sincerity—such as verbal expressions of remorse and nonverbal cues such as tone and eye contact—may be processed heuristically (e.g., Bobocel, McCline, & Folger, 1997; Shapiro, Buttner, & Barry, 1994) and taken as an indication of explanation adequacy. In support of this idea, researchers have found ratings of adequacy and sincerity to be highly related in correlational research (e.g., Shapiro et al., 1994, study 1).

found that these factors combine additively, such that explanations are most effective when they contain detailed information and the communicator is interpersonally sensitive. In related research, Shapiro and her colleagues (1994) examined the roles of communicator sensitivity and specificity of the message content. Similar to Greenberg, Shapiro et al. found that both explanation features contributed to judgments of explanation adequacy. It is interesting to note that expressions of remorse, as in an apology, are often included as part of the operationalization of communicator social sensitivity (e.g., Greenberg, 1994), consistent with the notion that apologies may have beneficial effects.

In conceptually related work on message content, researchers have suggested recently that multiple explanations may be more effective than a single explanation. For example, in an investigation of company responses to customer complaints, Conlon and Murray (1996) found that the combination of an apology and a justification was more effective in mitigating customer complaints than was either account alone (see also Gilliland et al., 2001). In still other work in this vein, researchers have found that explanations for selection decisions are more influential when they contain personalized information compared with when they do not (Gilliland, 1994; Ployhart & Ryan, 1997; Ployhart et al., 1999).[4]

Recently, Manscour-Cole and Scott (1998) found that the source of the message may be influential. In a longitudinal field study, the researchers found that layoff survivors' perceptions of the fairness of a restructuring and layoff process were greater for those who indicated that they had first heard of the layoff in discussions with their direct managers as opposed to other sources, including the official company announcement. The researchers found that this was especially true for those employees who had, 15 months earlier, indicated that they had a high-quality relationship with their direct supervisor. There are several plausible interpretations of this effect, one being that employees who first heard the news from their direct manager perceived greater information or more sensitive treatment.

In addition to message content and communicator characteristics, some research has examined the communication medium, namely, whether the explanation is delivered orally versus in writing. Drawing on research in the area of nonverbal communication, Shapiro and her colleagues (1994, study 2) hypothesized that, compared to explanations delivered in writing, those delivered orally might raise perceptions of the account giver's sincerity due to subtle cues that accompany oral de-

---

[4]It is noteworthy that Ployhart et al. (1999) found that personalized information exacerbates both positive and negative effects of explanations. Possible negative effects are discussed in the next section.

livery. Shapiro et al. also suggested that verbal and nonverbal cues might serve as a heuristic in judgments of account reasonableness. As expected, the researchers found that the explanation features under investigation had a more pronounced influence on ratings of account adequacy when the explanation was delivered orally rather than in writing.

Does the timing of the message influence its effectiveness? Several theorists have suggested that timely feedback is one standard or criterion by which people evaluate fairness, suggesting that explanations should not be severely delayed vis-à-vis the event in question (Aram & Salipante, 1981; Bies & Moag, 1986; Folger & Bies, 1989; Greenberg, Bies, & Eskew, 1991; Tyler & Bies, 1990). There is some evidence to support this idea. In a field study of the editorial review process, Gilliland and Beckstein (1996) found that authors' distributive justice perceptions were positively correlated with both an objective measure of the time (number of days) it took editors to render their editorial decision and a measure of perceived timeliness. Similarly, Conlon and Murray (1996) found that customers were more satisfied with the explanation that they had received from a company in response to their letter of complaint, and had greater intentions to conduct future business with the company, when they were more satisfied with the speed of the company's reply. Unlike Gilliland and Beckstein (1996), however, an objective measure of the speed of the company's reply failed to influence recipients' reactions (see Shapiro et al., 1994, study 2, for a similar null effect). Thus, there is some support for the idea that timeliness may influence the effectiveness of explanations, but more definitive research is needed, given the inconsistent findings across objective and subjective indices.

Characteristics of the Receiver and the Social Context

As noted earlier, research into factors that enhance the efficacy of explanations is fundamentally motivated by theorists' early discovery that the provision of an explanation is itself not sufficient; instead, recipients' evaluations or interpretations of the explanation are crucial. Although the recipient was clearly recognized as having a key role in the process of account receiving, much of the empirical research to date has focused on identifying characteristics of the message (e.g., content, medium, source, timing) and characteristics of the account giver (e.g., sincerity, social sensitivity, relationship to recipient) that contribute to account efficacy. In recent years, research has begun to consider the role of the receiver more explicitly. Importantly, this work also acknowledges the role of social and contextual factors, such as the nature of the past relationship between the recipient and the account giver, as well as

the reactions of coworkers. Research on the roles of the receiver and the social context is particularly promising because it encourages the conceptualization of explaining as a reciprocal process rather than as a unidirectional event. Such a conceptualization is consistent with theorizing in the broader psychological and sociological literatures (e.g., Schönbach, 1990). As a consequence of this conceptualization, justice researchers are grappling increasingly with complex questions pertaining to the efficacy of managerial explanations.

A study by Rousseau and Tijoriwala (1999) highlights the role of the receiver in the study of managerial accounts. The authors conducted a field survey in a hospital implementing empowerment among nurses and examined factors that influenced nurses' interpretations of the social account offered by management. They found that trust in management, the nature of the psychological contract, and beliefs of coworkers influenced the degree to which nurses believed management's account of the change, as well as the alternative reasons that nurses generated for the change. The account was more readily accepted and successful in motivating employee participation for those who had a high-quality relationship with the organization, and for those whose coworkers accepted the account offered by management. Among other things, these findings highlight the important role of relational and social factors that can impinge on recipients' construals of explanations, in particular in the context of explaining a complex organizational change that occurs over a protracted period of time.

In other research highlighting the role of recipient, some researchers (e.g., Bobocel, McCline, & Folger, 1997; Frey & Cobb, 1999) have suggested that reactions may be influenced by receivers' cognitive processing strategy. As discussed by Bobocel et al., psychological research has delineated a continuum of processing strategies by which people make judgments (for reviews, see Chaiken & Trope, 1999; Petty & Cacioppo, 1986; Shiffrin & Schneider, 1977; Wegner & Bargh, 1998). At the *controlled* or *systematic* end, people engage in mindful, deliberate, and effortful processing. At the *automatic* or *heuristic* end, judgments are more mindless, less deliberate, and less effortful. When processing a communication more systematically, judgments are said to result from attending to, elaborating on, rehearsing, and integrating information contained in the message. In contrast, when processing a communication more heuristically, judgments are likely to be influenced by the quick application of well-learned decision rules or schemas, such as "in general, the experts are right," and "if others agree, the explanation is likely to be true." Drawing on this broad dual-process distinction, Bobocel et al. hypothesized that the features that contribute to an account's efficacy may be moderated by processing strategy. For example, as people move toward the systematic end of the processing contin-

uum—depending on their motivation and ability to process an account more or less deliberately—they may be relatively more influenced by the quality of arguments. In contrast, as people move toward the heuristic end of the processing continuum—either because they are unable to process more systematically or they are not sufficiently motivated to do so—they may be relatively more influenced by cues in the situation. Such cues can pertain to the message itself (e.g., number of arguments), the communicator (e.g., expertise, sensitivity), or the context (e.g., audience response). Future empirical research is necessary to test the viability of this model.

A study by Conlon and Murray (1996) also indirectly highlights the role of the receiver in determining the effectiveness of managerial accounts. Drawing parallels between Best and Andreason's (1977) life cycle of customer complaints and Felstiner, Albel, and Sarat's (1980–1981) model of grievances, Conlon and Murray hypothesized that apologies may be particularly effective in the context of customer complaints. According to Felstiner and colleagues, people are said to progress through three stages in the grievance process: (a) the perception of injury, (b) the attribution of responsibility and blame, and (c) the demand for some remedy, referred to as naming, blaming, and claiming, respectively. Conlon and Murray reasoned that apologies may be more effective than excuses or denials on the theory that, by the time people complain to an organization, they have already determined blameworthiness. As a consequence, people may be more resistant to excuses or denials and more receptive to an apology. Conlon and Murray's results were in line with their reasoning.

Although the researchers did not test the role of recipients' goals directly, we believe that their study has important theoretical implications: The effectiveness of particular types of accounts might be influenced by receivers' goals. When people are first deciding whether to name an event as an injustice, justifications may be more effective than excuses or apologies because justifications aim to reframe an event in more positive terms whereas both excuses and apologies admit that injury has occurred. Once people have decided that an injury has occurred and are next deciding whether to blame the offending party, excuses may be particularly effective because they aim to minimize responsibility. Finally, as argued by Conlon and Murray, once people have decided that an injury has occurred and that an actor or institution is responsible, apologies may be particularly effective. Admittedly, we suspect that people move through the naming, blaming, and claiming stages very rapidly, thereby blurring the distinctions just drawn. Clearly, our ideas will need to be validated in future research. Nevertheless, research that explicitly considers the goals of the recipient promises to shed light on why and when particular types of accounts may be

more or less effective, providing a more complete understanding of the account-receiving process.

Finally, research on third-party observer reactions to explanations has similarly highlighted the role of the receiver. For example, Davidson and Friedman (1998) found what they labeled a "persistent injustice effect," such that an excuse failed to mitigate perceived injustice among Black respondents who observed transgressions toward a hypothetical Black victim. The researchers suggest that the persistent injustice effect results from the combination of the observers' in-group identification and their personal experiences with injustice, factors that combine to produce the motivation and ability to empathize with the victim.

In summary, researchers have devoted a good deal of attention to the study of factors that contribute to the efficacy of explanations. Clearly, explanations are not all equally effective in assuaging negative reactions. Numerous factors have been studied; we classified these broadly as factors pertaining to the message, the actor, the receiver, and the situation, with the situation including the social context. It will be important to continue research into characteristics of the receiver and the social context that influence how people construe explanations. Further, it will be of interest to investigate the possible interactive effects of various factors that influence efficacy.

ARE THERE POTENTIAL DRAWBACKS TO USING REMEDIAL EXPLANATIONS?

As summarized earlier, on balance the evidence to date suggests that managerial explanations can potentially enhance perceived fairness and maintain employee morale. Moreover, the Shaw et al. (2003) meta-analysis showed that excuses may be particularly effective, a finding that is consistent with a large volume of psychological research on excuse making (e.g., Harvey, 1995). In their comprehensive review, Snyder and Higgins (1988) found that, relative to not using excuses, excuse making can have a host of beneficial effects, including intrapsychic benefits for the account giver (e.g., higher self-esteem and adjustment, reduced anxiety and negative affect, and even better task performance), and the recipient (e.g., restored self-esteem, reduced negative affect), as well as for interpersonal relations.

Although the benefits of explanations—in particular, excuses or mitigating accounts—have been emphasized in the justice literature, there has been less theory and research on the potential disadvantages. Several justice theorists have raised the possibility of adverse consequences of managerial accounts (e.g., Shapiro, 1991; Sitkin & Bies, 1993), but only recently are researchers beginning to study the potential risks of account giving systematically. For example, Bobocel and Farrell

(1996, study 1) found that providing an inadequate excuse for a diversity policy raised perceptions of unfairness among observers relative to a control condition in which no explanation was offered. Similarly, Skarlicki, Folger, and Gee (2004) found that providing recipients with a negative outcome accompanied by either a polite message or an apology—but no substantive content—resulted in greater perceptions of unfairness and attributions of manipulative intent relative to when participants received no message at all. Other research suggests that excuse-making may have trade-off effects for the actor's public image. For example, Bobocel et al. (1998) found that participants who imagined themselves as an employee who was denied a request by their manager evaluated their manager as more friendly and likeable as a person—but weaker as a leader—when he shifted responsibility to others compared with when he accepted responsibility or did not provide an account.

In a recent review of psychological literature on excuse making, Schlenker and his colleagues (Schlenker, et al., 2001) drew on their triangle model of responsibility (Schlenker, Britt, Pennington, Murphy, & Doherty, 1994) to elucidate the possible downsides. Schlenker et al. (2001) suggested that because excuses are self-serving explanations of events, they are vulnerable to creating a negative image of the excuse maker; in particular, excuses can undermine perceptions of the excuse maker's character as someone who has integrity, is effectual, and is concerned about the greater good. Thus, excuses have the potential to make the excuse maker appear to be deceitful, ineffectual, and self-absorbed. Schlenker et al. argued that excuses can therefore be harmful to the excuse makers' public identity, private views of the self, interpersonal relations, and possibly even future performance. According to Schlenker et al. (p. 25), the beneficial effects of excuse making likely accrue to the extent that excuses: (a) are credible, (b) maintain the actor's self-engagement in cases of important and recurring tasks, and (c) maintain goodwill and do not give the impression of narcissism. An important direction for future research on managerial explanations will be to investigate more systematically the potential downsides, in particular, of excuses, and when negative effects are likely to occur.

So far, we have been discussing several possible risks of explanations that are deemed by recipients as inadequate or disingenuous. But there is another way in which explanations—which are perceived as adequate and sincere—can have adverse effects. Research into the role of explanations in the employee selection process has revealed that adequate explanations for job rejections can lead to a diminished sense of self-efficacy (e.g., Gilliland, 1994; Ployhart & Ryan, 1997; Ployhart et al., 1999). Presumably, adequately and sincerely explaining the process enhances recipients' perceptions of fairness. In turn, the more fair that recipients perceive the job rejection, the more they are inclined to attribute

it to internal factors, such as their ability or effort, rather than to external factors, such as improper selection procedures. Such internal attributions result in lowered self-evaluations.

Martin, Parsons, and Bennett (1995) found a similar pattern in a natural field experiment that examined the influence of workers' membership in an employee involvement (EI) program on their reactions to being laid off. On the grounds that EI programs facilitate open communication between workers and management, including opportunities for management to adequately explain decisions, the researchers predicted that layoff victims who had been members of EI programs would react more favorably toward the layoff process than would nonmembers. Results confirmed their predictions. Additionally—although the overall level of self-blame was low regardless of EI membership—those employees who were members of EI programs placed significantly more blame on themselves for the impending layoff than did nonmembers.

Together, these findings highlight serious potential trade-off effects of "successful" explanations. On the one hand, offering an adequate explanation may yield several benefits for both the account giver and the account receiver, as well as for interpersonal relations. On the other hand, successful explanations may adversely affect receivers' self-evaluations. These findings are of course consistent with other justice research (discussed in detail elsewhere in this volume) that has demonstrated negative effects of perceived procedural fairness on self-evaluations (e.g., Brockner & Wiesenfeld, 1996; Brockner et al., 2003; Van den Bos, Bruins, Wilke, & Dronkert, 1999). Future research is needed to understand how managers can offset the potentially negative side effects of "good" explanations on receiver self-evaluations.

WHEN IS IT MOST IMPORTANT TO EXPLAIN?

As noted earlier, most studies have examined the efficacy of managerial explanations for mitigating negative reactions to unfavorable events. This focus follows directly from early sociological treatments of accounts (e.g., Scott & Lyman, 1968) and from psychological research on attribution processes. Attribution research indicates that people are more motivated to ask "why" questions, and consequently to search for causal information, when the outcome of an event is negative or unexpected, or when people are confronted with events that are stressful, novel, or personally important (Wong & Weiner, 1981). Similarly, fairness theory and its predecessor, referent cognitions theory, predict that explanations ought to have stronger effects when the event or behavior being explained is unfavorable rather than favorable.

Several studies have nevertheless manipulated or measured outcome favorability, as well as outcome severity, to examine the possible

moderating role directly. Although there are some exceptions, several studies support the idea that explanations have stronger effects on a variety of reactions when the event being explained is negative rather than positive (e.g., Daly, 1995; Folger & Martin, 1986; Greenberg, 1993b, 1994). Similarly, the effects of explanations tend to be stronger when the negative event is of greater rather than lesser severity (Brockner et al., 1994; Greenberg, 1994; Schaubroeck, May, & Brown, 1994; Shapiro, 1991; Shapiro et al., 1994, study 2). In their meta-analysis, Shaw et al. (2003) found that outcome favorability/severity indeed significantly moderated the relation between explanations and recipient responses. Explanations had a greater influence on recipient responses when the event being explained was more, rather than less, unfavorable/severe.[5]

Do these findings imply that there is no value in explaining favorable outcomes or less severe negative outcomes? No. Several studies have demonstrated that explanations enhance perceptions of process fairness regardless of the favorability or severity of the decision outcome (e.g., Daly, 1995; Folger & Martin, 1986; Gilliland & Beckstein, 1996; Greenberg, 1994). Furthermore, in the context of selection decisions, research has revealed that explaining the selection process to those who are selected for the job—a positive outcome—can bolster participants' self efficacy (e.g., Gilliland, 1994; Ployhart & Ryan, 1997; Ployhart et al., 1999).

Researchers have examined the moderating role of other variables that, like outcome favorability and outcome severity, presumably increase recipients' motivation to understand why an event occurred. The current evidence suggests that the influence of explanations on recipient responses is stronger when the event being explained is more important (e.g., Brockner et al., 1990), when the event violates one's expectations (e.g., Colquitt & Cherkoff, 2002; Greenberg, 1993b), and in conditions where people are more uncertain about the event being explained (Brockner et al., 1990). From the latter findings, several researchers have suggested that explanations may be crucial in managing organizational change, when it is likely that uncertainty is high (e.g., Cobb & Wooten, 1998; Rousseau & Tijoriwala, 1999). It is worth noting a parallel between this line of thinking and recent research in the broader justice literature testing fairness heuristic theory (e.g., Lind, 2002; Van den Bos, Lind, & Wilke, 2001) and the related uncertainty management model of fairness (Van den Bos & Lind, 2002), which shows that people are more influenced by manipulations of fairness under conditions of greater uncertainty.

In summary, the data are consistent with the idea that explanations have a greater potential to shape receiver reactions in situations in

---

[5]Shaw et al. (2003) appear to have combined studies that manipulated or measured outcome favorability with those that manipulated or measured outcome severity.

which the receiver is particularly motivated to understand why the event transpired or what its implications are. Past research on moderators has uncovered important situational factors that presumably influence receivers' motivation to understand. Future research should also examine the moderating role of person variables that might influence receivers' proclivity to ask why, regardless of the situation.

WHAT FACTORS INFLUENCE HOW PEOPLE EXPLAIN?

As is evident from the preceding sections, much of the research on managerial explanations has examined their effects, the factors that influence their efficacy, and the factors that moderate their influence. Recently, research has expanded to include consideration of the factors that determine an actor's use of explanations. In short, there has been a shift toward examining explanations as a dependent variable, as well as an independent variable.

Although research in this vein has gained favor recently, its potential value has been recognized for some time (e.g., Greenberg, 1990; Schlenker, 1980; Schönbach, 1990; Sitkin, Sutcliffe, & Reed, 1993). In one study, Greenberg (1990) examined the narrative comments provided by supervisors in their evaluations of subordinates' performance. He found that supervisors' explanations could be classified into four major categories, and that use of the different categories depended on the nature of the evaluation. Explanations focusing on the meritorious aspects of performance were typically used to explain high ratings, apologies typically accompanied low ratings, and average ratings received no explanation. Similarly, Sitkin et al. (1993) conducted a field study in which pharmacists had to decide whether to fill a potentially erroneous prescription, and how much information to share with their client. The researchers found that pharmacists drew selectively on a variety of institutionalized norms to make their potentially questionable action appear more just.

In several recent articles, Folger and his colleagues highlighted the topic of managerial account giving in the context of what they labeled the "Churchill effect" (see Folger & Pugh, 2002; Folger & Skarlicki, 2001). Citing anecdotal evidence, these researchers have suggested that managers are often the least interpersonally sensitive, paradoxically, when employees most need them to be sensitive—when rendering or implementing unfavorable decisions, such as layoffs. Drawing on existing psychological evidence, Folger and his colleagues highlighted several reasons why managers may distance themselves from employees during difficult times, and fail to provide adequate explanations. These reasons include negative emotions, avoidance of blame, and fear of being sued.

In an initial test of their ideas, Folger and Skarlicki (1998) examined the role of blameworthiness as one determinant of how managers explain decisions. The authors found that MBA students asked to imagine a layoff as due to personal mismanagement (rather than external conditions) indicated that they would spend less time explaining the layoff to their subordinates. Sitkin et al. (1993) reported a similar finding in their study of pharmacists discussed earlier: The more that pharmacists perceived filling a potentially erroneous prescription to threaten their legitimacy, the fewer explanations they offered to their client.

Psychological research in the area of interpersonal relations has examined characteristics of the actor that influence how they explain their actions. For example, drawing on the McLaughlin et al. (1983) mitigation–aggravation continuum of account types, several studies have found that women are more likely than men to proffer mitigating accounts, such as concessions, apologies, or excuses (e.g., Gonzales et al., 1990, 1992; Tata, 1998, 2000). In one series of studies by Gonzales and colleagues (1992), respondents were asked to read various hypothetical predicaments and to imagine themselves as the offending party. They then provided written accounts to the victim explaining what happened. Gonzales et al. found that women gave more complex accounts—comprising more than one type of explanation—than did men, especially more complex concessions, and that women told fewer lies.

In a recent workplace study, Tata (1998) asked nonmanagerial employees to recall a time when they were denied a request by their boss, and to describe any explanations provided by the manager. Tata found that female managers used more concessions and excuses compared to male managers, although there was no gender difference in the number of justifications or refusals. In addition, the gender of the employee (the account receiver) appeared to influence the type of account used by managers. In general, female managers provided more excuses and concessions to female employees than to male employees; male managers, however, provided excuses and concessions relatively equally between male and female employees. Unfortunately, because Tata's results rely solely on employees' recollections of their managers' explanations, they are open to alternative interpretations. For example, they may reflect memory biases resulting from respondents' implicit theories of gender differences in leadership rather than actual leader behavior. Although the results require replication to rule out alternative interpretations, they are consistent with the idea that both the gender of the account giver and the gender of the account receiver may influence how actors explain their actions.

A recent study by Korsgaard, Roberson, and Rymph (1998, study 1) more clearly illustrates the role of the receiver. Korsgaard and her colleagues hypothesized that employees who are more assertive in their

communication style would elicit more considerate behavior and better explanations from their managers. In an experiment conducted to test this idea, Korsgaard et al. had undergraduate students assume the role of an appraiser and deliver performance feedback to another participant (in reality an experimental confederate) who had performed poorly. The confederate's communication style was manipulated such that it was either assertive or unassertive. The results showed that appraisers were more likely to display consideration toward the appraisee, and to provide justifications for their evaluations, when the confederate's communication style during the meeting was assertive rather than unassertive.

In addition to the examination of situational factors, characteristics of the actor, and characteristics of the receiver, cross-cultural researchers have examined whether culture influences an actor's accounting behavior. Much of this research has compared the responses of people from individualistic cultures, such as North America, to those from collectivistic cultures, such as Asia. Generally speaking, within individualistic cultures, personal goals are given priority over goals of the collective, and behaviors are determined by one's attitudes and the perceived costs and benefits associated with performing a particular behavior. By contrast, within collectivistic cultures, group goals are given priority over personal goals, and behaviors are determined by group norms, duties, and obligations (e.g., Singelis, 1994; Triandis, 1996).

Several studies have demonstrated that, compared to people from individualistic cultures, those from collectivistic cultures are more likely to provide mitigating accounts. For example, Itoi, Ohbuchi, and Fukuno (1996) asked American and Japanese students first to read scenarios in which they assumed the role of a harm doer who unintentionally harmed someone and then to indicate the likelihood of using various account types in response to the harm done. They found that collectivists (relative to individualists) preferred more mitigating accounts, such as apologies and excuses, and less aggravating accounts, such as justifications.

In summary, research into the psychology of managerial account giving promises to enrich our understanding of the process considerably. A key direction for future research will be to continue to identify factors that influence how managers explain their own or others' actions. An important outgrowth of research on account giving will be to examine the effects on the actor. As noted earlier, by and large, justice researchers have focused on the empirical study of receiver reactions. There has been no systematic research on the repercussions of account giving for the actor, apart from his or her image in the eyes of the receiver. This is in stark contrast to the study of accounts in the broader psychology litera-

ture, where the emphasis has been on the benefits of account giving for the actor. As highlighted earlier, psychological research has demonstrated that there can be clear intrapsychic benefits of account giving, in particular of excuse making, for the actor. Of course, as also discussed earlier, Schlenker and his colleagues (2001) identified possible detrimental effects of excuse making for the account giver's private identity and future performance. It will be of interest to study both the potential benefits and the potential downsides of account giving for the actor in terms of his or her emotions, private evaluations of the self, and task performance.

CONCLUSION: WHERE HAVE RESEARCHERS BEEN AND WHERE IS THE FIELD GOING?

We began this chapter by asking the broad question: Do explanations influence perceived fairness in the workplace? Our review has revealed that explanations have the potential to enhance perceived fairness and to maintain employee morale during bad times. Yet it also revealed that the influence of explanations is not straightforward. After two decades of investigation, researchers have learned a great deal about managerial explanations. Still there are more questions to be addressed within the broad framework of Fig. 16.1, many of which we raised throughout this review. In particular, seven themes for future research emerged. These are summarized in Table 16.1. As indicated by these themes, research in the coming years must grapple with a number of challenging issues. To achieve a fuller understanding of the role of explanations, investigators will need to better delineate the many processes and factors that determine how both actors and receivers interpret and react to explanations, and why and when they do so. We hope that our explicit identification of themes will be of assistance, although we expect new themes to emerge as well.

In conclusion, it is our belief that explaining often does matter: It can help both parties in an exchange weather difficult times. But the process is complex, and much more remains to be discovered about the intricacies of explaining in the organizational context. Communication is crucial to the success of the organization, and explanation addresses the central question that people always ask—why? We look forward to continuing research on this issue, as investigators delve into the many important and intriguing questions that are as yet unanswered.

ACKNOWLEDGMENTS

Preparation of this chapter was supported by a grant from the Social Sciences and Humanities Research Council of Canada. We thank Colin M. MacLeod for his helpful comments on an earlier draft of this chapter.

REFERENCES

Aram, J. D., & Salipante, P. F. (1981). An evaluation of organizational due process in the resolution of employee/employer conflict. *Academy of Management Review, 6*, 197–204.

Baron, R. A. (1990). Countering the effects of destructive criticism: The relative efficacy of four interventions. *Journal of Applied Psychology, 75*, 235–245.

Best, A., & Andreasen, A. R. (1977). Consumer responses to unsatisfactory purchases: A survey of perceiving defects, voicing complaints, and obtaining redress. *Law and Society Review, 11*, 701–742.

Bies, R. J. (1987). The predicament of injustice: The management of moral outrage. *Research in Organizational Behavior, 9*, 289–319.

Bies, R. J., & Moag, J. F. (1986). Interactional justice: Communication criteria of fairness. In R. J. Lewicki, B. H. Sheppard, & M. H. Bazerman (Eds.), *Research on negotiations in organizations* (Vol. 1, pp. 43–55). Greenwich, CT: JAI Press.

Bies, R. J., & Shapiro, D. L. (1987). Interactional fairness judgments: The influence of causal accounts. *Social Justice Research, 1*, 199–218.

Bies, R. J., & Shapiro, D. L. (1988). Voice and justification: Their influence on procedural fairness judgments. *Academy of Management Journal, 31*, 676–685.

Bies, R. J., Shapiro, D. L., & Cummings, L. L. (1988). Causal accounts and managing organizational conflict: Is it enough to say it's not my fault? *Communication Research, 15*, 381–399.

Blumstein, P. W., Carssow, K. G., Hall, J., Hawkins, B., Hoffman, R., Ishem, E., Maurer, C. P., Spens, D., Taylor, J., & Zimmerman, D. L. (1974). The honoring of accounts. *American Sociological Review, 39*, 551–566.

Bobocel, D. R., Agar, S. E., Meyer, J. P, & Irving, P. G. (1998). Managerial accounts and fairness perceptions in conflict resolution: Differentiating the effects of minimizing responsibility and providing justification. *Basic and Applied Social Psychology, 20*, 133–143.

Bobocel, D. R., & Debeyer, M. (1998). Explaining controversial organizational decisions: To legitimize the means or the ends? *Social Justice Research, 11*, 21–40.

Bobocel, D. R., & Farrell, A. C. (1996). Sex-based promotion decisions and interactional fairness: Investigating the influence of managerial accounts. *Journal of Applied Psychology, 81*, 22–35.

Bobocel, D. R., & Holmvall, C. M. (2001). Are interactional justice and procedural justice different? Framing the debate. In S. Gilliland, D. Steiner, & D. Skarlicki (Eds.), *Theoretical and cultural perspectives on organizational justice* (Vol. 1, pp. 85–108). Greenwich, CT: Information Age.

Bobocel, D. R., McCline, R. L., & Folger, R. (1997). Letting them down gently: Conceptual advances in explaining controversial organizational policies. In C. L. Cooper & D. M. Rousseau (Eds.), *Trends in organizational behavior* (Vol. 4, pp. 73–88). New York: Wiley.

Brockner, J., DeWitt, R. L., Grover, S., & Reed, T. (1990). When is it especially important to explain why: Factors affecting the relationship between mangers' explanations of a layoff and survivors' reactions to the layoff. *Journal of Experimental Social Psychology, 26*, 389–407.

Brockner, J., Konovsky, M., Cooper-Schneider, R., Folger, R., Martin, C., & Bies, R. J. (1994). Interactive effects of procedural justice and outcome negativity on victims and survivors of job loss. *Academy of Management Journal, 37*, 397–409.

Brockner, J., Heuer, L., Magner, N., Folger, R., Umphress, E., Van den Bos, K., Vermunt, R., Magner, M., & Siegel, P. (2003). High procedural fairness heightens the effect of outcome favorability and procedural fairness on self-evaluations: An attributional analysis. *Organizational Behavior and Human Decision Processes, 91,* 51–68.

Brockner, J., & Wiesenfeld, B. M. (1996). An integrative framework for explaining reactions to decisions: Interactive effects of outcomes and procedures. *Psychological Bulletin, 120,* 189–208.

Chaiken, S., & Trope, Y. (Eds). (1999). *Dual-process theories in social psychology.* New York: Guilford Press.

Cobb, A. T., & Wooten, K. C. (1998). The role social accounts can play in a "justice intervention." *Research in organizational change and development, 11,* 73–115.

Cody, M. J., & McLaughlin, M. L (1990). Interpersonal accounting. In H. Giles & W. P. Robinson (Eds.), *Handbook of language and social psychology* (pp. 227–255). Oxford: John Wiley & Sons.

Colquitt, J. A., & Chertkoff, J. M. (2002). Explaining injustice: The interactive effect of explanation and outcome on fairness perceptions and task motivation. *Journal of Management, 28,* 591–610.

Conlon, D. E., & Murray, N. M. (1996). Customer perceptions of corporate responses to product complaints: The role of expectations. *Academy of Management Journal, 39,* 1040–1056.

Conlon, D. E., & Ross, W. H. (1997). Appearances do account: The effects of outcomes and explanations on disputant fairness judgments and supervisory evaluations. *International Journal of Conflict Management, 8,* 5–31.

Daly, J. P. (1995). Explaining changes to employees: The influence of justifications and change outcomes on employees' fairness judgments. *Journal of Applied Behavioral Science, 31,* 415–428.

Davidson, M., & Friedman, R. A. (1998). When excuses don't work: The persistent injustice effect among Black managers. *Administrative Science Quarterly, 43,* 154–183.

Felstiner, W. F., Abel, R., & Sarat, A. (1980–1981). The emergence and transformation of disputes: Naming, blaming and claiming. *Law and Society Review, 15,* 631–654.

Folger, R. (1986). A referent cognitions theory of relative deprivation. In J. M. Olson, C. P. Herman, & M. P. Zanna (Eds.), *Relative deprivation and social comparison: The Ontario symposium* (Vol. 4, pp. 33–55). Hillsdale, NJ: Lawrence Erlbaum Associates.

Folger, R. (1993). Reactions to mistreatment at work. In K. Murnighan (Ed.), *Social psychology in organizations: Advances in theory and research* (pp. 161–183). Englewood Cliffs, NJ: Prentice Hall.

Folger, R., & Bies, R. J. (1989). Managerial responsibilities and procedural justice. *Employee Responsibilities and Rights Journal, 2,* 79–89.

Folger, R., & Cropanzano, R. (2001). Fairness theory: Justice as accountability. In J. Greenberg & R. Cropanzano (Eds.), *Advances in organizational justice* (pp. 1–55). Palo Alto, CA: Stanford Press.

Folger, R., & Martin, C. (1986). Relative deprivation and referent cognitions: Distributive and procedural justice effects. *Journal of Experimental Social Psychology, 22,* 531–546.

Folger, R., & Pugh, S. D. (2002). The just world and Winston Churchill: An approach/avoidance conflict about psychological distance when harming victims. In M. Ross & D. Miller (Eds.), *The justice motive in everyday life* (pp. 168–186). New York: Cambridge University Press.

Folger, R., Rosenfield, D., & Robinson, T. (1983). Relative deprivation and procedural justifications. *Journal of Personality and Social Psychology, 45,* 268–273.

Folger, R., & Skarlicki, D. P. (1998). A popcorn metaphor for employee aggression. In R. Griffin, A. O'Leary-Kelly, & J. Collins (Eds.), *Dysfunctional behavior in organizations: Violent and deviant behavior* (pp. 43–81). Stanford, CT: JAI Press.

Folger, R., & Skarlicki, D. P. (2001). Fairness as a dependent variable: Why tough times can lead to bad management. In R. Cropanzano (Ed.), *Justice in the workplace: From theory to practice* (Vol. 2, pp. 97–118). Mahwah, NJ: Lawrence Erlbaum Associates.

Frey, F. M., & Cobb, A. T. (1999, August). *What constitutes an "acceptable" social account: An investigation of content and source factors.* Paper presented at the Annual Meeting of the Academy of Management, Chicago, IL.

Gilliland, S. W. (1994). Effects of procedural and distributive justice on reactions to a selection system. *Journal of Applied Psychology, 79,* 691–701.

Gilliland, S. W., & Beckstein, B. A. (1996). Procedural and distributive justice in the editorial review process. *Personnel Psychology, 49,* 669–691.

Gilliland, S. W., Groth, M., Baker, R. C. IV., Dew, A. F., Polly, L. M., & Langdon, J. C. (2001). Improving applicants' reactions to rejection letters: An application of fairness theory. *Personnel Psychology, 54,* 669–703.

Gonzales, M. H., Manning, D. L., & Haugen, J. A. (1992). Explaining our sins: Factors influencing offender accounts and anticipated victim responses. *Journal of Personality and Social Psychology, 62,* 958–971.

Gonzales, M. H., Pederson, J. H., Manning, D. J., & Wetter, D. W. (1990). Pardon my gaffe: Effects of sex, status, and consequence severity on accounts. *Journal of Personality and Social Psychology, 58,* 610–621.

Greenberg, J. (1990). Looking fair vs. being fair: Managing impressions of organizational justice. *Research in Organizational Behavior, 12,* 111–157.

Greenberg, J. (1993a). The social side of fairness: Interpersonal and informational classes of organizational justice. In R. Cropanzano (Ed.), *Justice in the workplace: Approaching fairness in human resource management* (Vol. 1, pp. 79–103). Hillsdale, NJ: Lawrence Erlbaum Associates.

Greenberg, J. (1993b). Stealing in the name of justice: Informational and interpersonal moderators of theft reactions to underpayment inequity. *Organizational Behavior and Human Decision Processes, 54,* 81–103.

Greenberg, J. (1994). Using socially fair treatment to promote acceptance of a work site smoking ban. *Journal of Applied Psychology, 79,* 288–297.

Greenberg, J., Bies, R. J., & Eskew, D. E. (1991). Establishing fairness in the eye of the beholder: Managing impressions of organizational justice. In R. A. Giacalone & P. Rosenfeld (Eds.), *Applied impression management: How image-making affects managerial decisions* (Vol. 135, pp. 111–132). Thousand Oaks, CA: Sage.

Harvey, J. H. (1995). Accounts. In A. R. Manstead & M. Hewstone (Eds.), *Blackwell encyclopedia of social psychology* (pp. 3–5). Cambridge, MA: Blackwell.

Itoi, R., Ohbuchi, K.-I., & Fukuno, M. (1996). A cross-cultural study of preferences of accounts: Relationship closeness, harm severity, and motives of account making. *Journal of Applied Social Psychology, 26,* 913–934.

Konovsky, M. A., & Cropanzano, R. (1991). Perceived fairness of employee drug testing as a predictor of employee attitudes and job performance. *Journal of Applied Psychology, 76,* 698–707.

Konovsky, M. A., & Folger, R. (1991). The effects of procedures, social accounts, and benefits level on victims' layoff reactions. *Journal of Applied Social Psychology, 21,* 630–650.

Korsgaard, M. A., Roberson, L., & Rymph, R. D. (1998). What motivates fairness? The role of subordinate assertive behavior on managers' interactional fairness. *Journal of Applied Psychology, 83*, 731–744.

Leventhal, G. S. (1980). What should be done with equity theory? New approaches to the study of fairness in social relationships. In K. Gergen, M. Greenberg, & R. Willis (Eds.), *Social exchange: Advances in theory and research* (pp. 27–55). New York: Plenum Press.

Lind, E. A. (2002). Fairness judgments as cognitions. In M. Ross & D. T. Miller (Eds.), *The justice motive in everyday life* (pp. 416–431). New York: Cambridge University Press.

Lind, E. A., & Tyler, T. R. (1988). *The social psychology of procedural justice.* New York: Plenum Press.

Mansour-Cole, D. M., & Scott, S. G. (1998). Hearing it through the grapevine: The influence of source, leader-relations, and legitimacy on survivors' fairness perceptions. *Personnel Psychology, 51*, 25–54.

Martin, C. L., Parsons, C. K., & Bennett, N. (1995). The influence of employee involvement program membership during downsizing: Attitudes toward the employer and the union. *Journal of Management, 21*, 879–890.

McLaughlin, M. L., Cody, M. J., & O'Hair, H. D. (1983). The management of failure events: Some contextual determinants of accounting behavior. *Human Communication Research, 9*, 208–224.

Mellor, S. (1992). The influence of layoff severity on postlayoff union commitment among survivors: The moderating effect of the perceived legitimacy of a layoff account. *Personnel Psychology, 45*, 579–600.

Ohbuchi, K.-I., Kameda, M., & Agarie, N. (1989). Apology as aggression control: Its role in mediating appraisal of and response to harm. *Journal of Personality and Social Psychology, 56*, 219–227.

Petty, R. E., & Cacioppo, J. T. (1986). The elaboration likelihood model of persuasion. In L. Berkowitz (Ed.), *Advances in Experimental Social Psychology* (Vol. 19, pp. 123–205). New York: Academic.

Ployhart, R. E., & Ryan, A. M. (1997). Toward an explanation of applicant reactions: An examination of organizational justice and attribution frameworks. *Organizational Behavior and Human Decision Processes, 72*, 308–335.

Ployhart, R. E., Ryan, A. M., & Bennett, M. (1999). Explanations for selection decisions: Applicants' reactions to informational and sensitivity features of explanations. *Journal of Applied Psychology, 84*, 87–106.

Rousseau, D. M., & Tijoriwala, S. A. (1999). What's a good reason to change? Motivated reasoning and social accounts in promoting organizational change. *Journal of Applied Psychology, 84*, 514–528.

Schaubroeck, J., May, D. R., & Brown, F. W. (1994). Procedural justice explanations and employee reactions to economic hardship: A field experiment. *Journal of Applied Psychology, 79*, 455–460.

Schlenker, B. R. (1980). *Impression management: The self-concept, social identity, and interpersonal relations.* Monterey, CA: Brooks/Cole.

Schlenker, B. R. (Ed.). (1985). *The self and social life.* New York: McGraw-Hill.

Schlenker, B. R., Britt, T. W., Pennington, J., Murphy, R., & Doherty, K. (1994). The triangle model of responsibility. *Psychological Review, 101*, 632–652.

Schlenker, B. R., Pontari, B. A., & Christopher, A. N. (2001). Excuses and character: Personal and social implications of excuses. *Personality and Social Psychology Review, 5*, 15–32.

Schönbach, P. (1990). *Account episodes: The management or escalation of conflict.* Cambridge: Cambridge University Press.

Schweiger, D. M., & DeNisi, A. S. (1991). Communication with employees following a merger: A longitudinal field experiment. *Academy of Management Journal, 34,* 110–135.

Scott, M. B., & Lyman, S. M. (1968). Accounts. *American Sociological Review, 33,* 46–62.

Shapiro, D. L. (1991). The effects of explanations on negative reactions to deceit. *Administrative Science Quarterly, 36,* 614–630.

Shapiro, D. L., Buttner, E. H., & Barry, B. (1994). Explanations: What factors enhance their perceived adequacy? *Organizational Behavior and Human Decision Processes, 58,* 346–368.

Shaw, J. C., Wild, E., & Colquitt, J. A. (2003). To justify or excuse?: A meta-analytic review of the effects of explanations. *Journal of Applied Psychology, 88,* 444–458.

Shiffrin, R. M., & Schneider, W. (1977). Controlled and automatic human information processing: II. Perceptual learning, automatic attending and a general theory. *Psychological Review, 84,* 127–190.

Singelis, T. M. (1994). The measurement of independent and interdependent self-construals. *Personality and Social Psychology Bulletin, 20,* 580–591.

Sitkin, S. B., & Bies, R. J. (1993). Social accounts in conflict situations: Using explanations to manage conflict. *Human Relations, 46,* 349–370.

Sitkin, S. B., Sutcliffe, K. M., & Reed, G. L. (1993). Prescriptions for Justice: Using social accounts to legitimate the exercise of professional control. *Social Justice Research, 6,* 87–111.

Skarlicki, D. P., Ellard, J. H., & Kelln, B. R. C. (1998). Third-party perceptions of a layoff: Procedural, derogation, and retributive aspects of justice. *Journal of Applied Psychology, 83,* 119–127.

Skarlicki, D. P., Folger, R., & Gee, J. (2004). When social accounts backfire: The exacerbating effects of a polite message or an apology on reactions to an unfair outcome. *Journal of Applied Social Psychology, 34,* 322–341.

Snyder, C. R., & Higgins, R. L. (1988). Excuses: Their effective role in the negotiation of reality. *Psychological Bulletin, 104,* 23–35.

Tata, J. (1998). The influence of gender on the use and effectiveness of managerial accounts. *Group and Organization Management, 23,* 267–288.

Tata, J. (2000). She said, he said. The influence of remedial accounts on third-party judgments of coworker sexual harassment. *Journal of Management, 26,* 1133–1156.

Tedeschi, J. T., & Reiss, M. (1981). Predicaments and verbal tactics of impression management. In C. Antaki (Ed.), *Ordinary language explanations of social behavior* (pp. 271–309). San Diego, CA: Academic Press.

Thibaut, J. W., & Walker, L. (1975). *Procedural justice: A psychological analysis.* Hillsdale, NJ: Lawrence Erlbaum Associates.

Triandis, H. C. (1996). The psychological measurement of cultural syndromes. *American Psychologist, 51,* 407–415.

Tyler, T. R., & Bies, R. J. (1990). Beyond formal procedures: The interpersonal context of procedural justice. In J. S. Carroll (Ed.), *Applied social psychology and organizational settings* (pp. 77–98). Hillsdale, NJ: Lawrence Erlbaum Associates.

Tyler, T. R., & Blader, S. L. (2000). *Cooperation in groups: Procedural justice, social identity, and behavioral engagement.* Philadelphia, PA: Psychology Press.

Tyler, T. R., & Lind, E. A. (1992). A relational model of authority in groups. In M. P. Zanna (Ed.), *Advances in experimental social psychology* (Vol. 25, pp. 115–191). San Diego, CA: Academic Press.

Van den Bos, K., & Lind, E. A. (2002). Uncertainty management by means of fairness judgments. In M. P. Zanna (Ed.), *Advances in experimental social psychology* (Vol. 34, pp. 1–60). San Diego, CA: Elsevier.

Van den Bos, K., Lind, E. A., & Wilke, H. A. M. (2001). The psychology of procedural and distributive justice viewed from the perspective of fairness heuristic theory. In R. Cropanzano (Ed.), *Justice in the workplace: From theory to practice* (Vol. 2, pp. 49–66). Mahwah, NJ: Lawrence Erlbaum Associates.

Van den Bos, K., Bruins, J., Wilke, H. A. M., & Dronkert, E. (1999). Sometimes unfair procedures have nice aspects: On the psychology of the fair process effect. *Journal of Personality and Social Psychology, 77,* 324–336.

Wanberg, C. R., Bunce, L. W., & Gavin, M. B. (1999). Perceived fairness of layoffs among individuals who have been laid off: A longitudinal study. *Personnel Psychology, 52,* 59–84.

Wegner, D. M., & Bargh, J. A. (1998). Control and automaticity in social life. In D. T. Gilbert & S. T. Fiske (Eds.), *The handbook of social psychology* (4th ed., Vol. 1, pp. 446–496). New York: McGraw-Hill.

Weiner, B., Graham, S., Peter, O., & Zmuidinas, M. (1991). Public confession and forgiveness. *Journal of Personality, 59,* 281–312.

Wood, R. E., & Mitchell, T. R. (1981). Manager behavior in a social context: The impact of impression management on attributions and disciplinary actions. *Organizational Behavior and Human Decision Processes, 28,* 356–378.

Wong, P. T., & Weiner, B. (1981). When people ask "why" questions, and the heuristics of attributional search. *Journal of Personality and Social Psychology, 40,* 650–663.

17

How Can Training Be Used to Foster Organizational Justice?

Daniel P. Skarlicki
University of British Columbia

Gary P. Latham
University of Toronto

Empirical research investigating whether leaders can be trained to be fair is reviewed. An argument is made for why leaders should be trained in organizational justice. Given the potential difficulties in such an endeavor, the pitfalls to be avoided in executing this training are described. Finally, a step-by-step summary of "how to train" leaders in justice principles is provided.

Can leaders be trained to be fair? Based on the limited number of studies that have been conducted to date, the answer to this question would appear to be yes. In this chapter, we review the empirical evidence that supports this answer. Second, we explain why leaders *should* be trained in organizational justice. We contend that organizational justice principles are an important aspect of leadership training, and we provide examples of organizational issues where such training is or should be beneficial. Third, because training in justice principles is more difficult than it may initially seem, pitfalls for researchers in executing this training are identified. Gaining access to a research site, for instance, can be a difficult obstacle. Consequently, we take the reader "behind the scenes" and discuss, from a researcher's perspective, pitfalls that can be avoided when designing and implementing a training intervention in organizational justice.

A fourth issue addressed in this chapter is the training principles in the preceding studies that can be extrapolated to increase the likelihood of success of future training programs. We provide a step-by-step summary of "how to train" leaders in justice principles. These steps include: (a) conducting a needs analysis, (b) maximizing the trainees' learning, (c) ensuring the transfer of training, and (d) evaluating the training's effectiveness. We close with ideas for future research.

EXISTING EVIDENCE

The first published empirical study to test whether leaders can be trained to be fair was conducted in a Canadian public sector labor union (Skarlicki & Latham, 1996). Principles of organizational justice were taught to union leaders (a) to see whether a training intervention impacts union members' assessment of their leaders' fairness, and (b) to assess whether such an intervention increases the union members' organizational citizenship behavior (OCB) toward their union organization. The training consisted of four 3-hour sessions conducted over a 3-week period. We focused on procedural and interactional justice principles. For

example, the union leaders were taught the importance of *representation*. That is, union issues and principles should reflect the viewpoints of the membership rather than a chosen few. The membership must have *"voice."* Members must perceive that their opinions are taken into account before the union executive committee makes a decision. The union leaders must apply the rules and procedures consistently. The logic underlying the union leaders decisions must be explained to the rank and file. The sincerity of the leaders in working to advance the interests of the members must not be perceived as questionable.

The perceived fairness of the leaders was assessed anonymously by the union members. OCB was measured using anonymous peer evaluations. Measures of perceived fairness and OCB were collected from the training and the control group immediately before and again 1 month after the training intervention was completed.

The training intervention was conducted in a labor union for two reasons. First, union survival depends on members volunteering to serve the union (i.e., OCB). Thus, a program that addresses ways to increase citizenship behavior in the union directly benefits that organization. Previous research had shown that fairness perceptions were associated with OCB (Moorman, 1991). Consequently, we wanted to learn whether OCB could be increased by training leaders to be seen as fair. Second, a labor union provides a setting for collecting uncontaminated behavioral measures of OCB. Attending meetings, voting in union elections, and serving on union committees are indicators of citizenship behavior. They are discretionary behaviors that are not formally required or monetarily rewarded. Yet in the aggregate, they contribute to the effective functioning of the union.

The results of this study were threefold. First, we found that the training intervention increased the union members' perceptions of fairness on the part of their leaders relative to the members whose leaders had not been trained. Second, the intervention increased significantly the level of the members' citizenship behavior toward their union (e.g., attending union meetings, volunteering to serve on committees). Third, we found that fairness perceptions of the leadership by members explained (i.e., mediated) the effect of the training intervention on the members' OCB in this union.

We then replicated the training intervention in a private-sector union (Skarlicki & Latham, 1997).This second union provided a more stringent test than the first study of the effect of leadership training on OCB. This is because the union members in this second study were shareholders in the company that employed them. Labor union research suggests that union members who are shareholders tend to be more sympathetic and responsive to the company than to the union (Blasi & Kruse, 1991). The results of this second study, however, mirrored those obtained in

the first study—training union leaders in the principles of organizational justice increased their members' perceptions of their fairness. The training intervention also had a significant effect on members' citizenship behaviors in the union, despite the fact they owned shares in their company.

At least three additional studies provide evidence that leaders can be trained to be fair. Skarlicki and Jones (2002) trained managers and employees of a national retail store. The dependent variables were employees' perceptions of their supervisors' fairness, and peer ratings of the employees' OCB. Before the training, there were no differences in fairness perceptions or OCB between the employees in the store where the training took place and the employees in the store who served as a control group. Following the training intervention, employees' perceptions of the managers' fairness and the employees' OCB were significantly higher in the training than in the control group.

In a fourth study, Greenberg (1999) trained managers on ways of enhancing interpersonal justice in a discount store of a chain that was experiencing high levels of theft by employees. The training was administered to the managers for 2 hours per week over an 8-week period in one randomly selected store. The second and third stores served as control conditions. Managers in a second store, selected at random, were trained on an unrelated topic, namely, ways of improving customer service. Managers in a third store received no training. The dependent variables included job satisfaction, organizational commitment, turnover intentions, and theft. Greenberg found that the training intervention was effective at improving all four dependent variables. Most importantly, theft was reduced in the treatment group from 8% to less than 4%. No appreciable drop in theft was observed in the other two conditions.

Leadership training in organizational justice principles has also been found to improve perceptions of fairness of managers who administer discipline to employees. Cole and Latham (1997) trained supervisors on six aspects of procedural justice whose relevance to disciplinary settings had been established in prior research (see Ball, Trevino, & Sims, 1994, for a review). These principles included: (a) explanation of the performance problem, (b) positive demeanor of the supervisor, (c) subordinate influence over the process, (d) lack of arbitrariness, (e) employee counseling, and (f) privacy. The training consisted of role-playing exercises that were conducted in small groups over a period of 5 half-days. Labor lawyers, human resources (HR) managers, and union officers assessed the effectiveness of the training. They observed the supervisors' role-playing disciplinary action with their employees in a variety of scenarios without knowledge of who had been trained. Trained supervisors were seen as behaving

more fairly when administering discipline than the supervisors in the control group.

In summary, these five studies provide evidence, across different organizational settings, that leaders can indeed be trained to be fair. Moreover, these studies show that a training intervention that increases fairness on the part of leaders has a beneficial impact on theoretically relevant variables, including job attitudes (e.g., job satisfaction, organizational commitment) and behavior (e.g., OCB, turnover intentions, theft).

Despite the evidence that has been amassed within the past decade on the organizational benefits to be gained from organizational justice, there are few justice training studies in the scholarly research journals. In the subsequent section we argue the logic for subsequent research on training based on the principles of organizational justice.

WHY SHOULD LEADERS BE TRAINED IN ORGANIZATIONAL JUSTICE PRINCIPLES?

The answer to this question is at least fivefold. First, fairness contributes to effective organizational functioning. In addition to the dependent variables already discussed in the five training studies, perceptions of fairness are related to numerous attitudes, including trust in supervisors (Konovsky & Pugh, 1994), job satisfaction (McFarlin & Sweeney, 1992), organizational commitment (Konovsky, Folger, & Cropanzano, 1987), compliance with decision making (Kim & Mauborgne, 1993), and perceived organizational support (Rhoades & Eisenberger, 2002). Moreover, perceived fairness is related to employee cooperation in groups (see Tyler, this volume), whereas perceptions of unfairness are associated with retaliatory behavior (Skarlicki & Folger, 1997). These findings were obtained across cultures (e.g., Farh, Earley, & Lin, 1997). Thus, the evidence suggests that fairness can provide a competitive advantage: Companies that have leaders who are seen as fair are likely to be far more effective than companies whose leaders are seen as unfair.

Second, HR procedures are effective to the degree that they are accepted by the employees whom they impact (Noe, Hollenback, Gerhart, & Wright, 2003). The acceptability of procedures is highly dependent on whether the employees view the organizational policies as fair. Organizational justice principles provide the basis for HR professionals to develop procedures and systems that will be accepted and implemented in the organization. Fairness criteria have been identified for numerous HR functions, including selection (Cropanzano & Wright, 2003; Gilliland & Hale, this volume), performance appraisal (Greenberg,1986), training (Gilliland & Gilliland, 2001), and reward systems (Greenberg,

1996).Those leaders who apply these principles should be able to ensure that HR procedures are accepted by employees. Training in organizational justice should help leaders acquire the skills to do this.

Third, delivering bad news is arguably among the more difficult tasks of a leader. In challenging economic times, in which organizations are constantly changing, leaders are increasingly called upon to be "the messenger" on issues ranging from resource cutbacks to job layoffs to plant shutdowns. The way that this news is delivered affects the degree to which employees accept organizational change (Greenberg, 1994), react to salary cuts (Greenberg, 1990a) and layoffs (Brockner, Tyler, & Cooper-Schneider, 1992; Lind, Greenberg, Scott, & Welchans, 2000), and agree to the outcomes of dispute resolution (Cole & Latham, 1997; Lind, Kulik, Ambrose, & de Vera Park, 1993). Training in organizational justice principles provides leaders a framework for delivering this information in ways that are perceived as fair.

Fourth, an understanding of justice principles is critical for business ethics (Greenberg & Bies, 1992). In the wake of a series of high-profile corporate scandals (e.g., Enron) and reports of global employee mistreatment (e.g., Nike), national polls in Canada and the United States show that corporate executives have taken on the status of villains."Business leader" is viewed as an oxymoron (Latham & McCauley, in press). Leadership training in organizational justice principles provides a framework that can guide leaders to be ethical.

Fifth, the global organization requires leaders to cope with differences among countries regarding employee ethnicity and political ideology. Social identity differences will likely become a source of conflict in the workplace similar to what they are in society at large (Latham & McCauley, in press).Knowledge of and skill in the application of organizational justice principles may enable leaders to prevent or effectively manage identity-based conflict.

In summary, at least five reasons explain why leaders should be trained in justice principles. Moreover, justice training will likely be beneficial in those situations in which perceptions of unfairness are frequently experienced. Examples of situations where perceptions of unfairness exist are plentiful. In management and union relations, both parties often perceive the other party to be unfair. Layoffs and downsizing can be deemed unfair by layoff victims, survivors, and third parties. Mergers and acquisitions are usually seen as unfair when organizations undergo extensive change, and rank-and-file employees have minimal, if any, voice in the process. Because of the benefits associated with training in organizational justice principles, and the ease with which perceptions of unfairness can arise in organizations, we believe that fairness training should be an important component of MBA as well as executive education programs.

GUIDELINES FOR AVOIDING RESEARCH PITFALLS

Conducting research in leadership training in justice principles is not necessarily easy. As stated earlier, only five training studies have been conducted on ways of inculcating justice principles. Collectively we have conducted four of these five (Cole & Latham, 1997; Skarlicki & Jones, 2002; Skarlicki & Latham, 1996, 1997). Thus, we point out "pitfalls" that can sabotage a researcher's efforts.

Proposing training for leaders on fairness principles can be met with resistance. By agreeing to participate, managers might believe that they are admitting to the need to improve the fairness of their practices. We believe that the following four principles will increase the probability that an organization's leaders will agree to training in organizational justice.

Focus on Expected Outcomes

Arguably, what has allowed us relatively easy access to organizations for the purpose of investigating the effects of an independent variable has been our focus on the dependent variable. It is the dependent variable that is usually of far greater interest to organizational decision makers than is the proposed intervention. For example, in the Skarlicki and Latham (1996, 1997) and Skarlicki and Jones (2002) studies, the dependent variable of interest was OCB. OCB includes such behaviors as volunteering to serve on committees, helping one's coworkers, and providing excellent customer service. Consequently, OCB is a dependent variable of interest to most, if not all, organizations.

To conduct our research, we needed to show decision makers how OCB could increase significantly as a result of the training intervention we were proposing to them. To accomplish this, we provided decision makers examples of ways that OCB can contribute to their effectiveness as leaders, as well as the effectiveness of their organization. We emphasized that increasing perceptions of their fairness by their organizations' members is highly likely to increase OCB in their organization.

Reduce Defensive Behavior

Most often, leaders believe they are fair, and deem fairness principles as mere common sense (Greenberg, 1996; Greenberg & Lind, 2000). Thus, we explain that it is necessary but not sufficient to *be* fair; in addition, it is necessary for them as leaders to *be seen as* fair. We explain that the purpose of training is on ways of increasing the probability that what they are doing will be seen as fair by others. Thus, the training is not necessarily an admission by them that they are unfair in their role as leaders.

Rather, the training is framed as designed to increase their understanding of how perceptions of fairness are formed.

Use Appropriate Language

It is critical for researchers to understand the language of the organization. Our experience with working in a union setting, although limited, illustrates this point. First, there are negative perceptions of a business school by many union members. For example, one union president stated: "Let me see if I have this right. You want my union to participate in a study with the Faculty of *Management*? You must be joking." Second, it took considerable learning on our part to use language that does not offend union officials. For example, in a telephone conversation with another union leader, we described justice as a way to "empower" union members with "voice." This was the wrong choice of words. Our statement was abruptly countered by a 10-minute lecture from the union leader on the drawbacks of empowerment to the union movement followed by a "click"; he hung up on us. We approached 30 unions before getting approval to implement the training program.

The points we are emphasizing here are twofold. First, researchers must understand not only what the organization's leaders care about, but also the organization's language. Second, researchers must be able to make explicit to decision-makers "what's in it for them" to support and/or participate in a training program. Understanding these issues from the organization's perspective is important to researchers in order to gain permission and support to collect data.

Practice What You Preach

Researchers need to "walk the talk" of fairness in the training design. Otherwise, trainees are likely to view the trainers as hypocritical, and decrease their acceptance of the training content (Gilliland & Gilliland, 2001). Fairness theories are rich with guidelines that can be applied by researchers to the research process. For example, anxiety is decreased and motivation to learn is increased when the trainee is given a choice of whether to attend a training program. In making this choice, people should be given the logic underlying the training program (Hicks & Klimoski, 1984). These training principles (i.e., giving people a voice in whether to attend the training program; providing trainees with a complete rationale for the program) are consistent with principles of fair treatment.

We made presentations to the union executive committee as well as to the members themselves at the union's annual general meeting. In our presentations we supported the union leadership's assertion that union

survival depends on members getting actively involved in the union. We explained that we could help the executive committee improve member participation in the union by training the union's leaders in the principles of organizational justice.

In summary, fairness training can be a sensitive issue for organizations and their leaders. Thus, it is especially important that researchers take steps to understand context. In the following section we provide a step-by-step description of how to increase the likelihood that (a) organizations will support a training program, and (b) the program will be effective at training leaders to be fair, and to be seen as fair.

TRAINING LEADERS IN ORGANIZATIONAL JUSTICE PRINCIPLES: KEY CONSIDERATIONS

In reviewing the five extant training studies on organizational justice, we distilled a series of principles that we believe are common across studies. These principles, which are listed next, are likely to contribute to a successful intervention to teach the principles of organizational justice.

Needs Analysis

The initial step in designing leadership training in organizational justice is to determine what the trainees need to learn, and what they will be expected to do at the completion of the training (Wexley & Latham, 1991). Based on a needs analysis, the researcher develops the content of the training. A needs analysis consists of an organization, person, and task analysis (McGehee & Thayer, 1961). The needs analysis is also important in determining how the training can benefit the organization, and to help decision makers understand "what's in it for them."

Organization Analysis. Training is accepted by an organization's decision makers to the extent that it is linked directly to the acceleration of the internalization and implementation of the organization's strategic plan (Latham, 2003). Gaining access to this plan can be difficult to obtain by outsiders. Nevertheless, it can be gleaned from a number of sources, including reading periodicals (e.g., newspaper articles, business magazines), interviewing individuals who work as consultants to organizations, and asking contacts such as participants in a business school's executive education programs. This analysis also involves gaining an understanding of the organization's culture and values.

For example, in the Skarlicki and Latham studies (1996, 1997) we determined that OCB is the *sine qua non* of a union. Union leaders cannot mandate members' union involvement. A union member can only be re-

quired to pay union dues. Yet without members actively supporting
their union through OCB (e.g., voting in elections, volunteering for union committees, serving as an officer of the union), the union risks de-
certification. In our discussions with members of the union executive
committee, we learned of their frustrations regarding the lack of OCB
on the part of their members. For example, some leadership positions
were left vacant because no member was willing to serve as a candidate.
As a result, union elections were often decided by acclamation.

Union members frequently complained that the union leadership
provided poor service and insufficient communication. Yet when union
leaders held information meetings, they were poorly attended. At one
annual general meeting, only six members attended, and one of the six
attendees resigned his post. Despite appeals and exhortations from union leaders, there was apathy among members. No OCB was forthcom-
ing from them.

Similarly, Greenberg's (1999) training program was based on the conclusion that the organization must reduce theft. Thus, this training program provided a way for leaders to address a specific problem that was
confronting them.

Person Analysis.   After analyzing the organization in terms of its
mandate and strategy, the next question to be addressed is: Who needs
the training? In the Skarlicki and Latham studies, we asked the question, who is critical for bringing about a significant increase in OCB in
the union? The initial answer to this question was the members themselves. But, why were the members not responding positively to their
elected leaders' ongoing requests and exhortations for the necessity of
OCB? In asking such questions, the answer as to whom the training
should be given emerged: The union leaders. Our conclusion was supported by empirical research. Kelloway and Barling (1993) found that
interventions by union leaders can increase union member participation in union activities.

Task Analysis.   The purpose of task analysis is to identify the behaviors that are critical to the effectiveness of a leader in meeting the
study's goals, be it fostering OCB, reducing theft, or administering
discipline. In Greenberg's (1999) study, an attitude survey that had
been completed storewide revealed that the employees were dissatisfied with management. They expressed feelings of underpayment,
dissatisfaction with their jobs, and a lack of commitment to the organization. Employees depicted their managers as being disrespectful, un-
caring, insensitive, and generally unconcerned about their welfare.
They reported a lack of voice in company procedures. In response,
Greenberg designed an interpersonal justice training program that in-

cluded techniques of delegation, supportive communication, and how to treat employees with respect and dignity.

In Skarlicki and Latham (1996), we met with individual union members and discovered that there were indeed perceptions by union members of unfair procedures and interpersonal treatment by union leaders. One member had received reimbursement for travel expenses to a union meeting whereas another member had not. The latter individual subsequently withdrew his support of the union by not attending further meetings. Few people understood the reimbursement policy, and it was perceived by the members as biased. Other members reported that they did not feel that they had a voice in union decisions. Still other members stated that they were not kept informed of union decisions, and they did not feel that their union leaders listened to them. Based on this information, the content of the training focused on the following principles of organizational justice: procedural, interactional, and informational justice, as well as managing impressions of justice.

Maximizing the Trainee's Learning

Once the content of the fairness intervention has been identified, and the question of who will be trained has been answered, the next step involves designing the training program itself. The studies to date maximized learning of the training principles by focusing on active participation, distributive practice, the meaningfulness of the presented material, feedback or knowledge of results (Wexley & Latham, 1991), and the setting of learning goals based on this feedback (Seijts, Latham, Tasa, & Latham, 2004; Winters & Latham, 1996). Each of these principles is essential to the success of a leadership fairness intervention.

Active Participation. Trainees require an opportunity to practice, in a risk-free environment, the principles being taught. They need to be encouraged to explore alternate solutions to problems. Errors in a risk-free setting provide information and motivation that enhances learning (Dormann & Frese, 1994). Active participation works best when trainees are given advice, before beginning practice, about the process or strategy that should be used for effective performance. This involves explaining the specific steps to trainees, and having them practice the skills in the training session. For example, in one session we demonstrated and explained the steps of active listening, and the union leaders practiced active listening skills with one another. Participants in Greenberg's (1999) as well as Cole and Latham's (1997) study were involved in a variety of role-playing exercises.

Distributed Practice.   Voluminous data in experimental psychology indicate that distributed practice sessions usually permit more effective learning than continuous practice (Wexley & Latham, 1991). In the Skarlicki and Latham studies (1996, 1997), we scheduled the training to take place in four 3-hour sessions, and the trainees, that is, the union leaders, were asked to practice the skills on the job with their union members between each session. In Greenberg's (1999) study, training was held 2 hours per week over an 8-week period. In Cole and Latham (1997), training occurred over a period of 5 half-days.

Feedback.   Martocchio and Dulebohn (1994) found that feedback that attributes performance to factors within the trainees' control increases their self-efficacy, that is, the belief that "I can do this." Most people are receptive to feedback that allows them the opportunity to make the necessary adjustments to improve their behavior regarding the goal that they are trying to attain. Negative feedback is usually accepted by trainees if they perceive the trainer as trustworthy and knowledgeable of the subject matter (Arvey & Ivancevich, 1980). Feedback is a moderator of goal-setting effectiveness (Locke & Latham, 1990).

In the Skarlicki and Latham (1996, 1997) studies, feedback for the trainees was provided in three ways. First, we (as trainers) provided the trainees feedback after they practiced their skills in the sessions. Second, after modeling and teaching the trainees principles in effective feedback, we had the trainees provide one another feedback in each training session. Third, at the beginning of each session, trainees reported on their homework experiences (i.e., practicing their skills with the union members), and they gave one another feedback on what they did well, and what they could do even better in the future. In this way, the trainees not only received feedback from the us and from one another, they learned how to provide each other feedback. Specifically, we taught them to provide feedback using the following framework: "Here is what you are doing well, and here is what you could start doing, stop doing, or do differently, to be more effective."

Meaningfulness of Material.   Neutral labeling is used in most training programs. That is, the training begins with such statements as: "The objectives of this training are as follows." Martocchio (1992) showed that anxiety can be reduced and learning increased by labeling the training as an opportunity for trainees, rather than merely using neutral descriptive language. For instance, "opportunity labeling" involves introductory statements as: "You can expect to gain quite a lot from this training." In the training in organizational justice, we explained that: "You will learn that perceptions of fairness are often determined by specific events. You will design strategies that can enhance members' per-

ceptions of fairness. You will gain specific skills that can contribute to your ability to be an effective union leader."

Learning Goals.   In the early stages of learning, setting a performance outcome goal can have a deleterious effect on performance (Kanfer & Ackerman, 1989). This is because in their focus on attaining a specific outcome, people often overlook the necessity of mastering the procedure or process necessary for attaining the goal. Consequently, specific difficult learning goals rather than outcome goals should be set (Seijts, Latham, Tasa, & Latham, 2004; Winters & Latham, 1996). Thus, in the fairness training we explained the learning goals at the beginning of each training session. For example, in session 1, the learning goal was to identify specific procedures that would positively impact the fairness of procedures. In session 2, the learning goal focused on discovering concrete ways to provide voice for union members. We explained that voice is often relevant to fairness perceptions both before and after decisions are made. We began each training session with a review of the learning goals that they had achieved. This contributed to the trainees' confidence that they could learn the principles and skills associated with fairness.

Transfer of Training

Although fairness training can contribute to leaders' understanding key principles, the training is effective to the degree that learning is transferred back to the organization. Five training principles contribute to transfer of training: self-efficacy, outcome expectancies, maximizing the similarity between the training situation and the job setting, providing a variety of examples that trainees are likely to encounter on the job, and relapse prevention.

Outcome Expectancies.   People need to see the relationship between what they do, and the desired outcomes that they can expect as a result of doing so (Latham, 2001). In Skarlicki and Latham (1996, 1997), the homework for session 1 was the goal of interviewing two or three union members. The task involved asking union members to (a) describe a time when they felt they were treated unfairly and to (b) describe how they reacted to the mistreatment, as well as (c) what needed to do done to rectify the unfairness. At the beginning of the next session, the trainees reported ways that they had discovered a direct link between unfair treatment and lack of union member participation. Through group discussion, they came to understand fairness principles, and ways they could address many of the concerns raised by the interviewees.

Self-Efficacy. Self-efficacy mediates the transfer of training to the job (Bandura, 1986). Four factors that contribute to self-efficacy are enactive mastery, vicarious experience, verbal persuasion, and emotional arousal. To give the trainees the confidence that they could attain the outcomes that they desired, we focused on *enactive mastery* by breaking down the challenge of increasing fairness perceptions into specific steps that the trainees could systematically learn. We increased *emotional arousal* by setting the learning goals described earlier. In addition, the trainees identified ways they were potentially creating a perception of in- versus out-groups among union members (e.g., sitting with the same union members each day at lunch). They set a goal to sit with different union members during each lunch and coffee break. *Vicarious experience* was facilitated by having the trainees themselves serve as models for one another to demonstrate these critical skills. *Verbal persuasion* was used by us as trainers to convince them that we were confident that they could (a) master each of the skills in the training, and (b) attain the overall goal of increasing perceptions of union fairness among the union membership.

Maximize the Similarity Between the Training Situation and the Job. To maximize the similarity between training and the work setting, we (Skarlicki & Latham, 1996) developed a case study for the trainees. The case was based on actual events that had occurred in the union. Throughout the sessions, the trainees were asked to discuss the relevance of each fairness principle to their union local. Because the grievance procedure is highly relevant to the role of a union representative, we dedicated an entire training session to focus on ways to enhance the fairness of the grievance procedure. The trainees made minor modifications to the grievance procedure to enhance its fairness. We also designed role plays to simulate leader-member interactions. In summary, the trainees worked with "real-time" issues that were relevant to their ability to lead effectively.

Provide Varied Examples. Through their interviews with union members, following session 1, the trainees identified instances where their union members felt unfairly treated. Several examples were generated and shared in the debriefing that began in session 2. We used these examples in the training sessions to illustrate and explain each of the different fairness principles. These examples were highly relevant because they were derived from events that took place in their union local. As a result, the trainees developed strategies and engaged in role plays on ways to address a variety of unfair situations. Similarly, Greenberg (1999) had leaders read and analyze several different cases and discuss relevant managerial problems in their respective stores.

Relapse Prevention. In the fourth and final session, (Skarlicki & Latham, 1996, 1997), we explained to the trainees why there was a possibility that they would return to their former style of union leadership subsequent to the training program. Thus, we asked them to discuss and design strategies on how to support one another in maintaining their "new" leadership style after the training program was completed. As a result, the trainees formed a support group that met on a weekly basis to discuss the application of the learning principles to upcoming union activities. In addition, we offered a refresher session to the union leaders after the training program was completed. In this session, the trainees discussed which of the newly acquired skills were most useful to them on a day-to-day basis, and identified how they could support one another to "stay on track."

Training Evaluation

Researchers need to be bilingual—not in the Anglophone/Francophone meaning of the term in Canada, but in "sense-making" terms for (a) client/practitioners and (b) fellow researchers. We have yet to be confronted by a client who refused our request as researchers to evaluate the effects of a training intervention. This is because we frame the evaluation in terms of the client's desire for documentation rather than the researchers' need for data. Rather than discuss the necessity of such things as a quasi-experimental design or the value of a training and control group, we discuss the impossibility of training everyone at once, and the fairness inherent in random selection as to who will be initially trained. We do not emphasize to clients that journal editors and reviewers look positively on seeing that a subsequent training intervention brought the control group to the same level of effectiveness as the original training group. It is of little or no interest to clients. Moreover, we usually seek the client's permission to publish the results after the training rather than prior to it. This is because there is little point in making a request to submit something that may turn out not to be worthy of a journal submission. When making the request of the client, we explain that journal publication is a strong indicator of the quality of the work that was performed. We also offer not to disclose the identity of the organization when publishing the study.

We argue for the collection of reaction, learning, and behavioral measures. We explain that reaction measures are important for at least three reasons (Wexley & Latham, 1991). First, measures regarding the practicality of the training often correlate with immediate learning (e.g., "To what extent will the training enable you to perform your job more effectively?"). Second, favorable reactions can influence other people to enroll in the program. Third, reaction data usually suggest ways that the

trainers can make needed adjustments to training content and the style with which it is presented so that the interest of the trainees is enhanced.

Greenberg (1999) administered measures of job satisfaction, commitment, turnover intentions, and theft at regular intervals before and after the training period. He found that the training was effective at improving employees' attitudes—at first only somewhat, then considerably more so after the training was completed. As noted earlier, theft dropped from 8% to 4% at 2 weeks after the training was completed, and remained low for 6 months. No appreciable changes were observed in the control groups. This study points to the importance of control groups without which the assessment of training effectiveness is difficult.

In Skarlicki and Latham (1996, 1997), we collected reaction measures 1 month after the completion of the program. Rather than only assessing whether the trainees liked versus disliked the training program, we also assessed the extent to which they reported using the fairness principles back on the job. The 1-month time frame was chosen to give the trainees sufficient opportunity to make that assessment. The measures focused on the relevance and usefulness of each of the four training sessions. For example, in each session, we asked trainees to respond to items such as: (a) "Were the principles covered in this section relevant to your union local?" (b) "Were you able to actually use the principles in dealing with union members?" Trainees responded to a 5-point Likert-type scale ranging from 1 (strongly disagree) to 5 (strongly agree). If the results had shown that the trainees were not using the justice principles, we would have designed a specific follow-up session to problem solve ways to correct the situation. Our data showed that each of the sessions was highly relevant to the role of a union leader, and that the training principles were used by them.

Learning measures were administered before and after the training to the union leaders in both the training and control groups. Examples of items included: (a) Describe six characteristics that influence perceptions that a decision is fair. (b) Identify five ways in which the union strives to be fair to its members. (c) How would you "de-fuse" a member who feels he or she has been treated unfairly? A graduate student who was blind to the study conditions graded the learning test. The results showed that before the training was conducted, there were no differences between the scores of the training and control groups. Following the intervention, however, the union leaders who were in the training group scored significantly higher than those who were in the control group.

The behavioral measures consisted of the union members' anonymous ratings of the fairness of their union leader. The behavioral measures were taken before and approximately 3 months following the training intervention. This allowed sufficient time for the leaders to in-

teract with a large number of union members. The fairness measures were reworded from Moorman's (1991) study so as to be applicable to a union setting. Examples included: "My union representative considers my viewpoint when making decisions." "My union representative listens to my personal concerns." "My union leader gives me an adequate explanation for union decisions." Responses ranged from 1 (strongly disagree) to 5 (strongly agree). The results showed that union leaders who had been trained were observed to be significantly fairer than those leaders who had not been trained.

Finally, we were interested in testing whether the training intervention had a positive impact on OCB. Behavioral observation scales (Latham & Wexley, 1977) were developed to define and measure citizenship behavior in the union. Examples of items included: "Does your coworker attend union meetings and information sessions?" "Does your coworker attend functions that are not required but that help show union strength?" and "Does your coworker distribute union information to others?" Responses ranged from 1 (almost never) to 5 (almost always). Union members nominated a peer to appraise their union citizenship behavior. OCB was assessed immediately before and three months after the leader training for union members in both the treatment and control groups. The results showed that union members whose leaders had been trained engaged in OCB significantly more than members whose leaders had not been trained.

For journal purposes, we used analysis of covariance (ANCOVA) with the pretest scores as the covariate to assess the effect of the training on both the learning and behavioral measures (see Arvey & Cole, 1989). We also conducted tests to determine whether perceptions of fairness mediated the effect of the training on the dependent variable, which in our case was OCB. Guidance on how to conduct these analyses is provided by Baron and Kenny (1986). In this way, the researcher can provide conclusive evidence whether it was the fairness perceptions that caused the change in the dependent variable or something else. We did not, however, present our results to the clients in terms of inferential statistics; rather, we explained them in terms of graphs, as the latter are easily understood by clients.

From an evaluation perspective, it is critical that researchers consider the numerous potential threats to the internal validity of the study such as mortality or history (for a review see Cook & Campbell, 1979). To offset the potential loss of statistical power due to mortality, we personally followed up with the participants to urge them to complete the measures.

In addition to the statistical results, we obtained qualitative evidence of the outcomes of the training. For instance, in the union elections that followed the training intervention, there were multiple candidates for

several union executive positions. As noted earlier, this had not been observed in previous elections. Nor did it occur in the control group where the candidate was once again reelected by acclamation. This positive effect for the union had also not occurred with previous training programs for union leaders (e.g., grievance handling, labor law, new steward training). This information provides additional evidence of the practical significance of training in organizational justice. Qualitative data, along with quantitative analysis, provide convergent validity for the conclusion that training union leaders in the principles of organizational justice increases the citizenship behavior of the union members.

PRACTICAL SIGNIFICANCE OF TRAINING

Prior to Skarlicki and Latham (1996), studies on the relationship between perceptions of fairness and OCB were based on cross-sectional designs, in which the direction of causality could not be inferred. It is plausible that the direction of causality could flow, for instance, from OCB to fairness perceptions. One explanation for this possibility is that managers tend to categorize their employees into an in-group or an out-group (Graen & Cashman, 1975). Supervisors tend to rate members of the in-group as higher on OCB than members of the out-group. Those in-group members, in turn, tend to rate their supervisors as high on fairness. Thus, whether fairness causes OCB or vice versa was not known. By using a training intervention, we were able to test causality and determine that increases in fairness result in higher levels of OCB.

Our finding regarding causality suggests that fairness training may be effective for achieving organizational goals over and above traditional HR strategies. Greenberg's (1999) study provides a case in point. The organization had tried to reduce theft by using such HR techniques as security cameras and preemployment screening for honesty. These previous attempts, however, were unsuccessful. Training leaders in interpersonal fairness, on the other hand, resulted in a significant reduction in theft.

Is Training Leaders in Fairness Different from General Management Training?

Many of the practices endorsed by popular management training literature are consistent with the principles derived from the organization justice research. Examples include giving employees voice in decisions, providing employees with explanations for decisions, and treating employees with dignity and respect (e.g., Kouzes & Posner, 2003). Similar principles appear in the literature on effective leadership, particularly on the leader's role as a facilitator (e.g., Quinn, Faerman, Thompson, &

McGrath, 2003), for empowering employees (e.g., Whetton & Cameron, 1998), and for introducing change effectively (e.g., Senge, 1994).

The training of leaders in organizational justice principles, however, differs in one primary respect from general management training. The primary focus of justice training is usually on enhancing the followers' perceptions of fairness. In most leadership training programs (e.g., Frayne & Latham, 1987; Latham & Saari, 1979), the dependent variable is an assessment of the leader's behavior subsequent to the intervention. In four of the five studies on training leaders in principles of justice, the primary dependent variable was an assessment of the behavior of the people whom the leaders led, rather than the behavior of the leaders themselves. That this is not always the case is shown in the Cole and Latham (1997) study, where the fairness of leaders in administering disciplinary action was evaluated.

Future Research

Research is needed regarding the structure of fairness. Previous research suggests that different types of fairness are related to different types of organizational outcomes. Masterson, Lewis, Goldman, and Taylor (2000), for example, found that interactional justice is related more to OCB directed at one's supervisor, whereas procedural justice is relatively more related to organizational commitment and job satisfaction. Training programs in which different aspects of justice are emphasized are likely to influence different dependent variables.

Informational and interpersonal justice principles have high relevance to trainees because they apply no matter where the leaders are in an organization's hierarchy. Most importantly, the principles associated with these two aspects of justice are under the trainees' control; a trainee's ability to demonstrate informational and interpersonal justice is not limited by organizational constraints. Training in informational justice, for example, not only helps leaders to understand the importance of providing an explanation and rationale for their decisions, but it also helps them to understand which type (e.g., penitential vs. causal vs. ideological accounts) will be most beneficial to subordinates' fairness perceptions.

From a training perspective, however, interpersonal justice is likely to be affected by informational fairness training. This is because aspects of informational justice (i.e., providing social accounts and explanations) also symbolize that the employee is deemed to be worthy of dignified treatment. Thus, we expect that by providing subordinates with complete and adequate explanations, leaders will also be seen as demonstrating dignity and respect for their subordinates. This warrants further study.

Interpersonal justice refers to treating subordinates with dignity, respect, and sensitivity (Bies, 2001). This definition, however, tends to be highly abstract. In order to enhance interpersonal justice, leaders need to understand what specifically they need to *do* to demonstrate sensitivity, dignity, and respect for their subordinates. For training in this aspect of justice to be effective, we believe it is critical that the trainer defines these concepts in terms of specific behaviors.

Studies are needed to determine the long-term effects of organizational justice training. In three studies (Skarlicki & Jones, 2002; Skarlicki & Latham, 1996, 1997), significant effects (OCB) were observed 3 months after the training was completed. In a fourth study (Greenberg, 1999), effects (theft reduction) emerged 2 weeks after the training and remained stable for 6 months afterward. Although the effects would be expected to dissipate over time, future research might investigate (a) the length of time before the effects appear, (b) how long the effects endured, and (c) what factors lead to a longer versus shorter duration.

Research is needed on the contextual factors that moderate the effectiveness of justice training. Schminke, Ambrose, and Cropanzano (2000), for example, found that organizational size hindered interpersonal justice, and centralization hindered procedural justice. Another potential moderator is the organization's climate. Is training effective, for example, under conditions where prior trust in leadership is extremely low? Skarlicki, Barclay, Pugh, and Patient (2003) found that attempts by leaders to provide an explanation for the downsizing to layoff victims were not effective. The explanation was perceived as "hollow justice"—an attempt to gain the benefits of fairness without actually being fair (Greenberg, 1990b). In addition to organizational climate, Colquitt, Noe, and Jackson (2002) found that differences in fairness perceptions were a function of procedural justice climate strength. Research is needed to determine whether climate strength can be influenced by training, and whether climate strength moderates training effectiveness.

Bowen, Gilliland, and Folger (2000) proposed that organizational justice can translate into higher company profits. They identified two potential linkages. First, employees who perceive they are treated fairly provide higher quality service and demonstrate greater OCB toward customers (relative to employees who feel less fairly treated). Second, customers reciprocate the fair treatment by demonstrating loyalty, and recommending the company to others, resulting in higher sales and higher profits for the company. Each of these paths should be tested through the use of a leadership training intervention in justice principles.

CONCLUSION

Leadership training in organizational justice might be viewed erroneously by some as manipulative—that leaders will use the training as a technique to be seen as fair while behaving unfairly. We believe that this concern is not warranted. To the degree that fairness is used as manipulation, most, if not all employees will view the leader's behavior as "window dressing" and see through it. On the other hand, if employees perceive that leaders are sincere, they are likely to acknowledge the importance to the organization of fairness in the workplace.

The burgeoning research on justice that has occurred over the past 30 years provides a foundation for understanding how fairness perceptions relate to organizational behavior. This research is important, however, insofar as fairness principles are actually used in the workplace to improve leadership and organizational practices. Leadership training in fairness principles provides a mechanism for behavioral science to have a positive effect on workplace practices.

REFERENCES

Arvey, R. D., & Cole, D. A. (1989). Evaluating change due to training. In I. L. Goldstein (Ed.), *Training and development in organizations* (pp. 89–117). San Francisco: Jossey-Bass.

Arvey, R. D., & Ivancevich, J. M. (1980). Punishment in organizations: A review, propositions, and research suggestions. *Academy of Management Review, 5,* 123–132.

Ball, G. A., Trevino, L. K., & Sims, H. P. (1994). Just and unjust punishment: Influences on subordinate performance and citizenship. *Academy of Management Journal, 37,* 299–322.

Bandura, A. (1986). *Social foundations of thought and action: A social cognitive theory.* Englewood Cliffs, NJ: Prentice Hall.

Baron, R. M., & Kenny, D. A. (1986). The moderator-mediator variable distinction in social psychological research: Conceptual, strategic, and statistical considerations. *Journal of Personality and Social Psychology, 51,* 1173–1182.

Bies, R. J. (2001). Interactional (in)justice: The sacred and the profane. In J. Greenberg & R. Cropanzano (Eds.), *Advances in organizational justice* (pp. 89–118). Stanford, CA: Stanford University Press.

Blasi, J., & Kuse, D. (1991). *The new owners: The mass emergence of employee ownership in public companies and what it means to American business.* New York: Harper Business.

Bowen, D. E., Gilliland, S. W., & Folger, R. (2000). HRM and service fairness: How being fair with employees spills over to customers. *Organizational Dynamics, 27,* 7–23.

Brockner, J., Tyler, T. R., & Cooper-Schneider, R. (1992). The influence of prior commitment to an institution on reactions to perceived unfairness: The higher they are, the harder they fall. *Administrative Science Quarterly, 37,* 241–261.

Cole, N. D., & Latham, G. P. (1997). Effects of training in procedural justice on perceptions of disciplinary fairness by unionized employees and disciplinary subject matter experts. *Journal of Applied Psychology, 82,* 699–705.

Colquitt, J. A., Noe, R.A., & Jackson, C. L. (2002). Justice in teams: Antecedents and consequences in procedural justice climate. *Personnel Psychology, 55,* 83–109.

Cook, T. D., & Campbell, D. T. (1979). *Quasi-experimentation: Design and analysis for field settings.* Boston: Houghton Mifflin.

Cropanzano, R., & Wright, T. A. (2003). Procedural justice and organizational staffing: A tale of two paradigms, *Human Resource Management Review, 13,* 7–39.

Dormann, T., & Frese, M. (1994). Error training: Replication and the function of exploratory behavior. *International Journal of Human Computer Interaction, 6,* 365–372.

Farh, J. L., Earley, P. C., & Lind, S. C. (1997). Impetus for action: A cultural analysis of justice and organizational citizenship behavior in Chinese society. *Administrative Science Quarterly, 42,* 421–444.

Frayne, C. A. & Latham, G. P. (1987). The application of social learning theory to employee self management of attendance. *Journal of Applied Psychology, 72,* 387–392.

Gilliland, S. W., & Gilliland, C. M. K. (2001). Justice of diversity training. In S. W. Gilliland, D. D. Steiner, & D. P. Skarlicki (Eds.), *Research in social issues in management: Theoretical and cultural perspectives on organizational justice* (pp. 139–160). Greenwich, CT: Information Age.

Graen, G., & Cashman, J. (1975). A role-making model of leadership in formal organizations: A developmental approach. J. G. Hunt & L. L. Larson (Eds.), *Leadership frontiers* (pp. 430–166). Kent, OH: Kent State University Press.

Greenberg, J. (1996). Determinants of perceived fairness of performance evaluations. *Journal of Applied Psychology, 71,* 340–342.

Greenberg, J. (1990a). Employee theft as a reaction to underpayment inequity: The hidden costs of pay cuts. *Journal of Applied Psychology, 72,* 55–61.

Greenberg, J. (1990b). Looking fair vs. being fair: Managing impressions of organizational justice. In B. M. Staw, & L. L. Cummings (Eds.), *Research in organizational behavior* (Vol. 12, pp.111–157). Greenwich, CT: JAI Press.

Greenberg, J. (1994). Using socially fair treatment to promote acceptance of a work-site smoking ban. *Journal of Applied Psychology, 79,* 288–297.

Greenberg, J. (1996). *The quest for justice on the job.* Newbury Park, CA: Sage.

Greenberg, J. (1999). *Interpersonal justice training (IJT) for reducing employee theft: Some preliminary results.* Unpublished manuscript. The Ohio State University, Columbus, OH.

Greenberg, J., & Bies, R. J. (1992). Establishing the role of empirical studies of organizational justice in philosophical inquiries into business ethics. *Journal of Business Ethics, 11,* 433–444.

Greenberg, J., & Lind, E. A. (2000). The pursuit of organizational justice: From conceptualization to implication to application. In C. L. Cooper & E. A. Locke (Eds.), *I/O psychology: What we know about theory and practices* (pp. 72–105). Oxford, England: Blackwell.

Hicks, W. D., & Klimoski, R. J. (1984, August). *The process of entering training programs and its effects on training outcomes.* Paper presented at the meeting of the Academy of Management, Boston.

Kanfer, R., & Ackerman, P. L. (1989). Motivation and cognitive abilities: An integrative/aptitude treatment interaction approach to skill acquisition. *Journal of Applied Psychology, 74,* 657–690.

Kelloway, E. K., & Barling, J. (1993). Members' participation in local union activities: Measurement, prediction, and replication. *Journal of Applied Psychology, 78,* 262–279.

Kim, W. C., & Mauborgne, R. A. (1993). Making global strategies work. *Sloan Management Review, 34*, 11–27.

Konovsky, M. A., Folger, R., & Cropanzano, R (1987). Relative effects of procedural and distributive justice on employee attitudes. *Representative Research in Social Psychology, 17*, 15–24.

Konovsky, M. A., & Pugh, S. D. (1994). Citizenship behavior and social-exchange. *Academy of Management Journal, 37*, 656–669.

Kouzes, J. M., & Posner, B. (2003). *The five practices of exemplary leadership.* San Francisco: Jossey-Bass.

Latham, G. P. (2001). The importance of understanding and changing employee outcome expectancies for gaining commitment to an organizational goal. *Personnel Psychology, 54*, 707–716.

Latham, G. P. (2003). *Training: A missing link in the strategic plan.* In J. Pickford (Ed.), *Mastering people management.* (pp. 219–222). London: Prentice Hall.

Latham, G. P., & McCauley, C. D. (in press). Leadership in the private sector: Yesterday versus tomorrow. In C. Cooper (Ed.), *The twenty-first century manager.* Oxford, England: Oxford University Press.

Latham, G. P., & Saari, L. M. (1979). The application of social learning theory to training supervisors through behavioral modeling. *Journal of Applied Psychology, 64*, 239–246.

Latham, G. P., & Wexley, K. N. (1977). Behavioral observation scales for performance appraisal purposes. *Personnel Psychology, 30*, 255–268.

Lind, E. A., Greenberg, J., Scott, K. S., & Welchans, T. D. (2000). The winding road from employee to complainant: Situational and psychological determinants of wrongful termination claims. *Administrative Science Quarterly, 45*, 557–590.

Lind, E. A., Kulik, C. T., Ambrose, M., & de Vera Park, M. W. (1993). Individual and corporate dispute resolution: Using procedural fairness as a decision heuristic. *Administrative Science Quarterly, 38*, 224–251.

Locke, E. A., & Latham, G. P. (1990). *A theory of goal setting and task performance.* Englewood Cliffs, NJ: Prentice Hall.

Martocchio, J. J. (1992). Microcomputer usage as an opportunity: The influence of context in employee training. *Personnel Psychology, 45*, 529–552.

Martocchio, J. J., & Dulebohn, J. (1994). Performance feedback effects in training: The role of perceived controllability. *Personnel Psychology, 47*, 357–373.

Masterson, S. S., Lewis, K., Goldman, B. M., & Taylor, M. S. (2000). Integrating justice and social exchange: The differing effects of fair procedures and treatment on work relationships. *Academy of Management Journal, 43*, 738–748.

McFarlin, D. B., & Sweeney, S. D. (1992). Distributive and procedural justice as predictors of satisfaction with personal and organizational outcomes. *Academy of Management Journal, 35*, 626–637.

McGehee, W., & Thayer, P. W. (1961). *Training in business and industry.* New York: Wiley.

Moorman, R. H. (1991). Relationship between organizational justice and organizational citizenship behaviors: Do fairness perceptions influence employee citizenship? *Journal of Applied Psychology, 76*, 845–855.

Noe, R. A., Hollenback, J. R., Gerhart, B., & Wright, P. M. (2003). *Human resource management: Gaining a competitive advantage.* Burr Ridge, IL: McGraw-Hill/Irwin.

Quinn, R. E., Faerman, S., Thompson, M., & McGrath, M. R. (2003). *Becoming a master manager* (3rd ed.). New York: John Wiley & Sons.

Rhoades, L., & Eisenberger, R. (2002). Perceived organizational support: A review of the literature. *Journal of Applied Psychology, 87,* 698–714.

Schminke, M., Ambrose, M., & Cropanzano, R. (2000). The effect of organizational structure on perceptions of procedural justice. *Journal of Applied Psychology, 85,* 294–304.

Seijts, G. H., Latham, G. P., Tasa, K., & Latham, B. W. (2004). Goal setting and goal orientation: An integration of two different yet related literatures. *Academy of Management Journal, 47,* 227–239.

Senge, P. M. (1994). *The fifth discipline.* New York: Currency.

Skarlicki, D. P., Barclay, L. J., Pugh, S. D., & Patient, D. L. (2003). *When explanations are not enough: Retaliation in layoffs.* Manuscript under review.

Skarlicki, D. P., & Folger, R. (1997). Retaliation in the workplace: The roles of distributive, procedural, and interactional justice. *Journal of Applied Psychology, 82,* 434–443.

Skarlicki, D. P., & Jones, D. (2002). *Training leaders in organizational justice principles to increase citizenship behavior in a retail setting.* Unpublished manuscript. University of Calgary.

Skarlicki, D. P., & Latham, G. P. (1996). Increasing citizenship behavior within a labor union: A test of organizational justice theory. *Journal of Applied Psychology, 81,* 161–169.

Skarlicki, D. P., & Latham, G. P. (1997). Leadership training in organizational justice to increase citizenship behavior within a labor union: A replication. *Personnel Psychology, 50,* 617–633.

Wexley, K. N., & Latham, G. P. (1991). *Developing and training human resources in organizations* (3rd ed.). Englewood Cliffs, NJ: Prentice Hall.

Whetton, D. A., & Cameron, K. S. (1998). *Developing management skills* (4th ed.). Reading, MA: Addison-Wesley

Winters, D., & Latham, G. P. (1996). The effect of learning versus outcome goals on a simple versus a complex task. *Group and Organization Management, 21,* 236–250.

VI

GENERALIZABILITY ISSUES

18

How, When, and Why Does Outcome Favorability Interact with Procedural Fairness?

Joel Brockner
Columbia Business School

Batia Wiesenfeld
New York University

The tendency for outcome favorability to interact with procedural fairness to influence employees' work attitudes and behaviors is an important and robust finding in the organizational justice literature. In an earlier review (Brockner & Wiesenfeld, 1996), we summarized studies showing that high procedural fairness reduced the effect of outcome favorability on employees' support for decisions, decision makers, and organizations, relative to when procedural fairness was low. More recent studies show that the interactive relationship between outcome favorability and procedural fairness takes a different form, particularly on measures of self-evaluation. Specifically, high procedural fairness heightens the effect of outcome favorability on employees' self-evaluations, relative to when procedural fairness is low. Guided by theoretical accounts of the two different interactive relationships, we present additional findings that show how people's status relative to the other party in an encounter determines whether the interactive relationship takes one form rather than the other, on the same dependent variable. Specifically, high procedural fairness reduced the effect of outcome favorability among lower status parties and heightened the effect of outcome favorability among higher status parties, relative to when procedural fairness was low. Finally, we suggest how future research may move toward broader conceptualizations of the interactive relationship(s) between outcome favorability and procedural fairness.

In everyday life, a number of expressions remind us of the dual importance of both the outcomes people receive and the processes or procedures that accompany them. For example, we are told that "life is not only a race, but also a journey," that we should pay attention to matters of both "substance and style," and that "it's not only what we say or do, but also how we say or do it" that determines our effectiveness in influencing others. It should therefore come as little surprise that the effects of outcomes and processes on social interaction have long been of interest to organizational psychologists. At first, theory and research tended to examine the role of outcomes. For example, social exchange theory (Blau, 1964) examined outcome favorability, that is, people's perceptions of how much they benefited (either tangibly or intangibly) from their social interactions and relationships. As might be expected, the more favorable the outcomes, the more positively people respond. For example, people have more of a desire to interact with others when the outcomes associated with their encounters are more rather than less favorable.

Subsequently, organizational psychologists turned their attention to more procedural concerns, such as the fairness of the processes used by

resource allocators to plan and implement decisions (Lind & Tyler, 1988; Thibaut & Walker, 1975). Originally, procedural justice was equated with the extent to which people were allowed to have voice, either in the form of providing input into the decision-making process (process control) or having a say in the actual rendering of the decision (outcome control). Subsequently, procedural fairness has been shown to depend on many other factors, such as whether decisions were enacted consistently, with adequate advance notice beforehand and with an opportunity to appeal afterward, whether people were given a clear and adequate explanation of why the decisions were made, and more generally, whether the affected parties were treated with dignity and respect during the planning or implementation of the decision (Bies, 1987; Blader & Tyler, 2003; Colquitt, 2001; Leventhal, Karuza, & Fry, 1980). Across a wide variety of decision-making contexts, various aspects of procedural fairness have proven to be positively related to people's willingness to support decisions, the parties who make them, and the organizations in which they are made (Greenberg, 1996).

THE INTERACTIVE EFFECTS OF OUTCOME FAVORABILITY AND PROCEDURAL FAIRNESS

That people generally react better to decisions, interactions, and relationships in which outcomes are more favorable and procedures are more fair is obvious—indeed, mundane. More interestingly, however, both theory (e.g., Folger, 1986) and research (e.g., Brockner & Wiesenfeld, 1996; Folger, Rosenfield, & Robinson, 1983) have suggested that outcome favorability and procedural fairness often *interact with one another* to influence employees' work attitudes and behaviors. Thus, the magnitude of the generally positive effects of outcome favorability on people's reactions depends on the level of procedural fairness accompanying the outcome. Moreover, the magnitude of the generally positive effects of procedural fairness on people's reactions depends on the level of outcome favorability accompanying the procedure.

The interactive relationship between outcome favorability and procedural fairness is noteworthy for at least four reasons. First, there are by now large literatures that have considered the effects of outcome favorability (e.g., Blau, 1964) and procedural fairness (e.g., Lind & Tyler, 1988) separately, that is, as "main effects." The interactive relationship between outcome favorability and procedural fairness suggests that the precise impact of each of these two factors may need to take the other one into account. At the very least, future research may be more enlightening if these two factors were to be examined jointly rather than separately. Second, the interactive relationship is less obvious (and hence more intriguing) than is an additive relationship, which

simply posits that both outcome favorability and procedural fairness are influential. In response to the criticism that social science research often merely proves what people already believed to be true, McGuire (1973) offered a number of ways to generate more thought-provoking empirical research questions. One suggestion was for researchers to take some well-established finding as their point of departure (e.g., people are more satisfied with decisions when their outcomes are more favorable) and then delineate the conditions under which the finding is more versus less pronounced. McGuire suggested that efforts to account for variations in the truth value of fairly obvious statements, such as "people respond better when their outcomes are more favorable," would contribute to a more nuanced understanding of the statement than would research that merely provided additional confirmatory evidence.

Third, by better understanding when (a) outcome favorability will be more or less impactful (e.g., depending on procedural fairness), or (b) procedural fairness will be more or less influential (e.g., depending on outcome favorability), we may gain insight into *why* these two factors influence people's reactions to decisions. The fact that procedural fairness has a moderating influence on outcome favorability may help to explain why outcome favorability affects people as it does. Similarly, the moderating influence of outcome favorability on procedural fairness may help to explain why procedural fairness is influential.

Fourth, the interactive relationship between outcome favorability and procedural fairness has applied or practical significance. Organizational authorities have tough challenges. They must gain the support of various constituencies for their decisions, themselves, and the institutions that they represent. To gain support, authorities must concern themselves with their constituencies' perceptions of outcome favorability. After all, it is only natural for constituents to evaluate whether they will be better off or worse off as a result of a certain decision. Furthermore, authorities need to concern themselves with their constituencies' perceptions of procedural fairness. Accordingly, authorities must pay attention to how they go about trying to gain their constituencies' support (e.g., Kim & Mauborgne, 1997). Creating perceptions of high outcome favorability and high procedural fairness are not cost free; they require time, money, and psychological energy, among other resources. The moderating influences of outcome favorability and procedural fairness on one another suggest that the extent to which authorities need to concern themselves with each of these factors depends on the perceived level of the other factor. For example, to gain the support of their constituents it may be more necessary for authorities to ensure high outcome favorability when procedural fairness is

low than when procedural fairness is high. Moreover, it may be more necessary for authorities to ensure high procedural fairness when outcome favorability is low rather than high.

Given the significant implications of the interactive relationship between outcome favorability and procedural fairness, it is important to address the closely related questions of how, when, and why outcome favorability and procedural fairness interact. The remaining sections of the chapter address these matters. First, we take as a point of departure the results of studies summarized in our earlier review article, which focused on one particular form of interactive relationship between outcome favorability and procedural fairness (Brockner & Wiesenfeld, 1996). One way to describe the earlier findings is that people's attitudes and behaviors (e.g., their support for decisions, decision-makers, and organizations) are *less* influenced by outcome favorability when procedural fairness is high rather than low. More recently, the results of a number of studies have shown that the interactive relationship between outcome favorability and procedural fairness may also take a very different form. Accordingly, the second section of this chapter reviews these findings, which show that people's evaluations of themselves are *more* influenced by outcome favorability when procedural fairness is high rather than low.

At first blush, the results presented in the first two sections seem contradictory, in that they suggest that high procedural fairness may either reduce or heighten the effect of outcome favorability, relative to when procedural fairness is low (Brockner, 2002). One obvious difference between these two sets of findings is that they emerged on different types of dependent variables. Of greater importance, the theoretical accounts (or "whys") of these two sets of findings help to delineate the conditions under which the interactive relationship between outcome favorability and procedural fairness will take one form rather than the other. Thus, in the third section of this chapter we describe recent findings that delineate when high procedural fairness reduces versus heightens the influence of outcome favorability, even on the same dependent variable. In particular, whether people are of lower or higher status than their interaction partner proves to be pivotal. The fourth section offers a call for future theory and research to conceptualize the interactive relationship(s) between outcome favorability and procedural fairness more broadly. Conceiving the interactive relationships(s) more broadly may help to identify (a) additional factors (besides procedural fairness) that have a moderating influence on outcome favorability, and (b) additional factors (besides outcome favorability) that have a moderating influence on procedural fairness.

WHEN DOES HIGH PROCEDURAL FAIRNESS REDUCE
THE INFLUENCE OF OUTCOME FAVORABILITY?

Beginning with Folger and his colleagues in the 1980s (Folger, 1986; Folger & Martin, 1986; Folger et al., 1983) and continuing into the 1990s, many researchers examined the interactive effect of outcome favorability and procedural fairness on people's beliefs and behaviors. The interactive relationship that we described in our earlier review is highly generalizable (Brockner & Wiesenfeld, 1996). It was found under highly diverse contexts, with a variety of operationalizations of both outcome favorability and procedural fairness, and across an assortment of dependent variables. Some studies were conducted under controlled laboratory conditions, in which the independent variables were experimentally manipulated (e.g., Folger & Martin, 1986; Folger et al., 1983), whereas others were done in the field (e.g., Greenberg, 1994; Schaubroeck, May, & Brown, 1994). Among the field studies, some examined citizens' reactions to their encounters with legal authorities (e.g., Lind & Tyler, 1988), whereas others investigated the effects of organizational events on employees' work attitudes and behaviors (Daly, 1995). Among the studies done in organizations, some examined employees' reactions to an organizational change affecting many employees, such as the introduction of a smoking ban (Greenberg, 1994), a pay freeze (Schaubroeck et al., 1994), and layoffs (Brockner, et al., 1994), whereas others looked at the effects of an event that was more individually targeted, such as an expatriate assignment (Garonzik, Brockner, & Siegel, 2000) or a recent performance appraisal (Magner, Welker, & Johnson, 1996).

The independent variable of outcome favorability was operationalized in a variety of ways. Most were of a tangible nature, such as the degree of economic hardship imposed by a pay freeze (Schaubroeck et al., 1994), the severity of the consequences associated with being either the victim or survivor of a layoff (Brockner et al., 1994), and whether the participant had been selected or rejected for a job (Van den Bos, Vermunt, & Wilke, 1997). Procedural fairness also was induced in many different ways, including voice (Cropanzano & Konovsky, 1995), explanation quality (Daly, 1995), social sensitivity (Greenberg, 1994), and judgments of the overall fairness of the process (Daly & Geyer, 1994). Although the dependent variables also were quite diverse, most referred to attitudes or behaviors reflecting participants' willingness to support the decision that was reached (Korsgaard, Schweiger, & Sapienza, 1995), the party who made the decision (Magner et al., 1996), and the organization in which the decision was made (Brockner et al., 1994).

Highly consistent results emerged among the 45 independent samples included in our earlier review, as well as in subsequent studies

(Brockner, Siegel, Daly, Tyler, & Martin, 1997; Garonzik et al., 2000; Skarlicki & Folger, 1997). Specifically, the tendency for people to respond more positively when outcomes were more favorable was less pronounced when procedural fairness was high rather than low. To state the interaction effect differently, the tendency for people to respond more positively when procedures were more fair was less pronounced when outcome favorability was high rather than low.

Explaining the Interaction Effect

Two explanations of the interaction effect have been conceptually developed and empirically confirmed within the past few years. These two explanations are not mutually exclusive. Moreover, they were not designed to explain the interactive relationship between outcome favorability and procedural fairness per se. Rather, and herein lies part of their appeal, they are more general frameworks that may account for a wide range of justice-related effects.

Relational Theories.   Relational theories of justice (e.g., Lind & Tyler, 1988; Tyler & Lind, 1992) posit that people are concerned with determining the nature of their relationships with other parties (Lind, 1995, 2001). One important relational judgment pertains to the extent to which the other party may be trusted, and one indicator of the other party's trustworthiness is his or her procedural fairness. The more the other party is procedurally fair, the more he or she will be trusted (Konovsky & Pugh, 1994). Trust, in turn, interacts with outcome favorability, such that when trust in the other party is high, outcome favorability will have less of an impact on people's support for decisions/ decision makers/organizations, relative to when trust in the other party is low.

Why might trust interact with outcome favorability? Note that the outcomes examined in most if not all of the studies that we previously reviewed referred to events that were *recent* and *tangible.* As Brockner (2002) suggested, trust influences people's perceptions along two dimensions—the time frame through which people view their relationship with the other party, and the "currency" of exchange in the relationship—that may account for the interactive relationship between trust and outcome favorability (such that outcome favorability is less influential when trust is relatively high).

In most exchange relationships, people care about the outcomes they receive in the present, as well as the outcomes that they can reasonably expect to receive in the future. When people trust their exchange partner, they are likely to feel reassured about the favorability of their future outcomes. As a result, they may assign less importance

to, and hence be less influenced by, the favorability of their current outcomes. However, when people do not trust their exchange partner, they have no such assurances about their future outcomes. This may lead them to assign greater significance to (and hence be more affected by) their current outcomes.

In most exchange relationships, people also care about both the tangible economic outcomes that they receive (whether they stand to gain or lose in a material way), as well as the intangible, symbolic outcomes (whether they are respected by the other party, which, in turn, may influence feelings of self-worth). In exchange relationships characterized by high levels of trust, both parties may believe that they are receiving favorable intangible outcomes. More trusting relationships symbolize to people that they are held in higher regard by the other party (Kramer & Tyler, 1996). Lind (2001) suggested that high procedural fairness "leads to a shift from responding to a social situation in terms of immediate self-interest ... to responding to social situations as a member of the larger social entity." In the latter case, "there is far less concern with ... the individual material payoffs associated with any given behavior" (p. 67).

Pulling together the effects of the time frame and currency of exchange factors suggests that the degree of favorability of recent tangible outcomes will be less influential when procedural fairness (as an elicitor of trust) is relatively high. However, when people do not trust the other party, they may define the relationship as more transactional, in which they assign less importance to intangible outcomes and more importance to tangible outcomes. If this were to occur, they should be more influenced by the favorability of their recent tangible outcomes.

The preceding reasoning makes two predictions, each supported by recent empirical research. First, it is not procedural fairness per se that interacts with outcome favorability to influence employees' support for decisions, decision makers, and organizations. Rather, it is the degree of *trust elicited by procedural fairness* that interacts with outcome favorability, such that outcome favorability is less likely to influence employees' support when trust is high rather than low (Brockner et al., 1997).

Second, although people generally are motivated to make inferences about their relationships with others (including how much to trust the others), the strength of this concern may vary. For example, the more that people attach significance to their relationships with others, the more likely they are to be concerned with determining the nature of the relationships (such as how much to trust the other). The conditions under which people attach greater significance to their relationships with others, in turn, should elicit more of an interactive relationship between outcome favorability and procedural fairness.

Recent findings confirm this prediction. One series of studies examined the moderating impact of between- and within-cultural differences in interdependent/independent self-construals (Markus & Kitayama, 1991) on the interactive relationship between outcome favorability and procedural fairness (Brockner, Chen, Mannix, Leung, & Skarlicki, 2000). In Asian cultures (or among people with more of an interdependent self-construal), the tendency for high procedural fairness to reduce the relationship between outcome favorability and employees' support for decisions and decision makers was stronger than it was in Western cultures (or among people with more of an independent self-construal). Presumably, those with more interdependent self-construals assigned greater significance to their ongoing relationships with others than did those with more independent self-construals. Another set of studies provided converging evidence by showing that the more people attached importance to their long-term relationship with the other party, the more likely they were to exhibit the interactive relationship between outcome favorability and procedural fairness (Kwong & Leung, 2002).

Fairness Theory.   A more recent extension of referent cognitions theory (Folger, 1986), fairness theory suggests that how people react to their outcomes depends on their judgments of accountability or responsibility (Folger & Cropanzano, 1998). The effect of outcome favorability on people's reactions depends on the degree to which they hold the decision maker accountable for the decision. Because prevailing ethical standards and norms mandate that exchange partners should behave in procedurally fair ways, behavior that violates such norms tends to be attributed to something about the actor (Jones & Davis, 1965). This reasoning suggests that people will view the other party to be more responsible for his/her behavior—and, by extension, more responsible for the outcomes of the exchange—when the other party exhibits lower procedural fairness. For example, if employees failed to receive a desired promotion due to the other party's use of unfair procedures, then employees are likely to see the other party as responsible for their failure to be promoted, leading to high feelings of resentment towards the other party.

The results of a series of laboratory studies by Folger and his colleagues are consistent with this reasoning (Cropanzano & Folger, 1989; Folger & Martin, 1986; Folger et al., 1983). These studies showed that when procedural fairness was high, outcome favorability had much less of an impact on resentment toward the other party, relative to when procedural fairness was low. Put differently, procedural fairness was strongly (and inversely) related to feelings of resentment when outcome favorability was low, whereas procedural fairness bore little relationship with resentment when outcome favorability was high.

Differentiating Between Explanations

One important difference between relational theory (Lind, 2001) and fairness theory (Folger & Cropanzano, 1998) consists of how people are posited to use procedural fairness information. According to the relational viewpoint, people use procedural fairness information for social sensemaking purposes. That is, procedural fairness informs people of the nature of their relationship with the other party. As Van den Bos, Bruins, Wilke, and Dronkert (1999) suggested, people want to know whether the other party can be trusted (trust), whether the other party will treat them in an honest and nonbiased way (neutrality), and whether the other party will accord them the appropriate standing as a member of their group (standing). Procedural fairness informs people about trust, neutrality, and standing. In other words, people make a number of important relational inferences on the basis of procedural fairness information. Of greatest current concern, the inferences they make about trust are particularly relevant to the interactive relationship between outcome favorability and procedural fairness.

According to fairness theory, people use procedural fairness information to make sense of the outcomes associated with the other party's behavior. As attribution theorists have noted (e.g., Kelley, 1972), one way in which people make sense of their outcomes is through attributions of responsibility. People interpret the meaning of their outcomes by determining the extent to which the other party is responsible, and procedural fairness information helps them to determine the other party's responsibility. Just as procedural fairness information may be used to make multiple relational inferences (not only about trust, but also about neutrality and standing), so too it may be used to make more than one attribution of responsibility. That is, in addition to helping people judge the other party's responsibility for their outcomes, procedural fairness information may be used to make self-attributions of responsibility.

The extent to which people make self-attributions of responsibility for their outcomes also has implications for the interactive relationship between outcome favorability and procedural fairness. However, as we explain in the next section, the interactive relationship to which self-attributions are relevant takes a form that is very different from the interactive relationship that has been discussed to this point.

WHEN DOES HIGH PROCEDURAL FAIRNESS HEIGHTEN THE INFLUENCE OF OUTCOME FAVORABILITY?

One way in which people make sense of their outcomes is by determining their own personal responsibility (in addition to that of the other

party). Theory and research in the achievement motivation literature (e.g., Weiner, 1985) have suggested that the more that people see themselves as responsible for their outcomes, the more likely is the favorability of the outcomes to influence their self-evaluations. Outcomes for which people perceive themselves to be more personally responsible elicit more positive self-evaluations when outcomes are favorable and more negative self-evaluations when outcomes are unfavorable, relative to when people view themselves as less responsible for their outcomes. Furthermore, theory and research in the justice literature suggest that low procedural fairness not only leads people to see *the other party* as more responsible for their outcomes (Folger & Cropanzano, 1998), but also that high procedural fairness induces people to see *themselves* as more responsible for their outcomes (Mark & Folger, 1984).

Previously, we suggested that people are more likely to externalize the causes of their outcomes when the other party is procedurally unfair. That is, they attribute their outcomes to the (unfair procedures of the) other party. In contrast, when procedural fairness is high people cannot as easily externalize the causes of their outcomes. As Brockner (2002) suggested, outcomes associated with fair procedures are likely to be viewed as deserved, that is, arrived at "fairly and squarely" (Heuer, Blumenthal, Douglas, & Weinblatt, 1999). Judgments of deservingness, in turn, are closely linked to perceptions of personal responsibility. When people believe that they received the outcomes they deserved, they are in essence saying that there was something about themselves (e.g., their personality, ability, or behavior) that was responsible for their outcomes. Indeed, several recent studies provide empirical evidence that people see themselves as more personally responsible for their outcomes when the other party is more procedurally fair (Leung, Su, & Morris, 2001; Van den Bos et al., 1999).

The preceding reasoning has important implications for the interactive relationship between outcome favorability and procedural fairness. Specifically, on dependent variables in which the object of evaluation is the self (e.g., temporary feelings of self-esteem, self-efficacy, or ratings of one's own job performance), or on dependent variables that may be related to people's self-evaluations (e.g., "self-conscious" emotions such as guilt and pride; Tangney & Fischer, 1995), there should also be an interactive effect of outcome favorability and procedural fairness. Note, however, that the nature of the interactive effect of outcome favorability and procedural fairness on self-evaluations is expected to be very different from the interactive relationship discussed in the preceding section. More specifically, high procedural fairness should *heighten* the influence of outcome favorability on self-evaluations, relative to when procedural fairness is low. The basis of

this assertion is twofold. First, higher procedural fairness leads people to see themselves as more personally responsible for their outcomes (Van den Bos et al., 1999). Second, outcomes for which people feel more personally responsible are more likely to influence their self-evaluations (Weiner, 1985). To state differently the expected interactive effect of outcome favorability and procedural fairness on self-evaluations, when outcomes are favorable, procedural fairness and self-evaluations should be positively related to each other. However, when outcomes are unfavorable, there should be less of a positive (and perhaps even an inverse) relationship between procedural fairness and self-evaluations.

Results consistent with this reasoning have been reported by Gilliland (1994), and in three studies conducted by Schroth and Shah (2000). These findings were reported in our earlier review article (Brockner & Wiesenfeld, 1996), in which they were described as "contrary interactions" because their nature was different from the vast majority of studies showing that high procedural fairness reduced rather than heightened the influence of outcome favorability. There is, by now, considerably more evidence that high procedural fairness heightens the influence of outcome favorability on people's self-evaluations, relative to when procedural fairness is low (Brockner et al., 2003; Koper, Van Knippenberg, Bouhuijs, Vermunt, & Wilke, 1993; Ployhart & Ryan, 1998; Ployhart, Ryan, & Bennett, 1999).

Moreover, several studies have shown that it was the effect of procedural fairness on perceptions of personal responsibility for outcomes that played a key role in accounting for these findings. For example, one study used a mediational analysis to demonstrate that it was not procedural fairness per se that interacted with outcome favorability to influence self-esteem. Rather, it was the perception of personal responsibility for one's outcomes *elicited by procedural fairness* that interacted with outcome favorability to influence participants' self-esteem (Brockner et al., 2003, Study 2).

In sum, an answer to the "how" question posed in the title of this chapter is that the interactive relationship between outcome favorability and procedural fairness may take multiple forms. Previously (Brockner & Wiesenfeld, 1996), we focused on the considerable evidence showing that high procedural fairness reduced the effect of outcome favorability on people's support for decisions, decision makers, and organizations, relative to when procedural fairness is low. Furthermore, there is now ample evidence that high procedural fairness heightens the effect of outcome favorability on people's self-evaluations, relative to when procedural fairness is low. Moreover, related findings provide an answer to the "why" question posed in the title of this paper. The interaction effects appear to be based on people's use of procedural fairness information for two related but conceptually distinct

sensemaking purposes: (a) to determine the nature of their relationship with the other party, in particular how much to trust the other, and (b) to determine their own as well as the other party's level of responsibility for their outcomes (Brockner, 2002).

A Potential Managerial Dilemma

The two different forms of interactive relationships also may pose a dilemma to managers, particularly when they must make "the difficult choices" (i.e., decisions yielding unfavorable outcomes). When employees perceive the outcomes of a decision to be relatively unfavorable, the managerial challenge is to maintain (i.e., minimize potential reductions in) employees' support for the decisions, the decision makers, and the organization. Furthermore, in most instances, managers probably would prefer to maintain (i.e., minimize the potentially harmful effects of the unfavorable outcomes on) employees' self-evaluations. To achieve both of these goals, the advice offered by practitioners (e.g., Kim & Mauborgne, 1997) and academics alike (e.g., Tyler & Lind, 1992) is to ensure relatively high levels of procedural fairness. Note, however, that when outcomes are unfavorable high procedural fairness may elicit greater employee support for the system, while simultaneously lowering employee self-evaluations.

The extent to which the combination of high procedural fairness and unfavorable outcomes poses a managerial dilemma depends on two considerations. First, it is important to specify the nature of the relationship between procedural fairness and self-evaluations. In studies showing an interactive effect of outcome favorability and procedural fairness on employees' self-evaluations, the results are quite consistent in showing that procedural fairness and self-evaluations are more positively related to each other when outcomes are favorable than when they are unfavorable. However, mixed results have been obtained *within* the condition in which outcomes are unfavorable. Some studies find that the relationship between procedural fairness and self-evaluations is weakly positive or nonsignificant (but significantly less positive than when outcomes are favorable; e.g., Brockner et al., 2003). Other studies actually show a significant *inverse* relationship between procedural fairness and self-esteem when outcomes are unfavorable (e.g., Schroth & Shah, 2000). Obviously, the latter findings make the use of high procedural fairness more controversial than the former, in that high procedural fairness actually may be damaging to self-esteem when outcomes are unfavorable. Thus, further research is needed to pinpoint the precise nature of the relationship between procedural fairness and self-evaluations in the face of unfavorable outcomes.

Second, it could even be argued that reductions in employees' self-evaluations (at least temporarily) may be a price that managers have to pay in order to elicit behavioral change in their employees. For example, suppose that a manager believed that the best way to motivate a particular employee was to give him or her unfavorable feedback.[1] If so, then the manager may be well advised to communicate that the procedures by which the feedback was arrived at were fair. The employee's perception that procedures were fair may lead him/her to take the feedback more seriously (i.e., make more personal attributions of responsibility), which may, in turn, elicit greater motivation to change.

However, if and when (a) procedural fairness and self-esteem are inversely related, and (b) managers want to avoid lowering employees' self-esteem, then they cannot simply rely on previous prescriptions to be procedurally fair (Kim & Mauborgne, 1997) when implementing decisions that yield unfavorable outcomes. This is not to suggest, of course, that managers should be procedurally unfair (to minimize reductions in employees' self-evaluations). Rather, we believe that managers need to be procedurally fair *and also* take other actions that would minimize any potential reduction in employees' self-evaluations, such as encouraging employees to engage in a self-affirming activity (cf., Wiesenfeld, Brockner, & Martin, 1999; Wiesenfeld, Brockner, Petzall, Wolf, & Bailey, 2001).

INTEGRATING THE TWO SETS OF FINDINGS

Taken together, the results presented in the previous two sections provide one answer to the "when" question posed in the title of this chapter. Across a wide variety of settings and samples, outcome favorability and procedural fairness interact (in two different ways) to influence people's reactions to their social exchanges. One way to interpret the findings to this point is that the form of the interaction effect depends on the nature of the reaction (or dependent variable) that is being assessed. When the dependent variable consists of people's support for decisions, decision makers, and organizations, high procedural fairness reduces the effect of outcome favorability, relative to when procedural fairness is low. However, when the dependent variable refers to people's self-evaluations, high procedural fairness heightens the influence of outcome favorability (e.g., Gilliland, 1994).

---

[1]Whether and when unfavorable feedback is motivating is itself a matter of considerable complexity. As Kluger and DeNisi (1996) suggested, unfavorable feedback can be demotivating as well as motivating, depending on the situation (and the person). For the purposes of the present example, let's assume that the manager is correct in his or her judgment that unfavorable feedback will lead to higher levels of employee motivation.

It could be argued that finding different interactive relationships on different types of dependent variables is not particularly surprising. After all, if people's responses to one type of dependent variable (e.g., organizational commitment) are either uncorrelated with or inversely related to their responses to the other type of dependent variable (e.g., self-esteem), then it stands to reason that the interactive relationship between outcome favorability and procedural fairness may take different forms on the different measures. What makes the findings all the more intriguing, however, is that reactions to the two different types of dependent variables tend to be *positively* related to one another (in the few studies that assessed both types). For example, Ployhart et al. (1999, study 1) showed that participants' appraisals of themselves and their organizations were positively correlated. Similarly, Brockner et al. (2003, study 4) observed a modest but significant positive correlation between employees' (a) self-appraisals and (b) organizational commitment, even though high procedural fairness *heightened* the effect of outcome favorability on the former, and *reduced* the effect of outcome favorability on the latter, relative to when procedural fairness was low.

Furthermore, a number of other related matters remain unresolved. For one thing, the preceding sections say little about the factors that elicit the sensemaking processes that may account for either or both of the two interaction effects. To better answer the "when" question posed in the title of this chapter, it is necessary to identify the elicitors of the sensemaking processes. In addition, the interaction effects in the two preceding sections are somewhat difficult to integrate. They take different forms, for possibly different reasons, on different types of dependent variables. If our analysis of the "whys"—that is, the reasons underlying the two different interactive relationships—is correct, then it may be possible to delineate the conditions under which the two different interactive relationships emerge on the *same* dependent measure.

More specifically, a variable that at one level makes salient concerns about trusting the other party and that at another level makes salient attributions of personal responsibility may elicit the two different interaction effects, on the same dependent variable, in the same study. One such variable is people's status relative to the other party in the encounter. For reasons to be set forth next, among people of lower status than the other party, evaluating the trustworthiness of the other party is likely to be more salient, relative to the (higher status) other. Moreover, among those of higher status than the other, evaluating their level of personal responsibility for their outcomes is likely to be more salient, relative to the (lower status) other.

Chen, Brockner, and Greenberg (2003) recently examined the moderating effect of people's relative status on the interactive relationship be-

tween outcome favorability and procedural fairness. The relational perspective on procedural fairness (e.g., Tyler & Lind, 1992) suggests that people use procedural fairness information to make inferences about the nature of their relationship with the other party, such as how much the other party may be trusted. The conditions that heighten the salience or importance of determining the trustworthiness of the other party should elicit more of the interaction effect in which high procedural fairness reduces the influence of outcome favorability on people's support for decisions, decision makers, and organizations (Brockner et al., 2000; Kwong & Leung, 2002).

People's status relative to the other party is likely to influence the extent to which they assign importance to evaluating the trustworthiness of the other party. More specifically, several literatures in social psychology have suggested that people who perceive themselves to be of lower status will be more concerned with determining how much to trust the other party (Brewer & Brown, 1998; Crocker, Major, & Steele, 1998). Kramer (1996), for example, suggested that lower status people often encounter considerable uncertainty not only about the quality of the outcomes they are receiving, but also about the fairness and integrity of the procedures used to generate those outcomes:

> As a result of these uncertainties, individuals in subordinate roles … lack precisely those types of information needed to make informed judgments about the trustworthiness (or lack of trustworthiness) of those exercising authority over them. Thus, from the standpoint of those on the bottom, decisions regarding how much trust should be conferred on a particular relationship become simultaneously more *consequential* and more problematic…. Those on the bottom of a hierarchical relationship routinely encounter both vulnerability and uncertainty, and these are the conditions that *make salient concerns about trust.* (Kramer, 1996, p. 223, emphasis added)

This reasoning suggests that people who perceive themselves to be of lower status should be especially likely to show the interactive relationship between outcome favorability and procedural fairness in which high procedural fairness reduces the influence of outcome favorability. Chen et al. (2003) tested this hypothesis in a series of studies in which the dependent variable was the same for all participants, namely, their desire for future interaction with the other party.

What about people who perceive themselves to be of higher status? Prior theory and research suggest that the salient concern for them is less about determining how much to trust the other party, and more about how to *maintain* their relatively high status, which brings about not only material benefits, but also psychological ones, such as

high self-esteem (e.g., Fiske, 2001; Pfeffer, 1992; Swann, 1996). If so, then higher status people should be particularly attuned to cues that inform them of whether they will be able to maintain their status in their interactions with (lower status) others. Moreover, the combination of outcome favorability and procedural fairness information is relevant to the higher status person's quest for status maintenance. Therefore, higher status people will use information about outcome favorability and procedural fairness to determine whether their interactions or relationships with other parties enable them to maintain their status. Interestingly enough, higher status people may use outcome favorability and procedural fairness information in ways that lead to an interactive relationship in which high procedural fairness *heightens* the influence of outcome favorability on desire for future interaction with the other party.

Here's how. It is reasonably self-evident that high-status persons will be more likely to maintain their status when the outcomes of their exchange with the other party are favorable rather than unfavorable. Therefore, all else being equal, they should be more attracted to interaction partners and relationships when outcome favorability is high rather than low. Moreover, given that procedural fairness information may be used to make judgments of personal responsibility for outcomes, the tendency of high-status persons to prefer interactions/relationships when outcomes are favorable should be stronger when procedural fairness is high rather than low. Favorable outcomes accompanied by fair procedures are particularly enhancing to one's self-esteem (and hence affirm high status); however, unfavorable outcomes accompanied by fair procedures may be damaging to self-esteem (Schroth & Shah, 2000), and hence threaten high status. Given that higher status people seek status maintenance in their interactions with lower status others, they should be considerably more attracted to interaction partners and relationships in which outcomes are favorable and procedures are fair than to those in which outcomes are unfavorable and procedures are fair.

What happens when procedures are unfair? Although the desire for future interaction should still be positively related to outcome favorability, the outcomes associated with unfair procedures are *less* self-relevant (than when procedures are fair). For example, outcome favorability has less of an influence on self-evaluations when procedures are relatively unfair (Brockner et al., 2003; Schroth & Shah, 2000). Put differently, the outcomes associated with unfair procedures are less relevant to the higher status party's desire to maintain his or her status. Thus, among higher status persons we would expect outcome favorability to have less of an influence on their desire for future interaction

with the (lower status) other when procedural fairness is low rather than high.[2]

Chen et al. (2003) recently tested the hypothesis that one's relative status in a social encounter would determine the nature of the interactive effect of outcome favorability and procedural fairness on participants' desire for future interaction with the other party. The independent variables of outcome favorability, procedural fairness, and relative status were conceptually similar across studies, as was the dependent variable of desire for future interaction with the other party. However, there were many contextual differences between studies, including the nature of the interaction (negotiations vs. reward allocation), the participants (MBA students vs. employees), and the ways in which the independent variables were operationalized. For example, in the negotiation setting perceived status was based on the prestige of the groups to which individuals belonged, whereas in the reward allocation setting status was based on participants' formal hierarchical position (supervisor vs. subordinate). In spite of the contextual differences between the studies, highly consistent results emerged. Among those who were of lower status, outcome favorability and procedural fairness interacted, such that high procedural fairness reduced the relationship between outcome favorability and desire for future interaction, relative to when procedural fairness was low. Among those of higher status, outcome favorability and procedural fairness interacted, such that high procedural fairness heightened the relationship between outcome favorability and desire for future interaction, relative to when procedural fairness was low. Among participants of equal status to the other party (i.e., when both parties were low in status or when both were high in status), outcome favorability and procedural fairness did not interact at all. Rather, the equal-status participants exhibited main effects of outcome favorability and procedural fairness on desire for future interaction.

These findings have several important theoretical implications. First, in the studies reviewed in our earlier paper (Brockner & Wiesenfeld, 1996), in which high procedural fairness reduced the effect of outcome favorability, the participants always were of relatively lower status (e.g., citizens, direct reports, and subjects), responding to the outcome

---

[2]For parties of equal status, neither maintenance of status nor concerns about trust are likely to be strongly salient. Thus, although each of procedural justice and outcome favorability may be expected to influence desire for future interaction, it is less likely that the sensemaking processes responsible for an interactive relationship between these two factors will be elicited, relative to when people are of differing status. That is, among equal-status people, both outcome favorability and procedural fairness may be positively related to their desire for future interaction with the (equal status) other. However, in this case the effects of outcome favorability and procedural fairness are expected to be additive rather than interactive.

favorability and procedural fairness of actions taken by parties of higher status (e.g., legal authorities, managers, and experimenters, respectively). Although little mention was made of this feature of the previous studies, the Chen et al. (2003) findings suggest that it was necessary to elicit the interactive relationship in which high procedural fairness reduced the effect of outcome favorability on employees' support for decisions, decision makers, and institutions, relative to when procedural fairness is low.

Moreover, although it is important to understand the reactions of lower status persons to outcome favorability and procedural fairness (which has been the focus of most previous studies), it is also worthwhile to delineate the combined effects of outcome favorability and procedural fairness on higher (and equal) status parties. Much if not most organizational research looks at the effects of the actions taken by managers (higher status parties) on their direct reports (lower status parties), rather than the other way around. In reality, the influence process between managers and their direct reports is bidirectional (e.g., Ginzel, Kramer, & Sutton, 1992). The Chen et al. studies suggest that it is indeed important to examine how outcome favorability and procedural fairness influence both lower and higher status parties. Although both lower and higher status parties' desire for future interaction with one another was influenced by the interaction between outcome favorability and procedural fairness, the nature of the interactive effect differed between the lower and higher status participants.

Second, the findings serve to integrate further the two different interactive relationships between outcome favorability and procedural fairness. Previous studies showed that the two different interactive patterns emerged on different dependent variables, raising questions about whether it was the sensemaking processes that accounted for the interactive relationships or some other factor inherent to the difference between the dependent variables. The Chen et al. (2003) findings suggest that the presence of different dependent variables is not necessary to bring about the two different interactive relationships between outcome favorability and procedural fairness. Existing theory suggested that the two different interactive relationships could emerge on the same dependent variable (desire for future interaction with the other, a likely indicator of overall relationship quality), depending on one's relative status in the situation. Relative status was presumed to influence the sensemaking consideration that was salient to participants, and in so doing, to determine the nature of the interactive relationship between outcome favorability and procedural fairness.

Third, in our earlier review (Brockner & Wiesenfeld, 1996), we noted that a number of studies failed to exhibit an interactive relationship between outcome favorability and procedural fairness (e.g., Dipboye & de

Pontbriand, 1981; Lind, Kurtz, Musante, Walker, & Thibaut, 1980). The Chen et al. findings are particularly integrative in that, guided by theory, they begin to shed light on whether the interactive relationship between outcome favorability and procedural fairness will emerge *at all*, and when it does, whether it will take one form rather than the other. These results imply that social encounters between parties of relatively equal status (both high or both low) are less apt to elicit the sensemaking processes that lead outcome favorability and procedural fairness to interact in either of the two ways that have been discussed in the present analysis.

TOWARD A BROADER CONCEPTUALIZATION OF THE INTERACTIVE RELATIONSHIP(S)

Although the interaction effects have proven to be robust findings in previous research, they may actually be subsumed by even broader theoretical perspectives. Hence, it may be useful for future researchers to evaluate this possibility. One way to conceive of the interaction effects more broadly is by asking the following questions: What is it about procedural fairness that causes it to have a moderating influence on outcome favorability? Moreover, what is it about outcome favorability that causes it to have a moderating influence on procedural fairness? Insight into the former question may unearth other factors (besides procedural fairness) that dictate when outcome favorability will be more versus less influential. Answers to the latter question may help identify other factors (besides outcome favorability) that dictate when procedural fairness will be more versus less influential.

What Is it About Procedural Fairness?

Here we consider why procedural fairness moderates the influence of outcome favorability—for example, why outcome favorability has more of an influence on self-evaluations (or related measures) when procedural fairness is relatively high. One possibility is that high procedural fairness leads people to experience their interactions (and associated outcomes) as more self-relevant, that is, as having more implications for their personal values, sense of identity, and self-esteem. For example, the more that people see themselves as personally responsible for their outcomes, the greater is the self-relevance of those outcomes. High procedural fairness, in turn, predisposes people to feel more personally responsible for their outcomes (Van den Bos et al., 1999). Indeed, it is the heightened sense of personal responsibility (elicited by high procedural fairness) that caused outcome favorability to have more of an impact on people's self-evaluations when procedural fairness was high rather than low (Brockner et al., 2003).

This reasoning suggests that other process-related variables (besides high procedural fairness) that induce people to make internal attributions for their outcomes may heighten the effect of outcome favorability on their self-evaluations. For example, suppose that many people applied for a highly coveted job. According to attribution theory (Kelley, 1972), the person who is selected for the position is more likely to make an internal attribution for being selected, relative to if fewer people had applied. Furthermore, making more of an internal attribution for the favorable outcome, the selected individual is likely to experience a more positive self-evaluation. Consider, on the other hand, the individual who applied for a less desirable job for which relatively few others had applied. If the person is rejected for the position, he or she is more likely to make an internal attribution than if many people had applied. Moreover, making more of an internal attribution for the unfavorable outcome, the rejected individual is likely to experience more negative self-evaluation.

Future research also should evaluate the possibility that factors other than making internal attributions for one's outcomes may increase the self-relevance of events in the workplace. For example, people may assign self-relevance to workplace events when their attention is self-directed. Inducements to self-directed attention include: (a) being new on the job (or otherwise unfamiliar with the task at hand), (b) being demographically different from the majority of one's coworkers, and (c) receiving negative feedback about one's recent task performance. Subsequent outcomes experienced under conditions of greater self-directed attention are likely to have more of an influence on people's self-evaluations, for better or worse. For example, we would expect that people who are relatively new at their jobs (and who are therefore feeling self-conscious about their ability to perform) will experience more of a boost in self-esteem in response to favorable performance feedback, relative to their counterparts who receive the identical feedback but who are more familiar with their task requirements. On the other hand, people who are demographically different from most of their coworkers (and, as a result, who are feeling self-focused) may experience more of a reduction in self-esteem in response to unfavorable outcomes, relative to those who receive the same unfavorable outcomes but who are more demographically similar to their coworkers (and are therefore feeling less self-focused).

In summary, when people go about doing their work, or interacting with other parties in the workplace, various factors may influence the self-relevance of the process. Previous research already has shown that the other party's procedural fairness is one inducement to self-relevance, by influencing the extent to which people make internal attributions for their outcomes (Van den Bos et al., 1999). Other process considerations

(besides procedural fairness) may influence people's tendencies to make internal attributions for their outcomes, and other psychological factors (besides making internal attributions for outcomes) may influence the perceived self-relevance of the process. We hypothesize that all of these factors will behave like procedural fairness in moderating the effect of outcome favorability on people's self-evaluations. Whenever the process of task engagement or interacting with others is perceived to be more self-relevant, outcome favorability should be more positively related to people's self-evaluations.

What Is It About Outcome Favorability?

Here we consider why outcome favorability moderates the influence of procedural fairness—for example, why procedural fairness has more of an influence on people's support for decisions, decision makers, and organizations when outcomes are unfavorable rather than favorable. We believe that unfavorable outcomes (more than favorable outcomes) elicit a sensemaking process in which people seek to evaluate how much to trust the other party, (particularly when people are of lower status than the other party). Mayer, Davis, and Schoorman (1995) defined trust as the "willingness of a party to be vulnerable to the actions of another party based on the expectation that the other will perform a particular action important to the trustor, irrespective of the ability to monitor or control that other party" (p. 712). Given this definition, it stands to reason that feelings of vulnerability (and therefore concerns about how much to trust the other party) will be greater in the face of unfavorable rather than favorable outcomes. One source of information that people use to evaluate how much to trust the other is procedural fairness. If unfavorable outcomes heighten the relevance of procedural fairness information (in inducing people to evaluate how much to trust the other), it follows that people's procedural fairness perceptions will have more of an influence on their support for the other party's decisions, for the other party, or for the organization, when outcomes are relatively unfavorable.

The reasoning just described suggests that other factors (besides unfavorable outcomes) that elicit a sensemaking process in which people seek to evaluate how much to trust the other party similarly should heighten the influence of procedural fairness information. By heightening feelings of vulnerability, unfavorable outcomes make it *important* for people to engage in a sensemaking process in which they evaluate the trustworthiness of the other party. A related inducement to engage in sensemaking is *uncertainty* about the trustworthiness of the other party. In other words, people may seek to determine the trustworthiness of the other party when (a) it is important for them to do so (e.g.,

when outcomes are unfavorable, eliciting feelings of vulnerability), and (b) they lack the ability to do so (e.g., when they are uncertain about the other's trustworthiness).

One important implication of this reasoning is that, like outcome favorability, people's level of uncertainty about how much to trust the other will have a moderating influence on procedural fairness, such that procedural fairness will have more of an effect on people's support for the other party and his or her decisions when uncertainty is relatively high. For example, in new relationships people may lack information about how much to trust the other. As a result, they may focus attention on (and be influenced by) the other party's level of procedural fairness.

Indeed, Van den Bos, Wilke, and Lind (1998) tested the hypothesis that procedural fairness is more influential in the face of greater uncertainty about how much to trust the other party. The dependent variable in this study was participants' satisfaction with a resource allocation decision made by another party. Independent variables included (a) the procedural fairness of the decision and (b) uncertainty about how much to trust the other party. The latter variable, in turn, consisted of three levels. One group was led to believe that the other party could be trusted (certain-positive condition), a second group was told that the other party could not be trusted (certain-negative condition), and a third group was given no information about how much to trust the other (uncertain condition). An interaction between procedural fairness and uncertainty emerged. In the uncertain condition, there was a highly positive and significant relationship between procedural fairness and satisfaction with the decision. In marked contrast, procedural fairness and satisfaction with the decision were unrelated in both the certain-positive and certain-negative conditions.

In short, the interactive relationship between outcome favorability and procedural fairness (in which unfavorable outcomes make procedural fairness information more impactful) may have much in common with a cornerstone finding of uncertainty management theory (Van den Bos & Lind, 2002), namely, the interactive relationship between uncertainty and procedural fairness in which higher uncertainty makes procedural fairness information more impactful. Future efforts to integrate the moderating effects of each of outcome favorability and uncertainty on procedural fairness information may help to refine our thinking about uncertainty management theory. For example, unfavorable outcomes and high uncertainty may heighten the salience of people's concerns about the trustworthiness of the other party, leading them to be attentive to and influenced by trust-related information such as procedural fairness. Alternatively, it could be more general concerns stimulated by uncertainty (including but not

limited to establishing the trustworthiness of the other party) that make people hungry for, and therefore affected by, procedural fairness information. If this were the case, then it may be possible to subsume the moderating effect of outcome favorability on procedural fairness under uncertainty management theory. That is, unfavorable outcomes are probably more likely than favorable outcomes to elicit a host of uncertainties in people (e.g., whether the unfavorable outcomes will continue, and if so, whether they will be able to muster the resources to address them), thereby making people more susceptible to influence by procedural fairness information.

In related fashion, an important question for future research pertains to the nature of the uncertainty that has a moderating influence on procedural fairness. On the one hand, research has already shown that uncertainty *about how much to trust the other party* moderates the impact of procedural fairness (Van den Bos et al., 1998). On the other hand, recent findings suggest that additional sources of uncertainty, such as being reminded of one's mortality (Van den Bos & Miedema, 2000), or merely being asked to contemplate uncertainty per se (Van den Bos, 2001), heightens the impact of procedural fairness on people's affective states. Whether certain sources of uncertainty have more of a moderating influence on procedural fairness and if so, why, are important questions for further research. For example, recent evidence suggests that although both mortality salience and uncertainty salience magnify the influence of procedural fairness information on people's level of anger, the moderating impact attributable to uncertainty salience is significantly greater than is the moderating influence of mortality salience (Van den Bos, Poortvliet, Miedema, & Van den Ham, 2004). These findings suggest that it is the uncertainty elicited by mortality salience (and not mortality salience per se) that moderated the influence of procedural fairness on people's level of negative affect in the Van den Bos and Miedema (2000; Van den Bos et al., 2004) studies.

CONCLUDING COMMENTS

In summary, the interactive relationship between outcome favorability and procedural fairness takes two different forms (Brockner, 2002; Brockner & Wiesenfeld, 1996). Across a wide variety of studies, high procedural fairness has been found to reduce the effect of outcome favorability on people's support for decisions, decision makers, and organizations, relative to when procedural fairness is low. Many other studies have shown that high procedural fairness heightens the effect of outcome favorability on people's self-evaluations, relative to when procedural fairness is low. These findings result from people's use of procedural fairness information for two (not mutually exclusive) purposes:

(a) to determine the nature of their relationship with the other party, in particular, how much to trust the other, and (b) to make attributions of responsibility to themselves and the other party for the outcomes of their encounters. These two reasons for the interactive relationships, in turn, suggest that people's relative status in their social encounters will dictate the form of the interactive effect of outcome favorability and procedural fairness on the same dependent variable (namely, people's desire for future interaction with the other party). Having demonstrated the forms (how), generality (when), and explanations (why) of the interaction effects, we now need to evaluate whether the interactive relationships may be subsumed by an even larger network of factors, some related to outcome favorability (e.g., uncertainty) and others related to procedural fairness (e.g., self-relevance of the process). We suspect that such future efforts will yield findings with a host of theoretical and practical implications for both the justice literature and related research in organizational and social psychology.

ACKNOWLEDGMENTS

We are grateful to Jerry Greenberg, Morela Hernandez, and Kees Van den Bos for their helpful comments on an earlier draft of the chapter.

REFERENCES

Bies, R. J. (1987). The predicament of injustice: The management of moral outrage. In L. L. Cummings & B. M. Staw (Eds.), *Research in organizational behavior* (Vol. 9, pp. 289–319). Greenwich, CT: JAI Press.

Blader, S., & Tyler, T. R. (2003). Testing the four component model of procedural justice. *Personality and Social Psychology Bulletin, 29,* 747–758.

Blau, P. (1964). *Exchange and power in social life.* New York: Wiley.

Brewer, M. B., & Brown, R. J. (1998). Intergroup relations. In D. T. Gilbert, S. T. Fiske, & G. Lindzey (Eds.), *The handbook of social psychology* (4th ed., Vol. 2, pp. 554–594). New York: Oxford University Press.

Brockner, J. (2002). Making sense of procedural fairness: How high procedural fairness can reduce or heighten the influence of outcome favorability. *Academy of Management Review, 27,* 58–76.

Brockner, J., Chen, Y., Mannix, E., Leung, K., & Skarlicki, D. (2000). Culture and procedural fairness: When the effects of what you do depend upon how you do it. *Administrative Science Quarterly, 45,* 138–159.

Brockner, J., Heuer, L. B., Magner, N., Folger, R., Umphress, E., Van den Bos, K., Vermunt, R., Magner, M., & Siegel, P. A. (2003). High procedural fairness heightens the effect of outcome favorability on self-evaluations: An attributional analysis. *Organizational Behavior and Human Decision Processes, 91,* 51–68.

Brockner, J., Konovsky, M., Cooper-Schneider, R., Folger, R., Martin, C. L., & Bies, R. J. (1994). The interactive effects of procedural justice and outcome negativity on the victims and survivors of job loss. *Academy of Management Journal, 37,* 397–409.

Brockner, J., Siegel, P. A., Daly, J., Tyler, T. R., & Martin, C. (1997). When trust matters: The moderating effect of outcome favorability. *Administrative Science Quarterly, 42*, 558–583.

Brockner, J., & Wiesenfeld, B. M. (1996). An integrative framework for explaining reactions to decisions: The interactive effects of outcomes and procedures. *Psychological Bulletin, 120*, 189–208.

Chen, Y., Brockner, J., & Greenberg, J. (2003). When is it "A pleasure to do business with you"? The effects of status, outcome favorability, and procedural fairness. *Organizational Behavior and Human Decision Processes, 92*, 1–21.

Colquitt, J. A. (2001). On the dimensionality of organizational justice: A construct validation of a measure. *Journal of Applied Psychology, 86*, 386–400.

Cropanzano, R., & Folger, R. (1989). Referent cognitions and task decision autonomy: Beyond equity theory. *Journal of Applied Psychology, 74*, 293–299.

Cropanzano, R., & Konovsky, M. A. (1995). Resolving the justice dilemma by improving the outcomes: The case of employee drug screening. *Journal of Business and Psychology, 10*, 221–243.

Crocker, J., Major, B., & Steele, C. M. (1998). Social stigma. In D. T. Gilbert, S. T. Fiske, & G. Lindzey (Eds.), *The handbook of social psychology* (4th ed., Vol. 2, pp. 504–554). New York: Oxford University Press.

Daly, J. P. (1995). Explaining changes to employees: The influence of justifications and change outcomes on employees' fairness judgments. *Journal of Applied Behavioral Science, 31*, 415–428.

Daly, J. P., & Geyer, P. D. (1994). The role of fairness in implementing large-scale change: Employee evaluations of process and outcome in seven facility relocations. *Journal of Organizational Behavior, 15*, 623–638.

Dipboye, R. L., & de Pontbriand, R. (1981). Correlates of employee reactions to performance appraisals and appraisal systems. *Journal of Applied Psychology, 66*, 248–251.

Fiske, S. T. (2001). Effects of power on bias: Power explains and maintains individual, group, and societal disparities. In A. Y. Lee-Chai & J. A. Bargh (Eds.), *The use and abuse of power: Multiple perspectives on the causes of corruption* (pp. 181–193). Philadelphia, PA: Psychology Press/Taylor & Francis.

Folger, R. (1986). Rethinking equity theory: A referent cognitions model. In H. W. Bierhoff, R. L. Cohen, & J. Greenberg (Eds.), *Justice in social relations* (pp. 145–162). New York: Plenum Press.

Folger, R., & Cropanzano, R. (1998). *Organizational justice and human resource management.* Thousand Oaks, CA: Sage.

Folger, R., & Martin, C. (1986). Relative deprivation and referent cognitions: Distributive and procedural justice effects. *Journal of Experimental Social Psychology, 22*, 531–546.

Folger, R., Rosenfield, D., & Robinson, T. (1983). Relative deprivation and procedural justification. *Journal of Personality and Social Psychology, 45*, 268–273.

Garonzik, R., Brockner, J., & Siegel, P. A. (2000). Identifying international assignees at risk for premature departure: The interactive effect of outcome favorability and procedural fairness. *Journal of Applied Psychology, 85*, 13–20.

Gilliland, S. W. (1994). Effects of procedural and distributive justice on reactions to a selection system. *Journal of Applied Psychology, 79*, 691–701.

Ginzel, L., Kramer, R., & Sutton, R. I. (1992). Organizational impression management as a reciprocal influence process: The neglected role of the organizational audience. In L. L. Cummings & B. M. Staw (Eds.), *Research in organizational behavior* (Vol.15, pp. 227–266). Greenwich, CT: JAI Press.

Greenberg, J. (1994). Using socially fair treatment to promote acceptance of a work site smoking ban. *Journal of Applied Psychology, 79,* 288–297.

Greenberg, J. (1996). *The quest for justice on the job: Essays and experiments.* Thousand Oaks, CA: Sage.

Heuer, L. B., Blumenthal, E., Douglas, A., & Weinblatt, T. (1999). The generality of procedural justice concerns: A deservedness model of group value and self-interest based fairness concerns. *Personality and Social Psychology Bulletin, 25,* 1279–1292.

Jones, E. E., & Davis, K. E. (1965). From acts to dispositions: The attribution process in person perception. In L. Berkowitz (Ed.), *Advances in experimental social psychology* (Vol. 2, pp. 219–266). New York: Academic Press.

Kelley, H. H. (1972). Attribution in social interaction. In E. E. Jones, D. E. Kanouse, H. H. Kelley, R. E. Nisbett, S. Valins, & B. Weiner (Eds.), *Attribution: Perceiving the causes of behavior* (pp. 1–26). Morristown, NJ: General Learning Press.

Kim, W. C., & Mauborgne, R. (1997). Fair process: Managing in the knowledge economy. *Harvard Business Review, 75,* 65–75.

Kluger, A. N., & DeNisi, A. (1996). Effects of feedback intervention on performance: A historical review. *Psychological Bulletin, 119,* 254–284.

Konvosky, M. A., & Pugh, S. D. (1994). Citizenship behavior and social exchange. *Academy of Management Journal, 37,* 656–669.

Koper, G., Van Knippenberg, D., Bouhuijs, F., Vermunt, R., & Wilke, H. (1993). Procedural fairness and self-esteem. *European Journal of Social Psychology, 23,* 313–325.

Korsgaard, M. A., Schweiger, D. M., & Sapienza, H. J. (1995). The role of procedural justice in building commitment, attachment, and trust in strategic decision-making teams. *Academy of Management Journal, 38,* 60–84.

Kramer, R. M. (1996). Divergent realities and convergent disappointments in the hierarchic relation: Trust and the intuitive auditor at work. In R. M. Kramer & T. R. Tyler (Eds.), *Trust in organizations: Frontiers of theory and research* (pp. 216–245). Thousand Oaks, CA: Sage.

Kramer, R. M., & Tyler, T. R. (1996). *Trust in organizations: Frontiers of theory and research.* Thousand Oaks, CA: Sage.

Kwong, J. Y. Y., & Leung, K. (2002). A moderator of the interaction effect of procedural justice and outcome favorability: Importance of the relationship. *Organizational Behavior and Human Decision Processes, 87,* 278–299.

Leung, K., Su, S., & Morris, M. W. (2001). When is criticism not constructive? The roles of fairness perceptions and dispositional attributions in employee acceptance of critical supervisory feedback. *Human Relations, 54,* 1155–1187.

Leventhal, G. S., Karuza, J., & Fry, W. R. (1980). Beyond fairness: A theory of allocation preferences. In G. Mikula (Ed.), *Justice and social interaction* (pp. 167–218). New York: Springer-Verlag.

Lind, E. A. (1995). *Social conflict and social justice: Some lessons from the social psychology of justice.* Leiden, the Netherlands: Leiden University Press.

Lind, E. A. (2001). Fairness heuristic theory: Justice judgments as pivotal cognitions in organizational relations. In J. Greenberg & R. Cropanzano (Eds.), *Advances in organizational justice* (pp. 56–88). Stanford, CA: Stanford University Press.

Lind, E. A., Kurtz, S., Musante, L., Walker, L., & Thibaut, J. (1980). Procedure and outcome effects on reactions to adjudicated resolutions of conflicts of interest. *Journal of Personality and Social Psychology, 39,* 643–653.

Lind, E. A., & Tyler, T. R. (1988). *The social psychology of procedural justice.* New York: Plenum Press.

Magner, N., Welker, R. B., & Johnson, G. G. (1996). The interactive effects of participation and outcome favourability on turnover intentions and evaluations of supervisors. *Journal of Occupational and Organizational Psychology, 69,* 135–143.

Mark, M. M., & Folger, R. (1984). Responses to relative deprivation: A conceptual
framework. In P. Shaver (Ed.), *Review of personality and social psychology* (Vol. 5,
pp. 192–218). Beverly Hills, CA: Sage.

Markus, H. R., & Kitayama, S. (1991). Culture and the self: Implications for cognition, emotion, and motivation. *Psychological Review, 98,* 224–253.

Mayer, R. C., Davis, J. H., & Schoorman, F. D. (1995). An integrative model of organizational trust. *Academy of Management Review, 20,* 709–734.

McGuire, W. J. (1973). The yin and yang of progress in social psychology: Seven
koan. *Journal of Personality and Social Psychology, 26,* 446–456.

Pfeffer, J. (1992). *Managing with power: Politics and influence in organizations.* Boston:
Harvard Business School Press.

Ployhart, R. E., & Ryan, A. M. (1998). Toward an explanation of applicant reactions:
An examination of organizational justice and attribution frameworks. *Organizational Behavior and Human Decision Processes, 72,* 308–335.

Ployhart, R. E., Ryan, A. M., & Bennett, M. (1999). Explanations for selection decisions: Applicants' reactions to informational and sensitivity features of explanations. *Journal of Applied Psychology, 84,* 87–106.

Schaubroeck, J., May, D. R., & Brown, F. W. (1994). Procedural justice explanations
and employee reactions to economic hardship: A field experiment. *Journal of Applied Psychology, 79,* 455–460.

Schroth, H., & Shah, P. (2000). Procedures, do we really want to know them? *Journal
of Applied Psychology, 85,* 462–471.

Skarlicki, D. P., & Folger, R. (1997). Retaliation in the workplace: The roles of distributive, procedural, and interactional justice. *Journal of Applied Psychology, 82,*
434–443.

Swann, W. B., Jr. (1996). *Self-traps: The elusive quest for higher self-esteem.* New York: W.
H. Freeman.

Tangney, J. P., & Fischer, K. W. (1995). *Self-conscious emotions: The psychology of shame,
guilt, embarrassment, and pride.* New York: Guilford Press.

Thibaut, J., & Walker, L. (1975). *Procedural justice: A psychological analysis.* Hillsdale,
NJ: Lawrence Erlbaum Associates.

Tyler, T. R., & Lind, E. A. (1992). A relational model of authority in groups. In M. P.
Zanna (Ed.), *Advances in experimental social psychology* (Vol. 25, pp. 115–191). New
York: Academic Press.

Van den Bos, K. (2001). Uncertainty management: The influence of uncertainty salience on reactions to perceived procedural fairness. *Journal of Personality and Social Psychology, 80,* 931–941.

Van den Bos, K., Bruins, J., Wilke, H. A. M., & Dronkert, E. (1999). Sometimes unfair
procedures have nice aspects: On the psychology of the fair process effect. *Journal
of Personality and Social Psychology, 77,* 324–336.

Van den Bos, K., & Lind, E. A. (2002). Uncertainty management by means of fairness
judgments. In M. P. Zanna (Ed.), *Advances in experimental social psychology* (Vol.
34, pp. 1–60). San Diego, CA: Academic Press.

Van den Bos, K., & Miedema, J. (2000). Toward understanding why fairness matters:
The role of uncertainty salience on reactions to procedural fairness. *Journal of Personality and Social Psychology, 79,* 355–366.

Van den Bos, K., Poortvliet, P. M., Maas, M., Miedema, J., & Van den Ham, E.-J. (2004). An enquiry concerning the principles of cultural norms and values: The impact of uncertainty and mortality salience on reactions to violations and bolstering of cultural worldviews. *Journal of Experimental Social Psychology, 40.*

Van den Bos, K., Vermunt, R., & Wilke, H. A. M. (1997). Procedural and distributive justice: What is fair depends more on what comes first than on what comes next. *Journal of Personality and Social Psychology, 72,* 95–104.

Van den Bos, K., Wilke, H. A. M., & Lind, E. A. (1998). When do we need procedural fairness? The role of trust in authority. *Journal of Personality and Social Psychology, 75,* 1449–1458.

Weiner, B. (1985). "Spontaneous" causal thinking. *Psychological Bulletin, 97,* 74–84.

Wiesenfeld, B. M., Brockner, J., & Martin, C. (1999). A self-affirmation analysis of survivors' reactions to an unfair organizational downsizing. *Journal of Experimental Social Psychology, 35,* 441–460.

Wiesenfeld, B. M., Brockner, J., Petzall, B., Wolf, R., & Bailey, J. (2001). Stress and coping among layoff survivors: A self-affirmation analysis. *Anxiety, Stress, and Coping: An International Journal, 14,* 15–34.

19

How Generalizable Are Justice Effects Across Cultures?

Kwok Leung

City University of Hong Kong

A three-stage model consisted of justice rules, criteria, and practices is used to organize the cross-cultural literature on organizational justice. Justice rules are abstract principles that guide justice decisions; justice criteria are specifications for implementing justice rules; and justice practices represent the concrete standards, verbal and nonverbal behaviors, and social arrangements for operationalizing justice criteria. A review of the cross-cultural literature shows that there are substantial cultural variations in the salience of and preference for justice rules, criteria, and practices. Individualism–collectivism and power distance provide the conceptual basis for organizing and interpreting most of the cross-cultural findings in organizational justice, although some results call for the development of alternative cultural frameworks for their interpretations. Common problems in cross-cultural research in organizational justice, implications of cross-cultural research for theory development, and directions for future research are discussed.

Justice has a long history in human civilizations. Twenty-five centuries ago, Confucius warned us in the *Analects* of the dire consequences of distributive injustice: "The head of state or a noble family worries not about poverty but about uneven distribution.... For where there is even distribution there is no such thing as poverty" (1992, p. 161). About a century later, Aristotle cautioned us in the *Ethics,* as many modern managers would, that "how actions are to be performed and distributions made in order to be just—to know that is a harder task than to know what one's health requires" (1976, p. 197). The Bible alludes to a proportionality norm for distributive and retributive justice: "For whatsoever a man soweth, that shall he also reap" (Galatians 6:7). A cursory reading of classics from different corners of the world would testify to the centrality of justice concerns in social life.

The ubiquity of justice is often explained by a functionalist view, which argues that for a social group to function properly, justice rules need to be developed to guide and regulate the behaviors of its members. To the extent that there are organized social activities, justice principles can be identified, regardless of the cultural contexts involved. In a recent interpretation of this functionalist view, Lind (1994) argued that people are confronted with a fundamental dilemma about how much to submit to a group, and how much to maintain a self-identity. These two goals are typically mutually exclusive, and a balance must be struck between them. The most efficient solution to this dilemma is, according to Lind (1994), to rely on principles of justice. "By specifying power-limit-

ing rules about how people should be treated, how decisions should be made, and how outcomes are to be allocated, rules of justice limit the potential for exploitation and allow people to invest their identity and effort in the group with confidence that they will not be badly used by the group" (p. 30). In short, the functionalist view suggests that justice norms and principles should be identifiable in any human groups.

It is interesting to note that the English words "justice" and "fairness" may not be easily translated into some languages. For instance, Van den Bos and Lind (2002) noted that these two English terms correspond well to their Dutch counterparts, but that the translation of these terms into French is problematic. Kidder and Muller (1991) raised some doubt about the importance of justice in Japan because there is no exact word for justice in Japanese. However, with Van den Bos and Lind (2002), I argue that linguistic variations in the slant and twist associated with the notions of justice and fairness across cultures do not invalidate the universality of the justice concern. Different linguistic populations just talk about justice and fairness in different ways.

A universal concern for justice, however, does not mean that all justice effects are necessarily generalizable across cultures. The purpose of this chapter is to review the organizational justice literature and identify both culture-general and culture-specific justice effects. Conclusions and implications for future research are discussed at the end.

THE THREE-STAGE MODEL OF JUSTICE

To provide a framework to organize cultural similarities and differences in justice processes, Morris and Leung (2000) proposed a two-stage model, in which justice rules, defined as abstract principles that guide a decision, are distinguished from justice criteria, which are specifications for the implementation of a justice rule. Leung and Tong (2004) noted that the two-stage model is pitched at an abstract level, and does not address cross-cultural differences in justice-related actions and arrangements. To address this inadequacy, Leung and Tong proposed the addition of a final stage of concrete actions, termed justice practices, that operationalize the justice criteria. A justice practice represents the concrete standards, verbal and nonverbal behaviors, and social arrangements with which justice criteria are operationalized and implemented. Another way to put it is that a justice practice represents how a justice criterion in a given situation is enacted. The three-stage framework of justice is shown schematically in Fig. 19.1.

Distributive justice is used to illustrate how the three-stage framework can illuminate cultural differences in organizational justice. Although people emphasize a fair allocation regardless of their cultural back-

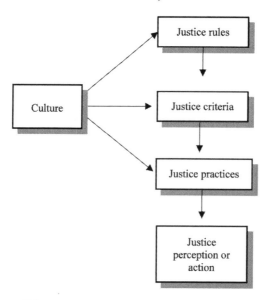

FIG. 19.1.   The three-stage model of justice.

grounds, they may differ in their preferences for allocation rules, such as equity, equality, and need. Even if similar justice rules are adopted, different cultural groups may use different justice criteria to implement a given rule. For instance, many forms of input are legitimate in implementing the equity rule, such as effort and contributions, and the allocation outcomes may vary drastically as a function of how input is defined. Finally, even if a certain input is chosen as the criterion, there are multiple ways to operationalize it. Contributions, for instance, may be defined by quantity, quality, or both.

When people are confronted with a justice situation and have to decide what is fair, they will first appraise the social situation to identify the appropriate principles of justice. In the second stage, they will select the specific criteria associated with these principles. In the final stage, concrete actions, standards, and arrangements will be selected to implement the chosen criteria. In this model, culture affects the interpretation of the social situation and the selection of justice principles, criteria, and practices. Cultural differences may occur in each of the three stages, and any such differences may lead to differences in the outcomes and perceived fairness of a justice decision.

Before I delve into the cross-cultural implications of this three-stage model, I first review briefly the widely accepted tripartite typology of organization justice. Distributive justice refers to the fairness of an allo-

cation; procedural justice, the fairness of decision-making procedures; and interactional justice, the fairness of interpersonal treatment during the implementation of the procedures. Recently, Colquitt (2001) proposed a more detailed taxonomy of procedural justice, which involves the splitting of interactional justice into an interpersonal and an informational dimension. Because most previous research is organized around the tripartite taxonomy, I employ this scheme in the chapter. In the following, the three-stage model is used to review the cross-cultural literature on organizational justice, and to evaluate the extent to which justice effects are generalizable across cultures.

JUSTICE RULES

Distributive Rules

Distributive justice dominated initial behavioral research on justice, and earlier works focus on the proportionality rule, or the equity rule (Adams, 1965). Many other allocation rules have been discussed subsequently, two of which, equality and need, have received the most attention (e.g., Deutsch, 1975). In general, equity is conducive to productivity, equality to interpersonal harmony, and need to individual well-being (e.g., Deutsch, 1975; Leung & Park, 1986).

Cross-cultural research on distributive rules attempts to link preferences for these rules to cultural dimensions (for reviews, see James, 1993; Leung, 1997). Although resources may be tangible or intangible (Foa & Foa, 1974), cross-cultural research is concerned mostly with tangible resources, and is guided primarily by the individualism–collectivism framework. This line of work began with Leung and Bond (1982), who found that the equality rule was preferred to a larger extent by Hong Kong Chinese than by Americans. To explain this result, they argued that because solidarity, harmony, and cohesion in a group are emphasized in collectivistic cultures, the equality rule is preferred. Because equity is conducive to productivity, competition, and self-gain, it is preferred in individualist cultures. Similar results have been reported by Bond, Leung, and Wan (1982), who found that Hong Kong Chinese showed a more egalitarian tendency in allocating both a tangible reward (assign a better grade) and a social-emotional reward (maintaining friendship) than did Americans. Kashima, Siegal, Tanaka, and Isaka (1988) also found that Japanese regarded an equal division as fairer, and were more willing to change to an equality rule than were Australians.

In collectivistic societies, in-groups are likely to be smaller (Wheeler, Reis, & Bond, 1989), and include only family members, close relatives,

and intimate friends, compared to in-groups in individualistic societies (e.g., Bellah, Madsen, Sullivan, Swidler, & Tipton, 1985). One consequence is that individualism is likely to be associated with a more universalistic application of justice principles, with fewer differences across in-groups and out-groups. In contrast, the emphasis on group boundaries in collectivistic societies is likely to lead to a contextual view of justice, and the application of different justice principles across group boundaries. In line with this argument, Leung and Bond (1984) found that compared with Americans, Hong Kong Chinese, who are collectivists, were more likely to favor a generosity rule (the tendency to allocate a generous share of a reward to others) with in-group members by employing either the equity or the equality norms, as a function of their inputs. With out-group members, however, both cultural groups followed an equity rule that is based on contributions.

Results from a few studies deviate from those just described and need some explanation. Individualism–collectivism and the preferences for distributive rules among American, Japanese, and Korean university students were examined by Leung and Iwawaki (1988), who, surprisingly, did not find any difference among these three groups. However, the individualism levels of the Japanese and American participants were measured and found to be similar. Leung and Iwawaki (1988) suggested that the absence of cultural differences may be attributable to the similar level in individualism among the three cultural groups. Kim, Park, and Suzuki (1990) asked Koreans, Japanese, and Americans to allocate grades among their classmates with whom they completed a group project. Koreans followed the equality rule more closely than did Japanese or Americans, but Japanese and Americans were similar in their distributive behavior. Because individualism–collectivism was not measured, it is unclear whether the pattern is also attributable to a similar level of individualism of the Japanese and Americans. These two studies make it clear that we cannot assume the applicability of cross-cultural value surveys (e.g., Hofstede, 1980) to any given sample, especially young people, who are likely to display value changes.

Chen (1995) asked employees from mainland China and the United States to role play the president of a manufacturing company and allocate rewards to its employees. Contrary to expectation, Chinese participants showed a stronger preference for equity than did the Americans. Chen (1995) attributed this unexpected result to the rapid shift to a market economy in China, and the concomitant emphasis on productivity rather than in-group harmony. However, Leung (1997) argued that the recipients depicted in the study were out-group members, and the Chinese preference for equity is consistent with the findings of Leung and Bond (1984).

McLean Parks, Conlon, Ang, and Bontempo (1999) found no difference in the rules used by American and Singaporean MBA students to
distribute and recover both tangible and intangible resources. However, in this study, as in the study of Chen (1995), participants were
asked to play the role of a manger and distribute or recover resources for
their subordinates. It is also possible that an out-group situation was
created in this situation, and the absence of a cultural difference is consistent with the argument of Leung and Bond (1984).

A few studies have actually correlated the preference for distributive
rules with individualism–collectivism in different cultures, and the
general finding is that collectivism correlates with the preference for
equality (for a review, see Leung & Stephan, 2001). Chen, Meindl, and
Hui (1998), however, reported a more complex pattern. Collectivism
was correlated with the preference for equality for Hong Kong Chinese
only, but no relationship was found for Americans.

Socioeconomic conditions may override the effects of culture on preferences for distributive rules. In work contexts, the use of the deservingness rule in allocating recourses is typically regarded as fairer than the
use of the need rule, as Cohn, White, and Sanders (2000) showed across
seven countries (Bulgaria, France, Hungary, Poland, Russia, Spain, and
the United States). This result is somewhat unexpected for the three
Eastern European countries because of their communist past. However,
Murphy-Berman, Berman, Singh, Pacharui, and Kumar (1984) and
Berman, Murphy-Berman, and Singh (1985) both found that Indians ad-
hered to the need norm more closely than did Americans. Leung (1988)
suggested that the scarcity of resources in India may have heightened
the concern for the well-being of fellow group members. Thus, although
equality should be preferred by Indians because of their collectivist orientation, the need norm should take priority because individual well-
being is more salient. Consistent with this argument, Murphy-Berman
and Berman (2002) found that in allocating a resource, Hong Kong Chinese regarded the use of the merit rule as fairer than the use of the need
rule, whereas the opposite was true for Indonesians. Again, resource
scarcity in Indonesia may have heightened the preference for the need
rule in Indonesia. Finally, Wegener and Liebig (1995) showed that
young people in the former East Germany were less favorable toward
egalitarianism than older people, whereas the pattern was reversed in
the former West Germany. One possible explanation is that older people
from Former East Germany were more receptive of egalitarianism man-
dated by communism, whereas young people were less socialized into
an egalitarian orientation. In former West Germany, however, younger
people perhaps were more receptive of socialist values that endorse a
more equal distribution of wealth. In sum, these results highlight the effects of socio-political conditions on distributive preferences.

Situational goals have also been shown to override the effects of culture. Leung and Park (1986) found that both Koreans and Americans
were more likely to adopt equality when the interactional goal was solidarity, and equity when the goal was productivity. Similarly, Chen et al.
(1998) found that both Hong Kong Chinese and American students
were more likely to adopt an equal allocation of a group reward when
task interdependence was high than low, and to adopt an equitable allocation when the goal was productivity or fairness rather than when it
was solidarity. It is also instructive to note that in a review of a number
of European studies on distributive norms, Miles and Greenberg (1993)
were unable to conform the relationship between individualism and the
use of the equity norm and between collectivism and the use of the
equality norm. Miles and Greenberg suggested that this disarray may
have been caused by a lack of information on the situational influence
on the salience of distributive norms in these studies. Obviously, the effects of culture need to be assessed along with any situational variables
that impinge on the salience of different distributive rules.

Procedural Rules

Procedural rules typically involve a set of steps and processes for decision making. Initial research in this area focused on conflict resolution
procedures in legal settings (Thibaut & Walker, 1975), and the major
finding is that people prefer conflict resolution procedures that grant
the disputants process control (opportunities to express opinions and
provide facts and evidence) but place the control over the outcome (decisions on how a dispute is resolved) in the hands of an impartial third
party. A prototypical example of a procedure that embodies these characteristics is the adversary adjudication system used in English-speaking courts. Research has shown that the preference for adversary
adjudication was found not only in United States and United Kingdom,
but also in France and Germany, which have a different legal system
(Lind, Erickson, Friedland, & Dickenberger, 1978). Thibaut and
Walker's (1975) theory contradicts a body of literature showing that
procedures that allow for compromises, such as mediation, are preferred in many non-Western countries (e.g., Gulliver, 1979; Nader &
Todd, 1978; Wall & Blum, 1991). Based on data from Hong Kong and the
United States, Leung (1987) proposed and confirmed that individualism was associated with a preference for adversary adjudication, and
collectivism with a preference for mediation and negotiation. Morris,
Leung, and Iyengar (2004) recently replicated this pattern again with
Chinese and Americans. Kozan and Ergin (1998) also found that in a
prisoner's dilemma game, Turkish college students were more likely to
use an intermediary, whereas U.S. students were more likely to engage

in direct communication. Tinsley (1998, 2001) showed that Japanese were more likely to co-opt a third-party authority figure to resolve a dispute, whereas Germans were more likely to rely on objective standards or standard operating procedures.

Subsequent research on procedural preferences has included informal conflict resolution procedures, which has yielded more or less similar results. With a set of both formal and inform procedures, Leung, Au, Fernández-Dols, and Iwawaki (1992) found that collectivists (Spanish and Japanese) were more likely to prefer negotiation and compromises than were individualists (Dutch and Canadians). Ohbuchi and Takahashi (1994) reported that Japanese were likely to rely on avoidance and indirect methods (suggesting, ingratiation, impression management, and appeasing) to handle a conflict, whereas Americans tended to adopt direct methods (persuasion, bargaining, and compromise). Chung and Lee (1989) reported that Japanese and Koreans were less likely to employ confrontational modes in conflict resolution in the workplace than were Americans. Graham, Mintu, and Rodgers (1994) found that across eight cultural groups, collectivism was correlated with a negotiation style that is characterized by cooperativeness and willingness to attend to the other party's needs.

Some cross-cultural studies are based on the dual concern model, which posits five basic styles of conflict resolution (Carnevale & Leung, 2001). The empirical results support a relationship between individualism-collectivism and conflict styles. Two collectivistic groups, Brazilians and Mexicans, showed a greater preference for styles of conflict resolution that are high in concern for others (collaboration and accommodation) than did Americans (Gabrielidis, Stephan, Ybarra, Pearson, & Villareal, 1997; Pearson & Stephan, 1988). Elsayed-Ekhouly and Buda (1996) found that Arab executives used avoiding more and dominating less than did U.S. executives. Morris et al. (1998) found that Chinese managers showed conflict avoidance more than did managers from the United States, India, and the Philippines, whereas U.S. managers used competing more than managers from China, India, and the Philippines.

As in distributive rules, the in-group–out-group distinction affected the procedural preferences of collectivists more than individualists. Leung (1988) found that compared with Americans, Chinese were less likely to pursue a conflict with in-group members than with out-group members. Probst, Carnevale, and Triandis (1999) reported a similar effect of individualism–collectivism in a social dilemma study.

The cultural dimension of power distance also impacts on procedural preferences. In high power distance societies, procedures that involve a high-status third party as the decision maker are more accepted. Leung and Lind (1986) found that compared to Americans, Chinese accepted an inquisitorial adjudication more, in which the judge plays a

key role in determining the facts and evidence used to arrive at a verdict. In line with this finding, Tse, Francis, and Walls (1994) found that executives from China were more likely to consult their superiors in a conflict than were Canadian executives. Chung and Lee (1989) found that Japanese and Koreans were more likely to appeal to authorities to resolve a conflict than were Americans. Finally, in a study of 23 national groups, Smith, Peterson, Leung, and Dugan (1998) found that participants from high power distance countries were less likely to rely on their peers and subordinates to resolve a dispute in their work group.

The literature on procedural rules focuses primarily on conflict resolution procedures, but other procedural rules exist in the workplace, such as those for recruitment and promotion. Unfortunately, cross-cultural research on these other procedures is limited. One interesting cultural difference in procedures is the notion of what a contract entails. In individualist societies, contracts are typically assumed to be binding, and tend to be precise and concrete. In collectivist societies, contracts often are taken as symbols of collaboration and general guidelines for future actions. Agreements stated in contracts tend to be abstract, and are subjected to future interpretations in light of unexpected situational changes (e.g., see Lubman, 1988, for the case of China; Sullivan, Peterson, Kameda, & Shimada, 1981, for a contrast between Japan and the United States). Leung and Stephan (2000) provided an analysis of a dispute between Britain and China over the handover of Hong Kong based on cultural differences in the notion of a contract.

Steiner and Gilliland (1996) examined the fairness of several selection tools in two cultures. French students were found to regard the use of graphology (handwriting analysis) and personality tests in selection as fairer than did American students. In contrast, American students regarded the use of interviews, resumés, biographical information, and honesty tests as fairer. Phillips and Gully (2002) extended the work of Steiner and Gilliland (1996) by comparing employees in Singapore and the United States in their perception of different selection tools. Americans perceived resumés as more favorable and personality tests, graphology, and ethnicality/nationality as less favorable selection tools than did Singaporeans. As a final example, McFarlin and Sweeney (2001) provided a review of how culture affects performance appraisal processes and noted some systematic cultural variations. For instance, individual feedback intended to differentiate employees is more common in individualist than in collectivist cultures. Systematic investigation of how performance appraisal is conducted across cultures has yet to begin, and such studies would definitely reveal cultural differences in preferences for procedural rules associated with performance appraisal. In sum, there is an obvious need to examine procedural preferences cross-culturally in domains other than conflict resolution.

Summary

The preceding review makes it clear that there are substantial cross-cultural variations in the preferences for justice rules. Individualism–collectivism and power distance provide the major frameworks for organizing the myriad of cultural similarities and differences in preferences for distributive and procedural rules. However, we know relatively little about the effects of other cultural variables, and about cultural differences in procedural preferences outside of the conflict resolution domain. Finally, it should be noted that interactional justice, often viewed as the interpersonal side of formal procedures, does not involve explicit rules. The effects of culture on this aspect of justice are concerned with justice criteria and practices.

JUSTICE CRITERIA

Distributive Criteria

Individualism–collectivism also provides a framework for organizing cultural differences in distributive criteria. In collectivist societies, given that loyalty is emphasized, seniority is an important distributive criterion because a long tenure signals high commitment to a group (Milliman et al., 1995). For instance, it is well known that seniority is more emphasized in compensations and promotion decisions in Japan than in the United States (e.g., Ouchi & Jaeger, 1978). Hundley and Kim (1997) reported that Americans emphasized performance more, and Koreans emphasized seniority, education, and family size more, in judging the fairness of pay levels. Another feature of individualism is the emphasis on the individual. In a comparison of banks in Hong Kong and Britain, White, Luk, Druker, and Chiu (1998) reported that in determining salary adjustments, individual performance was emphasized more in Britain than in Hong Kong.

In high power distance societies, people at the top of the organizational hierarchy are entitled to more privileges and deference than their counterparts in low power distance societies. Mendonca and Kanungo (1994) suggested that status and position are more likely to be regarded as a legitimate input in resource allocations in high power distance societies. One example comes from India, a high power distance society with in the past a caste system that organized people into four ranks. Although this system has been abandoned, caste characteristics are still used occasionally as a criterion for recruitment (Gopalan & Rivera, 1997). Education background may also be regarded as a status marker, which explains the emphasis on educational credentials in recruitment decisions in Confucian countries (e.g., Sarachek, 1990). For instance,

Hundley and Kim (1997) found that Koreans emphasized educational background more than Americans in judging the fairness of pay levels.

Mueller, Iverson, and Jo (1999) demonstrated the influence of culture on the criteria used in fairness judgments. Although in the United States, met expectations with regard to autonomy exerted a stronger influence on justice perceptions, justice perceptions were more influenced by met expectations with regard to advancement opportunities in South Korea. The cultural difference with regard to autonomy is consistent with the individualism–collectivism framework, but the explanation for the cultural difference in advancement opportunities is less obvious. Mueller et al. argued that the higher emphasis given to advancement opportunities by Koreans is consistent with their emphasis on status. We may conjecture that advancement opportunities should influence justice perception more in high than in low power distance societies.

As in distributive rules, socioeconomic factors may override the effects of culture on the preference for distributive criteria. A good example comes from the work of Leung and his colleagues on social comparison processes. Social comparison is pivotal to judgments of distributive justice, and similar others are hypothesized as a natural referent group for evaluating the fairness of one's share (e.g., Adams, 1965). However, socioeconomic factors may alter the choice of the referent group. In international joint ventures in China, the salary of local employees is drastically lower than that of expatriate managers who perform similar responsibilities. Leung, Smith, Wang, and Sun (1996) found that in these joint ventures, fairness perception based on a comparison with other local employees was related to job satisfaction, but fairness perception based on a comparison with expatriate managers was not. Furthermore, the Chinese employees did not perceive the astronomical salaries of the expatriate managers as unfair. Apparently, the locals did not compare themselves with the expatriates, who were seen as out-group members. When a similar survey was conducted 3 years later, however, drastically different results were obtained (Leung, Wang, & Smith, 2001). Fairness perception based on a comparison with expatriate managers was related to job satisfaction, and local employees regarded the high salary of the expatriate managers as very unfair. Leung, Wang, and Smith (2001) proposed that the growing perception of injustice of the high pay of expatriate mangers may be attributed to the increasing contact with them brought about by the surge in foreign direct investment in China. This contact may have led locals to see themselves as comparable to expatriate managers in terms of skills and know-how, resulting in a direct social comparison with them and a heightened sense of injustice. This result also runs counter to the view that Chinese have rigidly defined in-group–out-group

boundaries because of their collectivistic orientation. Against the influence of cultural orientations, economic variables are able to promote the use of out-groups as the referent group in this context.

Procedural Criteria

Research has documented a number of criteria that people use to evaluate the fairness of a procedure, and culture is able to shape the relative importance of some of these criteria. Drawing on the individualism–collectivism framework, Leung (1987, 1997) argued that "animosity reduction" is an important criterion for evaluating the fairness of conflict resolution procedures. Indeed, his research with Hong Kong Chinese and American students and adults showed that this criterion was employed by both cultural groups. Ohbuchi, Fukushima, and Tedeschi (1999) reported that in resolving a dispute, Japanese regarded a justice goal (to restore fairness) as less important and a relationship goal (to maintain a positive relationship with the other party) as more important than did Americans. Along this line of logic, Tinsley (1997) argued that the goals underlying the dual concern model for conflict management should include not only concerns for self and others, but also concern for the collective. In fact, Ohbuchi, Suzuki, and Yoichiro (2001) found that for Japanese employees, the attainment of group goals was related to perception of fairness, but not the attainment of individual goals, which showed a direct effect on outcome satisfaction without being mediated by justice perception.

Power distance has been found to moderate the effect of voice. Tyler, Lind, and Huo (2000) argued that, based on the relational model, cultural values may shift the significance of interpersonal treatment as an indicator of social standing in a group. Specifically, in high power distance cultures, people are accustomed to less positive interpersonal treatment by authority figures, and hence less positive treatment, should be more accepted and result in less negative consequences. In four studies, Tyler et al. showed that across students and employees from four cultures differing in power distance (Hong Kong, Japan, United States, and Germany) and across several ethnic groups in the United States, people with a higher level of power distance reacted less negatively to a lower level of interpersonal treatment in a decision-making process in terms of acceptance of the decision and the evaluation of the decision makers. In these studies, interpersonal treatment includes both opportunities to have voice in the decision-making process, which is an aspect of procedural justice, and the quality of the interpersonal treatment received, which falls into the domain of interactional justice. In a series of three studies, Brockner et al. (2001) focused on voice alone and showed that compared with people from low power distance cul-

tures (United States and Germany), people from high power distance cultures (China, Hong Kong, and Mexico) reacted less negatively to a lower level of voice in a decision-making process in terms of lower organizational commitment or satisfaction with the decision-making process. Several monocultural studies also yielded results consistent with the cross-cultural results reviewed before. Lee, Pillutla, and Law (2000) studied a group of Chinese employees in Hong Kong, and found that power distance moderated the effect of procedural and interactional justice on trust in supervisors in that the effects of these two aspects of justice were stronger for people with lower levels of power distance. Brockner et al. (2001, study 4) showed that among a group of employees in China, voice showed a stronger effect on job satisfaction, organizational commitment, intention to remain in the organization, and supervisory evaluation of performance for those with lower levels of power distance. Interestingly, Hui and Au (2001) found that in an encounter between customers and service providers, voice showed a stronger effect on perceived justice for mainland Chinese than for Canadians, which is opposite to what is expected from the power distance framework. One explanation for this unexpected pattern is that service providers are likely to be seen as having low status in high power distance societies, and the absence of voice from a low-status group may trigger a high level of perceived justice.

In a seven-country study, which included Bulgaria, France, Hungary, Poland, Russia, Spain, and the United States, the effect of impartiality and voice on fairness perception was examined in two contexts (Cohn, White, & Sanders, 2000). In one context, the decision was about the dismissal of an employee, whereas in the other context, the decision involved finding a job through an employment agency. Generally speaking, the effect of culture was minimal, and impartiality was a better predictor than voice in the dismissal case, whereas the opposite was true for the employment agency case. The lack of cultural difference in the voice effect may be due to the relatively similar power distance among these nations.

Finally, not all criteria are subjected to the influence of culture. The positive effect of perceived process control granted by a procedure on its perceived fairness has been replicated in many countries other than the United States, including Britain, France, Germany (Lind et al., 1978), Hong Kong (Leung, 1987), Japan, and Spain (Leung et al., 1992).

Interactional Criteria

The relationship between power distance and interpersonal justice was succinctly summarized by James (1993), who concluded that "cultures that inculcate an acceptance of power differences lead individu-

als to expect, take for granted and, therefore, not get angry about, injustices" (p. 23). His conclusion was based on a study by Gudykunst and Ting-Toomey (1988), who analyzed data on anger and justice from seven European countries (reported by Babad & Wallbott, 1986; Wallbott & Scherer, 1986). A strong correlation between power distance and the anger expressed in reaction to injustice was found in which the higher the power distance of a society, the less likely it was that perceptions of unjust treatment would trigger an angry reaction. In higher power distance cultures, people's acceptance of unequal social prerogatives appears to lead to a high tolerance of unfair interpersonal treatment. In a direct demonstration of this relationship, Bond, Wan, Leung, and Giacalone (1985) showed that compared to Americans, Chinese from Hong Kong were more willing to accept insulting remarks from a high-status in-group person, but no cultural difference was found when the insult came from a low-status individual. Leung, Su, and Morris (2001) put American and Chinese MBA students in the role of an employee whose suggestion was criticized by a manager in an interactionally unfair manner. That is, the manager interrupted, failed to listen closely, and was dismissive toward the employee. The manager was either someone of essentially equal level in the organization or someone substantially more senior. Compared to Americans, Chinese perceived a senior manager's actions as less unjust and were less negative toward the superior. Finally, Blader, Chang, and Tyler (2001) found that relational concern showed a larger influence on perceived procedural justice, and instrumental concern a larger effect, for Americans than for Taiwanese. Blader et al. (2001) provided an account for this pattern of results with the power distance framework. Because of a higher power distance, Taiwanese placed a smaller emphasis on interpersonal treatment, which explained the smaller effect of relational concern for them.

Summary

Again, most cross-cultural research on justice criteria is guided by individualism–collectivism and power distance. Compared with the research on justice rules, the scope, depth, and breadth of the cross-cultural research on justice criteria are less impressive. Many important justice criteria have yet to be subjected to cross-cultural investigation.

JUSTICE PRACTICES

The notion of justice practices is rather new, and systematic cross-cultural research in this area has yet to begin. Empirical results are fragmented and scarce, and hence the following review is speculative and

only focuses on the effects due to individualism-collectivism, which are more coherent.

Practices for Distributive Criteria

For applying a distributive rule, concrete justice practices need to be identified to implement the criteria associated with this rule. For instance, loyalty is sometimes used as a criterion for implementing the equity rule. Group membership characteristics that signal loyalty, such as length of service, should be used more often in collectivist than in individualist cultures. Indeed, Japanese and Koreans did emphasize length of service more than their American counterparts in compensation decisions (e.g., Hundley & Kim, 1997; Ouchi & Jaeger, 1978). With regard to justice practices that define contributions, effort exerted should be emphasized more by collectivists than by individualists, as it signals loyalty and commitment to the ingroup. For instance, Stevenson et al. (1990) reported a higher emphasis on the total time spent in lesson and revision by Chinese than by Americans in educational settings. On the other hand, individualists should emphasize objective indicators of performance, such as work output, more than effort in defining contributions. Collectivists should also emphasize contributions to interpersonal relationships, such as contributions to group harmony, more than individualists, although this argument has not been confirmed in a previous test (Bond et al., 1982).

In deciding on practices to implement the equality rule, when nondivisible or multidimensional resources are involved, collectivists, because of their emphasis on ingroup harmony, should prefer practices that allow compromises (e.g., turn-taking for sharing a resource among the recipients).

With regard to justice practices for the need rule, one obvious speculation is that given the group orientation of collectivists, they are likely to prefer practices that are group based. For instance, in meeting the learning needs of employees, arrangements that facilitate group learning rather than individual learning may be preferred. In fact, Hundley and Kim (1997) found that family size showed a larger effect on judgment of pay fairness for Koreans than for Americans.

Practices for Procedural Criteria

In decision-making procedures, collectivists should be more likely to prefer group-based process control (e.g., appointing a group representative to present the views of a group to decision makers) than are individualists, who should prefer individual process control (e.g., allowing

the parties affected by a decision to present their views to decision makers). Collectivists may prefer direct control over the outcome of a decision, so that compromises with other people are possible (Leung, 1988). In contrast, individualists may be more likely to cede outcome control to a neutral party for a win–lose verdict because of their emphasis on competition and sensitivity about due process (e.g., Finkel, Crystal, & Watanabe, 2001). Finally, individualists are more likely to employ absolute standards to evaluate the ethicality of a decision-making procedure, whereas collectivists are more likely to take into account their relationship with the target in deciding what standards to use (Vasquez, Keltner, Ebenbach, & Banaszynski, 2001). For instance, breaking a rule in order to help a friend is judged to be less unfair in India than in the United States (Miller & Bersoff, 1992).

Practices for Interactional Criteria

Compared with individualists, collectivists should display a higher level of respect toward ingroup members and attempt to protect their face. For instance, Cushner and Brislin (1996, pp. 188–189) suggested that it would be considered rude in Korea to criticize subordinates in front of their colleagues. In contrast, Wierzbicka (1991) noted that in Israel, open confrontation is encouraged and appreciated because it reflects spontaneity, closeness, and mutual trust. Individual rights, such as privacy, are emphasized more in individualist than in collectivist cultures. For instance, discussion of the problems of coworkers in their absence was considered less acceptable in the United States and Britain than in Japan and Hong Kong (Smith, Peterson, Misumi, & Tayeb, 1989).

In providing justifications for a decision, individualists are more likely to engage in a cost-benefit analysis, because of their emphasis on economic rationality associated with a market-pricing orientation (Fiske, 1992). Collectivists are more likely to involve normative arguments (Triandis, 1995, p. 155). Individualists, such as Americans, prefer a clear and explicit communication style, whereas an implicit communication style is more common in collectivist societies, such as in Japan (Gudykunst & Nishida, 1994). Consistent with this argument, communication is often tactful, modest, and polite in Thailand (Sriussadaporn-Charoenngam & Jablin, 1999). In negotiation, collectivists (Japanese, Hong Kong Chinese, and Russians) were more indirect in communicating their preferences, priorities, and suggestions than were Americans (Brett & Okumura, 1998; Brett et al., 1998). Triandis et al. (2001) also found that deception was more prevalent in negotiation in collectivist than in individualist cultures.

Summary

The notion of justice practices is new, and it is not surprising that relevant empirical results are scanty. In fact, the typology of justice practices is still rudimentary, and much of the review is guided by individualism–collectivism. Interestingly, this area may provide the arena for culture to play a critical role in shaping its development. Recall that the procedural criteria proposed by Leventhal (1980) over two decades ago did not consider any cross-cultural variations. A taxonomy of justice practices, with full consideration of culture at its inception, should be richer and more comprehensive.

JUSTICE PERCEPTIONS: PROCESSES, ANTECEDENTS, AND CONSEQUENCES

In this section, I explore the cultural generalizability of the antecedents and consequences of justice perception, and its underlying processes.

Processes Underlying Justice Perceptions

Several models have been proposed to explain the justice effect, but only the group value model (Lind & Tyler, 1988), which has subsequently been expanded into the relational model (Tyler & Lind, 1992), has been subjected to some cross-cultural examination. The relational model posits that justice is important because how justly one is treated reflects one's standing in a group, and this assertion has been supported by a wide array of empirical evidence, including cross-cultural results (Tyler, Boeckmann, Smith, & Huo, 1997). The prominence of relational aspects of procedural justice in influencing a wide range of reactions has been documented in a variety of cultures. More importantly, predictions based on the relational model have been confirmed in cross-cultural studies. Brockner, Chen, Mannix, Leung, and Skarlicki (2000) tested an interesting argument derived from the key assumption of the group value model, namely, that justice is important because it symbolizes one's social standing in a group. This assumption suggests that procedural justice should matter more for cultural groups that are more concerned with their relationship with in-group members. Brockner et al. tested this notion in three studies, with procedural justice operationalized by either procedural features or quality of interpersonal treatment. As expected, when the outcome was low, the effect of procedural justice on a variety of recipient reactions was stronger in collectivist cultures (China and Taiwan) than in individualist cultures (Canada and the United States). Furthermore, regression analyses showed that this cul-

tural difference was mediated by self-construal (independent vs. inter-dependent self). In other words, self-construal, a cognitive consequence of individualism–collectivism, seems to be driving the observed cultural differences in the effect of procedural justice.

In a similar logic based on the relational model, Kwong and Leung (2002) predicted that the significance of a relationship should moderate the interaction between procedural justice and outcome favorability. Procedural justice should show a stronger effect in interactions in which the interactants had a more significant relationship with each other, and this prediction was confirmed with both university students and employees in Hong Kong.

An Attributional Analysis of Justice Effects

Leung, Su, and Morris (2001) argued that dispositional attribution should mediate the negative effects of perceived injustice. Specifically, unfair treatment is able to trigger an ascription of negative traits to the perpetrator, which in turn leads to negative reactions from the recipient of the unfair treatment. Leung et al. (2001, first study) showed that for both American and Chinese MBA students, unfair criticism from a supervisor was indeed related to ascription of negative traits to the su-pervisor. In their second study, Leung et al. showed that negative dis-positional attribution partially mediated the negative reactions to unfair criticism among Chinese employees in Hong Kong.

Although Leung et al. (2001) reported cultural similarity in the attri-butional process associated with a justice actor, Au, Hui, and Leung (2001) revealed cultural differences in self-attribution, or self-blame, by customers in a service context. When a service problem occurred, the provision of voice resulted in less self-blame for Canadians, but showed no effect on the self-blame of Chinese. The explanation offered by these authors is that Canadians are more attuned to competition and maximi-zation of self-gain because of their individualistic orientation. In the event of a service problem, Canadians may be more likely to view the provision of voice on the part of the service provider as an acknowledg-ment of wrongdoing. Not much research has investigated the relation-ship between attributional processes and justice perception across cultures, and we are still a long way from a coherent account of how cul-ture shapes the link between attribution and justice.

Antecedents of Justice Perceptions

In previous sections, I reviewed some cultural differences in prefer-ences for justice rules, criteria, and practices, and such differences ob-

viously result in different antecedents of justice perception as well as different degrees of influence of similar antecedents on justice perception across cultures. In this subsection, I review a few other antecedents of justice perception that show both cultural similarities and differences. Pillai, Scandura, and Williams (1999) found that, across six cultural groups (Americans, Australians, Indians, Colombians, Arabians—Saudis, and Jordanians), transformational leadership was related to the perception of procedural justice, but not to distributive justice. Leader–member exchange (LMX), which captures the quality of the relationship between superiors and subordinates, was related to distributive and procedural justice across these cultural groups. The only exception is that LMX was not related to procedural justice for Indians.

Price et al. (2001) found that, consistent with prospect theory, the level of voice received showed a generally concave relationship with perceived fairness across judges from Mexico, the Netherlands, the United States, and Britain. Consistent with the power distance framework, a higher level of voice was needed for a similar level of fairness perception for Dutch and British participants than for Mexican participants. There was no difference between Mexican and American participants in the relationship between voice level and fairness perception, but the responses to the hierarchy of authority scale for these two cultural groups were also similar.

Finally, Gelfand et al. (2002) argued that in negotiation, the egocentric bias—the tendency to view one's own behavior and a larger share for oneself as fairer—should be more prominent for individualists than for collectivists, because of the need for individualists to "stand out" and achieve better outcomes than others. In four studies comparing Japanese and Americans by means of various methodologies, Gelfand et al. confirmed their prediction and found that Americans did show a stronger egocentric tendency than Japanese. In other words, justice perception is more tinted by egocentric processes for individualists that for collectivists. However, it should be noted that the Japanese in their studies did show some degree of egocentric bias. Leung, Tong, and Ho (2004) also reported some degree of egocentric bias in a negotiation context with Hong Kong Chinese participants, another collectivist group.

Consequences of Justice Perceptions

The positive effects of perceived justice on a variety of outcome variables have been supported across cultures. For instance, the positive effects of justice on evaluation of outcomes and decision makers documented in the United States (Lind & Tyler, 1988; Tyler & Bies, 1990) were replicated

with Chinese in Hong Kong, Taiwan, and mainland China (Blader et al., 2001; Fields, Pang, & Chiu, 2000; Leung, Chiu, & Au, 1993; Leung & Li, 1990; Leung et al., 1996). Pearce, Bigley, and Branyiczki (1998) reported that procedural justice was positively related to organizational commitment and trust in coworkers in Lithuania. Rahim, Magner, Antonioni, and Rahman (2001) reported that procedural justice was positively related to organizational commitment, and distributive and interactional justice was negatively related to turnover intention among U.S. and Bangladesh managers and academics.

Some cross-cultural research has examined whether distributive and procedural justice show differential effects on job attitudes across cultures. Pillai, Williams, and Tan (2001) evaluated the relative impact of procedural and distributive justice on three job attitudes: job satisfaction, organizational commitment, and trust, across Americans, Chinese in Hong Kong, Indians, and Germans. The procedural measure used included both elements of formal procedures and interpersonal treatment. Results showed that distributive justice was related to trust for all four groups, to job satisfaction except for Americans, and to organizational commitment for Indians only. Procedural justice was related to trust except for Chinese, to job satisfaction for Americans only, and to organizational commitment except for Indians. Pillai et al. (1999) found that in a causal model, procedural justice did not show any significant relationship with job satisfaction for Americans, Australians, Indians, Colombians, and Arabians—Saudis and Jordanians. These results are generally consistent with results previously reported in the United States, with procedural justice showing a larger impact on organizational commitment, and distributive justice showing a larger impact on job satisfaction (e.g., Folger & Konovsky, 1989).

Two studies uncovered cultural differences in the consequences of justice perception. Lam, Schaubroeck, and Aryee (2002) found that in a combined sample of Hong Kong Chinese and American employees, power distance moderated the effects of distributive and procedural justice on job performance, absenteeism, and job satisfaction. Justice effects were larger for respondents with lower levels of power distance. However, individualism–collectivism did not moderate the justice effects on any of the outcome variables. Note that the results associated with power distance are consistent with the moderating influence of power distance on the effects of voice and interpersonal treatment reviewed in a previous section. Finally, Farh, Earley, and Lin (1997) argued that individual modernity influences the effect of justice, and showed that among Chinese employees in Taiwan, justice effects on organizational citizenship behavior were weaker for those lower in modernity.

CONCLUSIONS

Cross-Cultural Research and Theory Development

In a recent comment on the cross-cultural literature on organizational justice, Greenberg (2001) posed the fundamental question of why we should study justice cross-culturally. His view is that cross-cultural research on justice should help us understand the notion of justice more. Using this yardstick, one may pose a more direct question: To what extent has cross-cultural research helped advance justice theories?

Theory advancement stimulated by cross-cultural research is clear in three areas. First, as this review has shown, guided by individualism–collectivism and power distance, cross-cultural research has demonstrated systematic, interpretable cultural differences across a wide range of nations that vary along these two dimensions. In addition, Greenberg (2001) noted that most social scientists, including organizational justice researches, tend to ignore social contexts, and I may add that this tendency perhaps reflects their desire for universal knowledge. One important goal of cross-cultural research is then to provide a reality check and force researchers to confront human diversity and develop richer, more comprehensive models and theories.

Second, cross-cultural research has generated some broad-bushed frameworks that are quite encompassing and comprehensive. The two-stage framework of justice developed by Morris and Leung (Leung & Morris, 2001; Morris & Leung, 2000), and its extension, the three-stage framework, proposed by Leung and Tong (2004) and briefly reviewed here, provides a comprehensive typology of justice constructs. With regard to specific constructs, cross-cultural research has also spawned several novel concepts, such as the generosity rule in distributive justice, the role of harmony in procedural justice, and the notion of face in interactional justice. These novel constructs have not caught the attention of monocultural researchers in any significant way, but when radical ideas are needed for revitalizing organizational justice, some of these culturally derived ideas will become popular. A case in point is individualism–collectivism and power distance, which are increasingly used as individual-level constructs in monocultural studies. The reason for their popularity is simple: Novel individual difference variables are rare, given the long history of research in this area, and individualism–collectivism and power distance open up a new window on linking individual differences to a wide array of social behavior.

Third, cross-cultural research has pointed to justice processes that would have been ignored in monocultural research. As an example, take identification with a group, which has not been researched much by monocultural researchers of organizational justice. Huo, Smith, Tyler,

and Lind (1996) utilized this notion to examine the antecedents of justice perception in a culturally diverse workplace, and discovered that identification showed a drastic effect on the relative importance of the antecedents of justice. For ethnic minorities who identified with their own group, justice perception was more driven by instrumental concerns, whereas for those who identified with the superordinate group, justice perception was more driven by relational concerns. Identification may turn out to be a "growth" area in the next phase of organizational justice research in monocultural studies, because people do identify with various units to different degrees in the workplace.

Methodological Issues

In this review, I note that a number of methodological issues are sometimes overlooked, adding confusion to the already fuzzy findings that is typical of much of cross-cultural research. First, in some studies employing regression techniques or structural equations modeling, beta or path coefficients for different cultural groups are not tested. If the coefficient is significant for one group, and nonsignificant for another group, a cultural difference is assumed without an actual test of the two coefficients (e.g., Pillai et al., 2001; Rahim et al., 2001). It is possible that the coefficients are not statistically different across cultures, and a simpler, more coherent picture may emerge based on the assumption of cross cultural generality.

Second, a related problem with the use of regression or causal analysis is that the size of a beta or path coefficient depends very much on what other variables are being considered together with the focal variables. The size of a coefficient is likely to decrease if a larger number of independent variables are being considered. In different cross-cultural studies, the number of independent variables being examined often varies, making it hard to compare the effect sizes of justice variables across these studies.

Third, cross-cultural studies may employ very different populations, ranging among undergraduates, MBA students, rank-and-file employees, managers, and academics, and the context of the research is also diverse, involving very different industries. Before we conclude that some genuine cultural differences really exist, we need to rule out the plausible effects of contextual variables, a task that has rarely been attempted.

Fourth, cultural differences may have been artificially created by differential reliabilities across cultural groups. If a concept is measured more reliably in one cultural than another, a cross-cultural difference may emerge when there is no difference in the true scores. This problem is common for research that employs an etic perspective, in which standardized instruments are used in different cultural groups. When mea-

578 19. JUSTICE EFFECTS ACROSS CULTURES

sures developed in one culture (typically the United States) are applied in other cultures (typically non-Western cultures), their reliability may be compromised. For instance, Rahim et al. (2001) reported that the alphas of their justice measures are higher for American than for Bangladesh respondents. One solution to this problem is to develop emic instruments that are appropriate for the cultures studied (e.g., Farh et al., 1997).

Fifth, main effects, whether they are based on cultural similarities or differences, are typically robust across cultures and highly replicable. Interaction effects, however, are hard to interpret and replicate. For instance, Fields et al. (2000) examined whether procedural justice moderated the effects of distributive justice on several job outcomes in a sample of Hong Kong employees, and reported some two-way interactions that differed from those reported by earlier studies in the United States. In a cross-cultural study of American and Bangladesh employees, Rahim et al. (2001) reported some cultural differences in the interaction effects between different aspects of justice on organizational commitment and turnover intention. However, without replications, it is uncertain whether these cultural differences are real or due to chance. Before we begin to grapple with the underlying meaning of cultural differences in interaction effects, we must be certain of their robustness.

Directions for Future Research

Globalization has awakened many social scientists to a multicultural world, and we have accumulated considerable knowledge about culture and organizational justice in the past two decades. Nonetheless, our understanding is still in its infancy, and in the following, I highlight a few "high-yield" areas for researchers to pursue in this decade.

Few would object to the conclusion that the cross-cultural findings guided by individualism-collectivism and power distance popularized by Hofstede (1980) are most robust, coherent, and interpretable. However, for the field to progress and remain vigorous, we must venture beyond these two familiar guideposts. There are other cultural dimensions in the literature, such as the value dimensions identified by Schwartz (1994), dimensions of social axioms (Bond et al., 2004), and leadership dimensions identified in the GLOBE Project (House, Hanges, Javidan, Dorfman, & Gupta, 2004). Systematic research to explore how these other dimensions are related to justice phenomena and processes should be underway.

Current research on organizational justice is mostly concerned with the allocation of tangible resources. McLean Parks et al. (1999) examined tangible as well as intangible resources, and their allocation as well as their recovery among Americans and Singaporeans. For both cultural

groups, the equality rule was more often used, and the equity rule less often used, when resources were recovered than when they were distributed. Resource types also affected the use of distributive rules, with the equity rule used more often for monetary and status resources, and the need rule used more often for goods, services, and information. A related issue to note is that retributive justice, that is, the allocation of penalty to wrongdoers, has not attracted much cross-cultural research in an organizational context (for a review of culture and retributive justice, see Leung & Morris, 2001). Interesting cultural similarities and differences will definitely emerge when researchers embark on new enquiries into different types of resources, the recovery of resources, and the allocation of disincentives.

Finally, returning to the challenge of Greenberg (2001) that cross-cultural research should play a key role in theory advancement, the potential for cross-cultural organizational justice research to invigorate and innovate justice theories has been largely untapped. Van de Vijver and Leung (1997, pp. 13–14) argued that the chance of radical theoretical innovation by testing a well-established theory around the world is low. To maximize the impact of cross-cultural research on theory development, an important strategy, termed the "decentered approach," should be adopted, which includes culture as a key element in the initial stage of theory development. Hopefully, future theoretical work in the justice area will routinely consider culture as a fundamental building block for maximal innovativeness and comprehensiveness.

ACKNOWLEDGMENTS

I thank Jerry Greenberg for his insightful comments on an earlier draft. This chapter was supported by a research grant provided by City University of Hong Kong.

REFERENCES

Adams, J. S. (1965). Inequity in social exchange. In L. Berkowitz (Ed.), *Advances in experimental social psychology* (pp. 267–299). New York: Academic Press.

Aristotle. (1976). *Ethics* (J. A. K. Thomson, Trans.). Middlesex, England: Penguin.

Au, K., Hui, M. K., & Leung, K. (2001). Who should be responsible? Effects of voice and compensation on responsibility attribution, perceived justice, and post-complaint behaviors across cultures. *International Journal of Conflict Management, 12*, 350–364.

Babad, E. Y., & Wallbott, H. G. (1986). The effects of social factors on emotional reactions. In K. S. Scherer, H. G. Wallbott, & A. B. Summerfield (Eds.), *Experiencing emotion: A cross-cultural study* (pp. 154–172). Cambridge, England: Cambridge University Press.

Bellah, R. N., Madsen, R., Sullivan, W. M., Swidler, A., & Tipton, S. M. (1985). *Habits of the heart: Individualism and commitment in American life*. Berkeley, CA: University of California Press.

Berman, J. J., Murphy-Berman, V., & Singh, P. (1985). Cross-cultural similarities and differences in perception of fairness. *Journal of Cross-Cultural Psychology, 16*, 55–67.

Blader, S. L., Chang, C. C., & Tyler, T. R. (2001). Procedural justice and retaliation in organizations: Comparing cross-nationally the importance of fair group processes. *International Journal of Conflict Management, 12*, 295–311.

Bond, M. H., Leung, K., Au, A., Tong, K. K., Reimel de Carrasquel, S., Murakami, F., et al. (2004). Culture-level dimensions of social axioms and their correlates across 41 cultures. *Journal of Cross-cultural Psychology, 35*, 548–570.

Bond, M. H., Leung, K., & Wan, K. C. (1982). How does cultural collectivism operate? The impact of task and maintenance contributions on reward allocation. *Journal of cross-cultural psychology, 13*, 186–200.

Bond, M. H., Wan, K. C., Leung, K., & Giacalone, R. (1985). How are responses to verbal insults related to cultural collectivism and power distance? *Journal of Cross-Cultural Psychology, 16*, 111–127.

Brett, J. M, Adair, W., Lempereur, A., Okumura, T., Shikhirev, P., Tinsley, C. H., & Lytle, A. (1998). Culture and joint gains in negotiation. *Negotiation Journal, 14*, 61–86.

Brett, J. M., & Okumura, T. (1998). Inter- and intracultural negotiation: U.S. and Japanese negotiators. *Academy of Management Journal, 41*, 495–510.

Brockner, J., Ackerman, G., Greenberg, J., Gelfand, M. J., Franscesco, A., Chen, Z., et al. (2001). Culture and procedural justice: The influence of power distance on reactions to voice. *Journal of Experimental Social Psychology, 37*, 300–315.

Brockner, J., Chen, Y. R., Mannix, E. A., Leung, K., & Skarlicki, D. P. (2000). Culture and procedural fairness: When the effects of what you do depend on how you do it. *Administrative Science Quarterly, 45*, 138–159.

Carnevale, P. J., & Leung, K. (2001). Cultural dimensions of negotiation. In M. A. Hogg & R. S. Tindale (Eds.), *Blackwell handbook of social psychology, Vol 3: Group processes* (pp. 482–496). Oxford, UK: Blackwell.

Chen, C. C. (1995). New trends in rewards allocation preferences: A Sino–U.S. comparison. *Academy of Management Journal, 38*, 408–428.

Chen, C. C., Meindl, J. R., & Hui, H. (1998). Deciding on equity or parity: A test of situational, cultural and individual factors. *Journal of Organizational Behavior, 19*, 115–129.

Chung, K. H., & Lee, H. C. (1989). National differences in managerial practices. In K. H. Chung & H. C. Lee (Eds.), *Korean managerial dynamics* (pp. 163–180). New York: Praeger.

Cohn, E. S., White, S. O., & Sanders, J. (2000). Distributive and procedural justice in seven nations. *Law and Human Behavior, 24*, 553–579.

Colquitt, J. A. (2001). On the dimensionality of organizational justice: A construct validation of a measure. *Journal of Applied Psychology, 86*, 386–400.

Confucius. (1992). *The analects* (D. C. Lau, Trans.). Hong Kong: Chinese University Press.

Cushner, K., & Brislin, R. W. (1996). *Intercultural interactions: A practical guide*. Thousand Oaks, CA: Sage.

Deutsch, M. (1975). Equity, equality, and need: What determines which value will be used as the basis of distributive justice? *Journal of Social Issues, 31*, 137–149.

Elsayed-Ekhouly, S. M., & Buda, R. (1996). Organizational conflict: A comparative analysis of conflict styles across cultures. *International Journal of Conflict Management, 7*, 71–80.

Farh, J. L., Earley, P. C., & Lin, S. C. (1997). Impetus for action: A cultural analysis of justice and organizational citizenship behavior in Chinese society. *Administrative Science Quarterly, 42*, 421–444.

Fields, D., Pang, M., & Chiu, C. (2000). Distributive and procedural justice as predictors of employee outcomes in Hong Kong. *Journal of Organizational Behavior, 21*, 547–562.

Finkel, N. J., Crystal, D. S., & Watanabe, H. (2001). Commonsense notions of unfairness in Japan and the United States. *Psychology, Public Policy, and Law, 7*, 345–380.

Fiske A. P. (1992). The four elementary forms of sociality: Framework for a unified theory of social relations. *Psychological Review, 99*, 689–723.

Foa, U., & Foa, E. (1974). *Societal structures of the mind.* Springfield, IL: Thomas.

Folger, R., & Konovsky, M. (1989). Effects of procedural justice and distributive justice on reactions to pay raise decisions. *Academy of Management Journal, 32*, 115–130.

Gabrielidis, C., Stephan, W. G., Ybarra, O., Pearson, V. M. S., & Villareal, L. (1997). Preferred styles of conflict resolution: Mexico and the United States. *Journal of Cross-Cultural Psychology, 28*, 661–677.

Gelfand, M. J., Higgins, M., Nishii, L. H., Raver, J. L., Dominquez, A., Murakami, F., Yamaguchi, S., & Toyama, M. (2002). Culture and egocentric perceptions of fairness in conflict and negotiation. *Journal of Applied Psychology, 87*, 833–845.

Gopalan, S., & Rivera, J. B. (1997). Gaining a perspective on Indian value orientations: Implications for expatriate managers. *International Journal of Organizational Analysis, 5*, 156–179.

Graham, J. L., Mintu, A. T., & Rodgers, W. (1994). Explorations of negotiation behaviors in ten foreign cultures using a model developed in the United States. *Management Science, 40*, 72–95.

Greenberg, J. (2001). Studying organizational justice cross-culturally: Fundamental challenges. *International Journal of Conflict Management, 12*, 365–375.

Gudykunst, W. B., & Nishida, T. (1994). *Bridging Japanese/North American differences.* Thousand Oaks, CA: Sage.

Gudykunst, W. B., & Ting-Toomey, S. (1988). Culture and affective communication. *American Behavioral Scientist, 31*, 384–400.

Gulliver, P. H. (1979). *Disputes and negotiations: A cross-cultural perspective.* New York: Academic Press.

Hofstede, G. (1980). *Culture's consequences: International differences in work-related values.* Beverly Hills, CA: Sage.

House, R. J., Hanges, P. J., Javidan, M., Dorfman, P., & Gupta, V. (Eds.). (2004). *GLOBE, cultures, leadership, and organizations: GLOBE study of 62 societies.* Newbury Park, CA: Sage.

Hui, M. K., & Au, K. (2001). Justice perceptions of complaint-handling: A cross-cultural comparison between PRC and Canadian customers. *Journal of Business Research, 52*, 161–173.

Hundley, G., & Kim, J. (1997). National culture and the factors affecting perceptions of pay fairness in Korea and the United States. *International Journal of Organizational Analysis, 5*, 325–341.

Huo, Y. J., Smith, H. J., Tyler, T. R., & Lind, E. A. (1996). Superordinate identification, subgroup identification, and justice concerns: Is separatism the problem, is assimilation the answer. *Psychological Science, 7*, 40–45.

James, K. (1993). The social context of organizational justice: cultural, intergroup, and structural effects on justice behaviors and perceptions. In R. Cropanzano (Ed.), *Justice in the workplace* (pp. 21–50). Hillsdale, NJ: Lawrence Erlbaum Associates.

Kashima, Y., Siegal, M., Tanaka, K., & Isaka, H. (1988). Universalism in lay conceptions of distributive justice: A cross-cultural examination. *International Journal of
Psychology, 23*, 51–64.

Kidder, L. H., & Muller, S. (1991). What is "fair" in Japan? In H. Steensma & R.
Vermunt (Eds.), *Social justice in human relations, Vol. 2: Societal and psychological
consequences of justice and injustice* (pp. 139–154). New York: Plenum Press.

Kim, K. I., Park, H. J., & Suzuki, N. (1990). Reward allocations in the United States,
Japan, and Korea: A comparison of individualistic and collectivistic cultures.
Academy of Management Journal, 33, 188–198.

Kozan, M. K., & Ergin, C. (1998). Preference for third party help in conflict management in the United States and Turkey: An experimental study. *Journal of Cross-
cultural Psychology, 29*, 540–558.

Kwong, J. Y. Y., & Leung, K. (2002). A moderator of the interaction effect of procedural justice and outcome favorability: Importance of the relationship. *Organizational Behavior and Decision Making Processes, 87*, 278–299.

Lam, S. S. K., Schaubroeck, J., & Aryee, S. (2002). Relationship between organizational justice and employee work outcomes: A cross-national study. *Journal of Organizational Behavior, 23*, 1–18.

Lee, C., Pillutla, M., & Law, K. S. (2000). Power-distance, gender and organizational
justice. *Journal of Management, 26*, 685–704.

Leung, K. (1987). Some determinants of reactions to procedural models for conflict resolution: A cross-national study. *Journal of Personality and Social Psychology, 53*, 898–908.

Leung, K. (1988). Theoretical advances in justice behavior: Some cross-cultural input. In M. H. Bond (Ed.), *The cross-cultural challenge to social psychology* (pp.
218–229). Newbury Park, CA: Sage.

Leung, K. (1997). Negotiation and reward allocations across cultures. In P. C. Earley
& M. Erez (Eds.), *New perspectives on international industrial/organizational psychology* (pp. 640–675). San Francisco: Jossey-Bass.

Leung, K., Au, Y. F., Fernández-Dols, J. M., & Iwawaki, S. (1992). Preferences for
methods of conflict processing in two collectivist cultures. *International Journal of
Psychology, 27*, 195–209.

Leung, K., & Bond, M. H. (1982). How Chinese and Americans reward task-related
contributions: A preliminary study. *Psychologia, 25*, 32–39.

Leung, K., & Bond, M. H. (1984). The impact of cultural collectivism on reward allocation. *Journal of Personality and Social Psychology, 47*, 793–804.

Leung, K., Chiu, W. H., & Au, Y. K. (1993). Sympathy and support for industrial actions. *Journal of Applied Psychology, 78*, 781–787.

Leung, K., & Iwawaki, S. (1988). Cultural collectivism and distributive behavior: A
cross-national study. *Journal of Cross-Cultural Psychology, 19*, 35–49.

Leung, K., & Li, W. K. (1990). Psychological mechanisms of process control effects.
Journal of Applied Psychology, 75, 613–620.

Leung, K., & Lind, E. A. (1986). Procedural justice and culture: Effects of culture,
gender, and investigator status on procedural preference. *Journal of Personality
and Social Psychology, 50*, 1134–1140.

Leung, K., & Morris, M. W. (2001). Justice through the lens of culture and ethnicity.
In V. L. Hamilton & J. Sanders (Eds), *Handbook of justice research in law* (pp.
343–378). New York: Plenum Press.

Leung, K., & Park, H. J. (1986). Effects of interactional goal on choice of allocation
rules: A cross-cultural study. *Organizational Behavior and Human Decision Processes, 37*, 111–120.

Leung, K., Smith, P. B., Wang. Z. M., & Sun, H. F. (1996). Job satisfaction in joint venture hotels in China: An organizational justice analysis. *Journal of International Business Studies, 27,* 947–962.

Leung K., & Stephen, W. G. (2000). Conflict and injustice in intercultural relations: Insights from the Arab-Israeli and Sino-British disputes. In J. Duckitt & S. Renshon (Eds.), *Political psychology: Cultural and cross-cultural perspectives* (pp. 128–145). London: Macmillan.

Leung, K., & Stephan, W. G. (2001). Social justice from a cultural perspective. In D. Matsumoto (Ed.), *The handbook of culture and psychology* (pp. 375–410). New York: Oxford University Press.

Leung, K., Su, S. K., & Morris, M. W. (2001). When is criticism *not* constructive? The roles of fairness perceptions and dispositional attributions in employee acceptance of critical supervisory feedback. *Human Relations, 54,* 1155–1187.

Leung, K., & Tong, K. K. (2004). Justice across cultures: A three-stage model for intercultural negotiation. In M. Gelfand & J. Brett (Eds.), *The handbook of negotiation and culture* (pp. 313–333). Stanford, CA: Stanford University Press.

Leung, K., Tong, K. K., & Ho, S. S. Y. (2004). Effects of interactional justice on egocentric bias in resource allocation decisions. *Journal of Applied Psychology, 89,* 405–415.

Leung, K., Wang, Z. M., & Smith, P. B. (2001). Job attitudes and organizational justice in joint venture hotels in China: The role of expatriate managers. *International Journal of Human Resource Management, 12,* 926–945.

Leventhal, G. S. (1980). What should be done with equity theory? New approaches to the study of fairness in social relationships. In K. Gergen, M. Greenberg, & R. Willis (Eds.), *Social exchange* (pp. 27–55). New York: Academic Press.

Lind, E. A. (1994). Procedural justice and culture: Evidence for ubiquitous process concerns. *Zeitschrift für Rechtssoziologie, 15,* 24–36.

Lind, E. A., Erickson, B. E., Friedland, N., & Dickenberger, M. (1978). Reactions to procedural models for adjudicative conflict resolution: A cross-national study. *Journal of Conflict Resolution, 2,* 318–341.

Lind, E. A., & Tyler, T. R. (1988). *The social psychology of procedural justice.* New York: Plenum Press.

Lubman, S. B. (1988). Investment and export contracts in the People's Republic of China: Perspectives on evolving patterns. *Brigham Young University Law Review, 3,* 543–565.

McFarlin, D. B., & Sweeney, P. D. (2001). Cross-cultural applications of organizational justice. In R. Cropanzano (Ed.), *Justice in the workplace: From theory to practice* (Vol. 2, pp. 67–95). Mahwah, NJ: Lawrence Erlbaum Associates.

McLean Parks, J., Conlon, D. E., Ang, S., & Bontempo, R. (1999). The manager giveth, the manager taketh away: Variation in distribution/recovery rules due to resource type and cultural orientation. *Journal of Management, 25,* 723–757.

Mendonca, M., & Kanungo, R. N. (1994). Motivation through effective reward management in developing countries. In R. N. Kanungo & M. Mendonca (Eds.), *Work motivation: Models for developing countries* (pp. 49–83). New Delhi: Sage.

Miles, J. A., & Greenberg, J. (1993). Cross-national differences in preferences for distributive justice norms: The challenge of establishing fair resource allocations in the European community. In J. B. Shaw, P. S. Kirkbride, & K. M. Rowland (Eds.), *Research in personnel and human resources management* (Supplement 3, pp. 133–156). Greenwich, CT: JAI.

Miller, J. G., & Bersoff, D. M. (1992). Culture and moral judgment: How are conflicts between justice and friendship resolved? *Journal of Personality and Social Psychology, 62,* 541–554.

Milliman, J., Nason, S., Von Glinow, M. A., Huo, P., Lowe, K. B., & Kim, N. (1995). In search of "best" strategic pay practices: An exploratory study of Japan, Korea, Taiwan and the United States. *Advances in International Comparative Management, 10,* 227–252.

Morris M. W., & Leung, K. (2000). Justice for all? Progress in research on cultural variation in the psychology of distributive and procedural justice. *Applied Psychology: An International Review, 49,* 100–132.

Morris, M. W., Leung, K., & Iyengar, S. S. (2004). Person perception in the heat of conflict: Negative trait attributions affect procedural preferences and account for situational and cultural differences. *Asian Journal of Social Psychology, 7,* 127–147.

Morris, M. W., Williams, K. Y., Leung, K., Larrick, R., Mendoza, M. T., Bhatnagar, D., Li, J., Kondo, M., Luo, J., & Hu, J. (1998). Conflict management style: Accounting for cross-national differences. *Journal of International Business Studies, 29,* 729–748.

Mueller, C. W., Iverson, R. D., & Jo, D. G. (1999). Distributive justice evaluations in two cultural contexts: A comparison of U.S. and South Korean teachers. *Human Relations, 52,* 869–893.

Murphy-Berman, V., & Berman, J. J. (2002). Cross-cultural differences in perceptions of distributive justice. *Journal of Cross-Cultural Psychology, 33,* 157–170.

Murphy-Berman, V., Berman, J. J., Singh, P., Pacharui, A., & Kumar, P. (1984). Factors affecting allocation to needy and meritorious recipients: A cross-cultural comparison. *Journal of Personality and Social Psychology, 46,* 1267–1272.

Nader, L., & Todd, H. F. (1978). *The disputing process: Law in ten societies.* New York: Columbia University Press.

Ohbuchi, K., Fukushima, O., & Tedeschi, J. T. (1999). Cultural values in conflict management: Goal orientation, goal attainment, and tactical decision. *Journal of Cross-Cultural Psychology, 30,* 51–71.

Ohbuchi, K., Suzuki, M., & Yoichiro, Y. (2001). Conflict management and organizational attitudes among Japanese: Individual and group goals and justice. *Asian Journal of Social Psychology, 4,* 93–101.

Ohbuchi, K., & Takahashi, Y. (1994). Cultural styles of conflict management in Japanese and Americans: Passivity, covertness, and effectiveness of strategies. *Journal of Applied Social Psychology, 24,* 1345–1366.

Ouchi, W. G., & Jaeger, A. M. (1978). Type Z organization: Stability in the midst of mobility. *Academy of Management Review, 3,* 305–314.

Pearce, J. L., Bigley, G. A., & Branyiczki, I. (1998). Procedural justice as modernism: Placing industrial/organizational psychology in context. *Applied Psychology: An International Review, 47*(3), 371–396.

Pearson, V. M. S., & Stephan, W. G. (1988). Preferences for styles of negotiation: A comparison of Brazil and the U.S. *International Journal of Intercultural Relations, 22,* 67–83.

Phillips, J. M., & Gully, S. M. (2002). Fairness reactions to personnel selection techniques in Singapore and the United States. *International Journal of Human Resource Management, 13,* 1186–1205.

Pillai, R., Scandura, T. A., & Williams, E. A. (1999). Leadership and organizational justice: Similarities and differences across cultures. *Journal of International Business Studies, 30,* 763–779.

Pillai, R., Williams, E. S., & Tan, J. J. (2001). Are the scales tipped in favor of procedural or distributive justice? An investigation of the U.S., India, Germany, and Hong Kong (China). *International Journal of Conflict Management, 12,* 312–332.

Price, K. H., Hall, T. W., Van den Bos, K., Hunton, J. E., Lovett, S., & Tippett, M. J. (2001). Features of the value function for voice and their consistency across participants from four countries: Great Britain, Mexico, the Netherlands, and the United States. *Organizational Behavior and Human Decision Processes, 84,* 95–121.

Probst, T., Carnevale, P. J., & Triandis, H. C. (1999). Cultural values in intergroup and single-group social dilemmas. *Organizational Behavior and Human Decision Processes, 77,* 171–191.

Rahim, M. A., Magner, N. R., Antonioni, D., & Rahman, S. (2001). Do justice relationships with organization-directed reactions differ across U.S. and Bangladesh employees? *International Journal of Conflict Management, 12,* 333–349.

Sarachek, B. (1990). Chinese administrative thought. *Advances in International Comparative Management, 5,* 149–167.

Schwartz, S. H. (1994). Beyond individualism/collectivism: New dimensions of values. In U. Kim, H. C. Triandis, C. Kagitcibasi, S. C. Choi, & G. Yoon (Eds.), *Individualism and collectivism: Theory, method, and applications* (pp. 112–143). Newbury park, CA: Sage.

Smith, P. B., Peterson, M. F., Leung, K., & Dugan, S. (1998). Individualism-collectivism, power distance, and handling of disagreement: A cross-national study. *International Journal of Intercultural Relations, 22,* 351–367.

Smith, P. B., Peterson, M. F., Misumi, J., & Tayeb, M. H. (1989). On the generality of leadership styles across cultures. *Journal of Occupational Psychology, 62,* 97–110.

Sriussadaporn-Charoenngam, N., & Jablin, F. M. (1999). An exploratory study of communication competence in Thai organizations. *Journal of Business Communication, October,* 382–418.

Steiner, D. D., & Gilliland, S. W. (1996). Fairness reactions to personnel selection techniques in France and the United States. *Journal of Applied Psychology, 81,* 134–141.

Stevenson, H. W., Lee, S. Y., Chen, C. S., Stigler, J. W., Hsu, C. C., & Kitamura, S. (1990). Contexts of achievement: A study of American, Chinese, and Japanese children. *Monographs of the Society for Research in Child Development, 55*(1–2, Serial no. 221).

Sullivan, J., Peterson, R. B., Kameda, N., & Shimada, J. (1981). The relationship between conflict resolution approaches and trust: A cross-cultural study. *Academy of Management Journal, 24,* 803–815.

Thibaut, J., & Walker, L. (1975). *Procedural justice: A psychological analysis.* Hillsdale, NJ: Lawrence Erlbaum Associates.

Tinsley, C. H. (1997). Understanding conflict in a Chinese cultural context. In R. Bies, R. J. Lewicki, & B. Sheppard (Eds.), *Research on negotiations in organizations* (pp. 209–225). Beverly Hills, CA: Sage.

Tinsley, C. H. (1998). Models of conflict resolution in Japanese, German, and American cultures. *Journal of Applied Psychology, 83,* 316–323.

Tinsley, C. H. (2001). How we get to yes: Predicting the constellation of strategies used across cultures to negotiate conflict. *Journal of Applied Psychology, 86,* 583–593.

Triandis H. C. (1995). *Individualism & collectivism.* Boulder, CO: Westview Press.

Triandis, H. C., Carnevale, P., Gelfand, M., Robert, C., Wasti, A., Probst, T., et al. (2001). Culture, personality and deception: A multilevel approach. *International Journal of Cross-Cultural Management, 1,* 73–90.

Tse, D. K., Francis, J., & Walls, J. (1994). Cultural differences in conducting intra- and inter-cultural negotiations: A Sino-Canadian comparison. *Journal of International Business Studies, 25,* 537–555.

Tyler, T. R., & Bies, R. J. (1990). Beyond formal procedures: The interpersonal context of procedural justice. In J. S. Carroll (Ed.), *Applied social psychology and organizational settings* (pp. 77–98). Hillsdale, NJ: Lawrence Erlbaum Associates.

Tyler, T. R., Boeckmann, R. J., Smith, H. J., & Huo, Y. J. (1997). *Social justice in a diverse society.* Boulder, CO: Westview.

Tyler, T. R., & Lind, E. A. (1992). A relational model of authority in groups. In M. Zanna (Ed.), *Advances in experimental social psychology* (pp. 115–191). New York: Academic Press.

Tyler, T. R., Lind, E. A., & Huo, Y. J. (2000). Cultural values and authority relations: The psychology of conflict resolution across cultures. *Psychology, Public Policy, and Law, 6,* 1138–1163.

Van de Vijver, F., & Leung, K. (1997). *Methods and data analysis for cross-cultural research.* Newbury Park, CA: Sage.

Van den Bos, K., & Lind, E. A. (2002). Uncertainty management by means of fairness judgments. In M. P. Zanna (Ed.), *Advances in experimental social psychology* (pp. 1–60). San Diego, CA: Academic Press.

Vasquez, K., Keltner, D., Ebenbach, D. H., & Banaszynski, T. L. (2001). Cultural variation and similarity in moral rhetorics: Voices from the Philippines and the United States. *Journal of Cross Cultural Psychology, 32,* 93–120.

Wall, J. A., & Blum, M. E. (1991). Community mediation in the People's Republic of China. *Journal of Conflict Resolution, 35,* 3–20.

Wallbott, H. G., & Scherer, K. R. (1986). The antecedents of emotional experiences. In K. S. Scherer, H. G. Wallbott, & A. B. Summerfield (Eds.), *Experiencing emotion: A cross-cultural study* (pp. 69–83). Cambridge, England: Cambridge University Press.

Wegener, B., & Liebig, S. (1995). Dominant ideologies and the variation of distributive justice norms: A comparison of East and West Germany, and the United States. In J. R. Kluegel, D. S. Mason, & B. Wegener (Eds.), *Social justice and political change: Public opinion in capitalist and post-communist states* (pp. 239–259). New York: Aldine.

Wheeler, L., Reis, H. T., & Bond, M. H. (1989). Collectivism-individualism in everyday life: The Middle Kingdom and the melting pot. *Journal of Personality and Social Psychology, 57,* 79–86.

White, G., Luk, V., Druker, J., & Chiu, R. (1998). Paying their way: A comparison of managerial reward systems in the London and Hong Kong banking industries. *Asia Pacific Journal of Human Resources, 36,* 54–71.

Wierzbicka, A. (1991). *Cross-cultural pragmatics: The semantics of human interaction.* Berlin: Mouton de Gruyter.

VII

INTEGRATION

20

Organizational Justice: Where Do We Stand?

Jason A. Colquitt
University of Florida

Jerald Greenberg
Ohio State University

Brent A. Scott
University of Florida

In an effort to characterize the current status of the field of organizational justice, we synthesize and integrate the principal themes expressed in this Handbook of Organizational Justice. Our remarks are organized around the major parts of this book: construct validity issues, the justice judgment process, justice effects, justice applications, and generalizability issues. Acknowledging the importance of these five themes for the field's healthy maturity, and with an eye toward avoiding potential pitfalls, we offer suggestions for further conceptual refinement and identify promising new research directions. These form the basis of our cautiously optimistic conclusions about the future of the field of organizational justice.

Two decades have passed since Greenberg and Folger introduced the concept of procedural justice to organizational scientists (Folger & Greenberg, 1985; Greenberg & Folger, 1983). In that time, over 500 articles have appeared with the keywords "justice" or "fairness" in a Web of Science search, along with some 20 books devoted to this topic (e.g., Cropanzano, 1993, 2001; Folger & Cropanzano, 1998; Greenberg, 1996; Greenberg & Cropanzano, 2001; Lind & Tyler, 1988). Now, this considerable body of work is chronicled by the first handbook devoted to summarizing this voluminous literature.

The purpose of this chapter is twofold. First, we summarize and comment on the major ideas expressed throughout the present volume. This discussion is organized around the five major themes addressed in this handbook: construct validity issues, the justice judgment process, justice effects, justice applications, and generalizability issues. Second, based on the discussions offered by the authors, we will offer some questions for future research and theory development in these areas. In so doing we identify where we believe the field of organizational justice currently stands and where it should be going.

CONSTRUCT VALIDITY ISSUES

The chapters in Part II of this handbook explore several important issues, including the number of distinct justice dimensions the literature should recognize and the exact manner in which justice should be conceptualized and measured. Schwab's (1980) recommendations about construct validity are relevant in this regard. Specifically, he emphasized the importance of construct definitions when judging the correspondence between a measure and the underlying construct it is meant

to assess. As a whole, organizational behavior scholars have been criticized for neglecting to offer such definitions and for offering definitions that are unnecessarily complex (Locke, 2003). Indeed, Locke (2003) suggested that dictionary definitions are preferable to the more complex definitions used in academic literatures. With this in mind, let us examine the definitions of *just* and *fair* found in the current edition of a popular dictionary (Merriam-Webster, 2003):

Just (p. 679):
- Having a basis in or conforming to fact or reason: reasonable.
- Conforming to a standard of correctness: proper.
- Acting or being in conformity with what is morally upright or good: righteous.
- Being what is merited: deserved.
- Legally correct: lawful.

Fair (p. 449):
- Marked by impartiality and honesty: free from self-interest, prejudice, or favoritism.
- Conforming with the established rules: allowed.
- Consonant with merit or importance: due.

To the field's credit, the multiple dimensions of organizational justice captured in the literature (its seminal, guiding theories, in fact) closely reflect the different facets of these dictionary definitions. For example, the notions of merit and deservingness are incorporated into conceptualizations of equity and distributive justice (Adams, 1965; Deutsch, 1975; Homans, 1961; Leventhal, 1976a). Many facets of the dictionary definitions, such as correctness, morality, impartiality, and conformity to established rules of conduct, also are addressed in Leventhal's (1980) treatment of procedural justice. Finally, an emphasis on adhering to standards of proper, honest, and morally appropriate behavior may be seen in Bies and Moag's (1986) discussion of interactional justice. Accordingly, all of the major dimensions of justice found in the organizational justice literature correspond to one or more facets of the dictionary definitions of *just* and *fair*.

This leads us to the issue addressed by the first two chapters of Part II: Are the multiple justice dimensions really distinct? In other words, if the constructs all fit the same set of definitions, are the distinctions among them of value? Ambrose and Arnaud tackle this important question with respect to distributive and procedural justice, examining this question from a variety of perspectives. They provide compelling evidence that these two constructs can be distinguished theoretically, that they can be measured and manipulated independently, and that their

effects and antecedents often differ. These arguments complement earlier treatments of the issue (Cropanzano & Ambrose, 2001) while also breaking important new ground.

Bies explores the analogous question with respect to procedural justice and interactional justice. However, the issue of their separation is more controversial, primarily because there was a time when combining them was accepted practice in the literature (Cropanzano & Greenberg, 1997; Tyler & Bies, 1990). Bies chronicles this period in his chapter and describes why he now believes that procedural justice and interactional justice should be kept separate. Like Ambrose and Arnaud, he approaches the question from a variety of perspectives, including the effects of these concepts on other variables, factor-analytic support, and meta-analytic results. Bies concludes that interactional justice is not merely a form of procedural justice, but that the two dimensions are, in fact, distinct (see also Bobocel & Holmvall, 2001).

Taken together, the chapters by Ambrose and Arnaud and by Bies suggest that the domain of organizational justice is characterized by at least three dimensions. Following Greenberg (1993a) and Colquitt (2001), both Bies and Colquitt and Shaw also discuss the merits of separating interactional justice into separate interpersonal and informational facets. The sincerity and respectfulness of communication is conceptually distinct from the honesty and adequacy of its content, and both factor-analytic and meta-analytic data support this separation (Colquitt, 2001; Colquitt, Conlon, Wesson, Porter, & Ng, 2001).

Although one may be tempted to believe that these chapters will put to rest the question of "How many forms of justice are there?," we do not expect that to occur. As Colquitt and Shaw discuss, the correlations among the justice types often fall between .60 to .70, a range where combination seems justified and separation seems problematic. Adding to this, Ambrose and Arnaud describe the multicollinearity problems created by such high correlations. Multicollinearity inflates standard errors, making independent effect and unique explained-variance estimates much more unstable across studies. This brings us to two critical questions, the answers to which may dictate the way organizational justice is conceptualized and measured over the next several years: (a) What are the merits of overall measures of justice? (b) Should the content and context of organizational justice be expanded?

What Are the Merits of Overall Measures of Justice?

Ambrose and Arnaud note that many of the earliest and most influential works in the justice literature emphasized the importance of an overall notion of justice (e.g., Leventhal, 1980; Lind & Tyler, 1988). They also review some recent calls for an increased emphasis on overall, ho-

listic, or total justice. Still, very few studies—either lab or field investigations—include such a measure. Colquitt and Shaw note that there are two ways in which overall justice may be conceptualized—as a higher order latent variable (with specific justice dimensions as indicators), and as a global, self-report measure that does not reference specific justice criteria or types (see also Colquitt & Greenberg, 2003).

As a thought exercise, imagine what the literature would look like if such overall justice measures were included in most studies over the next several years. As Ambrose and Arnaud suggest, few articles would focus on the unique variance associated with one particular form of justice, or on the differential effects of multiple justice dimensions. More attention would be focused instead on the total variance explained in important outcomes, irrespective of whether that variance stemmed from one dimension or another. Because the effect sizes for overall justice likely would be more stable than the independent effects of three or four highly related dimensions, results would accumulate more rapidly.

One also might expect that overall justice more often would be paired with other organizational behavior variables, a desirable state of affairs advocated by Greenberg (1996). As a practical matter, scholars tend to measure carefully the variables germane to their own literatures (e.g., by paying close attention to distinctions among dimensions) while glossing over such issues in other areas. Lewicki, Wiethoff, and Tomlinson make this point in their chapter, noting that justice scholars conceptualize trust more simplistically than justice, whereas trust scholars conceptualize justice more simplistically than trust. With this in mind, researchers interested in other literatures, who otherwise might be tempted to incorporate justice into their studies, may be reluctant to add three or four additional variables to their data collection and analysis efforts, leading them to shy away from considering justice at all. With the advent of a more unidimensional, less fragmented, measure of justice such reluctance might disappear, paving the way for organizational justice to become better integrated with other topics in the field of organizational behavior.

As an analogy, consider the literature on perceived organizational support (POS; Eisenberger, Huntington, Hutchison, & Sowa, 1986), which was introduced the same year in which Bies and Moag (1986) identified interactional justice. Now, assume that a leadership scholar wants to assess the degree to which an employee's organization treats him or her in a caring, respectful manner—possibly as a mediator of the effects of leadership styles or behaviors. Although that researcher may elect to measure interactional justice, he or she may be inclined to favor the simpler construct of POS for fear of drawing the ire of journal editors by omitting some key dimensions of organizational justice. Because an

overall justice measure would be less subject to this concern, its presence in other literatures, although not assured, would be more likely. This would be desirable insofar as it promises to broaden the nomological net within which the construct of organizational justice may be understood (Greenberg, 1996).

Despite this, there also are drawbacks of focusing on overall justice exclusively. As Colquitt and Greenberg (2003) noted, justice interventions may be limited in their scope and comprehensiveness. Which fairness criteria should interventions prioritize when resources such as money or time are issues (as is almost always the case)? Such questions require studies on justice facets, making an exclusive focus on overall justice less beneficial. Indeed, one may draw a parallel to the literature on job satisfaction, where measures of both specific dimensions (e.g., pay, coworker, leader) and overall satisfaction have both been used (e.g., Jackson & Corr, 2002; Wanous, Reichers, & Hurdy, 1997). The best approach, therefore, may be to examine specific dimensions and overall justice in combination. As Colquitt and Shaw recommend, field studies relying on structural equation modeling could examine a model's fit with an overall factor, allowing specific and overall effects to be analyzed simultaneously. Studies that measure or manipulate specific dimensions also could rely on overall justice as a mediator of dimension effects. In either case, the critical step would be to examine whether the specific dimensions have incremental effects over the more general factor.

Should the Content and Context of Organizational Justice Be Expanded?

Whether one focuses on overall justice or its dimensions, another key question arises with respect to construct validity: What is the content of organizational justice and in what context should it be explored? In many respects, the content of organizational justice has remained remarkably stable. As summarized by Colquitt and Shaw's Table 4.1, justice measures generally assess the same criteria identified by the seminal works in the field (Bies & Moag, 1986; Greenberg, 1986; Leventhal, 1980; Thibaut & Walker, 1975). Expansion of these criteria has occurred only when a specific context makes other criteria salient. For example, although Gilliland (1993) suggested that job relatedness is an important criterion for procedural justice in a selection context, its applicability to other contexts has not been established.

Although the content of justice has remained stable, the contexts within which justice effects have been examined have continued to expand. Over the years, studies have moved beyond dispute resolution (within which justice originally was studied) to such other areas as per-

formance evaluation, selection, compensation, and training contexts, to name but a few (for reviews, see Colquitt & Greenberg, 2003; Cropanzano & Greenberg, 1997; Greenberg & Lind, 2000). At the same time these extensions have broadened the generalizability of justice effects, they also represent situations in which an authority figure makes some sort of decision that impacts one or more members of a collective. From this perspective, the context of justice may be considered to have remained quite stable: It almost always is examined in a hierarchical decision-making context.

Advocating expansion of content of interactional justice, Bies recommends moving beyond the notions of respect, propriety, justification, and truthfulness identified originally by Bies and Moag (1986). Specifically, he has identified several new facets of interactional justice, including derogatory judgments, deception, invasion of privacy, abusive actions, and coercion (see also Bies, 2001). Although some of these may be subsumed by Bies and Moag's (1986) original four dimensions (e.g., deception by truthfulness, derogatory judgments by propriety), others (e.g., abusive actions and coercion) clearly expand the construct space.

Interestingly, some of Bies's additions create new sources of overlap with procedural justice, particularly the notions of deception and invasion of privacy subsumed under Leventhal's (1980) ethicality criterion of procedural justice. Ethicality remains one of the more ambiguous justice rules, however, and the assessment of ethicality in self-report measures of justice rarely specifies practices like privacy invasion. It also is notable that Bies's additions reflect the "darker side" of the construct insofar as privacy invasions, derogatory judgments, and abuse are qualitatively different than the mere absence of respect, propriety, truthfulness, and justification. Given the widespread nature of such considerations in organizations (Griffen & O'Leary-Kelly, 2004; Sackett & DeVore, 2001), such additions may be expected to boost the variance explained in key job attitudes and behaviors by these interactional facets.

A more fundamental type of expansion resides in Bies's notion of an "encounter perspective." Bies begins by noting that justice scholars typically focus on the fairness of discrete decision or resource allocation events, which Bies refers to as "exchanges." However, he notes that employees raise concerns about bosses who break promises, disclose secrets, and coerce employees even when no decision or resource allocation is relevant. In Bies's terms, these more general concerns are based in "encounters." While Bies makes an important observation, we contend that the distinction between exchanges and encounters is practically analogous to the distinction between events and entities made by Cropanzano, Byrne, Bobocel, and Rupp (2001). If employees

596   COLQUITT, GREENBERG, SCOTT

are asked to rate the sincerity shown during their last performance appraisal, then they are forming an event or exchange judgment. However, if employees are asked to rate the interpersonal justice shown by their bosses in general, then they are forming an entity or encounter-level judgment.

Thus, the event versus entity (or exchange vs. encounter) distinction represents not so much an expansion of justice contexts as a clarification of the multiple contexts studied. Yet a key question remains unanswered by Bies: To what extent is justice bounded by hierarchical authority relationships? Does it make sense to speak of procedural or interpersonal justice among coworkers? Just as they do with leaders, coworkers have encounters with one another and form entity judgments about one another. Likewise, coworkers can treat one another inconsistently, with bias, and disrespectfully. Furthermore, perceived fairness of one's coworkers also may be correlated significantly with key job attitudes and behaviors among employees.

In examining this issue beyond hierarchical authority relationships, we must be careful not to threaten the construct validity of organizational justice. The fine line between a coworker being interactionally just as opposed merely to being "nice" too easily may become blurred as contexts broaden. Likewise, it may be difficult to distinguish between a coworker who is procedurally unfair and one who is only "close-minded." The behaviors Bies discusses take on special importance when they occur in a hierarchical context, and it is within such a context that the initial theorizing on interactional justice was born (Bies & Moag, 1986). The presence of hierarchy also is central both to the initial conceptualizations of procedural justice (Leventhal, 1980; Thibaut & Walker, 1975) and to more recent theorizing such as the relational model of justice (Tyler & Lind, 1992) and fairness heuristic theory (Lind, 2001).

Although we acknowledge the potential importance of expanding the justice concept to nonhierarchical relationships, we encourage theorists to consider the challenges to construct validity posed by such an endeavor. Our ultimate concern is that by misapplying justice constructs or by casting our conceptual net too broadly, their essential nature may become so diffuse as to be meaningless. This was what happened in the early 1980s when equity theory experienced a decline in popularity (Greenberg, 1982). To some extent, it was the overstretching of equity theory beyond hierarchical relationships (Walster, Berscheid, & Walster, 1973) that led to questions about the validity of distributive justice as a whole (Leventhal, 1980). Now that we have expanded the construct space of organizational justice, it seems prudent to learn from the past by sidestepping further threats to construct validity.

THE JUSTICE JUDGMENT PROCESS

The matter of how people form judgments of justice has received the most theoretical attention in the justice literature. The most prominent theories of the justice judgment process are the instrumental model (Lind & Tyler, 1988; Thibaut & Walker, 1975); the relational model (Tyler & Lind, 1992); fairness theory (Folger & Cropanzano, 1998, 2001); the moral virtue, or deontic, model (Folger, 1998, 2001); and fairness heuristic theory (Lind, 2001), which recently has been subsumed by uncertainty management theory (Lind & Van den Bos, 2002; Van den Bos & Lind, 2002). These theories explore, with varying degrees of emphasis, why people attend to issues of fairness and the nature of the information they gather in making such judgments.

Both matters are explored in Part III of this handbook, which begins where the procedural justice literature originated—the concept of control. Shapiro and Brett review Thibaut and Walker's (1975) work linking process control and outcome control to perceptions of procedural fairness along with more recent work exploring how the various forms of control best could be combined. They then explore the multiple reasons why individuals attend to issues of control-based fairness, such as voice. These include instrumental reasons (i.e., voice will help further one's own economic interests) and noninstrumental reasons (i.e., voice reaffirms that one is respected by an authority figure).

Of course, one might argue that both these instrumental and noninstrumental reasons are indicative of self-interest. Carr and Greenberg explore this issue in depth by examining whether all justice concerns can be explained solely by self-interest. These authors review three reasons why individuals care about justice: (a) It reinforces feelings of esteem, (b) it improves control over outcome allocations, and (c) it signals a respect for morality. Using Greenberg's (2001) contention that all three reasons represent a form of self-interest as a starting point, the authors explore the commonalities among the three reasons. They eventually conclude that all three reasons support a higher order, ultimate (and self- interested) goal of "belonging"—the need to form and maintain lasting, positive relationships. The authors also introduce the concept of a goal hierarchy for justice, according to which individuals attend to the fairness of events and entities to monitor degree of achievement with the goal of belonging.

Carr and Greenberg's discussion of self-interest contrasts with Folger, Cropanzano, and Goldman's ideas about justice and morality. Taking a less cognitively oriented view of the justice judgment process, Folger and his associates note the emotional nature of reactions to injustice. Specifically, they suggest that individuals are "hardwired" to respond to injustice with emotional arousal and attempts at retribution or

reconciliation. In describing this so-called "deontic response," Folger et al. also explore the overlap between justice and morality—two concepts whose boundaries often are blurred.

The interplay of cognition and emotion underlying deontic responses to injustice also may be found in trust, a construct that in some ways is similar to justice. Lewicki, Wiethoff, and Tomlinson explore the often-blurred boundaries between justice and trust, and clarify the relative positioning of these constructs in models from both literatures. As these authors note, trust can be rooted in emotion and affect or in a cognitive analysis of the trustee's characteristics. Regardless of its origin, trust has assumed many roles within the justice judgment process, which has proven to be a source of confusion when attempting to reconcile multiple models. Lewicki et al. review these discrepancies in a manner that brings a more comprehensive understanding of trust to justice scholars.

As a whole, these chapters raise several important questions about justice judgments that are worthy of delineation: (a) Is belonging really the ultimate goal of justice? (b) How do justice rules fit with conceptualizations of the justice judgment process?

Is Belonging Really the Ultimate Goal?

Carr and Greenberg's notion of a goal hierarchy integrates the various reasons given for caring about issues of fairness (e.g., esteem, control, morality). Their approach opens up a variety of new research directions, such as individual and situational antecedents of goal weighting, individual differences in the importance of belonging, and empirical testing of the ultimate role of belonging. The latter is particularly important, given that there are two other intuitively plausible candidates for "ultimate status:" trust and uncertainty. Carr and Greenberg discuss trust and uncertainty in the context of managing discrepancies between entity judgments and expectations, but they do not position those goals within their hierarchy.

Lewicki et al. suggest that trust is one of the most salient indicators of the type of relationship existing between two parties (e.g., market, communal). In reading their discussion of the sources and origins of trust, we were struck by the overlap with the Cropanzano, Byrne, Bobocel, and Rupp (2001) multiple needs framework. For example, sources of trust in authorities include predictability, caring and benevolence, and moral integrity (e.g., Mayer, Davis, & Schoorman, 1995; Rousseau, Sitkin, Burt, & Camerer, 1998). Predictability fulfills many of the same needs as the control motive, whereas caring and benevolence improve feelings of status or esteem. Finally, moral integrity has much in common with the concepts of moral virtue or deonance. If those concepts are

indeed sources of trust, then it follows that trust may serve as an ultimate goal that is fulfilled by those lower order goals.

Positioning trust as the ultimate goal more closely parallels the logic of fairness heuristic theory, which argues that individuals attend to issues of fairness because ultimately they are concerned with trustworthiness (Lind, 2001). Recently, fairness heuristic theory has been subsumed by uncertainty management theory (Lind & Van den Bos, 2002; Van den Bos & Lind, 2002), which argues that uncertainty reduction is the ultimate goal—with the trustworthiness of an authority figure being one of several sources of uncertainty. In support of this notion, Van den Bos and Lind (2002) review studies showing that justice becomes especially important when uncertainty is primed within individuals by asking them to think about previous instances of pain or their own mortality (see also Lind & Van den Bos, 2002).

Trust and uncertainty (or, more accurately, security) may be alternatives to the ultimate goal of belonging. Of course, both goals are themselves related to belonging. Trust is vital to the forming and maintaining of interpersonal relationships, and those relationships are a powerful source of uncertainty reduction. It may be that belonging, trust, and security all fall somewhere within an expanded goal hierarchy, each affecting in its own way the multiple needs of control, esteem, and morality. This suggestion points to the utility of Carr and Greenberg's goal hierarchy as a mechanism for integrating a variety of distinct concepts within the justice literature.

Where Do Justice Rules Fit In?

A second question raised by the chapters in Part III concerns the role of the justice rules articulated by Leventhal (1976b, 1980) and by Bies and Moag (1986). Although the rules presented in Table 4.1 of Colquitt and Shaw are measured or manipulated in the vast majority of studies in the justice literature, their role remains unclear in recent theorizing. To help illustrate some important questions regarding justice rules, we present an overview of the justice judgment process in Fig. 20.1. This diagram should not be considered a causal model, but rather, a summary of the sequence of steps involved in forming justice judgments.

The process depicted in Fig. 20.1 begins with the triggering of justice concerns, as individuals attend to issues of fairness for some reason. That reason may pertain to concerns over belonging, as suggested by Carr and Greenberg, or instead it may revolve around issues of trust and uncertainty. More specifically, those concerns may refer to issues of control, esteem, or morality (Carr & Greenberg, this volume; Cropanzano, Byrne, Bobocel, & Rupp, 2001; Shapiro & Brett, this volume). Regardless, some assessment of the justice rules is now called for, with Fig. 20.1 rep-

600

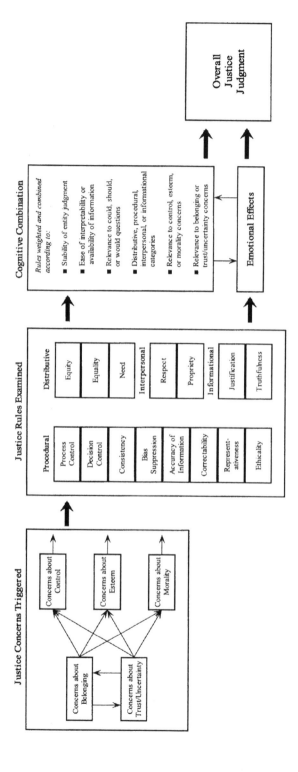

FIG. 20.1. Overview of justice rules in the justice judgment process.

resenting the four major categories of justice rules: distributive, procedural, interpersonal, and informational.

Are these rules (or categories of rules) equally relevant to concerns about control, esteem, and morality? Are they relevant to concerns about belonging, trust, or uncertainty? In some cases, the answers are straightforward. For example, research on the relational model suggests that procedural rules are relevant to both control and esteem needs (Tyler & Lind, 1992). With respect to specific procedural rules, one might expect that process control and decision control would be particularly relevant to control or instrumental concerns (Shapiro & Brett, this volume) whereas ethicality would be most relevant to morality concerns (Folger et al., this volume). Beyond these intuitive predictions, however, justice scholars know little about how the triggers of justice concerns shape the form that the justice-formation process takes.

Regardless of the kinds of concerns that trigger the process, theories of justice judgments agree that individuals do not assess each and every one of those individual rules independently when forming a fairness perception. Fairness heuristic theory, for example, suggests that the cognitive combination of the rules depends on whether a stable entity judgment already exists. If so, then the cognitive exercise is ended (Lind, 2001). If the process continues, however, then the theory suggests that rules are combined according to their ease of interpretability and/or the availability of information pertaining to them. These rules also may be combined according to conceptual similarity, whether in terms of the "would," "could," and "should" categories of fairness theory (Folger & Cropanzano, 1998, 2001) or the distributive, procedural, interpersonal, or informational categories supported by factor analyses (Colquitt, 2001; Colquitt & Shaw, this volume). Finally, the rules even may be combined according to their relevance to the very concerns that began the process (e.g., control, esteem, morality, belonging, trust).

Although each of these cognitive combinations is possible, we know very little about how the process actually works. Most of the laboratory studies on justice judgments manipulate a very narrow set of justice rules (e.g., process control, consistency), and most of the field studies combine those rules into larger justice dimensions. Both strategies leave several questions unanswered. Which rules are most interpretable? Which are most relevant to the critical question of "should this have happened differently" (Folger et al., this volume)? Aside from these cognitive issues, which rules are most capable of arousing the positive and negative emotions that can impact fairness perceptions so powerfully? Answering such questions requires more careful attention to the justice rules considered within the justice judgment process.

JUSTICE EFFECTS

From its inception, the justice literature has explored the effects of fair treatment on reactions to decisions and to the authority figures making those decisions. The so-called "fair process effect" illustrated that a fair decision-making procedure (i.e., one that affords individuals process control or voice) was associated with positive attitudinal reactions (Folger, Rosenfield, Grove, & Corkran, 1979). In organizational contexts, those attitudinal reactions have included boosts in job satisfaction, organizational commitment, and trust in management (Alexander & Ruderman, 1987; Folger & Konovsky, 1989; McFarlin & Sweeney, 1992). Fairness effects have been generalized to behavioral outcomes as well, including traditional measures of job performance (Konovsky & Cropanzano, 1991), turnover (Aquino, Griffeth, Allen, & Hom, 1997), employee citizenship behaviors (Moorman, 1991), and more negative reactions, such as theft (Greenberg, 1990) and retaliation (Skarlicki & Folger, 1997).

The ability of justice variables to explain variance in key organizational outcomes has no doubt fueled the popularity of the literature. The chapters in Part IV of this handbook make several important contributions to this critical area. For example, Van den Bos takes readers back to the field's foundations by reviewing the fair process effect found in some of the seminal works in the literature (e.g., Greenberg & Folger, 1983). Van den Bos also reviews what the fair process effect actually represents, as the term has been used somewhat inconsistently in the literature. Finally, he explores the intervening mechanisms that underlie the effect, drawing mediators from several key conceptualizations (e.g., the instrumental model, the relational model, referent cognitions theory). Particular attention is given to the mechanisms of uncertainty management theory (Lind & Van den Bos, 2002; Van den Bos & Lind, 2002), a recently introduced model that subsumes fairness heuristic theory (Lind, 2001).

The impressive breadth of the fair process effect is reviewed by Conlon, Meyer, and Nowakowski, who summarize the behavioral effects of organizational justice. Behavioral effects generally have been more variable than attitudinal effects, with relationships varying widely by the nature of the behavior. Notably, Conlon et al. organize their review around what they dub "the good, the bad, and the ugly" to emphasize how justice effects vary by the nature of the behavioral outcome. The authors then close with several important observations for scholars attempting to link justice to behavior, including the challenge of operationalizing key variables with precision.

Extending the Conlon et al. efforts to identify *what* the effects of justice are, Blader and Tyler explore *why* those effects occur. In so doing,

they review a broad spectrum of theories and use them to explain the effects of fair treatment. These authors discuss some of the same theories discussed by Van den Bos, while also reviewing social exchange, causal attribution, and fairness theory explanations, along with their own recent work on the group engagement model (Tyler & Blader, 2000). This chapter, therefore, represents the most comprehensive examination of fairness effect mechanisms to date. Like Conlon et al., Blader and Tyler also close by discussing the various ways to conceptualize the outcomes examined by justice scholars. In doing so, they position their discussion around the broad concept of cooperation.

The last chapter in Part IV, by Moorman and Byrne, also explores theoretical explanations for justice effects. These authors concentrate their analysis on organizational citizenship behavior (OCB) effects, which have a special importance to the history of the literature. Citizenship was the first behavioral outcome significantly linked to justice with any regularity (for a review, see Greenberg, 1993b). One might argue that the findings regarding citizenship opened the door for considering other behavioral effects of justice. Moorman and Byrne discuss social exchange and social-identity based mediators of justice effects, introducing a model that promises to shape future research on citizenship (in addition to other positive behavioral effects). As in the case of Blader and Tyler, Moorman and Byrne's chapter represents an important contribution toward our understanding of justice effects.

The chapters in Part IV go beyond merely summarizing the broad nature of justice effects by also proposing theoretical mechanisms underlying those effects. Past research has relied on "rule-of-thumb" models such as the two-factor and agent system models (Bies & Moag, 1986; Sweeney & McFarlin, 1993), which offer some useful predictions for attitudinal outcomes but are difficult to apply to behavioral outcomes (Colquitt et al., 2001; Colquitt & Greenberg, 2003). The chapters by Van den Bos, by Conlon et al., by Blader and Tyler, and by Moorman and Byrne also highlight two critical questions: (a) Which mediators are most worthy of study? (b) Does the relevance of those mediators vary across contexts?

Which Mediators Are Most Worthy of Study?

These chapters draw on much of the rich theorizing on the justice judgment process and apply it "downstream" to predict the effects of those formed judgments. The tendency has been to label a theory as relevant to the justice judgment process or to the pattern of justice effects, but never both (Blader & Tyler, this volume; Colquitt & Greenberg, 2003; Van den Bos, this volume). For example, the instrumental model routinely has been used to explain what triggers the

justice judgment process (i.e., concerns about the predictability of future economic outcomes). Yet perceptions of instrumentality or evaluations of outcomes rarely are used as explicitly measured mediators of justice effects (Blader & Tyler, this volume). This practice has created an asymmetry in the literature, allowing theorizing to prosper in analyses of justice judgments while remaining limited in analyses of justice effects.

Table 20.1 summarizes the mediators discussed by the authors in Part IV. Specifically, five families of theories are discussed: (a) the instrumental model, (b) the relational and group engagement models, (c) fairness heuristic and uncertainty management theories, (d) fairness theory and the deontic model, and (e) social exchange theories. Although the first four families have been applied most often to studying the justice judgment process (typically, explaining the types of concerns that trigger the formation of fairness perceptions), the fifth family of

TABLE 20.1

Potential Mediators of Justice Effects Organized by Theory

Theory	Applied to justice judgments?	Potential mediators of justice effects
Instrumental model (Thibaut & Walker, 1975)	Yes	Instrumentality Outcome evaluations
Relational model (Tyler & Lind, 1992) and group engagement model (Tyler & Blader, 2000)	Yes	Identification with group Pride in group Respect from group Esteem Legitimacy of authority
Fairness heuristic theory (Lind, 2001) and uncertainty management theory (Lind & Van den Bos, 2002; Van den Bos & Lind, 2002)	Yes	Trust Uncertainty perceptions
Fairness theory (Folger & Cropanzano, 1998) and the deontic model (Folger, 2001)	Yes	Emotions (anger, blame)
Social exchange theories (e.g., Blau, 1964; Gouldner, 1960)	No	Felt obligation Trust Affective commitment Normative commitment Leader–member exchange LMX quality

theories—social exchange theories—has been applied more frequently to studying justice effects. For example, Cropanzano, Rupp, Mohler, and Schminke (2001) presented a comprehensive application of social exchange theories to justice effects, discussing some of the same mechanisms reviewed by Moorman and Byrne.

It is important to note that the set of mediators in Table 20.1 is not parsimonious, and it is impractical to include 10 or more mediators in a single study. A potentially useful strategy for reduction is to identify the most important mediator from each theoretical family. Moorman and Byrne suggest that identification (from the relational model) and felt obligation (from social exchange theory) are the most proximal drivers of citizenship. It may be that those mediators could be paired with a single mechanism from each of the other families. On the other hand, it may be that all five families are not needed to explain justice effects. After controlling for other types of mediators, one or more may be redundant.

Another strategy for reduction might be to focus on mechanisms that are found in multiple theoretical frameworks. For example, the mediating role of trust can be grounded either in fairness heuristic theory or in social exchange theories, suggesting that its explanatory power may be greater than the other mediators. We also note that a justice ® trust causal order is consistent with trust models that cast justice as a criterion of trustworthiness (e.g., Mayer et al., 1995). Of course, we would be remiss if we neglected to repeat our suggestion that trust may serve as one of the higher order concerns that trigger the justice judgment process (recall our comments on Carr and Greenberg's goal hierarchy). In this regard, the key to identifying the most important mediators of justice effects may be to examine the hierarchy of concerns that explain why individuals care about justice.

Does the Relevance of the Mediators Vary?

After a subset of key mediators is identified, we need to consider whether the relevance of these factors varies systematically. It seems likely that the explanation of an effect will depend on the nature of the outcome, as noted by Van den Bos. In this regard, consider the "good, bad, and ugly" distinction made by Conlon et al. Are some of the mediators in Table 20.1 more relevant to the "good," others more strongly associated with the "bad," and still others more germane to the "ugly"? As an example, do high levels of affective commitment (due to fair treatment) explain subsequent citizenship in the same way that low levels of affective commitment (due to unfair treatment) explain subsequent counterproductive behavior? If the latter relationship is

weaker in effect size, or if it becomes nonsignificant statistically, then the mediating role of affective commitment varies across "good" and "ugly" outcomes.

Although the possibility of such variation must be determined empirically, most of the mediators appear to be more capable of explaining beneficial reactions than adverse reactions. As Van den Bos suggests, fairness theory and the deontic model are uniquely suited to explaining withdrawal or counterproductive behaviors. Presumably, low levels of key attitudes such as identification, felt obligation, and trust would be insufficient to trigger such outcomes. When paired with feelings of anger or blame, however, reactions like quitting, theft, or retaliation appear more likely. In other words, there may be an interactive effect of multiple mediators such that these attitude–behavior linkages are amplified by negative emotions. Such interactions are important to consider insofar as they winnow down a larger set of mediators to a more critical subset.

A related possibility is that the relevance of mediators varies for different justice variables. An example would be mediators that are more relevant to interpersonal and informational justice than to procedural or distributive (or vice versa). Such variation might be due to commonalities in referent, given that measures of both constructs reference one's leader. A more interesting speculation pertains to variation occurring within justice dimensions. For example, it is possible that respectful treatment might have different explanatory mechanisms than verbal abuse. Likewise, just as the most salient emotions (e.g., pride in the case of respectful treatment; anger in the case of verbal abuse) may differ, so too may the most important attitudinal mediators.

Finally, it is again worth considering how Cropanzano, Byrne, Bobocel, and Rupp's (2001) distinction between events and entities may come into play (see also Bies's encounter vs. exchange distinction). Emotional mediators may help explain reactions to single, discreet events (given that emotions, themselves, are short-term forms of affect; Lord & Kanfer, 2002), but as the lens moves from one event to more general, entity judgments, the mechanisms may become more cognitive. For example, anger may explain verbal retaliation following an unfair performance appraisal, whereas a lack of trust may explain voluntary turnover from an unfair organization. Of course, given that many of the mediators in Table 20.1 have both affective and cognitive components, such variation is particularly difficult to test.

JUSTICE APPLICATIONS

The wealth of attitudinal and behavioral effects of organizational justice that have been studied has led to a wide variety of applications. This

practical applicability is enjoyed by few other topics in the field of organizational behavior, doubtlessly contributing to the justice literature's growing popularity (Greenberg & Lind, 2000). When Greenberg and Folger introduced the construct of procedural justice to organizational behavior scholars over two decades ago, they discussed its applicability to participation initiatives, dispute resolution programs, performance evaluation methods, and compensation systems (Folger & Greenberg, 1985; Greenberg & Folger, 1983). In the decades that followed, justice principles also were applied to such contexts as employee selection (Gilliland, 1993), training implementation (Quinones, 1995), and the management of large-scale organizational change (e.g., Brockner & Greenberg, 1990; Daly & Geyer, 1994), among others (for a review, see Greenberg & Lind, 2000).

The articles in Part V of this handbook spotlight new and less widely explored areas of justice applications in addition to offering in-depth reviews of more well-examined areas. The first chapter, by Vermunt and Steensma, on justice and stress management, is an example of the former. The fact that this is an infrequently studied topic is noteworthy insofar as Adams's (1965) original conceptualization of equity theory was predicated on inequity as a source of distress in a social exchange relationship (although its role in this regard is controversial; see Greenberg, 1984). Vermunt and Steensma go beyond simply discussing the nature of inequity distress by applying many different principles of organizational justice to the management of stress in organizations. The specific dimensions examined in the justice literature overlap in content with many of the commonly studied stressors, and the mechanics by which justice judgments are made are in many ways similar to the processes involved in appraising stress. These analyses offer a promising new framework for understanding how justice may be used to manage reactions to work stressors.

Gilliland and Hale review personnel selection, which is of one of the more visible areas of industrial/organizational psychology within which justice applications have appeared (Gilliland, 1993; Gilliland & Steiner, 2001). These authors focus on antecedents of fairness perceptions in organizations by decomposing the selection process into three distinct stages: recruitment, screening and selection, and decision making and communication. This distinction is noteworthy insofar as it underscores how the determinants of fairness can change over time, thereby illustrating how, for example, fairness in recruitment contexts may differ from fairness in screening decisions.

Acknowledging that efforts to make the selection process equitable and unbiased may be imperfect, Stone-Romero and Stone consider how justice principles can be applied to reducing discrimination against out-group members or members of minority groups. After chronicling

the nature of discrimination and prejudice in the United States, these authors describe how its forms have evolved over the years from the overt to the subtle. They then detail how discrimination occurs along multiple justice dimensions, grounding their examples in social identity theory. Stone-Romero and Stone then introduce a "group-based differential justice model" that details how membership in a relevant in-group or out-group influences the various justice dimensions and eventual treatment received by employees. Finally, the authors close by identifying some practical implications derived from their analyses.

Bobocel and Zdaniuk review a concept touched upon by both Gilliland and Hale and by Stone-Romero and Stone—the use of explanations in organizations. Explanations are a key ingredient in the application of justice principles in several areas, most notably selection, performance evaluation, and the management of large-scale change. Explanations usually qualify the information on which evaluations of procedural justice are made. And merely offering an explanation is an important source of informational justice. Bobocel and Zdaniuk review the effects of explanations on fairness perceptions and detail the various types of explanations given (see also Shaw, Wild, & Colquitt, 2003). Importantly, they also explore factors that alter the effectiveness of explanations (e.g., characteristics of the message or the actor) as well as their perceived necessity (e.g., outcome favorability).

For the advice shared in Part V of this handbook to have the most profound practical impact, it may be necessary for managers to be trained to be fair—be it in methods of managing stress (Vermunt & Steensma, this volume), selecting employees fairly (Gilliland & Hale, this volume), reducing discrimination (Stone-Romero & Stone, this volume), or using explanations effectively (Bobocel & Zdaniuk, this volume). With this in mind, Skarlicki and Latham conclude Part V by reviewing the literature on how managers and leaders can be trained in principles of organizational justice. They review the empirical studies on this issue while also providing advice on how to design future studies. Notably, Skarlicki and Latham apply their discussion of justice principles to all phases of the training process, including the assessment of needs, the design of the instructional environment, and the encouragement of efforts to promote transfer of training to work environments.

Taken together, the chapters in Part V highlight the breadth and diversity of ways in which matters of justice apply to organizations. We see that justice principles are being applied to new areas of interest (e.g., stress management), in addition to being applied to more traditional practices (e.g., selection, explanations) with deeper levels of theoretical precision. Efforts of both types may prove to be useful in making organizations more fair. The notion of fair and unfair organizations leads us to two key integrative questions relevant to application: (a) Can justice

scholars create and assess justice interventions at the organizational level? (b) How do justice interventions affect the climate of the organizations in which they occur? We consider each of these in turn.

Can Justice Interventions Occur at the Organizational Level?

Most of the research and conceptual work applying organizational justice to decision making has focused on particular areas such as selection, training, or performance evaluation. This narrow focus is understandable given the complex nature of fairness in organizations. Unfortunately, this narrowness prevents us from taking a broader and more comprehensive organizational-level approach to fairness.

Researchers considering applications of justice principles in organizations may benefit by considering the approach taken in the literature on human resource management and firm performance (for a review, see Wright & Boswell, 2002). That literature links various human resource practices to organizational effectiveness (e.g., profitability, survival). Future justice scholars might assess the fairness of human resource practices in much the same manner. Specifically, employees could complete scales assessing their beliefs about the fairness of the procedures used for selection, training, performance evaluation, compensation, dispute resolution, and separation (for an example, see Huselid, 1995). Alternatively, such judgments could be made by content analyzing fairness in official company documents and manuals (for an example, see Welbourne & Andrews, 1996).

Although such research would not be easy to conduct, it would allow justice scholars to examine a variety of issues. For example, one might compare the importance of multiple organizational practices from a fairness perspective. In so doing, researchers would be able to consider the extent to which the fairness of performance evaluation systems has stronger effects on firm performance than the fairness of other practices (e.g., pay). The answers to such questions may provide organizations with a rationale for prioritizing the funding and sequencing of justice-based interventions. Scholars also could examine the interactive effects of fair practices, to see whether fair programs substitute for one another or whether they have synergistic effects (Delery, 1998). It may be that a single unfair practice or incident within an organization will prove sufficient to counteract the benefits of all other acts of fairness. The present state of our knowledge provides little insight into this intriguing possibility.

The larger question that such research could address is fundamental: "Are fairer organizations more effective than less fair organizations?" Welbourne and Andrews (1996) showed that the degree to which companies valued human resources and used appropriate rewards pre-

COLQUITT, GREENBERG, SCOTT

dicted their subsequent survival. The investigators assessed these two variables by examining company prospectuses. Drawing on this, the same kind of coding might be done to arrive at assessments of various justice dimensions. It is plausible that fairness has significant effects on organizational effectiveness given that firm-level level ratings of employee satisfaction have modest but significant correlations with financial outcomes (Harter, Schmidt, & Hayes, 2002). Of course, this is an empirical question—and, in our opinion, one worthy of future research attention.

How Do Justice Interventions Affect the Climate of Organizations?

A related question concerns *justice climate*—defined as an aggregate cognition about how a unit as a whole is treated (Colquitt, Noe, & Jackson, 2002; Mossholder, Bennett, & Martin, 1998; Naumann & Bennett, 2000). As in the case of other areas of climate (for a review, see Carr, Schmidt, Ford, & DeShon, 2003), justice climate may be studied by aggregating the perceptions of individual employees to the unit level and examining the effects of the aggregate perceptions on individual and unit-level outcomes. The degree of convergence in perceptions also may be assessed to demonstrate that a meaningful climate exists (making the unit average a meaningful variable) and to serve as a measure of climate strength (Colquitt et al., 2002). An obvious research question in this regard concerns the degree to which justice climates are linked to organizational effectiveness (as has been demonstrated in the case of perceptions of job satisfaction; Harter et al., 2002).

A more subtle question concerns the conceptualization of justice climate and its relationship to justice interventions and applications. The paradigm for studying organizational climate, reviewed earlier, may be contrasted with the paradigm for studying organizational culture (Ashkanasy & Jackson, 2001; Denison, 1996). Typically, culture scholars do not rely on aggregated survey responses to conceptualize organizational culture. Instead, they examine cultural "carriers" or "artifacts," such as practices, routines, rituals, symbols, and language, inferring culture indirectly from these indicants. It is an intriguing possibility that justice culture may be inferred the same way—that is, from coding the content of specific practices, ceremonies, and language used in selection, training, performance evaluation, compensation, dispute resolution, and separation systems.

Such an approach would provide several benefits. It would complement traditional survey-based measures, thereby making it possible to assess convergent validity. Alternatively, indirect inference of "justice culture" could be used as an antecedent of aggregate justice attitudes,

making it possible to model the impact of actual practices and interventions on employees' fairness perceptions. Aggregate justice attitudes also could be used as a mediating variable linking justice culture to organizational effectiveness. Given its focus on actual practices and applications, this culture paradigm could yield more obvious prescriptions for improving fairness in organizations than attitudinal measures whose antecedents are not always apparent. Work of this type also would underscore the importance of a system-wide commitment to justice, insofar as culture strength would be assessed by the degree to which all practices signal fair treatment to the same degree.

GENERALIZABILITY ISSUES

Having already explored how justice is conceptualized, how justice judgments are formed, and their effects and potential applications in organizations, Part VI of this handbook examines the extent to which these matters are generalizable. Issues of generalizability typically have revolved around two questions: (a) How do procedural effects vary from high to low levels of outcome favorability (and vice-versa)? (b) How do justice effects vary across cultures? Both issues are comprehensively reviewed in Part VI.

Brockner and Wiesenfeld summarize their extensive work on the interaction between procedural justice and outcome favorability (e.g., Brockner & Wiesenfeld, 1996). Typically, although there are positive effects of procedural fairness when outcome favorability is low, there are also less positive effects of procedural fairness when outcome favorability is high (Brockner, 2002; Brockner & Wiesenfeld, 1996). The explanation for this difference lies in the dependent variable, with the former pattern being demonstrated for organization or authority-referenced reactions and the latter pattern being demonstrated for self-referenced reactions. As such, these authors are examining generalizability in two different ways—how procedural effects generalize across levels of outcome favorability and how that specific interaction generalizes across different kinds of outcomes.

Leung examines the extent to which various justice rules and effects generalize across national cultures. He argues that although concerns over justice may be universal, justice effects may not take the same form across cultures. Leung organizes his examination of generalizability with respect to five distinct issues: the rules for judging justice (e.g., equity, equality, process control), the goals of fair treatment (e.g., enhancing solidarity, reducing animosity), the specific choices made when actually applying justice principles (e.g., what exactly qualifies as an "input," how process control should be implemented), the process by which justice judgments are formed, and the effects of justice on key

outcomes. These five foci allow for a more comprehensive, fine-grained analysis of cross-cultural generalizability than previously has been possible. In closing, Leung also examines some methodological issues that pose challenges for assessing the generalizability of justice effects across national cultures.

By articulating the various constructs that underlie outcome favorability and culture, the two chapters in Part VI touch on two important generalizability issues, which we now consider. Specifically, these are: (a) What are the most central moderators from a conceptual standpoint? (b) How may additional moderators be identified?

What Are the Most Central Moderators Conceptually?

Moderator variables play a vital role in the theory-building process. They describe where, when, or for whom a particular relationship between variables is expected to hold (Whetten, 1989), which often is a more interesting question than whether a relationship differs from zero (Campbell, 1990). However, moderator variables also may be problematic to the extent that they result in increasingly complex models involving an ever-widening list of potential boundary conditions. With this consideration in mind, it becomes important to identify the most conceptually important moderators and then to examine whether other moderators are subsumed by this central set. In other words, it may be helpful to view moderators in a hierarchical manner, with more central moderators occupying higher levels while subsuming the moderating role of less central variables.

In this vein, Brockner and Wiesenfeld note that the moderating role of outcome favorability might be subsumed by the moderating role of trust (Brockner, Siegel, Daly, Tyler, & Martin, 1997). By definition, trust is more salient when vulnerability is high or when risks are present, and negative outcomes increase both vulnerability and risk. Thus, consistent with fairness heuristic theory (Lind, 2001), trust may occupy a higher level in a moderator hierarchy. Brockner and Wiesenfeld also identify uncertainty as a means of reconceptualizing their outcome favorability effect, a possibility in keeping with uncertainty management theory (Lind & Van den Bos, 2002; Van den Bos & Lind, 2002).

Leung also distinguishes between more specific boundary conditions and the more general conceptual moderators that possibly subsume them. For example, differences between two specific countries may be explained by general differences in individualism–collectivism. Given that this variable has both within- and between-culture variance (Oyserman, Coon, & Kemmelmeier, 2002), this variable may also be relevant to justice effects in a single culture sample (Colquitt et al., 2002). Leung also identi-

fies other concepts that could occupy a higher rung in a moderator hierarchy, including power distance, situational goals (e.g., solidarity, animosity reduction), relationship strength, and group identification. Further studies on justice moderation would benefit from comparing the relative importance of such moderators, to see which variables represent the most important boundary conditions.

How May Additional Moderators Be Identified?

With the exception of research on outcome favorability and culture, the examination of moderators in the justice literature has been accused of being scattershot (Colquitt & Greenberg, 2003). A laundry list of specific variables has been examined, often in only a single study and with little or no theoretical grounding. As a result, our knowledge of the generalizability of justice principles has not accumulated as rapidly as other areas of the literature. The organizational justice literature therefore might benefit from a systematic plan or strategy for identifying additional moderators in future research.

The notion of a moderator hierarchy identified earlier may be especially beneficial in this regard. As an example, assume that a scholar is interested in personality variables that moderate the effects of justice on certain attitudes and behaviors. Assume further that trust is believed to occupy a lofty position in the moderator hierarchy of justice. That researcher might decide to focus on the construct of propensity to trust, defined as a general willingness to trust others (Mayer et al., 1995). Alternatively, he or she might examine the personality dimension of agreeableness, which subsumes the propensity to trust (e.g., Skarlicki, Folger, & Tesluk, 1999). In either case, that choice would be made in a more systematic fashion, thereby providing a theoretical basis for the predicted interactions.

Lacking such a moderator hierarchy, scholars also may draw on the framework proposed by Colquitt and Greenberg (2003), which distinguishes between two categories of individual and contextual moderators: sensitivity moderators (which make individuals more sensitive to justice information or judgments) and expectation moderators (which lead individuals to change their conceptualizations of fairness). Cast in these terms, Brockner and Wiesenfeld's discussion focuses primarily on sensitivity moderators, such as outcome favorability and trust. However, Leung describes cultural characteristics, such as collectivism and power distance, that alter expectations about what constitutes fair procedures and fair outcomes. We suspect that most of the moderators examined in the literature will be of the sensitivity variety, but caution that it is important to continue exploring how situational norms, cul-

tural variables, and individual differences alter people's beliefs about precisely what constitutes fairness.

CONCLUSION

To highlight the most critical issues bearing on the field of organizational justice, the chapters in this handbook were organized around a set of focal questions. Taken together, these contributions illustrate that much has been learned about such core issues as the construct validity of organizational justice, the manner in which justice judgments are made, the effects of perceptions of justice and injustice, the ways in which justice is applied in various organizational contexts, and the generalizability of these various issues. In view of the fact of scientific life that theory building and theory testing make up an iterative process, surely none of the contributors would claim that they have answered their assigned question completely. Despite this, as we consider the chapters in this book as a whole, we cannot help but be struck by the impressive nature of the accumulated knowledge within the field of organizational justice.

Based on our analyses in this chapter, we are prepared to hazard an answer to the question posed in our chapter subtitle, "Where do we stand?" At the risk of oversimplification (or corrupting a metaphor), our response is that organizational justice is now "a promising young adult" (Colquitt & Greenberg, 2003). Due to nurturing in the form of better theory, more refined conceptualizations, and more rigorous measurement techniques, the field has now bloomed out of the "intellectual adolescence" in which it was characterized little more than a decade ago (Greenberg, 1993c). Like any young adult, of course, this one has still more room to grow and mature. However, with the popularity of the organizational justice literature to propel it and an established set of core tenets to guide it, this young adult's promise is likely to be fulfilled in impressive fashion. In this regard, we are optimistic that the contributions to this handbook will shape the field's future as it enters its third decade—its intellectually most mature and productive years.

REFERENCES

Adams, J. S. (1965). Inequity in social exchange. In L. Berkowitz (Ed.), *Advances in experimental social psychology* (Vol. 2, pp. 267–299). New York: Academic Press.

Alexander, S., & Ruderman, M. (1987). The role of procedural and distributive justice in organizational behavior. *Social Justice Research, 1,* 177–198.

Aquino, K., Griffeth, R. W., Allen, D. G., & Hom, P. W. (1997). Integrating justice constructs into the turnover process: A test of a referent cognitions model. *Academy of Management Journal, 40,* 1208–1227.

Ashkanasy, N. M., & Jackson, C. R. A. (2001). Organizational culture and climate. In N. Anderson, D. S. Ones, H. K. Sinangil, & C. Viswesvaran (Eds.), *Handbook of industrial, work, and organizational psychology* (Vol. 2, pp. 398–415). Thousand Oaks, CA: Sage.

Bies, R. J. (2001). Interactional (in)justice: The sacred and the profane. In J. Greenberg & R. Cropanzano (Eds.), *Advances in organizational justice* (pp. 89–118). Stanford, CA: Stanford University Press.

Bies, R. J., & Moag, J. F. (1986). Interactional justice: Communication criteria of fairness. In R. J. Lewicki, B. H. Sheppard, & M. H. Bazerman (Eds.), *Research on negotiations in organizations* (Vol. 1, pp. 43–55). Greenwich, CT: JAI Press.

Blau, P. M. (1964). *Exchange and power in social life.* New York: Wiley.

Bobocel, D. R., & Holmvall, C. M. (2001). Are interactional justice and procedural justice different? Framing the debate. In S. Gilliland, D. Steiner, & D. Skarlicki (Eds.), *Theoretical and cultural perspectives on organizational justice* (pp. 85–110). Greenwich, CT: Information Age.

Brockner, J. (2002). Making sense of procedural fairness: How high procedural fairness can reduce or heighten the influence of outcome favorability. *Academy of Management Review, 27,* 58–76.

Brockner, J., & Greenberg, J. (1990). The impact of layoffs on survivors: An organizational justice perspective. In J. Carroll (Ed.), *Advances in applied social psychology: Business settings* (pp. 45–75). Hillsdale, NJ: Lawrence Erlbaum Associates.

Brockner, J., Siegel, P. A., Daly, J., Tyler, T. R., & Martin, C. (1997). When trust matters: The moderating effect of outcome favorability. *Administrative Science Quarterly, 42,* 558–583.

Brockner, J., & Wiesenfeld, B. M. (1996). An integrative framework for explaining reactions to decisions: Interactive effects of outcomes and procedures. *Psychological Bulletin, 120,* 189–208.

Campbell, J. P. (1990). The role of theory in industrial and organizational psychology. In M. D. Dunnette & L. M. Hough (Eds.), *Handbook of industrial and organizational psychology* (Vol. 1, pp. 39–74). Palo Alto, CA: Consulting Psychologists Press.

Carr, J. Z., Schmidt, A. M., Ford, J. K., & DeShon, R. P. (2003). Climate perceptions matter: A meta-analytic path analysis relating molar climate, cognitive and affective states, and individual level work outcomes. *Journal of Applied Psychology, 88,* 605–619.

Colquitt, J. A. (2001). On the dimensionality of organizational justice: A construct validation of a measure. *Journal of Applied Psychology, 86,* 386–400.

Colquitt, J. A., Conlon, D. E., Wesson, M. J., Porter, C., & Ng, K. Y. (2001). Justice at the millennium: A meta-analytic review of 25 years of organizational justice research. *Journal of Applied Psychology, 86,* 425–445.

Colquitt, J. A., & Greenberg, J. (2003). Organizational justice: A fair assessment of the state of the literature. In J. Greenberg (Ed.), *Organizational behavior: The state of the science* (pp. 165–210). Mahwah, NJ: Lawrence Erlbaum Associates.

Colquitt, J. A., Noe, R. A., & Jackson, C. L. (2002). Justice in teams: Antecedents and consequences of procedural justice climate. *Personnel Psychology, 55,* 83–109.

Cropanzano, R. (1993). *Justice in the workplace: Approaching fairness in human resource management.* Hillsdale, NJ: Lawrence Erlbaum Associates.

Cropanzano, R. (2001). *Justice in the workplace: From theory to practice.* Mahwah, NJ: Lawrence Erlbaum Associates.

Cropanzano, R., & Ambrose, M. L. (2001). Procedural and distributive justice are more similar than you think: A monistic perspective and a research agenda. In J. Greenberg & R. Cropanzano (Eds.), *Advances in organizational justice* (pp. 119–151). Stanford, CA: Stanford University Press.

Cropanzano, R., Byrne, Z. S., Bobocel, D. R., & Rupp, D. E. (2001). Moral virtues, fairness heuristics, social entities, and other denizens of organizational justice. *Journal of Vocational Behavior, 58,* 164–209.

Cropanzano, R., & Greenberg, J. (1997). Progress in organizational justice: Tunneling through the maze. In C. L. Cooper & I. T. Robertson (Eds.), *International review of industrial and organizational psychology* (Vol. 2, pp. 317–372). New York: John Wiley & Sons.

Cropanzano, R., Rupp, D. E., Mohler, C. J., & Schminke, M. (2001). Three roads to organizational justice. In G. R. Ferris (Ed.), *Research in personnel and human resource management* (pp. 1–113). San Diego: Elsevier.

Daly, J. P., & Geyer, P. D. (1994). The role of fairness in implementing large-scale change: Employee evaluations of process and outcome in seven facility relocations. *Journal of Organizational Behavior, 15,* 623–638.

Delery, J. E. (1998). Issues of fit in strategic human resource management: Implications for research. *Human Resource Management Review, 8,* 289–309.

Denison, D. R. (1996). What is the difference between organizational culture and organizational climate? A native's point of view on a decade of paradigm wars. *Academy of Management Review, 21,* 619–654.

Deutsch, M. (1975). Equity, equality, and need: What determines which value will be used as the basis for distributive justice? *Journal of Social Issues, 31,* 137–149.

Eisenberger, R., Huntington, R., Hutchison, S., & Sowa, D. (1986). Perceived organizational support. *Journal of Applied Psychology, 71,* 500–507.

Folger, R. (1998). Fairness as a moral virtue. In S. W. Gilliland, D. D. Steiner, & D. P. Skarlicki (Eds.), *Research in social issues in management* (Vol. 1, pp. 3–33). New York: Information Age.

Folger, R. (2001). Fairness as deonance. In S. W. Gilliland, D. D. Steiner, & D. P. Skarlicki (Eds.), *Theoretical and cultural perspectives on organizational justice* (pp. 3–34). Greenwich, CT: Information Age.

Folger, R., & Cropanzano, R. (1998). *Organizational justice and human resource management.* Thousand Oaks, CA: Sage.

Folger, R., & Cropanzano, R. (2001). Fairness theory: Justice as accountability. In J. Greenberg & R. Cropanzano (Eds.), *Advances in organizational justice* (pp. 89–118). Stanford, CA: Stanford University Press.

Folger, R., & Greenberg, J. (1985). Procedural justice: An interpretive analysis of personnel systems. In K. Rowland & G. Ferris (Eds.), *Research in personnel and human resources management* (Vol. 3, pp. 141–183). Greenwich, CT: JAI Press.

Folger, R., & Konovsky, M. A. (1989). Effects of procedural and distributive justice on reactions to pay raise decisions. *Academy of Management Journal, 32,* 115–130.

Folger, R., Rosenfield, D., Grove, J., & Corkran, L. (1979). Effects of "voice" and peer opinions on responses to inequity. *Journal of Personality and Social Psychology, 37,* 2253–2261.

Gilliland, S. W. (1993). The perceived fairness of selection systems: An organizational justice perspective. *Academy of Management Review, 18,* 694–734.

Gilliland, S. W., & Steiner, D. D. (2001). Causes and consequences of applicant fairness. In R. Cropanzano (Ed.) *Justice in the workplace* (Vol. 2, pp. 175–195). Mahwah, NJ: Lawrence Erlbaum Associates.

Gouldner, A. W. (1960). The norm of reciprocity: A preliminary statement. *American Sociological Review, 25,* 161–178.

Greenberg, J. (1982). Approaching equity and avoiding inequity in groups and organizations. In J. Greenberg & R. L. Cohen (Eds.), *Equity and justice in social behavior* (pp. 389–435). New York: Academic Press.

Greenberg, J. (1984). On the apocryphal nature of inequity distress. In R. Folger (Ed.), *The sense of injustice: Social psychological perspectives* (pp. 167–186). New York: Plenum Press.

Greenberg, J. (1986). Determinants of perceived fairness of performance evaluations. *Journal of Applied Psychology, 71,* 340–342.

Greenberg, J. (1990). Employee theft as a reaction to underpayment inequity: The hidden cost of pay cuts. *Journal of Applied Psychology, 75,* 561–568.

Greenberg, J. (1993a). The social side of fairness: Interpersonal and informational classes of organizational justice. In R. Cropanzano (Ed.), *Justice in the workplace: Approaching fairness in human resource management* (pp. 79–103). Hillsdale, NJ: Lawrence Erlbaum Associates.

Greenberg, J. (1993b). Justice and organizational citizenship: A commentary on the state of the science. *Employee Responsibilities and Rights Journal, 6,* 222–237.

Greenberg, J. (1993c). The intellectual adolescence of organizational justice: You've come a long way, maybe. *Social Justice Research, 6,* 135–147.

Greenberg, J. (1996). *The quest for justice on the job: Essays and experiments.* Thousand Oaks, CA: Sage.

Greenberg, J. (2001). The seven loose can(n)ons of organizational justice. In J.Greenberg & R. Cropanzano (Eds.), *Advances in organizational justice* (pp. 245–271). Stanford, CA: Stanford University Press.

Greenberg, J., & Cropanzano, R. (2001). *Advances in organizational justice.* Stanford, CA: Stanford University Press.

Greenberg, J., & Folger, R. (1983). Procedural justice, participation, and the fair process effect in groups and organizations. In P. B. Paulus (Ed.), *Basic group processes* (pp. 235–256). New York: Springer-Verlag.

Greenberg, J., & Lind, E. A. (2000). The pursuit of organizational justice: From conceptualization to implication to application. In C. L. Cooper & E. A. Locke (Eds.), *I/O psychology: What we know about theory and practice* (pp. 72–108). Oxford, England: Blackwell.

Griffen, R. W., & O'Leary-Kelly, A. (2004). *The dark side of organizational behavior.* San Francisco, CA: Pfeiffer.

Harter, J. K., Schmidt, F. L., & Hayes, T. L. (2002). Business-unit-level relationships between employee satisfaction, employee engagement, and business outcomes: A meta-analysis. *Journal of Applied Psychology, 87,* 268–279.

Homans, G. C. (1961). *Social behavior: Its elementary forms.* New York: Harcourt, Brace & World.

Huselid, M. A. (1995). The impact of human resource management practices on turnover, productivity, and corporate financial performance. *Academy of Management Journal, 38,* 635–672.

Jackson, C. J., & Corr, P. J. (2002). Global job satisfaction and facet description: The moderating role of facet importance. *European Journal of Psychological Assessment, 18,* 1–8.

Konovsky, M. A., & Cropanzano, R. (1991). Perceived fairness of employee drug testing as a predictor of employee attitudes and job performance. *Journal of Applied Psychology, 76*, 698–707.

Leventhal, G. S. (1976a). The distribution of rewards and resources in groups and organizations. In L. Berkowitz & E. Walster (Eds.), *Advances in experimental social psychology* (Vol. 9, pp. 91–131). New York: Academic Press.

Leventhal, G. S. (1976b). Fairness in social relationships. In J. W. Thibaut, J. T. Spence, & R. C. Carson (Eds.), *Contemporary topics in social psychology* (pp. 211–239). Morristown, NJ: General Learning Press.

Leventhal, G. S. (1980). What should be done with equity theory? New approaches to the study of fairness in social relationships. In K. Gergen, M. Greenberg, & R. Willis (Eds.), *Social exchange: Advances in theory and research* (pp. 27–55). New York: Plenum Press.

Lind, E. A. (2001). Fairness heuristic theory: Justice judgments as pivotal cognitions in organizational relations. In J. Greenberg & R. Cropanzano (Eds.), *Advances in organizational justice* (pp. 56–88). Stanford, CA: Stanford University Press.

Lind, E. A., & Tyler, T. R. (1988). *The social psychology of procedural justice.* New York: Plenum Press.

Lind, E. A., & Van den Bos, K. (2002). When fairness works: Toward a general theory of uncertainty management. In B. M. Staw & R. M. Kramer (Eds.), *Research in organizational behavior* (Vol. 24, pp. 181–223). Boston, MA: Elsevier.

Locke, E. A. (2003). Good definitions: The epistemological foundation of scientific progress. In J. Greenberg (Ed.) *Organizational behavior: The state of the science* (pp. 415–444). Mahwah, NJ: Lawrence Erlbaum Associates.

Lord, R. G., & Kanfer, R. (2002). Emotions and organizational behavior. In R. G. Lord, R. J. Klimoski, & R. Kanfer (Eds.), *Emotions in the workplace* (pp. 5–19). San Francisco, CA: Jossey-Bass.

Mayer, R. C., Davis, J. H., & Schoorman, F. D. (1995). An integrative model of organizational trust. *Academy of Management Review, 20*, 709–734.

McFarlin, D. B., & Sweeney, P. D. (1992). Distributive and procedural justice as predictors of satisfaction with personal and organizational outcomes. *Academy of Management Journal, 35*, 626–637.

Merriam-Webster, Inc. (2003). *Merriam-Webster's collegiate dictionary* (11th ed.). Springfield, MA: Author.

Moorman, R. H. (1991). Relationship between organizational justice and organizational citizenship behaviors: Do fairness perceptions influence employee citizenship? *Journal of Applied Psychology, 76*, 845–855.

Mossholder, K. W., Bennett, N., & Martin, C. L. (1998). A multilevel analysis of procedural justice context. *Journal of Organizational Behavior, 19*, 131–141.

Naumann, S. E., & Bennett, N. (2000). A case for procedural justice climate: Development and test of a multilevel model. *Academy of Management Journal, 43*, 881–889.

Oyserman, D., Coon, H. M., & Kemmelmeier, M. (2002). Rethinking individualism and collectivism: Evaluation of theoretical assumptions and meta-analyses. *Psychological Bulletin, 128*, 3–72.

Quinones, M. A. (1995). Pretraining context effects: Training assignment as feedback. *Journal of Applied Psychology, 80*, 226–238.

Rousseau, D. M., Sitkin, S. B., Burt, R. S., & Camerer, C. (1998). Not so different after all: A cross-discipline view of trust. *Academy of Management Review, 23*, 393–404.

619

Sackett, P. R., & DeVore, C. J. (2001). Counterproductive behaviors at work. In N. Anderson, D. S. Ones, H. K. Sinangil, & C. Viswesvaran (Eds.), *Handbook of industrial, work, and organizational psychology* (Vol. 1, pp. 145–151). Thousand Oaks, CA: Sage.

Schwab, D. P. (1980). Construct validity in organizational behavior. In L. L. Cummings and B. M. Staw (Eds.), *Research in organizational behavior* (Vol. 2, pp. 3–43). Greenwich, CT: JAI Press.

Shaw, J. C., Wild, R. E., & Colquitt, J. A. (2003). To justify or excuse?: A meta-analytic review of the effects of explanations. *Journal of Applied Psychology, 88*, 444–458.

Skarlicki, D. P., & Folger, R. (1997). Retaliation in the workplace: The role of distributive, procedural, and interactional justice. *Journal of Applied Psychology, 82*, 434–443.

Skarlicki, D. P., Folger, R., & Tesluk, P. (1999). Personality as a moderator in the relationship between fairness and retaliation. *Academy of Management Journal, 42*, 100–108.

Sweeney, P. D., & McFarlin, D. B. (1993). Workers' evaluations of the "ends" and "means": An examination of four models of distributive and procedural justice. *Organizational Behavior and Human Decision Processes, 55*, 23–40.

Thibaut, J., & Walker, L. (1975). *Procedural justice: A psychological analysis.* Hillsdale, NJ: Lawrence Erlbaum Associates.

Tyler, T. R., & Bies, R. J. (1990). Beyond formal procedures: The interpersonal context of procedural justice. In J. Carroll (Ed.), *Applied social psychology and organizational settings* (pp. 77–98). Hillsdale, NJ: Lawrence Erlbaum Associates.

Tyler, T. R., & Blader, S. L. (2000). *Cooperation in groups: Procedural justice, social identity, and behavioral engagement.* New York: Psychology Press.

Tyler, T. R., & Lind, E. A. (1992). A relational model of authority in groups. In M. P. Zanna (Ed.), *Advances in experimental social psychology* (Vol. 25, pp. 115–191). San Diego, CA: Academic Press.

Van den Bos, K., & Lind, E. A. (2002). Uncertainty management by means of fairness judgments. In M. P. Zanna (Ed.), *Advances in experimental social psychology* (Vol. 34, pp. 1–60). San Diego, CA: Elsevier.

Walster, E., Berscheid, E., & Walster, G. W. (1973). New directions in equity research. *Journal of Personality and Social Psychology, 25*, 151–176.

Wanous, J. P., Reichers, A. E., & Hurdy, M. J. (1997). Overall job satisfaction: How good are single-item measures? *Journal of Applied Psychology, 82*, 247–252.

Welbourne, T. M., & Andrews, A. O. (1996). Predicting the performance of initial public offerings: Should human resource management be in the equation? *Academy of Management Journal, 39*, 891–919.

Whetten, D. A. (1989). What constitutes a theoretical contribution? *Academy of Management Review, 14*, 490–495.

Wright, P. M., & Boswell, W. R. (2002). Desegregating HRM: A review and synthesis of micro and macro human resource management research. *Journal of Management, 28*, 247–276.

Author Index

Note: *f* indicates figure, *n* indicates footnote, *t* indicates table

A

Aarts, H., 222, *241*
Abel, R., 160, *175*, 484, *494*
Ackerman, G., 171, 172, *175*, 567, 568, *580*
Ackerman, P. L., 511, *520*
Acrey, B. P., 442, *461*
Adair, W., 571, *580*
Adams, J. S., 5, 8*f*, 16, 17, 18, 36, *46*, 61, 66, *79*, 115, 118*t*, 126, *147*, 278, 289, *294*, 358, *376*, 385, 386, 388, 394, 395, 406, *407*, 444, 450, 451, 455, 456, *461*, 559, 566, *579*, 591, 607, *614*
Adams-Roy, J., 128, *147*, 317, *323*
Agar, S. E., 276, *294*, 477, 486, *493*
Agarie, N., 479, *496*
Aiello, J. R., 304, 319, *324*
Alexander, S., 9*f*, 27, *46*, 63, *82*, 250, *266*, 276, *294*, 456, *461*, 602, *614*
Alge, B. J., 132, 133, *147*
Alicke, M. D., 195, *208*
Allegro, J., 384, 385, *407*, *410*
Allen, D. G., 38, *46*, 602, *614*
Allen, N. J., 137, *147*, 368, *378*
Allport, G. W., 441, 447, *461*
Ambrose, M., 11*f*, 35, 37*f*, 42, 43, 46, *52*, 60, 63, 66, 68, 77, *79*, *80*, *83*, 87, 89, 92, 97, 101, *107*, *109*, 129, 133, 136, *147*, *151*, 157, *176*, 190, 192, *208*, *209*, 222, 224, *239*, *297*, 306, 317, 319, *324*, *326*, 390, *408*, 425, *435*, *504*, *517*, *521*, *522*, 592, *616*
Anderson, C., 238, *242*
Anderson, N., 18, *48*, 413, 416, 419, *434*, *435*
Andersson, L. M., 87, *107*, 312, *324*
Andreasen, A. R., 484, *493*
Andrews, A. O., 609, *619*
Ang, S., 561, 578, *583*
Antonioni, D., 575, 577, 578, *585*
Aquino, K., 35, 38, *46*, 224, *239*, 313, 321, *324*, 602, *614*
Aram, J. D., 482, *493*
Aristotle, 556, *579*
Armeli, S., 365, 366, 370, 372, *377*
Arrow, K., 256, 257, *266*
Arvey, R. D., 424, *434*, 510, 515, *519*
Aryee, S., 87, 92, *107*, 250, *266*, 310, 311, *324*, *326*, 367, 368, *376*, 575, *582*
Ashkanasy, N., 236, *239*, 610, *615*
Ashmore, R. D., 441, *461*
Au, A., 578, *580*
Au, K., 568, 573, *579*, *580*, *581*
Au, Y. F., 563, 568, *582*
Au, Y. K., 575, *582*
Audi, R., 103, *107*
Austin, J. T., 187, 197, 198, *208*
Austin, W., 190, *208*
Avedon, M. J., 412, 415, 422, *436*
Avery, D. R., 135, 136, *147*, 160, 161, *175*
Aydin, O., 20, *46*

B

Babad, E. Y., 569, *579*
Baccino, T., *298*
Bacharach, S. B., 114, 134, 141, *147*
Bachman, R., 275, 276, *297*
Bachrach, D. G., 357, 358, *379*
Bailey, J., 538, *553*
Baker, B., 413, 427, *435*
Baker, R. C., IV, 11*f*, 39, *50*, 477, 481, *495*
Balkin, D. B., 119, 137, *152*
Ball, G. A., 65, *79*, 502, *519*
Banaszynski, T. L., 571, *586*
Bandura, A., 512, *519*
Barber, A. E., 416, 421, *434*

T

Tajfel, H., 251, 270, 338, *353,* 362, *380,* 445, 446, 447, 448, 458, 459, *466*
Takahashi, Y., 563, *584*
Tan, J. J., 575, 577, *585*
Tanaka, K., 63, 64, *81,* 559, *582*
Tangney, J. P., 206, *212,* 236, 237, *243, 244,* 535, *552*
Tanzer, N., 90, 98, 101, *111*
Taris, T. W., 395, 402, 405, *410*
Tasa, K., 509, 511, *522*
Tata, J., 475, 477, 478, 490, *497*
Tax, S. S., 87, 91, *108*
Tayeb, M. H., 571, *585*
Taylor, A. D., 5, *47*
Taylor, E. C., 359, *380*
Taylor, J., 479, *493*
Taylor, M., 34, *53,* 74, 76, 77, 78, *82, 83,* 87, 91, 99, *111,* 224, *243,* 305, 319, *326,* 335, *353,* 368, 373, *378,* 416, *438,* 517, *521*
Taylor, S. E., 280, *295*
Tedeschi, J. T., 257, *269,* 474, *497,* 567, *584*
Tellegen, A., 106, *112*
Tepper, B. J., 87, *112,* 136, *151,* 206, *212,* 314, *327,* 372, 373, *380,* 397, 398, 405, *410*
Tesluk, P., 87, *112,* 133, 134, *151,* 234, *244,* 314, *327,* 613, *619*
Tetrick, L. E., 250, *266,* 359, 368, *380*
Thaler, R. H., 216, 226, *242*
Thatcher, S. M. B., 222, 223, *242*
Thayer, P. W., 507, *521*
Thibaut, J., 5, 6, *9f,* 21, 22, 23, 24, 25, 26, 29, 30, 31, 39, 45, 46, *54, 56,* 61, 62, 63, 64, 68, 70, 71, 72, *82, 83, 84,* 105, *112,* 117, *118t,* 124, 126, 127, 130, 136, *151,* 156, 157, 158, 159, 160, *176, 177,* 190, *212,* 260, *270,* 275, 276, 277, 281, 282, 283, 284, 288, 293, *297, 298,* 300, 333, 335, 345, *353,* 431, *438,* 452, 455, *466,* 470, *497,* 527, 544, *551, 552,* 562, *585,* 594, 596, 597, *604t, 619*
Thibodeau, R., 18, *54*
Thompson, L., 72, *82*
Thompson, M., 516, *521*
Thoresen, C. J., 357, *378*
Thornton, G., 313, 318, *325,* 423, *436*
Thorsteinson, T. J., 428, *438*
Tijoriwala, S. A., 477, 483, 488, *496*
Ting-Toomey, S., 569, *581*
Tinsley, C. H., 170, 171, 172, *177,* 308, 320, *325,* 563, 567, 571, *580, 585*
Tippett, M. J., 574, *585*
Tipton, S. M., 560, *580*
Todd, H. F., 562, *584*
Tomaka, J., 386, 392, 396, 406, *410*

Tomlinson, E., 204, *210,* 261, *270*
Tong, K. K., 557, 574, 576, 578, *580, 583*
Tooby, J., 220, 235, *240, 244*
Topolnytsky, L., 137, 138, *150*
Törnblom, K., 71, 73, *83,* 334, *353,* 388, 406, *410*
Toyama, M., 574, *581*
Traupmann, J., 5, *51*
Treasure, F. P., 206, *209*
Trevino, L. K., 65, *79,* 234, *244,* 502, *519*
Triandis, H. C., 491, *497,* 563, 571, *585*
Tripp, T., 87, 90, 98, 99, 100, 106, *108, 110,* 216, 222, 223, 224, 226, 237, *239, 240,* 255, *266,* 393, *407*
Tröetschel, R., 199, *208*
Trope, Y., *243,* 483, *494*
Truman, H. S., 440, *466*
Truxillo, D. M., 412, 413, 416, 421, 422, 423, 426, 429, *434, 438*
Tse, D. K., 564, *586*
Tuchinsky, M., 254, 259, 260, *270*
Turillo, C. J., 180, 181, 183, *185t,* 188, 189, 191, 192, 194, 205, 208, *212,* 223, 226, 227, *244,* 433, *438*
Turnbull, W., 448, *465*
Turner, J., 251, *270,* 338, *353,* 362, *380,* 445, 447, 448, 450, 458, *466, 467*
Tversky, A., 234, *242,* 285, *296*
Tyler, T., 5, 6, *9f, 10f, 11f,* 23, 25, 26, 27, 30, 31, 33, 34, 35, *37f,* 39, 40, 41, 42, 46, *47,* 52, *54, 55,* 61, 62, 64, 65, 66, 68, 71, 73, 74, 76, *79, 82, 84,* 87, 88, 89, 99, 101, 105, *108, 110, 112,* 114, 115, 117, 120, 124, 125, 128, 133, 134, 141, *147, 150, 151, 152,* 159, 160, 161, 162, 163, 164, 165, 167, 168, 169, 171, 172, 173, *176, 177,* 180, 183, *185t,* 189, 190, 191, 193, *211,* 212, 233, *244,* 250, 251, 252, 253, 254, 256, 262, *267, 268, 269, 270,* 275, 276, 277, 278, 279, 280, 281, 282, 287, 288, 289, 292, *296, 297, 298,* 299, 304, 314, *324,* 330, 331, *326,* 334, 335, 336, 337, 338, 340, 343, 346, 347, 348, 350, 351, *351, 353, 354,* 362, 363, 364, 366, 369, 370, 374, *376, 378, 380,* 390, 392, 398, *410,* 419, *436, 438,* 444, 452, *465, 467,* 470, *470m1,* 477, 480, 482, *496, 497,* 504, *519,* 527, 530, 531, 532, 537, 540, *549, 550, 551, 552,* 567, 569, 572, 574, 575, 577, *580, 581, 583, 586,* 590, 592, 596, 597, 601, 603, *604t,* 612, *615, 618, 619*

U

Umphress, E. E., 180, 181, 183, *185t,* 188, 189, 191, 192, 193, 194, 205, 208,

Subject Index

Note: *f* indicates figure, *n* indicates footnote, and *t* indicates table

effects of justice on, 15
fair, 15
helping, 93, 191
illegal, 418
immoral, 217
justice-relevant, 222
leader, 103, 367, 492, 519, 521
mandatory, 42
moral, 230
negotiating, 87
norm-violating, 393
opportunistic, 87
proactive, 350
prosocial, 70
retaliation, 87, 97, 133, 234, 342, 505
unethical, 385
unjust, 195
voice, 161
withdrawal, 366
Behavioral
adjustments to work performance, 19
differences, 173
effects, 42
engagement, 42
intentions, 43
measures, 516–517
reactions, 395, 458–459
to inequity, 17
Belief in a just world (BJW), 406
Belonging, 203
Benevolence, 251, 254
Bias, 21, 39, 118*t*, 124, 126, 144–146, 159–160,
169, 204, 233, 316, 418, 443–462,
492, 511, 576, 600, 610
suppression, 24, 30–31, 33, 40, 62, 66,
120, 123, 128, 144, 454
Blame, 224, 226, 230–231, 235–237, 480, 486,
489, 492, 575, 608*t*, 610
lack of, 230
Bosses
abusive, 87
Boundary-spanning roles, 96
Brief Symptom Inventory, 398
Budget allocations, 87

C

Cahn, Edmond, 105
Calculus-based trust (CBT), 257–259, 263, 265
and market relationship, 260–261
Causal attribution processes, 343
Cheap talk, 255
Choice, 25
Citizenship behaviors, 77, 276
Codes of conduct, 15
Cognitive dissonance theory, 5
Commitment, 27–28, 32, 65, 76, 79, 87, 276,
320, 458, 483, 504–505, 510, 516,

519, 541, 567, 570, 572, 577, 580,
606, 608*t*, 609–610, 615
Communication
decision making and, 426–429
emotional, 235
initial, 415–416, 418
insufficient, 392, 510
nonverbal, 482
quality, 94
style, 493, 572
two-way, 103, 420–422
supportive, 511
Company policy, 276
Comparative expectations, 15
Compensation, 129, 405, 567, 572, 599, 611,
613–614
Competency, 254
Compliance, 26, 93, 302–303, 306–309,
319–320, 349, 505
Computer monitoring, 305
Configural justice, 93
Conflict, 98, 162, 221, 225, 237, 384, 397,
476–477, 505
avoidance, 565
management, 87, 96, 121, 129, 259, 276,
312, 569
resolution, 22, 62, 113, 121, 129, 156–157,
563, 566–567
suppression of, 311
Connectedness, 265, 356, 373–375
Consequences, 343
Consideration, 30–31, 33, 60, 75, 102–104,
160–161, 164–165, 167–168, 171,
184*t*
lack of, 391–392
Consistency, 24, 27, 66
Construct
discrimination, 89–91
validity, 60, 121, 122*f*
Contamination, 122*f*, 123–124
Control, 189, 346
model, 333–334
over outcomes, 180
Cooperation (*see also* Employee cooperation), 6, 42, 191, 204, 206, 331–332,
346, 412, 607
Corporate
fraud, 248
layoffs, 87
responses to consumer complaints, 87
Correctability, 27, 66
Counterfactual conceptualizations, 35–36, 37*f*
Counterproductive behavior, 349–350
Coworkers, 6, 190, 315, 318, 457, 600
connectedness with, 373
endangering, 317
harassing, 322–323
problems of, 572

Made in the USA
Lexington, KY
13 June 2019